# SUBSTANCE ABUSE, ASSESSMENT AND ADDICTION

# SUBSTANCE ABUSE ASSESSMENT, INTERVENTIONS AND TREATMENT

Additional books in this series can be found on Nova's website
under the Series tab.

Additional E-books in this series can be found on Nova's website
under the E-book tab.

SUBSTANCE ABUSE ASSESSMENT, INTERVENTIONS AND TREATMENT

# SUBSTANCE ABUSE, ASSESSMENT AND ADDICTION

### KRISTINA A. MURATI
### AND
### ALLISON G. FISCHER
#### EDITORS

**Nova Science Publishers, Inc.**
*New York*

For permission to use material from this book please contact us:
Telephone 631-231-7269; Fax 631-231-8175
Web Site: http://www.novapublishers.com

**NOTICE TO THE READER**

The Publisher has taken reasonable care in the preparation of this book, but makes no expressed or implied warranty of any kind and assumes no responsibility for any errors or omissions. No liability is assumed for incidental or consequential damages in connection with or arising out of information contained in this book. The Publisher shall not be liable for any special, consequential, or exemplary damages resulting, in whole or in part, from the readers' use of, or reliance upon, this material. Any parts of this book based on government reports are so indicated and copyright is claimed for those parts to the extent applicable to compilations of such works.

Independent verification should be sought for any data, advice or recommendations contained in this book. In addition, no responsibility is assumed by the publisher for any injury and/or damage to persons or property arising from any methods, products, instructions, ideas or otherwise contained in this publication.

This publication is designed to provide accurate and authoritative information with regard to the subject matter covered herein. It is sold with the clear understanding that the Publisher is not engaged in rendering legal or any other professional services. If legal or any other expert assistance is required, the services of a competent person should be sought. FROM A DECLARATION OF PARTICIPANTS JOINTLY ADOPTED BY A COMMITTEE OF THE AMERICAN BAR ASSOCIATION AND A COMMITTEE OF PUBLISHERS.

Additional color graphics may be available in the e-book version of this book.

LIBRARY OF CONGRESS CATALOGING-IN-PUBLICATION DATA

Substance abuse, assessment, and addiction / editors, Kristina A. Murati and Allison G. Fischer.
    p. cm. -- (Substance abuse assessment, interventions and treatment)
  Includes bibliographical references and index.
  ISBN 978-1-61122-931-8 (hardcover : alk. paper)
  1. Substance abuse. 2. Substance abuse--Treatment. I. Murati, Kristina A. II. Fischer, Allison G.
  HV4998.S828 2011
  616.86--dc22
                                                                 2010044717

*Published by Nova Science Publishers, Inc.* ✛ *New York*

# CONTENTS

# PREFACE

Substance dependence, or addiction, is a relapsing disorder characterized by the loss of control of drug or alcohol intake, or a compulsion to take the substance, associated with the appearance of a withdrawal syndrome after a discontinuation of its long-term use. This book presents and discusses research in the study of substance abuse, including drug abuse and education; binge drinking; the treatment of heroine and cocaine abuse; women and addictions; anabolic steroid abuse and alcoholism and pregnancy.

Chapter 1 - Drug dependence, or addiction, is a relapsing disorder characterized by the loss of control of drug intake, or compulsion to take the drug, associated with the appearance of a withdrawal syndrome after a discontinuation of its long-term use. Several authors have pointed out the need to define the phenomenon of addiction in behavioral terms establishing that, in a general way, addiction is a relapsing disorder that leads to a compulsive drug use, despite the harmful effects in some aspects of the person's functioning. Actually, with the progress in basic and clinical research, evidenced by the rapid advances at the molecular, cellular, neural and behavioral levels, the study of drug dependence has raised important conceptual issues that have helped the neurobiological research to better understand the changes in the neural mechanisms underlying the development of addiction, and the expression of the withdrawal symptoms.

Chapter 2 - In the following lines some historical and cultural aspects of the drug addiction are commented.

It is pointed out that it is not possible to eradicate this problem, specifing the reasons that support this affirmation.

Using a Maria Montessori's idea and the others ideas we consider nowadays that some mental functions have changed because of social phenomenons, and this has influence over pathologies like anorexia, border line personality, psychopathic personality and drug addiction.

Some aspects about prevention and education in drugs are reviewed.

It is proposed that education have to be planned according to the person to whom it is addressed. To people who is victim of poverty it is recommended working resilence. To people who does not have economical problems it is necessary reviewing and facing values, and also generating a conceptual change.

Prevention requires confronting the possibility af being responsible and reviewing the functions that have switched. It is also needed the community action of society.

Chapter 3 - Clinical research points out that there is a comorbid relationship between drug addiction and high-risk sexual behavior. Much of this relationship has been explained as the use of sexual behavior as a way to exchange for drugs of abuse. However, studies using animal models have implicated neural and psychological mechanisms that may link drug abuse and risky sexual behavior. Both drug taking and sexual behavior involve overlapping neural circuitry, and both events also evoke dopamine efflux in the nucleus accumbens. This neural overlap appears to be sufficient to induce cross-sensitization. However, this cross-sensitization appears to be unilateral with chronic drug exposure resulting in the enhancement of sexual motivation and sexual behavior, but not the reverse. In contrast to the cross-sensitization literature, the findings of reinstatement studies have suggested that the neural overlap and involvement of dopamine may not be sufficient for the reinstatement of drug-seeking behavior following a sexual event that presumably primes the system. The purpose of the present chapter is to review this empirical literature and to discuss the possible role of learning as a link between the two, with particular emphasis on the incentive sensitization view of drug addiction.

Chapter 4 - The term binge drinking is in common usage. Having gained some degree of international credibility, it is employed frequently in reports emerging from research and national agencies, but also within the media and popular press. Implicitly it is linked with the negative consequences of the excesses of alcohol consumption, particularly within the younger members of the population.

This chapter will consider the evolution of the term in the recent past, how it is interpreted and will discuss its value as society in general seeks to curb the excesses of alcohol consumption and address the short and longer term harm that ensues.

Chapter 5 - Although the behavioral healthcare field has increasingly emphasized the value of evidence-based practices, community-based settings are typically slow to modify their existing clinical practices. One strategy that has been found to accelerate the implementation of evidence-based practices in behavioral healthcare settings is the use of peer opinion leaders. The Tampa Practice Improvement Collaborative (PIC) project evaluated the relative effectiveness of an opinion leader model in implementing evidence-based practices related to treatment of co-occurring mental health and substance use disorders. Practitioners from ten diverse substance abuse treatment programs (n = 43) within the area's largest publicly funded agencies were trained to implement an evidence-based manualized treatment intervention with the assistance of peer opinion leaders. A comparison group of counselors (n = 28) working in a nearby geographic area received a more traditional, less intensive training approach. This paper describes use of opinion leaders and intensive training to implement an evidence-based treatment manual in several community-based treatment settings, and highlights a series of implementation strategies found to be effective in these settings.

Chapter 6 - This paper addresses controversial topics in the assessment and treatment of heroin addiction. Included in the discussion are issues of dose and outcome, difficulties with toxicology screens, the role of co-occurring Axis I and Axis II disorders, the introduction (and extinction) of newer medications to treat heroin dependence, difficulties of measuring treatment outcome, models of heroin dependence, the role of user personality, and the question of heroin maintenance treatment.

Chapter 7 - The Arrestee Drug Abuse Monitoring (ADAM) program identified almost half of all ADAM-Manhattan arrestees interviewed 2000-2003 as at risk of drug dependence

(RDD) for various street drugs. Higher rates were associated with using heroin and crack, more frequent use, being younger, and being arrested in 2001-02. More than two-fifths the marijuana-only users were RDD. Taken at face value, these findings support efforts to provide drug treatment to arrestees, even those that use only marijuana. There are two major caveats that suggest a need for much further research: there has been only one limited validity study of ADAM's screen for RDD, and research suggests that existing treatment modalities may be particularly ineffective for marijuana-only users. Despite the suggested need, only a quarter of arrestees with possible substance dependence problems received treatment in the past 12 months.

Chapter 8 - Despite huge advances in the neuroscience of substance abuse and dependence in the past twenty years, no approved pharmacological treatment exists for cocaine abuse.

The systematic reviews of treatments with available medications have found no evidence supporting the use of antidepressants, carbamazepine, or dopamine agonists in the pharmacotherapy of cocaine abuse. Dopamine receptor antagonists (neuroleptics) proved somehow effective in reducing cue-induced craving; however these medications are poorly tolerated, and record a significantly high dropout rate. Finally, high-dose methadone and buprenorphine were reported to promote cocaine abstinence in cocaine- and opioid-dependent patients, but their long-term effectiveness is still unknown.

Targeting symptoms might improve treatment effectiveness. Cocaine is thought to produce its addictive effect by four mechanisms basically: cocaine-induced euphoria; hedonic dysregulation; disruption of pre-frontal functioning; and cue-induced craving.

On the basis of the known neurochemistry of cocaine some target compounds have been studied, the most promising being BP897, a D3 partial agonist, and vanoxerine, a highly selective inhibitor of dopamine uptake. Results on humans, however, are pending. Recently modafinil, a glutamate-enhancing medication that inhibits GABA release too, proved effective in favouring cocaine abstinence in cocaine abusing people. Some open-label studies also reported the effectiveness of g-vinyl GABA, an irreversible inhibitor of GABA-transaminase, and of tiogabine, a GABA reuptake inhibitor, both compounds preventing relapse and thus increasing cocaine abstinence.

An alternative approach rests on the use of vaccines. Studies on rats showed that cocaine antibodies block cocaine from reaching the brain and prevent the reinstatement of cocaine self-administration. Ethical issues, however, are raised by the recourse to immunotherapy, particularly when proposed under legal coercion.

Psychosocial treatments are a useful companion in the pharmacotherapy of cocaine abuse, with group therapy and contingency management therapies capable to improve motivation and social functioning, particularly in patients abusing alcohol too.

Chapter 9 - Methadone maintenance is an effective means of preventing HIV transmission in drug users, through the reduction of injection and needle-sharing. In Hong Kong, a low threshold approach has been adopted in the introduction of methadone maintenance since over 30 years ago. The methadone treatment programme (MTP) now reaches about 9000 drug users regularly. HIV prevalence has remained low at below 1%.

The rising HIV prevalence in neighbouring cities calls for an enhancement of the MTP in Hong Kong. The provision of HAART (highly active antiretroviral therapy) in conjunction with counseling in a specialized care setting could potentially reduce the chance of virus dissemination from known positive drug users. Early diagnosis of HIV infection and their prompt referral to care are however the pre-requisites. A new programme was introduced to offer urine-based HIV testing on an opt-out basis. Over a three-month pilot in 2003, 74.7% (1834) of 2456 methadone users were tested. During the full-year programme in 2004, attendees of 20 methadone clinics were tested in four clusters. A total of 8905 tests were provided in the clinics, amounting to 90% of the active caseload during the testing periods. The coverage varied in different clinics, ranging from 71.9% to 100%. Large clinics with higher turnover were liable to have a lower coverage. The general acceptance of drug users to the new testing programme was high. Lack of motivation was determined to be the single most important reason for refusing the test.

The testing nevertheless has provided a new opportunity for arousing AIDS awareness in methadone users, including those who chose to opt out. Surveillance was enhanced: HIV prevalence was 0.5% in the 2003 pilot and 0.2% during the 2004 full-year programme. The difference might have arisen from the self-exclusion of known positive individuals in the second year. A total of 32 drug users, 24 of which newly diagnosed, were tested positive in the urine-based HIV testing programme. The provision of clinical management, and the linkage with public health interventions are additional benefits brought about by the programme, which may also lead to better control of the epidemic.

In conclusion, the incorporation of urine-based HIV testing in a conventional methadone clinic network is feasible. The testing would, in the next phase, be regularized by repeating in yearly cycles. The wide coverage, adoption of a routine but voluntary testing strategy, and the integration of clinical and public health intervention, are lessons learned from the programme. The maintenance of a low HIV prevalence in drug users, amidst potential changes in HIV epidemiology and pattern of drug use, remains a challenge for Hong Kong.

Chapter 10 - Drug and alcohol abuse impairs memory and such impairment is assessed with tests such as the California Verbal Learning Test. These tests, however, do not analyze the shape of the memorization curve itself. The authors propose that analyzing the shape of the memory curve can serve as a diagnostic tool to allow a clinician to better evaluate the effects of any treatment on drug addicts and alcoholics. In this article, the authors provide a mathematical model for analyzing the shape of either individual or group memorization curves. The model assumes that the memorization curve is exponential in shape and employs three parameters: B2 — the velocity of memorization; B4 — an asymptotic volume of memorized material and B3 — predisposition to the next memorization before the beginning of testing. The model is tested using data from drug addicts and alcoholics and provides convincing evidence of how a mathematical treatment of the learning curve reveals new insights when nootropics (Nootropil, Baclofen, Bemethyl, and Aethimizol) and vasorelaxants (Cinnarizine and Dibazol) are used.

Chapter 11 - Evidence suggests that individuals in substance use treatment become very preoccupied with food and their body shape and gain weight in recovery. Adolescents in substance use treatment evidence weight gain that cannot be explained by maturation factors alone. Many adolescents believe that various drugs have the power to keep them slim and this belief is associated with the persistent increase of substance use and treatment resistance. Women are more preoccupied with fear of gaining weight than men, and they use substances more often due to higher levels of weight and body image concerns than men. This chapter outlines the relationship between substance use, body shape and food preoccupation; provides the prevalence of body weight and shape concerns in women with addiction; reviews the literature on the various issues and struggles related to women's weight and shape issues and substance use initiation, treatment and recovery and the lack of treatment and support to address these issues; will render the significance and urgency to address this problem clear. This chapter also presents qualitative data linking substance use, food, and body weight and shape preoccupation in women and offers practical ways to address food, weight and shape concerns for women with addictions to enhance recovery, minimize relapse, and increase women's overall well being.

Chapter 12 - A large majority of women entering addiction treatment present significant symptoms of trauma related to physical or sexual abuse. Despite research indicating that trauma interventions are integral to women's successful recovery from addiction, many programs do not adequately address violence-related trauma. This chapter provides a review of the literature on trauma among women with addictive disorders and several manual based interventions developed to address co-occurring addiction and trauma-related disorders. One intervention, "Beyond Trauma," which has become increasingly popular among community based programs is described in detail. Beyond Trauma appears to have several advantages over other therapies for treating trauma and addiction in women, including 1) a theoretical foundation that draws on relational theory as a guide to the intervention, 2) a broad based approach that can be utilized by a variety of professional and paraprofessional staff members, 3) a focus that goes beyond treating women with a formal diagnosis of post traumatic stress disorder to include treatment for an array of symptoms and problems associated with trauma, and 4) gender-appropriate use of expressive arts in its curriculum. The chapter also discusses treatment program environment factors that may be critically important to treatment outcome for women: 1) whether the program is gender specific, 2) the degree of emphasis on peer involvement in recovery, 3) program recognition of the value of knowledge-based recovery experience, 4) program facilitation of cohesion, 5) the empowerment of clients in decisions affecting the program and 6) skills training relevant to managing moods, relationships and a variety of problems that women face during recovery. Possible mechanisms of change for Beyond Trauma are explored with particular emphasis on the variety of ways the intervention attempts to impact problem areas experienced by women (e.g., mental health functioning self esteem and social support). Recommendations for future research in the treatment of trauma and addiction-related disorders in women are outlined.

Chapter 13 - The abuse of anabolic steroids by teenagers—that is, their use without a prescription—is a health concern. Anabolic steroids are synthetic forms of the hormone testosterone that can be taken orally, injected, or rubbed on the skin. Although a 2006 survey funded by the National Institute on Drug Abuse (NIDA) found that less than 3 percent of 12th graders had abused anabolic steroids, it also found that about 40 percent of 12th graders described anabolic steroids as "fairly easy" or "very easy" to get. The abuse of anabolic steroids and behavioral changes in teenagers.

Chapter 14 - Nowadays, fingerprint analysis based on chromatography has become one of the approaches widely used for quality assessment of herbal medicine. In this paper, chromatographic fingerprint from high performance liquid chromatography-diode array detector (HPLC-DAD) and gas chromatography–mass spectrometry (GC-MS) is investigated. A pragmatic approach combining several well-established chemometric methods is developed for processing the data sets in order to assess the similarity/difference in chromatographic fingerprints obtained. The strategy includes baseline correction, peak alignment, variable selection, correlation analysis, principal co-ordinates analysis (PCO), principal component analysis (PCA) and Procrustes analysis. In order to demonstrate the advantages of chromatographic fingerprint with total profile, a previously used method of fingerprint analysis based on a chromatographic peak table is also investigated in this paper. In the real application to herbal samples of Rhizoma *chuanxiong*, Radix *angelicae*, Cortex *cinnamomi*, Herba *menthae*, Ginkgo *biloba* and Rhizoma *asarum* collected from different sources, fingerprint analysis based on total chromatograms coupled with chemometric data preprocessing and data analysis is a reliable method and thus it should be applicable for quality assessment of herbal medicine.

Chapter 15 - More than 35 years after its introduction into the therapy of pregnant heroin addicts methadone maintenance continues to be the standard therapy of opiate addiction in pregnancy. Benefit on pregnancy and neonatal outcome compared to the sole abuse of street heroin is evident.

However, there is ongoing need for clinical research to further improve the management of craving during pregnancy as well as the prevention and therapy of neonatal abstinence syndrome.

This chapter intends to review different approaches in improving these problems. Maternal maintenance therapy is discussed under consideration of recent insights into methadone metabolism and the physiological changes during pregnancy as well as under consideration of optimal therapy of concomitant infectious diseases highly prevalent in this risk group. Eventually actual therapy strategies in the management of neonates of opiate addicted women will be illustrated and critically commented.

An overview will be given to allow a better understanding of the specific needs of these women during pregnancy and their affected offsprings.

Chapter 16 - In this section the authors review historical aspects of the use of alcohol by women. Social and cultural characteristics are mentioned about of the ingestion of alcohol in different regions all over the world. Statistics figures are pointed out that give an image of the alcohol consumption in the general population and in women more specifically. The interactions among the biological, psychological and social traits of women are emphasized. It is analysed the pregnancy in adolescents and its relation with the pregnancy of high risk.

It is examined the fetal alcohol syndrome that is the first avoidable cause of mental retardation in U.S. Data about the use of alcohol during the pregnancy are revealed. We mention the problems in the diagnosis of the alcohol use, mainly during the pregnancy. It is proposed and justified the use of tests to the diagnosis of alcoholism. Treatment and ethical aspects are treated.

In:  Substance Abuse, Assessment and Addiction
Editors: Kristina A. Murati and Allison G. Fischer

ISBN: 978-1-61122-931-8
© 2011 Nova Science Publishers, Inc.

*Chapter 1*

# DRUG ABUSE

## *Manoel Jorge Nobre and Vanessa Moreno Castilho*

## INTRODUCTION

Drug dependence, or addiction, is a relapsing disorder characterized by the loss of control of drug intake, or compulsion to take the drug, associated with the appearance of a withdrawal syndrome after a discontinuation of its long-term use. Several authors have pointed out the need to define the phenomenon of addiction in behavioral terms establishing that, in a general way, addiction is a relapsing disorder that leads to a compulsive drug use, despite the harmful effects in some aspects of the person's functioning. Actually, with the progress in basic and clinical research, evidenced by the rapid advances at the molecular, cellular, neural and behavioral levels, the study of drug dependence has raised important conceptual issues that have helped the neurobiological research to better understand the changes in the neural mechanisms underlying the development of addiction, and the expression of the withdrawal symptoms.

Drugs of abuse produce, initially, a state of pleasure characterized by its positive reinforcing properties, and that is the reason they are taken. However, its repetitive administration leads to a natural adaptation of the central nervous system, including long-lasting changes. As the user's body adjusts to the drug, a bigger amount of it needs to be taken each time to get to the same first results. This can quickly lead to the use of more and more of the drug and, consequently, to addiction or dependence, characterized by the appearance of a behavioral repertoire toward an excessive drug intake, whenever the drug ingestion is interrupted. This means that, in addicts, drug-seeking behavior becomes compulsive. If a user stops taking the drug withdrawal symptoms appears, as the nervous system needs to adjust functioning without the drug. It may take weeks before the nervous system is back to normal, and during this time there is great temptation to use the drug again and then, discontinue the withdrawal symptoms. In fact, relapse is possible even after long periods of abstinence, even years after cessation of drug use (Figure 1). In this chapter, we will briefly discuss some basic neurobiological, motivational and behavioral processes that drive an individual from an impulsive to a compulsive disorder and, the importance of affective symptoms, such as fear and anxiety, as the promoting factors of relapsing.

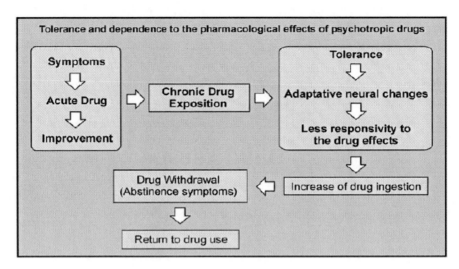

Figure 1. The addiction cycle from acute to chronic ingestion and its importance in relapse (return to drug intake after a period of abstinence).

## NEURAL ADAPTATION

Drug seeking behavior and drug self-administration in both animals and humans, can be triggered by drugs of abuse themselves, or can be facilitated by prolonged exposition to stressful events. Chronic ingestion of drugs of abuse leads to long-lived alterations in the brain function, and the fundamental types of mechanisms appear to be similar: chronic drug administration induces prolonged changes in the brain function (neural plasticity), by influencing the signal transduction pathways of the brain, including the regulation of neural gene expression. This type of functional organization reflects adaptation to the environment. In this sense, long-lasting activity-dependent changes in the efficacy of synaptic transmission, play an important role in the development of neural circuits and may mediate many forms of learning and memory that serves an adaptive process, shared by virtually all organisms. So, if the environment stays approximately the same, the functional organization also remains unaltered. On the other hand, any changes in the environment lead to a homeostatic imbalance reflected by physiological modifications in the neural systems that trigger plastic changes to facilitate re-adaptation. That is what drug abuse does: functional and probably structural changes in the brain functioning.

In parallel with drugs that produce physical addiction, many drugs of abuse also cause psychological dependence, that is, in some situations the individual maintains the behavior upon which their presentation is contingent. Most addictive drugs, like amphetamine, cocaine, morphine and ethanol, and in some cases benzodiazepines, support self administration. This pattern of responding may vary depending upon the schedule of delivery, the organisms' prior history and the type of stimuli presented (type of drug, cues presented during reinforcement, etc).

In a general way, the phenomenon of neural adaptation to continuous administration of any drug could be observed from the following hypothetical constructs: the appearance of tolerance or sensitization to the effects of the drug, the raising of an abstinence syndrome after the treatment has been discontinued (withdrawal), and the appearance of feelings of craving. We will see briefly now, each one of these constructs.

## TOLERANCE

Tolerance and physical dependence develop after chronic administration of any one of an array of mood-altering substances. Tolerance is a phenomenon often defined as a gradual decrease in responsiveness (over days or weeks) to a drug dose, after its continuous administration in such a way that the dose must be increased to produce the same initial effect and thus, more drug is needed. Tolerance and dependence develop as the nerve cells counteract the drug's psychoactive effects, chemically and structurally. Tolerance is a complex generalized phenomenon that involves many independent physiological and behavioral mechanisms (Figure 2).

The tolerance can be pharmacodynamic (or functional tolerance), physiological (or adaptation by homeostatic mechanisms), pharmacokinetic (metabolic) and conditioned (behavioral). Of importance for this chapter is the classically conditioned tolerance in which a stimulus repeatedly paired with the drug administration can evoke, alone, conditioned responses that are conflicting with the drug effect, by compensatory mechanisms. The conditioned tolerance can be explained by a compensatory response (CR) in which the conditioned stimuli presented during the drug administration acquire the capacity to elicit the compensatory response, by compensatory mechanisms, or the cues present in the context at the moment of the drug ingestion add to the drug effects generating a compensatory response, which is a tolerance response to the drug effects (Figure 3).

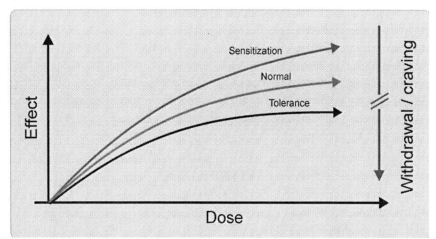

Figure 2. Shifts in a dose-response curve during tolerance and sensitization. There is a shift of the dose-response curve to the right or to the left in the tolerance and sensitization, respectively, that is, for a given dose there is a lower or a greater effect in comparison with the initial dose. Cessation of drug intake leads to craving and withdrawal syndrome.

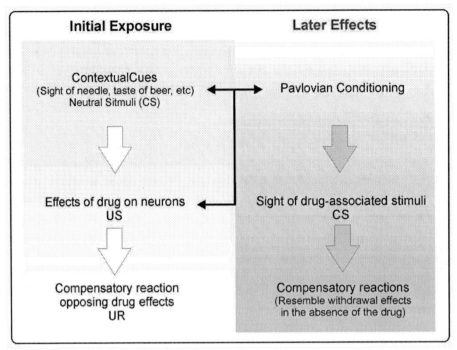

Figure 3. Main effects of chronic drug use and the importance of Pavlovian conditioning in the learned tolerance. An initial exposure to drug (on acute ingestion) leads to its reinforcing effects on the central nervous system that promotes a raised compensatory response, that is, a compensatory response of the organism opposed to the drug effect. In parallel, environmental cues, initially harmless (e.g. sight of a needle), begin to sum up to the drug effects. After a long-period administration and in function of a Pavlovian-like conditioning, the simple presentation of a cue-related drug raises a similar compensatory response and all the disagreeable effects, similarly to what happens during drug withdrawal.

## SENSITIZATION

Sensitization is defined as the enhancement of a directly elicited drug effect, through adaptive processes, and appears to represent facilitation within a system, making it easier to elicit the response in future occasions. Like tolerance, sensitization of a drug effect can become linked to the events that co-occurred when the effect was originally elicited, being thus possible to come under selective event control.

## WITHDRAWAL

The term withdrawal defines a group of symptoms that result from an abrupt interruption of a chronic drug treatment. The abrupt interruption of the chronic administration of a drug of abuse leads to the instatement of a withdrawal syndrome characterized by the raise of a lot of physical and negative affective symptoms, such as dysphoria, anhedonia and anxiety. This type of phenomenon can also be induced by pharmacological means or by the use of specific antagonists. For example, an opioid withdrawal syndrome can be induced in morphine-dependent rats by the administration of an opioid antagonist, such as naltrexone. In the same way, a benzodiazepine withdrawal syndrome can be produced by a single injection of flumazenil, a benzodiazepine antagonist.

During withdrawal of a drug of abuse, the individual becomes obsessed with obtaining the drug for a sense of well being. Chemically dependent people become inflexible in their behavior toward the drug, despite the adverse consequences. The intensity of this felt "need" or dependence may vary from mild craving, to an intense overwhelming obsession. In most cases, the withdrawal symptoms are opposed to the original symptoms, or represent an exacerbation of the symptoms which generated the need of that drug. Because of this, it is common to say that the withdrawal symptoms are a rebound effect in the physiological systems modified by the drug. For example, alcohol depresses the central nervous system, withdrawal stimulates it. Amphetamine is a stimulant of the central nervous system, so amphetamine withdrawal causes depression. Benzodiazepines are anxiolytic drugs; nevertheless diazepam withdrawal is characterized by intense anxiety.

The time required to produce physical dependence may vary among the drugs. Withdrawal symptoms can develop in a single day with large quantities of central nervous system depressants. For most drug users, development of physical dependence is gradual, occurring over weeks, months, or years of chronic administration.

## CRAVING

Generally, craving is defined as an excessive "yearning" to experiment the effects of some drug, or a very strong desire for a drug or for its intoxicating effects, and it is thought to develop, at least partially, as a result of associations resulting from Pavlovian conditioning that rise when the person is confronted with a conditioned stimulus associated with the drug effects. In fact, even stimuli presented during a single cocaine experience may elicit drug-seeking for up one year. Craving is one of the most important symptoms of the withdrawal syndrome and frequently represents the most common cause of relapse. Nevertheless, the occurrence of craving and relapse can be facilitated by other factors, like stress. In fact, stress plays a crucial role in relapse, although complex and influenced by multiple sources.

## NEURAL SYSTEMS AND DRUG DEPENDENCE

After a chronic exposition to drugs of abuse, many changes begin to occur in the brain, particularly at the brainstem and limbic structures. In fact, drugs of abuse act characteristically on a particular system in the brain to achieve its rewarding effects. Initially, the reinforcing properties of the drug seem to act according to the paradigm of the operant conditioning in which its rewarding effects facilitate further exposure to the drug.

In general, the factors that lead an individual from a simple acute ingestion of any psychoactive drug, to an incontrollable "craving" for it, could be described in three steps: Initially, almost always because of social or cultural pressures, the individual takes the drug (alcohol, for example). The contact and ingestion (acute use) of the drug raises an affective (psychological) and physical (somatic and autonomic) welfare that causes a temporary organic unbalancing. In this stage the subject responds to the drug and to the drug-related stimuli in a controlled manner, not dissimilar from normal motivated responding. Following repeated ingestion (chronic use), an homeostatic process begins to occur, promoting a neural adaptation. At the same time, all the cues presented during reinforcement (drug ingestion) begin to add to the drug effect leading to tolerance. With repeated drug exposure, the subject enters progressively in the stage of drug abuse. The repeated associations of drug reward and drug-related stimuli result in the attribution of excessive motivational value to the drug-associated stimuli. At this moment, the subject can still control the drug intake in the absence of the drug-related stimuli. Their presence, however, elicits drug-seeking, associated sometimes to mild drug need (craving). In this stage, abstinence results in a negative emotional state that maintains the motivational relationship between the subject and the drug in the intervals, when drug-conditioned incentives are not available. In the post-addiction stage, abstinence symptoms progressively disappear but Pavlovian associations remain as powerful incentives for reinstatement of drug self-administration, so that the presence of a mild drug-related cue is sufficient to evoke craving.

## THE DOPAMINERGIC SYSTEM

Most drugs of abuse act on ancient and remarkably conserved neural mechanisms, associated with positive emotions that evolved to mediate incentive behavior. Heroin, cocaine, alcohol, marijuana, amphetamine, and their synthetic analogs activate mesolimbic dopamine-containing neurons and associated opioid receptors, in mammalian brains, a system that may be a "common neural currency" for reward and a substrate for regulating motivation. In fact, the discovery of neural circuits responsible for the modulation of the reinforcing effects of drugs of abuse starts, initially, from a classical experiment conducted by Olds and Milner (1954) that, accidentally, revealed the involvement of the mesolimbic-dopaminergic pathway in the reward effects induced by electrical intracranial self-stimulation in rats (Figure 4). They found that electrical stimulation of this brain area has a potent reinforcing effect, which means that the subject will repeat any behavior which results in pleasurable sensation.

The reinforcing effects of brain electrical stimulation have been found in a variety of animals. The discovery has also been confirmed in humans. Since then, these regions are called pleasure or reward centers in the brain. There are reward centers in the hypothalamus, septal regions and in the temporal lobes of the cerebral hemispheres. For instance, when the septal region is stimulated in conscious patients undergoing neurosurgery, they experience feelings of pleasure, optimism, euphoria, and happiness.

Since the discovery that most drugs of abuse (except benzodiazepines) increase the release of dopamine in the brain, there has been an intense interest in the long-length mesolimbic-dopaminergic pathway, the main dopaminergic system in the brain. The most important source of dopaminergic innervation in the central nervous system is found in the mesencephalon, basically three cell groups named, A8, A9 and A10. The A8 and A10 groups compose the ventral tegmental area (VTA), and the A9 group belongs to the *substantia nigra pars compacta* (SNpc). It is well known that the mesencephalic dopaminergic neurons localized in these areas give rise to massive ascending projections, divided in two main systems: the *nigro-striatal* that originates mainly from A9 group neurons, and the mesolimbic dopaminergic system that originates from the A10 group.

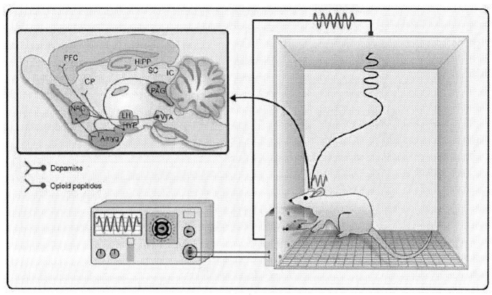

Figure 4. Brain self-stimulation in rats. Brain electrical stimulation by an electrode inserted into the medial forebrain bundle (the brain reward system) enhances rat lever pressing behavior. Since the animal prefers the region of the test apparatus where the stimulation is received, it may be inferred that the rat has a pleasurable experience. To test this hypothesis, researchers have elaborated an experiment to determine whether the rat would learn to perform arbitrary behaviors to obtain brief pulses of brain stimulation. Amyg = amygdala, CP= caudate-putamen, Hipp = hippocampus, Hyp = hypothalamus, IC = inferior colliculus, LH = lateral hypothalamus, Nac = nucleus accumbens, PAG = ventral periaqueductal gray, PFC = prefrontal cortex, SC = superior colliculus.

In a general way, the nigro-striatal pathway is a motor control pathway and the mesolimbic system is the so-called reward pathway (Figure 5).

The dopaminergic neurons from the VTA project to the basal forebrain, mainly to the prefrontal cortex, *nucleus accumbens* (NAcc), olfactory tubercle, amygdala and limbic cortices through the medial forebrain bundle (Figure 5). This system is commonly activated by natural reinforcers, such as water, food and sex, and is the primary site of action of drugs like alcohol, stimulants (such as cocaine) and opioids. As an example, the reinforcing effects of cocaine and amphetamines are the result of the drug-induced alterations in dopamine NAcc; opiates, nicotine and THC act by interacting with dopamine and opioid peptides systems in the ventral tegmental area, NAcc and amygdala.

Many studies have revealed the essential role of the ventral tegmental area in reward. Some works utilizing the self-administration technique showed that animals self-administer drugs directly in this structure while the rewarding properties of morphine are probably due to its action in opioid receptors present in the dopaminergic neurons.

The *nucleus accumbens* (NAcc) is the other structure clearly involved in the reinforcing effects of psychoactive drugs. This forebrain region is also known by the name of ventral striatum and is the main target of the dopaminergic projections from VTA, consisting of a ventral shell (target of the mesolimbic dopamine projections) and a dorsal core (the target for the nigro-striatal system). It is well documented that the activation of NAcc can facilitate or trigger consumatory behavior (eating) but, its primary role is in the motivational circuitry. Most researchers in the field of drug abuse believe that drug-induced pleasurable effects correlate with an increase in the extracellular dopamine levels within the NAcc and there is some agreement about the mainly function of dopamine in the reinforcing effects of drugs of abuse, but this is not true for benzodiazepines; just to remember, this class of anxiolytic drugs act on specific receptors called GABA-benzodiazepine receptors.

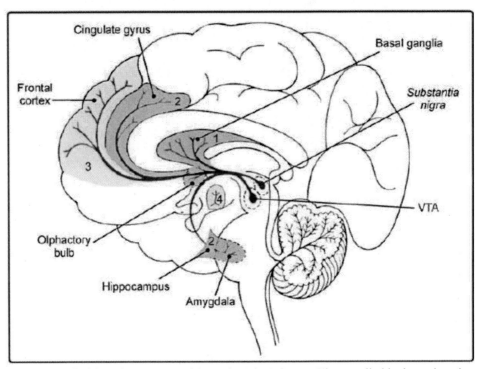

Figure 5. The mesolimbic and *nigro-striatal* dopaminergic pathways. The mesolimbic dopaminergic pathway has cell bodies located in the VTA and its axons ascend through the medial forebrain bundle to limbic and cortical structures innervating mainly the NAcc and also the amygdala, hippocampus, septum and olfactory tubercle. The mesolimbic pathway is involved in the control of motor behavior, as well as motivation, emotions and reward. The *nigro-striatal* dopaminergic pathway originates in the SNpc and terminates in the dorsal part of the striatum, the caudate-putamen, also known as the dorsal striatum. A minor part of this pathway projects to the ventral striatum. The *nigro-striatal* pathway contains about 75% of whole brain dopamine, and is involved in the control of posture and motor behavior, as well as learning motor programs and habits.

For example, differently from other psychoactive drugs, the withdrawal syndrome induced by abrupt interruption of chronic treatment with diazepam seems not to be linked to changes in dopamine transmission in the mesolimbic system. In this way, the behavioral, sensorial and autonomic effects observed during diazepam withdrawal could be a consequence of the activation of other neurotransmitter systems, like the glutamatergic or serotonergic, for example.

A lot of evidence has demonstrated the involvement of the mesolimbic system (comprised of the NAcc, amygdala, and VTA) in the reinforcing properties of drugs of abuse and it has already been demonstrated an increase of dopamine levels in the NAcc after direct electrical stimulation of some brain regions, or after self-administration of many drugs of abuse including ethanol. Thus, it has been of utmost importance to have knowledge on the multiple ways drugs of abuse act on the dopaminergic system. The disclosure of the particular dopaminergic circuit, the type of receptors with which a given drug interacts and its mechanism of action is of great importance in the understanding of the molecular mechanisms underlying its potential of abuse (Box 1). However, not all drugs have their potential of abuse related to the dopaminergic transmission. Indeed, it is very intriguing that though benzodiazepines and alcohol share virtually the same behavioral effects, the symptoms observed after benzodiazepine administration seem not to be related to alterations in dopaminergic processes. Our understanding of the mechanisms of action of benzodiazepines, alcohol and nicotine has been significantly enhanced by the discovery of their brain targets, the GABA$_A$ and the nicotine receptors.

## THE GABAERGIC SYSTEM, BENZODIAZEPINES AND ALCOHOL

When benzodiazepine drugs were first introduced in the clinical practice, they were thought to be free of addictive properties, until the 1970's decade, when it was clear that these types of compounds could produce a withdrawal syndrome after its discontinuation. The study of benzodiazepines and its propensity to produce abstinence is a relevant matter, since a substantial proportion of patients that receive both high and normal doses of benzodiazepines will develop some form of physiological dependence (neuroadaptation induced by a prolonged exposure to the drug).

Benzodiazepines have been prescribed basically by their hypnotic and anxiolytic properties and, also, as sedatives, anticonvulsants, muscle-relaxants, and to treat the symptoms of alcohol withdrawal. However, despite the clinical advantages (mainly their minimal side-effects and a very low risk of overdose), during chronic administration it has been reported physiological withdrawal syndrome, following their abrupt discontinuation, and the return of the original anxiety in a more potent form (named rebound anxiety) sometimes accompanied by psychological (anxiety, irritability, insomnia) and physiological (tremor, palpitations, muscle spasms, gastrointestinal disturbances and even, in some cases, convulsions) symptoms. It has also been reported marked catatonia induced by benzodiazepine abstinence, with high doses and/or long term treatment. The increased anxiety symptoms are not so easy to differentiate from the original pathology, but they can be distinguished in terms of intensity and severity. It is worth mentioning that the high levels of anxiety, and the somatic and autonomic changes, present during abstinence are among the most powerful reasons for resuming drug intake.

Tolerance to benzodiazepines has been mainly attributed to metabolic (pharmacokinetic) or adaptive (pharmacodynamic) changes within the central nervous system after a prolonged exposure to the drug. These effects are mainly an attempt of the central nervous system to return to homeostasis, and keep its normal physiological function. It is considered that the physiological dependence leads to a pattern of physical withdrawal (somatic and autonomic alterations) symptoms, and that the psychological dependence reflects the powerful desire (craving) to obtain the drug during abstinence. Many theories have been elaborated to explain these types of adaptative processes. One of the most widely known argues that chronic drug administration leads to the initiation of adaptive processes that counteract the acute effects of the drug, and that these processes persist after the drug has been cleared from the brain, leaving the opposing forces unopposed (Figure 6).

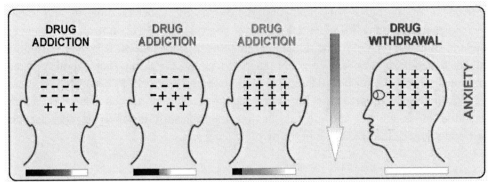

Figure 6. Schematic illustration of the main alterations induced by drug of abuse in the brain. In a "normal" condition, and regulated by homeostatic mechanisms, there is a balance between inhibitory and excitatory mechanisms. A long-term drug use (e.g. opioid drugs) leads to an enhancement of the excitatory systems in the brain, as opposed to the depressant effects of the drug. During abstinence, when the organism is drug-free, there is an overload in the brain areas where the drug acted induced by the excitatory mechanisms, mainly mediated by glutamate.

Up to now, not a single specific neurotransmitter binding site for alcohol in the brain has been identified, but it is thought that alcohol can affect the neuronal function by directly interacting with membrane proteins, such as receptors and ion channels. Current research also strongly suggests that alcohol, similar to other drugs of abuse such as benzodiazepines, affects multiple neurotransmitter systems in the brain, causing the neuron to react, by increasing or decreasing its normal functions. Research performed on the GABAergic system has demonstrated that both alcohol and benzodiazepines potentiate chloride influx induced by $GABA_A$ receptors in some regions of the brain. These types of effects can be blocked by previous administration of GABA antagonists, such as picrotoxin or bicuculline and even by benzodiazepine inverse agonists. However, it seems that the $GABA_B$ receptors are also involved in the alcohol effects. In fact, their blockade can powerfully enhance the acute effects of alcohol on $GABA_A$ receptor-mediated inhibitory postsynaptic currents (IPSCs) in the hippocampus of the rat. In this way, $GABA_B$ receptors seem to function as autoreceptors inhibiting $GABA_A$ IPSCs, suggesting that some $GABA_B$ receptor-dependent processes can play an important role in the alcohol sensitivity of GABAergic synapses.

The reinforcing effects of alcohol can explain its ability to function as discriminative stimulus in a lot of operant paradigms. In fact, alcohol is considered to be reinforcing because its ingestion, withdrawal following long-term use, or sometimes just the sight or smell of an alcoholic drink or associated cues, increase the drinking probability. These effects could be explained by the ability of alcohol to interact with the brain reward system, thus stimulating its continued use.

When alcohol is chronically administered, some neurons seem to adapt to its presence by enhancing or reducing their response to a normal stimuli, characterizing an organic form of tolerance. Also, chronic alcohol administration produces behavioral effects similar to that observed during chronic exposure to benzodiazepines and barbiturates. Indeed, chronic alcohol ingestion produces tolerance, dependence and a withdrawal syndrome after its interruption. These types of effects are associated with a decrease in the sensitivity of $GABA_A$ receptors in some areas of the brain, mainly the cerebral cortex, NAcc, the medial septal nucleus and, also, the spinal cord.

## THE OPIOID SYSTEM

Since 1806, when the German scientist Sertürner isolated morphine, a very important active principle of opium, this substance has been largely used in the entire world, basically by its anesthetic qualities. Morphine is a very potent analgesic, but it is as addictive as opium. Indeed, besides its analgesic effects, its acute administration produces euphoria, drowsiness and, in a chronic administration, it has a high potential to produce dependence.

The existence of endogenous opioid-like molecules produced by the organism itself was demonstrated in 1970's, from the observation that the mammalian brain extracts possess opiate-like activity. This fact has stimulated the researches in this field, leading to the isolation and characterization of endogenous opioid peptides, such as the enkephalins (leu- and met-enkephalin), β-endorphins and dynorphins, each one of them derived from its precursors molecules Proenkephalin A (ProEnk), Pro-opiomelanocortin (POMC) and Proenkephalin B, also known by Prodynorphin (ProDyn), respectively.

Tolerance to opioids develops rapidly, although not all their pharmacological effects change with the same speed and magnitude. For example, whereas the analgesic and euphoric effects suffer rapid tolerance, miosis and constipation persist even after prolonged (chronic) use. The level of tolerance depends upon the frequency of use and doses of the drug. After three or four months of use, the dose consumed can be ten times higher than the initial. In fact, the dose utilized by a regular user can be enough to kill a non-tolerant user.

Tolerance to opioid substances seems to be mainly pharmacodynamic since the cells virtually "adapt themselves" to the drug presence. The chronic administration of opioids just moderately reduces the number of opioid receptors *in vivo*. For example, after 6 days of subcutaneous administration of morphine in guinea pigs, the number of μ receptors is 25% reduced, with no alterations in the number of δ or κ receptors. Therefore, the tolerance to opioids is not exclusively linked to the down-regulation of receptors, but mainly to the desensitization process.

Conditioning processes have also been implicated in the development of tolerance to opioids. An environmental stimulus associated with morphine administration elicits compensatory responses. This can be confirmed by some experiments in which rats have received morphine chronic treatment in a distinct environment. The tolerance to the analgesic effects occurred only when the animals were tested in the same context in which they had received the drug, but not when they were tested in a different context.

All the opioid substances produce psychological and physiological dependence expressed, respectively, by the emergence of affective and physical withdrawal symptoms, when the chronic administration of the drug is abruptly discontinued. These symptoms are so unpleasant that they constitute the most important factor that leads the user to persist taking the drug. The physical signs are restlessness, agitation, yawning and chills and a lot of autonomic and somatic changes. The severity of these symptoms depends on the dose utilized, the frequency of administration and the time of drug use. This set of symptoms is accompanied by emotional alterations, such as depression, irritability and high levels of anxiety. The peak of these symptoms generally occurs 26 h after the last administration and disappears between 7 to 10 days. During the abstinence phase, opioid administration blocks all symptoms. It is believed that the withdrawal syndrome occurs when the opioid receptors stop being occupied with the opioid. For this reason, the administration of an opioid antagonist, as naloxone, that removes abruptly the opioid from its receptors, promotes a withdrawal syndrome more severe than that caused by the simple abstinence of the drug.

## OPIOID REINFORCEMENT, DEPENDENCE AND WITHDRAWAL EFFECTS

There is some evidence showing that the positive reinforcement produced by opioids depends on the opioid receptors activation in the ventral tegmental area (VTA) and in the NAcc. In this way, rats rapidly learn to press a lever to get morphine injections in the VTA, but not in other areas. Besides, morphine microinjection in the VTA facilitates the intracranial self-stimulation (ICSS) and induces conditioned place preference (CPP). It is believed that exogenous opioids produce its positive reinforcement effects through activation of $\mu$ receptors present in the VTA, specifically. The same phenomenon is observed in the NAcc, but this type of behavior requires higher doses of morphine than the ones that maintain the self-administration in the VTA. Similarly to what occurs in the VTA, blockade of $\mu$ or activation of $\kappa$ receptors in the NAcc results in conditioned place aversion (Box 2).

It is believed that many brain regions are responsible for the development and expression of opioid dependence. Studies with microinjection of opioid antagonists in specific brain areas of opioid-dependent animals have been conducted to identify the structures involved in the physical and affective symptoms of abstinence.

The brain structures involved in the physical dependence to opioids seem to be, mainly, the locus coeruleus, central gray and lateral hypothalamus, since the administration of naloxone or metylnaloxonium (a hydrophilic opioid antagonist that is not quickly spread out in the brain), directly in these areas, precipitates the somatic symptoms of withdrawal in morphine-dependent animals.

On the contrary, microinjections of opioid antagonists in the VTA and, especially, in the NAcc and amygdala, precipitate only affective signs of abstinence in dependent animals, expressed by the conditioned aversion to the place, associated with the withdrawal. Moreover, the induction of the affective symptoms of morphine abstinence is correlated with increased activity of neurons in the central nucleus of amygdala and the NAcc (shell).

The chronic use of opioids produces changes in the endogenous opioid systems. In a clinical study, it was observed that human addicts in heroine present plasmatic levels of $\beta$-endorphin about 3 times lesser than normal subjects, suggesting that the endorphin system in chronic addicts in heroine is depressed. Morphine-dependent rats present diminished levels of $\beta$-endorphin in the plasma, pituitary, hypothalamus and mesencephalon. Thus, the tolerance to the analgesic effect of morphine, for example, could be developed because the reduction in the levels of endogenous opioids would imply in the necessity of greater amounts of morphine to inhibit the transmission in the pain pathways. In this point, abrupt withdrawal of morphine, in conjunction with low levels of endogenous opioid peptides, would disinhibit pain fibers, producing a typical symptom of withdrawal, the hyperalgesia. The same reasoning can be applied to other symptoms of abstinence.

Besides its crucial role in the mediation of positive reinforcing effects of the opioids, alterations in the mesolimbic dopaminergic system are also responsible for the expression of withdrawal symptoms. In morphine-dependent animals, the withdrawal of the drug reduces the rate of firing of the VTA-NAcc neurons in about 30%, decreasing significantly the amount of dopamine released in the NAcc, what possibly is correlated with the affective symptoms of abstinence. However, the importance of the decrease in dopaminergic activity during the expression of physical dependence to opioids also must be considered, since the somatic symptoms of withdrawal can be induced after the blockade of $D_2$ receptors in the NAcc, or reduced by its activation. As the administration of opioid antagonists in the NAcc does not precipitate somatic symptoms of abstinence, it becomes clear that this structure is not part of the main brain sites for the induction of physical dependence, but it can have an important role in the regulation of the circuits that fire the somatic and affective responses during the opioid withdrawal. The expressive reduction in the release of dopamine in the mesolimbic dopaminergic system can be influenced by the hyperactivity of the noradrenergic system, which exerts an inhibitory influence on the mesencephalic dopaminergic neurons. However, the relations among these systems still need to be elucidated.

## MARIJUANA, LYSERGIC ACID AND ECSTASY

Marijuana is one of the most utilized drugs of abuse in the world, even today. Its scientific name is *cannabis sativa* and the main chemical substance responsible for its psychomimetic effects is Δ-9-tetrahydrocannabinol (THC). The effects that marijuana produces in the central nervous system can be divided in physical and psychic effects. Its ingestion leads to very few physical effects like hyperemia, dry mouth and tachycardia Psychological effects will depend on the type of marijuana smoked, and the personal characteristics of the smoker, but generally feelings of welfare, calm, and easy laughing may appear (however, for some people the effects can be disagreeable and the individual may feel anxious, fearful of losing control, trembling and sweating). There is still evident disturbance in the person's capacity for calculating time and space, and also attention deficit and damages in learning and memory capacity. These types of cognitive deficiencies seem to persist after withdrawal. In few cases, chronic ingestion of marijuana produces paranoia and panic disorder.

So far, some studies have identified two cannabinoid-like receptors, the first named Type 1, CB1 (and another possible subtype called CB1A that mediates the acute effects of cannabinoids, as well as the development of tolerance) found in the brain, and the second, named type CB2, found in the immune system. CB1 receptors are found in highest concentration, in the brain neurons, are coupled via G proteins, and modulate adenylate cyclase and ion channels. CB2 receptors are found in cells of the immune system, are also coupled via G proteins, but inhibit adenylate cyclase. The CB1 receptor and its variant CB1A, are found mainly in the hippocampus, cerebellum and striatum. The CB2 receptor is found predominantly in the spleen and in haemopoietic cells, what could explain the immunosuppressive actions of marijuana. Similar to endogenous opiates, there is much evidence of the existence of an endogenous ligand for marijuana receptors in the brain, called *anandamide*. It is important to note that marijuana, as well as other drugs of abuse, also seems to generate its effects by increasing the activity of dopaminergic neurons in the VTA.

LSD is an abbreviation of diethylamide of lysergic acid, a synthetic drug that produces intense hallucinations when ingested, and is perhaps the most powerful psychedelic drug ever produced. LSD acts in the brain, producing a series of perceptual distortions that include hallucinations, illusions and disorders of thinking such as paranoia. Similarly to marijuana, its effects can be dependent on contextual and personal factors. In this way, some individuals experiment high excitation and euphoria while others become quiet and passive. LSD does not commonly lead to dependence, and there is not description of an abstinence syndrome if its chronic use is abruptly interrupted.

The chemical effects of LSD are not well understood, but several studies have demonstrated that LSD affects the serotoninergic systems in the brain. In this context, several proposals have emerged. One of them states that LSD is a serotonin (5-HT) receptor antagonist, acting specifically through these receptors, mainly in prosenchephalic structures, blocking 5-HT2 receptors, thus preventing the usual effects of 5-HT. Another possibility is that LSD is actually a 5-HT agonist instead of an antagonist, and also that LSD effects can be the result of 5-HT1 receptors in higher brain structures, which may result in an enhancement of positive mood state, such as euphoria and mood changes.

Ecstasy is the generic name of 3-4methylenedioxymethamphetamine (MDMA), a synthetic derivative of amphetamine that has stimulant, hallucinogenic and mood-improving qualities. Initially this substance was used basically as appetite moderator. To some authors, ecstasy should be considered as a central nervous system stimulant, like cocaine and amphetamine, but it is classified as a psychedelic drug by virtue of its potential for provoking hallucinations. As all psychomimetics, ecstasy is capable of promoting auditory, visual or tactile hallucinations and, at high doses, depersonalization, illusions and floating sensations, among other effects. Besides, the drug also increases the heart rate and blood pressure. Other symptoms such as dry mouth, loss of appetite and euphoria may also appear. During its continuous use the pleasurable affects tend to diminish while the negative ones (confusion, depression anxiety and paranoia) enhance.

Ecstasy is normally consumed in a pill form, and once it reaches its targets in the central nervous system, it virtually causes an explosion of 5-HT in the synapses, increasing the firing of post-synaptic neurons, faster than any other process. Together with serotonin changes, ecstasy also promotes a bizarre functioning of 5-HT transporters which tend to capture dopamine molecules in a neuron where they do not belong. Because dopamine is extremely harmful to serotonin cells, this reuptake error leads to a neural toxicity.

## STRESS, ANXIETY AND RELAPSE

Selye (1975) defined stress as the non-specific response of the body to any demand placed upon it to adapt, whether that demand produces pleasure or aversion. In any case, the sympathetic nervous system and the hypothalamic-pituitary adrenal axis are typically activated leading to an increase in the heart rate, rise in the blood pressure and a blood flow to skeletal muscles, increase in the blood glucose and rate of respiration, and dilatation of pupils, preparing the organism for flight or fight, when faced with the stressor.

The characteristic signs of the withdrawal or discontinuity of chronic use of psychostimulants, like d-amphetamine, courses with significant molecular adaptations in the neuronal circuitry of mesolimbic system, such as physiological alterations in the dopaminergic neurons that regulate motivational and emotional processes. This assumption may have a relationship with the fact that some stressful events also stimulate the dopaminergic mesolimbic system. Thus, the same dopaminergic circuits responsible for the pleasurable effects of a given drug acting on the mesolimbic system may also underlie the aversive effects of the drug withdrawal (see Box 3). It has been shown that the characteristic signs of the withdrawal or discontinuity of chronic use of psychostimulants, like d-amphetamine, courses with significant molecular adaptations in the neuronal circuitry of mesolimbic system, such as physiological alterations in the dopaminergic neurons that regulate motivational and emotional processes related to drug abstinence. In this context, it has been firmly demonstrated the ability of a variety of stressors to facilitate the acquisition of a drug self-administration procedure in rats. Rats exposed to tail-pinch, foot-shocks, social defeat, or neonatal isolation procedures, rapidly learn to self-administrate psychostimulants, such as cocaine and amphetamine, and opioids, such as morphine and heroin. In humans, it has been well documented that the reward effect of a drug is powerfully potentiated in individuals with previous history of stress. In fact, previous exposure to stressful situations is a strong factor that could lead an individual to relapse more easily, mainly because, as we shall see, withdrawal of drugs of abuse generates a lot of symptoms of somatic, autonomic and affective aversive nature. The conjunction of all these symptoms plus previous aversive experiences make the individual more predisposed to relapse after a long-term drug use.

In theory, it has been suggested that abstinence of many drugs of abuse that generate dependence, such as benzodiazepines, psychostimulants and opioids, also promotes a lot of aversive symptoms, as dysphoria and irritability accompanied by sensorial and autonomic alterations, similar to those verified in the anxiety. The abrupt discontinuation of a chronic treatment with diazepam, for example, results in a marked withdrawal syndrome characterized by high level of anxiety, insomnia, tremors, weight loss, muscle rigidity, sensorial disturbances and, sometimes, convulsion. These responses are the result of alterations in the $GABA_A$ receptor complex (as the self-administration of diazepam in rats is blocked after systemic injections of GABAergic or benzodiazepine antagonist) and, differently from other drugs of abuse, the emergence of these symptoms seems not to be related to changes in the release of dopamine in the mesolimbic system. In this way, it seems that the behavioral, sensorial and autonomic effects, consequent of benzodiazepine abstinence can be related to the activation of other systems of neurotransmitters, such as the glutamatergic and serotonergic. In fact, pharmacological experiments that utilize specific agonists and antagonists of glutamate receptors have confirmed that mechanisms mediated by excitatory aminoacids can underlie the expression of symptoms of benzodiazepine withdrawal. As an example, previous administration of GYKI-52466 (AMPA antagonist) prevents while CPP (NMDA antagonist) blocks anxiety, convulsion, and muscle spasms induced by withdrawal from chronic treatment with diazepam. These responses are initially modulated by AMPA receptors that, once activated, recruit NMDA receptors, resulting in the expression of withdrawal symptoms. Other studies have demonstrated that alterations promoted by benzodiazepine withdrawal are consequence of a deficit on the GABAergic inhibition exerted by the basolateral amigdaloid nucleus on central nucleus neurons. Chronic administration of benzodiazepines leads also to a decrease of the GABA ability to inhibit serotoninergic neurons, leading to an increase in its release in the basolateral amygdaloid nucleus. Thus, the altered states of fear and anxiety observed during withdrawal from benzodiazepines could be the consequence of a reduction of the control promoted by the neurons of the basolateral amygdala, on the neurons of the central nucleus. The central nucleus neurons project to midbrain areas mainly involved in the somatic and autonomic expression of fear and anxiety such as the periaqueductal gray. This structure participates actively in the expression of fear and defensive behaviors, as well as in vocalization and stress-induced analgesia.

Abstinence from opioids, such as morphine, also causes a similar pattern of affective and homeostatic imbalance. Some studies have demonstrated, for example, that abrupt interruption of opioids, in dependent humans, provokes irritability and extreme anxiety. In animals, opioid abstinence promotes anxiogenic effects in the plus-maze and conditioned place aversion.

The μ opioid receptors seem to have a fundamental role in the opioid addiction, as the knock-out mouse for this receptor do not present withdrawal symptoms after interruption of chronic morphine treatment. Other studies have revealed the involvement of neuropeptides, such as substance P, in the modulation of aversive effects induced by opioid withdrawal. In fact, it is well known that the reward effects of morphine are absent in the knock-out mouse for NK1 neurokininergic receptor. Besides, these receptors are expressed in great number in brain regions involved in depression and anxiety, as well as in other regions, such as the NAcc, that mediates the motivational properties of drugs of abuse, including opioids. There is also much evidence showing that NK1 receptors could be involved in the morphine-related reward processes.

All of these studies pointed out that the abrupt interruption of chronic ingestion of drug of abuse, that has mainly a negative reinforcing effect, induces an homeostatic imbalance leading, as a consequence, to the emergence of a great variety of symptoms, amongst which a pronounced increase in anxiety levels that could underlie the compulsive motivational behavior (craving) observed during withdrawal from drugs of abuse. Still, it is suggested that the symptoms observed during withdrawal from drugs of abuse, that are commonly observed in animals exposed to aversive stimulation, as for instance when facing natural predators, or after electrical or chemical stimulation of brainstem regions belonging to the so-called brain aversive system, such as the amygdala, medial hypothalamus and dorsal periaqueductal may share the same neurobiological mechanisms that are involved in anxiety/fear and, probably, in characteristic aversive states of the withdrawal from drug of abuse. These elements have been taken into account in an integrative model of drug dependence, outlined below.

# A THEORETICAL MODEL OF DRUG ABUSE

In the view of the operant learning theory, drug use can be viewed as a behavior that is maintained by its consequences. Consequences that strengthen a behavior pattern are reinforcers. Some drugs may reinforce the antecedent drug-taking behavior by terminating some aversive or unpleasant situation (negative reinforcement), as for example, when they alleviate pain or anxiety. Likewise, drugs may reinforce drug abuse by inducing pleasurable effects (positive reinforcement). It has been proposed that the same neural system is responsible for both the negative and positive reinforcing aspects of drug abuse. To support this assumption it appears that people take drugs primarily to avoid the discomfort of drug withdrawal rather than to experience pleasure. Dopaminergic projections from the VTA to the NAcc seem to be the main component of this system. Based on this view, the NAcc would be the main target for both psychostimulant and opiate reinforcement, with both classes activating the dopaminergic pathways linking these two brain structures.

Most studies that have implicated dopamine mechanisms in the reinforcing effects of drugs have used animal models that measure the direct self-administration of the drug, its effects on reward thresholds using intracranial self-stimulation in the medial forebrain bundle, particularly in its connections with the NAcc, and measure also the preferences for the environment paired with the drug administration (place preference). It has been found that psychostimulants and opiate drugs are self-administered intravenously. Decrease in the dose of drugs available to the animal will change the pattern of self-administration so that the interinjection interval decreases and the number of injections increase. Selective agonists and antagonists of these drugs decrease or increase the self-administration respectively, as if the rats were trying to compensate for the gain or the reduction in the reinforcement magnitude. Lesion of the NAcc, with 6-hydroxidopamine, produces a significant reduction in cocaine self-administration. This effect seems to be due to a cooperative action of dopamine on D1 and D2 receptors in the NAcc. Likewise, cocaine injected acutely has been reported to lower self-stimulation thresholds in rats. During cocaine withdrawal following prolonged use, reward thresholds are elevated. Thresholds of intracranial self-stimulation have been hypothesized to reflect the hedonic state of an animal because the animal will readily self-administer stimulation to its own brain. Intracranial self-stimulation is thought to activate the same neural substrates that mediate the reinforcing effects of natural reinforcers (e.g., water and food). Thus, it has been suggested by these findings, that cocaine can alter the function of the reward system in the medial forebrain bundle, and that during the course of cocaine withdrawal, there may be some hypoactivity in the functioning of the dopaminergic reward system.

Regarding opiates drugs, it has been shown that heroin, similarly to cocaine, is readily self-administered intravenously by rats. Rats have been found to maintain stable levels of drug intake on a daily basis, without any major indices of physical dependence. Likewise cocaine decreases in the doses of heroin available to the animal change the pattern of self-administration, i.e. the interinjection interval decreases and the number of injections increases. Similar increases in the number of injections have been obtained by both systemic and central administration of competitive opiate antagonists, such as methylnaloxoniun in the NAcc, suggesting that the animals attempt to compensate for the opiate antagonism, by increasing the amount of drug injected. Opiates are self-administered directly into the source of the mesolimbic dopamine system, the ventral tegmental area, and microinjections of opioids into the VTA lower brain stimulation reward thresholds and produce significant place preference.

It has also been shown that rats self-administer opioid peptides into the region of the nucleus accumbens. Furthermore, place preferences produced by opioids appear to have a major dopaminergic component. These results suggest that neural elements in the region of the nucleus accumbens are responsible for both the reinforcing properties of opiates and psychostimulants. However, the neurochemical mechanisms of these effects seem to be different. Rats trained to self-administer cocaine and heroin every day, receiving 6-hydroxidopamine (6-OHDA) lesions of the NAcc, have shown a time-dependent decrease or extinction of cocaine self-administration, whereas heroin self-administration was not disturbed by this procedure. Thus, the reinforcing actions of opiates may involve both a dopamine-dependent (VTA) and dopamine independent (NAcc) mechanism.

From the evidence obtained so far, it has not been possible to define clearly the neural substrates of the negative reinforcing properties of opiate withdrawal. As stated in the beginning of this chapter, dependence on opiate drugs is defined by a characteristic withdrawal syndrome that appears with the abrupt termination of the opiate administration, or that can be precipitated by the administration of competitive opiate antagonists. Opiate withdrawal in humans is characterized by both motivational symptoms and physical correlates such as nausea, gastrointestinal disturbances, chills, sympathetic reactions, painful flu-like dysphoric state, anxiety, depression, anhedonia, dysphoria, and drug craving. As these subjective symptoms are shared by several drugs of abuse, such as alcohol, morphine, cocaine and amphetamine, and based on the fact that in general, during precipitated withdrawal syndrome of these drugs, a dopamine reduction occurs in the NAcc, it has been suggested that a common neurochemical substrate may underlie the aversive subjective symptoms of drugs of abuse. In rats, opiate physical dependence has been characterized by an abstinence syndrome that includes the appearance of ptosis, teeth chattering, wet dog shakes and diarrhea, and this syndrome can be dramatically precipitated in dependent animals by systemic injections of opiate antagonists. Among motivational measures, the disruption of trained operant behavior for food reward, and the development of place aversion following precipitated withdrawal with systemic opiate antagonist administration have been studied.

In opposition to the notion of a same neural system underlying positive and negative reinforcement, it has been proposed that there are two distinct brain systems responsible for drug induced pleasure, and the alleviation of aversive stimulation. A schematic diagram of the functioning of these neural systems is depicted in Figure 7. This assumption in based on the observation that non dependent on morphine rats self-administer the drug directly in the VTA, in the absence of subsequent concomitants of abstinence. However, repeated administration of morphine into the periaqueductal gray, but not VTA, causes withdrawal syndrome after challenge with the opioid antagonist naloxone. Thus, drugs of abuse apparently act on this VTA-NAcc pathway to potentiate the drug taking behavior. On the other hand, opiate drugs act in the periaqueductal gray to alleviate three kinds of pain – physical pain, pain of loneliness and social withdrawal, and drug-induced pain of opiate withdrawal. It has been well documented that separate brain sites are responsible for the motivational symptoms and physical correlates of opiate withdrawal, and that some physical correlates may be mediated by peripheral (gut) opiate receptors. For example, the search for neural substrates for motivational symptoms and physical correlates of the withdrawal syndrome has identified several brain structures as being particularly important. Microinjection of methylnaloxoniun into the periaqueductal gray and locus coeruleus precipitates withdrawal syndrome in opiate-dependent rats, characterized by jumping, rearing, and increased locomotor activity. In a recent study using the place aversion paradigm by pairing methylnaloxoniun injection in several brain sites of dependent rats with a particular environment, it has been found that NAcc is the most sensitive site for the intracerebral injections of methylnaloxoniun produce place aversion in dependent rats. In view of these results, it has been suggested that the neurobiological basis for the motivational symptoms is localized in the NAcc, while the physical correlates may be mainly localized in regions such as the periaqueductal gray and *locus coeruleus*.

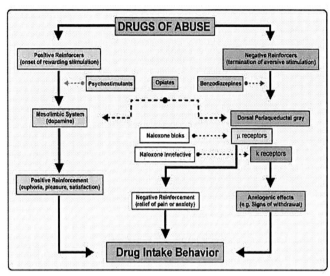

Figure 7. A hypothetical model of drug dependence.

From what has been discussed in this chapter it is clear that the positive and negative reinforcing effects of opioids seem to be mediated by different neural systems. In each system, the drug effects also depend on the type of opioid receptor on which it interacts. Activation of μ or δ receptors induces conditioned preference place in the NAcc. Injection of low doses of morphine, directly in the periaqueductal gray, activates only μ receptors and attenuates the aversive consequence of the electrical stimulation of this structure. On the other hand, the activation of κ or the blockade of μ receptors promotes conditioned place aversion. In function of these results many studies have suggested the involvement of opioid mechanisms in the modulation of the aversive behavior in the dorsal mesencephalon. Both autonomic and behavioral consequences, resultant of electrical stimulation of this region are attenuated by the administration of minor tranquilizers, probably through facilitation of GABAergic neurotransmission, that exert a tonic inhibitory control over the neural circuits responsible for the mediation and expression of the defensive behaviors elicited by stimulation of this brain region. Thus it is likely that several neurotransmitters systems may interact to produce the complex array of actions inherent to the positive and negative reinforcing effects of drugs of abuse.

# BOX 1. DOPAMINE RECEPTORS

Dopamine is a neurotransmitter that acts as a modulator of the neuronal activity, regulating important and different functions in the brain, such as sensory perception (in the retina and olfactory bulb), prolactin release in the pituitary gland, body temperature, food intake and sexual behavior in the hypothalamus, tuning of sensory motor cues in the basal ganglia, and importantly, the maintenance and expression of qualitative values of novelty in life experiences and, thus motivation and aversion. Dopamine belongs to a group of neurotransmitters called catecholamines. The precursor for the synthesis of DA is the aromatic amino acid tyrosine that is transformed in L-DOPA (L-3,4-dyhidroxyphenylalanine) by the enzyme tyrosine hydroxilase. The decarboxylation of L-DOPA by the enzyme aromatic L-amino acid decarboxylase transforms L-DOPA in dopamine.

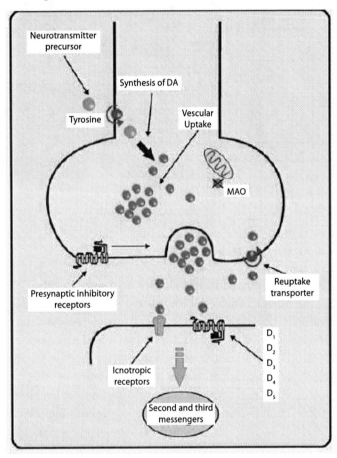

Figure A. Schematic representation of a dopaminergic (DA) synapse with the main steps involved in the neurotransmission. It can be seen the synthesis of DA from the amino acid tyrosine (TH) and the storage of DA in vesicles on the pre-synaptic neuron. On the synaptic cleft it is depicted the releasing of the neurotransmitter by exocytose, interaction of the neurotransmitter with the various receptors located on the post-synaptic neuron membrane. The enzymatic degradation of DA by the monoamine oxidase (MAO) and reuptake transporter sites are illustrated on the pre-synaptic neuron. Five types of DA receptors located on the post-synaptic neuron membrane are also indicated (D1, D2. D3, D4, D5).

Drugs of abuse produce their effects interacting with autoreceptors or postsynaptic dopaminergic receptors. There are, at least, five dopamine receptors (D1 to D5), divided in two subfamilies based on its pharmacological and biochemical properties, the D1-like (D1, D5) and the D2-like (D2, D3, D4) receptors. The D1-like receptors (D1 and D5) show pharmacological properties similar to those of the original pharmacologically defined D1 receptor, that is, a high affinity for selective antagonists of this subtype, SCH 23390 and SKF 83566. These receptors also show moderate affinity for typical and selective dopamine agonists, such as apomorphine and SKF 82526, respectively. A D1 receptor antagonist prevents the activation of the dopamine D1 receptor. The D1 receptor is coupled to stimulatory G-proteins, which dissociate from the receptor due to agonist binding, and initiate secondary messenger signaling mechanisms and stimulation of adenylyl cyclase. This causes cell depolarization, which is inhibited by antagonist binding. High levels of D1 receptors are found in the typical dopamine rich neurons of the brain, such as the neostriatum, substantia nigra, NAcc and tubercle olfactory, whereas the distribution of D5 receptors has a much more restricted distribution, and is not well understood.

The D2 receptors are the predominant D2-like subtypes in the brain and are found at high levels in dopamine brain areas. D3 and D4 receptors are found at much lower levels, in a more restricted distribution pattern and almost predominantly in limbic areas of the brain. The D2 receptor is coupled to inhibitory G-proteins, which dissociate from the receptor, due to agonist binding, and inhibit secondary messenger signaling mechanisms. In this way, a D2 receptor antagonist prevents the activation of the dopamine D2 receptor, causing inhibition of down-stream signaling mechanisms. Contrary to the D1-, the D2-like dopamine receptors have been shown to inhibit adenylyl cyclase. This type of receptor is important for mediating the effects of dopamine to control movement, some aspects of behavior in the brain and the prolactin secretion. Whilst the functions of the D3 and D4 receptors are less known, their localization in the limbic areas suggest that they play a role in cognitive, emotional and behavioral functions. The mesolimbic dopaminergic pathway has been implicated in the control of reward mechanisms and in the psychomotor effects of drugs of abuse. This is extended not only to drugs that affect directly the DA receptors, such as cocaine or amphetamines, but also to opiates and alcohol. Cocaine and amphetamines are the most common drugs that affect the DA pathways in the brain, and these drugs reach their effects in a similar manner.

## BOX 2. THE REINFORCING PROPERTIES OF OPIOIDS ALSO DEPEND OF OTHER NEUROTRANSMITTERS

Lots of evidence has implicated the mesolimbic dopaminergic system, specially the VTA – NAcc pathway, in the reinforcing effects of opioids. Intra-VTA morphine or intracerebroventricular β-endorphin microinjections increase the cell firing of dopaminergic neurons in the VTA and, consequently, increase DA release in the NAcc. This increase is mediated by μ receptors located in the cell bodies of VTA neurons. In contrast, the κ receptors activation in NAcc produces the opposite effect, reducing the local DA activity at the same time that produces conditioned place aversion. In agreement with studies utilizing specific dopaminergic ligands, several research groups have proposed that the tonic release of DA, activating mainly $D_1$ receptors in the NAcc, is necessary to maintain a neutral motivational state. Any alteration that reduces the DA activity mediated by $D_1$ receptors in this region, for example, the κ pre-synaptic receptors activation in the NAcc, produces aversive effects. On the other hand, any alteration that increases the DA activity, such as the activation of the μ receptors in the VTA, promotes positive reinforcement.

The involvement of dopamine in the opioid reinforcement has been widely confirmed. Neurotoxic lesions of the DA neurons in VTA or NAcc, produced by the neurotoxin 6-OHDA, reduce the CPP induced by μ agonists, as well as the conditioned aversion induced by κ agonists. However, while the self-administration of psychostimulants, like cocaine and amphetamine, is eliminated by VTA and NAcc 6-OHDA lesions, self-administration of heroin is only partially reduced, suggesting the involvement of other neurotransmitter systems in the mediation of the positive reinforcement effects of opioids.

Excitatory amino acids (EAA) seem also to have some involvement in the mediation of opioid reinforcement, but their function is less known. In models of ICSS and self-administration, the blockade of NMDA receptors increases the reinforcing effects of morphine and inhibits the CPP induced by the same drug, perhaps in virtue of the deleterious effects of the NMDA antagonists on learning.

The positive reinforcing effects of opioids must be also dependent on the cholecystokinin (CCK) action, which seems to produce different effects depending on the type of receptor that is activated. The activation of CCK-A receptors favors the establishment of the opioid reinforcement, while the activation of CCK-B receptors disrupts it. However, secure conclusions about this are difficult, because negative results about the role of CCK-B receptors in the opioid reinforcement have just been reported.

Other neurotransmitter systems are probably involved in the positive reinforcing effects of opioids. Histamine, for example, inhibits the positive reinforcement produced by morphine. On the other hand, substance P, acting on NK1 receptors, stimulates the rewarding processes related to morphine. The rewarding effects of morphine are absent in knock-out mice lacking the NK1 receptor. Moreover, these receptors are expressed in brain regions such as the NAcc that mediates the motivational properties of opioids. Serotonin seems to facilitate the reinforcing action of opioids. The NAcc is possibly, the main region involved in this effect, as suggested by the fact that lesions of 5-HT terminals in this area inhibit the CPP induced by morphine.

The development of the opioid dependence is characterized by alterations in other neurotransmitter systems. Much evidence also implicates the noradrenergic system in the expression of the physical dependence. In this respect, the most important cerebral area seems to be the *locus coeruleus*, the greatest group of noradrenergic neurons in the brain. This is the most sensitive region for the precipitation of physical symptoms of withdrawal after microinjection of metylnaloxonium, in dependent animals. The acute morphine administration, that activates $\mu$ receptors, hyperpolarizes the neurons of the *locus coeruleus*, reducing the release of noradrenaline (NA) in some areas of the CNS. With its chronic use, it develops tolerance for this effect and normalization of the NA release. During the opioid withdrawal occurs the rebound effect on the release of NA that increases significantly, mainly due to hyperactivity of the *locus coeruleus*. This increase is correlated with the occurrence of the somatic symptoms of abstinence.

The $\alpha_2$-adrenergic agonists, that inhibit the activity of the *locus coeruleus* neurons, just by acting in inhibitory autoreceptors, reduce the autonomic manifestations and the majority of the somatic symptoms of abstinence. Beyond its role in the physical dependence, the NA system also seems to be involved in the psychological dependence of opioids. In fact, affective symptoms of abstinence, expressed by the conditioned aversion to the place associated with the withdrawal, are blocked by the reduction of the central NA activity, through the administration of $\alpha_2$-adrenergic agonists or $\beta$-adrenergic antagonists.

The hyperactivation of *locus coeruleus* during the morphine withdrawal could be due, mainly, to the afferent excitatory projections, even though intrinsic modifications, consisting in an "up-regulation" of the CAMP pathway, can also be involved. It is believed that these afferent projections originate from the paragigantocelullaris nucleus that excites the *locus coeruleus* neurons through EAA release. The EAA favors the expression of physical dependence of opioids, as the blockade of NMDA receptors attenuates the severity of the somatic symptoms of withdrawal in dependent animals. Moreover, NMDA antagonists also prevent the development of physical dependence when administered together with morphine. The EAA also seems to contribute to the psychological dependence, since the blockade of NMDA receptors reduces the affective symptoms of morphine abstinence.

# BOX 3. THE SPIRALING DISTRESS MODEL

As noted earlier in this chapter the establishment of drug dependence involves the raise of an adaptive process aimed to counter the acute effects of the drug that persist even after the end of the drug treatment. In this condition, to inhibit the action of the drug in the brain there are the raise of neural processes with opposed signs that counteract the drug action so as when the drug administration is interrupted the withdrawal symptoms are expressed.

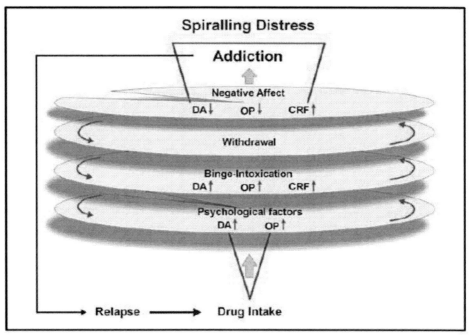

Figure B. The spiraling distress model of drug abuse. This model has been proposed by Koob and Le Moal (1997) to explain the involvement of different neural systems in the addiction cycle. The main site for the positive reinforcing effects of drugs of abuse (including psychostimulants, opiates, nicotine, cannabinoids and alcohol) is the mesolimbic dopaminergic system. Initially, there is an enhancement in the activity of this system. During drug withdrawal the brain reward function may be depressed in that the absence of the drug leads to several negative emotional-motivational states as dysphoria, stress, anxiety and even depression. In parallel with a decrease in dopamine levels there is also a decrease in opioid peptides, 5-HT, GABA levels with a concomitant increase in glutamatergic transmission and in CRF levels. DA: dopamine; OP:opioid peptides; CRF: corticotrophin releasing factor.

As proposed by Koob and Le Moal (1997), drug addiction is not only a static or unitary phenomenon but mainly a composition of several elements that constitutes what he called an ever-growing spiral-like pathology. In this case, multiple sources of reinforcement are identified in this cycle suggesting addiction as a break in the homeostatic organic levels induced by a dysregulation in the hedonic homeostatic process. During this process changes in the levels of some neurohormones and neurotransmitters systems have been identified suggesting an organic substrate for addiction that could mediate the appearance of addiction and the symptoms of withdrawal.

The theory considers three main components of the addiction cycle named *preoccupation-anticipation, binge-intoxication and withdrawal negative affects*. Each one of these constructs is linked to specific sources of reinforcement and different neurochemical and endocrine systems that, together, could explain the addiction cycle in a spiraling distress model used to describe the progressive imbalance of the brain-reward dopaminergic-system induced by the continuity of the addiction cycle. It is also possible that the cues present during drug ingestion can generate a secondary reinforcing-like effect, through Pavlovian conditioning. In this context, all the cues present during drug ingestion will be summed up to the drug effects.

It is well-known that the mesocorticolimbic system is the main responsible by the positive-reinforcing effects of drugs of abuse, as demonstrated by the fact that drugs such as opioids and psychostimulants enhance the dopamine transmission in this system. The major components of this circuit are the basal forebrain (mainly composed by NAcc, amygdala, limbic and frontal cortices) and the VTA (A10), the most important source of dopamine in the brain. There are also the presence of opioid peptides, GABA, glutamate and 5-HT neurons in this system.

Stress also plays an important role in the development of addiction since it is well demonstrated that individuals submitted to stressful events or with a previous history of stress are predisposed to drug dependence.

The state of stress induces a lot of physiological changes, amongst them the activation of the hypothalamic-pituitary-adrenal axis, which leads to an increase in the glucocorticoid levels in the bloodstream, the activation of the sympathetic system and the appearance of an emotional behavior in virtue of the activation of the brain emotional systems. The negative reinforcing effect of drugs of abuse is believed to occur through the alleviation of an existing aversive state (e.g. stress, pathological anxiety, or anxiety induced by withdrawal).

The spiraling distress model proposed by Koob assumes that the positive reinforcing effects are largely associated with the binge-intoxication stage and the negative one with negative affects that raise during withdrawal condition. Indeed, withdrawal of drugs of abuse leads to the expression of many negative affective states (a homeostatic dysregulation of the reward systems), amongst which extreme anxiety and a parallel activation of the stress system in the brain. These counteradaptative within-system changes include decreases in dopamine and opiate levels associated with decreases in GABA functions and increase in the glutamatergic transmission in the NAcc during abstinence.

## REFERENCES

Alexander EJ. Withdrawal effects of sodium amytal. *Dis Nerv Syst* 12:77-82, 1951.

Ariwodola OJ, Weiner JL. Ethanol potentiation of GABAergic synaptic transmission may be self-limiting: role of presynaptic GABA(B) receptors. *J Neurosci* 24:10679-10686, 2004.

Bals-Kubik R, Ableitner A, Herz A, Shippenberg TS. Neuroanatomical sites mediating the motivational effects of opioids as mapped by the conditioned place preference paradigm in rats. *J Pharmacol Exp Ther* 264:489-495, 1993.

Bozarth MA, Wise RA. Anatomically distinct opiate receptor fields mediate reward and physical dependence. *Science* 224:516-517, 1984.

Cohen BM, Baldessarini RJ. Tolerance to therapeutic effects of antidepressants. *Am J Psychiatry* 142:489-490, 1985.

Di Chiara G, North RA. Neurobiology of opiate abuse. *TIPS* 13:185-193, 1992.

Falk JL. Drug dependence: myth or motive? *Pharmacol Biochem Behav* 19:385-391, 1983.

Givens B, McMahon K. Effects of ethanol on nonspatial working memory and attention in rats. *Behav Neurosci* 111:275-282, 1997.

Graeff FG, Audi EA, Almeida SS, Graeff EO, Hunziker MH. Behavioral effects of 5-HT receptor ligands in the aversive brain stimulation, elevated plus-maze and learned helplessness tests. *Neurosci Biobehav Rev* 14:501-506, 1990.

Harris GC, Aston-Jones G. Involvement of $D_2$ dopamine receptors in the nucleus accumbens in the opiate withdrawal syndrome. *Nature* 371:155-157, 1994.

Kalant H, LeBlanc AE, Gibbins RJ, Wilson A. Accelerated development of tolerance during repeated cycles of ethanol exposure. *Psychopharmacology* (Berl) 60:59-65, 1978.

Koob GF, Bloom FE. Cellular and molecular mechanisms of drug dependence. *Science* 242:715-723, 1988.

Koob GF. Drugs of abuse: anatomy, pharmacology and function of reward pathways. *TIPS* 13:177-184, 1992.

Koob FG, Le Moal M. Drug abuse: hedonic homeostatic dysregulation. *Science* 278:52-58, 1997.

Koob GF, Le Moal M. Drug abuse: hedonic homeostatic dysregulation. *Science* 278: 52-58.oob GF, Le Moal M (2001) Drug addiction, dysregulation of reward, and allostasis. *Neuropsychopharmacology* 24:97-129, 1997.

Koob GF. Neuroadaptative mechanisms of addiction: studies on the extended amygdala. *Eur Neuropsychopharmacol* 13:442-452, 2003.

Lu L, Shepard JD, Hall FS, Shaham Y. Effect of environmental stressors on opiate and psychostimulant reinforcement, reinstatement and discrimination in rats: a review. *Neurosci Biobehav Rev* 27:457-491, 2003.

Markou A, Kosten TR, Koob GF. Neurobiological similarities in depression and drug dependence: a self-medication hypothesis. *Neuropsychopharmacology* 18:135-174, 1998.

McKim WA. *Drugs and behavior: an introduction to behavioral pharmacology (4th edition)*. New Jersey: Prentice-Hall, p. 246-267, 2000.

Narita M, Funada M, Suzuki T. Regulations of opioid dependence by opioid receptor types. *Pharmacol Ther* 89:1-15, 2001.

O'Brien CP. Drug addiction and abuse. In: *Goodman and Gilman's The Pharmacological Basis of Therapeutics*, Hardman J, Limbird L (eds.). New York: McGraw-Hill, pp. 557-577, 1996.

Oei TPS, Singer G, Jeffreys D, Lang W., Latiff A. Schedule induced self-injection of nicotine, heroin and methadone by naive animals. In: *Stimulus properties of drugs: ten years of progress* (Colpaert FC, Rosencrans JA, eds), pp 503-516. New York: Elsevier, 1978.

Olds J, Milner P. Positive reinforcement produced by electrical stimulation of septal area and other regions of rat brain. *J Comp Physiol Psychol* 47:419-427, 1954.

Pilotto R, Singer G, Overstreet D. Self-injection of diazepam in naive rats: effects of dose, schedule and blockade of different receptors. *Psychopharmacology* (Berl) 84:174-177, 1984.

Ramos BM, Siegel S, Bueno JL. Occasion setting and drug tolerance. *Integr Physiol Behav Sci* 37:165-177, 2002.

Remington B, Roberts P, Glautier S. The effect of drink familiarity on tolerance to alcohol. *Addict Behav* 22:45-53, 1997.

Rosebush PI, Mazurek MF. Catatonia after benzodiazepine withdrawal. *J Clin Psychopharmacol* 16:315-319, 1996.

Sante AB, Nobre MJ, Brandão ML. Place aversion induced by blockade of μ or activation of κ opioid receptors in the dorsal periaqueductal gray matter. *Behav. Pharmacol* 11:583-589, 2000.

Schulteis G, Koob GF. Reinforcement processes in opiate addiction: a homeostatic model. *Neurochem Res* 21:1437-1454, 1996.

Selye, H. Confusion and controversy in the stress field. *J.Hum.Stress* 1:37-44, 1975.

Siegel S. Evidence from rats that morphine tolerance is a learned response. *J Comp Physiol Psychol* 89:498-506, 1975.

Siegel S, Hinson RE, Krank MD, McCully J. Heroin "overdose" death: contribution of drug-associated environmental cues. *Science* 216:436-437, 1982.

Ungerstedt U. Stereotaxic mapping of the monoamine pathways in the rat brain. *Acta Physiol Scand Suppl* 367:1-48, 1971.

Van Ree JM, Gerrits MAFM, Vanderschuren LJMJ. Opioids, reward and addiction: an encounter of biology, psychology and medicine. *Pharmacol Rev* 51:341-396, 1999.

Waldhoer M, Bartlett SE, Whistler JL. Opioid receptors. *Annu Rev Biochem* 73:953-990, 2004.

Woods JH, Katz JL, Winger G. Benzodiazepines: use, abuse, and consequences. *Pharmacol Rev* 44:151-347, 1992.

Woods JH, Winger G. Current benzodiazepine issues. *Psychopharmacology* (Berl) 118:107-115, 1995.

In: Substance Abuse, Assessment and Addiction                    ISBN: 978-1-61122-931-8
Editors: Kristina A. Murati and Allison G. Fischer            © 2011 Nova Science Publishers, Inc.

Chapter 2

# DRUG ABUSE, EDUCATION AND ERADICATION

## *Eduardo Montesinos\* and Angèlica Calderòn\*\**

Psiquiatra Hospital General de Zona N° 1, IMSS. Tapachula Chiapas. Mèxico*
Consejo Mexicano de Medicina General**

## ABSTRACT

In the following lines some historical and cultural aspects of the drug addiction are commented.

It is pointed out that it is not possible to eradicate this problem, specifing the reasons that support this affirmation.

Using a Maria Montessori's idea and the others ideas we consider nowadays that some mental functions have changed because of social phenomenons, and this has influence over pathologies like anorexia, border line personality, psychopathic personality and drug addiction.

Some aspects about prevention and education in drugs are reviewed.

It is proposed that education have to be planned according to the person to whom it is addressed. To people who is victim of poverty it is recommended working resilence. To people who does not have economical problems it is necessary reviewing and facing values, and also generating a conceptual change.

Prevention requires confronting the possibility af being responsible and reviewing the functions that have switched. It is also needed the community action of society.

## INTRODUCTION

Man can be destroyed by the violence of his passions or his wishes, or by the accumulation and the abroupt elimination of the subterranean forces that imagination has stored in him. Balzac. [1]

In the next lines we will explore aspect related to the phenomenon of drugs and the drug dependence. Considering that it is not possible to eradicate drugs and their consumption , we will support this affirmation with objective data, we will also analyze from the point of view of education and medicine. The factors that can aid to prevent or to moderate this phenomenon. Education and Medicine have a close connection each other from the far distant part. Plato used to say education must pass men from bad state to another one good, medicine does the same. In this purpose physicians use remedies and sophists speeches. [2]

It is known that through the human history people who had lived in each time have considered their own time like the most stormy and most dangerous of all times, even some fanatics keep expecting the end of world especially at the end of each millennium although the risk of this paper seems to be elaborated in a line as the one previously described, and exaggerating the risk that we take our time as a modern prophet, that is not like that we will try to show that the modern dangers like the bloody wars in differents countries terrorism, inequality and injustice in the sharing out of wealth all over the world, with every time a larger number of poor people, ecological changes and new diseases as AIDS and others that are emerging again with a great virulence, now it is aggregating a lash that can exterminate the human species or at least, changing in a involutive sense the process our own development.

It is also possible that this work seems to be moralistic, but that is not the purpose, it is necessary to mention what Doctor Edwards, a widely acknowledged addiction specialist, says; there are 75 journals dedicated to study addictions, these have to take the responsibility of approaching the ethical topics and establishing the connection between science and intervention politics [3] the neurobiologist Dr. Damasio thinks that one goal of neurobiology and physicians in general must be to relieve the body suffering or an objective not less important to biomedical efforts must be to mitigate the suffering of the mental disease.

But an issue completely different and not enterely resolute is how to treat the suffering when it arises from the personal and social conflicts out of medical environment, it means to use the medical approach to relief any conflict.The risk is that to try of giving relief to the individual and social suffering eluding its causes in the social and individual dimensions, makes litlle probable that the solution lasts long time, it can treat a sympton but it do not do something against the roots disease [4]

The drug use is so important that many countries, Mèxico among them consider it a risk to the national security and a global problem. This generates a state policy that has the intention of finishing the problem, a even some times we think to eradicate it definitely, situation that is very desirable but not very probable in our western societies, Afganistan for example left of being the largest opiate producer in the world when it was under the Taliban regime who imposed a strict prohibition to the opiate cultivation, after wars Afganistan return to increment its production after the fall of the Taliban government. [5]

Drugs and the consequences that its use produces can not be separated of the rest of problems that humanity lives, there is a mistake in our cosmovision, that have led us to changes in the mental process that are manifested the appeerence of new pathologies or through the increase of the frecuency of presentation of other pathologies that were rarely observed in the past.

## DRUGS AND MEDICINE

A situation that provokes harsh criticism is: That the control over the drugs of abuse , it means the medicalitation of addictions coincided clearly with the birth of a new specialty the psychiatry, wich begins thanks to a situation of marketing: In England in 1868 was itroduced the Farmacy Act, that restricted the cocaine sale. What impulsed the promulgation of that act was the question: why allowing the shopkeepers monopolizing a market so profitable. In the international lecture of the Hague and Shanghai it was proposed that the thirty member countries legislated to restrict the opiate and cocaine sale, wich could be supplied only by a medical prescription. [6]

People who nowadays defended that to study and to treat the drug dependences, these must be considered as diseases they mention that there are two definitions.: Esenciallist, which try to explain the nature of "the definited", these are of hard demonstration. Nominalist are funtionals labels (operatives) that are awarded to a group of phenomenons. According to a nominalist definition, dependences share with others diseases three characteristics: There are disorders in the physical and mental functions, there is a weakening in the control of some aspects of behavior and there are also structural changes in addicts organism and a fall in the life expectation.

In spite of everything there are arguments that limit using only the disease model, to explain addictions; among others; it does not explain entirely the common factors between the pharmacological addictions and other addictions for example gambling addiction and the latest described addiction to internet. The disease model considers that the person that has an addiction is not responsible of this, therefore it does not explain how and why an important number of people get over their addictions without any treatment of professional help, neither does it explain how some people are benefited from some therapeutical approach and others for any other different. [7]

Who have elaborated this document think that the drugs phenomenon and the pharmacological dependence both them surpass to medicine and education, each one in the individual, they are problems that must be approach from many different angles, but there is not doubt both have a lot to say about of these problems, their prevention and treatment.

## HISTORICAL ASPECTS

We comment in this part, very concise datum to situate in the line of time some of the substance and when making the correlation, to support the affirmation that it is not possible to eradicate drugs.

Drugs have always existed in nature.In the odyssey is mentioned the "nepente" which means without grief and probably used to contain opium [8]

Some of the drugs exist in the planet in a natural way and have been considered as sacred drugs by the autochthonous cultures example of these are fungus and cactus from wich is obtained for example the peyote. The peyote named of god by the huicholes from the north of Mexico who use it, with a symbolic function, that reminds how is the ostia used by the Catholics.

The marijuana is probably described for the first time by Herodoto, who mentions that in the country of the scytas, grows the kannabis, he compares it with the linen and says that scytas like to feel the drunkenness that is produced by the fumigation of the seed of kannabis. [9]

## ENVIROMENTAL ASPECTS

Revising this way drugs, we can realize that several of them are vegetables that have existed in the planete from inmemorial time, belong to the regional ecosystems and extermining them can provoke some ecological changes.On the other hand, what useful would be destroy these plants? Whether everyday new synthetic drugs are being elaborated, which come to replace the drugs of natural origin and to all this is added the fact that the technology cooperates with new inventions generating addictions which do not require the use of substances.

Friedman comments that there is a changing pattern in the use of drugs by adolescents and youngs, who are using drugs by medical prescription, like sedatives, somniferous, anxiolytics and narcotic analgesics, that they get at home or from friends who share or sell them or well they get them with a medical prescription from little careful physicians [10]

In addition, if we see objetively the pharmacological dependence phenomenon we can observe that there are whole communities in wich drugs have been used without generating the serious problems that are lived nowadays because of its use. This take us to consider that the problem is not only each substance neither each person, but a social atmosphere that favours the use and the misuse of these substance, and has to be confronted from differents points of view.

The drug problems not are generally the only mental disorders that seem to be in a close relationship with the social aspects we also have to mention: The feeding disorders even when there are reports of women with symptoms of anorexia from ancient times for example, among some Catholic Saints, nowadays this problems reach epidemic levels [11] Some personality disorders also have this characteristic, in the X psychiatry congress of Valencia Univesity "psychiatry and post – modernity" professors Josè Giner and Ma Dolores Franco consider that is a pathology post – modern and it shows that the problems that some people present in front of what Lilpovetsky called the empty age. About the psycopathic personality disorder in its more dangerous version, the serial killers, Collin [12] he thinks it began in the XVIII century, although others authors as Carr. C [13] believe that have existed from the ancient times what seems to be true is they have increased their number in an alarmant way, it is also necessary to underline the increase in the statistics of the depressive disorder since the baby boom generation and in prospectives studies depression shows tendency to an alarming rise. This disorder has a complex and close connection with dependences, it is interesting to try to answer the question: what has happened in our communities that has generated this situations?

## THE CHANGE OF AWARENESS

What happens to us today? We are in a situation in wich thanks to the technological advances, it seems we can change everything and nothing like us neither is enough, people who can change their appearance, do it, almost every anatomical region can be modified with the intention of getting fame and money sportsmen and sportswomen risk their healt and/or life, using substances that finally harm them. The death view has varied so that the American sociologist G. Gorer talks of the "pornography of death"[14] in wich the consumption society manipulates and enjoys the violent death in videogames and through the media whereas on the other hand the real death is hidded, keeping away the moribunds from their families. We can consider death as our maximum limit and we wish we could avoid it and in that way to become inmortals. In the extreme to deny the facts of life, we can use drugs thus all this behavior look for satisfyng a wish that can in this sense to be considered, the man`s narcissism, Balzac would say that the subterranean forces that the imagination has accumulated in man seem to have been released.

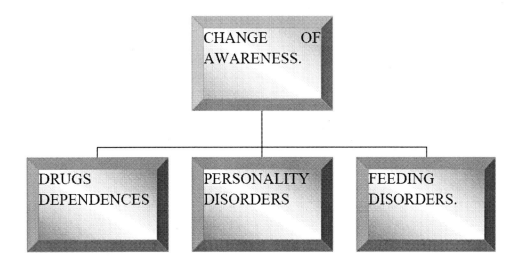

## ORIGIN OF CHANGING

The authors from whom we synthetize some ideas have tried to explain this changing according to Glucksmann the changing begins with Flaubert who "has changed the planet more than the atomic bomb" Glucksmann explains that the personage of Madame Bovary looks for the absolute instant that heaven seems to descended to land and leave the humans exhausted, with nothing for wishing, the creation gets lighted up by it self and emits a sovereign "fiat lux"; besides he thinks this point was beginning of a nihilism what is active, not reactive. [15] He also mentions Dostoievsky who asks where come from nihilistics? And he answers to himself from nowhere, they have been always with us inside us, near to us. Nihilism is an exercise of cruelty, he says to us that a nihilistic finds pleasure in intensity and not in results, coments that nihilism is a world enterprise of demoralization which is protected by the sequestration of the three magic devices of modern world: The circulation of weapons, money and feelings, and has a program that is the intrusion in the conciencius of another one.

There is no a bad part that organizes the evil, there is a general anesthesia that affects everybody. The modern submission is a despotism based in the voluntary servitud.

There are a humans creations like state and markets that own the characteristic of not having a incorporated brake sistem. Another author Collin says that Richardson with his novel "Pamela" teached the Europeans not only to dream but to take refuge in the Aladino cave of subjectivity he seems to have said "forget for some hours your everyday life and come with me to the imagination life" we should wonder is not that the function of any addiction?

He uses this idea to explain the sexual perversions, he also says that there is something mystical in them, the craving of becoming intimate with the nature forces and he comments too that they bring nothing to the biological evolution, they have negative sign, does not seem to happen the same with addiction?.

Collin says us that before the romantic rebellion man considered that he was part of enviroment and he depended of the world that surrounded him, but after he started to generate an interesting but terrifying idea; that he can be master of world and not its servant, he wishes he could to act with absolute egoism; and in the most extreme limit he thinks that reality does not exist. [12]

From the perspective of education Marìa Montessori mentioned that the social OMBIUS, dominates the child and with him all humanity such an OMBIUS is according Montessori an Evil Organization that takes the appearance of good and it is imposed the entire humanity by the environment because of suggestion. The good is really a masked evil. Nobody wants evil, everybody wants good, but that good is evil. [16]

The Argentinean Sabato tell us that the education that we give to our children, generates evil because we teach it like good.

## DRUGS AND BRAIN

According to the United Nations in its division to attention to drugs ONUDD [17] in the world, the use of cannabis has risen in 5% in the population of 15 to 64 years, from 2000 to 2005, 5% of world population have used illegal drugs at least one time in the last 12 months, the interaction between drugs and brain have great importance which explains the dependence phenomenon and the serious consequences of this interaction, this relationship is so important that some authors insist that addiction must be considered as a brain disease. There are different hypothesis about how addiction occurs. The hypotesis more accepted nowadays is the one that says that drugs stimulate the center of pleasure and provoke changes in different neurotransmitters mainly the dopamine, provoking sensations of wellfare to which brain gets adapted and for that looks for repeating the experience, this is the hedonistic explanation.

From a evolutionist perspective is said that there is a capacity to the self perceived survival ability and rerpoductive fitness (ESPSAR) such sistem prioritizes and organizes the motivation and the human behavior. Drugs increase the function of the system, they deceive this way; animals get oriented and fixed over positive stimulus and avoid the aversive , the emotions like the initial pleasure and the possible anxiety and rage posterior would epiphenomenon that occur after activiting the (ESPSAR), this is a teleological explanation. [18]

In this hypothesis must be underlined that the sistem has genetic and environmental components. The psychosocial characteristics could be transmited from one generation to another one by not genetic processes that would depend of the natural selection. Drugs deceive to the system, making it to identify them like preferables whatever be the hypothesis that we accept, we know that when addiction is present it generates neurochemical, molecular and genetic changes in the addict person's brain [19,20] the repeated use of drugs of abuse, provokes brain genetic changes. The changes to synaptic level generate variations in the intracellular signposting producing in the transcription factors what can provoke a correlation in the behavioural phenotype of addiction. Some factors of transcriptions studied are: CREBC (AMP Respose Elemental Binding protein) it is related with a behavioural syndrome characterizad by a diminution in the interest to natural recompenses DELTA FOSB increase the sensibility to drugs of abuse and the behavior of looking for recompenses [21]

We can not avoid asking, can these new characteristics be inherited as changes of novo?.

## FIRST CONCLUSION

We get this conclusion considering the changes that drugs provoke in the brain function, and the fact that every time there are more persons that use drugs. What will happen if the number of users continues increasing? We propose an example let's think in two youn men with potential to investigate, one of them in the inmunological field and the another one in the drugs field, if the first one got infected by the HIV even with that condition, he could find the cure to AIDS, but if the another one with potential in the drugs field become addict he would not develop any capacity. On the other hand the society in which we live seems to be the origin of the increment in the use and permanence of the problems, ideally societies are characterized by the plurality of ideas; and it is the dynamics of forces of the society which provoks the changes, but one characteristic of the modern society as we have mentioned before, is the homogenization of the thought and the general anesthesia in wich we are living. Kristeva describes it in this way "the modern man is on the point of losing the capacity of representing and judging the cosmos" and to the other human, [22] beings to judge the evil, it is required freedom, drugs probably anaesthetize us, and even more let's make another comparison. Although some people deny the ecological problems, because of their profit it is the reality what face us to need of accepting that reality and changing it, but if apart from who get great profits in keeping the drugs business and use lobbys to make their propaganda, what would happen if many of us who could lead the fight against drugs, are trapped in any dependence? And the rest of us keep anaesthetized, without judging the matter.

Conclusion: We consider what we have already mentioned, supports the idea that drugs and the drug dependence are serious risks to the humanity as we know it until now.

## PREVENTION

At the level of not specific primary prevention in which we think is the key to face this serious problem, the not specific primary prevention has a goal to act over all the elements and determinant factors of the problem, if we have considered that the situation that is lived with drugs nowadays is one more pathological manifestation of our society, the prevention not specific must try to change this situation.

Education can orient and help to change such reality. Education implies not only the formal and academical education, but also the not formal educaction, and awakening of people's awareness.

Brain changes its architecture as an answer to stimulus that it receives in a critical time to this changes, is the early childhood, is in this stage when it is defined the essential design of brain [23] on which the superior mental functions will settle.

This design will be the base on which continues the brain develop, in accordance with Dr: Post, a positive or negative stimulation with changes the brian microstructure in any time [23]

From the womb the brain of the fetus changes because of situations that affect, from the environment, to the mother , for example violence in couple this produces neurohormonal changes, like the rise of the cortisol what could explain the increase in depression in the present generations a disease that can get complicated with dependences, generating dual pathologies according to this information, is in this stage in which we must start the educational programs that tend to increase the positive , intellectual and the affective potentials. It is necessary to detect children vulnerable to the environment in order to profit the neuroplasticity with a preventive purpose. Specific programs that take into account the develop of the nervous system in accordance with the stimulus and the develop of emotions in addiction to the previous.

Despite the fact that the educational measures are general, it is convenient to differentiate some contents according to the kind of groups to whom them are addressed, without this be a - sine - qua - non condition, with children and youngs in vulnerable conditions it must be developed aspects that increase the resilency this kind of work has already been used in some groups in Mèxico. Resiliency can be understood, with a Ernesto Sabato's sentence: "world can nothing against a man who sings in misery". [24] One of the essential pillars of resiliency is developing the students' critical conscience, and this is also an objetive in the modern pedagogical systems. But it requires besides of developing the critical conscience, moving the will too, if this does not occur , then only is possible to keep intellectual and incessantly, the culture of dissatisfaction, complain and/or empty non conformism that even could take people to any dependences. Cytrulik commented that resiliency can not be conceptualized only in terms of the persons. It is required a collective vision of the word, which is referred to a change of the human being, who inscribes his developing in an environment and writes his history in a culture. It is needed a rational commitment with transformation and the will to accomplish it.

In this sort of strategy is accepted that school not any more monopolizes the knowledge, it is necessary that school works with the social organizations and institutions that produce knowledge. Musique, plastic arts, and cinema are useful to wake up curiosity, concern and wish to educate people involved with a change, that combats the social anesthesia and the nihilism. [25]

We must underline that more than anything also is necessary "teaching the teacher" which means that we are who must modify our cultural practices in the process teaching – learning, if we want to modify reality and not only watching and interpreting it with skepticism.

It is not about having heros, but keeping the sense of generosity and responsability to the others it is about being citizens and acting like that.[26]

This does not mean that children and youngs that present less factors of vulnerability this strategy has to be avoided, but in people like them it would be better to emphazise strategies that improve the values. It is important to mention the classification made by the creator of the logotherapy Dr Viktor Frankl, who described values of creation, wich are reached through acts of creation, it means how they works and whether or not occupy the place where they are situated, experientials involved or based in experience they are of welcoming to the universe for example: the delivery to beauty. Of attitude, these can help us to bear in a exemplary way the irreversible destiny, it is the how to bear the misfortune. [27]

It has been observed that relating variables there are an association between the family and interpersonal atmospheres and both of them are correlated with the teenagers` values. The interpersonal relationships, as well as the young people`s values can predict in a negative way the antisocial behavior [28]

Even university level, prestigious educador like Doctor Latapì coments "I have horror of a education which excludes the compassion, that gives up of looking for meanings or that closes the door to the possibilities of transcendency [29]

From the point of view of education it is important to comment the constructo to implicit theories. It is about the personal theories of the students who are characterized for being of difficult communication and underlying to the action. When comparing these with the scientic theories we find that the implicit theories can predict or decribe very well daily events, whereas the scientific knowledge can be less predictive in the daily aspects what can provoke that the student makes wrong decisions in spite of having the necessary information, we find examples in the teenagers` sexual habits and increase in the use of tobaco principally by women.

It is needed to foment the awareness about these ideas to get a conceptual change [30].

It is necessary to consider that the implicit theories of the students refer to specific facts, they are descriptives and look for the success, on the other hand the scientific theories look for not the specific but the general facts, they are explicatives and look for understand not for getting succes. All this influences the called conceptual change that consist in changing from one wrong idea to another specific idea (scientific) for getting this change, according to some authors it is required a change in the way of conceptualizing or in the conceptual schemes, that are used to interpret the problems. It is necessary to investigate in a wide way all these processes, in order that the education influences over addictions the conceptual change obtains a great importance whether we have to take into account models like the one of "the planned behavior" that incorporates cognitives and attitudinals factors directly related with the begining of use of drugs.

To Mexican students it was concluded that the preventive program addressed to modify behaviourals belives that be in favour of drugs consuming and to intensify the perception of the social rejection to the consumption. [31]

It is convenient to mention the Colombian Restrepo`s ideas who tell us that should exist a right to tenderness, these means a paradigm of the coexistence that must be gained in the loving, productive and political fields in which have dominated for centuries the values of revange, subjection and conquest. In order to reach this right we must educate in values, this education must be articulated to a suggestive aesthetics that allows to abandon the edicts and arrives to a education of taste and sensibility. In the end of a teaching cycle not only there is knowledge but also habits, moral scruples and behavioural routines that exert a great power of cognitive regulations on the pupil. [32]

In the tenderness we move in the dimension of the social aesthetic, that transcends the collective and sinks its roots in the affective, familiar and interpersonal dimensions from which is fed the citizen ethical. It is the daily routine signed by the affective dynamic where the public is produced. In the public and the private are articulated, the macrosocial with the psychology of the intimacy can be understood mental problems that are increasing.

Restrepo tell us is necessary revising the warrior ethics, which gets manifested in the executive and searcher of power ideologies who are afraid of falling in tenderness. He compares the executive with the addict, two both run away from intimacy and tenderness, the first one is example of a successful paranoid, caricature of the wish of success and the second one of the fear to the tenderness.

Children are manipulated in order to be teached, without allowing them being dragged by the singularity of their own experiences, that way is education, it is not allowed to be distracted in the charm of the sensibility, the interpersonal aspects are forbidden in order to favor to productivity, says Restrepo this author considers that even when we can not convince multitud we can appeal to tenderness, the same tell us Sabato; he explains that is needed to defend the tradition, which tell us how much of sacred a man has. They are not rational facts, but it is not important that they be we will be saved by the affection.

This coincides with the idea of resiliency of using arts or instrument, and there is a point of contact between the personal and the social, it is about sensibility, tenderness requires being developed, in order to not run away from reality, the not specific primary prevention is more related to a determined problem and influences directly over the factors that generate it, to study the problem let us make preventive srategies. We have already information to know drugs and their negative effects to human beings; for example we are trying the develop strategies thinking in the person and comunity, with the support of a voluntary net which includes neighbors, specific groups; work of group of develop attitudes and habilities of protection and self evaluation with systematized instruments of results of process and of impact that allow to observe the diminution of the experimental consumption, to avoid the first contact and reduce the abuse. The program named "Chimalli" works in four areas, drugs use and antisocial behavior, negative events of life and life style. It proposes the develop of several actions among others psychocorporal techniques, pychosocial techniques using vignettes in third person, psychoeducative techniques expressed in community practices.[33]

At this level we have to return to the argument that is generated by the society nowadays this is a series of information, a lot of them even presented in a brillant way in which the use of drugs is seen a something inevitable even valuable the use drugs has even compared with the masturbation [34], this last one has been critized by the medical guild in the past, without having been proved that it causes real problems. It is defended the idea that who not agree in the use of drugs are just defending the customs, letting the impression that using drugs, should be part of the freedom of human being, there are reports which say that youngs who use drugs in a experimental way are healthier than these that refuse to try them or those who became addicts [6] some criticism make to see how litlle scientific are the arguments against drugs; what is again to want to explain from the dimension of medicine the process health – disease and this criticism also call the attention about how physicians want to keep the control about what has to be used or not.

It is so interesting this argumentation that takes even the physicians to consider if we are not exaggerating, and if some physicians have used them (statistically thiswould not be surprising),maybe we could think that the use of drugs is not a big problem. It is said that the medical model trys the situation continues like it is, and it depends of the concern of the medical institution in keeping the power and being medicine a social institution, it represents the interests of certain conservative sectors that are against drugs without having justified scientifically such rejection . When they mention freedom, we ask it is not dangerous for freedom using sustances that have been described as cognitive authoritative, prepotent and totalitarian objects that convert to whom use them in slave [35] It is intersting to bring to the argumentation, another behavior that has risen among the youngs, it is the youngs who hurt themselves, if we consider that some of injuries are slight and that is just a minority which continues hurting itself after a while; May be we arrive soon to the conclusion that who explore this behavior are who want to keep the present situation previously described, situation in which people`s health is been destroyed not only because of drugs, but through of the alimentary and personality disorders, and this interpretation depends too of the vision of one sector of the society that has its ows interests and that in a precise moment are so subjective like the physician's.

We think that all these arguments must be valued and we have to find the positive aspects that are in them but physicians are obligated to make clear we disagree the use of drugs. It is not about demanding their dissaparence, fact that as we have already commented is very difficult, much less to be against the patients that depend on drugs, who deserve our best medical care and support, but looking for criticizing the social conditions that allow that every time a bigger number of persons feel the need of proving experiences that can put in risk their health and do not get minimized a series of behaviors that are generating serious problems in population.

This polemic has a lot of importance, we have seen to develop preventive interventions, we must avoid arguments that promote the use of drugs.

In the specific prevention we are looking for developing abilities of behavioural control in front of situations of risk, among them abilities of resistance in face of the pressure of group and developing of assertiveness.

Genetics with its fantastic development is used to try to prevent diverses pathologies. Genetics is also being studied in the drug dependences, it is considered that a polymorphism of unique nucleotide, which consists in the substitution of alleles one G by ane A (A1 18G) would be a locus to addiction to heroin, we would try to make prevention to this level for avoiding addictions [36]

The use of vaccines is being tried it means that when some one gets in contact with a drug (cocaine for example) it wakes up a reaction of antibodies that blockade the drug effect. This management receives a lot of critics, which include those of the medical guild, according this reasoning huge amount of money to investigate,pathent and fabricate vaccines and after sell them and make enourmous profit, all this generates that every time more and more people become addict and new drugs arise that will require specific new vaccines and in this way the problem is just perpetued.

In secondary prevention, the problem is already present and it is tried to solve it partial or totally. The firts step is a early diagnostic to get it, it is need that a bigger number of people know to recognize the signs and sympton that drugs produce in whom use them.

It is required too the developing of proofs every time cheaper and easy to apply to detect the users, proofs that must be reliables.In this point is necessary to arrive to social agreements to do those proofs without affecting person`s dignity. Another part of secondary prevention is the opportune and adecuate treatment.

Second Conclusion: The primary not specific prevention is the base that can avoid the dependences.

**Table 1. Levels of Prevention in drugs use**

| | |
|---|---|
| Not especificy<br>Primary<br>Prevention | Is the key to face the serious problem of drugs<br>Is necesary to detect children`s vulnerables conditions.<br>Increase Resilency.<br>School works with social organizations.<br>To teach the teacher |
| Especificy<br>Primary<br>Prevention | Use de Genetics to prevent dependences.<br>Vaccines |
| Secondary<br>Prevention. | Recognition the signs and symptoms that are produced by<br>drugs.<br>Specifical proofs.<br>Different treatments, emphasys in spiritual aspects.<br>Diminution of risks. |

## TREATMENT

There are different therapeutic approachings to offer to drug users. In many cases are necessary several modalities of integral treatment; individual, familiar and therapies of group. Besides it can be used differents approaches and therapeutic alternatives. There are studies that consider that is convenient to treat to teenagers who experience with drugs. Some authors have observed that adolescents who do not receive therapy do not abandon groups of addicts, and when they become adults, are drug dependents, their partners influence provokes an epidemic. The use of drugs is related with an important comorbidity, psychological and health risks. It is more probable to get therapeutic success in this stage than in adults. Treating adolescents with problems is preventive, and it will reduce the service demand by adults. [37]

The use of drug antagonists substance of drugs has shown to be useful in the opiate, alcohol, and tobacco dependences. It is very important to recognize and treat other pathologies that are presented at the same time, which we name dual pathologies.

We have insisted in to say the cultural factors, are influencing in the way to see life and world by some persons, that generates the need of using drugs or having behaviors that are noxiuos for themselves.

Among the different psycotherapies that can be used we think that without neglecting the physical and psychological factors of the dependences the spiritual factor its very important too.

A lot of people who fall in dependences could be looking for trascendence. William James used to say the real cure to drinking alcohol in excess is the passionate religion. Carl Jung used to comment that against the evil that prevails in world we should oppose the authentic religious vision or the protective contention of the human comunity. [38]

This factor is being taked into account by various groups of self help in which it is speaked about a superior power, when talking about spiritual aspect and different philosophies, we prefer to refer to spiritual dimension in the same sense that Frankl does it, who also names it the "noetic" dimension. It is not only the man`s own dimension, but it is a specific dimension, the spiritual aspect is by definition only the free in man and allows him to confront with all the social, the corporal and even the psychical. Frankl establishes a series of characteristics of the human: It is pure power, is just the possibility of manifestation it offers unity and totality to human person. It is a dialogue with oneself. It is the person's nucleus. It does not get sick it. Is the dimension where are located the specific human phenomenons. It instrumentalizes the psychophysical organism, using it as mechanism of expresion.. This dimension is not transmited from parents to children, but education can canalize and make easier the expression of the spiritual. Education from this point of view helps to form a person and person according Frankl, can be have free in any state of things. He is able to offer opposition, and is able to oppose always, of opposing to external and even internal position. His action can be restricted, for example because of the psychophysical damage that are caused by drugs, but the therapist keep a blind faith in the invisible but indestructible person.

This therapy looks for getting manifested the spiritual contents; and developing the being in his essence and sense. [39]

Even whitin of the secondary prevention it is promoted the reduction of damage. This proposed is contened in the believe that is possible to influence powerfully in the morbidity and mortality without need of insisting in the abstinence. This began when contacting to a group users of infections by HIV, besides offering support about health, housing and children care. Later trying of convencing some of them of using oral substitutes of drugs followed of detoxification and rehabilitation. [6]

Third conclusion: The therapy against dependence requires to attend the spiritual.


## REHABILITATION

In what is the third prevention we see rehabilitation which can be accomplished from different focus and strategies.One of them in accordance to our point of view use like arts tools and the sensibility develop, motivating the addicts to make values of creation according to the Frankl's terminology and according to the proposal of the right to tenderness, of reducing in the addict the fear to intimacy, to sensibility and to tenderness.

In the strategy besides of a psychotherapeutic treatment the patients are incorporated to ateliers of creative expression in wich they put name to their phantoms, make them of their own possesion and dialogue with themselves. Diction combats to the fact to compulsion and addiction. [40]


## REFERENCES

[1]   Balzac. H. *Le père Goriot*. Presses Pocket. 1978.

[2]   Platòn. Dialogos. *UNAM*. SEP. Mèxico. 1ª.1988

[3]   Edwards. G. *Adicciones; Revista Sociodrogalcohol*. 2005; 17 (2): 9 – 98

[4]   *El error de Descartes*. Damasio. A. 1ª.2006. Drokontos bolsillo.

[5]   Medina –Mora. M. Rojas. G. (2003). *La demanda de drogas: Mèxico en laperspectiva internacional.* 26, 2. 1 - 12

[6]   Gelder. G. M. Lòpez.Ibor.J.J. Andreassen.N. *Tratado de psiquiatrìa.* 1ª. España; Psiquiatrìa Editores. S. 2003.)

[7] Ayala .V. Càrdenas. G. Echeverria. L. Gutièrrez. L. M. First results of a self –control program to problem drinkers in Mèxico. *Salud Mental.* V 18 N ° 4.18 -24.)

[8] Katzung. farmacologìa bàsica y clìnica. Mèxico. *ElManual Moderno* 2002. Cap Abuso ded drogas 599 – 616

[9] Dornbierer.M. *La guerra de las drogas.*4ª. Mèxico; Grijalbo. 1991)

[10] Friedman. R. A, the changing Fac of teen age drug abuse. *N. Egl. J. Med.* 2006. Apr 6; 354: 1448 -50

[11] *Psicologìa.com* Vol 1 N° 1 Julio. 1997

[12] Colin.W. *Los inadaptados.* Buenos Aires; Planeta. 1989

[13] Carr. C. El Alienista. España; *Pnto de Lecura.* 2000.

[14] *Bioetica temas y perspectivas OPS.* Washington. D.C. 1990. 87 – 94

[15] Glucksmann. A. *Dostoievski en Manhattan.* 1ª. España; Taurus. 2000.

[16] Montessori.M. Formaciòn del hombre. Mèxico. Diana 1986, *cap La evoluciòn social del niño,* 69 – 78.

[17] *www.incb.org.pdf/5/ar/2005/incb_repot_2005*

[18] San Juan. J. Cela .C. *La profecia de Darwin.*1ª. Mèxico; Ars Medica.2006.

[19] Leff. P. Medina Mora. M. Calva. J.Valdès. A. Acevedo. R. Et al. Neurobilogy of addiction neuroanatomical, neurochemical, molecular and genetic aspect of morphine and cocaine addiction. *Salud Mental.*V. 23. N° 3. Junio 2000.

[20] Leff.P. Medina Mora. M. Calva. J.Valdès. A. Acevedo. R. Et al. Neurobilogy of addiction neuroanatomical, neurochemical, molecular and genetic aspect of morphine and cocaine addiction. *Salud Mental* V 23. N° 4. Agosto. 2000. 38 – 44.

[21] De la Gàndara M.S. Micò. S. Olivares. D. Szerman. B. Depresiòn en pacientes de riesgo. Ars Mèdica. 2004. Mèxico. Cap 4. *Depresiòn y acohol u otras drogas.* Patología dual. Szerman. B. 89 -110.

[22] Sichere B. *Historias del mal.* España; Gedisa. 1996.

[23] Kotulak. R. *El cerebro por dentro.* Mèxico; Diana. 2003.

[24] *Sabato. E.La resistencia. 1ª. Mèxico; Seix –Barral. 2004.*

[25] Melillo. A. Suàrez.O. E. Rodríguez. D. *Resiliencia y subjetividad.* 1ª. Buenos Aires; Paidos. 2004

[26] Monsivàis. C. *Del rancho al Internet.* Biblioteca del ISSSTE. 1999. Mèxico.

[27] Frankl. V. *Psicoanalisis y existencialismo.* Fondo de Cultura Econòmica. Mèxico. 2ª. 1978.

[28] Juàrez. F.Villatoro J. Fleiz. C. Medina – Mora. M. Carreño. S. Amador. N. Bermúdez.. P. Conducta antisocial, ambiente familiar e interpersonal en estudiantes adolescentes del Distrito Federal. *La Psicología Social en Mèxico.* 2002. 305 – 311. Amepso.

[29] *La Jornada.* 03. Marzo. 2007.Mèxico. p.17)

[30] Pozo. J. I. *La psicologìa cognitiva y laeducaciòn cientìfica.www.if.ufrgs.br/ publiclensino/n2/pozohtm*

[31] Rodríguez – Kuri .S. E. Dìaz. N. D. Gracia- Gutiérrez. S. E. Guerrero. H. J. A. Gòmez. M. E. Capacidad predictiva de la Teoría de la Conducta Planificada en la intenciòn y uso de drogas ilìcitas entre estudiantes mexicanos. *Salud Mental.* Vol 30. N° 1.2007. 68 – 81.

[32] Restrepo. L. C. *El derecho a la ternura.* Océano; Mèxico. 1994.

[33] Castro.M. Llanes. J. Modelo preventivo de riesgos psicosociales. Chimalli in Anonymous. Modelos preventivos. Mèxico. *CONADIC.* 45- 50.

[34] Cebriain. J. *Prohibicion.blogspot.com*

[35] Gòmez. D. Alonso − Fernàndez. F. Consideraciones psicobiològicas sobre las adicciones alimentarias. *Salud Mental.* Vol 24. N° 2.Abril. 2001.16 − 24.

[36] Opioid receptor Al 18G polymorpismin association with striatal opioid neuropeptide gene expresions in heroin abusers Batl. *Acad. Sci. U.S.A.* 2006. May 16; 103: 7883 - 7888.

[37] Swadi. H. Abuso de sustancias en adolescentes. *Avances en Psiquiatrìa.* Vol 6. N° 3. Diciembre. 2000. 35 − 43.

[38] Chopra. D. *Vencer las adicciones.* Ed: Javier Vergara; Argentina.1997.

[39] *www.logoforo.com/anm/templates/*

[40] *Berber. H. R. Cebada. M. ¿Què son las adicciones y como tratarlas?. A tu Salud. IMSS. 35. 2007. 81- 85.*

In: Substance Abuse, Assessment and Addiction  ISBN: 978-1-61122-931-8
Editors: Kristina A. Murati and Allison G. Fischer  © 2011 Nova Science Publishers, Inc.

*Chapter 3*

# SEXUAL EFFECTS AND DRUGS OF ABUSE: POSSIBLE LINKS THROUGH LEARNING

## *Chana K. Akins[a]\* and Neil Levens[b]*

[a]Department of Psychology, University of Kentucky,
Lexington, KY 40506-0044, USA
[b]Department of Psychology, University of South Carolina,
Columbia, SC 29208, USA

## ABSTRACT

Clinical research points out that there is a comorbid relationship between drug addiction and high-risk sexual behavior. Much of this relationship has been explained as the use of sexual behavior as a way to exchange for drugs of abuse. However, studies using animal models have implicated neural and psychological mechanisms that may link drug abuse and risky sexual behavior. Both drug taking and sexual behavior involve overlapping neural circuitry, and both events also evoke dopamine efflux in the nucleus accumbens. This neural overlap appears to be sufficient to induce cross-sensitization. However, this cross-sensitization appears to be unilateral with chronic drug exposure resulting in the enhancement of sexual motivation and sexual behavior, but not the reverse. In contrast to the cross-sensitization literature, the findings of reinstatement studies have suggested that the neural overlap and involvement of dopamine may not be sufficient for the reinstatement of drug-seeking behavior following a sexual event that presumably primes the system. The purpose of the present chapter is to review this empirical literature and to discuss the possible role of learning as a link between the two, with particular emphasis on the incentive sensitization view of drug addiction.

---

\* Address correspondence to: Chana K. Akins, Department of Psychology, University of Kentucky, Lexington, KY 40506-0044. e-mail: ckakin1@uky.edu; phone: (859) 257-1103; fax: (859) 323-1979

# INTRODUCTION

There is increasing clinical evidence for a comorbidity between psychostimulant abuse and compulsive sexual behavior (e.g., Kall, 1992; Kall and Nilsonne, 1995; Washton, 1989). For example, psychostimulant use has been linked to increased sexual activity, multiple sex partners (Ross, Hwang, Zack, Bull, and Williams, 2002; Weatherby, Shultz, Chitwood, McCoy, McCoy, Ludwig, and Edlin, 1992) and unprotected sex (Booth, Kwiatkowski, and Chitwood, 2000). Moreover, psychostimulant abusers have a higher than normal incidence of sexually transmitted diseases (Washton, 1989).

One contributing factor to this comorbid relationship between drug abuse and risky is clearly that drug addicts are exchanging sexual favors for drugs and/or money to support their drug habit. Another possible contributing factor for the drug abuse-sex relationship may be based on the incentive sensitization view of addiction (Robinson and Berridge, 2000, 2003). This view proposes that potentially addictive drugs may induce neural adaptations in the brain – e.g., in the neural reward circuitry (i.e., nucleus accumbens) and as a result, the brain systems involved in motivation and reward become hypersensitized to drugs. This sensitization induced by repeated psychostimulant administration may also be manifest as enhanced motivation toward natural rewards such as sex since the same brain systems involved in drug-induced adaptations are also known to be involved in sexual motivation and sexual behavior (Fiorino and Phillips, 1999a; Fiorino, Coury, and Phillips, 1997; Levens and Akins, 2004). The role of Pavlovian conditioning in incentive sensitization is becoming more evident. As a result of a hypersensitized reward-related brain system, cues that have become associated with drug-taking, via Pavlovian conditioning, may thereby activate the incentive-salience process (Robinson and Berridge, 2003). That is, the cues that are now conditioned stimuli (CSs) may increase in value and evoke approach responses or "wanting" (Berridge and Robinson, 2003). These physiological and psychological processes could contribute to our understanding of why some drug addicts also engage in risky sexual behavior.

# EFFECTS OF DRUGS OF ABUSE ON SEXUAL MOTIVATION AND SEXUAL BEHAVIOR

Behavioral sensitization is defined as enhanced responding to a drug after repeated administration of the drug. The incentive-sensitization theory (Robinson and Berridge, 2000, 2003) proposes that prolonged use of certain drugs creates neural adaptations in the limbic-motor circuitry, specifically the mesolimbic dopamine system, and that these adaptations are expressed as behavioral sensitization. The same circuitry involved in the expression of behavioral sensitization is also known to play a role in natural motivated behaviors such as sexual behavior (Phillips, Pfaus, and Blaha, 1991). Thus, repeated psychostimulant administration that leads to behavioral sensitization may be manifest as enhanced sexual motivation. Indeed, the incentive sensitization theory predicts that drug sensitization should facilitate responding to classes of naturally rewarding stimuli, a phenomenon referred to as cross-sensitization.

Evidence for cross-sensitization of drugs of abuse on sexual behavior has been investigated in a limited number of experiments. Fiorino and Phillips (1999a) investigated the effects of behavioral sensitization induced by amphetamine on sexual arousal in sexually naive male rats. Rats were placed in bilevel chambers that contained a set of ramps that allowed movement from one platform to the other. After 30 minutes, they were injected with either amphetamine (1.5 mg/kg i.p.) or saline and placed back into the bilevel test chambers. Two hours after the injection, they were returned to their home cages. Injections were given every other day for a total of 10 injections. Twenty-one days after the 10th injection, male rats were tested for sexual behavior in the bilevel test chambers. Activity counts, as measured by level changes, were recorded for 5 minutes before a receptive female rat was introduced for 30 min. Various measures of sexual interaction were recorded during the 30 min test. Ten sexual behavior tests were conducted, one every 4 days.

Results showed that rats that were given amphetamine every other day displayed enhanced activity on the 10th injection compared to the first one. In addition, they had progressively greater activity across injections compared to saline controls, confirming that sensitization had occurred. When tested for sexual behavior, sensitized rats made significantly more level changes than the control group on the 10th test during the first 5 minutes before the female was introduced. In addition, amphetamine-sensitized rats demonstrated shorter latencies to mount and a greater number of mounts, intromissions, and ejaculations compared with saline control rats. The findings demonstrate that prior chronic exposure to amphetamine facilitated sexual responding.

In a similar experiment, Levens and Akins (2004) investigated the effect of cocaine-induced behavioral sensitization on male sexual learning using a Pavlovian sexual conditioning paradigm. In this paradigm, an initially neutral object, a conditioned stimulus (CS), is presented to a male for several seconds followed by an opportunity to copulate with a receptive female, the unconditioned stimulus (US). After several pairings of the CS and US, the CS comes to elicit approach behavior. This conditioned approach behavior is indicative of learning and of the establishment of an association between the CS and the US.

Levens and Akins (2004) also tested for a drug-sex cross sensitization using an alternative species, Japanese quail. We wanted to test for the generality of the phenomenon across species with the assumption that if this phenomenon occurs similarly in birds as in mammals, it may also be more likely to also occur in humans. Additionally, sexual conditioning in male Japanese quail is a well-studied phenomenon (see Domjan, Cusato, and Krause, 2004 for review).

To test whether cocaine-induced behavioral sensitization would influence conditioned approach behavior and other aspects of learned sexual behavior, male quail were randomly assigned to one of four groups: Paired Cocaine ($n = 6$), Unpaired Cocaine ($n = 6$), Paired Saline ($n = 6$), or Unpaired Saline ($n = 6$). During sensitization training, both paired and unpaired cocaine groups received a daily injection of cocaine (10 mg/kg intraperitoneally or ip) and were immediately placed into a locomotor chamber for 30 min. This occurred once a day for 6 consecutive days. Saline groups received the same treatment except they were given an injection of saline (ip) once a day for 6 days. Following a 10-day withdrawal period, 10 sexual conditioning trials were conducted. During conditioning, paired subjects were presented with the CS object ( a small wooden block lowered from the ceiling of the test cage) and the amount of time subjects spent in an area marked off that contained the CS (the CS zone) was recorded. After 30 sec, the CS was raised and a door that led to a small chamber adjacent to the test cage and that contained a receptive female quail was opened. During the last 5 conditioning trials, a taxidermically-prepared model of a female bird was presented behind the door rather than the live female. This was done to reduce the variability of male sexual responding that might occur as a result of the female's behavior. Once males entered the cage, the door was closed, and they were given 5 min to interact with the female or model (US). During the 5 min interaction period, latency to copulate (beginning when the door was opened) and the frequency of cloacal contacts made toward the female was recorded. Unpaired subjects received the same treatment as paired subjects except that they were given 5 min to interact with the female bird (first 5 trials) or a taxidermic model of a female (last 5 trials) 3 hr prior to the CS presentation and in their home cages, in an unpaired fashion. Figure 1 represents mean photobeam breaks during the 30 min locomotor activity trials. Cocaine administration resulted in significantly greater locomotor activity than saline on each trial and across trials. Thus, providing evidence that behavioral sensitization had occurred.

The mean time birds spent in the CS zone during the 30 sec CS presentation across sexual conditioning trials is represented in Figure 2. The paired cocaine and paired saline groups both increased the amount of time they spent near the CS, an indication of conditioned approach behavior. However, group Paired Cocaine had enhanced conditioned approach responding compared to the paired saline group across trials and overall.

Because of differences in how paired and unpaired groups received the female US (i.e., for paired groups, a door was opened allowing paired males to interact with the female, whereas, for unpaired groups, the female was placed in the cage with the male), comparisons for latency to copulate were only measured in paired subjects. Figure 3 represents mean latency to first copulation with a female for the paired groups.

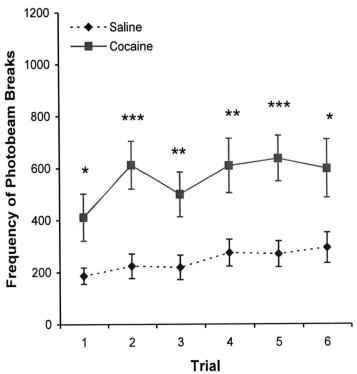

Figure 1. Mean frequency of photobeam breaks across 6 locomotor activity trials, each for 30 min.* = significantly different from saline, p<0.05; ** = p<0.01; *** = p<0.001. (Reprinted with permission).

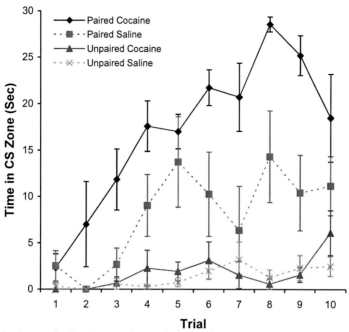

Figure 2. Time (sec) spent in the CS zone (+SEM) during the 30 sec presentation of the CS across 10 sexual conditioning trials. (Reprinted with permission).

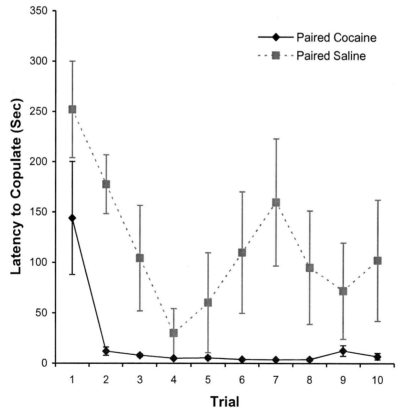

Figure 3. Latency to copulate (±SEM) during a 5 min test for paired subjects that received a CS foll followed by Copulatory opportunity across sexual conditioning trials (Reprinted with permission).

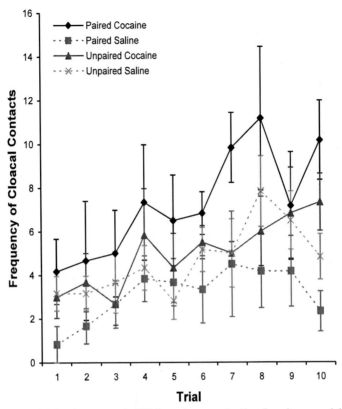

Figure 4. Frequency of cloacal contacts (±SEM) made toward a live female or model of a female during 5 min of each sexual conditionin trial (Reprinted with permission).

Latency to copulate decreased across trials for both paired groups, however group Paired Cocaine had a shorter overall latency than group Paired Saline. Mean frequency of cloacal contacts with the female during the 5 min US period is presented in Figure 4. Although, these data appear to be highly variable at each trial, overall, Group Paired Cocaine made more cloacal contacts than Groups Paired Saline.

In summary, Levens and Akins (2004) found that cocaine-induced behavioral sensitization facilitated conditioned approach behavior, latency to copulate with a female, and increased the frequency of copulation. These findings concur with other studies on the effect of drug-induced sensitization on naturally-rewarding stimuli (Fiorino and Phillips, 1999a; Nocjar and Panksepp, 2002), and they suggest that learning may play an important role in the enhancement of naturally rewarding stimuli by psychostimulants. Harmer and Phillips (1999) reported evidence for the role of learning in a food conditioning paradigm. Using a conditioned inhibition paradigm, rats that were sensitized to amphetamine were given excitatory conditioning in which a stimulus signaled the presentation of sucrose. Then they were presented with a compound stimulus that contained the excitatory stimulus and a new one in the absence of sucrose presentation (inhibitory conditioning). Harmer and Phillips (1999) found that prior repeated exposure to amphetamine facilitated both excitatory and inhibitory conditioning. Together, these results suggest that chronic psychostimulant exposure may enhance future Pavlovian learning.

## CONTEXT-SPECIFICITY OF DRUG EFFECTS ON SEXUAL MOTIVATION AND SEXUAL BEHAVIOR

In the previously discussed experiments (Fiorino and Phillips, 1999a; Levens and Akins, 2004), drug administration and sensitization occurred in a context that was distinct from the context in which sexual responding was allowed to occur. However, Fiorino and Phillips (1999a) also proposed that not only did chronic exposure to amphetamine enhance later sexual responding but that it may have increased the incentive value of the test chamber cues once these cues became associated with the female through learning.

To determine whether their findings were the result of a conditioned association formed between the drug and the test environment, Fiorino and Phillips (1999a) conducted a second experiment in which rats were sensitized with amphetamine in unilevel chambers that were the same size as the bilevel chamber but received a sexual behavior test in the bilevel chambers. The results of this experiment were similar to those in the first experiment. Amphetamine-sensitized males demonstrated shorter mount latencies and a greater number of intromissions and ejaculations than saline controls. Therefore the sexual behavior that was facilitated by behavioral sensitization occurred independently of the environment in which drug had been administered. Rather, behavioral sensitization may have enhanced the incentive qualities of the receptive female, such as the female's pheromones, sounds, earwiggling, and darting behaviors.

This supports the notion that motor sensitization that later enhances sexual responding is context-independent.

In another experiment designed to explore context-specificity of drug conditioning effects, Mitchell and Stewart (1990) injected male rats with morphine (10 mg/kg ip) immediately before placement into a mating arena, with no female present, for 1 hour. On alternate days, they were given saline injections in the animal colony. An unpaired group received the opposite; morphine injections in the animal colony and saline injections in the mating arena. A third group, the control group, received saline injections in both environments. All groups received 4 injections in the arena and 4 in the animal colony. Two days after the last injection of morphine, all rats were injected with saline and given a 30 minute copulation test while in the mating arena.

Results showed that the paired group demonstrated significantly more female-directed behavior (including anogenital exploration, pursuing, sniffing, grooming, and climbing over the female) than either the unpaired group or the control group. Similar results occurred when the rats were tested again for sexual behavior one week later. In addition, latencies to initiate copulation in the environment previously paired with morphine decreased. Thus, rats that were tested for sexual behavior in the same environment where they previously received cocaine showed more sexual motivation than male rats that were tested for sexual behavior in a place other than where they received morphine. This suggests that the context that became associated with the drug state may have later facilitated or modulated behaviors toward the naturally rewarding stimuli of the female such as ear wiggling, etc. It also suggests that under some conditions, cross sensitization may be context specific.

## EFFECTS OF SEXUAL EXPERIENCE ON DRUG RESPONDING

The literature on the effects of psychostimulant exposure and sexual motivation and behavior supports the notion that the overlapping dopaminergic circuitry and reward-related structures may be sufficient to result in enhancement of drug effects on sexual responding. A related question of interest is whether sexual experience or multiple sexual events enhances later responding to drugs of abuse, also referred to as cross-sensitization. There is evidence that similar to repeated drug administration, sexual experience or multiple sexual events sensitize neurons in the dopamine pathway (Kohlert and Meisel, 1999; Bradley and Meisel, 2001). Bradley and Meisel (2001) investigated whether sexual experience would facilitate drug-induced sensitization. They found that when sexually experienced female hamsters were given an amphetamine challenge (1.0 mg/kg) and tested for locomotor activity, they showed an increase in locomotor activity within the first 10 min after injection whereas sexually naïve female hamsters responded to amphetamine 20 min after injection. These findings support the incentive sensitization theory in that there may be converging neural mechanisms mediating responses to drugs and sexual behavior (Robinson and Berridge, 1993).

To date, no experiments have replicated Bradley and Meisel (2001). Levens (2003) attempted to replicate this experiment in using the same procedure in which they previously found that chronic cocaine enhanced sexual conditioning (Levens and Akins, 2004), except presenting cocaine and sexual conditioning trials in reverse order. Male quail were given 10 sexual conditioning trials, one per day. Sexual conditioning trials consisted of presentation of a CS object for 30 sec followed by 5 minutes to interact with a receptive female quail (Group Sex-Paired) or 5 minutes of visual exposure to a receptive female quail (Group No Sex-Paired). Comparable unpaired groups (Groups Sex-Unpaired and No Sex-Unpaired) received similar treatment as their paired counterpart, however, they were given copulatory opportunity or visual access to a female bird for 5 minutes, 3 hours prior to the presentation of the CS object. After the 10 conditioning trials, all birds were given a 10 day withdrawal period, followed by an injection of cocaine and placement into a locomotor activity chamber, once a day for 6 days.

There was virtually no evidence for sexual conditioning in this experiment. All groups showed similar approach behavior toward the CS object, and there were no differences in the frequency of cloacal contact movements made toward the female. Perhaps the only evidence for a conditioned effect is that the sex-paired group had a decrease in latency to copulate with the female.

Figure 5 shows the frequency of photobeam breaks across locomotor activity trials. Although activity increased across trials, there were no significant group differences either overall or across trials. One apparent explanation for this lack of finding is that, although all of the groups copulated with the female, the paired groups may not have been sexually conditioned. This might suggest the importance of learning for the occurrence of this phenomenon.

Another possibility is that males may be less respondent to psychostimulants than females. For example, female rats demonstrate greater levels of psychostimulant-induced locomotor activity (Camp and Robinson, 1988) and demonstrate a more robust behavioral sensitization to cocaine than male rats (van Haaren and Meyer, 1991). Bradley and Meisel (2001) found enhancement of psychostimulant-induced locomotor activity in female hamsters that were sexually experienced. It is possible that if we had used females as subjects, we may have demonstrated this effect.

Finally, it is possible is that the amount of sexual experience male quail were given in our experiment may not have been sufficient to sensitize neurons in the dopamine pathway and therefore not sufficient to induce a cross sensitization. Bradley and Meisel (2001) gave female hamsters 6 weeks of copulatory experience with a male hamster. Male quail in our experiment only received 10 days of experience.

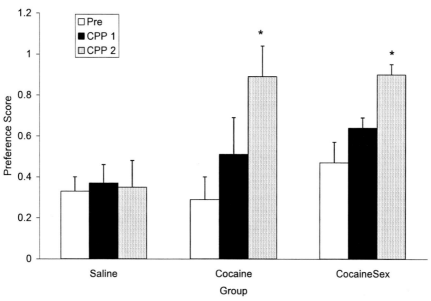

Figure 5. The preference score for groups saline, cocaine, and cocaine-sex during pre-exposure, and CPP tests 1 and 2. * = significantly different from saline, p < 0.05.

## REINSTATEMENT OF DRUG-SEEKING BY A SEXUAL EVENT

Another learning paradigm that has been used to study drug and sex interactions is the reinstatement procedure. The reinstatement procedure has typically been used to investigate events that induce drug relapse or drug-seeking behavior in animals that have been chronically exposed to drugs. In one variation of this procedure, male rats are trained to press a lever to self-administer drugs intravenously. The rats are then subjected to extinction in which lever pressing no longer results in drug administration. Subsequently, when these rats are re-exposed to the previously self-administered drug, reinstatement of drug-reinforced behavior occurs (deWit and Stewart, 1983). Previous research with drugs of abuse has demonstrated reinstatement of heroin-reinforced behavior following prolonged drug free periods (deWit and Stewart, 1983; Shaham, Rodaras, and Stewart, 1994). It has also been demonstrated that exposure to intermittent footshock stress reinstates heroin and cocaine-seeking behavior using this procedure (see Shaham, Erb, and Stewart, 2000 for review).

Shaham and colleagues (Shaham, Puddicome, and Stewart, 1997) used this reinstatement procedure to investigate whether sexual arousal could reinstate heroin-taking behavior in male rats. Rats were trained to self-administer heroin by pressing an active lever. They were then given extinction during which saline was substituted for heroin when the active lever was pressed. Following extinction, male rats were given exposure to a receptive female rat in the self-administration chamber. Under these conditions, male rats failed to reinstate heroin-taking behavior, thus indicating that sexual arousal may not be sufficient to reinstate drug-taking behavior.

Akins and Harris (unpublished) recently conducted a similar study using a variation of the reinstatement procedure that relies more heavily on Pavlovian conditioning rather than operant conditioning. In their experiment, male quail were trained to demonstrate a cocaine-induced conditioned place preference (CPP). They were then given 21 extinction trials that consisted of access to the entire chamber without cocaine or saline injections, similar to prior CPP tests. The day after the last extinction trial, a reinstatement test was conducted in which subjects were given 1 of 3 treatments: subjects that previously received saline received a saline injection (group saline), and those that received cocaine were either given a cocaine injection (group cocaine) or copulatory opportunity with a female bird in the home cage for 5 min (group cocaine-sex). Each treatment was followed immediately by placement into the center chamber with access to the entire chamber for 15 min.

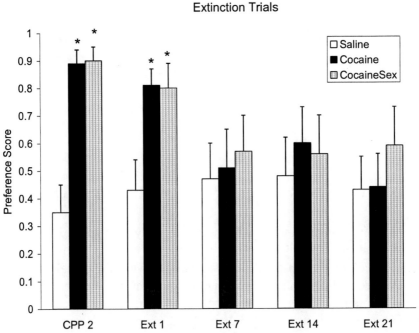

Figure 6. Preference score for groups saline, cocaine, and cocaine-sex for the last CPP trial and extinction trials 1, 7, 14, and 21. * = significantly different from saline, $p < 0.05$.

A preference score was calculated for each group to assess whether subjects increased the amount of time in their initially their trained context or their initially nonpreferred context. For both cocaine groups, the calculation was time in drug-paired chamber divided by time in drug paired chamber plus time in saline-paired chamber. For the saline group, this was time in initially least preferred chamber divided by least preferred plus preferred chamber. The greater the preference score, the more time the subjects spent in the drug paired chamber or for saline controls, the more time they spent in the initially least preferred side.

Figure 6 illustrates the preference score for each group during pre-exposure and the two CPP tests. Cocaine and cocaine-sex groups had significantly greater preference scores than the saline group during the last CPP test, suggesting a shift in preference for the compartment in which they had been placed after receiving an injection of cocaine.

The preference score for each group during the last CPP test and for extinction trials 1, 7, 14, and 21 is represented in Figure 7. Cocaine and cocaine-sex groups demonstrate a decrease in preference score across trials, meaning they were spending decreasing the amount of time they spent in the drug-paired chamber across extinction trials. The asterisks on this figure represents a significant difference for groups during each trial. Cocaine and cocaine-sex groups had a higher preference score on the last CPP test, and on extinction trial 1 but not by the 7th extinction trial.

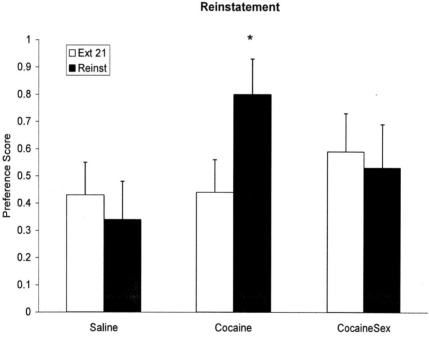

Figure 7. Preference score for groups saline, cocaine, and cocaine-sex during the reinstatement test in which subjects were given an injection of saline, and injection of cocaine, and copulatory opportunity in their home cage, respectively. * = significantly different extinction trial 21.

To determine whether the preference for the drug-paired chamber was reinstated, we compared preference scores for the last extinction trial with the reinstatement test. The results as shown in Figure 8 indicate a significant increase in time spent in the cocaine-paired chamber relative to time spent in the chamber after extinction for the group that received a priming dose of cocaine. However, there was no significant increase in preference score from the last extinction trial to the reinstatement trial when subjects were given copulatory opportunity with a receptive female quail.

Together, the findings of the reinstatement studies with rodents and quail suggest that sexual arousal and sexual conditioning may not be sufficient to elicit a drug reinstatement. Alternatively, one might argue that the experimental manipulations in Akins and Harris (unpublished) were not adequate to alter the dopaminergic system. Although we did not measure dopamine efflux to determine this, Shaham et al. (1997) used a similar procedure as that used by Pfaus and colleagues (Pfaus, Damsma, Nomikos, Wenstern, Blaha, Phillips, and Fibiger, 1990) who found a reliable increase in dopamine output in the nucleus accumbens. Another possibility is that although a sexual event and a drug-taking event activate similar brain systems, there are other significant differences that contribute to their differences in functionality. For example, the opioid system as well as areas of the brain that are not involved in drug reward, such as the mPOA, may mediate sexual motivation and behavior.

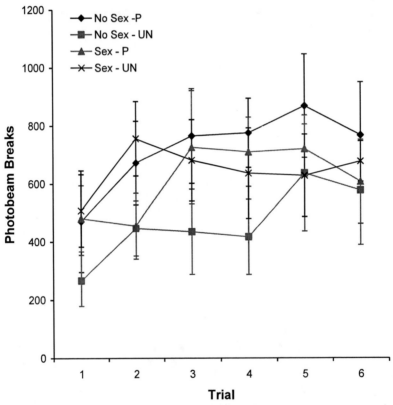

Figure 8. Mean frequency of photobeam breaks for groups No Sex-Paired, No Sex-Unpaired, Sex-Paired, and Sex-Unpaired, axross trials.

Finally, as suggested by Shaham et al. (1997), it is possible that although copulation with a female activates brain systems involved in both sexual behavior and reinstatement of cocaine-seeking behavior, the activation of these systems by sexual stimuli may result in behaviors directed toward sexual stimuli not toward drug-related stimuli. In other words, there might be an increase in interest in sexual-related cues rather drug cues as a result of priming the reward system with sexual behavior. Further research is needed to explore this possibility.

## DISCUSSION

It is well accepted that there is a link between drug abuse and compulsive and high-risk sexual behavior. Clinical studies have consistently found correlations and indicators between drug-related activities and risky sexual behaviors, as well as their relationship to sexually transmitted diseases (e.g., Brooks, Adams, Balka, Whiteman, Zhang, and Sugarman, 2004; Tapert, Aarons, Sedler, and Brown, 2001). Controlled studies using animal models have provided valuable information about the neural and psychological mechanisms that might link drug abuse and high-risk sexual behavior.

The neurochemical events that underlie drug taking behavior and sexual behavior are similar. Both behaviors typically induce increases in extracellular dopamine in the nucleus accumbens. Repeated administration of psychotimulants and discontinuation of drug exposure elicits augmented efflux of dopamine in the NA (Robinson and Becker, 1986; Pierce and Kalivas, 1997). Increases in dopamine efflux have also been associated with sexual interactions in male and female rats (Fiorino et al., 1997; Pfaus, et al., 1990; Mermelstein and Becker, 1995; Pfaus, Damsa, Wenkstern, and Fibiger, 1995) and female hamsters (Meisel, Camp, and Robinson, 1993). In addition, there is augmented dopamine efflux in the NA of amphetamine-sensitized male rats during sexual behavior compared to nonsensitized male rats (Fiorino and Phillips, 1999b).

Repeated administration of psychostimulants results in long-term neural adaptations in the limbic-motor circuitry that are manifest as behavioral sensitization (Robinson and Becker, 1986; Kalivas and Stewart, 1991; Robinson and Berridge, 1993; Pierce and Kalivas, 1997). This same limbic-motor circuitry is believed to be involved in other motivated behaviors such as sexual behavior (e.g., Phillips, et al., 1991). Current research on drug-induced behavioral sensitization and sexual behavior corroborates the data from neurochemical studies. Several studies have demonstrated the enhancing effects of chronic drug exposure on later sexual motivation and sexual behavior (Fiorino and Phillips, 1999a; Levens and Akins, 2004; Nocjar and Panksepp, 2002; Mitchell and Stewart, 1990). This literature supports the incentive sensitization view of addiction which suggests that neural adaptations occur in reward-related brain areas and become sensitized, and that this sensitization appears to increase the incentive value of natural rewards.

Learning has also been proposed to play a role in the psychological process of cross-sensitization (Berridge and Robinson, 2003; Robinson and Berridge, 2003). Stimuli acquire increased incentive salience as a result of Pavlovian associations formed between the stimuli and drug taking. These stimuli may then drive individuals to "want" or have cravings for the drug or, perhaps, other natural rewards. Indeed, the dopaminergic circuitry involved in reward has been thought to play an important role in Pavlovian associations and incentive salience of cues (Berridge and Robinson, 1998; Dickinson, Smith, and Mirenowicz, 2000). Therefore, it may be, at least in part, the sensitization of incentive salience to the drug cues that results in drug-seeking behavior and perhaps, even sex-seeking behavior.

Not all of the literature supports the notion of overlapping systems or of a link of sex and drug-taking behavior though learning. The findings of studies investigating the reverse of drug-sex cross sensitization, that is, whether sexual experience alters subsequent responding to drugs are not in agreement. One study, to date, has demonstrated that sexual experience sensitizes amphetamine-induced locomotor activity in female hamsters (Bradley and Meisel,

2001). The findings of two other studies (Levens, 2003; Shaham et al., 1997) failed to demonstrate that multiple sexual events were sufficient to sensitize later responding to drugs. However, these studies are difficult to compare because the former used female hamsters and the latter two used male quail and male rodents, respectively. In addition, the three studies used different behavioral paradigms (see above). It could also be argued that the findings of Bradley and Meisel (2001) were not very robust since they only found an augmentation of locomotor activity in amphetamine-sensitized female hamsters during the first 10 min, after which difference in locomotor activity was not evident.

Reinstatement studies also do not suggest a simple overlap between sexual behavior and drugs. Exposure to a receptive female and copulation do not appear to be sufficient to reinstatement of drug-seeking behavior (Shaham et al., 1997; Akins and Harris, unpublished). This appears to be the case even though exposure to an estrus female has been shown to provoke activity in both the dopamine (Hull, Lorraine, and Matuszewich, 1995) and opioid systems (Agmo and Berenfeld, 1990). It is possible that the surge in dopamine that occurs as a result of a sexual event is not sufficient to evoke a reinstatement. Another possibility as described by Shaham et al. (1997) is that the lack of finding might that stimuli associated with a sexual event may result in behaviors directed toward those stimuli but not drug-related stimuli. In this case, a sexual event is not likely to increase interest in drug-related cues. Alternatively, perhaps in order to observe evidence of reinstatement of drugs on sexual behavior and vice versa, exposure to the drug and to the sexual event need to occur in the same context. There is some evidence that cross-sensitization of sex and drugs is context-specific (Mitchell and Stewart, 1990). Further studies are needed to investigate the latter two possibilities.

In conclusion, in spite of some disparity in findings about the complementary nature of drugs and abuse and sexual behavior, growing evidence suggests that learning may be involved. Pavlovian associations can occur between stimuli related to drug taking, a sexual event, and/or other environmental cues. These associations can alter conditioned responding to drug-taking and/or sexual cues to induce "drug-seeking" or "sex-seeking" (referred to by Berridge and Robinson, 2003, as "wanting"). These behaviors may lead to relapse, or in the case of drugs and risky sexual behavior, a reciprocal relapse pattern in which drug addicts experience a drug binge episode, followed by risky sexual behavior, and another binge.

# REFERENCES

Agmo, A., and Berenfeld, R. (1990). Reinforcing properties of ejaculation in the male rat: Role of opioids and dopamine. *Behavioral Neuroscience*, 104, 177-182.

Akins, C. K., and Harris, E. (unpublished). Reactivation of cocaine conditioned place preference by cocaine and sexual reinforcement.

Berridge, K. C., and Robinson, T. E. (1998). What is the role of dopamine in reward: Hedonic impact, reward learning, or incentive salience? *Brain Research Review*, 28, 309-369.

Berridge, K. C., and Robinson, T. E. (2003). Parsing reward. *TRENDS in Neurosciences*, 26(9), 507-513.

Booth, R. E, Kwiatkowski, C. F., and Chitwood, D. D. (2000). Sex related HIV risk behaviors: differential risks among injection drug users, crack smokers, and injection drug users who smoke crack. *Drug and Alcohol Dependence*, 58, 219-26.

Bradley, K. C., and Meisel, R. L. (2001). Sexual behavior induction of c-Fos in the nucleus accumbens and amphetamine-stimulated lomocotor activity are sensitized by previous sexual experience in female Syrian hamsters. *Journal of Neuroscience*, 21(6), 2123-2130.

Brooks, J. S., Adams, R. E., Balka, E. B., Whiteman, M., Zhang, C., and Sugarman, R. (2004). Illicit drug use and risky sexual behavior among African American and Puerto Rican urban adolescents: the longitudinal links. *Journal of Genetic Psychology*, 165(2), 203-220.

Camp, D. M., and Robinson, T. E. (1988). Susceptibility to sensitization. I. Sex differences in the enduring effects of chronic d-amphetamine treatment on locomotion, stereotyped behavior, and brain monoamines. *Behavioural Brain Research*, 30, 55-68.

De Wit, H., and Stewart, J. (1983). Drug reinstatement of heroin-reinforced responding in the rat. *Psychopharmacology*, 79, 29-31.

Dickinson, A., Smith, J., and Mirenowicz, J. (2000). Dissociation of Pavlovian and instrumental incentive learning under dopamine antagonists. *Behavioral Neuroscience*, 114, 468-483.

Domjan, M., Cusato, B., and Krause, M. (2004). Learning with arbitrary versus ecological conditioned stimuli: Evidence from sexual conditioning. *Psychonomic Bulletin and Review*, 11,(2), 232-246.

Fiorino, D. F., Coury, A., and Phillips, A. G. (1997). Dynamic changes in nucleus accumbens dopamine efflux during the Coolidge effect in male rats. *Journal of Neuroscience*, 17, 4849-4855.

Fiorino, D. F., and Phillips, A. G. (1999a). Facilitation of sexual behavior in male rats following *d*-amphetamine-induced behavioral sensitization. *Psychopharmacology*, 142, 200-208.

Fiorino, D. F., and Phillips, A. G. (1999b). Facilitation of sexual behavior and enhanced dopamine efflux in the nucleus accumbens of male rats after D-amphetamine-induced behavioral sensitization. *Journal of Neuroscience*, 19(1), 456-463.

Harmer, C. J. , and Phillips, G. D. (1999). Enhanced conditioned inhibition following repeated pretreatment with *d*-amphetamine. *Psychopharmacology*, 142, 120-131.

Hull, E. M., Lorrain, D. S., and Matuszewich, L. (1995). Extracellular dopamine in the medial preoptic area: Implications for sexual motivation and hormonal control of copulation. *Journal of Neuroscience*, 15(11), 7465-7471.

Kalivas, P. W., and Stewart, J. (1991). Dopamine transmission in the initiation and expression of drug- and stress-induced sensitization of motor activity. *Brain Research Reviews*, 16, 223-244.

Kall, K. I. (1992). Effects of amphetamine on sexual behavior of male i.v. drug users in Stockholm—a pilot study. *AIDS Education and Prevention*, 1, 6-17.

Kall, K. I., and Nilsonne, A. (1995). Preference for sex on amphetamine: a marker for HIV risk behaviour among male intravenous amphetamine users in Stockholm. *AIDS Care*, 7, 171-188.

Kohlbert, J. G., and Meisel, R. L. (1999). Sexual experience sensitizes mating-related nucleus accumbens dopamine responses in female Syrian hamsters. *Behavioral Brain Rsearch*, 99, 45-52.

Levens, N. (2003). *Sex and drug interactions in male Japanese quail: Incentive sensitization and dopamine.* Unpublished dissertation.

Levens, N., and Akins, C. K. (2004) Cocaine induces conditioned place preference and increases locomotor activity in male Japanese quail. *Pharmacology, Biochemistry, and Behavior*, 68, 71-80.

Mermelstein, P. G., and Becker, J. B. (1995). Increased extracellular dopamine in the nucleus accumbens and striatum of the female rat during paced copulatory behavior. *Behavioral Neuroscience*, 109, 354-365.

Miesel, R. L., Camp, D. M., and Robinson, T. E. (1993). A microdialysis study of ventral striatal dopamine during sexual behavior in female Syrian hamsters. *Behavioral Brain Research*, 55, 151-157.

Mitchell, J. B., and Stewart, J. (1990). Facilitation of sexual behavior in the male rat in the presence of stimuli previously paired with systemic injections of morphine. *Pharmacology, Biochemistry, and Behavior*, 35, 367-372.

Nocjar, C., and Panksepp, J. (2002). Chronic intermittent amphetamine pretreatment enhances future appetitive behavior for drug- and natural-reward: Interaction with environmental variables. *Behavioral Brain Research*, 128, 189-203.

Pfaus, J. G., Damsma, G., Nomikos, G. G., Wenkstern, D., Blaha, C. D., Phillips, A. G., and Fibiger, H. C. (1990). Sexual behavior enhances central dopamine transmission in the male rat. *Brain Research*, 530, 345-348.

Pfaus, J. G., Damsma, G., Wenkstern, D., Fibiger, H. C. (1995). Sexual activity increases dopamine transmission in the nucleus accumbens and striatum of female rats. *Brain Research*, 693, 21-30.

Phillips, A. G., Pfaus, J. G., and Blaha, C. D. (1991). Dopamine and motivated behavior: Insights provided by in vivo analysis. In: Willner, P., and Scheel-Kruger, J. (Eds.). *The mesocorticolimbic dopamine system: From action to motivation.* Wiley, London, pp. 199-224.

Pierce, R. C. and Kalivas, P. W. (1997). A circuitry model of the expression of behavioral sensitization to amphetamine-like stimulants. *Brain Research Reviews*, 25, 192-216.

Robinson, T. E., and Becker, J. B. (1986). Enduring changes in brain and behavior produced by chronic amphetamine administration: A review and evaluation of animal models of amphetamine psychosis. *Brain Research Reviews*, 11, 157-198.

Robinson, T. E., and Berridge, K. C. (1993). The neural basis of drug craving: An incentive-sensitization theory of addiction. *Brain Research Reviews*, 18, 247-291.

Robinson, T. E., Berridge, K. C. (2000). The psychology and neurobiology of addiction: An incentive-sensitization view. *Addiction*, 95(Supl 2), S91-S117.

Robinson, T. E., Berridge, K. C. (2003). Addiction. *Annual Review of Psychology*, 54, 25-53.

Ross, M. W., Hwang, L. Y., Zack, L., Bull, L., and Williams, M. L. (2002). Sexual risk behaviours and STIs in drug abuse treatment populations whose drug of choice is crack cocaine. *International Journal of STD and AIDS*, 13, 769-774.

Shaham, Y., Erb, S., and Stewart, J. (2000). Stress-induced relapse to heroin and cocaine seeking in rats: A review. *Brain Research Reviews*, 33, 13-33.

Shaham, Y., Rodaros, D., and Stewart, J. (1994). Reinstatement of heroin-reinstated behavior following long-term extinction: Implications for the treatment of relapse to drug-taking. *Behavioral Pharmacology*, 5, 360-364.

Shaham, Y., Puddicombe, J., and Stewart, J. (1997). Sexually arousing events and relapse to heroin-seeking in sexually experienced male rats. *Physiology and Behavior*, 61(2), 337-341.

Tapert, S. F., Aarons, G. A., Sedlar, G. R., and Brown. S. A. (2001). Adolscent substance use and sexual risk-taking behavior. *Journal of Adolescent Health*, 28(3), 181-189.

Van Haaren, F., Meyer, M. E. (1991). Sex differences in locomotor activity after acute and chronic cocaine administration. *Pharmacology, Biochemistry, and Behavior*, 39 (4), 923-927.

Washton, A. M. (1989). Cocaine abuse and compulsive sexuality. *Medical Aspects of Human Sexuality, December,* 32-40.

Weatherby, N. L., Shultz, J. M., Chitwood, D. D., McCoy, H. V., McCoy, C. B., Ludwig, D. D., and Edlin, B. R. (1992). Crack cocaine use and sexual activity in Miami, Florida. *Journal of Psychoactive Drugs, 24,* 373–380.

In:  Substance Abuse, Assessment and Addiction    ISBN: 978-1-61122-931-8
Editors: Kristina A. Murati and Allison G. Fischer    © 2011 Nova Science Publishers, Inc.

*Chapter 4*

# BINGE DRINKING- A COMMENTARY

## *Jan Gill, Julie Murdoch and Fiona O'May*

Queen Margaret University, Edinburgh,
Scotland, UK

## INTRODUCTION

The term binge drinking is in common usage. Having gained some degree of international credibility, it is employed frequently in reports emerging from research and national agencies, but also within the media and popular press. Implicitly it is linked with the negative consequences of the excesses of alcohol consumption, particularly within the younger members of the population.

This chapter will consider the evolution of the term in the recent past, how it is interpreted and will discuss its value as society in general seeks to curb the excesses of alcohol consumption and address the short and longer term harm that ensues.

## HOW HAS THE TERM BINGE DRINKING (BD) EMERGED IN THE RECENT RESEARCH LITERATURE AND HOW IS IT DEFINED?

BD has been used by some within the alcohol research literature to describe a pattern of drinking which involves the intake of a large amount of alcohol within a relatively short period of time. Implicitly it is associated with negative health and behavioural repercussions i.e. it carries a 'risk'. Early work by Cahalan et al. (1969) suggested that drinking beyond 5 US drinks (i.e., 70g alcohol) on one occasion was linked to particular harm. This definition was adapted to include a time frame of drinking ; i.e. 5 drinks in a row within a two week period (O'Malley et al., 1984). An additional modification resulted from an appreciation of the differences between the genders in terms of body water composition and alcohol metabolic rates and the '4 drinks in a row for females and 5 drinks for males in a row within the past two weeks' (Wechsler et al. 1994) classification emerged from work related to the

USA College Alcohol Study. However several authors were critical because of the lack of specificity associated with the phrase 'in a row' and also because it failed to relate the biological consequences of BD to the blood alcohol levels known to be linked to intoxication e.g., Beirness et al., (2004) and Lange and Voas (2001). In 2004 the NIAAA National Advisory Council in the US attempted to address these concerns by defining BD as 'a pattern of drinking alcohol that brings blood alcohol concentration (BAC) to 0.08 gram percent or above. For the typical adult, this pattern corresponds to consuming 5 or more [US] drinks (male) or four or more drinks (female) in about two hours' (p. 3). (The council distinguished this pattern of drinking from a "bender" – two or more days of 'sustained heavy drinking'.)

Further clarification of the term binge drinking is evident within the literature. For example sub-classes of binge drinkers have been categorised. Weschler et al. (1994) suggested that those who binge drank one or two times in the last two weeks were 'infrequent' bingers while three or more times in the same time period categorised 'frequent' bingers. Valencia-Martin et al. (2007) sub-divided binge drinkers into 'frequent' (3 or more binge drinking episodes) or 'sporadic' ( one or two episodes) but within a 30 day time period. Cranford et al (2006) replaced the two week timeframe with 'one year' claiming that it was more effective at detecting 'risky drinkers'.

Townshend and Duka (2002) calculated a 'binge score' for their study based on questionnaire responses linking to pattern of drinking viz; speed of drinking, number of times drunk in the last 6 months and the percentage of times a drinking episode led to a participant's drunkenness. From their findings these authors suggest that their binge drinking score was more effective at distinguishing the binge from the non-binge drinker than the 5/4 measure of Weschler et al., (1994) which was more associated with the quantity of alcohol drunk.

## WHAT CLAIMS ARE MADE FOR THE USEFULNESS OF MEASURING INDIVIDUAL CONSUMPTION BY THIS MEANS?

There are two particular questions to address. Firstly what are the potential adverse effects and risks, of this form of drinking and secondly, does the 5/4 definition of BD with its various caveats, represent a useful measure with which to predict risk?

On the first point, it could be argued that the intake of a large amount of alcohol over a relatively short period of time could pose at least six categories of risk for a drinker; (i) immediate behavioural effects e.g., driving while under the influence, committing an act of vandalism etc, (ii) longer term behavioural effects e.g. dropping out of studies as a result of frequent absence from class, disqualification from driving, (iii) damaging effects on close friends, acquaintances or partners, (iv) short term physiological/health effects e.g. passing out, vomiting, immediate injury, (v) long term health actions e.g., on the liver resulting from regular exposure to large doses of alcohol and (vi) a predisposition to chronic forms of alcohol abuse.

If the incidence of BD can be accurately quantified and there is evidence linking this measurement to 'risk', then the argument for the early identification of this pattern of drinking and the subsequent development of appropriate harm reduction strategies seems clear.

The literature concerning the short and longer term physiological/ health risk is slowly accumulating. Additionally several reports have emerged to suggest that BD may incur an increased risk of developing a harmful pattern of consumption in later life (Bonomo et al., 2004; McCarty et al., 2004; Jefferis et al., 2005). Midanik et al. (1996) reported that the drinking of five or more drinks in a row 'ever' within the previous year was characterised by a greater risk of driving after drinking, alcohol-related employment problems and ICD-10 alcohol dependence. Among students, Weschler et al. (1994) reported that the odds of driving after drinking, of experiencing five or more alcohol-related problems in the past year, increased for binge drinkers compared to non-binge drinkers. Crucially the odds for the frequent binge drinkers were greater than those of the infrequent binge drinkers.

(For further discussion of alcohol misuse and its repercussions among university college students see Perkins, 2002; Wechsler and Austin,1998; Wechsler and Nelson, 2006; Wechsler et al., 1995, 2002;)

Certainly the 5/4 measure has gained some degree of credence within national survey tools e.g. the National Institute on Alcohol Abuse and Alcoholism (NIAAA), US National Institute of Health, Centers for Disease Control and Prevention, and the World Health Organisation. Wechsler and Nelson (2006) have argued that the 'purpose of the binge measure is for public health surveillance and not to diagnose alcohol use disorders for individuals' (p923) and 'as a screen to identify students who may need additional clinical assessment for intervention' (p922). They also suggest that the term BD is a summary measure which can be employed to predict the risk of some 'negative outcome' for populations and that it will permit comparison of drinking behaviour across research studies. (A point discussed further below.)

Naimi et al. (2003) argue that the term is useful to 'communicate concepts of risk to the general public' (p1636) suggesting that BD almost always leads to intoxication and subsequent impairment. They cite evidence that most drinkers engage in binge drinking behaviour with the intention of becoming drunk.

## ON WHAT GROUNDS HAS THE TERM BD BEEN CRITICISED?

The first problem refers to semantics. This criticism was articulated by the editor of a major US academic journal (Schuckit, 1998) who argued that the term binge drinking was · historically more commonly associated with the phenomenon seen in the clinical field where a person drinks over 'an extended period of time (often operationalized as at least 2 days) during which a person repeatedly administers a substance to the point of intoxication, and gives up his/her usual activities and obligations in order to use the substance' (p123). Consequently, he suggested, simply to avoid confusion, that the term *binge drinking* should be reserved for this extended drinking behaviour while the drinking pattern described by Wechsler et al. (1994), undoubtedly of importance should, (it is suggested in guidance later issued by the journal), be referred to as 'heavy drinking'/ 'heavy use' or 'heavy episodic drinking'/ 'heavy episodic use'. There are many individuals, particularly within the clinical field who endorse the view of Schuckit (1998) and several alternative terms have appeared within the literature over the years (see Table 1).

Despite these concerns the term binge drinking continues to be used to describe the sessional intake of alcohol. This is particularly evident in the media, (a current search of the UK 'Times' newspaper index reveals almost 500 'hits' for 'binge drinking' in the last three years) but also within official government publications and research literature. Critically this inconsistency extends also to the quantitative definition (see Table 2).

For example the World Health Organisation (WHO, 2004) define binge drinking as a 'risky single drinking occasion' (p28) but also use the descriptor 'Heavy episodic drinkers' to present international prevalence figures while the Alcohol Advisory Council of NZ (2005) define 'binge drinking' in the following manner; 'when you drink a lot more than usual on any one occasion'. In terms of amount of alcohol they advise 'No more than 6 drinks per occasion for men, no more than 4 for women'.

**Table 1. Examples of terms employed within the literature to describe the sessional drinking of alcohol**

| Term | Reference |
| --- | --- |
| Spree drinking | Brown and Gunn (1977) |
| Heavy episodic binge drinking | Nezleck et al (1993) |
| Frequent binge drinking | Schulenberg et al (1996) |
| Heavy sessional drinking | Measham (1996) |
| Risky single occasion drinking | Murgraff et al. (1999) |
| Concentrated Drinking Episode | Gill (2002) |
| Heavy Episodic Drinking | Makela and Mustonen (2007) |

In Australia the NHMRC (2001) report that 'Daily consumption should not exceed 4 standard drinks for men two for women, 4-6 should be viewed as hazardous for men, 2-4 for women'. In their later publication (NHMRC, 2007) the NHMRC make the following comment on the term binge drinking; 'This term is avoided as far as possible…because its meaning is ill defined and unclear'(p19). Statistics Canada (2004) define episodes of heavy drinking as five or more drinks on a single occasion. There is no gender distinction.

Within the UK, two measures of sessional intake have been described and both have been expressed in terms of the prevailing guidelines for safe drinking. The first (Moore et al., 1994) equated binge drinking with the sessional consumption of more than half of the *weekly* limits of consumption advocated by the Health Education Council (HEC,1985) i.e. half of 21 standard UK drinks for men, 14 for women. A later definition also emerged following the move within the UK to recommending 'Sensible Drinking' *daily* limits of consumption (Department of Health , 1995) i.e., daily limits of 3-4 standard drinks for men, 2-3 for women. Critically, it was suggested in this document that guidance on daily amounts could be 'helpful in deciding how much to drink on a single occasion and thus help people to avoid drunkenness' (p24). Following this reasoning many national agencies in the UK and researchers define BD as drinking more than double the recommended daily limit on any one day in the past week (8 standard UK drinks for men , 6 for women).

Many UK agencies add caveats to their definitions of binge or sessional drinking; the General Household Survey (Rickards et al., 2004) follows the above quantitative definition but describe it as 'heavy drinking that would be likely to lead to intoxication'. The

Parliamentary Office of Science and Technology (2005) state that binge drinking 'refers to the consumption of excessive amounts of alcohol within a limited time period. Such behaviour [BD] leads to a rapid increase in blood alcohol concentration (BAC) and consequently drunkenness' (p1). Alcohol Concern (2003) define BD as 'Drinking sufficient alcohol to reach a state of intoxication on one occasion or in the course of one drinking session' (p2).

However Anderson and Baumberg (2006) in their extensive report prepared for the European Commission, preface evidence relating to binge drinking levels in Europe with the following statement 'this chapter uses the term 'binge drinking' only when looking at reported drinking occasions above a given cut-off level of drinking, while 'intoxication' and 'drunkenness' are used to refer to self reports about how the individual perceived their state after drinking' (p93). They also state that drinking '5 or more 'standard drinks' on a single occasion is the most common definition of binge drinking but make no gender distinction.

Eurobarometer (2003) was also prepared for the European Commission and had the remit of interviewing over sixteen thousand European Union (EU) citizens aged 15 years or over. Participants were asked how often in the last month they had drunk the equivalent of one bottle of wine, 5 pints/bottles of beer or five measures of spirit on one drinking occasion. This was seen as 'excessive alcohol consumption'. A later study, Eurobarometer (2007) interviewed over twenty eight thousand EU citizens and defined the size of drinks more precisely (a 150ml glass of wine, one 330ml can of beer or 40ml of spirit). These definitions were used to monitor consumption at '5 or more drinks on one occasion'. No gender distinction was made nor was it specifically defined as 'binge drinking'.

**Table 2. Examples of International definitions of BD/Sessional intake of Alcohol**

| Publication | Limit of sessional intake of alcohol (g) for men | Limit of sessional intake of alcohol (g) for women |
|---|---|---|
| US (Wechsler et al.,1994) | 70 | 56 |
| Alcohol Advisory Council New Zealand (2005) | 60 | 40 |
| NHMRC Australia (2001) | 40-60 | 20-40 |
| Statistics Canada (2004) | 68 (both genders) | |
| UK (Moore et al., 1994) | 80 | 56 |
| UK (Rickards et al.,(2004) | 48-64 | 32-48 |
| Eurobarometer (2003) | 80 (beer) or 72 (wine) or 40 (spirit) (both genders) | |
| Eurobarometer (2007) | 53 (beer) or 72 (wine) or 64 (spirit) (both genders) | |

Using national definitions of the alcohol content of standard drinks, Table 2 describes the information presented in the above references contrasted with the definition of binge drinking proposed by Wechsler at al. (1994). The limits of sessional intake for men vary from 40g to 80g for men, 20-80g for women.

While there is evidence of some reluctance to adopt the term BD to describe sessional drinking, there is nevertheless clear disagreement as to how it should be quantified. This is also evidenced in Table 3 which summarises the disparity in the descriptors of sessional drinking employed within recent international research literature.

## PROBLEMS WITH QUANTIFYING SESSIONAL DRINKING

Thus the prevailing evidence suggests that use of the term BD as a descriptor of the sessional intake of alcohol is still favoured by the authors of some reports and scientific studies. Secondly, irrespective of favoured terminology, it is clear that there is considerable variation in the parameters used to define this pattern of drinking quantitatively and thereby, the associated dose of alcohol. The last point is crucial when the potential risk of this form of drinking is considered.

In truth this lack of consensus, in different guises, has bedevilled alcohol research for some time. There is a lack of clarity and agreement associated with much drinking measurement terminology and this can seriously restrict meaningful comparison between study findings. The terms 'safe' drinking, 'moderate' drinking, 'heavy' drinking can have a multiplicity of definitions. Additionally, when attempts are made to compare research evidence in terms of reported levels of sessional intake of alcohol the ineptitude of the term 'drink' is clearly evident. There is much disparity between how alcohol drinks are quantified and then reported in studies e.g. the terms millilitres, grams, fluid ounces of pure alcohol, fluid ounces of drink, standard units of drink are all employed. While it is true that the number of alcoholic drink varieties available to consumers has increased greatly, many researchers do little to facilitate the comparison of the drink quantities which they report. The elastic term 'drink' survives often without definition in spite of the fact the alcohol content of national standard drinks varies from 6 g in Austria to 19.75 g in Japan (over threefold) (ICAP,1998). Additionally, the '5/4 drinks' definition proposed by Wechsler et al (1994 ) to define binge drinking, is often applied without modification. The appeal by Brick (2006) to report all drinks and overall consumption in terms of grams of alcohol seems appropriate and somewhat overdue.

Many surveys designed to investigate sessional intake depend on the accurate account of a participant's drinking quantities usually from the previous week. The accuracy of this measure is threatened by poor recall (and given that the endpoint of an evening is often intoxication, this is an important point), poor understanding of drink sizes and the extensive range of 'designer drinks' with differing alcohol contents. Another problem which may contribute to the inaccurate quantification of the sessional intake of alcohol is the fact that self-poured drinks tend to be 'generous measures'. Gill and Donaghy (2004) and Gill and O'May (2007) suggested from studies conducted within the UK, that self-poured drinks of wine or spirit are likely to contain twice the assumed content of alcohol.

**Table 3. Examples from research of measures used to describe sessional alcohol intake**

| Country | Ref | Sessional Drinking definition | Term employed | Time period | Grams of alcohol for men | Grams of alcohol for women |
|---|---|---|---|---|---|---|
| New Zealand | Kypri et al. (2005)<br><br>(Asked how many of drinking episodes resulted in intoxication) | Consumption of 6 or more drinks per occasion for men. 4 or more for women | 'Binge Occasion' | 7 day retrospective diary. | 60g or more | 40g or more |
| Spain | Valencia-Martin et al. (2007)<br><br>(This group also calculated prevalence of frequent (3 or more episodes) or sporadic (1 or 2) episodes of binge drinking.) | Intake of 8 or more standard units of alcohol in men and 6 or more in women | Binge drinking | Drinking session in the preceding 30 days | 80g or more | 60g or more |
| Spain | Alvarez et al. (2006)<br><br>(Also asked if respondents had at least one episode of drunkenness in last year.) | 5 or more drinks on a single occasion | Episodes of 5 or more drinks | Preceding year | 50 g or more | 50 g or more |
| Canada | Murray et al. (2002) | Frequency of consumption of 8 or more drinks per occasion (no gender difference) | Binge drinking | 12 months | 104 g | 104 g |
| Netherlands | Van den Wildenberg et al. (2007) | 6 or more drinks on 1 occasion) (No gender distinction) | Binge drinking | 2 weeks | 60 g | 60 g |
| Finland | Kauhanen et al. (1997) | Over six bottles of beer. (men only) | Binging | week | 72 g | n/a |
| Sweden | Hansagi et al. (1995) | Half a bottle of spirit or 2 bottles of wine at one session. | Binge drinking | How often? | 112/144 g assuming 40% ABV spirit; 12% ABV wine | 112/144 g assuming 40% ABV spirit; 12% ABV wine |

**Table 3 – Continued**

| Country | Ref | Sessional Drinking definition | Term employed | Time period | Grams of alcohol for men | Grams of alcohol for women |
|---|---|---|---|---|---|---|
| Sweden | Selin (2003) | One bottle of wine or a corresponding quantity of other alcoholic beverages on one occasion. (no gender distinction) | Binge drinking | week | Assuming 12% ABV = 72 g | Assuming 12% ABV = 72 g |
| Denmark | Yuan et al. (2004) | 8 or more drinks for females. | Binge drinking | During pregnancy up to 36 weeks. | n/a | 96 |
| Norway | Alvik et al. (2005) | 5 or more standard drinks, (women) | Binge drinking | During pregnancy | n/a | 60-65 g or more |
| Norway | Alvik et al. (2006) | At least 5-7 standard drinks first antenatal visit, 8 or more at 30 weeks of pregnancy and 12 or more at 6 months after term (women). | Binge drinking | During pregnancy | n/a | 60-84 g; 96 g or more; 144 g or more. |
| Germany | Alte et al. (2004) | Five or more drinks (no gender distinction) | Binge drinking | month | More than 60 g | More than 60 g |
| Germany | Dietrich, A et al. (2004) | Number of days with 5 or more drinks. (No gender distinction) | Binge drinking | month | More than 60 g | More than 60 g |
| Russia | Kristjanson et al. (2007) | 5 or more drinks (women) | | An occasion in the past 30 days. | n/a | 70 g |
| Russia | Malyutina et al. (2002) | Consumption of 160g/day or more of pure ethanol usually lasting for a week and over'. (For males) | | n/a | 160 | n/a |
| France | Com-Ruelle et al. (2006) | Frequency of drinking 6 or more glasses on one occasion such that they are drunk. | | | 60 g | 60 g |

Thus drinking which takes place in the home setting or out with licensed premises may be particularly hard to quantify.

A further source of inaccuracy is highlighted by McAlaney and McMahon (2006). They suggest that the reported differences in the prevalence of binge drinking in different samples of the UK population may simply be explained by different interpretation of the 'same' binge drinking definition. The 8/6 measure referred to above was used in one national UK study to identify those drinking greater than this amount and by another to quantify drinkers drinking at this level *or* above. As might be expected the latter study reported higher values.

Surveys attempting to monitor levels of binge drinking should also consider the time point in the year when sampling occurs. Two US studies suggested that levels may be highest in the summer months, (Fitzgerald and Mulford, 1984; Cho et al., 2001) while Carpenter (2003) also from analysing US data reported similar findings but additionally applied them to January.

## What Is the Pharmacological Evidence to Support the Modifications Made to the Definition of Binge Drinking as Proposed by Wechsler et al. (1994)?

As noted above the NIAAA council (2004) approved a definition of binge drinking which equated it to resulting from drinking 5/4 US drinks drunk over a period of around two hours.

The BAC selected can be justified on the basis that Schuckit (2000) has linked a BAC of 0.08 to 0.15g/100ml to the symptoms of 'ataxia, decreased mentation, poor judgement and labile mood' (p69). Several countries have a BAC of 0.08g/100ml as the legal limit for driving (US, UK, Canada and New Zealand). The implication, it could be argued, is that this level of impairment increases 'risk' to an unacceptable level for a drinker and their associates i.e., the definition of binge drinking is appropriate.

The NIAAA council recognise that the definition cannot be correct for certain individuals with potentially altered alcohol metabolism e.g., the older person or those on medications. However, the definition has also been criticised for its failure to consider additional general factors known to influence the final BAC achieved, e.g., individual variations in alcohol tolerance, body weight, fat levels, food intake etc. This fact can be underscored by comparing the volume of distribution for a dose of alcohol for an 14 year old adolescent male and a 25 year old male. Using the algorithms of Watson et al. (1981), it is possible to calculate that the volume of distribution of the adolescent is 77% of that of the adult. The BAC resulting from a similar dose of alcohol will be proportionately different.

Several investigators have use field studies to investigate the BAC found in young adult drinkers drinking in a BD manner Three studies used actual BAC measurements ( Lange and Voas, 2001; Thombs et al., 2003 and Wright, 2006) while Kypri et al. (2005) estimated BAC from knowing a subject's gender, weight, alcohol metabolism rate and length of drinking period. In each study the quantity of drinks consumed predicted a greater proportion of 'binge drinkers' than the BAC values. Two of these studies were performed before the NIAAA published their definition of binge drinking which contains the additional caveat that the 4/5 drinks must be consumed in a 2 hour period. The 2 hour time interval in the definition is interesting. It is much shorter than the length of time many would spend socialising. The

NIAAA definition would imply that if the drinker has spread this intake i.e., consumed their drinks slowly then their BAC would not have reached the critical value and they would not be classified as binge drinkers. In practice, however, most research studies and surveys do not apply this condition and usually categorise BD simply on the basis of amount of alcohol consumed.

A comment made by Lange and Voas (2001) is interesting. They suggest that 'the use of this term [binge drinking] to describe drinking events that do not produce illegal BACs or significant impairment may affect the credibility of responsible drinking campaigns' (p315). Thus many who know that they have drunk 4/5 US drinks may also be aware that they have not experienced significant impairment. However there is an important counter argument; it is also crucial to stress that in the 'binge drinker' who spreads their consumption of alcohol, the liver will still have to process 70g/56g of alcohol. Spreading consumption may lower behavioural repercussions but our understanding of the long term health effects of frequently challenging the liver in this way at a relatively early stage in life, is still rather poor.

## ADDITIONAL CRITICISMS OF THE 5/4 MEASURE

Dimeff et al. (1995) have suggested that the term is dangerous for it labels responsible drinkers with a pathological term while the, Higher Education Center in the US has criticised the 5/4 measure as being too insensitive to detect changes in student drinking in response to new programs and policies which were nevertheless suggested by other measures e.g., BAC levels (US Department of Education, 2000).

Some have criticised the 5/4 definition of Wechsler because it effectively categorises all binge drinkers within one group (Gruenewald et al 2003). The range of consumption within the group may be very poorly described and heavily drinking individuals may be undetected but also given some degree of acceptability. White et al (2006) found that among male binge drinkers around half consumed twice the binge threshold 10+ (US) drinks (= 140 g of alcohol).

Gill and O'May (2007) found that the definition of binge drinking offered by female student drinkers ranged from 24 g to 448g of alcohol while a range of actual consumption equal to 56g to 192g was reported for consumption on the heaviest day in the previous week (Gill et al.,2007).

## ALTERNATIVE TERMINOLOGY FOR BINGE DRINKING

Inevitably there has been a concentration on the harmful and damaging repercussions of BD and the consequent need to quantify and measure it. However the US Department of Education (2000) suggest that definitions of heavy sessional intake of alcohol involving wording which relays the impact on people's lives might be more beneficial. Thus in the equation *750ml of alcohol (12%v/v) = 72 g of alcohol = intoxication = risk of harming self or important others*, it might be better to concentrate the wording of messages on the last two variables. Similarly the International Center for Alcohol Policies (ICAP, 2005) would prefer a definition which enunciated the ' implications for risk of health and social harm' (p 6-2 ). In this regard the terminology suggested by Murgraff et al. (1999) (Risky Single Occasion Drinking) has much to commend it.

It is also important to recognise the views of the drinker. For example Miller et al. (2005) in their analysis of previous UK survey data split respondents into 'spreaders' and 'bingers' on the basis of the number of times drinkers consumed alcohol each week. They recorded the negative and positive experiences reported by drinkers. Interestingly the highest level of positive experiences were reported by the binge drinkers at high levels of consumption – the consumption of 232 g of alcohol in one or two drinking sessions.

There is also evidence among the younger age groups that they identify very poorly with the quantitative BD definitions listed earlier. Guise and Gill (2007) found that for a group of female university students the quantity of drinks was perceived as being less important than the effects. Gill and O'May (2007) reported that first year university students favoured a more qualitative definition of BD, one that described a behavioural end point e.g. 'being drunk', 'sick' 'hammered'. The UK health education definition was seen as clinical, quantitative, favoured by researchers but not really relevant to the drinker (O'May and Gill (unpublished findings). The favouring of a more qualitative definition has been reported by others (WTAG, 2004). Another potential criticism of the mathematical rule to identify binge drinking is that it does not consider the social aspects of drinking. Drinking colleagues may act either positively or negatively in terms of making harm more likely. Furthermore several reports have identified some degree of self-management of sessional drinking; the initial drinks are taken to achieve a certain level of intoxication, later drinks to maintain it (Moore et al., 2007; Hammersley and Ditton, 2005).

An interesting perspective on the societal cost of 'binge drinking' to the UK , its impact on the night time economy and the government response to it, is presented by Hayward and Hobbs (2007). They suggest that 'the government continues an agenda of market led liberalization of the retailing of alcohol' (p450) and that 'Currently it is the logic of the market that informs government policy on alcohol, and it is in this chaotic environment the binge drinker has emerged from a plethora of definitions to capture the nation's headlines. Bingeing is central to the spectacle of the 'Night Time Economy' and 'is marketed as integral to the liminal quest' (p451).

## CONCLUDING REMARKS

Binge drinking is a term which can be justifiably criticised on several grounds. Its continued use is probably attributed in part to its popularity within the media. There is evidence of particular risks being associated with a heavy single occasion drinking pattern. However, there is a clear need within the research community to adopt standardised descriptive methods when quantitative tools are employed. Additionally, a further goal should be the greater understanding of the associated health impact in the short and longer term, particularly for certain groups e.g., the young underage drinker and females. From this knowledge a more widely accepted definition of heavy single occasion use, and one that has greater resonance with these critical groups, may emerge. A qualitative behavioural definition may have some merit.

# REFERENCES

Alcohol Advisory Council of NZ (2005) Low risk drinking. *http://www.alcohol.org.nz/ LowRiskDrinking.aspx*, accessed 12/12/07.

Alcohol Concern (2003) Factsheet 20: Binge Drinking. London, UK: Alcohol Concern.

Alte, D., Luedemann, J., Rose, H. J., and John, U. (2004) Laboratory Markers Carbohydrate-Deficient Transferrin, gamma-Glutamyltransferase, and Mean Corpuscular Volume Are Not Useful as Screening Tools for High-Risk Drinking in the General Population: Results From the Study of Health in Pomerania (SHIP), *Alcohol Clin. Exp. Res.*, 28, 931-940.

Alvarez, F.J., Fierro I. and del Rio ,M.C. (2006) Alcohol- related Social Consequences in Castille and Leon, Spain. *Alcohol Clin. Exp. Res.,* 30, 656-664.

Alvik, A., Haldorsen, T., and Lindemann, R. (2005) Consistency of Reported Alcohol Use by Pregnant Women: Anonymous Versus Confidential Questionnaires With Item Nonresponse Differences, *Alcohol. Clin. Exp. Res.,* 29, 1444-1449.

Alvik, A., Haldorsen, T., Groholt, B., and Lindemann, R. (2006) Alcohol Consumption Before and During Pregnancy Comparing Concurrent and Retrospective Reports, *Alcohol Clin. Exp. Res.*, 30, 510-515.

Anderson, P. and Baumberg, B. (2006) Alcohol in Europe. London. :Institute of Alcohol Studies, UK.

Alte, D., Luedemann, J., Rose, H. J., and John, U. (2004) Laboratory Markers Carbohydrate-Deficient Transferrin, gamma-Glutamyltransferase, and Mean Corpuscular Volume Are Not Useful as Screening Tools for High-Risk Drinking in the General Population: Results From the Study of Health in Pomerania (SHIP), *Alcohol. Clin. Exp. Res,.* 28, 931-940.

Beirness, D.J., Foss, R.D. and Vogel-Sprott, M. (2004) Drinking on campus: self reports and breath tests. *J. Stud. Alcohol* 65, 600-604.

Bonomo, Y.A., Bowes,G., Coffey, C., Carlin,J.B. and Patton,G.C. (2004) Teenage drinking and the onset of alcohol dependence: a cohort study over seven years. *Addiction* 99,1520-1528.

Brick, J. (2006) Standardization of Alcohol Calculations in Research. *Alcohol Clin. Exp. Res.* 30, 1276-1287.

Brown, C.N. and Gunn, A.D.G. (1977) Alcohol consumption in a student community. *The Practitioner* 219, 238-242.

Cahalan, D., Cisin,IH and Crossley,H.M. (1969) American Drinking Practices; A National Study of Drinking Behavior and Attitudes. Rutgers Center of Alcohol Studies, Monograph No.6, New Brunswick, NJ, US.

Carpenter, C (2003) Seasonal Variation in Self-Reports of Recent Alcohol Consumption: Racial and Ethnic Differences. *J. Stud. Alcohol.* 64, 415-418.

Cho,Y. I., Johnson, T.P. and Fendrich,M. (2001) Monthly Variations in Self-reports of alcohol consumption. *J. Stud. Alcohol* 62, 268-272.

Com-Ruelle, L., Dourgnon, P., Jusot, F., Latil, E. and Lengagne, P. (2005) Identification et mesure des problemes d'alcool en France: une comparaison de deux enquetes en population generale. Institute de Recherche et Documenattion en Economie de la Sante, Paris.

Cranford, J.A., McCabe,S.E. and Boyd,C.J. (2006) A New Measure of Binge Drinking: Prevalence and Correlates in a Probability Sample of Undergraduates. *Alcohol Clin. Exp. Res* 30,1896-1905.

Department of Health (1995) Sensible Drinking. The Report of an Inter-departmental Working Group. Department of Health London , UK.

Dimeff, L.A., Kilmer,J., Baer, J.S. and Marlatt, G.A. (1995) (Letter) Binge drinking in college. *JAMA* 273 (24) 1903-4.

Eurobarometer (2003) Special Eurobarometer 186. Health, Food and Alcohol and Safety. European Opinion Research Group EEIG, European Commission.

Eurobarometer (2007) Special Eurobarometer 272. Attitudes towards Alcohol, TNS Opinion and Social, European Commission.

Fitzgerald, J.L. and Mulford, H.A. (1984) Seasonal changes in alcohol consumption and related problems in Iowa, 1979-1980. *J. Stud. Alcohol* 45,363-368.

Gill, J. (2002) Reported levels of alcohol consumption and binge drinking within the UK undergraduate student population over the last 25 years. *Alcohol and Alcoholism* 37,109-120.

Gill, J. and Donaghy, M. (2004) Variation in the alcohol content of a sample of wine and spirit poured by a sample of the Scottish Population, *Health Education Research* 19, 485-491.

Gill, J and O'May, F. (2007) How 'sensible' is the UK Sensible drinking message? Factors which impact on levels of alcohol consumption among newly matriculated female university students. *J. Public Health* 29(1) 13-16.

Gill, J., Donaghy, M., Guise, J. and Warner P. (2007) Descriptors and accounts of female undergraduate drinking in Scotland. *Health Education Research* 22, 27-36.

Goudriann, A.E., Grekin, E.R. and Sher, K.J. (2007) Decision Making and Binge Drinking: A Longitudinal Study. *Alcohol Clin. Exp. Res.* 31,928-938.

Gruenewald, P.J., Johnson, F.W., Light, J.M. and Saltz,R.F. (2003) Drinking to extremes: theoretical and empirical analyses of peak drinking levels among college students. *J. Stud. Alcohol* 64, 817-824.

Guise, J and Gill, J (2007) "Binge drinking? It's good, it's harmless fun": A discourse analysis of accounts of female undergraduate drinking in Scotland. *Health Education Research* 22,895-906.

Hammersley, R and Ditton, J. (2005) Binge or bout? *Drug Education Prevention and Policy* 12, 493-500.

Hansagi, H., Romelsjö, A., Gerhardsson de Verdier, M., Andréasson, S. and Leifman, A. (1995) Alcohol Consumption and Stroke Mortality 20-Year Follow-up of 15 077 Men and Women. *Stroke* 26, 1768-1773.

Hayward, K.and Hobbs, D. (2007) Beyond the binge in 'booze Britain': market-led liminalization and the spectacle of binge drinking. *The British Journal of Sociology* 58, 437-456.

HEC (1985) *That's the Limit*. Health Education Council, London, UK.

ICAP (1998) *What is a "Standard Drink"?* International Center for Alcohol Policies ICAP Reports No. 5. ICAP, Washington, DC., US.

ICAP (2005) Binge drinking. International Center for Alcohol Policies ICAP Reports Module 6. ICAP, Washington, DC., US.

Jefferis, B.J., Power, C. and Manor, O. (2005) Adolescent drinking level and adult binge drinking in a national birth cohort. *Addiction* 100, 543-549.

Kauhanen, J., Kaplan, A. Goldgerg, D.E. and Salonen, JT. (1997) Beer drinking and mortality: results from the Kuopio ischaemic heart disease risk factor study, a prospective population based study. *British Medical Journal* 315,846-851.

Kristjanson, A. F., Wilsnack, S. C., Zvartau, E., Tsoy, M., and Novikov, B. (2007) Alcohol Use in Pregnant and Nonpregnant Russian Women *Alcohol Clin. Exp. Res.* 31, 299-307.

Kypri, K., Langley,J. and Stephenson, S. (2005) Episode-centred analysis of drinking to intoxication in university students. *Alcohol and Alcoholism*, 40, 447-452.

Lange, J.E. and Voas, R.B. (2001) Defining binge drinking quantities through resulting blood alcohol concentrations. *Psychology of Addictive Behaviors* 15, 310-316.

Malyutina, S., Bobak, M., Kurilovitch, S., Gafarov, V., Simonova, G., Nikitin, Y. and Marmot, M. (2002) "Relation between heavy and binge drinking and all-cause and cardiovascular mortality in Novosibirsk, Russia: a prospective cohort study", *The Lancet*, 360, 1448-1454.

McAlaney, J. and McMahon, J. (2006) Establishing rates of binge drinking in the UK: anomalies in the data. *Alcohol and Alcoholism* 41, 355-357.

McCarty, C.A., Ebel, B.E., Garrison, M.M., DiGiuseppe, D.L., Christakis, D.A. and Rivara, F.P. (2004) Continuity of Binge and Harmful Drinking from Late Adolescence to Early Adulthood. *Pediatrics* 114, 714-719.

Measham, F. (1996) The "Big bang" approach to sessional drinking. Changing patterns of alcohol consumption amongst young people in North west England. *Addiction Research* 4, 283-289.

Midanik, L.T., Tam, T.W., Greenfield, T.K. and Caetano, R. (1996) Risk functions for alcohol-related problems in a 1988 U.S. national sample. *Addiction* 91:1427-1437.

Miller, P, Plant, M. and Plant, M (2005) Spreading out or concentrating weekly consumption: alcohol problems and other consequences within a UK population sample. *Alcohol and Alcoholism* 40,461-468.

Moore, L., Smith, C. and Catford, J. (1994) Binge drinking: prevalence, patterns and policy. *Health Education Research 9, 497-505.*

Moore, S., Shepherd, J., Perham, N. and Cusens, B. (2007) The prevalence of alcohol intoxication in the night-time economy *Alcohol and Alcoholism* 42,629-634.

Murgraff, V., Parrott, A. and Bennett, P. (1999) Risky single-occasion drinking amongst young people – definition, correlates, policy and intervention: a broad overview of research findings. *Alcohol and Alcoholism* 34, 3-14.

Murray, R. P., Connett, J. E., Tyas, S. L., Bond, R., Ekuma, O., Silversides, C. K., and Barnes, G. E. (2002) Alcohol Volume, Drinking Pattern, and Cardiovascular Disease Morbidity and Mortality: Is There a U-shaped Function? *American Journal of Epidemiology*, 155, 242-248.

Naimi, T., Brewer, R., Mokdad, A., Denny, C., Serdula, M.and Marks, J. (2003) Letter. *JAMA* 289,1635-1636.

National Health and Medical Research Council [NHMRC] (2001) Australian Alcohol Guidelines: health Risks and Benefits. Commonwealth Department of Health and Aged Care, Australian Government. Canberra, Australia.

National Health and Medical Research Council [NHMRC] (2007) Australian Alcohol Guidelines for low-risk drinking. Draft for public consultation. October 2007. Australian Government. Canberra, Australia.

National Institute on Alcohol Abuse and Alcoholism (2004) NIAAA council approves definition of binge drinking. NIAAA Newsletter, No. 3, Winter. US Department of Health and Human services, National Institute of Health,US.

Nezlek, J.B., Pilkington, C.J. and Bilbro, K.G. (1993) Moderation in excess: binge drinking and social interaction among college students. *J. Stud. Alcohol* 55, 342-351.

O'Malley, P.M., Bachman, J.G. and Johnston, L.D. (1984) Period, age and cohort effects on substance use among American youth, 1976-1982. *Am. J. Public Health* 74, 682-688.

Parliamentary Office of Science and Technology. (2005) Postnote, Number 244. Binge Drinking and Public Health, London, UK.

Perkins, H.W. (2002) Surveying the Damage: A Review of research on Consequences of Alcohol Misuse in College Populations. *J. Stud. Alcohol,* Supplement No. 14:91-100.

Rickards, L., Fox, K., Fletcher, L. and Goddard ,E. (2004) Living in Britain: Results from the 2002 General Household Survey. National Statistics, London.

Schuckit, M.A. (1998) Editorial response. *Journal of Studies on Alcohol* 59, 123-4.

Schuckit, M.A. (2000) Drug and Alcohol Abuse: a Clinical Guide to Diagnosis and Treament. Kluwer Academic/Plenum Publishers, New York.

Schulenberg, J., O'Malley, P., Backman, J.G., Wadsworth, K.N. and Johnston, L.D. (1996) Getting drunk and growing up: trajectories of frequent binge drinking during the transition to young adulthood. *J. Stud. Alcohol* 56, 35-38.

Selin, K. H. (2003) Test-Retest Reliability of the Alcohol Use Disorder Identification Test in a General Population Sample. *Alcohol Clin. Exp. Res.* 27, 1428-1435.

Statistics Canada (2004) Health reports. How healthy are Canadians? 2004 Annual report. Canadian Institute for Health Information. Ottawa, Ontario, Canada.

Thombs, D.L., Olds, R.S. and Snyder, B.M. (2003) Field assessment of BAC data to study late-night college drinking. *J. Stud Alcohol* 64, 322-330.

Townshend, J.M. and Duka, T. (2002) Patterns of alcohol drinking in a population of young social drinkers: a comparison of questionnaire and diary measures. *Alcohol and Alcoholism* 37,187-192.

US Department of Education (2000) Higher Education Center for Alcohol and Other drug Abuse and Violence Protection. Note to the Field: On "Binge Drinking". Available at http://www.higheredcenter.org/press-releases/001020.html. Accessed 14/12/07.

Valencia-Martin, J.L., Galan, I and Rodriguez-Artalejo, F. (2007) Binge drinking in Madrid,Spain. *Alcohol Clin. Exp. Res.* 31, 1723-30.

van den Wildenberg, E., Wiers, R. W., Dessers, J., Janssen, R. G. J. H., Lambrichs, E. H., Smeets, H. J. M., and van Breukelen, G. J. P. (2007) "A Functional Polymorphism of the mu-Opioid Receptor Gene (OPRM1) Influences Cue-Induced Craving for Alcohol in Male Heavy Drinkers", *Alcohol Clin. Exp. Res.* 31, 1-10.

Watson, P.E., Watson, I.D. and Batt, R.D. (1981) Prediction of blood alcohol concentrations in human subjects: updating the Widmark equation. *J. Stud Alcohol* 42: 547-556.

Wechsler, H. and Austin, S.B. (1998) Binge Drinking: The Five/Four Measure. *J. Stud Alc* 59, 122-123.

Wechsler, H. and Nelson, T.F. (2006) Relationship Between Level of Consumption and Harms in Assessing Drink Cut-Points for Alcohol Research: Commentary on "Many

College Freshman Drink at Levels Far Beyond the Binge Threshold" by White et al. *Alcohol: Clin Exp Res* 30,922-927.

Wechsler, H., Davenport, A., Dowdell, G., Moeykens, B and Castillo, S. (1994) Health and Behavioral Consequences of Binge Drinking in College: A national survey of students at 140 campuses. *JAMA* 272, 1672-1677.

Wechsler, H., Moeykens, B., Davenport, A., Castillo, S. and Hansen, J. (1995) The Adverse impact of Heavy Episodic Drinkers on Other College students. *J. Stud Alcohol* 56, 628-634.

Wechsler, H., Lee, J.E., Kuo, M., Seibring, M., Nelson, T.F. and Lee, H (2002) Trends in college binge drinking during a period of increased prevention efforts. Findings from 4 Harvard School of Public Health College alcohol study surveys: 1993-2002. *J. Am Coll Health* 50,203-217.

White, A.M., Kraus, C.L. and Swartwelder, H.S. (2006) Many College Freshman Drink at Levels Far Beyond the Binge Threshold. *Alcohol Clin. Exp. Res.* 30, 1006-1010.

WHO Global status Report on Alcohol (2004) World Health Organization. Department of Mental Health and Substance Abuse, Geneva, Switzerland.

Wright, N.R. (2006) A day at the cricket: the breath alcohol consequences of a type of very English binge drinking. *Addiction Research and Theory* 14,133-137.

WTAG Binge Drinking Research (2004) Report of research and consultation conducted by MCM Research Ltd for Wine Intelligence. Oxford UK.

Yuan, W., Sorensen, H. T., Basso, O., and Olsen, J. (2004) Prenatal Maternal Alcohol Consumption and Hospitalization With Asthma in Childhood: A Population-Based Follow-Up Study, *Alcohol: Clin. Exp. Res.* 28, 765-768.

In: Substance Abuse, Assessment and Addiction
Editors: Kristina A. Murati and Allison G. Fischer

ISBN: 978-1-61122-931-8
© 2011 Nova Science Publishers, Inc.

*Chapter 5*

# Strategies for Implementing Evidence-Based Practice in Community Substance Abuse Treatment Settings

## *Roger H. Peters\*, W. Michael Hunt, Kathleen A. Moore, Holly A. Hills and M. Scott Young*

Florida Mental Health Institute, University of South Florida

## Abstract

Although the behavioral healthcare field has increasingly emphasized the value of evidence-based practices, community-based settings are typically slow to modify their existing clinical practices. One strategy that has been found to accelerate the implementation of evidence-based practices in behavioral healthcare settings is the use of peer opinion leaders. The Tampa Practice Improvement Collaborative (PIC) project evaluated the relative effectiveness of an opinion leader model in implementing evidence-based practices related to treatment of co-occurring mental health and substance use disorders. Practitioners from ten diverse substance abuse treatment programs (n = 43) within the area's largest publicly funded agencies were trained to implement an evidence-based manualized treatment intervention with the assistance of peer opinion leaders. A comparison group of counselors (n = 28) working in a nearby geographic area received a more traditional, less intensive training approach. This paper describes use of opinion leaders and intensive training to implement an evidence-based treatment manual in several community-based treatment settings, and highlights a series of implementation strategies found to be effective in these settings.

* Correspondence to: Roger H. Peters, Department of Mental Health Law and Policy, Florida Mental Health Institute, University of South Florida, 13301 Bruce B. Downs Blvd., Tampa, FL 33612. e-mail: peters@fmhi.usf.edu

# INTRODUCTION

Evidence from research and clinical practice in behavioral health settings highlights the disparity between the availability of evidence-based practices and implementation of these practices in the field (Institute of Medicine, 2001; Lamb, Greenlick, and McCarty, 1998; McCabe, 2004). For example, a number of empirically supported substance abuse treatment approaches have recently been developed (Galanter and Kleber, 1999; Lowinson, Ruiz, Millman, and Langrod, 2005), but have not been readily adapted into clinical practice (Sorensen, Rawson, Guydish, and Zweben, 2003). Some of the factors leading to this disparity include: (1) lack of information regarding newly developed treatment approaches, (2) difficulties understanding how to tailor evidence-based approaches for field settings, and (3) an absence of training and technical assistance related to these new interventions (Backer, 2000; Lamb, Greenlick, and McCarty, 1998; McLellan, 2002).

Other significant barriers to implementation of empirically supported practices include lack of organizational awareness about the need for change (Arthur and Blitz, 2000; Rogers, 2003), and lack of organizational readiness for change and staff reluctance to adopt new treatment approaches (Marinelli-Casey, Domier, and Rawson, 2002; Simpson, 2002). Many treatment agencies are inexperienced in how to apply technology transfer approaches, and may be unaware of effective implementation practices (Technical Assistance Collaborative, 2003). In the absence of organizational support and an articulated organizational implementation plan, the dissemination of evidence-based substance abuse treatment approaches has been poorly received by both staff and clients (Corrigan, et al., 2001; Lamb et al., 1998; McLellan, 2002). Inadequate technology transfer within substance abuse treatment agencies has been linked to poor outcomes related to client retention, substance use relapse, criminal recidivism, and staff turnover (Gerstein and Harwood, 1990).

A number of studies have begun to examine strategies for bridging the gap between empirically supported treatment approaches and practices implemented in the field (Marinelli-Casey, Domier, and Rawson, 2002; Sorensen et al., 2003). Simpson (2002) outlines a conceptual framework for understanding key principles related to technology transfer that includes interrelated factors of organizational readiness, dynamics, and supports; staff characteristics and attributes, and activities related to exposure, adoption, implementation, and practice of evidence-based approaches. Several key principles and strategies for encouraging technology transfer have emerged from the recent literature (Backer et al., 1986; Sorensen et al., 2003). Underlying principles of technology transfer include providing an accessible, user-friendly format for communicating new treatment approaches, credible evidence for new approaches, adequate resources for implementation, and incentives and other assistance to encourage staff to implement new approaches. Key strategies to accomplish effective technology transfer include methods designed to address potential staff and organizational barriers, personal contact with line staff during the adoption process, staff involvement in implementation efforts, and development of organizational champions to support the adoption of new treatment approaches (Corrigan, et al., 2001; Sorensen et al., 2003; Technical Assistance Collaborative, 2003). Additionally, interactive strategies that provide outreach to staff, and sequential and ongoing personalized consultation are more effective in promoting technology transfer than traditional classroom or continuing education trainings (Backer, 2000; Davis, et al., 1999).

Technology transfer approaches have increasingly focused on interpersonal strategies such as individualized consultation and inclusion of clinicians and administrators in the adoption process (Backer, 2003; Schmidt and Taylor, 2002). These strategies tend to be enhanced through use of credible peer leaders in the organization, or "opinion leaders", who often serve as central sources of information and help to stimulate innovation and change (Locock, Dopson, Chambers, and Gabbay, 2001; Rogers, 2003; Valente and Davis, 1999). Opinion leaders have increasing credibility and importance as organizations approach the point of implementing new practices (Locock, et al., 2001). Opinion leaders are easily identified through use of a "network analysis" conducted within a particular organization (Scott, 2000; Valente and Davis, 1999; Valente, 2000), and can help establish the credibility of evidence-based interventions and facilitate their diffusion and implementation (Kelly, et al. 1991; Lomas et al., 1991; Valente and Davis, 1999). Opinion leaders have been shown to be particularly effective in facilitating adoption of evidence-based approaches in substance abuse treatment and other health-related settings (Gingiss, Gottlieb, and Brink, 1994; Kelly et al., 1991; Lomas et al., 1991; Peters et al., in press; Sorensen and Clark, 1995).

Despite the identification of specific strategies for enhancing dissemination and adoption of evidence-based practices in the substance abuse treatment area, there have been few studies examining how these strategies are operationalized in community-based treatment settings. For example, although a conceptual framework has been developed to describe the technology transfer process in substance abuse treatment settings (Simpson, 2002), there are few studies that examine how this process is affected by different implementation strategies and by organizational variables. Although support for evidence-based substance abuse interventions is drawn primarily from randomized controlled trials, key evidence about the practicality and utility of these interventions is often achieved through "case-based" research (Edwards, Datillio, and Bromley, 2004) that employs narrative analysis and both qualitative and quantitative approaches.

The current study examines the process of implementing a structured series of training and consultation activities, coupled with use of peer opinion leaders in community-based substance abuse agencies, to implement an evidence-based treatment curriculum related to co-occurring mental health and substance use disorders. This was part of a larger study conducted in the Tampa Bay area as part of the Substance Abuse and Mental Health Administration's Center for Substance Abuse Treatment, Practice Improvement Collaborative (PIC) initiative. Eleven one-year developmental PIC projects were established between 1999-2000 and were funded for additional three-year implementation activities from 2000-2003. A total of 14 PIC projects have been developed throughout the country, with the goal of enhancing linkages between substance abuse researchers, practitioners, and policy makers, and of identifying effective strategies for disseminating evidence-based practices in the substance abuse treatment field (Center for Substance Abuse Treatment, 2003).

## METHOD

### Community Agency Partners

Four community-based agencies participated in the study, including the Hillsborough County Sheriff's Office's jail-based treatment program, and the three largest publicly funded substance abuse treatment agencies (ACTS, Inc., DACCO, Inc., Operation PAR, Inc.) in the Tampa Bay area. Each of the publicly funded treatment agencies provides a full range of outpatient, residential, and other services. Ten programs were selected from these four agencies to provide diversity across various different outpatient and residential programs that served clients who have co-occurring mental health and substance use disorders. A total of 43 counselors from the 10 treatment programs participated in the study, and all had primary work assignments related to direct client contact and other support activities. Participating agencies are briefly described in the following section.

### The Agency for Community Treatment Services (ACTS, Inc.)

ACTS is a non-profit organization in Tampa, Florida that provides substance abuse treatment to both adolescents and adults, the majority of whom are referred by or are involved with the criminal justice system. Ten counselors from one outpatient and two residential programs participated in the study.

### The Drug Abuse Comprehensive Coordination Office, Inc. (DACCO)

DACCO is a non-profit organization that provides substance abuse services in Tampa, Florida to adolescents and adults. Over half of their adult clients are court-ordered to treatment or have a criminal justice history. Fifteen counselors from one outpatient aftercare and two residential programs participated in the study.

### The Hillsborough County Sheriff's Office

The Hillsborough County Sheriff's Office (**delete italics for the previous five words) offers a voluntary in-jail substance abuse treatment program providing services to adult offenders. Three counselors participated in the study from this inpatient substance abuse program.

### Operation PAR, Inc (PAR)

PAR is a non-profit organization providing addiction and mental health services to a five-county area encompassing the Tampa Bay area. Over half of their clients are referred by the criminal justice system. Fifteen counselors from three residential programs participated in the study.

The Center for Drug-Free Living in Orlando, Florida was selected as the comparison site for the study. The Center for Drug-Free Living is the largest publicly funded substance abuse treatment provider in Orlando, and provides a full array of outpatient and residential services that are comparable to those provided in the Tampa treatment sites. The Center for Drug-Free Living serves a wide range of clients who have substance abuse and co-occurring mental health disorders, and has successfully participated in a number of federally funded research projects, including the NIDA Clinical Trials Network.

## Use of Evidence-Based Treatment Protocols

Prior to the study, a needs assessment was conducted to identify the most critical area for substance abuse treatment improvement in the community. The area of co-occurring disorders was selected on the basis of the needs assessment, and subsequent discussion between researchers and community constituents led to an agreement to implement a manualized treatment approach to address co-occurring disorders. An extensive literature review was then conducted, and an expert panel convened for the purpose of identifying an evidence-based co-occurring disorders treatment manual for use in the study. The panel included several national experts (Gary Field, Ph.D., Kim Mueser, Ph.D., Fred Osher, M.D.) in the co-occurring disorders area, in addition to administrators, counselors, and clients from the participating treatment agencies in the Tampa Bay area.

Based on a comprehensive literature review and recommendations from an expert panel, a psychoeducational treatment manual was selected for use in the study that was developed by the New Hampshire-Dartmouth Psychiatric Research Center (Mueser and Fox, 1998). The treatment manual was adapted for the current study through consultation with the expert panel, faculty at the New Hampshire-Dartmouth Psychiatric Research Center, and representatives from each of the participating treatment agencies in the Tampa Bay area. The treatment manual adapted for the current study included eight psychoeducational modules, and was intended for administration in a group treatment setting. Modules required 60 to 90 minutes to administer and each of the modules addressed a unique theme related to co-occurring disorders and described the interactive nature of the particular disorders (e.g., substance abuse and depression), pharmacological interventions for treating co-occurring disorders, and other types of treatment strategies. The treatment manual was field tested and revised through consultation with clients and staff from each of the participating treatment agencies, and a client workbook was also developed.

## Use of Peer Opinion Leaders for Training and Consultation

A network analysis (Valente, 2000) was conducted to identify peer opinion leaders within each of the 10 participating treatment programs. This was accomplished by surveying counselors to determine whom they would rely on among their co-workers to provide information regarding co-occurring mental health and substance abuse disorders. This process was designed to identify peers who were perceived as having the most expertise related to co-occurring disorders, and who were the most sought after by agency counselors for this purpose. One opinion leader from each program was selected, and recruited to participate in the study to provide training, consultation, and data collection.

Three different types of training were provided to counselors, prior to implementation of the evidence-based treatment manual. A 4-hour "Foundations" training focused on general principles of assessment and treatment of co-occurring disorders, and reviewed integrated treatment approaches that have proven effectiveness for clients with co-occurring disorders. A subsequent "Opinion Leader" training was provided only to designated opinion leaders from the 10 treatment programs. Opinion leaders participated in this two-day training to learn about the group content and format, and how to implement the treatment manual. This training was provided by a faculty member at the New Hampshire-Dartmouth Psychiatric Research Center who is an expert in the co-occurring disorders treatment area. The comparison group received only the 4-hour Foundations training, and received no additional training or opinion leader consultation. Participants in the comparison group were also mailed a copy of the co-occurring disorders treatment manual.

An additional 90-minute "Counselor" training was provided by opinion leaders to peer counselors within their own treatment agencies. This training reviewed the different psychoeducational modules, provided strategies for implementing the treatment manual in group treatment sessions, and provided clinical approaches for engaging clients in the treatment groups. Following implementation of the treatment manual, opinion leaders met weekly with their peer counselors to provide ongoing consultation regarding implementation of the treatment manual.

## Implementation of the Treatment Manual

Once the training sequence was completed, counselors in each of the participating agencies began implementing the manual in group treatment sessions during a three-month implementation period. In order to compile information regarding the implementation process, opinion leaders submitted weekly progress reports to verify use of the manual and to identify any problems that occurred during this process. Project staff observed randomly selected treatment sessions in each of the participating treatment agencies to assess fidelity in implementation of the treatment manual. To examine the effectiveness of the technology transfer intervention using opinion leaders and the structured training regimen, counselors in the intervention and comparison groups were asked about their use of the evidence-based treatment manual immediately following the three-month implementation period. Counselors in the intervention group were also re-assessed six months later to evaluate the short-term sustainability of this technology transfer approach.

### Key Findings Related to Strategies for Implementing Evidence-Based Practices

The following section highlights effective strategies in implementing the featured technology transfer intervention, which included use of a structured set of training workshops and deployment of peer opinion leaders, as previously described. Several sequential key steps in the implementation process are described, which we identified as essential in developing collaborative relationships with community-based substance abuse treatment agencies to implement evidence-based practices. Key steps included the following: (1) engagement of treatment agencies, (2) identifying an evidence-based treatment protocol, (3) developing and refining the treatment protocol, (4) mobilization of opinion leaders, (5) monitoring fidelity of training and implementation, and (6) collecting data to evaluate implementation outcomes. These key steps provide a heuristic framework by which to gauge the effectiveness of collaborative efforts to implement evidence-based practices in the behavioral health treatment field, and point to useful strategies for working with community partners to implement these practices. For each of the key implementation steps described in this section, we will review major activities and strategies used to enhance implementation of evidence-based treatment practices, challenges and obstacles faced, and key findings in implementing technology transfer approaches.

## Engagement of Treatment Agencies

Representatives from the four largest substance abuse treatment agencies in the Tampa Bay area were recruited and retained for this study. Membership included organizational leaders and administrators as well as staff who provided direct client services. Strategies to enhance agency commitment to the set of technology transfer activities included: (1) financial incentives to participating agencies, opinion leaders, and practitioners, (2) ongoing involvement of CEO's and agency site coordinators in all stages of the study implementation, (3) activities designed to develop the opinion leader network, and (4) involvement of national experts to promote the credibility and feasibility of evidence-based treatment protocols. These last two strategies will be discussed in more detail in subsequent sections.

### Financial Incentives

These were provided to each agency through subsidizing a portion of the salary of a site coordinator within each agency. Site coordinators were program directors and clinical coordinators who had immediate access to agency management staff and who were also tasked through their ordinary responsibilities with organizing clinical services within their agency. A modest yearly stipend ($500) was also provided to opinion leaders in each of the participating agency treatment programs, to support their involvement in the project. Participating agencies and site coordinators reported that these incentives were important in recognizing their ongoing efforts in the project, and were symbolic of shared resources between the university and partner agencies in pursuit of project goals.

### Ongoing Involvement of CEO's and Agency Site Coordinators in All Stages of the Study Implementation

Project staff also consulted with agency CEO's and other administrators prior to submitting the grant application to support the PIC project, which was a particularly important means to engage the participating agencies. In these discussions, consensus was reached regarding the following areas: (1) the importance of introducing evidence-based practices related to substance abuse treatment, (2) the purpose and importance of peer opinion leaders and structured training workshops as vehicles for implementing evidence-based practices, (3) involvement of site coordinators in the process, (4) strategies that would be used to identify evidence-based practice topics and manualized treatment protocols, and to refine these protocols, and (5) the type of data to be collected and the methods for data collection. Periodic email notes were sent to CEO's to update them on project activities and to solicit comments and information regarding the desirability and feasibility of various implementation approaches.

Several challenges were encountered in the process of engaging treatment agencies in project activities. Several agency administrators were concerned about the limited time that counselors had available to implement a new treatment curriculum, given existing obligations within their respective programs. To overcome this potential barrier, project staff met with treatment coordinators from each of the programs to identify a feasible setting and number of treatment sessions that could be dedicated to the evidence-based treatment protocols. In each case, it was determined that the appropriate vehicle for delivering the new treatment protocols was in the primary treatment groups provided in each of the programs. Given the range of participating outpatient and residential programs, it was necessary to organize the new treatment protocol in modules to accommodate the differing amounts of time available for group sessions in the various settings. This arrangement allowed counselors to present one or more modules at a time, depending on the time available during the treatment session.

Another issue that potentially threatened implementation of the manual was that site coordinators were reluctant to allow opinion leaders who were not clinical supervisors to serve in a training and advisory role for other counselors. They feared that this would create a duplicate supervisory structure, and that opinion leaders in some cases might be providing clinical supervision without the proper certification or licensure. To address these concerns, procedures were developed to specify that the role of opinion leaders would be limited to coaching and rehearsal of the curriculum, and that they would not provide supervision related to client treatment.

*Among the major findings from our activities to engage agencies in implementing evidence-based practices were the following:*

(1) As our project increasingly focused on activities related to implementation of the co-occurring disorders treatment protocol, involvement in project activities began to diminish among other community agencies that were not directly affiliated with the implementation study. We found that continued involvement in our community collaborative project could be sustained among these agencies by addressing their needs for staff training related to a range of clinical issues, and by providing free continuing education credits at these events.

(2) In addition to including agency CEO's in selected project activities, it was important to involve mid-level managers from the agencies (i.e., "site coordinators") in all project planning meetings, due to their unique knowledge of barriers to implementing technology transfer activities within their specific programs, and to their ability to leverage the implementation process within their programs.

## Identifying an Evidence-Based Treatment Protocol

As indicated previously, treatment of co-occurring disorders was selected as the focal area for the projects' implementation study, based on a needs assessment of community treatment agencies. In order to identify existing evidence-based treatment protocols related to co-occurring disorders and to develop credibility for use of these approaches, a two-day expert panel meeting was convened. Three national experts in co-occurring disorder treatment were invited to the meeting, who were distinguished through their research, training, and development of clinical programs. Approximately 25 other individuals were invited to attend this meeting, including CEO's, site coordinators, and consumers from the four participating substance abuse treatment agencies.

Following a review of the purpose and goals of the meeting, staff from each agency described the services they were currently providing for clients with co-occurring disorders. The national experts then proceeded to identify evidence-based assessment and treatment protocols related to co-occurring disorders. Through the expert panel meeting, the group identified a range of evidence-based approaches that were suitable for potential implementation in the current study, including protocols involving assessment of motivation and engagement in treatment, and treatment interventions related to relapse prevention, drug coping skills, life skills, and medication management. The national experts recommended implementing either a protocol to assess motivation for treatment of co-occurring disorders or a psychoeducational treatment protocol to be administered with clients with co-occurring disorders.

The group then reviewed practical implications for implementing each of these protocols, and developed consensus regarding the use of a group treatment manual that emphasized development of psychoeducational skills. It was determined that a manualized curriculum would provide the most effective means to disseminate a standardized protocol throughout the four participating agencies, and that this type of curriculum would also facilitate measurement of treatment fidelity and sustainability of implementation. The expert panel meeting was also useful in identifying individuals to consider as trainers in implementing this particular evidence-based treatment protocol, and strategies and instruments for evaluating implementation of the protocol, fidelity of implementation, and for sustainability of implementation.

*Among the major findings from our activities to develop consensus regarding evidence-based treatment protocols were the following:*

(1) The use of national experts on co-occurring disorders was well received by staff from the community substance abuse treatment agencies. As indicated by prior research, the use of national and external experts appeared to significantly enhance the credibility of the proposed interventions selected for dissemination, and assisted in developing consensus and support for the dissemination strategy.

(2) Many of the participants in the expert panel meeting did not have significant prior familiarity with the national experts, the treatment protocols, or this type of consensus-building activity. As a result, some of the ensuing discussion at the expert panel meeting was unfocused and tangential to the task at hand. The consensus-building activities might have been expedited and streamlined somewhat by dissemination of participant materials in advance of the meeting, describing the range of available evidence-based approaches. A detailed agenda with clearly specified goals and outcomes would also have helped to provide greater focus in the expert panel discussions.

(3) Despite the emergence of co-occurring disorders treatment as a significant topic addressed in the research literature and at training conferences, it became clear through the literature review conducted prior to the expert panel, and from the findings of the panel that there was not a wide range of existing evidence-based treatment protocols in this area. In fact, the only standardized curriculum identified in this area had been developed for psychoeducational groups with family members of individuals with serious mental illness, who also had co-occurring disorders. As a result of the expert panel, it became clear that a client treatment manual would need to be adapted from existing materials.

## Developing and Refining the Treatment Protocol

Once the expert panel meeting was completed and consensus reached regarding the use of a manualized protocol for delivering co-occurring disorders treatment, the next step was to identify and refine this protocol. As indicated previously, given the limited array of available resources, it was necessary to adapt materials from evidence-based treatments for use with clients who have co-occurring disorders. The family group psychoeducational manual developed by Meuser and colleagues (1998) at Dartmouth University was identified as the most suitable material for this purpose. The effectiveness of this manual had been established through previous studies conducted by the Dartmouth research team. Examination of this manual indicated that there was significant material that was relevant for clients in substance abuse treatment programs, and the format and organization were also of great potential value.

A first task in adapting the manual for dissemination in the project was to determine what content needed to be refined, and an appropriate length for the manual. Consensus was reached during the expert panel meeting that from six to eight modules of approximately 60 to 90 minutes in length would provide an intervention of similar intensity to the original family group treatment manual developed at Dartmouth University. Upon closer review, it was determined that eight modules would be needed to provide coverage of the full range of topics included in the Dartmouth manual. This level of material was of reasonable scale to allow the participating community agencies to add this material to their existing groups in each of the various treatment programs. As with the original family treatment manual, it was decided that each module, while thematically related, should be functionally independent, so that new clients entering a particular treatment program could immediately join a treatment group that was already in progress.

The second task involved selecting a series of topics to address in each of the modules. Based on feedback from the participating agencies, it was determined that the modules should focus on the interaction between substance use and mental health disorders, and as with the original manual, should provide a special emphasis on major mental health disorders such as depression, bipolar disorder, anxiety, and schizophrenia. One variation from the original manual was that there was now an emphasis on mental health disorders as they affected individuals with substance use disorders. This approach appeared to be reasonable given that the majority of participating treatment counselors had more experience with substance abuse issues than with mental health issues, and that a focus on substance use topics would be redundant with existing interventions provided within the treatment programs.

The work to adapt the evidence-based manual was conducted primarily by project staff, who were assisted by staff from the participating agencies. Project staff consisted of researchers with clinical training and experience, and agency staff included clinical managers, counselors, and former consumers of services. The family psychoeducational manual required significant adaptation, including expansion of handouts and exercise material, and the addition of material describing the interaction of co-occurring disorders. However, the organizational approach of the manual remained intact, with a general overview of the particular mental health disorder, a case study to illuminate clinical and behavioral features of the co-occurring disorders, self-assessment exercises, treatment approaches, and a resource guide that included bibliographical materials.

While the project staff took primary responsibility for revising the content of the manual, regular meetings were held with clinical staff from the participating agencies to refine the manual content for appropriate language, content, format, and sequence. After an initial draft of each module was completed, two staff consultants from participating agencies provided an extensive review and provided a set of recommended revisions. Following completion of necessary revisions, a group of clients from one of the participating agencies reviewed the modules, and provided comments and recommendations to project staff about the relevance and utility of the material, and identified examples of language and concepts that needed adaptation for use with clients in substance abuse treatment programs. Finally, a co-occurring disorders work group provided a final review of each module. This work group consisted of research staff, agency supervisors, and counselors as well as Dartmouth faculty who had authored the original family psychoeducational manual. Each of the modules was revised substantially during this process, and was then printed and distributed for use by each of the participating agencies.

Upon reviewing the final version of the treatment manual, agency staff recommended that a companion workbook be created for the clients. In its original form, this workbook was a condensed version of the treatment manual, and was composed primarily of exercises and case studies. However, based on client feedback, the workbook was eventually expanded to incorporate most of the content from the manual, including didactic material, case studies, self-assessment exercises, and bibliographic and resource material. Counselor notes and directives were the only materials not included in the client workbooks.

*Among the major findings from activities to develop and refine the treatment protocol were the following:*

(1) The size and modular format of the proposed treatment manual was of critical importance to the participating treatment agencies. Each of the agencies had a range of materials that had been developed for use in their treatment groups, and it was impractical to ask the agencies to replace the entirety of these materials with the new co-occurring disorders treatment curriculum. It was also important to divide the curriculum into eight freestanding modules, so that clients entering treatment at different times could benefit from this material.

(2) Although there was not a preexisting evidence-based treatment manual that was determined to be suitable for use in the current project, it was quite feasible to adapt such a manual from existing resources in the field, through collaboration of researchers, counselors, clients, and national experts. The adapted evidence-based manual was developed through an iterative process that involved identification of key features related to content and format, refining material to match the needs of the client population, review by counselors and clients, and development of ancillary materials following this review.

(3) Language used in the treatment manual was significantly adapted to eliminate psychological jargon and to provide vocabulary that was appropriate and accessible to the client population.

## Mobilizing Opinion Leaders

This study employed use of peer opinion leaders to disseminate the evidence-based treatment protocols within their treatment organizations. Opinion leaders are identified as persons who most influence the opinions, attitudes, beliefs, and motivations of others (Rogers and Cartano, 1962) and who have demonstrated effectiveness in disseminating information about new ideas or clinical practice techniques. Prior studies indicate that knowledge dissemination methods that use direct personal contact are more likely than printed materials alone to facilitate the adoption of treatment innovations in community settings, including substance abuse facilities (Backer, Liberman, and Kuehnel, 1986; Sorensen et al., 1988; Valente, 1996).

Network analysis techniques provide the most rigorous approach for identifying opinion leaders (Valente, 1996, 2000). This technique involves identification of a sample of respondents who then nominate opinion leaders through use of several key questions. Opinion leaders from 10 programs within the participating agencies in the current study were identified by asking all counselors the following question: *"From among your co-workers, whom would you go to if you had questions about a client with co-occurring mental health and substance abuse problems?"*

Opinion leaders participated in a specialized two-day training workshop on the co-occurring disorders treatment curriculum manual that included review of approaches to delivering the curriculum, and methods for training peer counselors in use of the curriculum. Once this training was completed, each opinion leader conducted a 90-minute training for all counselors in their treatment program that focused on the purpose, content, and delivery of the co-occurring disorders treatment protocol. Opinion leaders also provided weekly consultation to their peer counselors in use of the protocol, which included rehearsal of treatment techniques, review of progress in administering treatment sessions, debriefing critical incidents, and identifying strategies for overcoming barriers and obstacles.

*Among the major findings from our activities to mobilize peer opinion leaders included the following:*

(1) Contrary to predictions by agency CEO's, opinion leaders selected for the study were not always clinical supervisors. Although over half of opinion leaders were clinical supervisors, several non-supervisors were selected as peer opinion leaders who were mental health consultants to the treatment programs, or who had specialized training in mental health services. In comparison to their peer counselors, opinion leaders had more vocational experience and were more likely to have advanced degrees in the mental health area (Moore et al., 2004).

(2) On two occasions, individuals nominated as opinion leaders were not able to serve in that capacity. In one instance, the identified individual had administrative duties that prevented involvement in the study. Another nominated individual left the treatment agency soon after the selection process. In both cases, the individual ranked by counselors in the network analysis process as the second most important source of information related to co-occurring disorders served as the opinion leader for the study.

(3) Satisfaction surveys completed following the two-day opinion leader training indicated that the training was too long, and could be condensed to a single day. Subsequent projects involving training of peer opinion leaders have successfully trained staff during a one-day workshop.

(4) Opinion leaders indicated that the $500 stipend they received for participating in the study was an important engagement strategy, and reflected the scope of work that they had invested in training and consultation with peer counselors.

(5) Opinion leaders reported that their professional status within the treatment agency was enhanced by serving in this capacity, and that their role in the study and contributions to the study were widely known throughout the agency.

## Monitoring the Fidelity of Training and Implementation

Fidelity in implementing treatment interventions has been found to be quite important in assessing treatment outcomes (Moncher and Prinz, 1991), and fidelity measures have been increasingly used to monitor treatment activities in substance abuse (Orwin, 2000) and mental health (McGrew, Bond, Dietzen, and Salyers, 1994) settings. The current project assessed the fidelity of training workshops and implementation of the evidence-based treatment protocol. Training fidelity surveys assessed the extent to which each training session covered the intended material and whether the information was presented clearly. This information was important in verifying the effectiveness of training activities. Observational measures also were used to monitor whether the co-occurring disorders treatment groups were provided as intended. The observational measures were completed independently by two project staff, who provided ratings for the following: (1) coverage of specific content for modules assessed, (2) duration and size of the groups, and (3) degree of client participation in the treatment groups. Raters observed a broad range of sessions in order to monitor how each treatment module was implemented across agencies throughout the three-month implementation period.

In addition to independent fidelity ratings obtained from project staff, opinion leaders also submitted weekly progress reports regarding the groups that were provided by their peer counselors in their treatment program. These reports documented the sequence in which individual modules were presented, and provided information regarding how well the modules were received by the counselors and clients. These reports also included an open-ended item to describe counselors' reactions to the individual modules. A data manager from the research team created detailed data tracking logs to monitor the ongoing data collection process.

*Among the major findings from activities designed to monitor the fidelity of training and of implementation of the evidence-based treatment protocol included the following:*

(1) Completion of weekly opinion leader reports simplified the process of tracking completion of assignments and co-occurring disorders groups across the various different treatment programs.
(2) Observing treatment groups provided valuable data regarding implementation of the evidence-based treatment protocol and helped to identify portions of modules that were difficult for counselors to implement. These observations led to several recommendations for additional revisions of the treatment manual, and highlighted the need for additional staff training in several areas.

## Collection of Data to Evaluate Implementation Outcomes

A range of data was collected before, during, and after the implementation process to capture information regarding the effectiveness of the technology transfer approach examined in this study. Sources of information included agency administrators, counselors, and opinion leaders, and included data relevant to the process and outcomes of the implementation study, and to both individual participants in the study and to participating organizations. Data were collected at the following four time periods to assess organizational and counselor characteristics and outcomes related to the implementation process: (1) prior to implementation of the opinion leader training model (baseline), (2) post-implementation, following administration of the eight-module manual in group treatment settings, (3) at six months following implementation of the group treatment manual, and (4) at eighteen months following implementation of the group treatment manual.

Baseline survey data were gathered prior to presentation of the training workshops and to implementation of the treatment groups. These data included demographic and background information describing counselors and opinion leaders, including knowledge related to co-occurring disorders, attitudes towards treating clients with co-occurring disorders, and work activities related to assessment and treatment of co-occurring disorders. Counselors and opinion leaders also completed measures at each of these time periods to assess the amount of time allocated to working with clients who have co-occurring disorders. Organizational baseline measures were completed by counselors, opinion leaders, and agency administrative staff, including CEO's, administrators, program directors, program managers, supervisors, training coordinators, and human resources personnel. The organizational measures provided an indication of degree of counselor autonomy, motivation for changing assessment and treatment procedures, agency resources (e.g., access to the internet), and organizational climate. A follow-up counselor self-report instrument was developed to obtain information regarding counselors' past and current implementation of the treatment manual and to assess the level of adoption of these materials.

One goal of this study was to detect changes over the course of the study in counselors' attitudes and practices related to treatment of co-occurring disorders, with a specific focus on implementation of the evidence-based treatment protocol. Post-implementation, six-month, and eighteen-month follow-up surveys included the same items that were measured at baseline in order to assess changes in counselors' knowledge and attitudes regarding clients with co-occurring disorders. Additionally, items at these three time periods assessed whether counselors were currently using the co-occurring disorders treatment manual, whether they had plans to use the manual in the future, and whether they believed that the manual provided information useful in treating clients with co-occurring disorders. Comparison of baseline and post-implementation measures allowed for examination of changes in clinical practices occurring during the implementation phase of this study. The six-month and eighteen-month follow-up data assessed whether any of these changes were sustained over time.

*Among the major findings from activities designed to collect data to evaluate implementation outcomes included the following:*

1. A number of difficulties were encountered in obtaining baseline and follow-up data from participating program staff. This included incomplete compliance in returning mail surveys. As a result, counselor data at baseline and follow-up points were gathered on-site whenever possible. When this was not possible, it was necessary to use follow-up phone calls and mailings to remind counselors to return baseline and follow-up measures. These follow-up data collection approaches were only moderately successful, and the rate of return on mail-in survey forms was quite low, resulting in loss of data for some individuals.

2. As part of the on-site data collection efforts, staff were able to share information with counselors and other participants regarding the purpose and operational aspects of the research project. These efforts appeared to enhance compliance with completion and mailing of evaluation data forms.

# DISCUSSION

An emerging behavioral health services literature points to the need for specialized approaches to bridge the gap between practitioners, researchers, and policymakers to more effectively implement evidence-based practices (Institute of Medicine, 2001; Lamb, et al., 1998), particularly in substance abuse treatment and other related settings (McLellan, 2002; Moore et al., 2004; Simpson, 2002). One promising area for specialized approaches to technology transfer is the use of peer opinion leaders to promote dissemination of evidence-based approaches (Gingiss, Gottlieb, and Brink, 1994; Lomas et al., 1991; Valente and Davis, 1999).

The current study examined effective strategies for deploying a network of peer opinion leaders to facilitate structured training and consultation activities to support the implementation of an evidence-based co-occurring disorders treatment manual. This technology transfer approach appeared to be quite successful in encouraging dissemination and use of the evidence-based treatment manual, as evidenced by significantly higher rates of manual implementation among counselors receiving this intervention, as contrasted with counselors in the comparison group who received only a 4-hour training and a copy of the manual. Among the intervention group, there was also sustained implementation of the manual over a six-month follow-up period.

A series of key steps was identified as essential in implementing the opinion leader network and intensive training activities, and involved significant collaboration between community-based substance abuse treatment agencies. Key steps included: (1) engagement of treatment agencies, (2) identifying an evidence-based treatment protocol, (3) developing and refining the treatment protocol, (4) mobilizing opinion leaders, (5) monitoring fidelity of training and implementation, and (6) collecting data to evaluate implementation outcomes. Taken together, these key steps provide a conceptual framework by which to understand the process of developing collaborative community partnerships to implement evidence-based behavioral health practices, and to gauge the effectiveness of these collaborative efforts.

Findings from this study indicate that effective community-based collaboration to implement evidence-based behavioral health treatment interventions requires involvement at all levels of the various partner agencies. This includes involvement of CEO's, middle managers/program coordinators, clinical supervisors, and counselors. For most of these tiers of agency staff, recruitment and engagement to implement evidence-based practices is most effectively conducted on an individual basis, and includes review of the rationale for introducing these practices and a discussion of the practical implications for deployment within the agency. Preliminary discussions may also be needed with CEO's to identify the types of evidence-based practices that are suitable and desirable for use in their agency.

Multiple strategies can be used to engage community behavioral health agencies in the process of implementing evidence-based treatment practices. These include use of needs assessments, focus groups, and discussions with CEO's to identify shared goals and clinical targets. Important agency incentives to participate in this process include resources to support staff time invested in coordinating implementation, collecting data, and other related tasks. Availability of low cost training activities, and opportunities to work closely with research staff and their related academic institutions can also be rewarding to agency staff, although these benefits are moderated by the time commitments related to implementation.

Engagement in implementing evidence-based practices also appears to be facilitated by the use of staff embedded within the agency, such as "site coordinators" and "opinion leaders." These individuals can promote the implementation process and market the treatment protocol among their peer counselors, and can organize and provide staff training and consultation activities. Site coordinators are centrally located in community agencies so that they have visible contact with CEO's and counselors and other staff who provide client services, and can also serve as liaison with research staff. Site coordinators appear to be of particular importance within larger treatment agencies, in which there is a need to provide strategic planning and monitoring of evidence-based practices that are deployed across different programs.

Peer opinion leaders are not usually identified as such, nor do they always have designated responsibility within a treatment agency to serve in this capacity, but often operate informally as credible sources of information regarding evidence-based practices. Opinion leaders can provide an effective vehicle to disseminate technical information and consultation regarding evidence-based practices, and tend to expedite the technology transfer process. Agencies can readily and inexpensively identify existing opinion leaders through network analysis survey techniques.

National experts also can play an important role in facilitating implementation of evidence-based practices within community treatment agencies. In the current study, a small panel of experts was convened to identify and recommend particular evidence-based approaches related to treatment of co-occurring disorders. This approach helped to establish the credibility of the treatment protocol used in the study, and provided an opportunity for engagement of treatment agency staff in a dialogue regarding effective practices, feasibility of these practices within their agency settings, and to identify potential barriers to implementation. Some preparation may be needed to inform agency staff of external consultants' areas of expertise and field experience, prior to convening this type of consensus-building meeting.

Findings from the current study indicate that there are several stages of consensus-building relevant to the implementation of evidence-based treatment practices in the behavioral health area, particularly when implementation occurs across different treatment agencies and communities. Where existing treatment protocols are available that can be feasibly implemented in identified practice settings, the format and content of the protocols may need to be significantly adapted to address time constraints, special needs of client populations, and other considerations. In some cases, evidence-based treatment protocols may not be readily available for use in various practice settings, and consensus is needed to identify strategies for developing new materials derived from existing evidence-based practices. Those who design substantial adaptations to evidence-based protocols bear an important responsibility to conduct outcome research evaluating the effectiveness of the newly adapted intervention in the particular practice setting. Without these data, it is difficult to confirm that the evidence-based intervention is suitable for use in the new practice setting. Consensus is also needed among agencies implementing evidence-based practices to establish common approaches for disseminating and sustaining the use of these practices.

The effective deployment of evidence-based practices in behavioral health settings is predicated to a large extent on the integrity of the clinical intervention, and on the technology transfer approach. For example, material from treatment protocols that are poorly received by clients may lead to counselors discontinuing use of these protocols. These same results may be obtained if training and consultation approaches do not provide counselors with sufficient skills to implement treatment protocols effectively. Use of observation and objective rating forms are useful strategies in assessing fidelity of the evidence-based practices and of the technology transfer approach. On-site data collection is also the most effective technique for assessing the effectiveness of implementation trials involving technology transfer approaches. These activities can provide opportunities to augment staff's awareness of the goals and objectives of the implementation project.

Additional research is needed to identify the most effective strategies for identifying opinion leaders in different treatment settings, and to determine specific opinion leader characteristics and activities that influence the technology transfer process in these settings. Further investigation is also needed to examine organizational factors that may influence the technology transfer process, such as administrative support, counselor access to the internet, and availability of other agency resources. Research has not yet attempted to measure the independent contribution of different factors that may influence the technology transfer process in the behavioral health field, such as involvement of opinion leaders, application of intensive training and consultation activities, or other interventions such as sustained involvement with content experts.

For agencies enlisting the support of opinion leaders, it would be helpful to understand the optimal ratio of opinion leaders to assigned counselors, the most effective level of opinion leader involvement with peer counselors, and the impact of differing lengths of opinion leader involvement with peer counselors on implementation of new practice approaches. It would also be useful to identify organizational strategies to promote the credibility of opinion leaders in disseminating evidence-based substance abuse treatment practices.

## ACKNOWLEDGMENTS

Funding for this project was supported by the Substance Abuse Mental Health Services Administration, Center for Substance Abuse Treatment, Practice Improvement Collaborative (PIC) network grant #: 5 UD1 TI12662-03.

## REFERENCES

Arthur, M.W., and Blitz, C. (2000). Bridging the gap between science and practice in drug abuse prevention through needs assessment and strategic community planning. *Journal of Community Psychology*, *28*(3), 241-255.

Backer, T. (2000). The failure of success: Challenges of disseminating effective substance abuse prevention programs. *Journal of Community Psychology, 28*(3)*,* 363-373.

Backer, T. (2003). Science-based strategic approaches to dissemination. In J. L. Sorensen, R. A. Rawson, J. Guydish, and J. E. Zweben (Eds.), *Drug abuse treatment through collaboration: Practice and research partnerships that work*, (pps. 269-286). Washington, D.C: American Psychological Association.

Backer, T.E., Liberman, R.P., and Kuehnel, T.G. (1986). Dissemination and adoption of innovative psychosocial interventions. *Journal of Consulting and Clinical Psychology, 54*, 111-118.

Center for Substance Abuse Treatment (2003). *Building Practice Improvement Collaboratives: Eleven Case Studies*. Rockville, MD: U.S. Department of Health and Human Services.

Corrigan, P.W., Steiner, L., McCracken, S.G., Blaser, B., and Barr, M. (2001). Strategies for disseminating evidence-based practices to staff who treat people with serious mental illness. *Psychiatric Services, 52*(12), 1598-1606.

Davis, D.A., O'Brien, M.T., Freemantle, N., Wolf, F.M., Mazmanian, P., and Taylor-Vaisey, A. (1999). Impact of formal continuing medical education: Do conferences, workshops, rounds, and other traditional continuing education activities change physician behavior or health care outcomes? *Journal of the American Medical Association, 282* (9), 867-874.

Edwards, D.J., Dattilio, F.M., and Bromley, D.B. (2004). Developing evidence-based practice: The role of case-based research. *Professional Psychology: Research and Practice, 35* (6), pps. 589-597.

Galanter, M. and Kleber, H.D, (1999). *Textbook of substance abuse treatment*. Washington, D.C: American Psychiatric Press.

Gerstein, D., and Harwood, H. (1990). *Treating drug problems: Volume 1*. Washington, D.C: Institute of Medicine, National Academy Press.

Gingiss, P.L., Gottlieb, N.H., and Brink, S.G. (1994). Measuring cognitive characteristics associated with adoption and implementation of health innovations in schools. *American Journal of Health Promotion, 8*, 294-301.

Institute of Medicine (2001). *Crossing the quality chasm: A new health system for the 21$^{st}$ century*. Washington D.C: National Academy of Sciences.

Kelly, J.A., St. Lawrence, J.S., Diaz, Y.E., Stevenson, L.Y., Hauth, A.C., Brasfield, T.L., Kalichman, S.C., Smith, J.E., and Andrew, M.E. (1991). HIV risk behavior reduction following intervention with key opinion leaders of population: An experimental analysis. *American Journal of Public Health, 81(2)*, 168-171.

Lamb, S., Greenlick, M.R., and McCarty, D. (1998). *Bridging the gap between practice and research: Forging partnerships with community-based drug and alcohol treatment*. Washington, D.C: National Academy of Sciences, Institute of Medicine.

Locock, L. Dopson, S., Chambers, D., and Gabbay, J. (2001). Understanding the role of opinion leaders in improving clinical effectiveness. *Social Science and Medicine, 53*, 745-757.

Lomas, J., Enkin, M., Anderson, G.M., Hannah, W.J., Vayda, E., and Singer, J. (1991). Opinion leaders vs. audit and feedback to implement practice guidelines. *Journal of the American Medical Association, 265(17)*, 2202-2207.

Lowinson, J.H., Ruiz, P., Millman, R.B., and Langrod, J.G. (2005). *Substance abuse: A comprehensive textbook – 4th edition*. Baltimore: Williams and Wilkens.

Marinelli-Casey, P. Domier, C.P., and Rawson, R.A. (2002). The gap between research and practice in substance abuse treatment. *Psychiatric Services, 53* (8), 984-987.

McCabe, O.L. (2004). Crossing the quality chasm in behavioral health care: The role of evidence-based practice. *Professional Psychology: Research and Practice, 35* (6), pps. 571-579.

McGrew, J. H., Bond, G. R., Dietzen, L., Salyers, M. (1994). Measuring the fidelity of implementation of a mental health program model. *Journal of Consulting and Clinical Psychology, 62(4)*, p. 670-678.

McLellan, A.T. (2002). Technology transfer and the treatment of addiction: What can research offer practice? Journal of Substance Abuse Treatment,(** insert italics for previous five words - journal title) 22, 169-170.

Moncher, F. J., and Prinz, R. J. (1991). Treatment fidelity in outcome studies. *Clinical Psychology Review, 11(3)*, p. 247-266.

Moore, K.A., Peters, R.H., Hills, H.A., LeVasseur, J.B., Rich, A.R., Hunt, W.M., Young, M.S, and Valente, T.W. (2004). Characteristics of Opinion Leaders in Community-Based Substance Abuse Treatment Agencies. *The American Journal of Drug and Alcohol Abuse, 30*(1), 1-17.

Mueser, K.T., and Fox, L. (1998). *Stage-wise family treatment for dual disorders treatment manual.* Concord, NH: New Hampshire-Dartmouth Psychiatric Research Center.

Orwin, R. G. (2000). Assessing program fidelity in substance abuse health services research, *Addiction, 95*(Supp. 13), p. S309-S327.

Peters, R.H., Moore, K.A., Hills, H.A., Young, M.S., LeVasseur, J.B., Rich, A.R., Hunt, W.M., & Valente, T.W. (in press). Use of opinion leaders and Intensive training to implement evidence-based co-occurring disorders treatment in the community. In Edmundson, E., & McCarty, D. (Eds.), *Implementing evidence-based practices for treatment of alcohol and drug disorders.* New York: The Haworth Press.

Rogers, E.M. (2003). *Diffusion of innovations, 5th edition.* New York: Free Press.

Rogers, E.M. and Cartano, D.G. (1962). Methods of measuring opinion leadership. *Public Opinion Quarterly, 26,* 435-441.

Schmidt, F. and Taylor, T.K. (2002). Putting empirically supported treatments into practice: Lessons learned in a children's mental health center. *Professional Psychology: Research and Practice, 33* (5) 483-489.

Scott, J. (2000). *Network Analysis: A Handbook, Second Edition.* Newbury Park, CA: Sage.

Simpson, D.D. (2002). A conceptual framework for transferring research to practice. *Journal of Substance Abuse Treatment, 22,* 171-182.

Sorensen, J.L. and Clark, W.W. (1995). A field-based dissemination component in a drug abuse research center. In T.E. Backer and S. L. David (Eds.) *Reviewing the behavioral science knowledge base on technology transfer,* (pp. 186-197). (NIH Publication No. 95-4035) Rockville, MD: National Institutes of Health.

Sorensen, J.L., Hall, S.M., Loeb, P., Allen, T., Glaser, E.M., and Greenberg, P.D. (1988). Dissemination of a job seeker's workshop to drug treatment programs. *Behavior Therapy, 19,* 143-155.

Sorensen, J.L., Rawson, R.A., Guydish, J., and Zweben, J.E. (Eds.) (2003). *Drug Abuse Treatment Through Collaboration: Practice and Research Partnerships that Work.* Washington, D.C: American Psychological Association.

Technical Assistance Collaborative (2003). *Turning knowledge into practice: Am manual for behavioral health administrators and practitioners about understanding and implementing evidence-based practices.* Boston, MA: Technical Assistance Collaborative, Inc.

Valente, T.W. (1996). Social network thresholds in the diffusion of innovations. *Social Networks, 18(1), 69-89.*

Valente, T.W. (2000). Methods for identifying opinion leaders. *Unpublished manuscript.*

Valente, T.W., and Davis, R.L. (1999). Accelerating the diffusion of innovations using opinion leaders. *ANNALS, 566,* 55-67.

In: Substance Abuse, Assessment and Addiction            ISBN: 978-1-61122-931-8
Editors: Kristina A. Murati and Allison G. Fischer        © 2011 Nova Science Publishers, Inc.

*Chapter 6*

# CURRENT CONTROVERSIES IN THE ASSESSMENT AND TREATMENT OF HEROIN ADDICTION

## *Robert J. Craig*[1]

### Jesse Brown VA Medical Center, Chicago, IL USA

## ABSTRACT

This paper addresses controversial topics in the assessment and treatment of heroin addiction. Included in the discussion are issues of dose and outcome, difficulties with toxicology screens, the role of co-occurring Axis I and Axis II disorders, the introduction (and extinction) of newer medications to treat heroin dependence, difficulties of measuring treatment outcome, models of heroin dependence, the role of user personality, and the question of heroin maintenance treatment.

## HEROIN DEPENDENCE: DEFINITION AND OVERVIEW OF THE SYNDROME

Heroin is morphine treated with acetic acid, so technically it is diacetylmorphine and considered a semi-synthetic opioid. Historically it was developed to treat morphine dependence and thought not to be addictive. Official diagnostic nomenclature (e.g., DSM-IV) (APA, 1994) says "The essential feature of Substance Dependence is a cluster of cognitive, behavioral, and physiological symptoms...(with) continued use ...despite significant substance-related problems" (p176). This use results in tolerance, withdrawal and compulsive drug-taking behavior. By tolerance we mean the need for more of the drug to achieve the intended effect or substantially reduced effects when using the same amount of the drug. Withdrawal is a pattern of stage-specific patterns of signs and symptoms associated with the

---

[1] Address inquiries concerning this paper to rjcraig41@comcast.net

discontinuance of the drug. Compulsive substance use is manifested by continued use in the presence of adverse consequences, taking more of the drug than originally intended, manifestation of a persistent desire to cut down followed by continued use, daily behavior consumed by activities designed to procure the drug, and reduced social, occupational, recreational, and spiritual activities.

While opiates are used medically to treat pain, diarrhea, and cough, heroin has no accepted medical use. Heroin is usually taken intraveneously (IV – "mainlined"), or nasally (.e.g., "snorted" (insufflation). It is also administered by subcutaneous injections – a process known as "skin-popping".

Heroin intoxication is manifested by initial euphoria and impaired judgment followed by pupillary constriction (or pupillary dilation due to anoxia from an overdose), drowsiness ("nodding") (or coma if severe), slurred speech, impairment in memory or attention and motor disturbance. Medically, it causes dry mouth, a slowing of gastrointestinal activity and constipation. Chronic IV use can result in sclerosed veins and puncture marks at the injection sites giving the appearance of "railroad tracks". Abscesses are also possible, as is bacterial endocarditis, Hepatitis, and HIV infections, and positive PPD tests. Erectile dysfunction in males and irregular menses in females may occur, but loss of desire is probably the most common effect of chronic use. In addition to deaths from diseases, heroin addicts also die from overdose, accidents, and murder.

Heroin withdrawal is often stage-sequenced and occurs following cessation of use. Depending on habit strength and amount of the drug taken, this pattern of withdrawal occurs anywhere from hours to three days following the discontinuance of the drug. The individual experiences yawning, muscle aches, lacrimation or rhinorrhea, diaphoresis, fever, insomnia, nausea and vomiting. These symptoms are nearly identical to symptoms associated with influenza.

The most common laboratory test used to detect the presence of heroin is the urine toxicology screen. The acetic acid is metabolized and excreted and the urine tests positive for morphine. Urine samples are likely to test positive for morphine for up to three days following use in heroin-dependent patients. This will depend, however, on many other factors, including the specific procedures use to detect the drug (see section below on urine toxicology screens). Liver enzymes may also be elevated, and many heroin-addicted patients will test positive for Hepatitis C antibody (indicating past infection) or for the hepatitis antigen indicating an active infection.

Prevalence of heroin abuse/addiction will vary according to the population sampled. In the *Monitoring the Future (2004)* – a survey of drug abuse reported by high school teenagers, the prevalence of lifetime use of heroin was generally 1.5% among 8th, 10th, and 12th graders. According to the National Survey on Drug Use and Health (2003), among the general population age 12 and older, 404,000 had used heroin annually. NIDA estimates that there are over 1,000,000 heroin addicts in the U. S.

## Pharmacology and Pharmacokinetics

Heroin is transformed into MAM (6-momo-acetylmorphine) by hydrosis and then metabolized into morphine once it reaches the brain. Because of greater lipid (fat) solubility, heroin easily crosses the blood-brain barrier and acts on the same receptors as the natural opioid system (i.e., endorphins). The areas of the brain that are most sensitive to morphine and therefore also most sensitive to heroin are the hypothalamus, thalamus, and the amygdala.

# MODELS OF ETIOLOGY

Researchers have invoked biological, psychological, and sociological theories to explain why some people become addicted to opiates while others do not. Biological and pharmacological variables form the necessary but perhaps not the sufficient explanation for addiction.

## Biological Theories

Biological explanations for understanding of the central processes associated with addiction, especially tolerance, the addictive euphoria, and withdrawal are well-understood at the physiological level and at the anatomical level. We understand and can explain in microscopic detail what happens in the brain when molecules of heroin enter the brain, act upon the brain, and distributed through the body and finally metabolized and excreted. Where we are deficient is in biological understandings as to why some gravitate and become addicted in the first place. While variables of dose are relevant as a physical explanation, it is also true that most patients do not become addicted when given opiates for medical conditions. It is only a small percentage that develop an addiction.

The heroin "high" occurs when heroin molecules enter the brain and occupy the mu receptors activating the mesolimbic (midbrain) system that signals the ventral tegmental (VTA) area causing the release of dopamine in the nucleus accumbens. This results in feelings of pleasure. Tolerance occurs when the opiate receptors become less responsive to opiate stimulation so that more opiates are required to stimulate the VTA cells to release the same amount of dopamine in the nucleus accumbens.

Intoxication occurs when opiate molecules link to the mu receptors on brain cells in the locus cerulus. This linkage system activates an enzyme that converts adenosine triphosphate (ATP) into cyclic adenosine monophosphate (cAMP), which then triggers the release of noradrenaline. This linkage also results in the inhibition of the enzyme that converts ATP to cAMP, so that less cAMp is produced and hence less noradrenaline is released. This results in the classic symptoms associated with the heroin "rush" –slowed respiration, drowsiness, low blood pressure, and shallow breathing.

When opiates are not present to suppress the locus cerulus' enhanced activity, the neurons produce abnormally high levels of cAMP, leading to an excessive amount of noradrenaline, resulting in anxiety, muscle cramps and diarrhea – the classic opiate withdrawal syndrome. (Other areas of the brain also contribute to these symptoms, including the mesolimbic reward system.)

## Classical Conditioning

Classical conditioning involves a process whereby a neutral stimulus, called the unconditioned stimulus, is paired with a stimulus that evokes a response that is either rewarding or punishing. This process usually occurs several times until the neutral stimulus has the power to evoke the response alone. In the classic example, a hungry dog is presented with meat (the unconditioned stimulus) which evokes salivation (the unconditioned response). In the next phase, the presentation of the meat is preceded by a tone – perhaps a bell. After multiple pairing, the presentation of the bell is able to produce the response. The bell is now termed the conditioned stimulus and salivation after the bell is now termed the conditioned response.

Classical conditioning contributes to the perceived effects of heroin and also to withdrawal. Heroin is taken within certain environments and preceded by a series of behaviors (i.e., deciding to get the drug, driving to the spot where drugs are sold, reaching into one's pocket for the money to pay for the drug, giving the money to the dealer, seeing and receiving the bag of heroin, getting out one's "works" (i.e., needle if one is using IV), or preparing the drug to be sniffed, and finally receiving the rush as the drug impacts on the brain). This sequence is referred to as a "behavioral chain" and each behavior in the chain can be classically conditioned to cues in the environment that becomes associated with taking the drug. As one prepares to engage in this behavioral chain, these classically conditioned interoceptive (internal sensory receptors) and exteroceptive (stimuli in the environment) cues emerge. The patient has become conditioned to learn that a certain feeling will be associated with the end result of this chain and begins to feel anticipatory excitement (Wikler, 1973).

Classical conditioning also contributes to withdrawal. As one approaches an environment previously associated with the use of drugs, the presence of these environmental cues is sufficient enough to begin to experience a withdrawal syndrome that is relieved upon use of the drug. This explains why patients, following release from prison, have been known to go into withdrawal when re-entering their previous copping area even though they have not used heroin in several years.

Classical conditioning is more of an explanatory model to relapse than it is for onset of addiction in the first place.

## Psychodynamic Theories

Several psychodynamic theories have been proposed to explain why some, growing up in the same environment, and with similar parentage, develop a problem with heroin addiction while others do not (Blatt, McDonald, Sugarman, & Wilber, 1984; Lettieir, Sayers, & Perason, HW, 1980). These theories argue that heroin addiction is (a) related to feelings of childhood emotional deprivation and use heroin to experience a soothing, infantile, symbiotic bond, (b) an attempt to deal with excessively aggressive impulses and thereby preventing their expression, (c) a reaction to guilt, shame, and feelings of worthlessness, or (d) an attempt to self-medicate an underlying psychiatric disorder (Khantzian, 1985).

## Family Functioning Theories

It has been recognized for some time that the families of opiate addicts function differently than most other families (Alexander & Dibb, 1975;Harbin & Mazier, 1975). These theories have changed little in the intervening years (Stanton, 1997).This research has concluded that addict families are characterized by poor communication, unsuccessful attempts of parents to control the addict behavior combined with an unsuccessful attempt by the addict to emotionally separate from the nuclear family, a tendency of the father to dominate the mother or to be seen a week and submissive and subordinate to an aggressive wife. The addict's mother is described as enmeshed with the son (the addict) in a dyad that perversely excludes the father, who feels emasculated. From a family systems perspective the addict's behavior within the family is an attempt to maintain overall family homeostasis and related to an intense fear of separation and individuation. The addict's role is to act in ways to bring the familial dysfunction to the attention of mental health specialists through the addictive behavior.

## Socioeconomic Theories

Socioeconomic theories emphasize environmental variables that presage the onset of addiction. These include such factors to poverty, lack of economic opportunities, poor role models within the community, embattled and gang-infested neighborhoods, inadequate schools, estrangement from community instructions such as churches, etc.

## Summary and Conclusions

Theories of addiction have changed little in the past fifty years. It is also likely that all of these factors – biological, psychological, sociological, and in some cases, familial – play a role in the phases of addiction (onset, continuation, addiction, cessation, relapse, abstinence). Attention has changed from testing these theories to developing more effective treatment interventions for the disorder

# THE ASSESSMENT OF OPIATE ADDICTION

## Urine Toxicology Screens

Besides clinical examinations and evaluations, the toxicology screen for drugs of abuse is the most common physical test to aid in the diagnosis of heroin abuse (Craig, 2004). After ingestion, the acetic acid is metabolized and the excreted urine results in a positive finding for the presence of morphine in urine. While this is a simple principle, there are several factors to consider when evaluating the toxicology screen results.

1)   The urine sample should be taken under direct observation and chain of custody of the sample must also be assured. Drug addicts – especially males – have many ways to falsify a urine sample to avoid detection. For example, they purchase "clean" urine from a non-user and then switch urine prior to returning it to the technician. This is quite easily done if the sample is unobserved. Even when observed, unless the area is free from blind spots, addicts can substitute the urine by placing it in a balloon under the arm with a tube leading to the genital area. While appearing to urinate, they are

actually squeezing the bulb thereby allowing the contents (i.e., clean urine) to flow into the test vial. Sometimes addict work in pairs, distracting the technician while the partner makes the switch on the urine cart. Some may make the switch by accidentally dropping the real sample and then substituting the forged sample.

2) A number of products are available on the internet and are available for purchase (Cleartest.com, 2006). All of these products allege an ability to be able to falsify the urine results. Many of these products have clever and alluring names. For example, "The Urinator" consists of a small electric, self-contained module containing thermostatically controlled water maintained at the correct temperature for up to four hours. The water is mixed with a concentrated clean synthetic urine substitute. The device is small enough to hold in your hand and thereby easy to conceal. "Urine Luck" is a chemical solution which allegedly destroys unwanted substances (i.e., heroin). Similar products, such as "Zip-n-Flip, "Ready Clean", XXtra Clean" purport similar outcomes. "Clear Choice Shampoo" is available if hair testing is done instead of urine testing. It is questionable whether or not any of these devices or products can beat a toxicology screen. They are probably most often used for pre-employment physicals rather than for routine use in drug treatment programs.

3) Addicts try to add water brought from home or drink an excessive amount of water or substitute water scooped from the toilet bowl to try and change the Ph level of urine and thereby diluting the sample. Adding a colorant to the toilet bowl will defeat these attempts. They also have been known to drink vinegar, which theoretically would be effective except that the patient would have to ingest such a large amount that it would become toxic. Addicts also try and add chemicals or bleach, or water-purification tablets to the urine however these products have a recognizable odor.

4) Some addicts make a small pinhole in the collection tube (if plastic). This hole is too small to be detected at the collection site, but during shipping to the lab, the fluid slowly leaks out, resulting in an insufficient volume for testing.

Thus it is imperative that the technician be fully trained on these methods and make a conscientious effort to ensure that the sample analyzed is the actual specimen taken from the patient. The best method to defeat these efforts is a competent and well-trained technician, who directly observes the specimen collected with no distractions. A blue colorant may be added to the toilet bowl, and urine collection bottles are available for purchase which automatically records the temperature of the urine in the bottle, which should be the same as body temperature. Finally, one may test for the specific gravity of the sample, which, if less than 1.010, then the specimen is suspect.

While urine screens are the most common method to detect drugs of abuse, blood, hair, sweat, and saliva can also be used. Blood is more invasive - one needs about 40 strands of hair for each sample, thereby creating patient resistance, and use of sweat and saliva has collection problems. Urine toxicology tests are either screening tests or confirmatory tests. A good lab will employ both types of methods when reporting the results. Screening tests are used to rule out negative results. They are usually quick and cost-effective. When a positive result if found on a screening test, the sample should be tested by a more sensitive method, referred to as a confirmatory test. The likelihood that these two methods will result in a false positive is next to zero. Also, there are different laboratory techniques to assay the sample, each with advantages and disadvantages. These are presented in Tables 1 and 2.

**Table 1. Overview of Drug Use Detection Methods**

| Method | Cost | Detection Period | Detection of Poppy Seed | Cheating Potential | Problems |
|---|---|---|---|---|---|
| Urine | About 6$ for each unconfirmed test | 1-5 days for most drugs; up to 1 month for marijuana | Will test positive for opiates | Problematic | Testing methods differ in sensitivity and specificity |
| Hair | About $40/test | Up to 90 days 1 one 1/2" sample | Will not test positive for opiates | Impervious to cheating | Does not detect methadone, alcohol or semi-synthetic opiates* |
| Sweat | variable | undetermined | Distinguishes between opiates and poppy seed | Impervious to cheating | Does not detect methadone, or semi-synthetic opiates* |
| Saliva | Similar to costs of urine tox screens | undetermined | Depends on method used | Resistant to Cheating | Less effective in identifying marijuana |
| Blood | variable | Days | Able to differentiate opiates from poppy seed | Not susceptible to cheating | Invasive |

* Labs have screens set up for the five commonly sued drugs required for workplace drug testing, which is a big source of revenue. These methods could detect methadone and other opiates if someone was willing to pay the additional costs. Hospital-based labs could also detect these drugs when so requested.

Most labs use immunoassays because they are reliable, easy-to-use, and have ways to eliminate the vast number of negative tests from the few that will be positive. However, this method cross-reacts with chemically similar drugs in the same class and that can result in false positive findings. Most labs use a combination of gas chromatography (GC) and mass spectrometry as a confirmatory technique.

The sensitivity of a drug is that level of concentration of a drug in urine below which the assay can no longer detect it. The laboratory technician will set the threshold level for a positive finding with different labs possibly setting different threshold levels and thereby reporting different results.

The results will be reported as either positive or negative. The clinician needs to know what method was used to obtain the results and whether they were confirmed. I am personally aware of one situation where results were coming back which contradicted what the patients were telling their counselors and physicians. In many cases the patient was observed drinking methadone but then the results came back negative for methadone. When this was brought to the attention of responsible officials, we were chastised for not believing the lab results and charged with succumbing to the "charm" and manipulations of our patients.

## Table 2. Common Methods Used for Urine Toxicology Screens

| Method | Use | Turn-Around Time | Sensitivity | Specificity | Benefits | Problem |
|---|---|---|---|---|---|---|
| **Chromatography** | | | | | | |
| Thin-Layer (TLC) | Mass Screening | 2 hrs | reasonable | reasonable | Useful for large volume operations | Qualitative results only (pos.neg); results need confirmation; Specificity affected by environmental condition |
| Gas Liquid (GLC) | Used as a confirming test | 2 hrs | Greater than TLC but time-consuming | Utmost specificity | Low incidence of false positives; | Only a single specimen can assay a sample at any one time; more costly overall |
| **Spectral Methods** | | | | | | |
| Spectro-photo-fluometry | Often used to confirm results from immuno-Assays | | | | Can handle high volume output; simple to use | High false positive rates; virtually used for morphine detection only. |
| **immuno-assays (in general)** | | rapid | Very sensitive | poor | Adaptable to high volume operations; can detect smaller amounts of drug in urine than TLC | Cross-reactive with similar drugs, resulting in false positives |
| Free Radical Assay | Used for mass screening | 5 seconds to 2-3 minutes | High rate of false positives | low | Relatively inexpensive and requires little technical expertise | High equipment costs; results need confirmation by GC/TLC |
| Enzyme Multiplied ImmunoAssay | Allows for high-volume testing | 5 seconds to 2-3 minutes | High sensitivity | High specificity | Detects a wide range of substances; results very reliable when confirmed by GC/TLC | High instrument costs; results need confirmation by another method |
| Radio ImmunoAssays | Intended for screening with another method to confirm the results | 1-2 hours | | Doesn't detect a full range of drugs | More sensitive that FRAT/EMIT; low rate of false positives | Very costly; doesn't detect a wide range of drugs |
| Hemaglutination | High volume | 90 minutes | High | Not able to detect a wide range of drugs | Inexpensive; uses uncomplicated equipment | Limited number of samples assayed each day; high equipment costs. |

Accordingly, we split the next day's collection and sent them down as separate samples (without telling the lab) and then compared the results. The evidence was clear. The results were generally unreliable. When this evidenced was reported to these same responsible officials, it was then learned that the lab was not confirming the results due to costs and lack of personnel.

This is not necessarily an isolated occurrence. In a study reported in *JAMA*, the performance of 13 laboratories, serving 262 methadone maintenance treatment facilities, was evaluated by submitting pre-tested patient urine samples for blind testing. The false positive and false negative error rates for samples containing (or not containing) morphine, amphetamines, methadone, codeine, and barbiturates, ranged from 0% to 100% depending on the drug tested. These very same labs had detection rates in the 99% percentile for samples submitted to the Center for Disease Control (CDC) as quality checks. The results suggested that greater care was taken for samples to be submitted to CDC than for routine samples, and laboratories were often unable to detect the presence of illicit drugs at levels required of in their contracts. The authors recommended that drug treatment facilities monitor the performance of their laboratories with quality control samples and blind testing (Hansen, Caudill, & Boon, 1985). Subsequently NIDA developed proficiency standards for accrediting laboratories based on this study and others (Davis, Hawks, & Blanke, 1988).

In our own program, periodically we become suspect of urine results. Fortunately we have the cooperation of laboratory personnel to detect the source of the problem. Occasionally it is due to improper cleaning of the equipment between uses resulting in traces of drugs (usually cocaine), remaining in the equipment and thereby pickup up a positive reading for cocaine. At other times the standard is not able to detect the presence of methadone at extremely low doses. The point here is that one needs to have a good working relationship with the lab and the results from the lab require continued scrutiny.

## ASI (and its Problems)

The Addiction Severity Index (McLellan et al, 1992) was developed under contract from NIDA as a screening measure to assess the domains known to be effected by alcohol and drug abuse. These domains are medical, employment, family/social, legal, and psychological/psychiatric. The instrument also provides severity levels for both alcohol and drug abuse. It is questionnaire-based and takes about 45-minutes to administer. At the end of each section the patient provides a severity ranking for each domain and a rating of importance for inclusion in treatment. The clinician also provides a severity rating. Where there is agreement, then that would lead to congruent treatment goals, whereas widely discrepant ratings between clinician and counselor suggest probable denial and treatment resistance.

The ASI has consistently demonstrated its concurrent and predictive validity for both alcohol and drug-dependent patients. For example, in a recent study, low ASI severity scores in drug predicted good outcomes for patients on methadone maintenance treatment after one year of treatment; low scores on ASI psychological/psychiatric predicted attendance at counseling sessions, and low scores on ASI employment predicted full time employment. Correspondingly, high scores in those domains predicted continuing drug abuse, unemployment and treatment non-compliance in counseling (Craig & Olson, 2004).

The ASI has become the standard instrument to assess severity levels in addiction, at least in research studies, and the Department of Veterans Affairs require it as a standard measure at treatment intake as well as every six months thereafter, to assess treatment progress. However, its use has not become a mainstream assessment instrument among most treatment programs, despite its demonstrated validity. This is a concern to NIDA, which lists it as one area of technology transfer that remains lacking in treatment programs.

## Role of Personality

A datum in medicine is that it is just as important to know the person who has the disease as it is to know what disease the person has. In the case of psychiatric disorders, this datum is ever more true. In the Diagnostic Manual of Mental Disorders, 4 edition (1994) of the American Psychiatric Association, Axis I disorders (i.e., clinical syndromes) put one at risk for developing Axis II disorders (i.e., personality disorders). Similarly, having an Axis II disorder increases the risk of having certain Axis II disorders. This is referred to as comorbidity. For example, having an Axis II antisocial personality disorder increases the likelihood that the person will also develop a substance use disorder, either alcohol or drugs. Having a dependent personality disorder increases the risk of developing a clinical depression or a panic disorder.

Researchers have extensively evaluated the relationship between substance abuse and various Axis II disorders and this research has recently been summarized (Craig, 2003). Whether one uses a structured clinical interview or a self-report questionnaire to make a personality diagnosis, the personality disorder of Antisocial is the most common personality disorder associated with heroin addict, with prevalence rates ranging up to 62%, depending on the setting and the method used to make the diagnosis.

## TREATMENT OF HEROIN ADDICTION

### Methadone Maintenance Treatment

Methadone is D,1-4, 4-diphenyl-6-dimethyl-amino-3-hepatone, with the L isomer accounting for much of its activity (Weddington, 1995). It is available in tablet/wafer, power and injectable forms but oral use is the most common. It was initially developed as an analgesic but now is more currently used for opiate detoxification and for the treatment of the opiate abstinence syndrome and for maintenance treatment of opiate addiction. Its subjective effects include sedation, analgesia and changes in mood and is not substantially different form those of other opiates except for a longer duration. It depresses the respiratory center, has antitussive actions, inhibits gastrointestinal tone and propulsion, and produces mild hyperglycemia and hypothermia.

Methadone is absorbed quickly and plasma levels can be detected within 30 minutes of oral ingestion. Peak plasma levels are attained in about four hours. In non-tolerant patients, the mean half-life of the drug is about 15 hours, whereas after chronic administration the mean half-life is 22 hours (Weddington, 1995).

In 1964, Vincent Dole MD, an internist at Rockefeller University and Marie Nyswander MD, a New York psychiatrist began treating patients addicted to heroin with methadone hydrochloride. Patient were accepted into the treatment protocol if they were 20 and 40 years of age, had been using heroin for at least four years with repeated relapses, had no psychosis or serious medical illness, and were no coerced into treatment by the courts. They were hospitalized and placed on a gradual stabilizing dose of methadone.

Methadone induction began with low doses of 10 to 20mg/day and gradually increased over a period of from four to six week. This was done to avoid narcotic against effects. After patients had been stabilized on doses from 80 to 120mg/day, they were maintained on a single oral daily dose without further dose increases and, at the end of the six week trial, the patients were discharged to outpatient clinics where they continued to receive daily methadone. Urine toxicology screens were taken as a means to determine treatment effectiveness. These clinician/researchers were quick to add that, while counseling was available, the essential treatment was a medical approach to the heroin addiction.

Of the 1007 applicants interviewed as possible candidates, 60% were accepted.

Their initial report was based on 304 of these patients. The authors found dramatic improvement in patients treated with methadone. A total of 91% remained in treatment, 70% were employed or were in school, while the remaining 30% had discontinued heroin use and antisocial behavior, although they had not yet become socially productive. This favorable response to a medical therapy was not expected in a sample of patients with slum backgrounds, school dropouts, prison records, and minority group status. The authors questioned psychogenic theories of addiction etiology that stressed character defects in these patients as the seminal etiology of the disorder. Instead, they argued that heroin addiction was a metabolic disease caused by repeated exposure to narcotic drugs (Dole, Nyswander, & Kreek, 1966; Dole & Nyswander, 1967).

Over the past 40 years, methadone has become one of the most studied medications. This research has documented its effectiveness as well as the absence of any long-term side effects or complications in over 300 published studies (Hubbard & Marsden, 1986; Sells, Demaree, & Hornick, 1979). While on methadone, consumption of all illicit drugs declines to less than 40% of pre-treatment levels during the first year of treatment and to 15% of pre-treatment levels for patients who remain on methadone for two or more years (Ball & Ross, 1991). Furthermore, crime is substantially reduced. In the most detailed study of treatment outcome, Ball and Ross (1991) found that criminal activity was reduced by more that 70% during the first four months of treatment. Patients on methadone showed reduced rates of HIV infection – an outcome referred to as harm reduction. In one study, 5% of patients on methadone contracted HIV compared to a cohort of patients not on methadone whose rate of HIV infection was 26% (Metzger, 1993). It is also comforting to know that there is no difference in methadone treatment outcomes between Hispanic and African-American men and women. Both of these minorities of both genders achieve similar treatment outcomes after six months of treatment (Mulvaney et al, 1999). While methadone maintenance patients have high rates of alcohol abuse, ranging between 13% to 25%, these rates were not substantially different from the rates of heavy drinking reported in the general population (Ottomanelli, 1999). However, research has found that heavy drinking was not a major factor in treatment retention or outcome (Kreek, 1991).

Keep in mind that simply giving methadone is rarely sufficient to achieve these kinds of outcomes. Programs must also offer supportive services, such as counseling, vocational rehabilitation and social and psychological/psychiatric services in a comprehensive treatment plan. The addition of basic counseling services is associated with major increases in clinical efficacy (McLellan et al, 1993).

## Controversies with Methadone Maintenance

Despite its general acceptance in medicine and its effectiveness documented by researchers, a number of controversies continue to be associated with its use. These include methadone diversion, what is the most effective therapeutic dose, the quality of staff in methadone programs, its isolation from other health-care institutions, nonspecific interventions or poorly integrated interventions from other substances of abuse such as alcohol and cocaine, its opposition from abstinence-oriented treatment programs, such as 12-step programs and therapeutic communities. Also, heroin addicts often have high rates of psychiatric co-morbidities, particularly anxiety and affective disorders (Milby et al, 1996) and personality disorders especially antisocial personality disorders (Craig, 2003). Many of these patients are also the very ones who are non-responders to methadone and who continued to be negatively visible around the clinic. Hence, methadone maintenance programs, especially those which are not hospital-based but which are housed in the community, have not achieved full acceptance by their surrounding community.

## The Dosage Controversy

Here we will explore one of the more contentious controversies associated with methadone.

Despite the success often achieved with methadone and supportive services, not all patients or programs attain such outcome. The US General Accounting Office (GAO) studied 24 programs comprising 5600 active patients. They found that many patients on methadone continue to use heroin as well as other drugs. In 10 of the clinics over 20% of the patients ere still using heroin after six months of treatment and at two clinics over 50% were using heroin. The dosage levels at 21 of 24 clinics were below 60mg, which many clinicians believe to be the minimally therapeutic maintenance dose (GAO, 1990). Ball and Ross (1991) cited evidence that an adequate dose of methadone should be between 60mg – 100mg daily, since these dosages were associated with the highest rates of treatment retention and the lowest rates of illicit heroin use. Similar findings have been reported by other researchers (D'Aunno & Vaughn, 1992). These findings were included in the position statement of the American Psychiatric Association on methadone maintenance which stipulated that an adequate dose of methadone was between 60mg – 100mg/day (APA, 1994b). (See Figure 1).

While the preponderance of research does show that higher doses are generally associated with better outcomes than are lower doses, there are reports in the literature showing that low dose methadone (averaging 30mg/day) attained "outcome" rates (i.e., illicit heroin use) comparable to rates of high-dose programs, it did so at the expense of lower treatment retention (Craig, 1980). Other researchers found little difference in toxicology screens for heroin use between patients maintained on doses above or below 50mg/day and suggested that other variables may affect heroin use other than dose (Maddux et al, 1991).

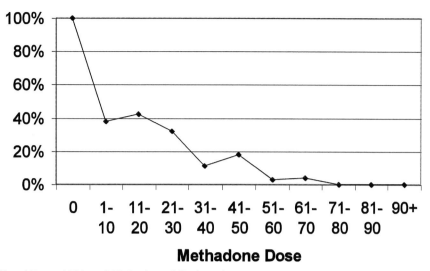

From Ball and Ross, 1991, p. 248. In the public domain.

Figure 1. Heroin Use in Past 30 Days (N=407)

In a naturalistic study, high versus low dose methadone maintenance patients (N=265) were compared on the outcome variables of illicit drug use, treatment retention, missed medication days, and ratings of counselors of patient progress. Initial results found no significant differences on any outcome variable associated with methadone dose. However, there were significant differences on these same variables by assigned therapists. Some counselors got better results with their patients than other counselors and these findings were independent of dose (Blaney & Craig, 1999).

Studies show that patients show marked improvement in illicit use of heroin compared to their use prior to admission. These improvements are generally maintained during methadone maintenance treatment. However, success rates are very low after methadone treatment. As many as 90% relapse within one year of discharge and range from 9% to 21% drug-free at following after five years post-treatment (Weddington, 1995).

## Harm Reduction vs. Abstinence

Research continues to demonstrate that methadone maintenance treatment is associated with reduced risks of criminality, reduced onset of HIV and TB, and reduction of sexually transmitted disorders. This is referred to as harm reduction. Proponents of harm reduction argue that patients should remain in methadone maintenance, even though they continue to use heroin because studies show that these patients are using less heroin than prior to methadone induction and this reduction of use is associated with reduction in risks of developing the aforementioned diseases.

In contrast to this are proponents of an abstinence model of treatment. There are two forms of this model. First, there are those who argue that being on methadone is not abstinence since they are using a (legal) narcotic. Rather they argue that patients should be off all drugs. Some staff in therapeutic communities (i.e. residential treatment programs), half-way houses and some Narcotics Anonymous chapters want patients to be off methadone and drug free. In other words, they want patients totally abstinent. A second form of this are some methadone maintenance programs, who, while understanding the harm reduction benefits of methadone maintenance, argue that the goal of methadone maintenance is the elimination of illicit heroin, Therefore, the patient must be totally abstinent from heroin or face administrative detoxification and eventual discharge. Proponents of this model differ in the length of time they give a patient before enacting this provision.

There is no immediate way to resolve this controversy, as it is really a matter of the philosophical belief system of program staff. The position statement of the American Psychiatric Association on Methadone Maintenance Treatment (1994) states that many patients need two or more years of methadone maintenance treatment before adequate outcome rates have been attained and some may need this treatment for the rest of their lives.

## Diversion

Initially the Food and Drug Administration regulated methadone maintenance treatment programs (MMTPs) and issued rules for the issuance of take-home methadone privileges. These rules stipulate eight conditions before methadone pick-up schedules are reduced. Initially patients must attend the clinic daily and ingest the methadone at the clinic for at least three months before take-home privileges can be considered. (Patients may be given a Sunday take-home dose if the clinic is closed on Sunday). Additional requirements include such things as an absence of criminal activity, adherence to program rules, regular attendance at counseling, an ability to safely store methadone away from children, etc. The Substance Abuse and Mental Health Service Administration (SAMHSA) now has regulatory oversight over MMTPs and has retained these same restrictions. Currently patients may be given up to a one month supply of take-home methadone after meeting clean time requirements and the other stipulations.

All this has meant that methadone has been diverted to the streets where it is sold. This has created an additional public health problem and generated neighborhood complaints about drug selling in and around the clinic and contiguous neighborhoods. Although many programs require methadone ingestion in front of a staff member (patients are then required to say something after swallowing), and test for methadone in toxicology screens to ensure ingestion, this does not impact the problem of methadone diversion. SAMHSA now requires MMTPs to have a Diversion Control Plan as part of their accreditation review. These Diversion Control Plans stipulate the steps program take to minimize methadone diversion. These steps include such things as (a) requiring only one patient at a time in front of the methadone dispensing window with other patients maintaining a stipulated distance between the ingesting patient and the next patient in line, (b) requiring a picture ID before dosing, convex mirrors placed in the dosing area allowing the methadone dispensers (pharmacists, nurses) to view peripheral activity, randomly "calling back" for bottles for patients on reduced pick-ups to verify responsible use, cameras placed within the pharmacy area, and continued monitoring and verification that patients continue to meet the SAMHSA regulations for continuation on reduced pick-up.

## Detoxification

Another issue is when and how to detoxify a patient on methadone. The position statement by APA (1994) states that detoxification should not be considered until at least two years of methadone maintenance treatment, assuming that the patient is stable in other areas of their life. Proponents of harm reduction might even argue that the patient shouldn't be detoxed at all, since doing so increases their risk of exposure to HIV, TB and STDs. This is contentious for staff operating from an abstinent oriented model.

While medical ethics gives the right for a patient to know their medication dose at any time, blind dose reductions is far preferable to non-blind detoxification. In blind dose procedures, the patient doesn't know whether or not their dose has been reduced, nor how much of a reduction has occurred. Clinical experience indicates that blind dose reduction tends to be more successful than open dosing.

A far more serious question pertains to the outcome studies of patients who have been detoxed off methadone. These studies show that, on average, most of these patients relapse and return to heroin use within one year of getting off methadone (Ball & Ross, 1991; Hser, Hoffman, Grella, & Anglin, 2001; Sells, Demaree, & Hornick, 1979). Many had died and many others were incarcerated. With this kind of outcome evidence, there is debate as to whether it is even advisable for a patient to be withdrawn from methadone, whether or not they are doing well on this therapy.

## LAAM and its Aftermath

Levo-alpha-acetyl-methadol (LAAM) is a synthetic opiate approved by the FDA in 1993 as a Schedule II controlled substance and sold under the name of ORLAAM. It was initially developed in 1948 as an analgesic but was subsequently found to be able to suppress the opiate withdrawal syndrome for more that 72 hours. Subsequently 27 separate studies allegedly established the safety and efficacy of LAAM as a maintenance treatment for opiate addiction. LAAM was dispensed three days a week with an increased dose for the weekend. It was metabolized into two active metabolites, nor-LAAM and dinor-LAAM.

LAAM was similar in action to other narcotics in the same class and hence was cross-reactive and tolerant to these drugs. Its major benefit was a reduced frequency of administration and visits to the clinic, and an alleged easier ability to detoxify a patient from LAAM compared to methadone e (NCADI, 1995)

After several years of use, it was learned that LAAM had an adverse effect on the QT interval in the heart. The medication was withdrawn and is no longer in use. The issue here is whether the early enthusiasm for Buprenorphine (see below) will suffer the same fate?

## Buprenorphine

Buprenorphine HCL is a partial opiate agonist developed and approved to treat opiate addicts in a doctor's office, thereby bypassing the extensive federal regulations required for patients enrolled in a methadone maintenance program. However, methadone maintenance programs can also use Buprenorphine but patients must then conform to these federal regulations. The drug purportedly minimizes withdrawal symptoms, decreases cravings, and partially blocks the effects of other opiates.

The drug is available in two forms. Subutex contains only Buprenorphine, while Suboxone contains Buprenorphine HCL/naloxone HCL dehydrate in a ration of 4:1. Both forms come in sublingual tablets. The drug binds to the opiate receptors in the brain thereby satisfying the addict's need for an opiate and also suppressing withdrawal symptoms. However, this drug only partially excites these receptors and so the patient does not get the full agonist effects caused by other opiate drugs. The drug affixes to and occupies these receptors for several days making it more difficult for other opiate drugs to excite these receptors. Buprenorphine is a partial agonist at the mu-opioid receptor and an antagonist at the kappa-opioid receptor; Naloxone is an antagonist at the kappa-opioid receptor. It is a Scheduled III narcotic in the *Controlled Substances Act*. It also has a ceiling effect making it more difficult to overdose on this drug. However, it does have sedating effects that interact with other drugs, such as benzodiazepines making these combinations potentially dangerous. Buprenorphine is metabolized to nonbuprenorphine byCYP3A4.Those wanting detailed information about the drug's pharmacokinetics should consult the package insert.

Generally patients are initially started on methadone maintenance or are transferred to Subutex. After stabilization, they are switched to Suboxone. Buprenorphine is metabolized to nonbuprenorphine by CYP3A4.

Buprenorphine cost more than methadone so one question is whether there is a cost-benefit ratio is favor of this drug. The Health Economics Resource center of the Department of Veterans Affairs developed an economic model comparing the effects of buprenorphine maintenance to methadone maintenance in terms of incremental costs, health care costs, and incremental effectiveness. They determined that the drug was cost effective in terms of its effects at reducing the health care costs associated with HIV infection. However, they also concluded that methadone maintenance was more cost effective than any scenarios developed by the authors. Methadone should remain the treatment of choice for patients addicted to opiates unless methadone maintenance treatment programs are not conveniently available within a community, or not attain the desirable clinical effectiveness, is not tolerated by the patient or when the patient has difficulty meeting the methadone clinic's hours of operation. In such cases, Buprenorphine is another treatment option and it was deemed safer and more effective for certain types of patients (Barnett, Zaric, & Brandeau, 2001). Additionally, it was found to be well tolerated by patients for short-term hospital-based detoxification (DiPaula, Schwartz, R., Montoya, I. D., Barrett, D., & Tang, 2002).

## Naltrexone: Theory and Outcome

Naltrexone hydrochloride was the first drug developed by NIDA in the treatment of opiate addiction (Ginzburg, 1984). It is an orally administered narcotic antagonist which blocks the physiological (but not the psychological) effects of opiates from 48 to 72 hours after an oral dose. It works by preferentially occupying the opiate receptor sites (i.e., mu, kappa, delta) in the brain, displacing agonists if present, and blocks the effects of any subsequent use of opiates as long as the drug is present in the body. Displacing agonists will result in a precipitate opiate withdrawal syndrome so that patients would have to be free of opiates for at least 24 hours prior to administration of this drug. It's principal metabolite 6-

beta-naltrexol have peak plasma levels within 1 to 4.5 hours. The plasma half-life is about 8 hours.

Trexan or revia (the brand name for Naltrexone) is a near-ideal pharmacological treatment of opiate dependence. It absolutely is effective when taken as prescribed. The patient will not feel the effects of heroin while on naltrexone. In addition to physiological explanations, at the theoretical level, the laws of learning also should explain why naltrexone is effective. When a patient is on naltrexone and uses heroin, the patient does not feel any effects from the heroin. In other words, there is a lack of reward. Upon repeated trials of using heroin and getting no reward, the paradigm of extinction is occurring which would predict that ultimately the patient would eventually stop using heroin.

Guess what? The patient tends to stop using the naltrexone so that they can use and feel the effects of heroin. Hence the drug has a low acceptability within the addict population. It is best used for patients who have a lot to lose if they relapse (i.e., physicians, lawyers, accountants, etc).

## ASSESSING CLIENT OUTCOMES

What outcome criteria should we use to measure success. We have all heard the phrase "the operation was a success but the patient died". Historically, total abstinence has been the criteria of treatment success, but many argue that reduction in use is just a valid measure of treatment success. Is reduction in sexually transmitted diseases, TB, and HIV/AIDS a treatment success even though there is no diminution of heroin use? Is employment a valid measure of good outcome? If a patient remains free from illicit drugs but still has problems with the law, is that treatment success? You can see that this is a value judgment of those that define success and policy makers that distribute money to successful programs.

### Heroin Maintenance?

Perhaps the most controversial proposal is to give heroin addicts prescribed heroin. Most recently this has been proposed by a few politicians as a way to combat crime in urban areas. Actually, this is an old idea (Drug Abuse Council, 1977). Since the United States policy views heroin as primarily a criminal problem, the idea of heroin maintenance is given little consideration in America. Because The United Kingdom viewed heroin as primarily a medical problem, the idea of heroin maintenance is less controversial and has been tired there. English doctors report that many addicts try to obtain higher doses of heroin and/or supplement their dose with street heroin. Also, the demand for heroin did not abate even with the presence of prescription heroin and the heroin black market continues to flourish in England. In a more recent study emanating from the united Kingdom, it was found that co-prescription of heroin combined with methadone was more effective than methadone maintenance alone (Metrebian, 2004; Metrebian, Shanahan, & Wells, 1998). To date, with concerns of spreading heroin addiction, the notion of heroin maintenance in America is not presently viable. Furthermore, England is relying more on methadone maintenance as the treatment of choice for heroin addiction.

Heroin addiction has shown some resilience to drug fads and continues despite drug epidemics of psychedelics in the 1960s, cocaine free-basing in the 1980s and is likely to remain when the current methamphetamine epidemic subsides. Therefore we need to continue to develop and research more effective treatments for this disorder and focus less of the controversies.

# REFERENCES

Alexander, BK; and Dibb, GS: Opiate addicts and their parents. *Fam. Proc.* 14, 499-514. 1975.

American Psychiatric Association. *Diagnostic and Statistical Manual of Mental Disorders.* 4th ed. Washington, DC: APA, 1994.

American Psychiatric Association. Position statement on methadone maintenance treatment. *American Journal of Psychiatry. 151, 792-793. 1994b.*

Author. *National Survey on Drug Use and Health.* Rockville, MD: National Institute on Drug Abuse, 2003.

Author. *Monitoring the Future.* Rockville, MD: National Institute on Drug Abuse, 2004.

Ball, JC; and Ross, A. *The Effectiveness of Methadone Maintenance Treatment: Patients, Programs, Services, and Outcomes.* New York: Spring-Verlag, 1991.

Barnett, PG; Zaric, GS; and Brandeau, ML. The cost-effectiveness of Buprenorphine maintenance therapy for opiate addiction in the United States. *Addict.* 96: 1267-1278, 2001.

Blaney, T: and Craig, RJ: Methadone maintenance: Does dose determine differences in outcome? *J. Sub. Ab. Treat.* 16, 221-228. 1999

Blatt, SJ; McDonald, C: Sugarman, A; and Wilber, C. Psychodynamic theories of opiate addiction: New directions for research. *Clin. Psychol. Rev.* 4, 159-189. 1984

Craig, RJ: *Counseling the Alcohol and Drug Dependent Client: A Practice Approach.* Boston, Mass: Allyn & Bacon. 2004.

Craig, RJ: Prevalence of personality disorders among cocaine and heroin addicts. *Directions in Addiction Treatment and Prevention.* 7, 33-42. 2003.

Craig, RJ: Effectiveness of low-dose methadone maintenance for the treatment of inner-city heroin addicts. *Int. J. Addict..* 15, 791-710. 1980.

Craig, RJ, and Olson, RE. Predicting methadone maintenance treatment outcomes using the Addiction Severity Index and the MMPI-2 content scales (Negative Treatment Indicators and Cynicism scales). *Am. J. Drug & Alc. Abuse.* 30, 823-839. 2004

Davis, KH; Hawks, RL; and Blanke, RV. Assessment of laboratory quality in urine drug testing: A proficiency testing pilot study. *JAMA,* 260, 1749-1754. 1988

D'Aunno, T: and Vaughn, TE: Variations in methadone treatment practices. *JAMA.* 267, 253-258. 1992.

DiPaula, BA; Schwartz, R; Montoya, ID; Barrett, D; and Tang, C. Heroin detoxification with Buprenorphine on an inpatient psychiatric unit. *J. Sub. Ab. Treat* 23, 163-169.

Dole, VP; Nyswander, M. E.. Heroin addiction – a metabolic disease. *Arch Intern Med* 120: 19-24, 1967

Dole, VP; Nyswander, M. E.; and Kreek, M. J. Narcotic blockade. *Arch. Intern Med* 118: 304-309, 1966

Drug Abuse Council. *What's happening with Heroin maintenance?* Washington, DC. 1977.

General Accounting Office: M*ethadone Maintenance: Some Treatment Programs are Not Effective; Greater Federal Oversight Needed.* Washington, DC: U.S. Government Printing Office. 1990.

Ginzburg, HM. *Naltrexone: Its clinical utility.* Rockville, MD: NIDA Treatment Research Report. 1984

Hansen, HJ; Caudill, SP: and Boone, J. Crisis in drug testing. *JAMA*, 253, 2382 – 2387. 1985

Harbin, HT: and Maziar, HM: The families of drug abusers: A literature review. *Fam. Proc.* 14 411-431. 1975

Hser, Y-I; Hoffman, V: Grella, CE: and Anglin, MD: A 33-year follow-up of narcotic addicts. *Arch. Gen. Psychiat.* 58, 503-508. 2001

Hubbard, RL: and Marsden, ME: Relapse to use of heroin, cocaine and other drugs in the first year of treatment: In *Relapse and Recovery in Drug Abuse.* NIDA Research Monograph 72. Rockvile, MD: U. S. Government Printing Office. 1986

Khantzian, EJ. The self-medication hypothesis of addictive disorders: Focus on heroin and cocaine dependence. *Am. J. Psychiat.* 142, 1259-1264. 1985.

Kreek, MJ: Using methadone effectively: Achieving goals by application of laboratory, clinical, and evaluation research and by development of innovative programs. In R. W. Pickens, C. G. Leukefeld, and C. R. Schuster (Eds). *Improving drug abuse retention.* Research Monograph 106, pp 136-151. Rockville, MD: NIDA

Lerrieri, DJ; Sayers, M; and Pearson, HW: *Theories on Drug Abuse: Selected Contemporary Perspectives.* Rockville, MD: NIDA, 1980.

Maddux, JF: Esquivel, M: Vogtsberger, KN: and Desmond, DP: methadone dose and urine morphine. *J. Sub. Ab. Treat.* 8, 195-201. 1991

McLellan, AT: Arndt, IO: Metzger, DS: woody, GE: and O'Brien, CP. The effects of psychosocial services in substance abuse treatment. *JAMA.* 269, 1953-1959. 1993.

McLellan, AT, Kushner, H., Metzger, DS, Peters, R, Smith, I, Grissom, G, Pettinati, H, Argeriou, M. The fifth edition of the Addiction Severity Index. *J. Subst. Abuse Treat*, 9, 199-213. 1992

Metrebian, N. Supervised co-prescription of heroin to treatment-resistant heroin addicts is more effective than treatment with methadone alone. *Evidence-based Ment. Hlth.* 7m 23, 2004.

Metrebian, N, Shanahan, W., and Wells, B. feasibility of prescribing injectable heroin and methadone to opiate dependent drug users; associated health gains and harm reductions. *Med. J. Aust.* 168, 596-600. 1998.

Metzger, J: HIV seroconversion among in and out of treatment intravenous drug users: An 180month prospective follow-up. *AIDS,* 9, 1049-1056. 1993.

Milby, JB; Sims, MK: Khuder, S; Schumacher, JE; Huggins, N; McLellan, AT; Woody, G and Haas, N. Psychiatric comorbidity: Prevalence in methadone maintenance treatment. *Am. J. Drug & Alc. Ab.* 22, 95-107. 1996.

Mulvaney, FD: Brown, LS: Aletrman, AI: Sage, RE: Cnaan, A: Cacciola, J: and Rutherford, M. Methadone-maintenance outcomes for Hispanic and African-American men and women. *Drug and Alc. Depend.* 54, 11-18. 1999.

National Clearinghouse for Alcohol and Drug Information. *LAAM in the Treatment of Opiate Addiction*. Rockville, MD: Substance Abuse and Mental Health Services Administration. 1995

Sells, SB:, Demaree, RG: and Hornick, CW: *Comparative Effectiveness of Drug Abuse Treatment Modalities*. NIDA Services Research Administrative Report. Washington, DC: NIDA. 1979.

Stanton, MD: The role of family and significant others in the engagement and retention of drug-dependent individuals. In LS Onken, JD Blaine, & JJ Boren (Eds). *Beyond the therapeutic alliance: Keeping the Drug-Dependent Individual in Treatment*. NIDA Research Monograph No. 165, pp. 157-180). Rockville, MD: National Institute on Drug Abuse. 1997

Weddington, WW. Methadone maintenance for opioid addiction. In N.S> Miller and M.S. Gold (Eds). *Pharmacological Therapies for Drug and Alcohol Addiction*. New York: Marcell Dekker (pp 411-417). 1995

Wikler, A. Dynamics of drug dependence: Implications of a conditioning theory for research and treatment. *Arch. Gen. Psychiat.* 28: 611-616.

*WWW.cleartest.com/products/index.html* (2006).

In:  Substance Abuse, Assessment and Addiction
Editors: Kristina A. Murati and Allison G. Fischer

ISBN: 978-1-61122-931-8
© 2011 Nova Science Publishers, Inc.

*Chapter 7*

# DEPENDENCE ON AND TREATMENT FOR STREET DRUGS AMONG MANHATTAN ARRESTEES

## *Bruce D. Johnson and Andrew Golub*
National Development and Research Institutes, Inc.

## ABSTRACT

The Arrestee Drug Abuse Monitoring (ADAM) program identified almost half of all ADAM-Manhattan arrestees interviewed 2000-2003 as at risk of drug dependence (RDD) for various street drugs. Higher rates were associated with using heroin and crack, more frequent use, being younger, and being arrested in 2001-02. More than two-fifths the marijuana-only users were RDD. Taken at face value, these findings support efforts to provide drug treatment to arrestees, even those that use only marijuana. There are two major caveats that suggest a need for much further research: there has been only one limited validity study of ADAM's screen for RDD, and research suggests that existing treatment modalities may be particularly ineffective for marijuana-only users. Despite the suggested need, only a quarter of arrestees with possible substance dependence problems received treatment in the past 12 months.

**Keywords:** Dependence, marijuana, arrestees, treatment, UNCOPE, ADAM

## INTRODUCTION

Extensive research has established the existence of a strong nexus between illicit use of street drug use and crime [1,2]. This finding holds out the hope that crime can be greatly reduced through criminal justice programs that emphasize drug treatment such as referral, diversion and drug courts. Such programs may be essential to reducing persistent criminal offending to the extent that offending is embedded within a lifestyle involving drug dependence. However, the potential success of any criminal-justice drug-treatment initiatives may depend on a variety of factors including the prevalence of use of different drugs among offenders, frequency of use, the extent of drug-related problems, the nature of the drugs-crime connection, the existence of other problems affecting both persistent criminal offending and drug use, and the efficacy of available treatment programs.

The Arrestee Drug Abuse Monitoring (ADAM) program has been a key source of information regarding use of street drugs among arrestees, most of whom are presumably criminal offenders. Given the drugs-crime nexus, ADAM data provide excellent information about drug use among many of the most serious drug users. Moreover, many criminal justice, drug treatment and allied agencies have been keenly interested in illicit drug use within this particular population. However, not all drug users are necessarily dependent. In 2000, ADAM introduced use of UNCOPE a short screen that identifies which arrestees are at risk of drug dependence (hereafter RDD). The term *risk for drug dependence* (RDD) emphasizes that an UNCOPE score is not a clinical diagnosis. In a clinical setting, these persons would almost surely receive a more thorough evaluation before admission to treatment. To the extent that UNCOPE provides a reasonably accurate determination it can prove useful for estimating the prevalence of RDD and its covariates.

This paper examines the prevalence of RDD among drug-users arrested in Manhattan, covariates of RDD, and the extent to which arrestees with possible dependence problems have been receiving treatment. The discussion explores the policy implications of the findings and makes explicit recommendations for additional research into the validity of ADAM's dependence scale in light of the newness of its use with arrestees and the importance of its accuracy for effective policy planning. The remainder of this introduction discusses key trends in drug use and RDD among arrestees and previous findings regarding the prevalence of RDD among illicit drug users in the general population.

## DRUG USE AND RDD AMONG ARRESTEES

The ADAM program has documented that illicit drug use is widespread among arrestees, that the types of drugs used vary widely across locations, and that the prevalence of various drugs has changed dramatically over time [3,4]. Golub and Johnson identified three distinct generations of drug users passing through Manhattan's booking facility [5]. Further research identified that similar patterns were occurring in arrestee populations across much of the country (with variations in timing and intensity) and to a lesser extent among the general population [6]. Among Manhattan arrestees, the heroin injection generation born primarily 1945-54 initiated use during the Heroin Injection Epidemic of the 1960s and early 1970s. During the 1980s, many of the heroin users that had persisted in their habits also became involved with crack cocaine. The crack generation born 1955-69 initiated use in the 1980s during the height of the Crack Epidemic. Americans born since 1970 have been much less likely to use cocaine powder, crack and heroin than their predecessors but increasingly likely to use marijuana. Many of these youths and young adults prefer to smoke marijuana in a blunt, an inexpensive cigar in which the tobacco filler has been replaced with marijuana. Hence, we refer to the generation of drug users among arrestees born since 1970 as the marijuana/blunts generation.

These findings indicate that the criminal justice system in Manhattan, and much of the rest of the country, has been dealing with an aging population of persistent crack and heroin users and increasingly with youthful marijuana-only users. Marijuana is often viewed as less dangerous and much less likely to cause dependence than other illicit drugs [7,8]. Marijuana use, sales, and subcultural activities have been associated with much less violence than the prominent and violent crack subcultures of the 1980s and 1990s [9]. On the other hand, Dennis et al. [10] counseled that public policy needs to focus on the pressing need for treatment of various cannabis use disorders. They noted that marijuana users comprise an increasing proportion of the persons entering publicly-funded treatment programs and being referred to treatment by the criminal justice system.

The ADAM 2000 report presents the first official publication of RDD estimates based on use of the UNCOPE scale [3]. It examines RDD among adult males arrested in 2000 at 35 ADAM sites across the nation. A substantial portion of Manhattan arrestees (42%) was RDD, slightly more than the median (37%) across sites. RDD varied across type of illicit drug used. Among ADAM-Manhattan adult male arrestees, those that had used heroin (81%) in the past 12 months were more likely to be RDD than those that had used crack (75%), powder cocaine (75%), or marijuana (51%). The ADAM program identified similar variation with drug type for other sites. Among Manhattan arrestees, RDD was higher among older arrestees and black arrestees. ADAM did not include a multivariate analysis of RDD [3]. The higher rates among older and black arrestees might be attributable to variation in the drug used. Additionally, the drug use categories were not mutually exclusive. Hence, many of the marijuana users that ADAM identified as drug dependent were likely also users of cocaine powder, crack, or heroin. Their drug dependence may have been a result of their use of drugs other than marijuana. The analyses in this paper deals with this difficulty using multivariate statistical procedures and a typology of mutually-exclusive drug-user types.

Among Manhattan arrestees identified as RDD, only a few had received any type of drug treatment in the past 12 months [3]: 14% had received inpatient treatment, and 22% had received outpatient treatment. Somewhat more had received lifetime treatment: 42% inpatient, and 40% outpatient. These rates were slightly higher than the median rates for the nation: 12% past-12-months inpatient, 8% past-12-months outpatient, 40% lifetime inpatient, and 27% lifetime outpatient.

## RDD IN THE GENERAL POPULATION

Since 1991, National Household Survey on Drug Abuse (NHSDA) has asked members of the general population that report use of illicit drugs to complete a short screen designed to assess drug dependence in the past 12 months. The screen is based on the criteria defined by the American Psychiatric Association first as DSM-III-R and then DSM-IV [11]. In this paper, we refer to persons as RDD when the NHSDA designated them as likely dependent to emphasize that they had not received a clinical diagnosis. This contrasts with the policy of the Substance Abuse and Mental Health Services Administration (SAMHSA) to refer to them as dependent in their publications [e.g., 11-13]. Using the same screener, the NHSDA assesses risk for alcohol dependence (RAD).

In the general population, RDD among past-12-month users varied across drugs and with frequency of use. Table 1 presents the rates of use and RDD for various substances measured by the NHSDA in 2001 [13]. Overall, RDD for an illicit drug was relatively uncommon (1.6%) in the general population, much less common than use (12.6%). Only a modest percentage of illicit drug users (13%) were RDD. The rate of RDD among users varied across drugs. Heroin had the highest rate (46%). The rates were lower for cocaine (18%) and marijuana (10%). A greater proportion of the general population drank alcohol (63.7%) than used any illicit drug (12.6%), but the rate of RAD was much lower for alcohol drinkers (4%).

**Table 1. A Comparison of Past-12-Month Substance Use
and Risk of Dependence among Persons Age 12 or
Older in the General Population, NHSDA 2001 (SAMHSA, 2002)**

|  | Drug[a] | | | | |
|---|---|---|---|---|---|
|  | Any Illicit Drug | Heroin | Cocaine (any form) | Marijuana | Alcohol |
| Use | 12.6% | 0.2% | 1.9% | 9.3% | 63.7% |
| RDD or RAD | 1.6% | 0.1% | 0.3% | 0.9% | 2.4% · |
| RDD or RAD /Use | 13% | 46% | 18% | 10% | 4% |

[a]Categories are not mutually exclusive.

These data suggest that many members of the general population could be in need of drug treatment. SAMHSA estimated that a substantial gap between treatment need and receipt of treatment services prevailed in 2000 [13]. They designated respondents as in need of drug treatment if they were identified as either RDD, were identified as at risk of drug abuse, or reported having received drug treatment in the past 12 months. The majority (60%) of respondents in need of drug treatment were also RDD. Only 17% of persons in need of drug treatment reported having received it in the past 12 months. SAMHSA did not report the extent to which the treatment gap varied across substances nor with frequency of use [13].

Prior research has identified frequency of use as an important covariate of RDD. Using NHSDA 1991-93 data for cocaine users, Chen and Kandel found that RDD increased steadily from 3% among respondents reporting use on 1-2 occasion in the past 12 months up to 74% for daily users [14]. Similarly, using NHSDA 1991-93 data for marijuana users, Chen et al. found that RDD increased steadily from 1% among respondents reporting use on 1-2 occasions, up to 20% among daily users [15]. The fact that the NHSDA is a cross-sectional survey complicates the interpretation of this finding. It could be the case that persons that use more frequently experience a greater risk of dependence. Alternatively, drug dependence could lead to more frequent use.

Frequency of use was the strongest covariate of RDD among cocaine users. After controlling for frequency of use, Chen and Kandel found that RDD among cocaine users did not vary significantly with gender, race/ethnicity nor age with the exception of one cross-term [14]. The rate of RDD increased more quickly with frequency of use among respondents age 12-17 than among respondents age 18 and above. Mode of consumption also proved important. Crack users were more likely to be RDD than powder cocaine users. Among marijuana users, age but not gender was associated with significant variation in RDD [15]. Marijuana users age 12-17 were also more likely to be RDD.

## METHODS

This section describes the ADAM program, discusses the structure and limitations of ADAM's new measure for RDD, and explains the multivariate procedure used to identify covariates of RDD.

# ADAM

In 1987, the National Institute of Justice established the Drug Use Forecasting [DUF] program to measure trends in illicit drug use among booked arrestees in most large cities (or counties) with a total population of at least 1 million, as well as many smaller cities for geographic diversity [3,4,16]. The program obtained both self-report and urinalysis data from arrestees. Urine tests provide a particularly valid indicator of recent drug use. The EMIT test employed can detect use of cocaine and opiates within 2-3 days and marijuana up to 30 days after use depending on the frequency of use. The test used does not distinguish between powder cocaine and crack use; hence, we refer to detected cocaine/crack use in this paper. Similarly, the test does not distinguish between various opiates. Heroin is the most commonly used opiate on Manhattan's streets; hence, we refer to detected opiates/heroin use.

In 1997, the program was retitled ADAM. In 2000, ADAM introduced significant changes to the sampling procedures, survey instrument, and public-use datafiles [16]. Since January 29, 2004, the ADAM program has been on hiatus as a Federal cost-saving measure [17]. At the time of this analysis, ADAM-Manhattan data were available through 2003. During the 2000-03 period, the ADAM-Manhattan program approached a random sample of 5,455 arrestees, 69% agreed to participate yielding 3,741 respondents. The ADAM public-use data files include post-sampling stratification weights for adult male arrestees to account for differential probability of sampling associated with time of arrest and booking facility. Since not all ADAM respondents provide urine samples, ADAM provides two sets of separate sample weights for use with the survey and urine data.

For this analysis, the ADAM-Manhattan sample weights were modified. Even though the ADAM sampling procedure introduced in 2000 is unbiased, the sample obtained could be biased due to systematic differences in who chooses to participate. Logistic regression was used to develop revised weights to control for non-participation in each year for male and female arrestees (eight separate models) accounting for variation across age, race/ethnicity and arrest charge. Sample weights were further adjusted so that female arrestees accounted for 15% in 2000 and 2001. Females comprised from 15.6%-16.6% of Manhattan arrestees from 1996 through 2001 [18]. This adjustment was not made for 2002 and 2003, in which ADAM-Manhattan obtained interviews with fewer than 50 females.

## MEASURING RISK OF DRUG DEPENDENCE

The UNCOPE scale assesses RDD and RAD based on answers to questions related to six substance-related problems [3,19]. The name UNCOPE is an acronym identifying these problems: **U**nintended use, **N**eglect of responsibilities, wanting to **C**ut-down, **O**thers object to use, **P**reoccupation with use, and use to relieve **E**motional distress. Respondents are designated as RDD if they report experiencing any three factors in the past 12 months, as long as they include either preoccupation or emotional distress, or if they report only two factors but they are preoccupation and emotional distress.

The scale also screens respondents for *risk of drug abuse*. However, we chose to focus on dependence and not abuse in this study. Based on a review of the literature, Hoffman et al. [19] concluded that, "[T]he majority of those meeting *abuse* criteria have no further problems over a five year period, the norm for those who are *dependent* is to have continued and persistent problems." (our emphasis). Unfortunately, the literature they cited pertains to alcohol-related problems. It is not clear whether this distinction between abuse and dependence holds for illicit drugs, particularly marijuana. A factor analysis by Teesson et al. found that abuse and dependence did not represent distinct disorders with respect to marijuana use [20]. Teesson et al. cited extensive prior empirical research that identified two very distinct factors associated with alcohol abuse and dependence. Teesson et al. suggested that abuse and dependence could represent different degrees along a single continuum of marijuana-related dysfunction.

There has been only limited research into the validity of the UNCOPE screen. The most convincing approach to establishing the accuracy of the screen would be to compare UNCOPE designations with clinical diagnoses for the same arrestees. This type of an analysis has not yet been performed. Hoffmann et al. did compare the UNCOPE designations to those from a much longer structured diagnostic interview, SUDDS-IV. The UNCOPE instrument had sensitivity of 88% and specificity of 83% [19]. This provides some evidence to suggest that UNCOPE provides a reasonable assessment of RDD, at least as good as other non-clinical instruments. However, we emphasize that there has been just one validity study of UNCOPE that we are aware of and that study has the following significant limitations: the sample was relatively small (310 arrestees from 4 locations). This study did not include analysis of the extent to which the validity of UNCOPE varied across arrestee characteristics such as race/ethnicity, gender and drug-user type. The report examined risk of dependence on alcohol and/or drugs (RDAD) but did not analyze RDD and RAD separately. The UNCOPE assessments were not compared to a clinical diagnosis—the arrestees interviewed could have provided inaccurate but consistent responses to both surveys.

## LOGISTIC REGRESSION OF VARIATION IN RDD

Logistic regression was used to examine the extent to which RDD varied across arrestees. This statistical procedure has the highly desirable ability to potentially identify spurious associations by measuring whether the variation associated with each independent variable is statistically significant after controlling for all of the other independent variables included in the analysis [21]. Wald statistics were used to test statistical significance and to approximately identify variables associated with the largest amount of variation. The $\alpha=.01$ level was used for assessing statistical significance.

Three independent variables were included in the model to assess how RDD varied with the nature of each arrestee's drug use: drug-user type (based on past-12-month use), frequency of use in the past 30 days, and injection of heroin. Other arrestee characteristics were included as independent variables to identify if RDD was more prevalent among some groups even after controlling for drug-use characteristics: gender, race/ethnicity, and birth cohort. Top charge for the current arrest was included for policy purposes to identify whether RDD was more common among arrestees for some crimes than for others. Interview year was included in the model to test for period effects.

## FINDINGS

This section describes the demographic composition of the ADAM-Manhattan sample, explores the variation in drug use, identifies key factors associated with variation in RDD, and presents the rate at which arrestees identified as RDAD received treatment.

## DEMOGRAPHICS

Table 2 presents the demographic and arrest characteristics of the sample. All estimates in this and subsequent tables were calculated using the revised sample weights. By construction, 10% of the weighted sample was female. The majority of the Manhattan arrestee sample was black (52%) or Hispanic (33%). A modest minority was white (10%). More than one third of all arrests were for a drug crime (35%). Just under half (47%) were for generally less serious offenses including trespassing, farebeating, forgery, simple assault and disturbing the peace. Arrestees' birth years were grouped into three birth cohorts: pre-1955 (10%), 1955-69 (42%), and 1970+ (48%), consistent with prior research on generations of drug users.

**Table 2. Demographic and Arrest Characteristics
for ADAM-Manhattan 2000-03 (N=3,741)**

| Gender | | Top Charge | |
|---|---|---|---|
| Male | 90% | Drug possession | 25% |
| Female | 10%[a] | Drug sale | 10% |
| | | Rob/burg/larc/auto | 14% |
| *Race* | | Murder/rape/aggr. assault | 6% |
| Black (non-Hispanic) | 52% | Other | 46% |
| Hispanic | 33% | | |
| White (non-Hispanic) | 10% | ***Interview Year*** | |
| Other/missing | 5% | 2000 | 30% |
| | | 2001 | 24% |
| *Birth Year* | | 2002 | 26% |
| Pre-1955 | 10% | 2003 | 20% |
| 1955-69 | 42% | | |
| 1970+ | 48% | | |

[a] Weights were adjusted so that females comprised no more that 15% of the weighted sample in each year.

# VARIATION IN DRUG USE

Respondents were grouped into a hierarchical drug-user typology based on self-reported use of marijuana, powder cocaine, crack and heroin in the past 12 months (see Table 3). Just under a third (30%) reported using none of these illicit drugs in the past 12 months. The largest percentage (31%) reported using only marijuana. Less than half (39%) of the Manhattan arrestees reported past-12-month use of powder cocaine, crack or heroin, illicit drugs that are broadly perceived by many as particularly dangerous and whose use and sale carry substantial penalties. Powder cocaine, crack and heroin users were classified according to their past-12-month use of these controlled substances, irrespective of their marijuana use. Some reported use of powder cocaine (7%) or heroin (6%) but no other controlled substances. A substantial proportion reported use of crack cocaine (16%) but not heroin (arrestees were designated as crack users irrespective of whether they also reported use of powder cocaine). A very modest percentage (3%) of the sample reported use of heroin and powder cocaine. A more substantial percentage (7%) reported both heroin and crack use (again, irrespective of their reported powder cocaine use).

### Table 3. Variation in Drug-User-Types across Birth cohorts

| Birth Cohort | Non-user | Marij-only | Powder cocaine | Crack | Heroin | Heroin+ cocaine | Heroin+ crack | Total |
|---|---|---|---|---|---|---|---|---|
| Total | 30% | 31% | 7% | 16% | 6% | 3% | 7% | 100% |
| | | | | | | | | |
| Pre-1955 | 37% | 9% | 8% | 24% | 7% | 4% | 10% | 100% |
| 1955-69 | 27% | 15% | 8% | 27% | 9% | 4% | 11% | 100% |
| 1970+ | 31% | 47% | 6% | 6% | 4% | 2% | 4% | 100% |

*% of Birth Cohort of each Drug-User Type*

Marijuana-only users were much more common among arrestees born since 1970 (47%) than among those born before 1970 (9-15%). Crack user (the sum of the crack and heroin+crack classifications) were much less common among those born since 1970 (10%) than among those born before 1970 (34-38%). Arrestees born before 1955 and arrestees born 1955-69 were similarly likely to use crack and heroin, despite observed variation across birth cohorts detected in previous studies [5]. Heroin users (the sum of the heroin, heroin+cocaine and heroin+crack classifications) were more common among arrestees born before 1970 (21-24%) than among those born since 1970 (10%).

The accuracy of this drug-user typology is limited by the accuracy of the arrestee's self reports. Prior literature indicated that rates of disclosure for drug use can be as low as 50% [22,23]. Accordingly, some individuals were probably classified in the lower levels of the drug-user hierarchy as non-users and marijuana-only users because they had not disclosed the full extent of their drug use. Urinalysis results can partially identify such misclassification (see Table 4). About a quarter of the arrestees classified as non-users (25%) or marijuana-only users (23%) were detected as recent cocaine/crack users by urinalysis. A relatively small proportion of arrestees classified as non-users (7%), marijuana-only (4%), powder cocaine (7%) and crack (5%) users were detected as recent opiates/heroin users. Some arrestees classified as non-users (15%) were detected as marijuana users. These misclassification rates quite possibly undercount non-disclosers because some respondents may have used a drug in the past 12 months, not reported its use, and not used the drug within the last few days. On the other hand, the misclassification rates could overcount non-disclosers to the extent that the urine tests produced false positives. We chose to base the drug-user typology on past-12-month use despite potential underreporting for several reasons: some of the apparent misclassifications could be false positives; any correction based on urinalysis results would probably be incomplete because of the limited window of detection associated with urinalysis; and, arrestees were not asked screener questions for RDD for use of drugs they did not disclose, self-professed non-users were not asked any questions related to RDD.

**Table 4. Variation across Drug-User-Types in Detected Drug Use and Frequency of Use**

| | Drug-User Type[a] | | | | | | | |
| | Non-user | Marij-only | Powder cocaine | Crack | Heroin | Heroin+ cocaine | Heroin+ crack | Total |
|---|---|---|---|---|---|---|---|---|
| Prevalence | (30%) | (31%) | (7%) | (16%) | (6%) | (3%) | (7%) | (100%) |
| *Variation in Recent Drug Use Detected by Urinalysis* | | | | | | | | |
| Marijuana | 15% | 80% | 45% | 27% | 32% | 25% | 26% | 41% |
| Cocaine/crack | 25% | 23% | 76% | 92% | 37% | 82% | 89% | 45% |
| Opiates/heroin | 7% | 4% | 7% | 5% | 85% | 82% | 64% | 17% |
| *Variation in Frequency of Use[b] in Past 30 Days* | | | | | | | | |
| 0 days | 100%[c] | 7% | 21% | 7% | 9% | 1% | 1% | 37% |
| 1-3 days | | 11% | 24% | 13% | 13% | 9% | 8% | 9% |
| 4-24 days | | 38% | 40% | 42% | 30% | 29% | 28% | 25% |
| 25-30 days | | 44% | 15% | 37% | 49% | 61% | 62% | 29% |

[a] Based on self-report of past-12-month use
[b] Drug used depends on drug-user type.
[c] By definition.

Frequency of drug use was operationalized as the number of the past 30 days the arrestee reported using illicit drugs, modified according to the drug-user hierarchy. For marijuana-only users, this variable measured the number of days they used marijuana. For the remaining illicit drug users, it was based on the drug they used most frequently from among powder cocaine, crack and heroin, irrespective of any marijuana use. More than a third of all arrestees reported no drug use in the past 30 days; this included all of the non-users (30% of the sample) plus an additional 7% of the sample that had reported some illicit drug use in the past 12 months but none in the past 30 days. Relatively few (9%) arrestees reported use on only 1-3 of the past 30 days, 25% reported use on 4-24 of the past 30 days and 29% on 25-30.

There was some variation in frequency of drug use across drug-user types. The majority of heroin users reported near daily use (49-62%), and most of the rest reported use on 4-24 of the past 30 days (28-30%). Crack-only users were more likely to use on 4-24 of the past 30 days (42%) than on 25-30 days (37%). Comparatively few powder-cocaine-only users reported near daily use (15%). These users were the most likely to report use on 0-3 day (45%), with the exception of non-users. Only 18% of the marijuana-only users reported use on fewer than 4 of the past 30 days. Hence, most of these arrestees were not involved with occasional recreational use of marijuana. On average, they smoked marijuana about as frequently as heroin and crack users consumed their drugs of choice.

The ADAM survey asked respondents to report their mode of consumption the last time they used a drug. A relatively modest percentage (32%) of heroin users reported injecting as opposed to sniffing or smoking.

## COVARIATES OF RDD

Type of drug user (Wald=280.9, see Table 5) was by far the most important covariate of RDD. Frequency of use (Wald=91.4) was the next most important followed by interview year (Wald=24.0) and Birth Cohort (Wald=9.3). There was no statistically significant variation in RDD associated with gender, race/ethnicity, top arrest charge, and heroin injection.

**Table 5. Covariates of Risk of Drug Dependence**

|  | Odds Ratio (Wald) |
|---|---|
| **Drug User Type** | (280.9) |
| Marijuana-only | 0.1 |
| Powder-cocaine-only | 0.4 |
| Crack | 1.0[a] |
| Heroin | 1.1 |
| Heroin+Cocaine | 2.1 |
| Heroin+Crack | 2.9 |
| *Frequency of Use* | (91.4) |
| 0 of past 30 days | 0.2 |
| 1-3 of past 30 days | 0.3 |
| 4-24 of past 30 days | 0.6 |
| 25-30 of past 30 days | 1.0[a] |
| *Interview Year* | (24.0) |
| 2000 | 1.0[a] |
| 2001 | 1.8 |
| 2002 | 1.7 |
| 2003 | 1.3 |
| *Birth Cohort* | (9.3) |
| Pre-1955 | 0.7 |
| 1955-69 | 1.0[a] |
| 1970+ | 1.3 |
| **Base Odds** | 4.8 |
| **Sample Size** | 2,388 |

Note: Estimates presented for those variables for which the Wald Statistic was statistically significant at α=.01 level. The variation associated with *Gender*, *Race/Ethnicity*, *Top Charge*, and *Heroin Injection* did not meet this criterion.

[a] Reference category

Table 6 presents the estimates for RDD as it varies across the characteristics identified as statistically significant in Table 5. Overall, more than two-fifths (44%, Table 6) of all arrestees were RDD. Nearly all (94%) arrestees that had used both heroin+crack in the past 12 months were RDD. Rates were slightly lower among other heroin and crack users (81-

92%), much lower among powder-cocaine-only users (58%) and just over two-fifths for marijuana-only users (42%).

**Table 6. Variation in RDD across Drug-User-Types, Frequency of Use, Interview Year and Birth Cohort**

| | Drug-User Type | | | | | | | |
| | Non-user[a] | Marij-only | Powder cocaine | Crack | Heroin | Heroin+ cocaine | Heroin+crack | Total[b] |
|---|---|---|---|---|---|---|---|---|
| Prevalence | (30%) | (31%) | (7%) | (16%) | (6%) | (3%) | (7%) | (100%) |
| RDD | 0% | 42% | 58% | 81% | 83% | 92% | 94% | 44% |
| *RDD by Frequency of Use in Past-30 Days* | | | | | | | | |
| 0 days | 0% | 17% | 43% | 68% | -- | -- | -- | 6% |
| 1-3 days | | 22% | 57% | 66% | 60% | -- | -- | 48% |
| 4-24 days | | 43% | 59% | 82% | 80% | 96% | 91% | 63% |
| 25-30 days | | 50% | 78% | 88% | 91% | 92% | 97% | 72% |
| *RDD by Interview Year* | | | | | | | | |
| 2000 | 0% | 37% | 58% | 75% | 81% | 81% | 92% | 43% |
| 2001 | | 47% | 64% | 84% | 81% | 96% | 97% | 48% |
| 2002 | | 44% | 56% | 84% | 87% | 93% | 92% | 47% |
| 2003 | | 41% | 51% | 82% | 83% | -- | 93% | 36% |
| *RDD by Birth Cohort* | | | | | | | | |
| Pre-1955 | 0% | 35% | 44% | 73% | 81% | -- | 86% | 41% |
| 1955-69 | 0% | 43% | 55% | 80% | 80% | 96% | 95% | 53% |
| 1970+ | 0% | 42% | 65% | 91% | 88% | 95% | 95% | 38% |

--Estimate not presented when based on fewer than 25 cases.
[a] By construction, non-users were not asked RDD questions.
[b] Total includes non-users.

The prevalence of RDD varied moderately with frequency of use. The rate of RDD among arrestees that had used on 1-3 of the past 30 days (48%) was lower than among more frequent users (63-72%). The variation with frequency of use for each drug-user type was more moderate. The rate of RDD was lowest among less frequent (0 and 1-3 days) marijuana-only users (17-22%) and twice as high among more frequent marijuana-only users (43-50%). The majority of all powder cocaine, crack and heroin users were RDD, for all levels of frequency of use (43-97%). Interestingly, a substantial proportion of powder cocaine (43%) and crack (68%) users that had not used in the past 30 days were still RDD.

The overall prevalence of RDD increased by 5 percentage points from 2000 (43%) to 2001 (48%) and declined substantially in 2003 (36%). The variation in RDD with birth cohort was rather modest, primarily because relatively few of the arrestees were born before 1955 (11%, Table 2), the oldest category. The 1955-69 birth cohort had the highest overall rate of RDD (53%, Table 6), much higher than the 1970+ birth cohort (38%), but this was primarily explained by a difference in drug-of-choice. Relatively more arrestees born before 1970 smoked crack; relatively more arrestees born after 1970 smoked marijuana (see Table 3).

Within each drug-user category except marijuana-only, the rate of RDD tended to increase with birth cohort (Table 6). This variation was quite noticeable among crack users. Older crack users (born before 1955) were less likely to be RDD (73%) than those born 1955-69 (80%) and the highest rate was among those born since 1970 (91%). It is possible that younger users of powder cocaine, crack and heroin were more likely to be dependent. However, it seems logical that older arrestees would have been more likely to have developed dependence over time.

## DRUG TREATMENT

Respondents were asked about their lifetime and past-12-month histories of inpatient drug/alcohol treatment, outpatient drug/alcohol treatment (excluding Alcoholics Anonymous or Narcotics Anonymous), and inpatient mental health treatment for problems not related to drug or alcohol use (see Table 7). The questions did not differentiate whether treatment was for drug or alcohol use. To have a parallel basis for comparison, we designated respondents as RDAD if they were either RDD, RAD or both. 22% of the ADAM-Manhattan arrestees were RAD. However, most of these respondents were also RDD. Consequently, RDAD (49%) was only 5 percentage points more prevalent than RDD (44%). Table 7 indicates that for each drug-user type the prevalence of RDAD was only a few percentage points higher than RDD. Among non-users of illicit drugs, only 10% were RAD.

### Table 7. Variation in Treatment History across Drug-User-Types

| | Drug-User Type | | | | | | | |
| | Non-user | Marij-only | Powder cocaine | Crack | Heroin | Heroin+ cocaine | Heroin+crack | Total |
|---|---|---|---|---|---|---|---|---|
| Prevalence | (30%) | (31%) | (7%) | (16%) | (6%) | (3%) | (7%) | (100%) |
| ***Risk of Dependence on*** | | | | | | | | |
| Drugs (RDD) | 0% | 42% | 58% | 81% | 83% | 92% | 94% | 44% |
| Alcohol (RAD) | 10% | 16% | 39% | 39% | 17% | 32% | 47% | 22% |
| Either (RDAD) | 10% | 45% | 65% | 82% | 84% | 94% | 95% | 49% |
| Received any drug/alcohol treatment in past 12 months | | | | | | | | |
| RDAD | 0% | 10% | 18% | 29% | 40% | 51% | 45% | 25% |
| Not RDAD | 0% | 5%[**] | 11% | 25% | 32% | -- | -- | 5%[**] |
| Received any drug/alcohol treatment in lifetime | | | | | | | | |
| RDAD | 47% | 29% | 60% | 72% | 75% | 83% | 81% | 59% |
| Not RDAD | 23%[**] | 20%[**] | 34%[**] | 60% | 65% | -- | -- | 26%[**] |
| *Treatment modality received in past-12-month[b]* | | | | | | | | |
| *(all arrestees that received treatment)[a]* | | | | | | | | |
| Inpatient drug/alc | -- | 44% | 53% | 62% | 53% | 56% | 63% | 57% |
| Outpatient drug/alc | -- | 59% | 66% | 50% | 67% | 74% | 59% | 59% |
| Other[c] | -- | 19% | 8% | 15% | 3% | 6% | 27% | 15% |

Estimate not presented when based on fewer than 25 cases.

[**]ANOVA test of the variation in prevalence between RDAD and not RDAD respondents was statistically significant at the $\alpha$=.01 level.

[a] There were too few arrestees that received treatment to simultaneously divide the subsample by both drug-user type and RDAD.

[b] Reports of treatments received are not mutually exclusive.

[c] Inpatient mental health treatment not for drug/alcohol use.

Most of the RDAD respondents had not received any treatment in the past 12 months (only 25% had). Heroin users were the most likely to have received treatment (40-51%), followed by crack (29%), powder-cocaine-only (18%) and marijuana-only (10%) users. No non-users that were RAD (0%) reported past-12-month treatment. Treatment was much more common among arrestees identified as RDAD than not-RDAD both in the past 12 months (25% versus 5%) and ever (59% versus 26%). However, this was primarily a composition effect because most heroin, crack and powder cocaine users (60-83%) were RDAD. For crack and heroin users, the difference in past-12-month and lifetime rates of treatment between arrestees designated RDAD and not-RDAD were not statistically significant. Thus, crack and heroin users were just as likely to have received past-12-month and lifetime treatment whether ADAM identified them as RDAD or not. Among those respondents that received treatment in the past 12 months, outpatient drug/alcohol treatment (59%) was somewhat more common than inpatient drug treatment (57%) and much more common than inpatient mental-health treatment for problems not related to drug or alcohol use (15%).

## DISCUSSION

This analysis suggests that dependence on street drugs is common among Manhattan arrestees, to the extent that the UNCOPE screen provides a reasonable indication of possible drug dependence. If true, the findings have important implications for public policy. However, further research into the validity of UNCOPE scale may be warranted. The one study published to date [19] provides limited documentation about the validity of the scale for use in the current arrestee context.

## COVARIATES OF RDD

Overall, this study found vast differences between Manhattan arrestees and the general population in the prevalence of RDD, and even the prevalence of RDD among illicit drug users. The 2001 NHSDA designated 1.6% of the general population as RDD, 13% of all illicit drug users. In contrast, ADAM-Manhattan 2000-03 designated 44% of all arrestees as RDD, 63% of all illicit drug users in this study. These aggregate differences are straightforwardly reconciled through consideration of the covariates to RDD and the differences in the compositions of the general and arrestee populations. The covariates of RDD identified in this study correspond closely with those identified in prior studies using the NHSDA. Consistent with SAMHSA [12], RDD varied substantially across drugs, with the highest rate among heroin users and the lowest among marijuana-only users. Consistent with Chen and Kandel [14], we found that RDD among cocaine users increased with frequency of use and was higher among crack users than powder-cocaine-only users. Interestingly, our estimate for RDD among near-daily powder-cocaine-only users (78%) was remarkably similar to Chen and Kandel's estimate for daily cocaine users (74%). Consistent with Chen et al. [15], we found that RDD among marijuana users increased with frequency of use. However, the RDD prevalence among near-daily marijuana-using Manhattan arrestees (50%) was much higher than among daily users in the general population (20%). Overall, much of the difference in the prevalence of RDD between the general population and the Manhattan arrestee populations can be accounted for by the following factors: much higher rates of drug use among arrestees; more use of powder cocaine, crack and heroin among arrestees; and more frequent drug use among arrestees. This convergence between different studies, different populations, and different measures, provides some support to the idea that UNCOPE and the NHSDA RDD scales provide consistent results.

## NEED FOR DRUG TREATMENT AMONG ARRESTEES

The high rate of RDD among Manhattan arrestees suggests that many of them are in need of drug treatment and that drug treatment might help reduce subsequent offending. ADAM-Manhattan designated 44% of arrestees as RDD. This is almost surely an underestimate since respondents that did not disclose their drug use were not even asked the UNCOPE questions.

The vast majority of self-reported heroin, crack and powder cocaine users were identified as RDD. These rates were so high as to suggests that perhaps nearly all arrestees that self-report use in the past 30 days need help in addressing their drug dependence. Moreover, even the crack and heroin users who were not-RDAD were almost as likely to report lifetime and past-12-month treatment involvement as their RDAD counterparts.

Perhaps a screener like the UNCOPE is unnecessary and possibly inaccurate for heroin, crack, and cocaine powder. Perhaps almost all of these arrestee drug-users are dependent, irrespective of whether they disclose drug-related problems. Perhaps even non-disclosers detected by urinalysis might be in need of treatment too. It would be interesting to determine using clinical diagnoses the extent to which dependence on heroin, crack and powder cocaine varied with disclosure of recent use based on a urinalysis test and with RDD based on the UNCOPE scale.

Exceedingly few Manhattan arrestees were identified as RAD that were not also RDD. Thus, extensive screening for alcohol problems would not substantially increase the number of Manhattan arrestees served. Rather, the data suggest that alcohol dependence is most often a comorbid condition that would need to be addressed in potentially serving a substantial portion of Manhattan arrestees' other drug dependence problems.

## A TEMPORAL SHIFT IN RDD

Curiously, RDD among ADAM-Manhattan arrestees increased in 2001 and then declined in 2003. There are a variety of possible explanations for this temporal shift. It could reflect a shift in policing priorities. One possibility is that police may have stopped arresting less serious offenders (this is often colloquially referred to as casting a narrower net). This changing priority could have led to an increase in prevalence of seriously-troubled persons among arrestees, persons more likely to be drug dependent. This study however provides some evidence that this was not the case. The multivariate analysis for covariates of RDD found that top arrest charge was not associated with significant variation in RDD, which implies that even if the proportion of arrests for less serious offenses had changed that it would not have caused a temporal shift in the prevalence of RDD.

Another possibility is that Manhattan arrestees' perspectives changed in 2001 due to historical events. The year 2001 was marked by terrorist destruction of the World Trade

Center in New York City on 9/11 and by a weakening economy. Two studies documented substantial increases in substance use and demand for treatment in the period after the attacks [24,25]. Although few arrestees were directly involved in the World Trade Center collapse, they may have increased their frequency of use in response to the stress. As a result, a modest increase in drug use and perceived symptoms of dependence may have occurred within a short space of time and then returned to more usual levels by 2003.

## RDD AMONG MANHATTAN ARRESTEES THAT USE ONLY MARIJUANA

The interpretation of RDD findings concerning marijuana-only users is somewhat more complicated than for heroin, crack, and cocaine users. Nearly a third of Manhattan arrestees reported using only marijuana in the past 12 months. This percentage may increase in the future, because marijuana has been the drug-of-choice among inner-city youths coming of age since 1990 [6]. The rate of RDD among marijuana-only users was 42%, much lower than among other illicit drug users but still substantial. Interestingly, about a quarter of even the least frequent (1-3 days in past 30 days) marijuana-only users were identified as RDD. There are several possible alternative explanations including: the potent marijuana being used today may be more likely to result in dependence; dependent marijuana users may be more likely to sustain arrests than others; and UNCOPE may not be appropriately calibrated for marijuana use among arrestees. Further validation research could lend considerable insight regarding the value of the UNCOPE scale.

The use of UNCOPE for identifying dependence on marijuana use among arrestees has not yet been directly validated. Accordingly, we strongly recommend an explicit comparison of UNCOPE measures of RDD with clinical diagnoses of dependence for marijuana-only using arrestees. The ADAM data indicated that marijuana-only using arrestees were likely to report behaviors such as preoccupation with use and use to relieve emotional distress on a short questionnaire. Perhaps preoccupation with marijuana use is qualitatively different, less severe, than preoccupation with drugs like crack or heroin. In which case, RDD would provide only a weak indication of possible drug dependence for marijuana users.

## RECEIPT OF TREATMENT

Receipt of treatment does not appear to be keeping up with the need among Manhattan arrestees, presuming that dependence as assessed by UNCOPE indicates a need for treatment. Only one quarter of the Manhattan-arrestees identified as RDAD reported having received treatment in the past 12 months. This lack of treatment may be due to service unavailability or because persons are not availing themselves of the services.

The disjunction between RDD and treatment received was most pronounced for marijuana-only users. Only 10% of marijuana-only users identified as RDAD reported having received treatment, less than half the overall rate. Treating marijuana dependent arrestees would appear to be an important priority given the widespread prevalence of marijuana use, especially among younger arrestees. During 2000-03, nearly a third of the Manhattan arrestees reported they used marijuana-only. If youths continue to avoid heroin, crack and cocaine powder, the prevalence of marijuana-only users among arrestees will likely increase in future years. On the other hand, providing treatment to marijuana-dependent arrestees could prove particularly difficult. Dennis et al. noted that current treatment modalities appear to be least effective at dealing with marijuana use [10]. Clearly more research is needed into understanding the extent to which marijuana-using arrestees are dependent, the nature of any disorders, and possible treatments for their problems.

## ACKNOWLEDGMENT

This analysis was supported a grant from the National Institute on Drug Abuse, "Marijuana/Blunts: Use, Subcultures, Markets" (1R01 DA/CA13690-02), by the Arrestee Drug Abuse Monitoring program (National Institute of Justice and National Opinion Research Corporation: OJP-2001-C003, Subcontract 6073) and by a grant from the National Institute on Drug Abuse for the evaluation of the Expanded Syringe Access Demonstration Program (R01 DA12809). Points of view and opinions expressed do not necessarily reflect the positions of the National Institute on Drug Abuse, the National Institute of Justice, nor National Development and Research Institutes.

## REFERENCES

[1]     Nurco, D.N. A Long-Term Program of Research on Drug Use and Crime. *Subst. Use Misuse* 1998, 33 (9), 1817-1837.

[2]     Tonry, M.; Wilson, J.Q., Eds.; *Drugs and Crime.* University of Chicago Press. Crime and Justice Series, volume 13, Chicago. 1990.

[3]     Arrestee Drug Abuse Monitoring (ADAM). *2000 Arrestee Drug Abuse Monitor: Annual Report.* NCJ 193013. National Institutes of Justice: Washington, DC.

[4]     Golub, A.; Johnson, B.D. Arrestee Drug Abuse Monitoring (ADAM) Program. In *Encyclopedia of Crime and Punishment*, volume 1; Levinson, D., Ed.; Sage: Thousand Oaks, CA, 2002; 62-64.

[5]     Golub, A.; Johnson, B.D. Cohort Changes in Illegal Drug Use among Arrestees in Manhattan: from the Heroin Injection Generation to the Blunts Generation. *Subst. Use Misuse* 1999, 34 (13), 1733-1763.

[6]     Golub, A.; Johnson, B.D. The Rise of Marijuana as the Drug of Choice among Youthful Arrestees. *National Institute of Justice Research in Brief*, NCJ 187490.

[7]     Grinspoon, L.; Bakalar, J.B. Marihuana. In *Substance Abuse: A Comprehensive Textbook*, third edition; Lowinson, J.H., Ruiz, P., Millman, R.B., Langrod, J.G., Eds.; Williams and Wilkins: Baltimore, 1997; 199-206.

[8]     Zimmer, L.; Morgan, J.P. *Marijuana Myths Marijuana Facts: A Review of the Scientific Evidence.* The Lindesmith Center: New York, 1997

[9]     Johnson, B. D.; Golub, A.; Dunlap, E. The Rise and Decline of Hard Drugs, Drug Markets and Violence in New York City; In *The Crime Drop in America*; Blumstein, A., Wallman, J., Eds.; Cambridge: New York, 2000; 164-206.

[10] Dennis, M.; Babor, T.F.; Roebuck, M.C.; Donaldson, J. Changing the Focus: The Case for Recognizing and Treating Cannabis Use Disorders. *Addiction*, 2002, 97 (supplement 1), 4-15.

[11] Epstein, J.F. *Substance Dependence, Abuse, and Treatment: Findings from the 2000 National Household Survey on Drug Abuse*, NHSDA Series A-16, DHHS Publication No. SAM 02-3642. Substance Abuse and Mental Health Services Administration, Office of Applied Studies: Rockville, MD, 2002.

[12] Substance Abuse and Mental Health Services Administration (SAMHSA). *Results from the 2001 National Household Survey on Drug Abuse: Volume II: Technical Appendices and Selected Data Tables*, NHSDA Series H-18, DHHS Publication No. SMA 02-3759. Office of Applied Studies: Rockville, MD, 2002

[13] Substance Abuse and Mental Health Services Administration (SAMHSA). *National and State Estimates of the Drug Abuse Treatment Gap: 2000 National Household Survey on Drug Abuse*, NHSDA Series H-14, DHHS Publication No. SMA 02-3640. Office of Applied Studies: Rockville, MD, 2002.

[14] Chen, K.; Kandel, D. Relationship between Extent of Cocaine Use and Dependence among Adolescents and Adults in the United States. *Drug Alcohol Depend.* 2002, 68, 65-85.

[15] Chen, K.; Kandel, D.B.; Davies, M. Relationship between Frequency and Quantity of Marijuana Use and Dependence among Adolescents and Adults in the United States. *Drug Alcohol Depend.* 1997, 46, 53-67.

[16] Hunt, D.; Rhodes, W. *Methodology Guide for ADAM*. National Institute of Justice: Washington, DC, 2001.

[17] National Institute of Justice. NIJ provides further information on ADAM Program decision. Retrieved April 13, 2004, from *www.ojp.usdoj.gov/nij/pdf/adam_letter.pdf*.

[18] Eterno, J. Personal communication on October 11, 2002, with the Commanding Officer of the New York City Police Department Mapping Support Unit.

[19] Hoffmann, N.G.; Hunt, D.E.; Rhodes, W.M.; Riley, K.J. UNCOPE: A Brief Substance Dependence Screen for Use with Arrestees. *J. Drug Issues* 2003, 33 (1), 29-44.

[20] Teesson, M.; Lynskey, M.; Manor, B.; Baillie, A. The Structure of Cannabis Dependence in the Community. *Drug Alcohol Depend.* 2002, 68, 255-262.

[21] Hosmer, D.W.; Lemoshow, S. *Applied Logistic Regression*. Wiley, New York, 1989.

[22] Harrison, L. The Validity of Self-Reported Drug Use in Survey Research: An Overview and Critique of Research Methods. In *The Validity of Self Reported Drug Use: Improving the Accuracy of Survey Estimates*; Harrison, L., Hughes, A., Eds.; National Institute on Drug Abuse Research Monograph 167, Washington, DC, 1997; 17-36.

[23] Magura, S.; Kang, S.Y. Validity of Self-Reported Drug Use in High Risk Populations: A Meta-Analytical Review. *Subst. Use Misuse* 1996, 31 (9), 1131-1153.

[24] Deren, S.; Shedlin, M.; Hamilton, T.; Hagan, H. Impact of the September 11th Attacks in New York City on Drug Users: A Preliminary Assessment. *J. Urban Health*, 2002, 79 (3), 409-412.

[25] Vlahov, D.; Galea, S.; Resnick, H.; Ahern, J.; Boscarino, J.A.; Bucuvalas, M.; Gold, J.; Kilpatrick, D. Increased Use of Cigarettes, Alcohol, and Marijuana Among Manhattan, New York, Residents after the September 11th Terrorist Attacks. *Am. J. Epidemiol.* 2002, 155 (11): 988-996.

In: Substance Abuse, Assessment and Addiction                ISBN: 978-1-61122-931-8
Editors: Kristina A. Murati and Allison G. Fischer          © 2011 Nova Science Publishers, Inc.

*Chapter 8*

# THE TREATMENT OF COCAINE ABUSE: PROBLEMS AND PERSPECTIVES

## *Antonio Preti*[1]
University of Cagliari, Italy

## ABSTRACT

Despite huge advances in the neuroscience of substance abuse and dependence in the past twenty years, no approved pharmacological treatment exists for cocaine abuse.

The systematic reviews of treatments with available medications have found no evidence supporting the use of antidepressants, carbamazepine, or dopamine agonists in the pharmacotherapy of cocaine abuse. Dopamine receptor antagonists (neuroleptics) proved somehow effective in reducing cue-induced craving; however these medications are poorly tolerated, and record a significantly high dropout rate. Finally, high-dose methadone and buprenorphine were reported to promote cocaine abstinence in cocaine- and opioid-dependent patients, but their long-term effectiveness is still unknown.

Targeting symptoms might improve treatment effectiveness. Cocaine is thought to produce its addictive effect by four mechanisms basically: cocaine-induced euphoria; hedonic dysregulation; disruption of pre-frontal functioning; and cue-induced craving.

On the basis of the known neurochemistry of cocaine some target compounds have been studied, the most promising being BP897, a D3 partial agonist, and vanoxerine, a highly selective inhibitor of dopamine uptake. Results on humans, however, are pending. Recently modafinil, a glutamate-enhancing medication that inhibits GABA release too, proved effective in favouring cocaine abstinence in cocaine abusing people. Some open-label studies also reported the effectiveness of g-vinyl GABA, an irreversible inhibitor of GABA-transaminase, and of tiogabine, a GABA reuptake inhibitor, both compounds preventing relapse and thus increasing cocaine abstinence.

An alternative approach rests on the use of vaccines. Studies on rats showed that cocaine antibodies block cocaine from reaching the brain and prevent the reinstatement of

[1] Address for correspondence: Dr Antonio Preti: Centro Medico Genneruxi via Costantinopoli 42, I-09129 Cagliari – ITALY; e-mail: apreti@tin.it

cocaine self-administration. Ethical issues, however, are raised by the recourse to immunotherapy, particularly when proposed under legal coercion.

Psychosocial treatments are a useful companion in the pharmacotherapy of cocaine abuse, with group therapy and contingency management therapies capable to improve motivation and social functioning, particularly in patients abusing alcohol too.

**Keywords:** Cocaine, Treatment, Substance abuse, Investigational compound

# INTRODUCTION

Cocaine abuse is a serious health problem; its impact on society entails a heightened burden of illness, crime, domestic violence, lower productivity, inability to work and death (Gawin & Kleber, 1986; Hanzlick & Gowitt, 1991; Marzuk, Tardiff, & Leon, 1992; Marzuk, Tardiff, Leon, et al, 1998; Stein, 1999). The costs deriving from this health-hazarding behaviour depend directly upon the strong reviving properties of cocaine, which can cause dependence in the abuser through its stimulating and rewarding effects.

In addition to personal consequences, which include a higher prevalence of cardiovascular accidents (stroke and myocardial infarction), pulmonary diseases, trauma and violent death (by both homicide and suicide), cocaine use affects the life of all the people exposed to the environments where it is abused through a wider spread of infectious diseases (HIV, hepatitis B and C, tuberculosis) and increased exposure to violence (Stein, 1999). On the whole the financial costs due to untreated substance abuse are estimated, in the USA only, at about $400 billion per year, with untreated cocaine abuse contributing to the burden substantially (Schneider Institute for Health Policy, 2001).

Because of these reasons cocaine abuse has become a focus of medical, social and political concerns worldwide, encouraging research on the mechanisms of cocaine action and on the development of effective pharmacotherapies for the treatment and the prevention of cocaine abuse (Carroll, Howell, & Kuhar, 1999; Kreek, 1997; Mello, & Negus, 1996).

# PSYCHOPHARMACOLOGY OF COCAINE

Cocaine is a powerful stimulant of the nervous system that increases alertness, energy and motor activity, and induces feelings of well-being and euphoria, as well as enhancing personal sensations of competence and sexual ability. Activation of the sympathetic nervous system occurs concomitantly with the behavioural stimulatory effects of cocaine, with tachycardia, hypertension and an enhanced risk of myocardial infarct and cerebrovascular haemorrhages in case of cocaine overdosing. At higher doses, anxiety, paranoia and restlessness can result from the over-stimulation of monoaminergic receptors.

Cocaine, indeed, is thought to produce its effects by blocking the monoamine system of re-uptake, with equipollent affinities for dopamine, serotonin, and norepinephrine transporters (Ritz, Cone, & Kuhar, 1990). Because of antagonism at the re-uptake site, more monoaminergic neurotransmitters become available for both pre- and post-synaptic receptors. As subjective effects fade away dysphoria, tiredness, depression, and irritability replace the stimulating action of cocaine, prompting subsequent drug re-use to regain the previously experienced positive sensations.

There is considerable evidence that most of cocaine reinforcing effects are mediated by its blocking the dopamine reuptake at the presynaptic terminals (Kuhar, Ritz, & Boja, 1991; Ritz, Lamb, Goldberg, & Kuhar, 1987). The resulting increase in dopamine at its receptors is thought to produce most cocaine effects (Carboni, Imperato, Perezzani, & Di Chiara, 1989; Koob, Caine, Parsons, Markou, & Weiss, 1997; Pontieri, Tanda, & Di Chiara,1995; Roberts, Corcoran, & Fibiger, 1977; Wise & Bozarth, 1987). In fact dopamine uptake inhibitors and direct-acting dopamine agonists can maintain drug self-administration in laboratory animals; dopamine uptake inhibitors and, partially, direct-acting dopamine agonists also substitute for cocaine; conversely dopamine antagonists can attenuate specific behavioural effects of cocaine including its reinforcing, locomotor activity, and discriminative stimulus effects (Carroll, Howell, & Kuhar, 1999; Kuhar, Ritz, & Boja, 1991).

In humans, increases in brain dopamine and D2 receptor occupancy associate to the reinforcing effects of cocaine, as well as of other psychostimulants (Volkow, Wang, Fowler, et al., 1999). However the occupancy of both D1 and D2 receptors is thought to be implicated in the reinforcing properties of cocaine, and in animal studies D1 and D2-like receptor antagonists attenuated cocaine self-administration (Caine, & Kook, 1994) whereas D1 and D2-like receptor agonists maintain it (Platt, Rowlett, & Spealman, 2001).

To date the mechanisms through which cocaine induces all its effects and produces the brain adaptations leading to dependence are not well understood yet. The molecular carrier of dopamine that is responsible for dopamine up-take, and thus for the termination of dopamine effects at the synapse, was isolated and cloned (Giros, El-Mestikawy, Godinot, et al., 1992; Kilty, Lorang, & Amara, 1991; Shimada, Kitayama, Lin, et al., 1991), allowing a better determination of the binding properties and activities of many ligands that are thought to exert their effects by interacting with this transporter (Preti, 2000a).

However dopamine might not be the sole mediator of the reinforcing properties of cocaine, since dopamine transporter knock-out mice, lacking the gene expressing the dopamine re-uptake carrier, were found to keep self-administering cocaine (Rocha, et al., 1998).

## MECHANISMS OF TOLERANCE, WITHDRAWAL AND ADAPTATION TO LONG-TERM USE

Cocaine can be taken intranasally, it can be smoked or injected intravenously. This drug has a relatively short half-life and its symptoms and signs of intoxication, and the pleasurable effects as well, usually decrease within 60-120 minutes (Table 1). The short duration of its effects is likely to contribute to the addictive power of cocaine, together with its ability to induce a rapidly mounting sensation of euphoria. The rate at which cocaine enters the brain seems associated with the "high" sensations (Volkow, et al., 1999).

Little tolerance to the effects of cocaine was reported and, generally, cocaine withdrawal syndrome is not so severe as classical opioid withdrawal. However, tolerance to cocaine sexual stimulation develops rapidly, sometimes resulting in impotence or sexual frigidity (Gold, 1992).

Withdrawal symptoms manifest themselves as the inverse of cocaine effects, and include decreased energy, limited ability to experience pleasure, and reduced interest in the environment (Gold, 1992). Cocaine abusers, and crack consumers particularly, feel anxious, depressed and sometimes paranoid as the "high" sensations subside. Such a rapid shift may trigger a sudden strong desire for reuse. These feelings, classified under the "craving" label, form a distinct part of the withdrawal syndrome in cocaine users.

**Table 1. Pharmacokinetics of Cocaine According to the Route of Administration**

| Route | Onset of action | Duration of the effects |
|---|---|---|
| Oral (by licking) | 1 hour | Several hours |
| Intranasal | 3-5 minutes | 45-60 minutes |
| Intravenous | 1-2 minutes | 10-20 minutes |
| Inhalation (by smoking) | 30 seconds | 5-10 minutes |

Despite low levels of tolerance and the limited extent of the withdrawal syndrome, even "recreational" users (once or twice a week; weekend users) report severe problems stemming from their drug use. Most of those who developed long-term or heavy usage of the substance are unable to "say no" to cocaine when available. Clearly the addictive power of cocaine goes well beyond its tolerance and withdrawal effects. The route of administration influences the ability to quit use: cocaine smokers are less likely to complete a treatment program than intranasal users, and intravenous users are even less able to achieve abstinence. Also doses influence the ability to reach and maintain abstinence, with higher doses and/or higher purity of the substance increasing the chance of reuse.

Chronic use of cocaine also associates to observable and measurable neuropsychological adaptations. Cognitive deficits were reported in long-term users, which mainly concerned executive functions such as decision-making and judgement (Rogers & Robbins, 2001). These deficits could also interfere with rehabilitation programmes (Rogers & Robbins, 2001). Impaired performance in motor-system functioning tests and slower reaction times were also reported in chronic cocaine abusers.

Persistent neurological and psychiatric impairments seem a feature of long-term cocaine abuse. Neurological and psychiatric symptoms could be as well the result of pre-existing abnormalities, revealed by chronic usage, as are the result of neuronal degeneration stemming from multifocal cerebral ischaemia, cerebral haemorrhages and/or infarction, and cerebral atrophy following cocaine use and/or health complications of substance abuse. Cocaine is an epileptogenic agent, too: with repeated administration, the risk of clonic convulsion increases (Merriam, Medalia, & Levine, 1988).

Neurobiological adaptations to prolonged use are also accounted for in some psychiatric disorders occurring in chronic abusers. The "crash" syndrome reported by some consumers when the psychostimulant effects of the compound cease, an extreme exhaustion that follows a binge immediately, may exhibit major depressive-like features with an enhanced risk of suicide (Gawin & Kleber, 1986).

Following a prolonged binge, symptoms of sleeplessness, irritability, paranoia, and acute toxic psychosis may develop (Vereby & Gold, 1988). Chronic cocaine usage can also produce a depletion of dopamine supply; since dopamine inhibits the secretion of prolactin, hyperprolactinemia could result leading to sexual dysfunctions in both males and females.

Many neurobiological changes are described in animal studies as a consequence of acute and chronic cocaine use, principally in the dopaminergic circuits (Woolverton, & Johnson,

1992). Dopaminergic mechanisms are known to mediate the incentive motivational properties of perceptual stimuli, and to contribute to the attributional salience of incentive stimuli (Schultz, Dayan, & Montague, 1997). Sensitisation, i.e. the incremental augmentation of motor and behavioural effects with a repeated administration of the drug, is the main finding resulting from the enhanced dopamine release induced by cocaine blocking the dopamine re-uptake carrier (Panikkar, 1999; Robinson & Berridge, 1993). Among other consequences, sensitisation is thought to mediate the higher likelihood of relapse in people sensitised to the psychotic effects of the compound (Panikkar, 1999).

A major change following cocaine long-term use is the so-called hedonic dysregulation, which shows as apathy, irritability, depression and suicidality. Such negative mood states are likely to instate and reinforce cocaine craving, because they are alleviated by cocaine use (Dackis & O'Brien, 2002). Hedonic dysregulation results from a cycle of addiction alternating negative and positive reinforcements due to withdrawal and euphoria enhancement respectively, that are consequent to cocaine reuse (Kalivas & McFarland, 2003). Disruption of the integrity of the mesolimbic dopaminergic pathway is thought to contribute to hedonic dysregulation significantly (Dackis & O'Brien, 2002).

Another target of cocaine effects, the prefrontal cortex, seems to mediate many aspects of addiction (Goldstein & Volkow, 2002). In particular, an activator of G protein signalling (AGS3) is persistently up-regulated in the prefrontal cortex after cessation of chronic cocaine treatment (Bowers, McFarland, Lake, et al., 2004).

## TREATMENT OF COCAINE ABUSE

Despite huge advances in the neuroscience of substance abuse and dependence in the past twenty years, no approved pharmacological treatment was found for cocaine abuse (Dackis, 2004; Shearer, & Gowing, 2004; Lima, Soares, Reisser, & Farrell, 2002).

On the basis of the known psychopharmacology of cocaine, some existing psychotropic compounds were tested for treatment effectiveness. Substitution therapy with dopamine agonists was experimented by analogy with methadone substitution therapy for heroin dependent patients. Antidepressants were used because of the high occurrence of symptoms of depression among chronic cocaine users. On the other hand the anti-epileptic drug carbamazepine, also effective as a mood stabilizer in a subgroup of patients with bipolar disorders, and neuroleptics, effective as antipsychotic agents, were tested for they ability to overcome mood swing (carbamazepine) or to antagonize dopamine stimulation (neuroleptics).

Several systematic reviews of the treatment with available medications found no evidence supporting the use of antidepressants, carbamazepine, or dopamine agonists in the pharmacotherapy of cocaine abuse (Table 2).

Antidepressants were tested on the assumption that, by increasing monoamine levels, they may alleviate cocaine abstinence symptomatology, and relieve dysphoria with associated craving by a general antidepressant action. Compared to other drugs, desipramine performed better in promoting abstinence (six trials), but it showed just a non-significant trend (Levin & Lehman, 1991; Lima, Reisser, Soares, & Farrell, 2003). One single trial saw imipramine performing better than placebo in terms of clinical response according to the patient's self-report. The results of some trials also suggest that patients on fluoxetine are less likely to dropout (Batki, Washburn, Deluchi, & Jones, 1996; Covi, Hess, Kreiter, & Haertzen, 1995). On the whole no evidence was found indicating the clinical efficacy of antidepressants compared to placebo in the treatment of cocaine abuse. Antidepressant medications, however, exert modest beneficial effects on patients with both depression and substance use disorders, though the rates of sustained abstinence are low in this population (Nunes, & Levin, 2004).

## Table 2. Systematic Reviews of Known Available Pharmacological Treatments of Cocaine Abuse

| Author/year | Participants | Intervention | Outcome | Results |
|---|---|---|---|---|
| Lima, et al., 2003 | 18 studies, with 1177 people randomised | Antidepressants | Positive urine sample for cocaine metabolites | No evidence supporting the clinical effectiveness of antidepressants |
| Lima, et al., 2002 | 5 studies, with 455 people randomised | Carbamazepine | Positive urine sample for cocaine metabolites | No evidence supporting the clinical effectiveness of carbamazepine |
| Soares, et al., 2003 | 17 studies, with 1224 people randomised | Dopamine agonists | Positive urine sample for cocaine metabolites, retention in treatment | No evidence supporting the clinical effectiveness of dopamine agonists |

The effectiveness of carbamazepine in the treatment of cocaine abuse was suggested by positive open label trials on 35 patients, such result being replicated in a cross-over randomized controlled study on 32 subjects (Halikas, Crosby, Pearson, & Graves, 1997). After pooling data from 5 randomized controlled trials, however, Lima and co-workers (2002) found no evidence of the efficacy of carbamazepine, with high dropout rates for both people taking the active compound (61%) and placebo (69%).

Among dopamine agonists, amantadine, bromocriptine, and pergolide were evaluated against positive urine sample for cocaine metabolites and retention in treatment. Again, no evidence was found on the clinical efficacy of these compounds, and a high rate of dropouts was observed in this population (Soares, Lima, Reisser, & Farrell., 2003). However the administration of methylphenidate to a small group of patients (12 individuals) with attention-deficit hyperactivity disorder led to a significant improvement in both primary psychopathology and cocaine use (Levin, Evans, & Kleber, 1998).

Dopamine receptor antagonists (neuroleptics) proved somehow effective in reducing cue-induced craving; however these medications are poorly tolerated, and record a significantly high dropout rate (Mello & Negus, 1996). Moreover neuroleptics are contraindicated because of acute reactions, since these compounds lower the seizure threshold. On the other hand, persistent symptoms of psychosis following cessation of cocaine use prompt a trial with antipsychotic medication. In these cases atypical anti-psychotics were marked as effective in reducing craving and relapse in patients dually diagnosed with schizophrenia and cocaine abuse (Smelson, Losonczy, Davis, et al., 2002). However the use of atypical neuroleptic drugs such as olanzapine in people lacking the relevant psychotic symptoms may be hazardous, since olanzapine may reduce treatment retention with no significant improvement in abstinence or craving (Kampman, K.M., Pettinati, H., Lynch, et al., 2003).

## PERSPECTIVES ON TREATMENT OF COCAINE ABUSE

Treatment retention and compliance with prescriptions are two critical factors in the recovery from substance abuse (Meyer, 1992). Impulsivity was found to be a significant predictor of cocaine use and treatment retention, suggesting the need to target this personality dimension in cocaine pharmacotherapy (Moeller, Dougherty, Barratt, et al., 2001; Patkar, Murray, Mannelli, et al., 2004). Motivation for behaviour change is another key element in the treatment of people abusing psychoactive substances (Margolin, Avants, Rounsaville, et al., 1997). Testing a pharmacologic agent in a motivationally inappropriate sample might not provide a good estimate of the agent's effectiveness.

Clinical observations are an invaluable source of information on cocaine pharmacotherapy, also because the animal models that yielded valuable contributions to research sometimes offer a questionable utility on a clinical ground (Carter, & Tiffany, 1999; Modesto-Lowe, & Kranzler, 1999; Siegel, 1999). Indeed, trials based on preclinical findings often yielded poor results in patient samples (Mello & Negus, 1996). Moreover the paradigms that are effective in animals, which cannot refuse to take the drug administered by the experimenter, fail when tested in a clinical sample, composed of people with the power to refuse to follow the clinician's advice. Dopamine antagonists, for example, are expected to be effective in reducing the reinforcing effects of cocaine, and in fact chronic treatment with low doses of flupenthixol was reported to decrease both cocaine craving and cocaine use in cocaine smokers (Gawin, Allen, & Humblestone, 1989). However due to unacceptable adverse side effects, pure dopamine antagonists are unlikely to become the ideal treatment of cocaine abuse unless this co-exists with a psychotic disorder, and compliance to treatment with a dopamine antagonist is expected to be poor.

## PATTERNS OF USE AND DUALLY DIAGNOSED POPULATION

Patterns of use influence sensitivity to treatment: a fraction of those abusing cocaine also abuse one or more other psychoactive substances (Table 3). Some abuse alcohol or sedatives to overcome the hyper-arousal induced by cocaine; others discover cocaine when they are already addicted to another psychotropic compound, opioids frequently (Leri, Bruneau, & Stewart, 2003). Another fraction of poly-drug abusing people suffers from a mental disorder, and cocaine is used together with legally prescribed drugs and other illegally available compounds to overcome some of the symptoms of the disorder or the unwanted side effects of medications (Khantzian, 1985).

Multiple substance use seems to be the predominant pattern of cocaine use. In a recent multi-centre cross-sectional study carried out in Europe, about 96% of all participants had used at least another substance in addition to cocaine in the previous 30 days (Prinzleve, Haasen, Zurhold, et al., 2004).

Cocaine abuse complicates the course of heroin dependence, leading to poorer response to methadone substitution therapy and lower treatment retention. Methadone doses were increased in some trials to improve both retention and efficacy, but other studies recorded negative results (Kreek, 1997; Margolin, Avants, Rounsaville, et al., 1997). However a recent meta-analysis, including 11 randomized controlled trials with 2279 randomised people and 10 controlled prospective studies with 3715 followed-up people, found a significantly higher chance of urine-based cocaine abstinence at higher doses of methadone (60 to 100 mg/die) in heroin dependent patients also abusing cocaine, with a Reduced Risk=1.81 (c.i. 1.15 – 2.85) (Faggiano, Vigna-Taglianti, Versino, & Lemma, 2004).

**Table 3. Typologies of Cocaine-Abusing People**

| Type of use | - occasional<br>- recurrent, on the basis of availability<br>- week-end user<br>- remitting-relapsing user<br>- chronic user |
|---|---|
| Pattern of drug use | - cocaine only<br>- cocaine and alcohol<br>- cocaine, alcohol, and sedatives<br>- heroin and cocaine<br>- poly-drug user |
| Co-morbidity | - no co-morbidity<br>- physical co-morbidity<br>- psychiatric co-morbidity<br>- physical and psychiatric co-morbidity |
| Dually diagnosed | - mental disorder preceding cocaine abuse<br>- mental disorder co-occurring with cocaine abuse<br>- mental disorder subsequent to cocaine abuse |
| Legal complications | - absent<br>- present |

Also buprenorphine proved an effective intervention in the maintenance treatment of heroin dependence, as effective as methadone at adequate dosages (Mattick, Kimber, Breen, & Davoli, 2003). Buprenorphine was reported to promote cocaine abstinence in cocaine- and opioid-dependent patients, but its long-term effectiveness is still unknown (Montoya, Gorelick, Preston, et al., 2004).

Alcohol and cocaine use was found to be highly correlated in a subpopulation of patients. Disulfiram, prescribed with active psychosocial therapy, was found to lead to higher retention rates and longer abstinence periods from both alcohol and cocaine (Carroll, Nich, Ball, et al., 1998; Carroll, Fenton, Ball, et al., 2004). However heroin-dependent patients also abusing cocaine and alcohol were less likely to obtain positive support from disulfiram (George, Chawarski, Pakes, et al., 2000; Patrakis, Carroll, Nich, et al., 2000).

Mixed results were found for naltrexone, another adjunctive therapeutic bullet in the treatment of alcohol abuse and dependence. Prescription of naltrexone (50 mg/die) together with active psychosocial therapy (relapse prevention or drug counselling) proved no more effective than placebo in reducing cocaine or alcohol use in cocaine-alcohol dependent patients (Schmitz, Stotts, Sayre, et al., 2004).

## END POINT AND OUTCOME MEASURES

Establishing adequate and sensitive measures to ascertain the efficacy of a therapy in the treatment of cocaine abuse is mandatory because of the heterogeneity of samples and the high dropout rate in this population. Appropriate diagnostic criteria to standardise cocaine abuse in terms of type (single- or poly-drug abuse), severity and co-morbidity (co-occurring mental and/or personality disorders), together with a profile of the patient according to the five major axes in DSM-IV are a useful procedure to define samples. Gold standard studies are prospective, parallel-group, double-blind, randomised controlled clinical trials; however due to the high costs of cocaine abuse, investigational safety trials can also offer important elements for evaluation, despite small sample size and the frequent lack of an appropriate control group.

Effective treatments are thought to achieve one or more goals out of five major objectives:

1.  reducing drug use or inducing abstinence;
2.  relieving the symptoms of withdrawal;
3.  preventing relapse and restoring functioning;
4.  reducing high-risk behaviours;
5.  reducing morbidity and mortality due to substance abuse.

On the basis of these end-point criteria, several outcome measures were established to evaluate the efficacy of currently available as well as of novel compounds in the treatment of cocaine abuse (Table 4).

Due to the high drop-out rates among people seeking treatment for cocaine abuse, treatment retention and acceptability are as relevant as any other outcome measure based on abstinence or reduction of use. Ideally the best treatment should be acceptable to the patients, retain them in treatment, engender measurable levels of cocaine abstinence and be adaptable to the different typologies of cocaine abuse.

It is unlikely that a single pharmaceutical compound may achieve all these effects, or even any intermediate stage towards their fulfilment without a concurrent appropriate integrative psychosocial programme (Bobes & McCann, 2000; Nathan, Bresnick, & Batki, 1998). The treatment of cocaine abuse requires the activation of a complex programme including detailed diagnostic assessment, evaluation of patients needs, and the settlement of active psychosocial interventions aimed at reinforcing treatment retention and therapy compliance. On the other hand, relying on psychosocial or behavioural procedures only is likewise unlikely to achieve full efficacy nor even any substantial result as far as complete cocaine abstinence is concerned, due to the high craving potential of the substance.

**Table 4. Measures of Outcome in the Study of the Efficacy of Cocaine Abuse Treatment**

| Main outcome | Type of measure |
|---|---|
| Efficacy | - urine samples positive for metabolites<br>- self-reported use<br>- self-reported relapse<br>- frequency of drug intake<br>- changes in craving for the drug<br>- severity of dependence (using scales such as the Addiction Severity Index, Symptoms Checklist 90) |
| Acceptability and retention | - total number of dropouts at the end of the trial<br>- side effects<br>- number of subjects who dropped out because of lack of efficacy |
| General outcomes | - death<br>- medical problems<br>- legal problems<br>- social and family relations<br>- employment and support |

Pharmacotherapy, therefore, preserves its primacy in the treatment of cocaine abuse, although currently available therapeutics have shown scanty effectiveness or are effective on limited groups of patients, such as methylphenidate for patients with attention-deficit hyperactivity disorder.

Targeting symptoms might improve treatment effectiveness. Cocaine is thought to produce its addictive effect by four mechanisms basically: cocaine-induced euphoria; hedonic dysregulation; disruption of pre-frontal functioning; and cue-induced craving.

**Table 5. Major Pathways to Addiction in Cocaine Abuse**

| Mechanism | Neurotransmitter(s) | Area or circuitry |
|---|---|---|
| Cocaine-induced euphoria | Dopamine<br>Glutamate | Nucleus accumbens |
| Hedonic dysregulation | Dopamine<br>Glutamate<br>GABA [?] | Mesolimbic pathways<br>Orbitofrontal cortex<br>Ventral tegmental area |
| Disruption of pre-frontal functioning | Glutamate | Prefrontal cortex<br>Anterior cingulated<br>Orbitofrontal cortex |
| Cue-induced craving | Glutamate<br>Dopamine<br>Norepinephrine<br>CRF | Anterior cingulated<br>Nucleus accumbens<br>Basolateral amygdala<br>Orbitofrontal cortex<br>Bed of the stria terminalis |

These cocaine effects involve different neurochemical pathways and cerebral areas (Table 5). Neurotransmitters dopamine and glutamate are mainly involved in the addictive effects of cocaine, as they act on a wide and interconnected network of circuits including the nucleus accumbens, the ventral tegmental area, the mesolimbic pathways, the orbitofrontal cortex, the anterior cingulated, the basolateral amygdala, and the bed of the stria terminalis (a synthesis in Dackis, 2004).

Despite some shortcomings, pre-clinical models remain invaluable tools in the development of effective therapeutic compounds. Efficacy, indeed, should be firstly demonstrated by the models predicting a clinical outcome. Though no indisputable animal model exists for cocaine treatment efficacy, pre-clinical studies point to some requisites a desired medication should posses: high potency and selectivity to limit unwanted side effects, the main reason for discontinuation of treatment together with lack of efficacy; an active action when administered according the most appropriate route, with oral administration preferred to any other method. A long-lasting action, to allow for reasonable dosing schedule, and slow penetration in the brain to avoid any 'high' sensation, are the two major pharmacokinetic requirements (Carroll, Howell, & Kuhar, 1999).

## SCREENING AND TESTING NOVEL COMPOUNDS IN THE TREATMENT OF COCAINE ABUSE

The scanty efficacy of currently available psychotropic drugs in the treatment of cocaine abuse urges novel compounds to be screened and tested for efficacy. Drug screening for novel compounds to be tested as putative anti-cocaine agents consists in a sequence including selection by neurochemical assays, to ascertain the pertinence of the compound to the neurobiological networks implied in cocaine actions; then exploration in behavioural models testing the influence of the novel substance on cocaine drug discrimination and self-administration (Table 6).

**Table 6: Preclinical Pharmacological Models for Drug Screening and Testing**

| Neurobiological assays | Behavioural assays |
| --- | --- |
| Receptor binding | Locomotor activity |
| Receptor autoradiography | Conditioned place preference |
| Immuno-cytochemistry | Drug discrimination |
| In situ hybridization | Drug self-administration |
| Microdialysis | Schedule-controlled responding |
| Voltametry | Intracranial self-stimulation |
| Gene cloning | |
| Antisense technology | |
| Knock-out procedures | |

The dopamine hypothesis of cocaine abuse is generally at the basis of neurochemical and behavioural assays for the screening of new effective therapeutic compounds for cocaine treatment. This hypothesis holds that cocaine produces most of its effects by blocking dopamine reuptake at the presynaptic side of the inter-neuron synapse (Kuhar, Ritz, & Boja, 1991). Cocaine interaction with the dopamine transporter would block the inward carrying action on the neurotransmitter, thus causing more dopamine molecules to be available for the activation of postsynaptic receptors (Figure 1).

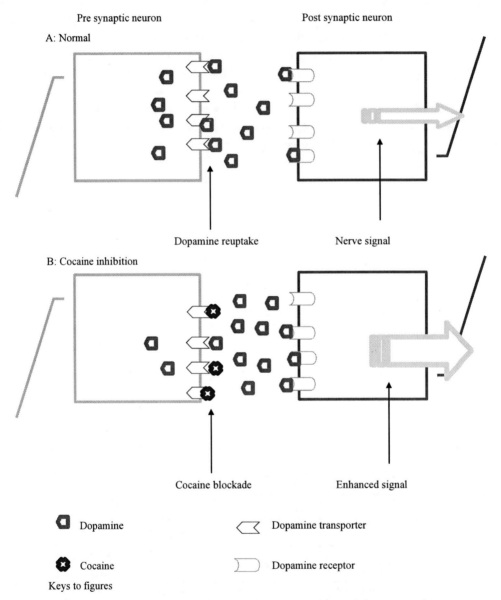

A): Stimulation of neuron releases dopamine from the presynaptic terminal into the synapse, where it binds to dopamine receptors and results in postsynaptic nerve signal; termination of dopamine action occurs by reuptake of dopamine by a specific transporter. B): Cocaine blocks the reuptake of dopamine by binding to the dopamine transporter, resulting in a dopamine excess at the synapse, thereby causing an enhanced postsynaptic nerve signal.

Figure 1: The dopamine hypothesis of cocaine abuse

Dopamine, however, is not the whole story in cocaine abuse, and a wide range of neurotransmitters was proved to contribute to the development of cocaine addictive properties (Carroll, Howell, & Kuhar, 1999; Dackis, 2004; Dackis, & O'Brien, 2003; Gorelick, Gardner, & Xi, 2004; Vetulani, 2001).

On the basis of the known neurochemistry of cocaine, the following target compounds have been studied: dopamine uptake inhibitors, dopamine receptor partial agonists, serotonergic drugs, glutamatergic agents, GABA receptor agonists, GABA-transaminase inhibitor, opioid sigma ligands, calcium channel blockers, CRF antagonist (Table 7).

**Table 7. Classes of Compounds Studied as Potential Medications of Cocaine Abuse**

| Target | Class of agent | Type of compound |
|---|---|---|
| Dopamine | Uptake inhibitors | Selective: Vanoxerine<br>Non-selective: PTT, Mazindol<br>Dopamine sparing: 4-Cl-BZT |
| | Dopamine agonists | D2-like agonists: Bromocriptine, Quinpirole<br>D3-selective: 7-OH-DPAT<br>D1-like agonists: Adrogolide |
| | Dopamine antagonists | Non-selective D2-like antagonists: Flupenthixol<br>Selective D3 antagonists: Nafadotride<br>D1-like antagonists: SCH39166 |
| | Partial agonists | D2-like partial agonists: SDZ208-911<br>Selective D3 partial agonists: BP897<br>D1-like partial agonists: SKF38393, SKF83959 |
| | Indirect agonists | Monoamine oxidase B inhibitor: Selegiline |
| Serotonin | Uptake inhibitors | Selective: Fluoxetine |
| | Serotonin agonists | Non selective (also 5-HT2 antagonist): Quipazine |
| | Serotonin antagonists | Selective 5-HT3 antagonists: Ondansentron |
| Glutamate | NMDA antagonists | Noncompetitive antagonists: MK801, Ibogaine |
| | Glutamaergics | Glutamate enhancing agents: Modafinil |
| GABA | Uptake inhibitors | Selective: Tiagabine |
| | Transaminase inhibitors | Irreversible: G-vinyl-GABA (Vigabatrin) |
| | Gabaergic | GABA enhancing agents: Gabapentin<br>Mixed action: Topiramate |
| | GABA agonists | Selective GABA-B agonists: Baclofen |
| Calcium channel | Blockers | L-type calcium channel blockers: Nimodipine |
| Opioids | Antagonists | Non selective antagonists: Naltrexone<br>Sigma antagonists: BMY14807, DuP734 |
| CRF | Antagonists | Putatively selective CRF1 antagonists: |

# DOPAMINERGIC AGENTS

The research following the dopamine paradigm of cocaine action focused on three major mechanisms: antagonism and extinction of cocaine-trained self-administration; prevention of drug-seeking reinstatement; reduction of cue-induced and stress-triggered craving (Carroll, Howell, & Kuhar, 1999; Platt, Rowlett, & Spealman, 2002).

Maintenance medications, able to replace the subjective effects engendered by cocaine, are thought to alleviate cocaine craving and to contribute to patient compliance and treatment retention. Dopamine uptake inhibitors and direct dopamine receptor agonists are being explored as candidate maintenance medications.

Both dopamine selective and non-selective uptake inhibitors were tested for their potential usefulness in the treatment of cocaine abuse. The phenyl-substitute piperazine derivative GBR12909, also known as vanoxerine, was studied most extensively for its promising properties (Preti, 2000a; Stafford, Rice, Lewis, & Glowa, 2000; Wong, Cantilena, Elkashef, et al., 1999). Vanoxerine binds with a high affinity at the dopamine transporter site, with affinity in the nanomolar range, and inhibits dopamine reuptake with high selectivity compared to the other monoamine uptake sites (Andersen, 1989). Vanoxerine was shown to decrease cocaine-maintained response without decreasing food-maintained responding in cocaine and food self-administration studies in rhesus monkeys (Glowa, Wojnicki, Matecka, et al., 1995a; 1995b). Vanoxerine, indeed, is able to occupy the dopamine transporter site persistently, to attenuate cocaine-induced increases in extracellular dopamine, and to decrease cocaine self-administration without interfering with other goal-directed behaviours (Rothman, Mele, Reid, et al., 1991; Villemagne, Rothman, Yokoi, et al., 1999). Thanks to its slow onset, long-lasting action, lower in-vivo efficacy as a motor stimulant as compared to cocaine, and with a non-stimulant profile of action in normal human beings following oral administration, vanoxerine could be an ideal candidate for the treatment of cocaine abuse (Matecka, Rothman, Radesca, et al., 1996).

Vanoxerine could work by virtue of its cocaine-like effects, preventing craving for cocaine and attenuating cocaine withdrawal symptoms, on the one hand; exerting a "blocking" effect on superimposed cocaine by virtue of its high affinity and slow dissociating binding mixed with low intrinsic activity as a stimulant, on the other. Results in animals are promising, and phase I studies on healthy volunteers predict a good safety and tolerability profile for vanoxerine (Preti, 2000a). Definitive results, however, are pending. Moreover some unwanted effect of the compound was reported: vanoxerine was found to induce a reinstatement of extinguished cocaine-seeking behaviour in animal models of relapse (De Vries, Schoffelmeer, Binnekade, & Vanderschuren, 1999), and to enhance the behavioural stimulant and discriminative stimulus effects of cocaine (Holtzman, 2001). Such effects, however, are dose-mediated: low doses of vanoxerine seem unable to elicit drug-seeking behaviours (Schenk, 2002).

The substitution of direct dopamine agonists for cocaine-enhanced dopamine action produced less straightforward results, with D1-like dopamine agonists able to reduce both cocaine self-administration and cocaine and/or cue-induced reinstatement in animal models, but at the price of adverse side effects (Platt, Rowlett, & Spealman, 2002).

The enhancement of dopamine action through indirect agonists is another direction of research that attempts at normalizing cocaine-induced dysregulation of dopaminergic pathways rather than replacing the addictive substance. Long-term cocaine use, indeed, reduces extracellular dopamine levels in the nucleus accumbens, but acute cocaine administration is able to produce a markedly enhanced dopamine signal due to a sudden hyper-stimulation of post synaptic receptors under low baseline levels (Zhang, Schlussman, Ho, et al., 2003). Such effect is likely to participate to the sensitisation observed after chronic cocaine use, and might also contribute to cue-induced craving. The administration of selegiline (20 mg/day), which inhibits monoamine oxidase B - a dopamine metabolic enzyme - and results in heightened baseline dopamine levels, was found to substantially reduce the euphoric effects of intravenous cocaine in 12 chronic consumers (Houtsmuller, Notes, Newton, et al., 2004). A randomized, 16-week placebo controlled study found that amantidine, another dopamine enhancing agent, significantly favoured abstinence in cocaine abusers (100 mg twice a day; Shoptaw, Kintaudi, Charuvastra, et al, 2002). The success reported in some trials with disulfiram (250 mg/day) in patients abusing both cocaine and alcohol was also attributed to the dopamine enhancing properties of the compound, which can inhibit dopamine-beta hydroxylase, an enzyme involved in the catabolism of the neurotransmitter (Carroll, Fenton, Ball, et al., 2004). An agonist approach, however, is believed to be potentially problematic because of effects on cardiovascular functions and temperature regulation (Klein, 1998).

Antagonizing cocaine effects by blocking its action at the dopamine reuptake site, or suppressing its enhancement of dopaminergic neurotransmission, is another strategy in the screening of putatively therapeutic compounds. Some evidence suggests that the binding profile of dopamine does not overlap with the binding profile of cocaine fully: theoretically it could be possible to design a compound able to block cocaine binding without interfering with dopamine transport, the so-called dopamine-sparing cocaine antagonist (Uhl, Lin, Metzger, & Dar, 1998). Compounds with a "binding/inhibition" ratio greater than 1 would be suitable for specific cocaine antagonism. Some putatively dopamine-sparing cocaine antagonists were proposed, but none has undergone extensive testing (Platt, Rowlett, & Spealman, 2002).

The use of nonselective dopamine receptor antagonists has produced some positive results in a selected sample of cocaine-abusing patients (Gawin, Allen, & Humblestone, 1989). However undesirable side effects and the possibility that direct dopamine antagonism could be overcome by higher doses of cocaine make their large-scale use unlikely. Nevertheless some D1-like selective antagonists, such as SCH39166, proved able to reduce the euphoric and stimulant effects of i.v. administered cocaine significantly, although under chronic conditions SCH39166 was unable to decrease cocaine subjective effects (Nann-Vernotica, Donny, Bigelow, & Walsh, 2001). So far no putatively cocaine antagonist was found to posses an effect profile favourable enough to justify clinical trials in patients (Platt, Rowlett, & Spealman, 2002).

In between substitution therapy and cocaine antagonism there are some compounds provided with a partial dopamine agonist profile of action. A partial dopamine agonist is able to mimic some effects of cocaine without producing the relevant toxic effects, due to the full blockade of dopamine receptors: partial agonists could act as synaptic "buffers" by reducing the dopaminergic activity when this is excessive and by promoting it when it is too low. Therefore in the presence of cocaine, a partial dopamine agonist should function as a cocaine antagonist; in the absence of cocaine, the partial dopamine agonist should act as a weak agonist primarily.

In this class the most promising compound is BP897, a ligand selective at the D3 receptor (Pilla, Parachon, Sautel, et al., 1999; Preti, 2000b). In animal models BP897 was shown to inhibit the cocaine-seeking behaviour that depends on the presentation of drug-associated cues, without having any intrinsic reinforcing properties (Cervo, Carnovali, Stark, & Mennini, 2003; Pilla, Parachon, Sautel, et al., 1999). The potential usefulness of BP897 in the treatment of drug-seeking behaviour is further supported by its effects on drug conditioning models (Garcia-Ladona & Cox, 2003). The effects elicited by BP897 on cocaine-associated cues seem selective for the behaviour controlled by cocaine, since BP897 did not alter the behaviour maintained by other drugs such as heroin, or by non-drug reinforcers such as sucrose (Pilla, Hutcheson, Adib-Samil, et al., 2001). BP897 has entered phase II clinical studies recently. Detailed pharmacokinetic and toxicological data, however, have not been published yet.

## COMPOUNDS ACTING ON GLUTAMATE AND GABA CIRCUITS

Various types of NMDA receptor antagonists, competitive, noncompetitive, and glycine site antagonists, have the potential to counteract relapse and drug-seeking behaviour in drug-dependent animals (Popik & Skolnick, 1996; Vetulani, 2001). NMDA receptor antagonists also inhibit dopamine receptor sensitisation, a feature of cocaine addiction, mainly by preventing its development rather than its expression (Vetulani, 2001).

Memantine, a non-competitive NMDA antagonist approved for use in acute and chronic neurodegenerative diseases, inhibits cocaine self-administration and suppresses cocaine-conditioned motor response in a dose-dependent manner, though without blocking cocaine cue-induced craving (Bespalov, Dravolina, Zvartau, et al., 2000; Hyytia, Backstrom, & Liljequist, 1999). However in humans memantine enhances the subjective feeling of pleasure induced by cocaine (Collins, Ward, McDowell, et al., 1998).

Another substance acting on the glutamate NMDA receptor, ibogaine, was reported to abolish heroin and cocaine craving in addicted poly-users (Vetulani, 2001). The ibogaine compound, as commonly used by inhabitants in Gabon, is subject to abuse and it exerts some NMDA receptor antagonism, but it also enhances glutamate effects by inhibiting its uptake by glial cells and enhancing its release from cortical synaptsomes (Popik, Layer, & Skolnick, 1996). One might wonder whether it is safe to replace cocaine with a potentially addictive compound, which was also reported to induce neurotoxic effects (O'Hearn & Molliver, 1993), with the risk of treating a bad disorder with a remedy that is worse than the disease. At the beginning of his career, indeed, Sigmund Freud (1884; 1984) proposed cocaine as a remedy for morphine and alcohol dependency. The effects were so devastating, that these early pharmacological writings were excluded from the *Standard Edition* of his complete works.

Glutamate, nevertheless, is a most likely target in the treatment of cocaine abuse. The dopaminergic bundle arising from the ventral tegmental area creates glutamatergic synaptic contacts in the nucleus accumbens, a major site of cocaine action. Cocaine increases glutamate levels in the nucleus accumbens sharply (Dackis & O'Brien, 2002); conversely, mice lacking glutamatergic mGluR5 receptors are unable to self-administer cocaine (Chiamulera, Epping-Jordan, Zocchi, et al., 2001).

It is known that chronic cocaine exposure lowers glutamate levels in the nucleus accumbens, but it sensitises the release of glutamate after acute administration (Dackis, 2004). Such an enhanced glutamate release from low baseline levels could partially explain the stronger rewarding effects of acute cocaine administration after some time of cocaine abstinence, resulting in cocaine reinstatement (Kalivas, McFarland, Bowers, et al., 2003). It is the same mechanism thought to be involved in dopamine signal potentiation after chronic cocaine use, where a markedly enhanced dopamine signal occurs despite reduced extracellular dopamine levels in the nucleus accumbens, due to a sudden hyper-stimulation of post synaptic receptors under low baseline levels (Zhang, Schlussman, Ho, et al., 2003). Given this scenario, some authors proposed that normalizing baseline levels in the dopamine and/or glutamate circuitry could contribute to blunt cocaine euphoria (Dackis, 2004).

Recently some small sample trials found that modafinil, a glutamate enhancing agent approved for the treatment of narcolepsy, reduces the euphoric effect of intravenous cocaine (Dackis, Lynch, Yu, et al., 2003; Dackis, 2004). Modafinil was well tolerated, thus leading to valid treatment retention. The authors of these studies proposed that modafinil would promote cocaine abstinence by reversing cocaine-induced dopamine dysregulation through its ability to restore glutamate normal baseline levels in the nucleus accumbens (Dackis, 2004).

More recently a report on a double-blind, placebo-controlled trial of modafinil (400 mg, single dose in the morning) in 62 cocaine dependent patients free of significant medical and psychiatric conditions found significantly more negative urine samples over the 8-week trial when compared to placebo, and a higher chance of achieving prolonged cocaine abstinence in the sample, with no serious adverse events and a high retention rate (no dropout) (Dackis, Kampman, Lynch, et al., 2004).

Modafinil exerts its action by enhancing glutamate effects and by inhibiting GABA release too (Ferraro, Tanganelli, O'Connor, et al., 1996). Cocaine dependence alone can decrease GABA levels in humans (Ke, Streeter, Nassar, et al., 2004); conversely, GABAergic agents were proved able to modulate the neurochemical and behavioural effects of cocaine (Brebner, Childress, & Roberts, 2002; Cousins, Roberts, & de Wit, 2002). GABA-B are particularly effective in promoting abstinence and reducing the use of cocaine, as well as that of heroin, alcohol and nicotine (Brebner, Childress, & Roberts, 2002; Cousins, Roberts, & de Wit, 2002).

Baclofen, a selective GABA-B agonist licensed as an antispasmodic for patients with spinal cord injuries or multiple sclerosis, is the most promising compound of this class, and the unique available for experimentation in humans. Baclofen attenuates cocaine- and heroin-seeking behaviour in rodents (Di Ciano & Everitt, 2003). Baclofen also inhibits self-administration of cocaine in animals dose-dependently, at doses that do not influence responding for food (Brebner, Froestl, Andrews, et al., 1999; Roberts, Andrews, & Vickers 1996). The agents that selectively bind to the GABA-B receptors with antagonist properties attenuate baclofen effects on cocaine self-administration, further confirming the specificity of baclofen action on the GABA-B receptor (Brebner, Froestl, & Roberts, 2002).

Baclofen might act by modulating dopamine neurotransmission in the mesolimbic pathways: injecting baclofen in the ventral tegmental area, indeed, decreases extracellular dopamine in the nucleus accumbens and in the medial prefrontal cortex (Yoshida, Yokoo, Tanaka, et al., 1994). Anecdotic reports indicate that the main effect of baclofen is to deprive cocaine of its peculiar 'taste' (the 'high' sensation), and this effect was also reported in the case of nicotine smoking (reported in Brebner, Childress, & Roberts, 2002). Unlike the similar cocaine blunting produced by neuroleptic drugs, so far no progressive escalation in cocaine use was reported following baclofen administration in cocaine-dependent subjects.

Both open-label studies and controlled trials showed the effectiveness of baclofen (20 mg, three times a day) in reducing cocaine usage (Brebner, Childress, & Roberts, 2002). Higher dosage, in the range of 20 mg four times a day, seems able to blunt the reinforcing properties of cocaine. A randomized, double-blind, placebo-controlled trial in 70 cocaine-dependent patients (16 weeks, 20 mg baclofen, three times/day) showed statistically significant reductions in cocaine use among baclofen-assigned subjects over those receiving the placebo, as indicated by urine drug screening results (Shoptaw, Yang, Rotheram-Fuller, et al., 2003). No significant adverse effects were reported and in general baclofen seems to be well tolerated, despite its muscle relaxant and sedative properties.

It has been proposed that baclofen may help against cue-induced craving (Di Ciano & Everitt, 2003) preventing relapse into use after abstinence, but the placebo-controlled trial showed no statistically significant advantage in terms of cocaine craving for the active compound over the placebo (Shoptaw, Yang, Rotheram-Fuller, et al., 2003). The short-lived action of baclofen (3-4 hours) is the major limitation for its use in large scale samples, since the motivation to take the medication is likely to wax and wane in the course of the day, particularly for such an instable population as that of cocaine abusers. Slow release preparations, or depot combinations, are likely to circumvent this limitation. Moreover the sedative and muscle relaxant effects of baclofen could be enhanced by alcohol and/or commonly prescribed sedatives, frequently co-abused with cocaine by a fraction of abusers. Careful evaluation of the pattern of abuse could aid in avoiding unhelpful drug interactions.

Other GABA enhancing agents have been tested as putatively anti-cocaine agents, many having already been approved as anticonvulsant therapeutics. An 8-week, open-label trial of 1,200 mg/day of gabapentin, a GABA agonist, found it effective in decreasing cocaine use without significant side effects or adverse events (Myrick, Henderson, Brady, & Malcolm, 2001). However in a 48-day double-blind, crossover design study gabapentin (600 to 1200 mg/day) was found to decrease some subjective effects of cocaine, though without affecting cocaine self-administration significantly (Hart, Ward, Collins, et al., 2004).

Gamma-vinyl-GABA (vigabatrin), an irreversible inhibitor of GABA-transaminase, another approved antiepileptic drug, showed a favourable profile in preclinical studies, suppressing elevation of the nucleus accumbens extracellular dopamine levels induced by the administration of addictive substances (Brodie, Figueroa, E., & Dewey, 2003; Gerasimov, Ashby, Gardner, et al., 1999). An open-label study showed some improvement in cocaine abusers (Brodie, Figueroa, E., & Dewey, 2003), but gamma-vinyl-GABA bears a high risk of undesirable side effects (drop in visual acuity due to irreversible concentric visual field constriction; gingival overgrowth), limiting its use as an anti-addictive agent (Vetulani, 2001). In a recent 9-week open-label trial, however, gamma-vinyl-GABA did not produce significant alterations in visual acuity in 30 polydrug abusers, favouring cocaine abstinence in the subgroup (18/30) who completed the study (Brodie, Figueroa, Laska, & Dewey, 2005).

In a ten-week randomized, placebo-controlled study in 45 cocaine-dependent methadone-treated patients tiagabide, another approved anticonvulsant drug (12-24 mg/day), was found able to moderately decrease (around 30%) both self-reported and urine-measured cocaine use at the higher dose (24 mg), with very few adverse effects (Gonzalez, Sevarino, Sofuoglu, et al., 2003). Even higher doses (24 mg) of tiagabide, however, did not alter the acute effects of oral cocaine (150 mg) in individuals who were used to cocaine (Lile, Stoops, Glaser, et al., 2004).

Topiramate, another licensed antiepileptic drug, is a more complex compound among those acting on the GABA circuitry. Topiramate, indeed, is a GABA-promoting agent that antagonizes the AMPA receptors too, thus interfering with the glutamatergic system (Gryder & Rogawski, 2003). In a 13-week, double-blind, placebo-controlled pilot trial in 40 cocaine abusing subjects topiramate, gradually titrated up to a dose of 200 mg/day, favoured the achievement and maintenance of abstinence from cocaine over placebo (Kampman, Pettinati, Lynch, et al., 2004). Adverse effects to topiramate, however, were reported (Bootsma, Coolen, Aldenkamp, et al., 2004), and the efficacy of the compound in long-term use by cocaine-addicted subjects has still to be demonstrated.

Finally the antiepileptic drug valproate, approved for the treatment of migraine headaches, epilepsy and bipolar affective disorder, was tested for the treatment of substance abuse disorders in individuals with co-occurring bipolar disorder and yielded positive results (Myrick & Brady, 2003). Valproate, as other antiepileptic agents, proved useful in the treatment of affective and anxiety disorders (Davis, Ryan, Adinoff, & Petty, 2000), which often complicate the course of substance abuse, including cocaine abuse. Unlike other psychotropic therapeutics it is unlikely to develop an additive interaction with alcohol, often co-abused with cocaine, and is devoid of any abuse potential. It seems particularly promising in relapse prevention and in the treatment of impulsivity and irritability, two personality dimensions that increase the risk of cocaine abuse reinstatement (Moeller, Dougherty, Barratt, et al., 2001). An 8-week open-label trial of valproate in cocaine dependent patients found a substantial reduction in cocaine use, measured by urine drug screens (from 64% to 28% at week 8), with a good retention in treatment (Myrick, Henderson, Brady, & Measom, 2001). Another open-label trial in 55 cocaine abusing subjects found promising results for valproate serum levels higher than 50 mg/ml (Halikas, Center, Pearson, et al., 2001).

Valproate possesses a limited liability to cause a benign decrease in platelet count, thus requiring careful monitoring of platelet count in treated patients, and some cases of hepatotoxicity have been reported in children treated for seizure disorder. Adults, however, seem less subject to this adverse effect of the treatment and a study on comorbid bipolar disorder and alcoholism found valproate to be safe and well tolerated (Myrick & Brady, 2003).

## OTHER COMPOUNDS UNDER EVALUATION
## FOR THE TREATMENT OF COCAINE ABUSE

On the whole, data from clinical studies seem to suggest that GABA-promoting agents might promote abstinence from cocaine by alleviating cue-induced craving associated to the hyper-activity of glutamatergic neurons in prefrontal regions, thus preventing relapse into use (Dackis, 2004). Activation of GABAergic systems in the prefrontal cortex, indeed, can decrease glutamatergic activity.

The role of drug-related cues in substance abuse is relevant to the development of dependence. Indeed, some researchers think that all addictive substances share the property of activating dopaminergic circuits in a specific limbic area involved in the storage of memory, and linked to cues possessing survival value (Di Chiara, 1999). By directly activating the dopaminergic circuits involved in associative learning, addictive drugs escape adaptive modulation of dopamine transmission, though inducing tolerance to their effects after long-term use (and sometimes also producing sensitisation). As a consequence, the stimuli paired to drug reward become able to control behaviour, eliciting desire for the drug (craving) and inducing relapse into use. A role for environmental and also for internal (psychological and physiological) cues in drug abuse has long been acknowledged in the history of the medicine of addiction (O'Brien, Childress, McLellan, & Ehrman, 1992; Siegel, 1999). This paradigm yielded valuable contributions to research (Carter, & Tiffany, 1999), but clinical utility was questioned and the consistency of results on cocaine dependence has been variable and inconstant (Modesto-Lowe, & Kranzler, 1999).

The brain circuits implicated in cue-induced craving overlap with those involved in stress-induced craving, stress being a powerful promoter of relapse into substance abuse. The hypothalamic-pituitary-adrenocortical (HPA) axis is the main system involved in stress response, via a corticotropin-releasing factor (CRF) regulatory mechanism (Stratakis, & Chrousos, 1995). A significant activation of the CRF-HPA axis and of the noradrenergic/sympatho-adreno-medullary (SAM) system response occurs during stress-induced and drug cue-induced cocaine craving states in cocaine dependent individuals (Sinha, Talih, Malison, et al., 2003).

Considerable evidence supports the notion that the CRF brain systems are critically involved in behavioural and physiological manifestations of drug withdrawal and in relapse into drug-taking behaviour induced by environmental stressors (Sarnyai, 1998; Sarnyai, Shaham, & Heinrichs, 2001). Preclinical data provide a rationale for the development of CRF-based pharmacotherapy for the treatment of substance abuse in humans. It is likely, indeed, that CRF antagonists may produce significant therapeutic effects in those disorders where the CRF contributes to the onset or to the maintaining of symptoms. At present some types of non-peptidergic CRF antagonists, able to cross the blood-brain barrier, are being developed for the treatment of mental disorders characterized by a CRF-HPA axis dysregulation (Kehne, & De Lombaert, 2002; Preti, 2001). A water-soluble pyrrolopyrimidine CRF antagonist, R121919, that binds to human CRH(1) receptors with high affinity and is well absorbed in humans, was found - in 24 patients with a major depressive episode - to significantly reduce depression and anxiety scores in both patient and clinician ratings at oral doses between 5-40 and 40-80 mg/die (Zobel, Nickel, Kunzel, et al., 2000).

But preliminary investigations on CRF antagonists in animal models of cocaine seeking-behaviour were disappointing (Lee, Tiefenbacher, Platt, & Spealman, 2003).

The calcium ion plays a crucial role in neuron discharge. Calcium crosses the neuronal membrane via two types of membrane channel: Voltage-dependent channels and Ligand-dependent ones. Among voltage-sensitive channels, L-type calcium channels play a relevant role in regulating adaptive changes in the central nervous system. In animals, infusion with ionophores – that facilitate calcium entry into neuronal cells – enhances the rewarding properties of morphine (Kuzmin, Patkina, & Zvartau, 1994).

Conversely the blockade of L-type calcium channels results in the blunting of the rewarding properties of morphine, cocaine, and amphetamine (Biala & Langwinski, 1996; Kuzmin, Zvartau, Gessa, et al. 1992). The combination of isradipine, an L-type calcium channel blocker, and naltrexone, an opiate receptor blocker, sensibly reduced the rewarding effects of the joint administration of cocaine and alcohol, a 'cocktail' frequently occurring in a subclass of cocaine abusers (Cramer, Gardell, Boedeker, et al., 1998).

Nifedipine, another calcium channel blocker, was reported to decrease subjective cocaine-induced effects in humans (Muntaner, Kumor, Nagoshi, & Jaffe, 1991). However when administered to 2 opiate dependent patients to treat opiate withdrawal precipitated by naltrexone, calcium channel antagonist nifedipine was found to cause confusion, casting some doubts on its use in substance abuse treatment (Silverstone, Attenburrow, & Robson, 1992). On the other hand opposite evidence suggests that nifedipine could alleviate cognitive disturbance in heroin, cocaine, alcohol and marihuana poly-users (Herning, Guo, & Lange, 1995). The verdict on calcium channel blockers, therefore, remains open to further reconsiderations.

Also the verdict on the use of naltrexone in cocaine abusers is still open. Acutely, naltrexone did not antagonize cocaine euphoria in humans, nor did maintenance therapy at full doses (200 mg/day) produce measurable effects on cocaine use (Sufuoglu, Singha, Kosten, et al., 2003; Walsh, Sullivan, Preston, et al., 1996). Despite negative results, some studies reported that abstinent cocaine-dependent patients showed less relapse into cocaine use over time when receiving naltrexone in combination with relapse-prevention therapy, a finding that underpins the need for the combination of pharmacotherapy with appropriate psychosocial intervention (Schmitz, Stotts, Rhoades, & Grabowski, 2001).

Work is in progress also in the field of serotonin-selective reuptake inhibitors (SSRIs) since these are, among antidepressants, the best tolerated and accepted by patients, and trials with fluoxetine showed that patients on this medication are less likely to dropout from treatment (Lima, Soares, Reisser, & Farrell, 2002). The class of SSRIs keeps growing with new compounds, the latter being likely to find their way in trials concerning patients with co-occurring major depression, or who abuse alcohol too, or as a potential treatment of impulsivity. Positive results were reported also for venlafaxine, a mixed norepinephrine and serotonin inhibitor, which produced a small but consistent reduction in cocaine euphoria (225 mg/day; Foltin, Ward, Collins, et al., 2003).

## TREATMENT ALTERING THE PHARMACOKINETIC OF COCAINE

Altering the pharmacokinetic of cocaine is another strategy pursued in the search for a treatment able to antagonize cocaine abuse. Both the promotion of cocaine catabolism, by enhancing the activity of the enzymes that can metabolise the compound, and the prevention of its entry in the central nervous system, by blocking its crossing the blood-brain barrier by means of anti-cocaine antibodies, were attempted with variable results (Vetulani, 2001).

Patients with low blood levels of butyrylcholinesterase (BchE) bear an enhanced risk of acute cocaine poisoning, and the natural variability of BchE activity is likely to contribute to the diversified sensitivity to cocaine (Mattes, Belendiuk, Lynch, et al., 1998). The artificial increase of BchE levels in animals was found to decrease the psychostimulatory action of cocaine, concurrently to a change in cocaine metabolism (Carmona, Schindler, Shoaib, et al., 1998). A higher-functioning mutant of human BchE was achieved by genetic engineering, but results are pending (Vetulani, 2001; Xie, Altimirano, Bartels, et al., 1999).

The use of cocaine-selective antibodies was attempted in order to block the compound peripherally and to prevent its crossing of the blood-brain barrier. Immunotherapy, with antibodies used to neutralize the drug, was developed for phencyclidine, nicotine and, precisely, cocaine. Anti-cocaine antibodies are expected to form heavy complexes with the substance unable to cross the blood-brain barrier, thus keeping it in the periphery where it is metabolised and excreted. Immunotherapy is thought to serve as a supplement to the programs aimed at preventing relapse and acute intoxication (Vetulani, 2001).

The production of selective antibodies against cocaine, however, is not an easy task: small molecules, like the ones of cocaine, generally do not alarm the immune system. However coupling cocaine to a protein carrier resulted in strong stimulation of the immune system in the animal. Such a mechanism, for analogy with common vaccination, is promoted as a 'vaccine'. Initial experiments in mice showed that such a 'vaccine' for cocaine prevented the entry of the substance in the central nervous system effectively, with long-lasting effects and a significant reduction in animals' cocaine self-administration (Fox, 1997; Fox, Kantak, Edwards, et al., 1996). The initial success prompted the development of more selective vaccines (Carrera, Ashley, Wirsching, et al., 2001), leading to a specific programme of experimentation in humans (Kosten, Rosen, Bond, et al., 2002).

The perspective of inducing immunization against cocaine use, also without the consent of the subject (compulsory treatment following a court judgement), has raised an intense and still alive debate on the ethical implications of immunotherapy for substance abuse (Cohen, 1997; World Health Organization, 2004). The currently shared vision is that, if the trials prove the safety and tolerability of anti-cocaine vaccines in humans, immunotherapy could be used in adults who voluntarily decide to commit themselves to such a programme after being carefully informed of any risk (World Health Organization, 2004). However, the possibility that long-lasting antibodies against cocaine are detected in the blood of treated patients even after many years raises the issue of the risk of violating privacy and discrimination laws. Preserving privacy and confidentiality should, therefore, become mandatory for any program based on vaccination and/or immunotherapy.

## THE NEED FOR AN ALL-EMBRACING APPROACH

The most effective drug cannot be fully effective without the patient's following prescriptions: compliance with therapy and treatment retention are two major supports to treatment effectiveness. The need for long-term treatment should also be adequately addressed in the case of patients suffering from a chronic, remitting-relapsing disorder such as cocaine abuse and dependence.

An accurate diagnosis and ascertainment of disorder severity is a pre-requisite to define adequate treatments: not all cocaine abusing patients are identical. Cocaine dependence severity, for example, was found to predict the outcome in patients with both cocaine and alcohol dependence (Kampman, Pettinati, Volpicelli, et al., 2004).

Multiple morbidities, including social instability, co-occurring psychiatric illness, infectious diseases and other organic complications of addiction require proper care and interventions. For dually diagnosed patients aggressive treatment of the co-occurring mental disorder is mandatory, even though its effectiveness is unlikely to produce cocaine abstinence per se. Similarly, the use of substitution therapy with methadone is appropriate in patients abusing both opioids and cocaine to the aim of improving compliance and retention, two major and often unachieved goals in the pharmacotherapy of cocaine abuse.

Psychosocial treatments are a useful companion in the pharmacotherapy of cocaine abuse, with group therapy and contingency management therapies being able to improve motivation and social functioning, particularly in patients abusing alcohol as well (Bobes & McCann, 2000). Programs aimed at improving retention in treatment, increasing compliance, providing services that address the patient's comorbid psychosocial problems, and encouraging involvement in self-help groups have been found to correlate with a higher chance of a positive outcome (Carroll, 2000; Crits-Christoph, Siqueland, Blaine, et al., 1999; Weiss, Griffin, Gallop, et al., 2000). Also the community reinforcement approach with abstinence-contingent incentives was found effective at achieving cocaine abstinence (Roozen, Boulogne, van Tulder, et al., 2004).

Other approaches including cognitive-behavioural therapy, 12 Steps, and 28 day Minnesota Model have been suggested to improve the outcome of cocaine treatment (Carroll, Rounsaville, & Gawin, 1991; Marlatt, & Gordon, 1985; Wells, Peterson, Gainey, et al., 1994), but there is lack of a systematic overview of psychosocial and rehabilitation treatments. A large meta-analysis is under way at the Cochrane inter-collaborative *Drugs and Alcohol Group* (Soares, Lima, & Farrell, 2004), and results are awaited to improve knowledge on the psychosocial treatment of cocaine abuse and dependence.

## CONCLUSION

The rapidly increasing knowledge of the mechanisms underlying cocaine abuse, as well as the foreseeable tremendous advances in the understanding of the neurobiology of substance abuse and its related disorders to come in the following years thanks to the continuing improvement in neuroscience-related technology, will have a likely positive impact on the settlement of evidence-based treatments. The deeper our knowledge of the neurochemistry of cocaine effects, the higher our chance to screen potentially therapeutic compounds.

Improving the clinical description of patients' characteristics will further enhance clinicians' ability to select sub-samples that are likely to respond to specific medications or treatment protocols. A more precise definition of sensitive outcome measures will favour the individuation of critical passages in the therapeutic process: side effects and adverse events influence compliance with therapy and treatment retention, as well as the pharmacological effectiveness of the compound under investigation.

Open-label trials and small-sample safety studies may contribute to research into effective treatments: supporting and financing the systematic review of small-scale investigations (meta-analysis) will allow saving on funds for larger randomized, placebo-controlled trials, which are generally more expensive and time-consuming.

Substance abuse and dependence impose high direct and indirect costs on society: the spreading of cocaine abuse in wealthy Western countries is expected to increase in the next years. Investments are therefore required and appropriate on the part of both public health authorities and private companies involved in drug development and research.

## Acknowledgment

The Author wishes to thank Miss Vittoria Rubino for her help in the revision of the English translation.

## References

Andersen, P.H. (1989). The dopamine uptake inhibitor GBR 12909: selectivity and molecular mechanism of action. *European Journal of Pharmacology*, 166, 493-504

Batki, S.L., Washburn, A.M., Deluchi, K., & Jones, R.T. (1996). A controlled trial of fluoxetine in crack cocaine dependence. *Drug & Alcohol Dependence*, 41, 137-142

Bespalov, A.Y., Dravolina, O.A., Zvartau, E.E., Beardsley, P.M., & Balster, R.L. (2000). Effects of NMDA receptor antagonists on cocaine-conditioned motor activity in rats. *European Journal of Pharmacology*, 390, 303-311

Biala, G., & Langwinski, R. (1996). Effects of calcium channel antagonists on the reinforcing properties of morphine, ethanol and cocaine as measured by place conditioning. *Journal of Physiology & Pharmacology*, 47, 497-502

Bobes, J., & McCann, U.D. (2000). Developments in the treatment of drug dependence. *Current Opinion in Psychiatry*, 13, 333-338

Bootsma, H.P., Coolen, F., Aldenkamp, A.P., Arends, J., Diepman, L., Hulsman, J., Lambrechts, D., Leenen, L., Majoie, M., Schellekens, A., & de Krom, M. (2004). Topiramate in clinical practice: long-term experience in patients with refractory epilepsy referred to a tertiary epilepsy center. *Epilepsy & Behavior*, 5, 380-387

Bowers, M.S., McFarland, K., Lake, R.W., Peterson, Y.K., Lapish, C.C., Gregory, M.L., Lanier, S.M., & Kalivas, P.W. (2004). Activator of G protein signalling 3: a gatekeeper of cocaine sensitization and drug seeking. *Neuron*, 42, 269-281

Brebner, K., Childress, A.R., & Roberts, D.C. (2002). A potential role for GABA(B) agonists in the treatment of psychostimulant addiction. *Alcohol & Alcoholism*, 37, 478-484

Brebner, K., Froestl, W., Andrews, M., Phelan, R., & Roberts, D.C.S. (1999). The GABA(B) agonist CGP44532 decreases cocaine self-administration in rats: demonstration using a progressive ratio and a discrete trials procedure. *Neuropharmacology*, 38, 1797-1804

Brebner, K., Froestl, W., & Roberts, D.C.S. (2002). The GABAB antagonist CGP56433A attenuates the effect of baclofen on cocaine but not heroin self-administration in the rat. *Psychopharmacology*, 160, 49-55

Brodie, J.D., Figueroa, E., & Dewey, S.L. (2003). Treating cocaine addiction: from preclinical to clinical trial experience with gamma-vinyl GABA. *Synapse*, 50, 261-265

Brodie, J.D., Figueroa, E., Laska, E.M., & Dewey, S.L. (2005). Safety and efficacy of gamma-vinyl GABA (GVG) for the treatment of methamphetamine and/or cocaine addiction. *Synapse*, 55, 122-125

Caine, S.B., & Koob, G.F. (1994). Effects of dopamine D-1 and D-2 antagonists on cocaine self-administration under different schedules of reinforcement in the rat. *Journal of Pharmacology & Experimental Therapeutics*, 270, 209-218

Carboni, E., Imperato, A., Perezzani, L., & Di Chiara, G. (1989). Amphetamine, cocaine, phencyclidine, and nomifensine increase extracellular dopamine concentrations preferentially in the nucleus accumbens of freely moving rats. *Neuroscience*, 28, 653-661

Carmona, G.N., Schindler, C.W., Shoaib, M., Jufer, R., Cone, E.J., Goldberg, S.R., Greig, N.H., Yu, Q.S., & Gorelick, D.A. (1998). Attenuation of cocaine-induced locomotr activity by butyrylcholisterinase. *Experimental & Clinical Psychopharmacology*, 6, 274-279

Carrera, M.R.A., Ashley, J.A., Wirsching, P., Koob, G.F., & Janda, K.D. (2001). A second-generation vaccine protects against the psychoactive effects of cocaine. *Proc. Natl. Acad. Sci. USA*, 98, 1988-1992

Carroll, K.M. (2000). Implications of recent research for program quality in cocaine dependence treatment. *Substance Use & Misuse*, 35, 2011-2030

Carroll, K.M., Fenton, L.R., Ball, S.A., Nich, C., Frankforter, T.L., Shi, J., & Rounsaville, B.J. (2004). Efficacy of disulfiram and cognitive behavior therapy in cocaine-dependent outpatients: a randomized placebo-controlled trial. *Archives of General Psychiatry*, 61, 264-272

Carroll, F.I., Howell, L.L., & Kuhar, M.J. (1999). Pharmacotherapies for treatment of cocaine abuse: preclinical aspects. *Journal of Medicinal Chemistry*, 42, 2721-2736

Carroll, K.M., Nich, C., Ball, S.A., McCance, E., & Rounsaville, B.J. (1998). Treatment of cocaine and alcohol dependence with psychotherapy and disulfiram. *Addiction*, 93, 713-728

Carroll, K.M., Rounsaville, B.J., & Gawin, F.H. (1991). A comparative trial of psychotherapies for ambulatory cocaine abusers: relapse prevention and interpersonal psychotherapy. *American Journal of Drug & Alcohol Abuse*, 17, 229-47

Carter, B.L., & Tiffany, S.T. (1999). Meta-analysis of cue-reactivity in addiction research. *Addiction*, 94, 327-340

Cervo, L., Carnovali, F., Stark, J.A., & Mennini, T. (2003). Cocaine-seeking behavior in response to drug-associated stimuli in rats: involvement of D3 and D2 dopamine receptors. *Neuropsychopharmacology*, 28, 1150-1159

Chiamulera, C., Epping-Jordan, M.P., Zocchi, A., Marcon, C., Cottiny, C., Tacconi, S., Corsi, M., Orzi, F., & Conquet, F. (2001). Reinforcing and locomotor stimulant effects of cocaine are absent in mGluR5 null mutant mice. *Nature Neuroscience*, 4, 873-874

Chuhma, N., Zhang, H., Masson, J., Zhuang, X., Sulzer, D., Hen, R., & Rayport, S. (2004). Dopamine neurons mediate a fast excitatory signal via their glutamatergic synapses. *Journal of Neuroscience*, 24, 972-981

Cohen, P.J. (1997). Immunization for prevention and treatment of cocaine abuse: legal and ethical implications. *Drug & Alcohol Dependence*, 48, 167-174

Collins, E.D., Ward, A.S., McDowell, D.M., Foltin, R.W., & Fischman, M.W. (1998). The effects of memantine on the subjective, reinforcing and cardiovascular effects of cocaine in humans. *Behavioural Pharmacology*, 9, 587-598

Cousins MS, Roberts DC, & de Wit H. (2002). GABA(B) receptor agonists for the treatment of drug addiction: a review of recent findings. *Drug & Alcohol Dependence*, 65, 209-220

Covi, L., Hess, J.M., Kreiter, N.A., & Haertzen, C.A. (1995). Effects of combined fluoxetine and counselling in the outpatient treatment of cocaine abusers. *American Journal of Drug & Alcohol Abuse*, 21, 327-344

Cramer, C.M., Gardell, L.R., Boedeker, K.L., Harris, J.R., Hubbell, C.L., & Reid, L.D. (1998). Isradipine combined with naltrexone persistently reduces the reward-relevant effects of cocaine and alcohol. *Pharmacology, Biochemistry & Behavior*, 60, 345-356

Crits-Christoph, P., Siqueland, L., Blaine, J., Frank, A., Luborsky, L., Onken, L.S., Muenz, L.R., Thase, M.E., Weiss, R.D., Gastfriend, D.R., Woody, G.E., Barber, J.P., Butler, S.F., Daley, D., Salloum, I., Bishop, S., Najavits, L.M., Lis, J., Mercer, D., Griffin, M.L., Moras, K., & Beck, A.T. (1999). Psychosocial treatments for cocaine dependence: National Institute on Drug Abuse Collaborative Cocaine Treatment Study. *Archives of General Psychiatry*, 56, 493-502

Dackis, C.A. (2004). Recent advances in the pharmacotherapy of cocaine dependence. *Current Psychiatry Reports*, 6, 232-331

Dackis, C.A., & O'Brien, C.P. (2002). Cocaine dependence: the challenge for pharmacotherapy. *Current Opinion in Psychiatry*, 15, 261-268

Dackis, C.A., & O'Brien, C.P. (2003). Glutamatergic agents for cocaine dependence.. *Annals of the New York Academy of Sciences*, 1003, 328-345

Dackis, C.A., Kampman, K.M., Lynch, K.G., Pettinati, H.M., & O'Brien, C.P. (2004). A Double-Blind, Placebo-Controlled Trial of Modafinil for Cocaine Dependence. *Neuropsychopharmacology*, Epub ahead of print, doi:10.1038/sj.npp.1300600

Dackis, C.A., Lynch, K.G., Yu, E., Samaha, F.F., Kampman, K.M., Cornish, J.W., Rowan, A., Poole, S., White, L., & O'Brien, C.P. (2003). Modafinil and cocaine: a double-blind, placebo-controlled drug interaction study. *Drug & Alcohol Dependence*, 70, 29-37

Davis, L.L., Ryan, W., Adinoff, B., & Petty, F. (2000). Comprehensive review of psychiatric use of valproate. *Journal of Clinical Psychopharmacology*, 20 (Suppl. 1), 1S-17S

De Vries, T.J., Schoffelmeer, A.N., Binnekade, R., & Vanderschuren, L.J. (1999). Dopaminergic mechanisms mediating the incentive to seek cocaine and heroin following long-term withdrawal of IV drug self-administration. *Psychopharmacology*, 143, 254-260

Di Chiara, G. (1999). Drug addiction as dopamine-dependent associative learning disorder. *European Journal of Pharmacology*, 375, 13-30

Di Ciano, P., & Everitt, B.J. (2003). The GABA(B) receptor agonist baclofen attenuates cocaine- and heroin-seeking behavior by rats. *Neuropsychopharmacology*, 28, 510-518

Faggiano, F., Vigna-Taglianti, F., Versino, E., & Lemma, P. (2004). Methadone maintenance at different dosages for opiod dependence. *Cochrane Database of Systematic Reviews*, 3, CD002208

Ferraro, L., Tanganelli, S., O'Connor, W.T., Antonelli, T., Rambert, F., & Fuxe, K. (1996). The vigilance promoting drug modafinil increases dopamine release in the rat nucleus accumbens via the involvement of a local GABAergic mechanism. *European Journal of Pharmacology*, 306, 33-39

Foltin, R.W., Ward, A.S., Collins, E.D., Haney, M., Hart, C.L,, & Fischman, M.W. (2003). The effects of venlafaxine on the subjective, reinforcing and cardiovascular effects of cocaine in opioid-dependent and non opioid-dependent humans. *Experimental & Clinical Psychopharmacology*, 11, 123-130

Fox, B.S. (1997). Development of a therapeutic vaccine for the treatment of cocaine addiction. *Drug & Alcohol Dependence*, 48, 153-158

Fox, B.S., Kantak, K.M., Edwards, M.A., Black, K.M., Bollinger, B.K., Botka, A.J., French, T.L., Thompson, T.L., Schad, V.C., Greenstein, J.L., Gefter, M.L., Exley, M.A., Swain,

P.A., & Briner, TJ. (1996). Efficacy of a therapeutic vaccine in rodent models. *Nature Medicine*, 2, 1129-1132

Freud, S. (1884). Über Koka. *Wiener Zentralblatt fur die gesamte Therapie*, 2, 289-314

Freud, S. (1984). Über Coca (classics revisited). *Journal of Substance Abuse Treatment*, 1, 206-217

Garcia-Ladona, F.J., & Cox, B.F. (2003). BP 897, a selective dopamine D3 receptor ligand with therapeutic potential for the treatment of cocaine-addiction. *CNS Drug Reviews*, 9, 141-158

Gawin, F.H., & Kleber, H.D. (1986). Abstinence symptomatology and psychiatric diagnosis in cocaine abusers. *Archives of General Psychiatry*, 43, 107-113

Gawin, F.H., Allen, D., & Humblestone, B. (1989). Outpatient regulation of "crack" cocaine smoking with flupenthixol decanoate. *Archives of General Psychiatry*, 46, 322-325

George, T.P., Chawarski, M.C., Pakes, J., Carroll, K.M., Kosten, T.R., & Schottenfeld, R.S. (2000). Disulfiram versus placebo for cocaine dependence in buprenorphine-maintained subjects: a preliminary trial. *Biological Psychiatry*, 47, 1080-1086

Gerasimov, M.R., Ashby, C.R. Jr., Gardner, E.L., Mills, M.J., Brodie, J.D., & Dewey, S.L. (1999). Gamma-vinyl GABA inhibits methamphetamine, heroin, or ethanol-induced increases in nucleus accumbens dopamine. *Synapse*, 34, 11-19

Giros, B., el-Mestikawy, S., Godinot, N., Zheng, K., Han, H., Yang-Feng, T., & Caron, M.G. (1992). Cloning, pharmacological characterization, and chromosome assignment of the human dopamine transporter. *Molecular Pharmacology*, 42: 383-390

Glowa, J.R., Wojnicki, F.H.E., Matecka, D., Bacher, J., Mansbach, R.S., Balster, R.L., & Rice, K.C. (1995a). Effects of dopamine reuptake inhibitors on food and cocaine maintained responding. I: dependence on unit dose of cocaine. *Experimental & Clinical Psychopharmacology*, 3, 219-231

Glowa, J.R., Wojnicki, F.H.E., Matecka, D., Rice, K.C., & Rothman, R.B. (1995b). Effects of dopamine reuptake inhibitors on food and cocaine maintained responding II: comparison with other drugs and repeated administration. *Experimental & Clinical Psychopharmacology*, 3, 232-239

Gold, M.K. (1992). Cocaine (and crack): clinical aspects. In: Lowinson, J.H., Ruiz, P., Millman, R.B., & Langrod, J.G., Eds, *Substance abuse. A comprehensive textbook*. Baltimore, Williams & Wilkins, Pp. 205-221

Gold, M.K., & Vereby, K. (1984). The psychopharmacology of cocaine. *Psychiatric Annals*, 140, 714-723

Goldstein, R.Z., & Volkow, N.D. (2002). Drug addiction and its underlying neurobiological basis: Neuroimaging evidence for the involvement of the Frontal Cortex. *American Journal of Psychiatry*, 159, 1642-1652

Gonzalez, G., Sevarino, K., Sofuoglu, M., Poling, J., Oliveto, A., Gonsai, K., George, T.P., & Kosten, T.R. (2003). Tiagabine increases cocaine-free urines in cocaine-dependent methadone-treated patients: results of a randomized pilot study. *Addiction*, 98, 1625-1632

Gorelick, D.A., Gardner, E.L., & Xi, Z.X. (2004). Agents in development for the management of cocaine abuse. *Drugs*, 64, 1547-1573

Gryder, D.S., & Rogawski, M.A. (2003). Selective antagonism of GluR5 kainate-receptor-mediated synaptic current by topiramate in rat basolateral amygdala neurons. *Journal of Neuroscience*, 23, 7069-70-7

Halikas, J.A., Center, B.A., Pearson, V.L., Carlson, G.A., & Crea, F. (2001). A pilot open clinical study of depakote in the treatment of cocaine abuse. *Human Psychopharmacology*, 3, 257-264

Halikas, J.A., Crosby, R.D., Pearson, V.L., & Graves, N.M. (1997). A randomised double-blind study of carbamazepine in the treatment of cocaine abuse. *Clinical Pharmacology & Therapeutics*, 62, 89-105

Hanzlick, R., & Gowitt, G.T. (1991). Cocaine metabolite detection in homicide victims. *JAMA*, 265, 760-761

Hart, C.L., Ward, A.S., Collins, E.D., Haney, M., & Foltin, R.W. (2004). Gabapentin maintenance decreases smoked cocaine-related subjective effects, but not self-administration by humans. *Drug & Alcohol Dependence*, 73, 279-287

Herning, R.I., Guo, X., & Lange, W.R. (1995). Nimodipine improves information processing in substance abusers. *Annals of the New York Academy of Sciences*, 765, 152-159

Holtzman, S.G. (2001). Differential interaction of GBR12909, a dopamine uptake inhibitor, with cocaine and methamphetamine in rats discriminating cocaine. *Psychopharmacology*, 155, 180-186

Houtsmuller, E.J., Notes, L.D., Newton, T., van Sluis, N., Chiang, N., Elkashef, A., & Bigelow, G.E. (2004). Transdermal selegiline and intravenous cocaine: safety and interactions. *Psychopharmacology*, 172, 31-40

Hyytia, P., Backstrom, P., & Liljequist, S. (1999). Site-specific NMDA receptor antagonists produce differential effects on cocaine self-administration in rats. *European Journal of Pharmacology*, 378, 9-16

Kalivas, P.W., & McFarland, K. (2003). Brain circuitry and the reinstatement of cocaine-seeking behavior. *Psychopharmacology*, 168, 44-56

Kalivas, P.W., McFarland, K., Bowers, S., Szumlinski, K., Xi, Z.X., & Baker, D. (2003). Glutamate transmission and addiction to cocaine. *Annals of the New York Academy of Sciences*, 1003, 169-175

Kampman, K.M., Pettinati, H., Lynch, K.G., Dackis, C., Sparkman, T., Weigley, C., & O'Brien, C.P. (2004). A pilot trial of topiramate for the treatment of cocaine dependence. *Drug & Alcohol Dependence*, 75, 233-240

Kampman, K.M., Pettinati, H., Lynch, K.G., Sparkman, T., & O'Brien. C.P. (2003). A pilot trial of olanzapine for the treatment of cocaine dependence. *Drug & Alcohol Dependence*, 70, 265-273

Kampman, K.M., Pettinati, H.M., Volpicelli, J.R., Oslin, D.M., Lipkin, C., Sparkman, T., & O'Brien, C.P. (2004). Cocaine dependence severity predicts outcome in outpatient detoxification from cocaine and alcohol. *American Journal of Addiction*, 13, 74-82

Ke, Y., Streeter, C.C., Nassar, L.E., Sarid-Segal, O., Hennen, J., Yurgelun-Todd, D.A., Awad, L.A., Rendall, M.J., Gruber, S.A., Nason, A., Mudrick, M.J., Blank, S.R., Meyer, A.A., Knapp, C., Ciraulo, D.A., & Renshaw, P.F. (2004). Frontal lobe GABA levels in cocaine dependence: a two-dimensional, J-resolved magnetic resonance spectroscopy study. *Psychiatry Research*, 130, 283-293

Kehne, J., & De Lombaert, S. (2002). Non-peptidic CRF1 receptor antagonists for the treatment of anxiety, depression and stress disorders. *Current drug targets. CNS and neurological disorders*, 1, 467-493

Khantzian, E.J. (1985) The self-medication hypothesis of addictive disorders: focus on heroin and cocaine dependence. *American Journal of Psychiatry*, 142, 1259-1264

Kilty, J.E., Lorang, D., & Amara, S.G. (1991). Cloning and expression of a cocaine-sensitive rat dopamine transporter. *Science*, 254, 578-579

Klein, M. (1998). Research issues related to development of medications for treatment of cocaine addiction. *Annals of the New York Academy of Sciences*, 844, 75-91

Koob, G.F., Caine, S.B., Parsons, L., Markou, A., & Weiss, F. (1997). Opponent process model and psychostimulant addiction. *Pharmacology, Biochemistry & Behavior,* 57, 513-521

Kosten, T.R., Rosen, M., Bond, J., Settles, M., Roberts, J.S., Shields, J., Jack, L., & Fox, B. (2002). Human therapeutic cocaine vaccine: safety and immunogenicity. *Vaccine*, 20, 1196-1204

Kreek, M.J. (1997). Opiate and cocaine addictions: challenge for pharmacotherapies. *Pharmacology, Biochemistry & Behavior*, 57, 551-569

Kuhar, M.J., Ritz, M.C., & Boja, J.W. (1991). The dopamine hypothesis of the reinforcing properties of cocaine. *Trends in Neurosciences,* 14, 299-302

Kuzmin, A.V., Patkina, N.A., & Zvartau, E.E. (1994). Analgesic and reinforcing effects of morphine in mice. Influence of Bay K-8644 and nimodipine. *Brain Research*, 652, 1-8

Kuzmin, A., Zvartau, E., Gessa, G.L., Martellotta, M.C., & Fratta, W. (1992). Calcium antagonists israpidine and nimodipine suppress cocaine and morphine intravenous self-administration in drug-naïve mice. *Pharmacology, Biochemistry & Behavior*, 41, 497-500

Lee, B., Tiefenbacher, S., Platt, D.M., & Spealman, R.D. (2003). Role of the hypothalamic-pituitary-adrenal axis in reinstatement of cocaine-seeking behavior in squirrel monkeys. *Psychopharmacology*, 168, 177-183

Leri, F., Bruneau, J., & Stewart, J. (2003). Understanding polydrug use: review of heroin and cocaine co-use. *Addiction*, 98, 7-22

Levin, F.R., Evans, S.M., & Kleber, H.D. (1998). Prevalence of adult attention-deficit hyperactivity disorder among cocaine abusers seeking treatment. *Drug & Alcohol Dependence*, 52, 15-25

Levin, R.L., & Lehman, A.E. (1991). Meta-analysis of desipramine as an adjunct in the treatment of cocaine addiction. *Journal of Clinical Psychopharmacology*, 11, 374-378

Lile, J.A., Stoops, W.W., Glaser, P.E., Hays, L.R., & Rush, C.R. (2004). Acute administration of the GABA reuptake inhibitor tiagabine does not alter the effects of oral cocaine in humans. *Drug & Alcohol Dependence*, 76, 81-91

Lima, A.R., Lima, M.S., Soares, B.G., & Farrell, M. (2002). Carbamazepine for cocaine dependence. *Cochrane Database of Systematic Reviews*, 2, CD002023

Lima, M.S., Reisser, A.A., Soares, B.G., & Farrell, M. (2003). Antidepressants for cocaine dependence. *Cochrane Database of Systematic Reviews*, 2, CD002950.

Lima, M.S., Soares, B.G., Reisser, A.A., & Farrell, M. (2002). Pharmacological treatment of cocaine dependence: a systematic review. *Addiction*, 97, 931-949

Margolin, A., Avants, S.K., Rounsaville, B., Kosten, T.R., & Schottenfeld, R.S. (1997). Motivational factors in cocaine pharmacotherapy trials with methadone-maintained patients: problems and paradoxes. *Journal of Psychoactive Drugs*, 29, 205-212

Marlatt, G.A., & Gordon, J.R. (1985). *Relapse Prevention*. New York: Guilford Press

Marzuk, P.M., Tardiff, K., & Leon, A.C. (1992). Prevalence of cocaine use among resident of New York City who committed suicide during a one-year period. *American Journal of Psychiatry*, 149, 371-375

Marzuk, P.M., Tardiff, K., Leon, A.C., Hirsch, C.S., Portera, L., Iqbal, M.I., Nock, M.K., & Hartwell, N. (1998). Ambient temperature and mortality from unintentional cocaine overdose. *JAMA*, 279, 1795-1800

Matecka, D., Rothman, R.B., Radesca, L., de Costa, B.R., Dersch, C.M., Partilla, J.S., Pert, A., Glowa, J.R., Wojnicki, F.H.E., & Rice, K.C. (1996). Development of novel, potent, and selective dopamine reuptake inhibitors through alteration of the piprazine ring of 1-(2-(diphenylmethoxy)ethyl)– and 1 - (2-(bis(4-fluorophenyl)methoxy)ethyl)-4-(3-phenylpropyl) piperazines (GBR 12935 and GBR 12909). *Journal of Medicinal Chemistry*, 39, 4704-4716

Mattes, C.E., Belendiuk, G.W., Lynch, T.J., Brady, R.O., & Dretchen, K.L. (1998). Butyrylcholinesterase: an enzyme antidote for cocaine intoxication. *Addiction Biology*, 3, 171-188

Mattick, R.P., Kimber, J., Breen, C., & Davoli, M. (2003). Buprenorphine maintenance versus placebo or methadone maintenance for opioid dependence. *Cochrane Database of Systematic Reviews*, 2, CD002207.

Mello, N.K., & Negus, S.S. (1996). Preclinical evaluation of pharmacotherapies for treatment of cocaine and opioid abuse using self-administration procedures. *Neuropsychopharmacology*, 14, 375-424

Mendelson, J.H., & Mello, N.K. (1996). Management of cocaine abuse and dependence. *New England Journal of Medicine*, 334, 965-972

Merriam, A.E., Medalia, A., & Levine, B. (1988). Partial complex status epilepticus associated with cocaine abuse. *Biological Psychiatry*, 23, 515-518

Meyer, R.E. (1992). New pharmacotherapies for cocaine dependence … revisited. *Archives of General Psychiatry*, 49, 900-904

Modesto-Lowe, V., & Kranzler, H.R. (1999). Using cue reactivity to evaluate medication for treatment of cocaine dependence: a critical review. *Addiction*, 94, 1639-1651

Moeller, F.G., Dougherty, D.M., Barratt, E.S., Schmitz, J.M., Swann, A.C., & Grabowski, J. (2001). The impact of impulsivity on cocaine use and retention in treatment. *Journal of Substance Abuse Treatment*, 21, 193-198

Montoya, I.D., Gorelick, D.A., Preston, K.L., Schroeder, J.R., Umbricht, A., Cheskin, L.J., Lange, W.R., Contoreggi, C., Johnson, R.E., & Fudala, P.J. (2004). Randomized trial of buprenorphine for treatment of concurrent opiate and cocaine dependence. *Clinical Pharmacology & Therapeutics*, 75, 34-48

Muntaner, C., Kumor, K.M., Nagoshi, C., & Jaffe, J.H. (1991). Effects of nifedipine pre-treatment on subjective and cardiovascular responses to intravenous cocaine in humans. *Psychopharmacology*, 105, 37-41

Myrick, H., & Brady, K.T. (2003). The use of divalproex in the treatment of affective disorders. *Psychopharmacology Bulletin*, 37 (Suppl. 2), 89-97

Myrick, H., Henderson, S., Brady, K.T., & Malcolm, R. (2001). Gabapentin in the treatment of cocaine dependence: a case series. *Journal of Clinical Psychiatry*, 62, 19-23

Myrick, H., Henderson, S., Brady, K.T., & Measom, M. (2001). Divalproex in the treatment of cocaine dependence. *Journal of Psychoactive Drugs*, 33, 283-287

Nann-Vernotica, E., Donny, E.C., Bigelow, G.E., & Walsh, S.L. (2001). Repeated administration of the D1/5 antagonist ecopipam fails to attenuate the subjective effects of cocaine. *Psychopharmacology*, 155, 338-347

Nathan, K.I, Bresnick, W.H., & Batki, S.L. (1998). Cocaine abuse and dependence. Approaches to management. *CNS Drugs*, 10, 43-59

Nunes EV, & Levin FR. (2004). Treatment of depression in patients with alcohol or other drug dependence: a meta-analysis. *JAMA*, 291,1887-1896

O'Brien, C., Childress, A.R., McLellan, A.T., & Ehrman, R. (1992). Classical conditioning in drug-dependent humans. *Annals of the New York Academy of Sciences*, 654, 400-415

O'Hearn, E., & Molliver, M.E. (1993). Degeneration of Purkinje cells in parasaggital zones of the cerebellar vermis after treatment with ibogaine or harmaline. *Neuroscience*, 55, 303-310

Panikkar, G.P. (1999). Cocaine addiction: neurobiology and related current research in pharmacotherapy. *Substance Abuse*, 20, 149-166

Patkar, A.A., Murray, H.W., Mannelli, P., Gottheil, E., Weinstein, S.P., & Vergare, M.J. (2004). Pre-treatment measures of impulsivity, aggression and sensation seeking are associated with treatment outcome for African-American cocaine-dependent patients. *Journal of Addictive Diseases*, 23, 109-122

Patrakis, I.L., Carroll, K.M., Nich, C., Gordon, L.T., McCance-Katz, E.F., Frankforter, T., & Rousanville, B.J. (2000). Disulfiram treatment for cocaine dependence in methadone-maintained opioid addicts. *Addiction*, 95, 219-228

Pilla, M., Hutcheson, D.M., Adib-Samil, P., Potton, E., & Everitt, B.J. (2001). Seeking responses for cocaine, heroin and natural reinforcers are differentially modulated by dopamine D3 receptors. *Society for Neuroscience*, Abstract 647.16

Pilla, M., Parachon, S., Sautel, F., Garrido, F., Mann, A., Wermuth, C.G., Schwartz, J., Everitt, B.J., & Sokoloff, P. (1999). Selective inhibition of cocaine-seeking behaviour by a partial dopamine D3 receptor agonist. *Nature*, 400, 371-375

Platt, D.M., Rowlett, J.K, & Spealman, R.D. (2001). Discriminative stimulus effects of intravenous heroin and its mechanisms in rhesus monkey: opioid and dopaminergic mechanisms. *Journal of Pharmacology & Experimental Therapeutics*, 299, 760-767

Platt. D.M., Rowlett, J.K, & Spealman, R.D. (2002). Behavioral effects of cocaine and dopaminergic strategies for preclinical medication development. *Psychopharmacology*, 163, 265-282

Pontieri, F.E., Tanda, G., & Di Chiara, G. (1995). Intravenous cocaine, morphine and amphetamine preferentially increase extracellular dopamine in the "shell" as compared with the "core" of the rat nucleus accumbens. *Proc. Natl. Acad. Sci. USA*, 92, 12304-12308

Popik, P., Layer, R.T., & Skolnick, P. (1996). 100 years of ibogaine: neurochemical and pharmacological actions of a putative anti-addictive drug. *Pharmacological Reviews,* 53, 791-798

Popik, P., & Skolnick, P. (1996). The NMDA antagonist memantine blocks the expression and maintenance of morphine dependence. *Pharmacology, Biochemistry & Behavior*, 53, 791-798

Preti, A. (2000a). Vanoxerine. *Current Opinion in Investigational Drugs*, 1, 241-251

Preti, A. (2000b). BP-897. current *Current Opinion in Investigational Drugs*, 1, 110-115

Preti, A. (2001). CRF antagonist. *Current Opinion in Investigational Drugs*, 2, 274-279

Prinzleve, M., Haasen, C., Zurhold, H., Matali, J.L., Bruguera, E., Gerevich, J., Bacskai, E., Ryder, N., Butler, S., Manning, V., Gossop, M., Pezous, A.M., Verster, A., Camposeragna, A., Andersson, P., Olsson, B., Primorac, A., Fischer, G., Guttinger, F.,

Rehm, J., & Krausz, M. (2004). Cocaine use in Europe – a multi-centre study: patterns of use in different groups. *European Addiction Research*, 10, 147-155

Ritz, M.C., Cone, E.J., & Kuhar, M.J. (1990). Cocaine inhibition of ligand binding at dopamine, norepinephrine and serotonin transporters: a structure-activity study. *Life Sciences*, 46, 635-645

Ritz, M.C., Lamb, R.J., Goldberg, S.R., & Kuhar, M.J. (1987). Cocaine receptors on dopamine transporters are related to self-administration of cocaine. *Science*, 237, 1219-1223

Roberts, D.C.S., Andrews, M.M., & Vickers, G.J. (1996). Baclofen attenuates the reinforcing effects of cocaine in rats. *Neuropsychopharmacology*, 15, 417-423

Roberts, D.C.S., Corcoran, M.E., & Fibiger, H.C. (1977). On the role of ascending catecholaminergic systems in intravenous self-administration of cocaine. *Pharmacology, Biochemistry & Behavior*, 6, 615-620

Robinson, T.E., & Berridge, K.C. (1993). The neural basis of drug craving: an incentive-sensitization theory of addiction. *Brain Research & Brain Research Reviews*, 18, 247-291

Rocha, B.A., Fumagalli, F., Gainetdinov, R.R., Jones, S.R., Ator, R., Giros, B., Miller, G.W., & Caron, M.G. (1998). Cocaine self-administration in dopamine-transporter knokout mice. *Nature Neuroscience*, 1, 132-137

Rogers, R.D., & Robbins, T.W. (2001). Investigating the neurocognitive deficits associated with chronic drug misuse. *Current Opinion in Neurobiology*, 11, 250-257

Roozen, H.G., Boulogne, J.J., van Tulder, M.W., van den Brink, W., De Jong, C.A., & Kerkhof, A.J. (2004). A systematic review of the effectiveness of the community reinforcement approach in alcohol, cocaine and opioid addiction. *Drug & Alcohol Dependence*, 74, 1-13

Rothman, R.B., Mele, A., Reid, A.A., Akunne, H.C., Greig, N., Thurkauf, A., de Costa, B.R., Rice, K.C., & Pert, A. (1991). GBR 12909 antagonizes the ability of cocaine to elevate extracellular levels of dopamine. *Pharmacology, Biochemistry & Behavior*, 40, 387-397

Sarnyai, Z. (1998). Neurobiology of stress and cocaine addiction. Studies on corticotropin-releasing factor in rats, monkeys, and humans. *Annals of the New York Academy of Sciences*, 851, 371-387

Sarnyai, Z., Shaham, Y., & Heinrichs, S.C. (2001). The role of corticotropin-releasing factor in drug addiction. *Pharmacological Reviews*, 53, 209-243

Schenk, S. (2002). Effects of GBR 12909, WIN 35,428 and indatraline on cocaine self-administration and cocaine seeking in rats. *Psychopharmacology*, 160, 263-270

Schmitz, J., Stotts, A., Sayre, S., DeLaune, K., & Grabowski, J. (2004). Treatment of Cocaine-Alcohol Dependence with Naltrexone and Relapse Prevention Therapy. *American Journal of Addiction*, 13, 333-341

Schmitz, J.M., Stotts, A.L., Rhoades, H.M., & Grabowski, J. (2001), Naltrexone and relapse prevention treatment for cocaine-dependent patients. *Addictive Behaviors*, 26,167-180

Schneider Institute for Health Policy. Brandeis University. (2001). *Substance abuse: The Nation's Number One Health Problem*. Princeton, NJ: Robert Wood Johnson Foundation

Schultz, W., Dayan, P., & Montague, P.R. (1997). A neural substrate of prediction and reward. *Science*, 275, 1593-1599

Shoptaw, S., Kintaudi, P.C., Charuvastra, C., & Ling, W. (2002). A screening trial of amantidine as a medication for cocaine dependence. *Drug & Alcohol Dependence*, 66, 217-224

Shoptaw, S., Yang, X., Rotheram-Fuller, E.J., Hsieh, Y.C., Kintaudi, P.C., Charuvastra, V.C., & Ling, W. (2003). Randomized placebo-controlled trial of baclofen for cocaine dependence: preliminary effects for individuals with chronic patterns of cocaine use. *Journal of Clinical Psychiatry*, 64, 1440-1148

Silverstone, PH, Attenburrow, MJ, & Robson, P. (1992). The calcium channel antagonist nifedipine causes confusion when used to treat opiate withdrawal in morphine-dependent patients. *International Clinical Psychopharmacology*, 7, 87-90

Soares, B.G.O., Lima, M.S., & Farrell, M. (2004). Psychosocial treatments for psychostimulants dependence. *Cochrane Database of Systematic Reviews*. 4, [under process]

Stafford, D., Rice, K.C., Lewis, D.B., & Glowa, J.R. (2000), Response requirements and unit dose modify the effects of GBR 12909 on cocaine-maintained behavior. *Experimental & Clininical Psychopharmacology, 8*, 539-548

Shearer, J., & Gowing, L. (2004). Pharmacotherapies for problematic psychostimulant use: a review of current research. *Drug & Alcohol Reviews*, 23, 203-211

Shimada, S., Kitayama, S., Lin, C.L., Patel, A., Nanthakumar, E., Gregor, P., Kuhar, M., & Uhl, G. (1991). Cloning and expression of a cocaine-sensitive dopamine transporter complementary DNA. *Science*, 254, 576-577

Siegel, S. (1999). Drug anticipation and drug addiction. *Addiction*, 94, 1113-1124

Sinha, R., Talih, M., Malison, R., Cooney, N., Anderson, G.M., & Kreek, M.J. (2003). Hypothalamic-pituitary-adrenal axis and sympatho-adreno-medullary responses during stress-induced and drug cue-induced cocaine craving states. *Psychopharmacology*, 170, 62-72

Smelson, D.A., Losonczy, M.F., Davis, C.W., Kaune, M., Williams, J., & Ziedonis, D. (2002). Risperidone decreases craving and relapses in individuals with schizophrenia and cocaine dependence. *Canadian Journal of Psychiatry*, 47, 671-675

Soares, B.G., Lima, M.S., Reisser, A.A., & Farrell, M. (2003). Dopamine agonists for cocaine dependence. *Cochrane Database of Systematic Reviews*, 2, CD003352

Sofuoglu, M., Singha, A., Kosten, T.R., McCance-Katz, F.E., Petrakis, I., & Oliveto, A. (2003). Effects of naltrexone and isradipine, alone or in combination, on cocaine responses in humans. *Pharmacology, Biochemistry, & Behavior*, 75, 801-808

Stein, M.D. (1999). Medical consequences of substance abuse. *Psychiatric Clinics of North America*, 22, 351-370

Stratakis, C.A., & Chrousos, G.P. (1995). Neuroendocrinology and pathophysiology of the stress system. *Annals of the New York Academy of Sciences*, 771, 1-18

Uhl, G.R., Lin, Z., Metzger, T., & Dar, D.E. (1998). Dopamine transporter mutations, small molecules, and approaches to cocaine antagonist/dopamine transport disinhibitor development. *Methods in Enzymology*, 296, 456-465

Vetulani, J. (2001). Drug addiction. Part III. Pharmacotherapy of addiction. *Polish Journal of Pharmacology*, 53, 415-434

Villemagne, V.L., Rothman, R.B., Yokoi, F., Rice, K.C., Matecka, D., Dannals, R.F., & Wong, D.F. (1999). Doses of GBR 12909 that suppress cocaine self-administration in non-human primates substantially occupy dopamine transporters as measured by (11C)WIN 35428 PET scans. *Synapse*, 32:,44-50

Volkow, N.D., Wang, G.J., Fowler, J.S., Logan, J., Gatley, S.J., Wong, C., Hitzemann, R., & Pappas, N.R. (1999). Reinforcing effects of psychostimulants in humans are associated with increases in brain dopamine and occupancy of D2 receptors. *Journal of Pharmacology & Experimental Therapeutics,* 291, 409-415

Walsh, S.L., Sullivan, J.T., Preston, K.L., Garner, J.E., & Bigelow, G.E. (1996). Effects of naltrexone on response to intravenous cocaine, hydromorphone and their combination in humans. *Journal of Pharmacology & Experimental Therapeutics*, 279, 524-538

Weiss, R.D., Griffin, M.L., Gallop, R., Onken, L.S., Gastfriend, D.R., Daley, D., Crits-Christoph, P., Bishop, S., & Barber, J.P. (2000). Self-help group attendance and participation among cocaine dependent patients. *Drug & Alcohol Dependence*, 60, 169-177

Wells, E.A., Peterson, P.L., Gainey, R.R., Hawkins, J.D., & Catalano, R.F. (1994). Outpatient treatment for cocaine abuse: a controlled comparison of relapse prevention and twelve-step approaches. *American Journal of Drug and Alcohol Abuse*, 20, 1-17

Wise, R.A., & Bozarth, M.A. (1987). A psychomotor stimulant theory of addiction. *Psychological Reviews*, 94, 469-492

Wong, D.F., Cantilena, L., Elkashef, A., Yokoi, F., Dogan, S., Stephane, M., Gjedde, A., Rothman, R.B., Mojsiak, J., & Vocci, F. (1999). In vivo human dopamine transporter occupancy of a potential cocaine treatment agent, GBR 12909. *Society for Neuroscience*, Abstract 522.7

Woolverton, W.L., & Johnson, K.M. (1992). Neurobiology of cocaine abuse. *Trends in Pharmacological Sciences*, 13, 193-200

World Health Organization. (2004). Ethical issues in neuroscience research on substance dependence treatment and prevention. In: World Health Organization, *Neuroscience of psychoactive substance use and dependence.* (pp. 209-240). Geneve: World Health Organization

Yoshida, M., Yokoo, H., Tanaka, T., Emoto, H., & Tanaka, M. (1994). Opposite changes in the mesolimbic dopamine metabolism in the nerve terminal and cell body sites induced by locally infused baclofen in the rat. *Brain Research*, 636, 111-114

Xie, W., Altimirano, C.V., Bartels, C.F., Speirs, R.J., Cashman, J.R., & Lockridge, O. (1999). An improved cocaine hydrolase: The A328Y mutant of human butyrylcholinesterase is 4-fold more efficient. *Molecular Pharmacology*, 55, 83-91

Zhang, Y., Schlussman, S.D., Ho, A., & Kreek, M.J. (2003). Effect of chronic 'binge cocaine' on basal levels and cocaine-induced increases of dopamine in the caudate putamen and nucleus accumbens of C57BL/6J and 129/J mice. *Synapse*, 50, 191-199

Zobel, A.W., Nickel, T., Kunzel, H.E., Ackl, N., Sonntag, A., Ising, M., & Holsboer, F. (2000). Effects of the high-affinity corticotropin-releasing hormone receptor 1 antagonist R121919 in major depression: the first 20 patients treated. *Journal of Psychiatric Research*, 34, 171-181

In: Substance Abuse, Assessment and Addiction
Editors: Kristina A. Murati and Allison G. Fischer

ISBN: 978-1-61122-931-8
© 2011 Nova Science Publishers, Inc.

*Chapter 9*

# INCORPORATION OF REGULARISED URINE-BASED HIV TESTING IN METHADONE TREATMENT PROGRAMME FOR ENHANCING THE EFFECTIVENESS OF HIV PREVENTION IN DRUG USERS

## *S. S. Lee, K. C. K. Lee, W. Y. Wan and K. H. Wong**

Centre for Health Protection, Department of Health, Hong Kon

## ABSTRACT

Methadone maintenance is an effective means of preventing HIV transmission in drug users, through the reduction of injection and needle-sharing. In Hong Kong, a low threshold approach has been adopted in the introduction of methadone maintenance since over 30 years ago. The methadone treatment programme (MTP) now reaches about 9000 drug users regularly. HIV prevalence has remained low at below 1%.

The rising HIV prevalence in neighbouring cities calls for an enhancement of the MTP in Hong Kong. The provision of HAART (highly active antiretroviral therapy) in conjunction with counseling in a specialized care setting could potentially reduce the chance of virus dissemination from known positive drug users. Early diagnosis of HIV infection and their prompt referral to care are however the pre-requisites. A new programme was introduced to offer urine-based HIV testing on an opt-out basis. Over a three-month pilot in 2003, 74.7% (1834) of 2456 methadone users were tested. During the full-year programme in 2004, attendees of 20 methadone clinics were tested in four clusters. A total of 8905 tests were provided in the clinics, amounting to 90% of the

---

* Part of the contents have contributed to the dissertation of Dr. W. Y. Wan for the joint fellowship examination of the Hong Kong College of Community Medicine and the Faculty of Public Health of the Royal Colleges of Physicians of the United Kingdom in 2004. Some early data have also been presented at the XV International AIDS Conference on 11-16 July 2004 in Bangkok, Thailand.

Correspondence: Dr KH Wong. Special Preventive Programme Office, 5/F Yaumatei Jockey Club Clinic, 145 Battery Street, Yaumatei, Kowloon, Hong Kong; Email: khwong@dhspp.net; Tel: (852) 27804390; Fax: (852) 27808622.

active caseload during the testing periods. The coverage varied in different clinics, ranging from 71.9% to 100%. Large clinics with higher turnover were liable to have a lower coverage. The general acceptance of drug users to the new testing programme was high. Lack of motivation was determined to be the single most important reason for refusing the test.

The testing nevertheless has provided a new opportunity for arousing AIDS awareness in methadone users, including those who chose to opt out. Surveillance was enhanced: HIV prevalence was 0.5% in the 2003 pilot and 0.2% during the 2004 full-year programme. The difference might have arisen from the self-exclusion of known positive individuals in the second year. A total of 32 drug users, 24 of which newly diagnosed, were tested positive in the urine-based HIV testing programme. The provision of clinical management, and the linkage with public health interventions are additional benefits brought about by the programme, which may also lead to better control of the epidemic.

In conclusion, the incorporation of urine-based HIV testing in a conventional methadone clinic network is feasible. The testing would, in the next phase, be regularized by repeating in yearly cycles. The wide coverage, adoption of a routine but voluntary testing strategy, and the integration of clinical and public health intervention, are lessons learned from the programme. The maintenance of a low HIV prevalence in drug users, amidst potential changes in HIV epidemiology and pattern of drug use, remains a challenge for Hong Kong.

# INTRODUCTION

Methadone maintenance was introduced in 1964 as a research project by Dr Vincent Dole and Dr Marie Nyswander in New York City.[1] The prescription of methadone, a long-acting heroin agonist, has been shown to relieve craving, suppress withdrawal syndrome, and result in tolerance to its narcotic effects. Methadone maintenance has proven itself to be an effective treatment for narcotic addiction, a chronic medical illness that carries considerable adverse consequences in public health and to the society. The treatment was, however, often seen as just one of the many modalities of drug rehabilitation. Stigma and misconceptions had made it almost impossible to expand methadone treatment programme (MTP) centering on maintenance. Since the 1980s, the growth of the HIV epidemic has provided a new platform for revitalizing methadone maintenance, though not without difficulties. Around the world, HIV epidemic has been fuelled by the practice of needle-sharing in drug-taking communities. In a survey, an HIV prevalence of over 20% was reported in 25 developing and transitional countries.[2] Reviews of studies provided evidence for MTP to reduce HIV risk behaviours, leading to the prevention of HIV infection.[3][4] MTP is now an integral component of a harm reduction strategy recommended for achieving effective control of HIV. The challenge rests with how the principle can be turned into sustainable programme.

In Hong Kong [Table 1], MTP was introduced to the Government in 1972, first as a pilot project and subsequently expanded in 1975 to become an extensive network of methadone clinics serving thousands of drug users.[5] Two phases can be distinguished in describing the MTP in Hong Kong. The first phase began with the launching of MTP from the mid-seventies to the mid-eighties, before the territory's HIV epidemic took shape. Methadone maintenance was provided to heroin users who came to the doorstep of methadone clinics in the neighbourhood, at a nominal fee. This low threshold approach did ensure that effective treatment was offered without any waiting list.[6] Utilisation of other drug rehabilitation services was not jeopardised, while crime rate fell precipitously in the ensuing years. In the second phase spanning through the nineties to the turn of the century, diagnosis of the first cases of HIV infections have catalysed the development of surveillance and client education in the same venues. [Table 2] This new set of activities was introduced by the Department of Health's AIDS programme. The reduction of risk-taking behaviours in methadone users has enabled Hong Kong to attain a low HIV prevalence of below 0.5% in drug users over the years. [7][8]

### Table 1. Hong Kong Overview

| Area[1] | 1100 Km[2] | |
|---|---|---|
| Population[1] (mid-year 2004) | 6,841,900 | population density of 6300 persons / Km[2] |
| Health indices[2] (2003) | Life expectation at birth | 78.6(M); 84.3 (F) |
| | Crude birth rate (per1000 population) | 7.0 |
| | Crude death rate (per 1000 population) | 5.4 |
| | Leading causes of death (top three) | Malignant neoplasm Heart diseases Cerebrovascular diseases |
| Per capita GDP at current market prices in 2003[1] | HK$179,333 (US$1=HJK$7.8) | |
| Pattern of drug use in 2003[3] | No. of reported drug users | 15605 |
| | No. of reported heroin users | 10330 |
| | Proportion of heroin users in reported drug users | 74.2% |
| | Proportion of male heroin users | 87.7% |
| | Proportion of injectors in heroin users | 54.9% |
| | Average daily expenditure on heroin | HK$250 (US$1=HK$7.8) |

[1]Hong Kong statistics. Hong Kong SAR Government Census and Statistics Department. www.info.gov.hk/censtatd/eng/hkstat/index.html accessed on 1 February 2005

[2]Vital statistics. Hong Kong SAR Government Department of Health. www.info.gov.hk/dh/useful/index.htm accessed on 1 February 2005

[3]Narcotics Division. Central registry of drug abuse 53rd report. Hong Kong: Government Logistics Department, 2004.

The MTP in Hong Kong has evolved to build a unique model characterized by the humanistic approach in the protection of public health on a population scale. The strategy for responding to two medical problems – narcotics addiction and HIV infection – has become one. Knowingly the programme itself is not perfect. There are gaps in the systematization of MTP on one hand, and the need to face new challenges on the other. Notably since the nineties, HIV rates in drug users in South East Asia [2] and Mainland China have been escalating.[9] While the contribution of MTP in the prevention of HIV infection is now well substantiated, its role in the control of HIV spread and the treatment of HIV infected drug users remains to be established. In order to maintain a low HIV prevalence, it's desirable to introduce clinic-based HIV intervention programme, a strategy that has been proposed in other low-prevalence health authorities.[10] A pre-requisite of such programme is to identify as many as possible HIV infected individuals in the community. This paper presents the programmatic and supoorting research efforts in the development of a urine-based HIV testing mechanism at Hong Kong's network of methadone clinics. This initiative tests the hypothesis of integrating clinical and public health strategies by expanding access of drug users to HIV testing on an opt-out basis.

**Table 2. Activities Introduced at Methadone Clinics between 1990 and 2000**

| surveillance | Unlinked anonymous HIV screening using urine samples collected at methadone clinics |
|---|---|
| HIV diagnosis | Voluntary HIV testing for drug users with risk behaviours |
| | Referral to AIDS counselling clinics for HIV testing |
| Education and training | IEC on HIV and drug users Posters, leaflets, videos and broadcasts on HIV and drug use |
| | Condom distribution |
| | Regular training workshops for methadone clinic staff on HIV and drug use |

## DEVELOPMENT OF A URINE-BASED HIV TESTING PROGRAMME FOR METHADONE USERS

The objectives of a urine-based HIV testing programme for drug users attending methadone clinics are fourfolds, to: (a) promote early HIV detection in infected drug users; (b) enhance surveillance; (c) provide information on HIV/AIDS and drug use; and (d) link HIV detection with treatment services for facilitating the provision of care and public health intervention. To achieve these objectives, the Programme was introduced in phases. The first phase was a pilot one to test the feasibility. It was conducted in three clinics over a three-month period in 2003. The second phase comprised the first one-year programme covering all clinics. Finally, the yearly programme was rolled out as a continuous effort taking reference from experiences of the first two phases, as well as studies conducted in the course of their implementation. These studies were: (a) evaluation based on the output statistics collected in the pilot and the one-year programme; (b) a questionnaire survey conducted at the end of the pilot for examining the reasons of attendees who refused the test; and (c) a focus group interview with front-line workers, organised between the pilot and the first-year's programme. This manuscript is a report of the programme in its first and second phases, plus lessons learned in the effort to enhance access of drug users to HIV testing.

### Methadone Clinic Operations in Hong Kong

Methadone clinics are operative under the Department of Health of the Hong Kong Special Administrative Region Government. There are currently a total of 20 methadone clinics – 7 day clinics (opening between 0700h and 2200h in 5, shorter hours in remaining two) and 13 evening clinics (opening between 1800h and 2200h in all except one) [Figure 1]

All clinics are open seven days a week. All opiate dependent clients, regardless of age, gender and ethnicity are accepted. Daily attendance at the clinics is expected. Any client who has defaulted for more than 28 days are required to re-register. At each visit, a drug user takes the prescribed methadone under supervision of an Auxiliary Medical Service staff, who is a volunteer that has received training to provide the service. The clinic charges HK$1 (US$0.13) for each visit for Hong Kong residents. The simple procedure consumes about one-minute for each attendance normally. Part-time doctors and social workers provide the medical and counselling support as appropriate. In 2004, the effective registration (defined as the number of methadone users attending the service at least once in the preceding 28 days) of methadone clinics was 9325 (as of June for the year). The daily attendance was 6791.

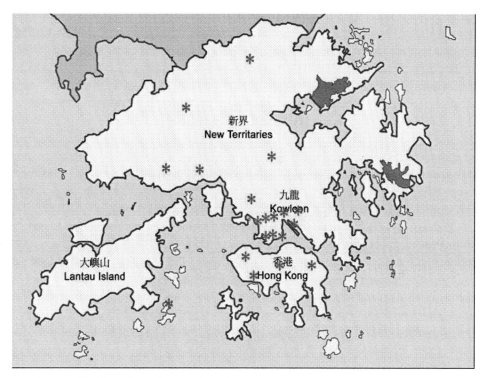

Figure 1: Geographical locations of methadone clinics in Hong Kong

Since 1990, HIV prevention and surveillance activities have been introduced through the collaboration with the Department's AIDS programme. Unlinked anonymous screening for HIV antibody was performed yearly on urine samples collected for drug monitoring. About 3000 tests were performed each year. Voluntary testing was offered to those presenting with risk behaviours, with an uptake of between 300 to 600 per year. HIV related risk behaviour monitoring was conducted. Information on HIV/AIDS (leaflets, posters, video and audio broadcast) are provided. An outreach project has been introduced since 2000 to access drug users, through the involvement of peer counsellors. The clinics work closely with the AIDS programme in the development of media campaigns that bring the message of methadone treatment to members of the public.

## Framework for the Pilot and the First-year Programme

The planning of the pilot programme and the first year programme required from the outset a thorough assessment of the pre-existing MTP. A SWOT (Strengths, Weaknesses, Opportunities, Threats) analysis was undertaken to assess the appropriateness of using methadone clinics and urine testing as the foundation of the new programme. [Table 3] Apparently, methadone clinics were considered well positioned to take on the new challenge. The following strategies were developed, with the objective of promoting HIV testing in an otherwise hard-to-reach population: (a) a provider-initiated approach was adopted, in contradistinction to the conventional client-initiated HIV testing; (b) an opt-out principle was built into the programme, while the test remained a voluntary one; (c) urine rather than blood or other body fluid was used for the test, taking advantage of the acceptance that drug users had already shown to the pre-existing urine testing for unlinked anonymous screening and drug monitoring; (d) a co-operative arrangement was recommended to bring the methadone programme in partnership with the HIV treatment service.

### Table 3. SWOT Analysis for Undertaking Voluntary Urine-Based HIV Testing in Methadone Clinics

| **A. Strengths** |
|---|
| – MTP is a well-established system with good coverage of drug users. |
| – Pre-existing unlinked anonymous screening mechanism involving urine samples collection can be utilized, obviating the need for new administrative arrangement. |
| – Acceptance of drug users would likely be good as they might have already been accustomed to urine testing for opiates and HIV. |
| **B. Weakness** |
| – Multiple lines of accountability may create difficulties in programme coordination. |
| – Clients' motivation and mobility could be low in a low threshold programme, which carries a potential risk of irregular coverage. |
| – The programme covers opiate dependent persons only without access for users of other psychotropic substances who may have practised risk behaviours. |
| **C. Opportunities** |
| – Collection of urine specimen is relatively simple compared to other body fluids, which can be managed by non-medical staff, give flexibility to future expansion of programme should need arises. |
| – Sustainability in terms of funding and administration is guaranteed for a government-run programme with policy support. |
| – HIV treatment is provided by a service within the same Department, making cross referral possible. |
| **D. Threats** |
| – Low motivators could easily default follow-up visits for HIV results or clinical consultation, making public health intervention difficult. |
| – Non Hong Kong residents can take part in the testing but are not eligible for affordable HIV treatment. |
| – The changing pattern of drug use and HIV epidemiology may become pressure points for a modification of the MTP, which may lead to changes in the mode of operation. |

A pilot programme was designed in line with these strategies. The pilot was meant to test the hypothesis that a wide coverage and high acceptance can be achieved in a busy clinic using the existing framework. Three methadone clinics (A, B and C) were chosen, each with a different profile in terms of the location, size of clienteles, and opening hours. [Table 4] In support of the pilot, IEC (information, education and communication) materials were produced, viz, video show, audio broadcast, pamphlets for distribution and posters/mini-posters for posting on walls in clinics. Information cards were produced to be given to drug users to deliver the specific messages on the programme. [Figure 2] The materials were revised after evaluation of the pilot programme. The first full-year programme was rolled out three months after completion of the pilot, allowing time for the necessary evaluation and the studies on acceptance. The 20 methadone clinics were grouped in four clusters, each for the introduction of urine-based HIV testing over a three-month period. Training workshops were conducted to explain the details of the programme to clinic staff. A set of protocols was established between the AIDS programme and the MTP.

**Table 4. Pilot Programme for Introducing Urine-Based HIV Testing, 2003.**

(a) Profile of selected methadone clinics

|  | Clinic A | Clinic B | Clinic C |
|---|---|---|---|
| Effective registration before pilot | 1678 | 420 | 175 |
| Average daily attendance before pilot | 1241 | 281 | 129 |
| Opening hours | 0700 – 2200h | 0700 – 2200h | 1800 – 2200h |
| Urine tests performed in the last round of unlinked anonymous screening | 614 | 224 | 105 |

(b) Coverage of testing

|  | Clinic A | | Clinic B | | Clinic C | | Total | |
|---|---|---|---|---|---|---|---|---|
|  | No. | (%) | No. | (%) | No. | (%) | No. | (%) |
| Total registration over three months* | 1767 |  | 512 |  | 177 |  | 2456 |  |
| Total no. of drug users who had been given an information card | 1767 | (100) | 512 | (100) | 177 | (100) | 2456 | (100) |
| Total no. tested | 1226 | (69.4) | 431 | (84.2) | 177 | (100) | 1834 | (74.7) |
| No. refusing the test | 551 | (31.2) | 78 | (15.2) | 10 | (5.6) | 639 | (26.0) |

* *Total registration over three months* is defined as the number of drug users who had used the methadone service at least once during the three months' pilot period

For each drug user, consent was obtained when one's newly admitted or on re-admission, with explanations provided on the rationale and the procedures involved in the urine testing. During the testing period, video and/or audio announcements were broadcast in the registration area. An information card was delivered to the attendee.[Figure 2] An Auxiliary Medical Service volunteer staff explained the mechanism in accordance with a standard checklist. The drug user was then given a specimen bottle and asked to produce a urine sample for HIV antibody testing, unless he/she opted out of the procedure. The sample was transported to the Public Health Laboratory Centre of the Department of Health where HIV antibody was tested by ELISA, followed by Western Blot for preliminary positive results.
a) poster.

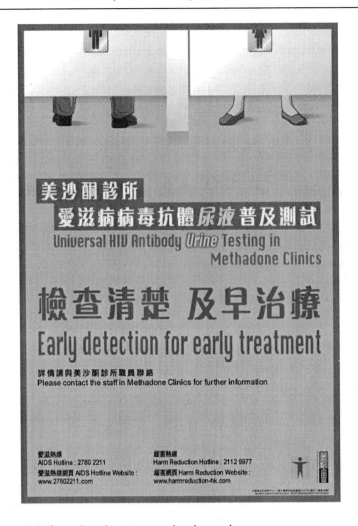

b) Information card delivered to drug user under the testing programme

### Universal HIV (Urine) Testing in Methadone Clinic – Information Card

1) Drug users have increased risk of HIV infection. Early diagnosis and treatment can improve prognosis.

2) Voluntary urine HIV test is offered to all methadone users on an annual basis. All methadone users are strongly advised to undergo testing.

3) You will be informed of the result in the subsequent visit. Referral to the Integrated Treatment Centre for treatment will be arranged for positive tested cases.

4) Result will be kept confidential.

5) If you have enquiries concerning HIV/AIDS, please call the AIDS Hotline at 27802211.

Figure 2: IEC materials developed in support of the urine-based HIV testing programme for drug users attending the methadone clinics.

The result was given to each person on his/her subsequent visit as soon as the result became available. A newly diagnosed HIV positive case was counselled by the clinic doctor or medical social worker, and then referred to the Integrated Treatment Centre, the Government's specialist HIV service where highly active antiretroviral therapy (HAART) was prescribed according to clinical indication.

## Studies on the Acceptance of Drug Users and Process Evaluation

A questionnaire survey was conducted at the end of the pilot testing period to identify reasons for refusal of the test. The survey was administered by clinic staff (Auxiliary Medical Service volunteers) over a one-week period on drug users who refused the test. A list of reasons was produced from previous formative research before piloting the programme, and were grouped in categories: (a) physical barrier precluding urine collection, or (b) inconvenience, or lack of time; (c) not wanting to know one's HIV status; (d) low perceived risk of infection; (e) not wanting to return for followup; and (f) refusal to provide an answer. Open answers were allowed.

A focus group interview was conducted involving the participation of front-line workers, with the objective of evaluating the process of the pilot programme. Interviewees were selected to represent a spectrum frontline staff in the methadone clinics. The interview was participated by 8 Auxiliary Medical Service volunteers (2 from Clinic A, 3 from each of Clinic B and C) and one medical social worker from Clinic A. The discussion framework was constructed with the incorporation of the following key questions: (a) how, if appropriate, had the programme achieved its original objectives; (b) how could the follow-up care of positive cases be improved; (c) means for increasing coverage; and (d) other comments relating to programme improvement.

## COVERAGE OF URINE-BASED HIV TESTING IN DRUG USERS

The coverage was high for this new approach of enhancing access of drug users to voluntary HIV testing. During the pilot phase, 1834 of the 2456 registered drug users over the three-month period were tested, yielding a coverage rate of 74.7%. The coverage was the lowest for the largest clinic (Clinic A: 69.4%), but higher for the smaller two clinics – Clinic B (84.2%) and Clinic C (100%). [Table IV] The situation was similar when the full one-year programme was in operation. The coverage was higher at an average of 90%, with a range from 71.9% to 100% across the twenty clinics. The programme resulted in the performance of 8812 tests. This is equivalent to an overall coverage of 90% (no. of tests delivered at the clinic divided by summation of attendance of 20 clinics over the respective three-month testing period). Table 5 shows the number of tests, coverage and results of the full-year programme.

While the coverage rate was in general high, it did vary from one clinic to another. It's noted that larger clinic, for example, those looking after 500 or more clients regularly, were more liable to have a lower coverage of below 90%. The turnover rate was also implicated. Numerically, turnover is defined as the annual sum of new admission, re-admission and terminations (those who drop out, have been absent for 28 days consecutively, died or opted to joined other rehabilitation programmes). An index was created by the ratio of turnover to the active registration as of the end of the year. A low coverage rate was associated with both a bigger turnover number ($p=0.001$) and higher turnover index ($p=0.648$), though the latter did not reach statistical significance. Similarly a lower registration number per opening hour was associated with a better coverage ($p<0.05$). Apparently the higher client number and the intensive turnover made it impossible to access all persons for HIV tests over a three-month period. Another factor related to coverage was the opening hours. Clinics which opened in the mornings (at 7am) were convenient to those who dropped in before heading for work (statistically not significant). These were also the same places where coverage was lower, as clients were often in a hurry. Interestingly, the number of hours of opening alone did not seem to bear any relationship with coverage. [Table VI]

### Table 5. Results of the Full-Year Programme, 2004.

|  | Total registration | No. tested for HIV antibody[¶] | No. opt out | Coverage (%) | No. positive |
|---|---|---|---|---|---|
| Clinic 1 | 41 | 41 | 0 | 100 | 0 |
| Clinic 2 | 174 | 157 | 17 | 90.2 | 0 |
| Clinic 3 | 190 | 178 | 12 | 93.7 | 1 |
| Clinic 4 | 488 | 468 | 20 | 95.9 | 1 |
| Clinic 5[*] | 307 | 273 | 34 | 88.9 | 0 |
| Clinic 6[*] | 1042 | 886 | 156 | 85.0 | 2 |
| Clinic 7 | 1159 | 1062 | 97 | 91.6 | 3 |
| Clinic 8 | 179 | 179 | 0 | 100 | 0 |
| Clinic 9 | 282 | 279 | 3 | 98.9 | 0 |
| Clinic 10[*] | 570 | 410 | 160 | 71.9 | 1 |
| Clinic 11 | 405 | 397 | 8 | 98.0 | 6 |
| Clinic 12[*#] | 1782 | 1546 | 236 | 86.8 | 5 |
| Clinic 13 | 274 | 273 | 1 | 99.6 | 0 |
| Clinic 14 | 157 | 151 | 6 | 96.2 | 0 |
| Clinic 15[*] | 246 | 211 | 35 | 85.8 | 1 |
| Clinic 16[#] | 412 | 407 | 5 | 98.8 | 0 |
| Clinic 17[*] | 1003 | 900 | 103 | 89.7 | 0 |
| Clinic 18[#] | 161 | 161 | 0 | 100 | 0 |
| Clinic 19[*] | 672 | 577 | 95 | 85.9 | 0 |
| Clinic 20 | 355 | 349 | 6 | 98.3 | 1 |
| Total | 9899 | 8905 | 994 | - - | 21 |

[¶] The number tested as reflected in the clinic statistics (used here for defining coverage) differs from that of the actual number of tests performed in the laboratory because of the difference in timeframe.

[*] clinics with less than 90% coverage.

[#] same clinics as the pilot phase.

**Table 6. Factor Associated with Coverage of Urine-Based
HIV Testing in Methadone Clinics**

| | | Coverage at or above 90% | Coverage below 90% | p | |
|---|---|---|---|---|---|
| (a) attendance in the 3-month testing period | | | | | |
| | ≥500 | 0 | 6 | 0.001 | * |
| | <500 | 12 | 12 | | |
| (b) annual turn over | | | | | |
| | ≥1000 | 0 | 6 | 0.001 | * |
| | <1000 | 12 | 2 | | |
| (c) turnover index | | | | | |
| | ≥1.5 | 8 | 4 | 0.648 | |
| | <1.5 | 4 | 4 | | |
| (d) inclusion of morning sessions | | | | | |
| | Yes | 2 | 4 | 0.161 | |
| | no | 10 | 4 | | |
| (e) night clinics | | | | | |
| | Yes | 9 | 3 | 0.167 | |
| | no | 3 | 5 | | |
| (f) registration/opening hour | | | | | |
| | ≥50 | 5 | 8 | 0.015 | * |
| | <50 | 7 | 0 | | |
| (g) median age of attendees | | | | | |
| | ≥40 | 7 | 1 | 0.07 | |
| | <40 | 5 | 7 | | |

* statistically significant by two tail Fischer Exact test.

a: turn over is the annual summation of new admissions, readmissions and terminations (patient who have dropped out or are absent for consecutive 28 days, died, or have joined other rehabilitation programmes).

b: effective registration as of the end of December 2004.

c: morning sessions were those beginning at 7am.

d: night clinics opened from 6pm to 10 pm only.

e: median age was obtained from a separate survey on risk behaviours conducted on all new or readmitted cases in a one month period in 2003.

While the urine-based testing system was designed to be implemented in three-month cycles, the programme has provided additional opportunities for HIV tests to be performed outside the standard testing period. After the three-month pilot in 2003, an additional 311 cases were tested, a 17% increase on top of the original number tested. For the full-year programme of 2004, 409 (4.6%) more drug users were tested after the three-month periods. It could be argued that three months was too short to be effective, especially in the case of busy clinics, for the HIV test to be offered to each and every person during the specified testing period. However, an extension of the time period for testing may make it difficult for focused promotion to be made to methadone users. Another alternative would be to offer testing the whole year round. Such practice may suffer from a lack of focus, and the consumption of additional resources in manpower, transportation of specimens, and communication between various parties.

## ACCEPTANCE OF HIV TESTING

While introduced as a provider-initiated routine system, drug users attending the methadone clinics were free to opt out of the test. To evaluate the acceptance of the new programme, the opt-out rate was determined. It was 26% during the pilot phase [table IV]. During the full-programme, the opt-out rate ranged from 0% to 28%. One hundred and seventy-nine drug users participated in the questionnaire survey to study the reasons for refusing the test. A majority of the respondents were male (90.5%). The commonest reason was perceived inconvenience, or the lack of time (68%), followed by physical barrier for collecting urine samples (5%). Examples of physical barriers included: old age, immobility, or being wheel-chair bound. A minority (1.7%) did not "want to know" his/her HIV status. A quarter (24%) refused to offer an answer.

Results of the questionnaire could be supplemented by the focus group interview. Staff were of the opinion that the main reason for refusal was the lack of motivation. Many drug users were in a hurry to leave, and were apparently uninterested in offering an answer to the question. Staff attributed the phenomenon to the lack of motivation. This lack of motivation might be an integral part of the addiction behaviour. Informants were convinced however that the programme had encouraged HIV testing in drug users who would otherwise not be accessing the procedure. The programme had also provided a new opportunity for conveying health messages to drug users. Staff were generally satisfied with the IEC materials, which had achieved in the delivery of clear messages to clients. On grading (1 to 10) satisfaction with IECs, all provided the grades of 6 to 10 for individual items.

## ENHANCEMENT OF HIV SURVEILLANCE

The determination of HIV prevalence in risk-taking communities is one important means of assessing population risk, especially for low prevalence populations like Hong Kong. Before introduction of the new programme, HIV surveillance in drug users was undertaken by two mechanisms: voluntary testing and unlinked anonymous screening. Voluntary testing has been offered to drug users joining residential rehabilitation services and methadone clinics. The numbers were however too small for meaningful analysis to be made (148 from methadone clinics in the year 2003). Unlinked anonymous screening of methadone clinic clients was performed yearly since 1992, using urine collected for drug monitoring. Between 2000 and 4000 samples were tested each round. The yearly prevalence had ranged between 0% to 0.27%. In 2003, it was 0.257% (95% CI: 0.083 – 0.599). [7] While this has remained a robust system, there were two main problems: firstly, there were no means of establishing the route of transmission for individual case as the results cannot be linked to the tested subjects; secondly, samples were collected from clinics in cycles. Each cycle covering all clinics would take about two years. Duplication is possible and comparability across years is difficult.

Unlinked anonymous screening was also undertaken in other drug rehabilitation services from 1998, but the mechanism was less consistent.

The voluntary urine-based HIV testing programme offered a new opportunity for determining HIV prevalence in drug users, using again the methadone clinics as the base for sample collection. During the pilot phase, the prevalence was 0.49% (9/1834, 95% CI: 0.224% to 0.932%). For the full year programme, 18 of the 8812 samples were positive, giving a figure of 0.2% (95% CI: 0.121% – 0.323%). The prevalence was comparable to the 0.257% from unlinked anonymous screening in 2003. The new figure is more robust in that a higher sample size, double that for unlinked anonymous screening, has become available. A systematic approach of going over all clinics in the course of one year has also enabled more meaningful interpretation to be made.

The new system is, of course, not without flaws in surveillance terms. The higher number of samples now means that up to 80% of heroin users known to the register have been tested. It's noted however that the representativeness of the samples may not necessarily be higher than that under unlinked anonymous screening. It can be argued that higher risk individuals might have opted out, though there's no evidence that such was happening in the pilot or the first full-year programme. Another potential problem is that as a voluntary testing programme, known infected individuals may tend to opt out, especially if one had already been tested positive in the same clinic. This might not be of any importance in the pilot round. In the first full year programme in the following year, it was found that only one previously positive case (out of nine) was detected, despite the provision of urine-based testing in the same clinics in both 2003 and 2004 (Pilot Clinic A, B and C were Clinic 12, 16 and 18 in the full-year programme – Tables IV and V). When testing is organised as a yearly exercise, it's possible that known positives may regularly opt-out. The function of the system to provide prevalence data may fall, though it may continue to function effectively in the identification of new cases. This phenomenon may account for the discrepancy between prevalence in the pilot and the full year programme. It's important therefore that analysis based on surveillance results collected from multiple sources would enable a picture to be painted for better describing the HIV situation in Hong Kong.

## REALISING PREVENTION-TREATMENT CONTINUUM

The 20 methadone clinics have over the years evolved to become an extensive network of public health services for drug users. With a total number of attendance at over 2.5 millions per year [11], the introduction of urine-based HIV testing has further transformed these clinics into a natural focal point for the identification of HIV infected drug users, where clinical management and public health intervention can be offered. It would be important to determine if the new programme could effectively identify previously undiagnosed drug users.

A total of 34 positive tests were obtained by combining the results of the pilot (11 positives) and the first full-year programme (23 positives) on urine-based HIV testing at methadone clinics. Two of the 11 in the pilot and 4 of the 23 in the full-year programme were detected after the designated three-month period. After exclusion of two repeat samples, one of which was tested positive in both rounds of 2003 and 2004, and the other repeated by the patient's request, the total number of HIV infected persons was 32. A majority (22/32, 68.8%) came from two of the clinics. The characteristics of these cases are in Table 7. Eight (25%) of these had been previously diagnosed positive outside the methadone urine testing programme. The transmission routes of 18 of the 32 cases were subsequently established as injection drug use. Seven were heterosexually acquired, and the routes of transmission for the remaining seven were yet to be established. The 24 newly diagnosed cases together accounted for about 5% of the all reported cases in Hong Kong for 2003 and 2004. If injection drug use alone as the transmission route is considered, the programme has so far added 15 cases to the total of the 32 reports of HIV infected drug users (46.9%) In other words, in the absence of the programme, a significant proportion of HIV infected drug users in Hong Kong would not have been identified.

**Table 7. Characteristics of HIV Infected Drug Users Detected Through the Pilot and Full-Year Urine-Based HIV Testing Programme Introduced at the Methadone Clinics in 2003 and 2004. (n=32)**

|  |  | n | (%) |
|---|---|---|---|
| *Gender* | Male | 27 | (84.4) |
|  | Female | 5 | (15.6) |
| *Age (year)* | Median | 33.5 |  |
|  | [Range 19-51] |  |  |
| *Ethnicity* | Chinese | 29 | (90.6) |
|  | Non-Chinese | 3 | ( 9.4) |
| *First diagnosis* | Newly reported | 24 | (75) |
|  | Previously reported | 8 | (25) |
| *Subsequent clinical Referral* | Integrated Treatment Centre | 24 | (75.0) |
|  | Other clinical service | 1 | (3.1) |
|  | Left Hong Kong | 4 | (12.5) |
|  | Referral not made | 3 | (9.4) |
| Speculated route of infection | Injection drug use | 18 | (56.2) |
|  | Heterosexual contact | 7 | (21.9) |
|  | Not established | 7 | (21.9) |

Referral of positive cases to the Department of Health's HIV clinic (Integrated Treatment Centre) forms the next important step towards achieving clinical and public health goals. As of the end of the year 2004, 25 of the 32 cases (78%) detected in the programme had attended the Integrated Treatment Centre. One attended follow-up at a major hospital in the territory. As for the rest, four had left Hong Kong, one was in prison and the rest (2) refused to be referred. The clinical consultation provided an opportunity for the planning of clinical care, which included the provision of HAART when clinically indicated. Other activities that could contribute to the control of infection were: risk reduction counselling, partner counselling and referral, and the collaboration with methadone clinics to promote adherence to methadone substitution treatment. On a population scale, adherence to HAART carries the potential of a reduction of viral load, which would further minimise the chance of viral dissemination.

# LESSONS FROM COMBINING METHADONE SUBSTITUTION TREATMENT WITH ROUTINE URINE-BASED HIV TESTING PROGRAMME

Over the last thirty years, the methadone clinics in Hong Kong have gone through two phases in its development, from the provision of substitution treatment as a means of drug rehabilitation since its inception (1970s to 1980s), to the incorporation of health promotion activities on HIV prevention (1980s onwards) for methadone users. The introduction of voluntary urine-based HIV testing represents a step towards a third phase, the objective of which is to add value by specifically enhancing the capacity of methadone clinics in supporting HIV diagnosis and control. The new phase shall see the dual role of effective clinical management and public health intervention at the clinic levels. Lessons learned, as detailed in the following paragraphs, may be useful for the reference of countries contemplating strategies on addressing the rising problem of HIV infection in drug users.

First of all, wide coverage is crucial. One unique characteristic of Hong Kong's methadone system is that of its extensive coverage. Its geographical spread and access to over 60% of registered drug users imply that this in fact is the service with broadest coverage of drug users, a conventional "hard-to-reach" population. In 2003, the total number of attendance stood at 2 575 324. [11] The population-based mode ensures that methadone clinics are positioned to make public health impacts. Knowingly substitution treatment is only one of the many modalities of treatment which can be offered to narcotic dependent persons.[12] The humble existence of the network of methadone clinics had not overtaken initiatives developed by other agencies, which have managed to offer assistance to drug users through other means of support.[5] A truly multi-modality approach has therefore been in place as the backdrop. When HIV landed in Hong Kong in the mid-eighties the extensive network of methadone clinics became the first line of defence in protecting the population from the infection. Advice against needle-sharing, information on HIV/AIDS and referral for counselling and testing were swiftly provided to thousands of drug users in the following years. Unlinked anonymous screening using urine samples was piloted in the clinics, contributing to the territory's understanding of the HIV situation. When enhancement of HIV testing was contemplated at the turn of the millennium, the same clinics emerged as the location of choice, taking advantage again of its wide coverage.

The second lesson that has been learned is the feasibility of new testing strategy in a hard-to-reach population. The Joint United Nations Programme on HIV/AIDS (UNAIDS) and World Health Organisation (WHO) [13] described four types of provider-initiated testing in its latest strategies: (a) voluntary counselling and testing (VCT), (b) diagnostic testing, (c) routine testing, and (d) mandatory testing. In Hong Kong, conventional VCT was provided by methadone clinics on a referral basis, but has met with limited response. Urine-based testing was introduced as one form of routine tests which is meant to access as many drug users as possible. While methadone clinics have offered the best possible location, the challenge was for the service providers to design a feasible and sustainable programme, against the background of minimal clinic support, high number of clients and the very short contact time each person had anticipated. To solve these problems, urine samples were used, obviating the need for blood-taking in a busy clinic. Information was provided and consent obtained when one presents for drug treatment, rather than just prior to sample collection. Such protocol has enabled routine sample collection to be organised during the very short contact time between the client and the clinic. As each person is expected to come to the clinic daily, opportunities have in fact been created cumulatively for each to be made aware of the testing programme. In 2002, a media campaign was launched to arouse awareness of the public as regards the use of methadone treatment as a harm reduction approach.[14] These collateral programmes have contributed to the support of voluntary urine-based HIV testing in drug users.

Thirdly, attention to both clinical and public health effectiveness is possible in the development of an intervention programme targeting drug users. The methadone clinic provides a convenient venue where HIV infected drug users are identified, diagnosed and referred for clinical consultation and followup management. The HIV testing contributes to surveillance and control on one hand, while functions as the gateway to clinical care. The clinical setting provides an opportunity for developing treatment plan, while concurrently risk reduction counselling and partner referral/referral are offered. In Hong Kong, Integrated Treatment Centre, a specialist HIV service, also operative under the Department of Health, is working in collaboration with the methadone clinics in the clinical management of HIV infected drug users. This cooperative approach is the foundation of the strategy to strengthen HIV prevention in drug users, using methadone clinic as the setting. In a place like Hong Kong where HIV caseload is small (and most patients not being drug users), the centralisation of HIV treatment in a specialist service outside methadone clinic is a more efficient model of clinical management. In localities with a higher HIV prevalence, especially in drug users, appropriate modification would be desirable. The same strategy of integrating clinical and public health management should however hold true.

## FUTURE CHALLENGES AND THE ROBUSTNESS OF THE HONG KONG MODEL

The methadone clinics in Hong Kong have so far served the purpose of protecting the territory from an explosive spread of HIV among drug users. The key features of its success are its vast coverage, low threshold, and the value-added components of patient education, counseling, and more recently, HIV diagnosis and referral. There is the argument however that the strategy has worked in light of a low HIV prevalence from the start, and the possible separation of drug users in Hong Kong from those in the neighbouring countries. One study suggested that there's no relationship between HIV epidemics in Hong Kong and that in Mainland China.[15] It's argued that if the equilibrium is disturbed, effectiveness of the programme could be at risk. The challenges faced by Hong Kong are, therefore, the potential impacts of a rising population of HIV infected drug users, and the changing pattern of drug use.

It's clear that while the HIV prevalence in Hong Kong has remained low to this day, the actual number of HIV positive drug users has been rising steadily. In and before 1998, no more than 3 cases of HIV infected drug users were reported each year. This rose to 6 in 1999, and ten or more yearly from 2000 onwards.[7] Some of the new diagnosis in 2003 and 2004 were made through the new urine-based HIV testing programme. So far all newly reported HIV positive drug users from the urine-based HIV testing programme had acquired the infections before they arrived in Hong Kong. While we take comfort that HIV spread in drug users has not yet occurred, the rising amount of viruses in the drug-taking communities is a cause for concern. Understandably the practice of risk behaviours in drug users in Hong Kong has been low, but they did occur. In fact some 50% of drug users in Hong Kong are infected with hepatitis C virus, an indicator of parenteral transmission that has probably occurred through needles.[16] The continued practice of injection and needle-sharing in even a small but rising number of drug users carries the potential risk of rapid dissemination in the course of time. This risk is particularly high knowing that many drug users from neigbouring cities in Mainland China (where HIV rate is high) may have come to Hong Kong for reasons unrelated to drug use, for example, family reunion. It would be a test of the existing low threshold programme for its effectiveness in minimising HIV spread when the prevalence has become higher.

If more drug users from outside Hong Kong are coming to settle locally, the other challenge is to address the health-seeking behaviours of the new comers. Currently, the network of methadone clinics is familiar to local drug users. The total attendance of methadone clinics was stable at between 2.3 to 3 million per year.[17] In 2000, 2001, 2002 and 2003, the number of new cases were 838, 654, 966 and 672 respectively [12] Using the active registration at the end of the year as the denominator, new cases account for less than 10% of methadone users. It's not known if these new attendees of methadone clinics represent a big, or small, fraction of people newly addicted to narcotics. Awareness of new drug users of the methadone system is likewise unknown. As a proportion of these new drug users could have originated from high prevalence localities, their mixing with local drug users would alter the existing equilibrium and the overall pattern of risk-taking behaviours. The access of new drug users to the methadone system would be one important factor in determining the effectiveness in HIV prevention and control.

# CONCLUSION

HIV infection in injection drug users is fast becoming a public health crisis that has drawn increasing international attention. The potential for HIV spread to occur rapidly over a relatively short timeframe is a cause for concern. Harm reduction is so far one most practicable public health strategy for preventing HIV spread through needle-sharing in drug users. Our Hong Kong model has, in the past three decades, been focusing on the application of methadone substitution, one facet of harm reduction, to minimise risk behaviours. The highly versatile MTP, characterised by broad coverage and easy access, has protected Hong Kong from massive HIV epidemic in drug users. The infrastructure in place has opened up the opportunities for health promotion activities, public health surveillance and targeted prevention to be incorporated, without the need for much additional resources. The piloting of a urine-based HIV testing programme would not have been possible without the network of methadone clinics over the territory.

Our studies in 2003 and 2004 have demonstrated that routine HIV testing on an opt-out basis using urine samples is a feasible approach for enhancing HIV diagnosis and care. The principles of voluntary testing, and the integration in routine clinic practice are the foundations of the new programme. These are the same principles, alongside the strategy of maximising acceptance to testing, that we learned from the universal antenatal HIV testing programme introduced in the public service in 2001.[18] Ensuring a high coverage is, understandably, an important goal of the programme. The variation of coverage in different clinics has provided us with insights of factors which might be associated with different levels of opt-out. The knowledge could be used for revising the programme's procedure when it is rolled out as a yearly exercise in the methadone clinics.

While the HIV epidemic in the neighbourhood of Hong Kong remains fluid, the following impacts of MTP, after incorporating routine HIV testing, can be anticipated: Firstly, the identification of HIV infected drug users will open up a new page in the introduction of clinic-based public health interventions. Provided a broad coverage is ensured, specific programme addressing the needs of HIV infected drug users can be designed, with the purpose of limiting the spread of the infection from persons known to be infected with the virus. The challenge is therefore for service providers to set a realistic target on coverage, and to develop programmes for achieving the target. This coverage would in future refer not only to that of the number submitting to testing, but the regular followup of those tested positive. Secondly, surveillance capacity is enhanced by the inclusion of a higher number of drug users in the methadone network. It must be cautioned, however, that interpretation must be made in context as drug users previously tested positive would tend to opt out in future. Nevertheless, the routine yearly programme would generate new data on newly acquired infections, or new infections that come into contact with the MTP. Finally, the clinical care of people with narcotics dependence and HIV infection would require new care models to be developed, taking into consideration behavioural, social and medical factors associated with the double disease. Such models would not only serve patients in Hong Kong but could become references for other services facing the similar dual problem of HIV and drug dependence.

## ACKNOWLEDGMENTS

The authors thank all Auxiliary Medical Service workers, social workers and doctors of the methadone clinics, public health and clinical staff of Special Preventive Programme (based in Integrated Treatment Centre and Red Ribbon Centre), for their assistance in introducing the urine-based HIV testing programme and the conduction of studies described in the manuscript. We are grateful to Dr WL Lim of the Public Health Laboratory Centre for organising the laboratory tests, Dr Robert Newman for his encouragement and advice in the past 30 years on methadone treatment, and Dr PY Lam, Director of Health, for his leadership and stimulation in initiating the range of public health activities in methadone clinics and on HIV/AIDS over the years. Contribution of drug users and volunteers of Project Phoenix are acknowledged, without which, the programme would not have been possible.

## REFERENCE

[1] Joseph H, Stancliff S, Langrod J. Methadone maintenance treatment (MMT): a review of historical and clinical issues. *Mt Sinai J Med* 2000;67:347-364.

[2]     Aceijas C, Stimson GV, Hickman M & Rhodes T on behalf of the UN Reference Group on HIV/AIDS Prevention and Control among IDU in Developing and Transitional Countries. Global overview of injecting drug use and HIV infection among injecting drug users. *AIDS* 2004;18:2295-2303.

[3]     Sorensen JL, Copeland AL. [Review] Drug abuse treatment as an HIV prevention strategy: a review. *Drug Alcohol Depend* 2000; 59:17-31.

[4]     Gibson DR, Flynn NM, MaCarthy JJ. Effectiveness of methadone treatment in reducing HIV risk behaviour and HIV seroconversion among injecting drug users. *AIDS* 1999;13:1807-1818.

[5]     Newman RG. Narcotic addiction and methadone treatment in Hong Kong: lessons for the United States. *J Public Health Policy* 1985;6:526-538.

[6]     Newman RG. Hong Kong: *Building a large scale, low threshold methadone programme. In: International Harm Reduction Development. Breaking down barriers – lessons on providing HIV treatment to injection drug users.* New York: Open Society Institute, 2004.

[7]     Special Preventive Programme. *HIV Surveillance Report 2003.* Hong Kong: Department of Health, 2004.

[8]     Wong KH, Lee SS, Lim WL, Low HK. Adherence to methadone is associated with a low level of HIV-related risk behaviours in drug users. *J Substance Abuse Treatment* 2003;24:233-239.

[9]     Zhang KL, Ma SJ. Epidemiology of HIV in China. *BMJ* 2002;324:803-804.

[10]   Institute of Medicine. *No time to lose – getting more from HIV prevention.* Washington: National Academy Press, 2000.

[11]   Department of Health. *Tables on health status and health statistics 2002 and 2003.* Hong Kong: Department of Health, 2004.

[12]   Narcotics Division and Action Committee Against Narcotics . Treatment and rehabilitation – helping with recovery. In: *Hong Kong Narcotics Report* 2004. pp 77-107. Hong Kong: Hong Kong SAR Government, 2004.

[13]   UNAIDS & WHO. UNAIDS/WHO Policy Statement on HIV testing. Geneva: UNAIDS, 2004. *www.unaids.org accessed on 31 January 2005.*

[14]   Lee KCK. How to sell the harm reduction concepts? – using social marketing to promote harm reduction concepts in Hong Kong. *Asian Harm Reduction network Newsletter* 2004; May-December: 14-15.

[15]   Lim WL, Xing H, Wong KH, Wong MC, Shao YM, Ng MH, Lee SS. The lack of epidemiological link between the HIV type 1 infections in Hong Kong and mainland China. *AIDS Res Hum Retroviruses* 2004;20: 259-262.

[16]   Special Preventive Programme. *Surveillance of viral hepatitis in Hong Kong – 2003 update report.* Hong Kong: Department of Health, 2004.

[17]   Director of Health. *Annual departmental report 2000/2001.* Hong Kong: Hong Kong SAR Government Department of Health, 2002.

[18]   Lee K, Cheung WT, Kwong VSC, Wan WY, Lee SS. Access to appropriate information on HIV is important in maximising the acceptance of the antenatal HIV antibody test. *AIDS Care* 2005;17(2):141-152.

In: Substance Abuse, Assessment and Addiction
Editors: Kristina A. Murati and Allison G. Fischer

ISBN: 978-1-61122-931-8
© 2011 Nova Science Publishers, Inc.

*Chapter 10*

# THE APPLICATION OF A MATHEMATICAL MODEL FOR THE ASSESSMENT OF THE MEMORIZATION CURVE IN DRUG ADDICTS AND ALCOHOLICS

## *Charles I. Abramson[1] and Igor I. Stepanov[*2]*

[1] Department of Psychology, Oklahoma State University, Stillwater, OK, USA
[2] Department of Neuropharmacology, Institute for Experimental Medicine,
St. Petersburg, Russia

## ABSTRACT

Drug and alcohol abuse impairs memory and such impairment is assessed with tests such as the California Verbal Learning Test. These tests, however, do not analyze the shape of the memorization curve itself. We propose that analyzing the shape of the memory curve can serve as a diagnostic tool to allow a clinician to better evaluate the effects of any treatment on drug addicts and alcoholics. In this article, we provide a mathematical model for analyzing the shape of either individual or group memorization curves. The model assumes that the memorization curve is exponential in shape and employs three parameters: B2 — the velocity of memorization; B4 — an asymptotic volume of memorized material and B3 — predisposition to the next memorization before the beginning of testing. The model is tested using data from drug addicts and alcoholics and provides convincing evidence of how a mathematical treatment of the learning curve reveals new insights when nootropics (Nootropil, Baclofen, Bemethyl, and Aethimizol) and vasorelaxants (Cinnarizine and Dibazol) are used.

**Keywords:** Memory, Memorization curve, Mathematical model, Drug addicts, Alcoholics.

---

[*] Correspondence concerning this article should be addressed to Igor I. Stepanov, Department of Neuropharmacology, Institute for Experimental Medicine, 12 Acad. Pavlov Street, St. Petersburg, 197376, Russia. E-mail: igorstep@is12044.spb.edu

It is well known that drug and alcohol abuse impairs memory (D'Argembeau, Van Der Linden, Verbanck and Noel, 2006; Ersche, Clark, London, Robbins, and Sahakian, 2006; Verdejo-Garcia, Bechara, Recknor, and Perez-Garcia, 2006; Pitel, Witkowski, Vabret, Guillery-Girard, Desgranges, Eustache and Beaunieux, 2007) and such impairment has been assessed with various tests including the California Verbal Learning Test (Delis, Kramer, Kaplan, and Ober, 1987), the "Mini-Mental State" (Folstein, Folstein, and McHugh, 1975), the Wechsler Memory Scale (Wechsler, 1987), and the Cambridge Neuropsychological Test Automated Battery (Robbins, James, Owen, Sahakian, McInnes and Rabbitt, 1994). No test, however, evaluates the shape of the memorization curve itself. We find this surprising because such an evaluation can supply additional information on early memory impairment and has a number of advantages including serving as a diagnostic tool, and providing an objective and quantitative measure of recovery. The purpose of this article is to propose a new approach in the assessment of memory based upon a mathematical analysis of the memorization curve.

The statistical analyses of learning/memorization data are typically restricted to the application of t-tests and ANOVA. These statistical treatments cannot assess the learning of a human as a "biological system." The system analysis, based on methods for system identification, have long existed and is widely used in the exact sciences, engineering (Sage and Melsa, 1971; Eykoff, 1974), biology (Grodins, 1963; Milsum, 1966) and in the ergonomic assessment of labor skills (Towill, 1976).

One of the methods for system identification is the analysis of transfer functions that assess reaction of the system on any input signal. The simplest input signal is the step function (Grodins, 1963; Milsum, 1966). From this point of view a memorization curve can be considered as the transfer function of the first order linear system in response to stepwise input action that results in the exponential mathematical model $Y = B3 * \exp(-B2 * X) + B4 * (1 - \exp(-B2 * X))$ (Stepanov, 1983). The output signal — the number of recalled words — is stochastic in nature because there are many factors (partly uncontrolled) that influence brain functioning. Therefore, from a mathematical point of view the nonlinear regression analysis should be used in evaluating the parameters of any mathematical model of the learning curve (Himmelblau, 1970; Draper and Smith, 1981).

The main goal of the current paper is to illustrate that analyzing the shape of a memorization or learning curve is a very informative estimator of learning. We do this by showing how a mathematical treatment of the learning curve reveals new insights when nootropics (Nootropil, Baclofen, Bemethyl, and Aethimizol) and vasorelaxants (Cinnarizine and Dibazol) are used.

## METHODS

### Subjects

The sample comprised 178 participants placed into one of four groups. The first group included 16 healthy volunteers of both genders (age range 25–35 years old). The second group included 20 male drug addicts (age 19–52). The third group included 80 male alcoholics (age 24–60). The fourth group included 62 alcoholics with a previous history of traumatic brain injury (age 29–57).

## Description of Drug Addicted Sample

All participants were intravenous drug users with heroin used in the majority of cases. Time of abuse ranged from 6 months to 15 years with a daily dose of 0.2 g to 1.0 g. Clinical symptoms included pronounced myalgia in extremities and back, arthralgiae, hyperhidrosis, tremor, psychomotor agitation, ataxia, headaches, a strong drive for the drug, and feelings of anxiety and dysphoria. The detoxification regime consisted of medication with B vitamins, non-narcotic analgesics, tranquilizers, and antipsychotic drugs. All participants expressed a desire for treatment.

## Description of Alcoholic Sample

These participants — 142 males — suffered from alcohol abuse for 10 to15 years. Eighty of the 142 showed no clinical acute form of mental impairment. The remaining 62 reported previous traumatic brain injury accompanied by loss of consciousness, vomiting, and headaches. The detoxification regime consisted of B vitamins and sedative medication with diazepam.

## Treatment

All participants received treatment for addiction in the Saint Petersburg city narcological dispensary (Russia). Drug addicts were treated with auricular acupuncture beginning 11 days after hospitalization and concluding 2 weeks later. Acupuncture needles were inserted into auricular points for "central nervous system", "sympathetic", "kidney", "liver", and "lung" bilaterally for 30 min.

The alcoholics without brain injury were randomly divided into 5 sub-groups. The first group — 20 participants — was treated with auricular acupuncture similar to the drug addicts. The second group — 15 participants — was treated with Nootropil and vitamins. The third group — 15 participants — was treated with Nootropil. The fourth group — 15 participants — was treated with Baclofen. The fifth group — 15 participants — was treated with Bemethyl.

The 62 alcoholics with traumatic brain injury were randomly divided into 7 sub-groups. The first group — 9 participants — was treated with placebo (tablets made of starch and sucrose). The second group — 9 participants — was treated with Cinnarizine (vasorelaxant). The third subgroup — 8 participants — was treated with Dibazol (vasorelaxant). The fourth group — 8 participants — was treated with Nootropil (nootropics). The fifth group — 13 participants — was treated with Baclofen (nootropics). The sixth group — 10 participants — was treated with Aethimizol (nootropics). The seventh group — 8 participants — was treated with Bemethyl (nootropics).

## Memory Test: Memorization of 10 Words

The nouns were selected from the "Russian language frequency vocabulary" with a frequency of not more than 12% (Lokhov and Stepanov, 1988). Recalled words, excluding repetitions, served as the dependent variable. Luriya (1962) developed this memory test and **it** is similar to the California Verbal Learning Test's memorization words from List A (Delis et al., 1987) with the exception that ten nouns were used and the test consisted of 7 trials.

## Description of the Mathematical Expression of the Transfer Function

The transfer function of the first order system in response to a stepwise external stimulus looks like $y = (y_0 - y_{ss}) \exp(-t/\tau) + y_{ss}$ , where $y_0 = y$ at $X=0$; $y_{ss} = y$ at $X=$Infinity; $\tau$ — the time constant of the system. The time constant reveals how much time is necessary for achievement of 63% from the difference between the initial ($y_0$) and asymptotic ($y_{ss}$) values (Grodins, 1963).

Stepanov (1983) proposed to use the transfer function for the first order system in the most obvious form as $Y = B3 * \exp(-B2*X) + B4*(1 - \exp(-B2*X))$. Y is the number of recalled words, excluding repetitions, and X is the trial number. The advantage of the model lies in estimating three parameters: B2 — the velocity of memorization; B4 — an asymptotic quantity of memorized items; B3 — predisposition to the next memorization before the beginning of testing, (i.e. at $X=0$). From a psychological point of view, coefficient B3 represents pretrial associative strength. The coefficient B4 can be treated as an estimator of the behavioral saturation level for associative strength or in other words ability for memorization.

Assessment of pretrial associative strength, or, in other words, predisposition to the next memorization of new information, is very important. Many mathematical models of learning and memorization (including the frequently used Weibull function) do not allow estimating the value of correct responses prior to next trial, since by definition $Y=0$ at $X=0$ (Gulliksen, 1934; Hull, 1943; Gallistel, Fairhurst, Balsam, 2004). Other memory models based on the theory of probabilities, also propose that $Y=0$ at $X=0$, because of how the term "probability" is defined $P \in [0,1]$ (Atkinson, Bower, and Crothers, 1965). Only the approach based on automatic control theory permits the initial and final system states to be arbitrary, so B3 is not permanently equal to zero. The initial value of the quantity of true responses (memorized objects) cannot be obtained directly from experimental data. It can be calculated only with the proposed mathematical model via parameter B3.

Our rationale for using coefficient B4 is that an individual cannot always correctly memorize every test item, so the model does not pre-fix B4 to the number of test items. Additionally, we restricted the value of coefficient B2 which must exceed zero by definition of the mathematical model. The upper limit we established for B2 is equal to 3.0. It is known that the first order system achieves 95% from the difference between B3 and B4 in $3\tau$ (Grodins, 1963; Milsum, 1966). Since $B2 = 1/\tau$, it means that if $B2=3$ then a subject can memorize all test items in one trial. In other words, we assume that the shape of the memorization curve is exponential if $0.005 < B2 < 3.0$. This limitation gives satisfactory results in practice.

## Estimation of the Parameters of the Model with Regression Analysis

The mathematical model we proposed is in the class of intrinsically nonlinear models. This means it is impossible to derive suitable formulas for calculating the coefficients of the model as is common for any linear regression model (Himmelblau, 1970; Draper and Smith, 1981). Most modern statistical packages (for example, SPSS or SAS) use iterative estimation algorithms (using input of start values) such as sequential quadratic programming or Levenberg-Marquardt in estimating the coefficients for a non-linear regression model and asymptotic standard errors of coefficients. However, if these starting values are very far from real model values, the least square method that calculates the sum of squares of difference between experimental and model values can get only a local minimum of this sum of squares. In this case, rather rough values of coefficients B2, B3, and B4 can be obtained. Stepanov (1983) used the method of direct search of the coefficients B2, B3, and B4 and derived all mathematical equations for calculation of their variances as well as for comparison of the same coefficients.

## Verification of the Model: Group Data

We verified the model with goodness of fit tests for both linear (Himmelblau, 1970) and non-linear models (Draper and Smith, 1981).The test of goodness of fit for linear models is based on calculation of the variance ratio of the residual variance to the variance of the error of the measurement: $F_{exp} = \dfrac{S_r^2}{S_e^2}$.

$S_r^2 = \dfrac{1}{n-3} \sum_{i=1}^{n} p_i (\overline{Y}_i - Y_{i\,mod})^2$, where i — the order trial number, $p_i$ is the number of cases (here $p_i$ is equal to the number of subjects in a group), $\overline{Y}_i$ — the mean value for every trial, $Y_{i\,mod} = B_3 e^{-B_2 X_i} + B_4(1 - e^{-B_2 X_i})$. $S_e^2 = \dfrac{\sum_{i=1}^{n} \sum_{j=1}^{p_i} (Y_{ij} - \overline{Y}_i)^2}{(\sum_{i=1}^{n} p_i) - n}$, where n — total number of trials.

Next, the significance level (p) for $F_{exp}$ is calculated with the number of degrees of freedom for the numerator is equal to (n-3) and with the number of degrees of freedom for the denominator is equal to $\left[\left(\sum_{i=1}^{n} p_i\right) - n\right]$, using the frequency function for F-distribution (see column 6 in table 1). If the significance level for $F_{exp}$ is p>0.2, it means that the mathematical model fits the learning data well. If 0.2>p>0.05, then only a tendency for fitting exists. If p<0.05, then the fit is not satisfactory. Strictly speaking, there is only an approximate estimator for the variance of measurement error for non-linear regression models (Draper and Smith, 1981). In other words, p>0.2 implies that the experimental data does not rule out the proposed mathematical model though other models may be also valid.

We also used an approximate test for goodness of fit for non-linear models (Draper and Smith, 1981). This test is based on calculations of the sum of square of the difference between experimental values and the values calculated with the mathematical model as well as the calculation of the sum of square of "pure errors." These values are placed in a special formula that gives a variance ratio belonging to Fisher's F-distribution and named "the ratio of averaged squares" (see column 7 in table 1). Next, the value of F-quantile with the confidence level P=0.95 is calculated (see column 8 in table 1). If the ratio of averaged squares is less than the appropriate F-quantile, then the mathematical model fits the data satisfactorily.

## Verification of the Model: Individual Data

If the regression analysis is applied to the memorization curve of an individual then the measurement error variance can not be estimated separately from residual variance. The residual variance is an estimation of the quality of the fit. The less residual variance the closer the experimental and model values are situated. In other words, in the case of fitting a single participant's learning curve, it is impossible to estimate quantitatively the quality of fit with the mathematical model. One way to estimate the strength of the correlation, however, is to calculate $R^2$ that is, the square of the correlation relation.

$$R^2 = 1 - \frac{\sum_{i=1}^{n}(Y_i - Y_{i\ mod})^2}{\sum_{i=1}^{n}(Y_i - \overline{Y})^2},$$

where n – the number of trials, $Y_i$ – the experimental value, $Y_{i\ mod}$ – calculated model value of true responses, $\overline{Y}$ – the average mean calculated over all experimental values. Excel, SPSS and other statistical package use $R^2$. Unfortunately, it is not possible to calculate significance with these statistics (Kendall and Stuart, 1975). Nevertheless, $R^2$ is useful for a quantitative estimate of the fit.

# RESULTS

## Healthy Volunteers

The results of the regression analysis of the mean values of recalled words for the group of healthy volunteers are given in table 1.1, and the memorization curve shown in figure 1, circles. Both tests for goodness of fit indicated that the mathematical model fitted the data well. Significance level for $F_{exp}$ was much greater than 0.2 (column 6, table 1.1) and the ratio of averaged squares was far less than the F-quantile (compare column 7 and column 8 in table 1.1). The value of the square of correlative relation is $R^2 = 0.98$ and is consistent with a satisfactory approximation of the memorization curve.

**Table 1. Results of the regression analysis**

| No. | Name of the group of subjects | The coefficients of the mathematical model | | | Significance level for the $F_{exp}$ p | The ratio of averaged squares | F-quantile for P=0.95 |
|---|---|---|---|---|---|---|---|
| | | B2 | B3 | B4 | | | |
| 1. | Healthy volunteers, 16 | 0.51±0.005 | 2.7±0.44 | 9.4±0.15 | 0.792 | 0.4224 | 2.4582 |
| 2. | Drug addicts before acupuncture treatment, 20 | 0.96±0.018 | 0.5±0.68 | 8.0±0.12 | 0.941 | 0.1831 | 2.4398 |
| 3. | Drug addicts after acupuncture treatment, 20 | 0.25±0.001 | 4.8±0.19 | 10.6±0.12 | 0.802 | 0.4119 | 2.4398 |
| 4. | Alcoholics before acupuncture treatment, 20 | 0.41±0.004 | 3.4±0.31 | 8.4±0.15 | 0.953 | 0.1732 | 2.4398 |
| 5. | Alcoholics after acupuncture treatment, 20 | 0.30±0.001 | 3.6±0.18 | 10.3±0.12 | 0.932 | 0.2121 | 2.4398 |
| 6. | Alcoholics before treatment with Nootropil and vitamins, 15 | 0.41±0.001 | 1.8±0.30 | 9.5±0.11 | 0.663 | 0.6005 | 2.4645 |
| 7. | Alcoholics after treatment with Nootropil and vitamins, 15 | 0.42±0.002 | 3.3±0.27 | 9.7±0.11 | 0.659 | 0.6063 | 2.4645 |
| 8. | Alcoholics before Nootropil treatment, 15 | 0.06±0.0001 | 4.0±0.08 | 19.5±0.27 | 0.524 | 0.8069 | 2.4645 |
| 9. | Alcoholics after Nootropil treatment, 15 | 0.23±0.0002 | 3.9±0.17 | 11.0±0.11 | 0.804 | 0.4055 | 2.4645 |
| 10. | Alcoholics before Baclofen treatment, 15 | 0.22±0.0002 | 3.7±0.15 | 10.7±0.11 | 0.840 | 0.3548 | 2.4645 |
| 11. | Alcoholics after Baclofen treatment, 15 | 0.23±0.0003 | 4.3±0.15 | 10.9±0.10 | 0.230 | 1.3147 | 2.4645 |
| 12. | Alcoholics before Bemethyl treatment, 15 | 0.09±0.001 | 4.1±0.10 | 14.9±0.22 | 0.197 | 1.5380 | 2.4645 |
| 13. | Alcoholics after Bemethyl treatment, 15 | — | — | — | | | |
| 14. | Alcoholics with traumatic brain injury; before treatment with placebo, 9 | 1.27±0.051 | 2.3±1.50 | 7.1±0.19 | 0.844 | 0.3485 | 2.5366 |
| 15. | Alcoholics with traumatic brain injury; after treatment with placebo, 9 | 0.94±0.158 | 3.1±0.76 | 6.9±0.19 | 0.997 | 0.0378 | 2.5366 |

**Table 1. (Continued).**

| No. | Name of the group of subjects | The coefficients of the mathematical model | | | | Significance level for the $F_{exp}$ p | The ratio of averaged squares | F-quantile for P=0.95 |
|---|---|---|---|---|---|---|---|---|
| | | B2 | B3 | B4 | | | | |
| 16. | Alcoholics with traumatic brain injury; before treatment with Cinnarizine, 8 | 0.18±0.005 | 5.1±0.30 | 8.6±0.31 | 0.615 | 0.6706 | 2.5611 |
| 17. | Alcoholics with traumatic brain injury; after treatment with Cinnarizine, 8 | 0.45±0.079 | 5.8±0.46 | 7.9±0.24 | 0.866 | 0.3166 | 2.5611 |
| 18. | Alcoholics with traumatic brain injury; before treatment with Dibazol, 8 | 0.51±0.039 | 4.8±0.47 | 7.4±0.17 | 0.902 | 0.2611 | 2.5611 |
| 19. | Alcoholics with traumatic brain injury; after treatment with Dibazol, 8 | 0.15±0.004 | 5.6±0.33 | 10.1±0.46 | 0.891 | 0.2776 | 2.5611 |
| 20. | Alcoholics with traumatic brain injury; before teatment with Nootropil, 6 | — | — | — | — | — | — |
| 21. | Alcoholics with traumatic brain injury; after treatment with Nootropil, 6 | — | — | — | — | — | — |
| 22. | Alcoholics with traumatic brain injury; before treatment with Baclofen, 13 | 0.20±0.005 | 3.9±0.29 | 7.4±0.27 | 0.986 | 0.0896 | 2.4803 |
| 23. | Alcoholics with traumatic brain injury; after treatment with Baclofen, 13 | 0.38±0.027 | 5.2±0.47 | 7.7±0.21 | 0.963 | 0.1487 | 2.4803 |
| 24. | Alcoholics with traumatic brain injury; before treatment with Aethimizol, 10 | 0.40±0.021 | 3.5±0.53 | 6.6±0.22 | 0.999 | 0.0110 | 2.5177 |
| 25. | Alcoholics with traumatic brain injury; after treatment with Aethimizol, 10 | 0.18±0.018 | 5.4±0.34 | 7.3±0.33 | 0.980 | 0.1056 | 2.5177 |
| 26. | Alcoholics with traumatic brain injury; before treatment with Bemethyl, 8 | 0.13±0.006 | 4.0±0.31 | 7.5±0.51 | 0.980 | 0.1060 | 2.5611 |
| 27. | Alcoholics with traumatic brain injury; after treatment with Bemethyl, 8 | 0.21±0.017 | 5.4±0.38 | 8.4±0.41 | 0.981 | 0.1036 | 2.5611 |
| 28. | Total alcoholics without traumatic brain injury; before treatment, 80 | 0.22±0.001 | 3.7±0.08 | 10.4±0.07 | 0.639 | 0.6561 | 2.3180 |
| 29. | Total alcoholics with traumatic brain injury; before treatment, 62 | 0.36±0.003 | 3.9±0.19 | 7.1±0.09 | 0.938 | 0.1536 | 2.3230 |

Comment: Values of the coefficients of the mathematical model are given with one standard error.

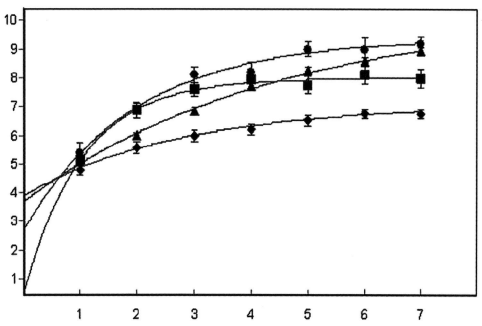

Figure 1. Memorization curves of the healthy participants (circles), drug addicts (squares), alcoholics without traumatic brain injury (triangles), and alcoholics with previous traumatic brain injury (diamonds). Vertical lines are S.E.M. Abscissa: trials, Ordinate: number of recalled words.

## Drug Addicts before Treatment

The results of the regression analysis of the mean values of recalled words of the participants suffering from drug addiction are given in table 1.2, and the memorization curve is shown in figure 1, squares. Both tests for goodness of fit indicated that the mathematical model provided an excellent fit. Significance level for $F_{exp}$ was much greater than 0.2 (column 6 in table 1.2) and the ratio of averaged squares was far less than the F-quantile (compare column 7 and column 8 in table 1.2). The value of the square of correlative relation is $R^2 = 0.99$ and is also consistent with a satisfactory approximation of the memorization curve.

## Alcoholics without Traumatic Brain Injury before Treatment

The results of the regression analysis of the mean values of recalled words for the group of participants suffering from alcoholism are given in table 1.28, and the memorization curve is shown in figure 1, triangles. Both tests for goodness of fit revealed that the mathematical model provided a good fit. Significance level for the $F_{exp}$ was much greater than 0.2 (column 6 in table 1.28) and the ratio of averaged squares was far less than the F-quantile (compare column 7 and column 8 in table 1.28). The value of the square of correlative relation is $R^2 = 0.99$ and consistent with a satisfactory approximation of the memorization curve.

## Alcoholics with Traumatic Brain Injury before Treatment

The results of the regression analysis of the mean values of recalled words of the group of participants suffering from alcoholism with previous traumatic brain injury are presented in table 1.29, and the memorization curve is shown in figure 1, diamonds. Both tests for goodness of fit showed that the mathematical model fitted the data well. Significance level for the $F_{exp}$ was much greater than 0.2 (column 6 in table 1.29) and the ratio of averaged squares was far less than the F-quantile (compare column 7 and column 8 in table 1.29). The value of the square of correlative relation is $R^2 = 0.99$ and is consistent with a satisfactory approximation of the memorization curve.

In participants suffering from drug addiction, the memorization curve is located below the curve for healthy subjects due to less pretrial associative strength — coefficient B3 ($p<0.05$) and asymptotic level — coefficient B4 ($p<0.001$). Drug addicted participants memorized the test items faster than healthy subjects did — coefficient B2 is greater ($p<0.001$), but memorized less words (8 in comparison with 9.4 for healthy subjects). In participants suffering from alcoholism, pretrial associative strength is greater than in healthy subjects ($p<0.05$), but they memorized the test words slower ($p<0.001$), so that seven trials is not enough to reach their asymptotic level. Participants with previous traumatic brain injury have difficulty memorizing the test items. Though the curves for both groups of alcoholics began from the same point (coefficients B3 do not differ), brain injury decreases the asymptotic level (coefficients B4 differ with $p=0.0001$).

## Treatment of Drug Addicted Participants

Treatment with auricular acupuncture led to a pronounce improvement in memory performance. The results of the group of participants suffering from drug addiction following auricular acupuncture treatment are given in table 1.3, and the memorization curves are shown in figure 2.A. Both tests for goodness of fit showed that the mathematical model provided an excellent fit. Significance level for the $F_{exp}$ was much greater than 0.2 (column 6 in table 1.3) and the ratio of averaged squares was far less than the F-quantile (compare column 7 and column 8 in table 1.3). The value of the square of correlative relation is $R^2 = 0.99$ and is consistent with a satisfactory approximation of the memorization curve. Comparison of the parameters of the memorization curves revealed that coefficient B3 was greatly increased following acupuncture treatment ($p<0.001$); coefficient B4 also increased ($p<0.001$). As a result, the initial and final portions of the memorization curve after acupuncture treatment was higher in comparison with the curve before treatment.

## Treatment of Alcoholic Participants without Previous Brain Damage

### Effect of Auricular Acupuncture

The results of the regression analysis of the mean values of recalled words of the group of alcoholics treated with auricular acupuncture are provided in table 1.4 (before) and 1.5 (after) treatment. The memorization curves are presented in figure 2.B. Both tests for goodness of fit revealed that the mathematical model fitted the data well. Significance level for the $F_{exp}$ was much greater than 0.2 (column 6 in table 1.4 and 1.5) and the ratio of averaged squares was far less than the F-quantile (compare column 7 and column 8 in table 1.4 and 1.5). The values of the square of correlative relation is $R^2 = 0.99$ before and after treatment and are consistent with a satisfactory approximation of the memorization curves. Comparison of the parameters of the memorization curves revealed that coefficient B3 was not altered, but coefficient B4 was increased (p<0.001). As a result, the memorization curve in alcoholics after acupuncture treatment began practically from the same initial value of recalled words, but rose up higher and higher with each succeeding trial.

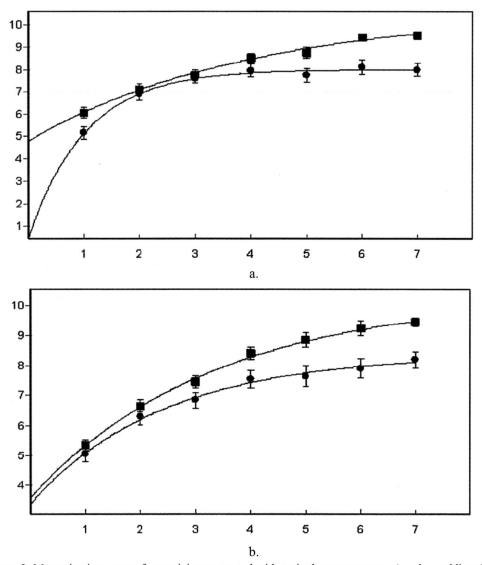

a.

b.

Figure 2. Memorization curves for participants treated with auricular acupuncture. A = drug addicts, B = alcoholics without traumatic brain injury. Circles = before acupuncture treatment, squares = after acupuncture treatment. Vertical lines are S.E.M. Abscissa: trials, Ordinate: number of recalled words.

### Effect of Nootropil and Vitamins

Other groups of alcoholic participants received treatment with nootropics. The results of the regression analysis of the mean values of recalled words of the group of alcoholics treated with Nootropil and vitamins are given in table 1.6 (before) and table **1.7** (after), and the memorization curves are shown in figure 3.A. Both tests for goodness of fit indicated that the mathematical model provided a good fit. Significance level for $F_{exp}$ was much greater than 0.2 (column 6 in table 1.6 and 1.7) and the ratio of averaged squares was far less than the F-quantile (compare column 7 and column 8 in table 1.6 and 1.7). The values of the square of correlative relation is $R^2 = 0.99$ before and after treatment. This too is consistent with a satisfactory approximation of the memorization curves. Comparison of the parameters of the memorization curves revealed that coefficient B3 increased (p=0.0003), but coefficient B4 did not changed. After treatment, the memorization curve began higher in comparison with the memorization curve before treatment, but the latter portions of both curves became closer in succeeding trials.

### Effect of Nootropil

The results of the regression analysis of the mean values of recalled words in the group of alcoholics treated only with Nootropil are given in table 1.8 (before) and 1.9 (after). The memorization curves are shown in figure 3.B. Both tests for goodness of fit revealed that the mathematical model fitted the data well. The significance level for $F_{exp}$ was much greater than 0.2 (column 6 in table 1.8 and 1.9) and the ratio of averaged squares was far less than the F-quantile (compare column 7 and column 8 in table 1.8 and 1.9). The values of the square of the correlative relation is $R^2 = 0.99$ both before and after treatment and consistent with a satisfactory approximation of the memorization curves. The velocity of memorization in this group of alcoholics was very low (B2=0.06) and indicates that these participants memorized words very slowly and that seven trials were not enough for them to reach their asymptotic level. Seventeen trials are necessary to reach 63% of (B4-B3). As a consequence, the asymptotic level (B4=19.5) does not reflect a real ability for memorization. This can be estimated by the mean value of true answers on trial seven, which is equal to 9.33. Comparing the parameters of the memorization curves revealed that coefficient B3 did not alter. The only effect of Nootropil was to increase the velocity of memorization (coefficient B2 increased from 0.06 to 0.23 with p<0.001). Hence, the memorization curve under the influence of Nootropil treatment bent upwards.

### Effect of Baclofen

The results of the regression analysis of the mean values of recalled words of the group of alcoholics treated with Baclofen are given in table 1.10 (before) and table 1.11 (after) with the memorization curves shown in figure 3.C. Both tests for goodness of fit indicated that the mathematical model fitted the data though fitting was better for initial testing then for testing after treatment (compare column 6 in table 1.10 and 1.11 and column 7 and column 8 in table 1.10 and 1.11). The values of the square of the correlative relation is $R^2 = 0.996$ before and $R^2 = 0.987$ after treatment. This is also consistent with a satisfactory approximation of the memorization curves. Comparison of the parameters of the memorization curves revealed that coefficient B4 did not alter. However treatment with Baclofen provided a moderate increase in the velocity of memorization (p<0.001) as well as increase of coefficient B3 from 3.7 to 4.3 (p=0.013). Hence, the memorization curve under the influence of Baclofen was located nearly in parallel with its initial curve though both curves should merge at Infinity (out of the range of the figure).

### Effect of Bemethyl

The results of the regression analysis of the mean values of recalled words for the group of alcoholics treated with Bemethyl are given in the table 1.12 (before) and table 1.13 (after) and the memorization curves are shown in figure 3.D. The memorization curve before treatment was fitted with the mathematical model, though the significance level for the $F_{exp}$ was equal to 0.2 (column 6 in table 1.12) and the ratio of averaged squares was less than the F-quantile (compare column 7 and column 8 in table 1.12). The values of the square of the correlative relation is $R^2 = 0.98$ and is consistent with a satisfactory approximation of the memorization curves. The velocity of memorization was very low (B2=0.09), so that the shape of the memorization curve was very close to a straight line. The effect of Bemethyl attracts attention to the unusual change in the shape of the curve, which was S-shaped. Comparing the parameters of the mathematical model with an S-shaped curve is not possible. In this case, the only way to asses the effect of Bemethyl was to compare the values of recalled words for every trial with a paired-samples t-test. Comparison revealed that the values after treatment were higher for trials 2, 4 and 6 (p<0.05). In other words, memorization was better, but the shape of the memorization curve was changed.

## Treatment of Alcoholic Participants with Previous Brain Injury

### Effect of Placebo

The results of the regression analysis of the mean values of recalled words of the group of alcoholics treated with placebo are given in the table 1.14 (before) and table 1.15 (after). Both tests for goodness of fit showed that the mathematical model provided a good fit. Significance level for $F_{exp}$ was much greater than 0.2 (column 6 in the table 1.14 and 1.15) and the ratio of averaged squares was far less than the F-quantile (compare column 7 and column 8 in table 1.14 and 1.15). The values of the square of correlative relation is $R^2 = 0.94$ before and 0.98 after treatment. This too is consistent with a satisfactory approximation of the memorization curves. Comparison of the parameters of the memorization curves revealed that coefficient B4 was not altered, but coefficients B2 and B3 increased (p=0.0501 and p=0.0019 accordingly). As a result, the memorization curve in alcoholics with previous traumatic brain injury after placebo treatment began higher in comparison with the memorization curve before treatment, but after the second trial both curves practically merged.

### Effect of Cinnarizine

The results of the regression analysis for the mean values of recalled words are given in table 1.16 (before) and table 1.17 (after) with the memorization curves shown in figure 4.A. Both tests for goodness of fit indicated that the mathematical model fitted the data well. Significance level for $F_{exp}$ was much greater than 0.2 (column 6 in table 1.16 and 1.17) and the ratio of averaged squares was far less than the F-quantile (compare column 7 and column 8 in table 1.16 and 1.17).

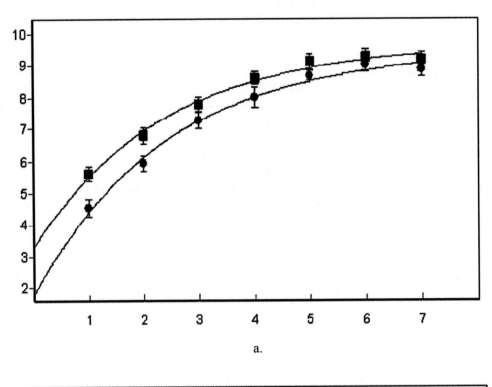

a.

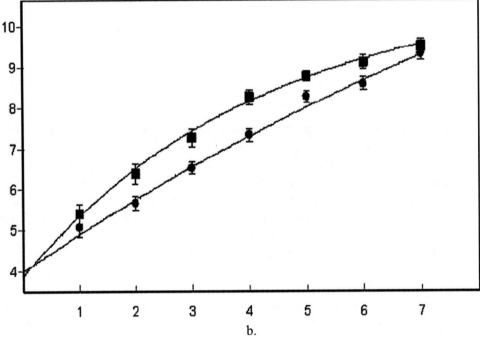

b.

Figure 3. Continued on next page.

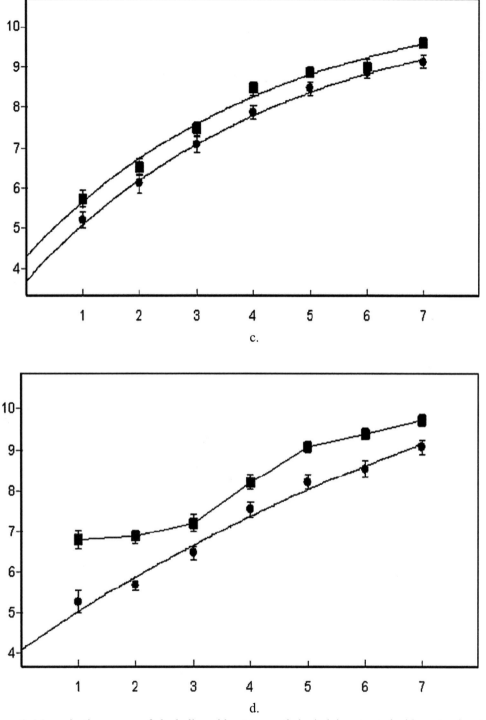

Figure 3. Memorization curves of alcoholics without traumatic brain injury treated with nootropics. A = treated with Nootropil and vitamins, B = treated with Nootropil, C = treated with Baclofen, D = treated with Bemethyl. Circles = before treatment, squares = after treatment. Vertical lines are S.E.M. Abscissa: trials, Ordinate: number of recalled words.

The values of the square of the correlative relation is $R^2 = 0.86$ before and 0.82 after treatment and is consistent with a satisfactory approximation of the memorization curves. Comparing the parameters of the memorization curves revealed that coefficients B3 and B4 were not altered, but coefficient B2 increased from 0.18 to 0.45 (p=0.0013), This means that the only difference between the memorization curves before and after treatment was a convex movement of the curve following treatment. Comparing the values of recalled words for every trial with a paired-samples t-test revealed that only the values for the second trial differed (p=0.049). This result illustrates an advantage of our model in that it was able to detect transient increases in the ability to memorize material. Hence, the effect of Cinnarizine was very weak.

### Effect of Dibazol

The results of the regression analysis of the mean values of recalled words are given in table 1.18 (before) and table 1.19 (after) and the memorization curves are shown in figure 4.B. Both tests for goodness of fit revealed that the mathematical model provided a good fit. Significance level for $F_{exp}$ was much greater than 0.2 (column 6 in table 1.18 and 1.19) and the ratio of averaged squares was far less than the F-quantile (compare column 7 and column 8 in table 1.18 and 1.19). The values of the square of the correlative relation is $R^2 = 0.93$ before and 0.92 after treatment and is consistent with a satisfactory approximation of the memorization curves. Comparing the parameters of the memorization curves revealed that coefficient B3 was not altered, coefficient B4 increased (p<0.001) and coefficient B2 decreased from 0.51 to 0.15 (p<0.001). As a result, memorization curves before and after treatment with Dibazol began at the same initial value of recalled words, but the memorization curve after treatment finished higher than the memorization curve before treatment. This means that Dibazol reduced the velocity of memorization and seven trials were not enough for reaching asymptotic values.

### Effect of Nootropil

The results of the regression analysis of the mean values of recalled words are given in table 1.20 and table 1.21. The data both before and after treatment were not fitted with the mathematical model because the memorization curves were of multangular shape (figure 5.A). In this case, the only way to evaluate the effect of Nootropil was to compare the values of recalled words for every trial with a paired-samples t-test. The comparison revealed that the values before and after treatment did not differ on any trial. Nootropil not only failed to restore the normal exponential shape of the memorization curve, but also did not improve memorization of the test items.

### Effect of Baclofen

The results of the regression analysis of the mean values of recalled words are given in the table 1.22 (before) and table 1.23 (after) and the memorization curves are shown in figure 5.B. Both tests for goodness of fit showed that the mathematical model fitted the data well. Significance level for the $F_{exp}$ was much greater than 0.2 (column 6 in table 1.22 and 1.23) and the ratio of averaged squares was far less than the F-quantile (compare column 7 and column 8 in table 1.22 and 1.23). The values of the square of the correlative relation is $R^2 =$

0.98 before and 0.95 after treatment and is consistent with a satisfactory approximation of the memorization curve. Comparing the parameters of the curves revealed that coefficient B4 did not increased, but coefficients B2 and B3 increased ($p<0.001$ and $p=0.0237$ accordingly). As the result, the memorization curve after Baclofen treatment began at higher level and approached closer to its asymptotic level. This means that Baclofen improved memorization in this group of alcoholics.

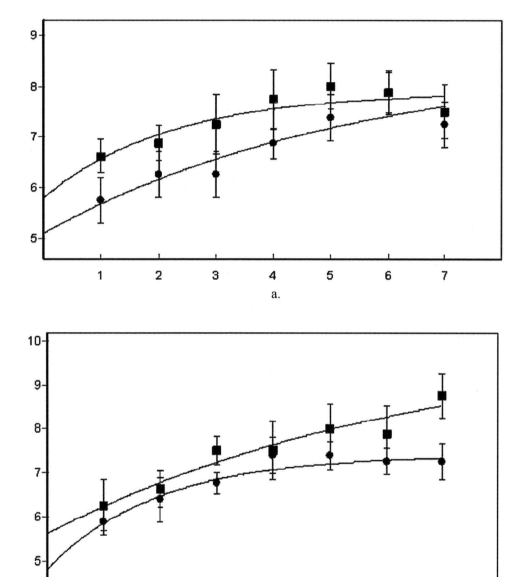

a.

b.

Figure 4. The memorization curves of the groups of alcoholics with traumatic brain injury treated with vasorelaxants. A = treated with Cinnarizine, B = treated with Dibazol. Circles = before treatment, squares = after treatment. Vertical lines are S.E.M. Abscissa: trials, Ordinate: number of recalled words.

## Effect of Aethimizol

The results of the regression analysis of the mean values of recalled words are given in the table 1.24 (before) and table 1.25 (after) and the memorization curves are shown in figure 5.C. Both tests for goodness of fit revealed that the mathematical model fitted the data well. Significance level for the $F_{exp}$ was much greater than 0.2 (column 6 in table 1.24 and 1.25) and the ratio of averaged squares was far less than the F-quantile (compare column 7 and column 8 in table 1.24 and table 1.25). The values of the square of the correlative relation is $R^2 = 0.99$ before and 0.90 after treatment and is consistent with a satisfactory approximation of the memorization curves. Comparing the parameters of the memorization curves revealed that there was a tendency to increase coefficient B4 (p=0.062), but coefficients B2 and B3 were increased (p<0.001 and p=0.0024 accordingly). As a result, the memorization curve after Aethimizol treatment began at higher level and was closer to its asymptotic level. This indicates that Aethimizol improved memorization in this group of alcoholics.

## Effect of Bemethyl

The results of the regression analysis of the mean values of recalled words are given in the table 1.26 (before) and table 1.27 (after) and the memorization curves are provided in figure 5.D. Both tests for goodness of fit showed that the mathematical model fitted the data well. Significance level for the $F_{exp}$ was much greater than 0.2 (column 6 in table 1.26 and 1.27) and the ratio of averaged squares was far less than the F-quantile (compare column 7 and column 8 in table 1.26 and 1.27). The values of the square of the correlative relation is $R^2 = 0.99$ before and 0.90 after treatment and is consistent with a satisfactory approximation of the memorization curves. Comparing the parameters of the memorization curves revealed that coefficient B4 was not increased and that coefficients B2 and B3 were increased (p<0.001 and p=0.0065 accordingly). The memorization curve after Bemethyl treatment began at a higher level and approached closer to its asymptotic level. This means that Bemethyl improved memorization in this group of alcoholics.

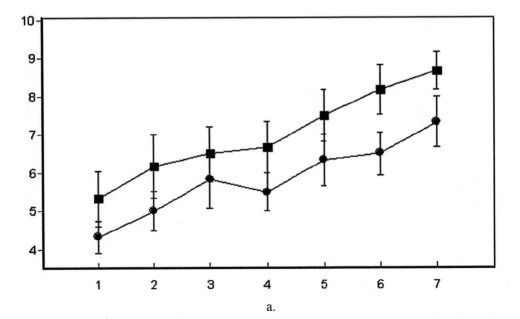

a.

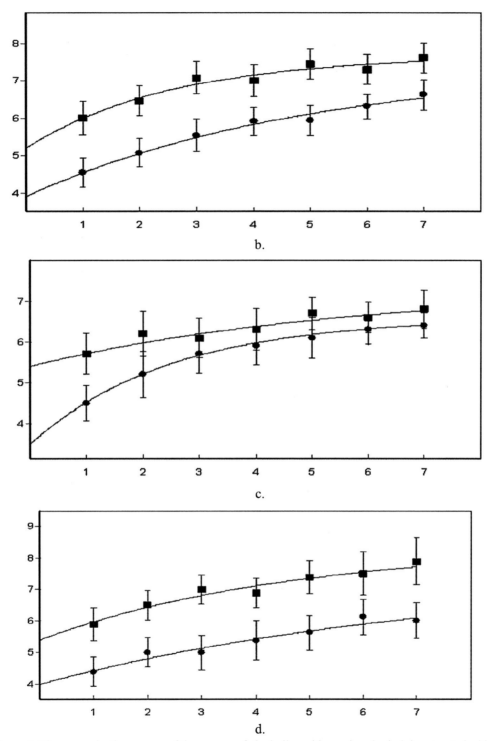

Figure 5. The memorization curves of the groups of alcoholics with previous brain injury treated with nootropics. A = treated with Nootropil, B = treated with Baclofen, C = treated with Aethimizol, D = treated with Bemethyl. Circles = before treatment, squares = after treatment. Vertical lines are S.E.M. Abscissa: trials, Ordinate: the number of recalled words.

## DISCUSSION

Our previous results showed that for some simple learning paradigms in land snails, rats, and humans the shape of the learning curve was exponential (Stepanov and Abramson, 2005). Our current results also support the view that the learning curve for memorization of words is also exponential. Hence, we put forward a hypothesis that the fundamental principles of the memory mechanisms are the same for all animals tested thus far and the shape of the learning/memorization curve is exponential. Deflections from the exponential shape are the result of disturbances of the memory mechanism, being functional and transient or pathological and stable.

We propose that by analyzing the shape of the memorization or learning curve allows a researcher or diagnostician to obtain more information on memory in comparison with the traditional simple calculation of the number of recalled words. Receiving additional information due to the use of the mathematical model can be explained by the fact that any mathematical model includes some coefficients that govern the behavior of the curve. We treat the coefficient B2 as the velocity of memorization; B4 — as an asymptotic volume of memorized words; B3 — as predisposition to the next memorization before the beginning of testing, (i.e. at X=0). In the future, we hope to link the coefficients with neuro-physiological processes.

Averaging across participants might give a misleading picture of what occurs in individuals (Wixted, 1997; Gallistel et al., 2004). To determine whether our model may provide such a misleading picture, we separately calculated individual memorization curves for each of 16 healthy participants. The shape of memorization curve was exponential in 13 of 16 participants. The quality of the fit differed among these individuals; however, $R^2$ exceeded 0.8 in nine of 13 participants. Among the three subjects that did not show an exponential curve, it was found that the test values for two subjects ranged from 7 to 10 true answers — the effect of "ceiling." This indicates that 10 test words happened to be too few for these individuals. That is why it is necessary to use more test words. For example, the California Verbal Learning Test uses 16 words (Delis et al., 1987). Our unpublished pilot data showed that the learning curve for memorization of 16 words from list A of the CVLT are fitting well with our mathematical model.

We must admit that the proposed mathematical model possesses some degree of robustness with respect to some non-exponential individual cases. However, if most of the individual cases are far from an exponential shape, then the group learning curve will be also of non-exponential shape. Thus, assessing the shape of the memorization curve using our model, for example, allows the researcher to better characterize memory function among volunteers and defining more accurately the values of the model coefficients. As applied to our data from healthy volunteers, excluding those participants without an exponential shape curve, revealed that the value of coefficient B2 was not changed (B2=0.51±0.0034), the value of the coefficient B3 became less (B3=1.8±0.45), and the value of coefficient B4 was slightly increased (B4=9.7±0.15).

Comparison of memorization curves in drug addicts and alcoholics with and without previous traumatic brain injury showed that addiction impairs memory functions. In drug addicts, the impairment is more prominent than in alcoholics. In alcoholics, on the contrary, readiness for memorization is higher than in healthy persons. Velocity of memorization is also lower in alcoholics. The influence of previous traumatic brain injury affects memorization the greatest. The memorization curve of these participants was situated well below all others.

The exponential shape of the memorization curve was found in all groups of alcoholics with the exception of the group of alcoholics with previous brain injury treated with Nootropil. Individual analysis of every participant's memorization curve in the Nootropil group revealed that the memorization curve was of the exponential shape in four participants before treatment, though the quality of the fit differed among individuals. The other two participants' curves differed greatly from an exponential shape so that the integrated data were not fitted with our mathematical model. This fact additionally emphasizes that the individual analysis of every participant's memorization curve is useful when taken together with a group curve analysis. Moreover, an analysis of the individual learning curve is important from a clinical poimt of view.

We would like to note that auricular acupuncture exerted a pronounced effect both on predisposition to the next memorization prior to testing and the ability for memorization. The same treatment in alcoholics without previous traumatic brain injury improved only the ability for memorization. This fact leads to the conclusion that brain memory mechanisms are more disturbed in the drug addict than in the alcoholic. Comparison of these two memorization curves showed that coefficients B4 did not differ after treatment in groups of drug addicts and alcoholics (p=0.11); in other words, improvement was of the same order. However, the predisposition to the next memorization before testing was better in drug addicts (p=0.0001). As a working hypothesis, we propose that auricular acupuncture activates natural brain mechanisms, not provoking any undesirable side effects.

In alcoholics without traumatic brain injury, Nootropil with vitamins and Baclofen increased the predisposition to the next memorization before the beginning of testing and increased the velocity of memorization. The influence on memorization following treatment with Baclofen was more pronounced. Nootropil alone only increased the velocity of memorization. Bemethyl changed the shape of the memorization curve from exponential to S-shape (see fig. 3. D). A similar effect on the learning curve was found in rats treated with beta-amyloid (Stepanov and Abramson, 2005; Stepanov and Abramson, unpublished data). We propose that alteration of the memorization curve's shape may reflect an initial disturbance of memory mechanisms. This fact indicates that an assessment of the shape of the learning/memorization curve should be included into the list of obligatory memory tests during development of novel nootropics.

Previous traumatic brain injury in alcoholics additionally disturbs memory mechanisms. Thus, Nootropil exerted a positive effect only in two participants out of six, so its effect was very weak. The effect of Baclofen was similar. However, Bemethyl improved memorization due to an increase in the velocity of memorization and the predisposition to the next memorization.

Our results suggest that nootropics mainly improve the predisposition to the next memorization whereas Dibazol and Cinnarizine (both are vasorelaxant drugs) do not affect the predisposition to the next memorization, but instead improved the ability for memorization. Auricular acupuncture treatment also led to improvement in memorization. Therefore, taken together the results of the regression analysis of the memorization curve demonstrate the expediency of combined treatment of alcoholics both with nootropics and with auricular acupuncture. This approach to treatment can significantly improve memory processes without any disturbance of fine physiological memory mechanisms.

In summary, we propose that the assessment of the shape of a participant's learning or memorization curve can provide important information to allow a clinician to assess the effects of any treatment on drug addicts and alcoholics.

## ACKNOWLEDGMENTS

The authors wish to thank their colleagues taking part in some aspects of this work. Dr. Oleg V. Goncharov, M.D., Ph.D. performed all participant examinations. Dr. Yuriy I. Usenko, M.D., Ph.D. performed acupuncture treatment of drug addicts and alcoholics groups. Dr. Peter D. Shabanov performed pharmacological treatment of alcoholics.

## REFERENCES

Atkinson, R. C., Bower, G. H., Crothers, E. J. (1965). *An introduction to mathematical learning theory*. New York-London-Sydney: John Wiley and Sons, Inc.

D'Argembeau, A., Van Der Linden, M., Verbanck, P., Noel, X. (2006). Autobiographical memory in non-amnesic alcohol-dependent patients. *Psychol Med., 36*, 1707–1715.

Delis, D. C., Kramer, J. H., Kaplan, E., Ober, B.A. (1987). *California Verbal Learning Test*. San Antonio, TX: The Psychological Corporation.

Draper, N. R., Smith, H. (1981). *Applied regression analysis*. New York: John Wiley and Sons, Inc.

Ersche, K. D., Clark, L., London, M., Robbins, T.W., Sahakian, B. J. (2006). Profile of executive and memory function associated with amphetamine and opiate dependence. *Neuropsychopharmacology, 31*, 1036 –1047.

Eykoff P. (1974). *System identification. Parameter and state estimation*. New York: Wiley.

Folstein, M. F., Folstein, S. E., McHugh, P. R. (1975). "Mini-Mental State". A practical method for grading the cognitive state of patients for the clinician. *J. Psychiatric Researches, 12*, 189-198.

Gallistel, C. R., Fairhurst, S., Balsam, P. (2004). The learning curve: implications of a quantitative analysis. *Proceedings of National Academy of Sciences USA, 101*, 13124-13131.

Grodins, F. S. (1963). *Control theory and biological systems*. New York and London: Columbia University Press.

Gulliksen, H. (1934). A rational equation of the learning curve based on Thorndike's law of effect. *Journal of General Psychology, 11*, 395-434.

Himmelblau, D. M. (1970). *Process analysis by statistical methods*. New York: John Wiley and Sons, Inc.

Hull, C. L. (1943). *Principles of Behavior*. New York: Appleton Century Crofts.

Kendall, M. G., Stuart, A. (1975). *The advanced theory of statistics. 3*. London: Charles Griffin and Company.

Lokhov, M. I., Stepanov, I. I. (1988). Metod opredeleniya funktsional'nogo sostoyaniya tsentral'noi nervnoi sistemi u tcheloveka [The method of estimation of a man CNS functional state]. Patent No 1377037 (USSR). *Byulleten' izobretenii*, No 8.

Luriya, A. R. (1962). *Vishye korkovye funktzii tcheloveka i ikh narusheniya pri lokal'nikh povrezhdeniyakh mozga [The higher cortical functions in humans and its dysfunctions at local brain injury]*. Moscow: Moscow State University Publishing House.

Milsum J. H. (1966). *Biological control systems analysis*. New York and London: McGraw-Hill Book Company.

Pitel, A. L., Witkowski, T., Vabret, F., Guillery-Girard, B., Desgranges, B., Eustache, F., Beaunieux, H. (2007). Effect of episodic and working memory impairments on semantic and cognitive procedural learning at alcohol treatment entry. *Alcohol. Clin. Exp. Res., 31*, 238–248.

Robbins, T., James, M., Owen, A., Sahakian, B., McInnes, L., Rabbitt, P. (1994). Cambridge Neuropsychological Test Automated Battery (CANTAB): A factor analytic study of a large sample of normal elderly volunteers. *Dementia, 5*, 266-281.

Sage, A. P. and Melsa, J. L. (1971). *System identification*. New York and London: Academic Pres.

Stepanov, I. I. (1983). Priblizhennii metod othsenivaniya parametrov krivoi obutcheniya [An approximate method of estimation of the learning curve parameters]. *Physiologiya Tcheloveka, 9*, 686–689.

Stepanov, I. I., and Abramson, Ch. I. (2005). A new mathematical model for assessment of memorization dynamics. *The Spanish Journal of Psychology, 8,* 142–156.

Towill, D. R. (1976). Transfer functions and learning curves. *Ergonomics, 19*, 623-638.

Verdejo-Garcia, A., Bechara, A., Recknor, E. C., Perez-Garcia, M. (2006). Executive dysfunction in substance dependent individuals during drug use and abstinence: an examination of the behavioral, cognitive and emotional correlates of addiction. *J. Int. Neuropsychol. Soc., 12*, 405–415.

Wechsler, D. (1987): *Wechsler Memory Scale* – Revised. San Antonio: Psychological Corporation.

Wixted, J. T. (1997). Genuine power curves in forgetting: a quantitative analysis of individual subject forgetting functions. *Memory and Cognition, 25*, 731-739.

In: Substance Abuse, Assessment and Addiction      ISBN: 978-1-61122-931-8
Editors: Kristina A. Murati and Allison G. Fischer      © 2011 Nova Science Publishers, Inc.

*Chapter 11*

# WOMEN AND ADDICTIONS: BODY WEIGHT AND SHAPE CONCERNS AS BARRIERS TO RECOVERY FROM SUBSTANCE USE DISORDERS. LET'S ADDRESS THESE ISSUES IN TREATMENT AND RECOVERY NOW!

## *Christine M. Courbasson[1] and Irina Schelkanova[2]*
[1]Concurrent Disorders Service, Centre for Addiction and Mental Health,
Department of Psychiatry, University of Toronto
[2]University of Toronto

## ABSTRACT

Evidence suggests that individuals in substance use treatment become very preoccupied with food and their body shape and gain weight in recovery. Adolescents in substance use treatment evidence weight gain that cannot be explained by maturation factors alone. Many adolescents believe that various drugs have the power to keep them slim and this belief is associated with the persistent increase of substance use and treatment resistance. Women are more preoccupied with fear of gaining weight than men, and they use substances more often due to higher levels of weight and body image concerns than men. This chapter outlines the relationship between substance use, body shape and food preoccupation; provides the prevalence of body weight and shape concerns in women with addiction; reviews the literature on the various issues and struggles related to women's weight and shape issues and substance use initiation, treatment and recovery and the lack of treatment and support to address these issues; will render the significance and urgency to address this problem clear. This chapter also presents qualitative data linking substance use, food, and body weight and shape preoccupation in women and offers practical ways to address food, weight and shape concerns for women with addictions to enhance recovery, minimize relapse, and increase women's overall well being.

# INTRODUCTION

It has been suggested that various forms of addictive behaviour, like eating and weight/shape issues and substance abuse, co-exist more frequently than would be expected by chance. Such co-morbidity may lessen the effectiveness of treatment and may not be recognized by clinicians who specialize in addictions. Prevalence of bulimic symptoms among inpatients at a chemical dependence clinic was measured and 17% of participants were diagnosable for eating disorders. Subjects were Caucasian and Native American women, and higher prevalence rate for both bulimia and for the combined eating disorders were noted among Caucasian women (Wilson, 1992). Research suggests that the more often and more severely an incoming college female diets, the more likely she is to use alcohol and other drugs (National Center on Addiction and Substance Abuse, 2003). Behaviour and attitudes characteristic of clinical eating disorders are over-represented in women receiving treatment for an alcohol problem, and further study of such co-morbidity is merited (Peveler, and Fairburn, 1990). Girls who smoke to suppress their appetites are among the largest group of new nicotine addicts. Among white teenagers who smoke, girls are 3 times likelier than boys to smoke to suppress their appetites (National Center on Addiction and Substance Abuse, 2003).

Birch, Stewart, and Brown (2007) explored the prevalence of eating disorders such as anorexia nervosa, bulimia nervosa, and a combination of anorexia and bulimia among women with substance use disorders. Various prevalence rates are given for each eating disorder type and women addicted to alcohol. The lowest estimates of the prevalence of SUD among women with eating disorders are substantially higher than 6.2% prevalence rate of SUD among women in the general population. Moreover, it is widely accepted that the prevalence rate of eating disorders is higher among women with SUD compared to the general population. The two types of behaviour, eating and substance related, overlap and may serve similar functions (Birch, Stewart, and Brown, 2007). The study examined the risk situations for heavy drinking vs. binge eating among women with a comorbid diagnosis. An interesting finding was that there was an interaction between heavy drinking and situation interaction. Heavy drinking occurred in these women in a social setting, when pleasant times were experienced and when happily interacting with others but also when in conflict with others. The study proposed that heavy drinking might be dependent on the status of social interaction.

Women with bulimia nervosa and anorexia nervosa have a higher prevalence rate for abusing substances than women in the general population. Women diagnosed with bulimia nervosa are found to be more likely to smoke, abuse laxatives and drink. Both smoking and drinking have an effect on appetite, with smoking believed to reduce appetite. The study concluded that the high rate of substance abuse may be related to the severe food deprivation in eating disorders, especially in patients with bulimia nervosa (Bulik, Sullivan, Epstein, McKee, Kaye, Dahl, and Weltzin, 1992). Gadalla and Piran (2007) conducted a meta-analysis of 41 studies published between January of 1985 and May of 2006, which examined the co-occurrence of eating disorders (ED) and alcohol use disorders (AUD) in women. Studies were reviewed and a quantitative synthesis of their results was carried out via the calculation of standardised effect sizes. Only 4 out of 41 studies reported negative associations between ED and AUD. The magnitude of the associations between eating-disordered patterns and AUD ranged from small to medium size and were statistically significant for any ED, bulimia nervosa (BN)/bulimic behaviour, purging, binge eating disorder (BED) and eating disorders not otherwise specified (EDNOS). No association was found between anorexia nervosa (AN) and AUD. The magnitude of the association between BN and AUD was the most divergent across studies and those between each of BED and dietary restriction and AUD were the most consistent across studies. Reported associations of different patterns of disordered eating and AUD were generally weakest and most divergent when participants were recruited from clinical settings and strongest and most homogeneous when participants were recruited from student populations.

Another study set out to investigate familial relations and transmittance of eating disorders and substance use disorders. The study found that there was no link between a mother's SUD and the daughter's disordered eating, and there was also no link between a mother's SUD and eating disorder and the daughter's SUD and eating disorder. Therefore the comorbidity of eating disorders and SUD may not have to do with familial relations based on studies so far. Furthermore the study also concludes that substance use or substance misuse is not cross-transmitted in families. An interesting finding, however, is that daughters of mothers with bulimic eating disorder symptoms show more disturbed eating attitudes and behaviours than daughters that have mothers without bulimic eating disorder symptoms (Von Ranson, McGue, Iacono, 2003).

## SUBSTANCE USE AS WEIGHT CONTROL

Specific substances are known for their weight management properties. This is a common concern as research has demonstrated that approximately 50% of female smokers and 25% of male smokers are weight concerned. Females with weight concerns have been shown to be heavy smokers, have significant body image concerns, have expectation for a 16-pound weight gain after quitting smoking, and have low confidence that they will be able to manage their eating (Clark et al., 2006). Similarly, in large sample experiment, at baseline, female smokers were more concerned with their weight than were men; 86% of women and 62% of men expressed concern about gaining weight if they quit smoking, and for 26% of women and 7% of men, that concern was extreme. More women (32%) than men (12%) were dieting. For women, smoking relates to weight gain concerns, negatively relates to quitting confidence and positively relates to general weight concerns (Razavi et al., 1999).

Findings of a study on cocaine use as a means of controlling weight shows that women who endorsed weight-related motivation for cocaine use also endorsed an average of three other substances for weight or appetite control. 85% of those with a current eating disorder endorsed using alcohol, either alone or in conjunction with cocaine, to control appetite or weight. Of the women who were using alcohol as an appetite control measure, half were alcohol dependent. Other women of the sample were alcohol abusers and 2 drank alcohol regularly, but not to the point of abuse or dependence. There is an association of heavy alcohol use in the eating disordered cocaine abuser. The alcohol use in this population may take the place of eating, separate from any interaction with cocaine. Those who identify alcohol as their primary substance of abuse and who also have an eating disorder need to be studied regarding the motivational relationship between alcohol and their eating disorder.

None of the 5 other women without eating disorders who endorsed use of cocaine for weight-related use endorsed using alcohol for weight-related use (Cochrane et al., 1998).

Another study reported that almost half of cocaine abusing women use both cocaine and alcohol as a weight control measure. Moreover 72% of women using substances to control their weight are diagnosed with an eating disorder. When taking these data into consideration it is important to consider that the sample size was rather small for the study; only 37 females were used as participants. The study also reported that 85% of the participants diagnosed with an eating disorder consumed alcohol in order to suppress their appetite (Cochrane, Malcolm, and Brewerton, 1998). There was also an obvious gender difference in the use of cocaine for weight control purposes; the ratio of women and men using cocaine for weight control purposes was 3:1.

The drug ecstasy has appetite suppressant and exercise promoting effects that may appeal to young women who are concerned about weight and body image. Curran and Robjant (2006) sought to determine whether young women who use ecstasy differ from those who do not use this drug in concerns about eating and weight, and in beliefs about how these are affected by recreational drugs. One hundred and thirty young women, all cigarette smokers, were recruited; 73 who used ecstasy were compared with 57 who did not. All were assessed on Garner's (1991) Eating Disorder Inventory (EDI-2), body mass index (BMI), depression and beliefs about the effects of different drugs on appetite, exercise and weight. The two groups did not differ on number of cigarettes smoked per day, depression scores, current BMI, lowest achieved BMI or ideal BMI. Ecstasy users had significantly higher scores than controls on four of the 11 sub-scales of the EDI: bulimia, impulse dysregulation, social insecurity and interpersonal distrust. For ecstasy users, scores on all four scales correlated positively with frequency of ecstasy use. However there were no group differences in 'drive for thinness' or 'body dissatisfaction' which may suggest that differences on other factors are related more to use of club drugs than to any specific eating pathology. Ecstasy users were more likely than controls to agree that ecstasy aids weight loss and that they exercise more when they use drugs. However, the findings suggested that women are not using ecstasy as a deliberate means of weight control (Curran, and Robjant, 2006). Thus, some girls take it for what they believe to be its weight loss properties and some don't – though we have observed in our clinical work that some might say it's not for weight loss even though it is.

## GENDER AND WEIGHT PREOCCUPATION

Women are more preoccupied with fear of gaining weight than men, and they use substances more often due to higher levels of weight and body image concerns than men. Body dissatisfaction and weight concerns are widespread among women in Western societies during adolescence and early adulthood, ages that are also associated with initiation and increased use of recreational drugs (Curran and Robjant, 2006). A number of studies indicate that women are less likely than men to enter treatment due to the fact that women are more concerned with their weight and less confident in their ability to control post-cessation weight gain (Jeffery et al., 2000). Also, high substance dependence, low motivation and confrontation with many stressful events should be considered as a possible explanation for this gender difference (Razavi et al., 1999).

It is already established that women who smoke cigarettes have higher levels of concern about weight and greater dissatisfaction with body shape than women who do not smoke. Further, tobacco smoking for the purpose of weight control has been consistently reported in studies of adolescent girls and young women (Curran and Robjant, 2006). Other drugs, such as ecstasy, also have appetite suppressant and exercise promoting effects and may appeal to young women who are concerned about weight and body image. Similar to smoking, it is reported that ecstasy users have higher total eating disorder index (EDI) scores, suggesting that women who use ecstasy have greater weight and body image concerns than those who do not use this drug. Specifically, their scores on the sub-scales of bulimia and impulse deregulation were significantly higher than controls (Curran and Robjant, 2006). Ecstasy users also agreed more than controls that 'ecstasy helps you lose weight', 'drugs help you eat less', 'I eat less when I take drugs but this is not deliberately for losing weight' and 'I exercise more when I take drugs but this is not deliberately for losing weight'.

Moreover, motivational use of cocaine related to weight concerns is also an important avenue of research, considering that research shows that females begin use 3 years earlier than males (females, 15 years; males, 18.6 years) and that males outnumber females in all age groups by a ratio of 3:1 except in the 12–17 age group, where females outnumber males (Substance Abuse and Mental Health Services Administration, 1995). The 12–17 age group is the prime age group for a female to develop an eating disorder (Cochrane et al., 1998). Also, women who take one substance (e.g., cocaine) to control their weight may be more likely to take a second, third, or more substances to have the same effect. There is a report on a large percentage of women with and without eating disorders using cocaine to control or lose weight. It confirms the results of Jonas et al. (1987) who found that 32% of the female callers to a cocaine hotline had eating disorders and that many of these women used cocaine to control weight or ameliorate their eating disorder symptoms (Cochrane et al., 1998).

Some research on co-use of several substances has shown that increasing dieting severity is positively associated with increasing severity of tobacco and marijuana use as well as alcohol use (Krahn et al., 1992). It is believed that self-deprivation of food increases susceptibility to frequent drug use. Deprivation, such as that seen in an eating disorder or in severe dieting, increases the likelihood of reinforcement for use of drugs such as cocaine, heroin, and alcohol (Krahn et al., 1992). The bottom line of many findings is that young women who use one or several substances to control their weight are more impulsive, more socially insecure and have more bulimic tendencies than young women who do not use these drugs.

## STRUGGLES RELATED TO WOMEN'S WEIGHT AND SHAPE ISSUES AND SUBSTANCE USE INITIATION, TREATMENT AND RECOVERY AND THE LACK OF TREATMENT

Arguably, women's struggle to maintain low weight and slim body shape leads them to engage into various weight control practices such as dieting, exercising, and purging. Consequently, increasing dissatisfaction with personal body image may influence the decision of some women to begin using various drugs implicated in appetite suppression. Numerous studies on tobacco use among women and young girls propose that increasing dieting severity is positively associated with increasing severity of tobacco and marijuana use as well as alcohol use, and self-deprivation of food increases susceptibility to frequent drug use. Deprivation, such as that seen in an eating disorder or in severe dieting, increases the likelihood of reinforcement for use of drugs such as cocaine, heroin, and alcohol. In comorbid conditions, bulimic women who have posttraumatic stress disorder and depression use alcohol and their eating disorder behaviours to cope maladaptively with depression and anxiety. Female cocaine abusers who abuse or are dependent on alcohol as a secondary diagnosis may even be more likely to have an eating disorder (Cochrane et al., 1998).

Tomeo et al. (1999) found that among girls, binge eating is positively associated with daily dieting and monthly purging and is positively associated with experimentation with substances. A study of tobacco use and unhealthy weight loss behaviours among 539 sixth-grade students revealed that already at that age girls who used unhealthy weight loss methods (vomiting or use of laxatives, water pills, or diet pills) were 14 times more likely to smoke than those who did not. In similar study, it was found that adolescent girls start to smoke after hearing that it increases metabolism and may induce weight loss. Once they start to smoke, some use cigarettes as a way to stave off hunger, as an alternative activity to eating, and/or to keep from gaining weight. Despite knowledge of the harmful health effects of smoking, many smokers cite fear of weight gain as a reason not to quit. Since many studies have indicated an association between smoking cessation and weight gain, it is difficult to allay the fear that quitting will ultimately result in an increase in weight (Forman and Morello, 2003).

Elevated dieting concerns were found to be a significant risk factor for smoking onset during college prior to smoking initiation in Saules et al. (2004) study. They offered that a possible explanation of smoking initiation is a response to a desire to control weight. Examinations of adolescent girls indicate that for many, smoking initiation is correlated with the belief that cigarette use will assist in weight, and a substantial number of women reported use of tobacco as a dieting strategy. Contrary to some reports (Fidler et al., 2007), Saules et al. (2004) found no evidence that smoking initiation decreased weight or prevented weight gain, because women in their sample were very light smokers on average.

Evidence suggests that individuals in substance use treatment become very preoccupied with food and their body shape and gain weight in recovery. Weight concerns may interfere with substance use treatment for females and, to a lesser degree, males, since people who use substances as an appetite suppressant and/or weight control device perceive greater difficulty in quitting. For example, some individuals refuse to quit smoking because of fear of weight gain. Many cross-sectional studies have reported that specific weight concerns about smoking cessation deter cessation, and some suggest that motivation to quit smoking is significantly lower in those with post-cessation weight concerns. Additionally, some prospective studies have found that cessation-related weight concerns are associated with reduced cessation success (Cooper et al., 2006; Fidler et al., 2007). Although about 70% of smokers want to quit their habit, with the majority citing health concerns as a primary reason to stop, there is widespread concern about the risks of gaining weight after quitting (Cahill and Ussher, 2007). In particular, female smokers who perceived difficulty in quitting were about 33% more likely to have weight concerns than female smokers who did not perceive difficulty in quitting. Among males, perceived difficulties in quitting and weight concerns were not highly significant (Forman and Morello, 2003).

Adolescents in substance use treatment evidence weight gain that cannot be explained by maturation factors alone. Many adolescents believe that various drugs have the power to keep them slim and this belief is associated with the persistent increase of substance use and treatment resistance. Strong positive associations between adolescent smoking and weight concerns, beliefs, and behaviors have been consistently identified in females (Forman and Morello, 2003). Thus, many adolescents believe that smoking helps to keep them slim. Furthermore, they are more likely to take up smoking if they perceive being thin as important, are concerned about their weight or are trying to lose weight (Fidler et al., 2007). Evidence suggests that independent of age, BMI, and known predictors of tobacco uptake, contemplation of cigarette use is positively related to concern about weight, whereas experimentation with cigarettes is positively related to engaging in weight control behaviors. Girls who moved beyond being concerned with their weight to actually engaging in extreme weight control behaviors are more likely to also move beyond thinking about smoking to experimenting with cigarettes (Tomeo et al., 1999). It appears that current female smokers are more likely to have a weight concern than female students who do not smoke. Although perceived fatness is not directly associated with smoking, females desiring to be thinner and/or who frequently diet are more likely to smoke than female students who do not have these weight concerns. The link between smoking and weight concerns in females thus may be partially attributable to having a negative, unrealistic, or unobtainable body image rather than actual body size (Forman and Morello, 2003).

Longitudinal findings support recent works in which it is found that weight, BMI and waist circumference are reduced in persistent female smokers over a 1-year period (Fidler et al., 2007). Having an example of regular smoking 15–16 years old adolescents who have a lower body mass index (BMI) than other students at the same age, some youth start to smoke hoping that it increases metabolism and may induce weight loss (Fidler et al., 2007). On one hand, smoking cessation may not only rob these females of the perceived physiological and social benefits of smoking, but quitting may also take away a weight control mechanism that has, in their view, kept them slim or prevented them from gaining even more weight. On the other hand, weight concerns may also prohibit effective smoking cessation programs for females and, to a lesser degree, males, since students who use smoking as an appetite suppressant and/or weight control device perceive greater difficulty in quitting. Many individuals refuse to quit smoking because of fear of weight gain (Forman and Morello, 2003).

## NEED FOR TREATMENT

Substance use treatment programs are increasingly including dieting advice in hopes of increasing the rate of women quitting -- but with little success. For example, treatment for female cocaine users poses a difficult problem for clinicians. It is unclear if the comorbid treatment of cocaine abuse and the eating disorder should be conducted simultaneously or sequentially. It also is unclear if relapse prevention efforts and treatment efforts must link the interaction between loss of sobriety and its effect on eating behaviour and the opposite effect of loss of control of eating and its effect on sobriety. Controlled studies using standardized treatments are needed to assess the best methods to treat these individuals (Cochrane et al., 1998).

Existence of an extra motivation such as physiological and social benefits of substance use clearly complicates the approach to the treatment regiment, that is, female smokers who use cigarettes as an appetite suppressant or to keep from gaining weight may be likelier to perceive difficulty in quitting (Forman and Morello, 2003). Also, there are certain beliefs about qualities of drugs, which influence decisions of individuals to administer them. Thus, the belief that ecstasy aids weight loss is not generalized to the other stimulant drugs, according to Curran and Robjant (2006). Rather it reflects users' greater experience of the appetite suppressant effects of ecstasy and of an increased ability to dance for prolonged periods and so expend energy.

## ADDRESSING FOOD, WEIGHT AND SHAPE CONCERNS FOR WOMEN WITH ADDICTIONS TO ENHANCE RECOVERY, MINIMIZE RELAPSE, AND INCREASE WOMEN'S OVERALL WELL BEING

Effective drug use preventive programs are needed. Psycho-educational programs should be delivered through the schools, since many recreational drugs are initiated and used during adolescent years. Moreover, 12-17 is an age group which is the most vulnerable to false beliefs about body image and ideal body shape; during this age there is the highest prevalence of eating disorders. Fidler et al., (2007) report that adolescents, especially girls, believe that smoking will help them to remain slim, and that weight concern and smoking behaviour tend to be associated. Fidler made recommendations that substance use prevention approaches among adolescents should work to alter perceptions of drugs as an effective weight control tool (2007). Additionally, positive results might be obtained by including counselling, since working with a therapist might help these young women to work through and alleviate their fears about increased weight.

The development of gender-specific substance use treatment programs may have more positive impact on motivation of sexes to quit intake of the drugs. Equipping participants of preventive programs with knowledge and behavioural skills to recognise and resist external cues that encourage initiation or continuation of drug use can have favourable outcome for the results of the program (Blechman and Brownell, 1999). Traditional divisions between treatment and prevention are becoming increasingly difficult to define in addiction. Short, intensive programs, which do not take a gender-oriented approach into consideration, are proven to be of a little effect (Blechman and Brownell, 1999).

Given the significant concerns about weight and shape in women with substance use problems it is crucial to address these in substance use treatment. The goal of treatment must be goal directed and. not exclusively symptom related. Improvement must be measured beyond the length of stay and symptom reduction, and focus on factors meaningful to the clients. The relationship must be with the person not with the diagnosis. A combination of individual psychotherapy and group work may be useful for these individuals, and medical monitoring may be required to minimize the possible medical complications in women who have a comorbid diagnosis of eating disorder. What is crucial is that the therapist pays special attention to the interrelationships amongst substance use and eating disordered behaviours.

As illustrated in Figure 1, weight concerns and problematic eating may be a prompting event to, or, a consequence of substance use.

Relationships:                                                                    Examples:

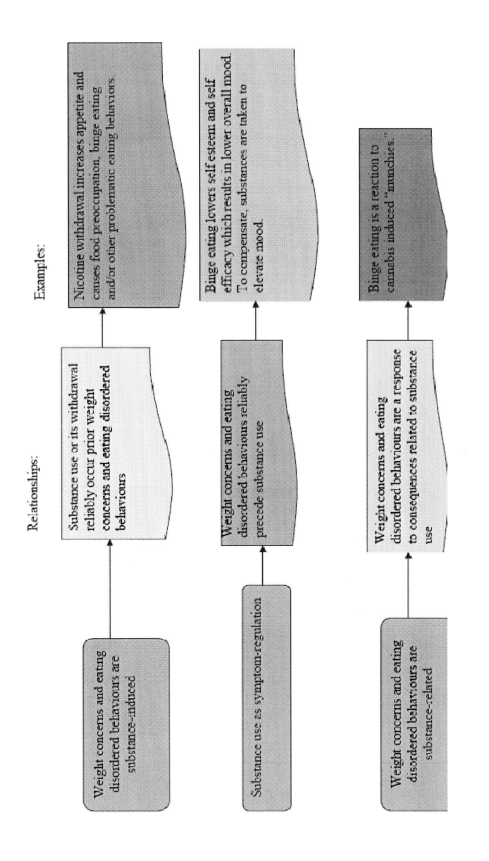

Weight concerns and eating disordered behaviors are substance-induced → Substance use or its withdrawal reliably occur prior weight concerns and eating disordered behaviours → Nicotine withdrawal increases appetite and causes food preoccupation, binge eating and/or other problematic eating behaviors.

Substance use as symptom-regulation → Weight concerns and eating disordered behaviours reliably precede substance use → Binge eating lowers self esteem and self efficacy which results in lower overall mood. To compensate, substances are taken to elevate mood.

Weight concerns and eating disordered behaviours are substance-related → Weight concerns and eating disordered behaviours are a response to consequences related to substance use → Binge eating is a reaction to cannabis induced "munchies."

**Figure 1. (Continued).**

Relationships:                    Examples:

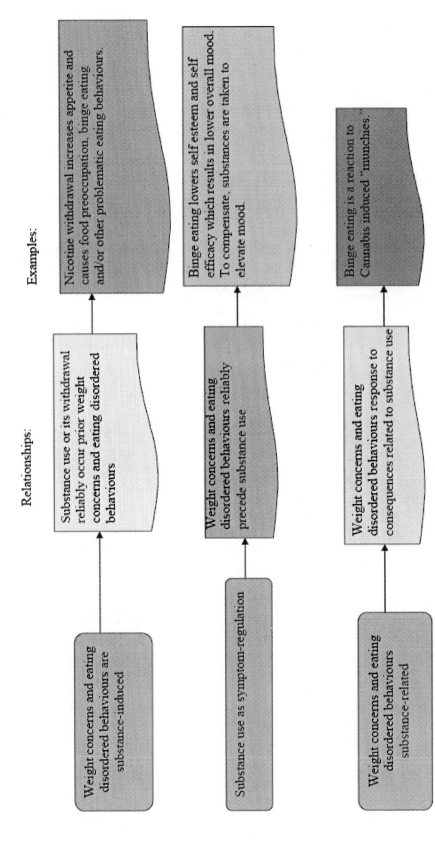

Figure 1. Connections among weight concerns, disordered eating and substance use behaviours.

An example is when weight concerns and problematic eating are substance induced and nicotine withdrawal increases a person's appetite and the person may become preoccupied by food, restrict, binge eat, or engage in other problematic eating behaviours as a result. Substance use may also serve as a symptom regulation. This can be identified when the weight concerns and disordered eating behaviours reliably precede substance use as in the case when a person binge eats, then becomes sad and depressed for having "done it again".

To compensate, she takes substances to elevate her mood. Another example of the relationship between weight concerns, problematic eating and substance use is illustrated when the weight concerns and disordered eating behaviours follow substance use. A woman may experience low mood, blame herself and feel discouraged after an alcohol binge. Subsequently she over eats to cope with her emotions but then feels more disappointed in herself and purges to get rid of the unpleasant feelings. In addition, weight concerns and problematic eating may be indirectly related to substance use. An example is a woman who experiences pain in her joints due to excess weight caused by binge eating. She uses narcotics to help her ease discomfort but often takes more than the prescribed amount because she feels that the pain is unbearable.

The woman's identity has to be addressed in treatment as it may be enmeshed with the weight concerns, problematic eating and substance use. Our clinical data confirms such a link and may be illustrated in drawings that individuals have done while in treatment. For example, a 23-year-old woman struggling with heroin and tobacco dependence and bulimia nervosa drew a picture of her upper body in grey and red with a "thought bubble" that contained packs of cigarettes, syringe, bungs and other substance related paraphernalia, a hamburger with a red cross on it and a face of a pig. She described the picture as representing her constant preoccupation with the substances she had used and her strong cravings for them. She stated that the number of substance related items was to emphasize the magnitude of her addiction and the hamburger represented the food she is "not allowed to eat" and that if she ate them she "would look like and feel like a pig". She stated that she used the red colour to represent alarm and anxiety she was feeling at the time. She used substances, restricted her food intake and self-induced vomiting to manage her weight. Once she stopped heroin use, her weight concerns became more prominent and her eating disordered behaviours increased substantially. She mentioned that she had noticed in the past that when she had been treated for her eating disorder, her substance use had increased substantially. The connection between weight concerns and substance use was essential to address in treatment.

Another example is that of a 42-year-old woman with problem gambling, nicotine dependence and binge eating disorder. To represent herself, she drew a scale of justice with the hand around 300 pounds, her actual weight, and a limit she would have never wanted to exceed. On one part of the balance, she drew herself like a crying face with a red closed mouth but without eyes. She stated that she drew the closed mouth because the opening of her mouth is a betrayal. On the other part of the balance, she drew what she considered unhealthy food that she strived to avoid. She reported that the food was winning, as the side of the scale with the food was lower. She also stated that she did not draw eyes on her face because she did not want to see this. She also drew a mouth linked to lungs. The mouth was smoking and the lungs were full of a black smoke. She clarified that this mouth was killing her and that smoking was "self-sabotage". She drew a "Rest in Peace" below the mouth-lung machine to express her ambivalence because she recognized she was killing herself by smoking but that she was smoking to find peace. She represented her problematic gambling through dollars burning. She expressed that she was angry with herself because she started the fire with very little money and she was "just throwing more and more". She reported that she was the fire and that she had to feed her urges with dollars. The client also acknowledged that money was burning too quickly and that she had to find a more stable source of pleasure in her life. In therapy she identified that she engaged in smoking, gambling, and problematic eating as emotion regulation strategies. Helping her practice adaptive emotion regulation strategies was crucial in treatment.

In terms of nutrition, it is fundamental that the therapist avoids rules around food and eating, watches specific terminology (i.e., using words such as good, bad, natural food, should) not only in the client but also in him/herself, and corrects any cognitive distortions about food. The therapist must frame facts about food and nutrition as guidelines and suggestions only, and acknowledge individual preferences, while challenging rigid beliefs and not forbidding specific food. A dietician trained in eating disorders may be a valuable source of advice who can teach clients to understand their hunger and satiety cues, help them remove labels and judgments attached to types and quantities of food, normalize eating, plan for weight restoration (as needed), and assist with medical monitoring. Residential treatment and medical stabilization may be required in cases when the problematic eating is so severe that the woman's life is severely compromised. Also of note is that alcohol use comorbid with anorexia nervosa is the largest predictor of mortality (Sullivan, 1995). A substance use therapist who identifies weight concerns and severe emaciation in a woman with alcohol use may suspect anorexia nervosa and should investigate further by asking the woman directly about her concerns, offer support as necessary, direct her to her family physician for further investigation and provide her with literature on comorbid substance use and eating disorders and their integrative treatment.

In cases when the woman is motivated with working on her substance use but is unwilling to address her problematic eating issue, it is important to identify the functional relationships amongst substance use, weight concerns and problematic eating, and use motivational interviewing techniques to help the client to consider these issues in substance use treatment.

## CONCLUSION

Many women believe that using various substances can help then control their weight and this belief is associated with the persistent increase of substance use and treatment resistance. Consequently, current directions in intervention must consider the links between substance use and weight and shape issues, particularly among young women, both in prevention and in treatment. Future clinical research must also address the functional relationships amongst substance use, weight concerns and disordered eating behaviours.

## ACKNOWLEDGMENTS

The authors thank Ms. Jenany for her assistance with the searches and Ms. Dixon for her assistance with the editing.

# REFERENCES

Blechman, E.A. and Brownell, K.D. (1999). *Behavioral Medicine and Women: A Comprehensive Handbook*. Published by Guilford Press.

Birch, C.D., Stewart, S.H., and Brown, C.G. (2007). Exploring differential patterns of situational risk of binge eating and heavy drinking. *Addictive Behaviors, 32,*433-448.

Bulik, C.M., Sullivan, P.F., Epstein, L.H., McKee, M., Kaye, W.H., Dahl, R.E., and Weltzin, T.E. (1992). Drug Use in Women with Anorexia and Bulimia Nervosa. *International Journal of Eating Disorders,* 11(3), 213-225.

Cahill, K; Ussher, M. (2007). Cannabinoid type 1 receptor antagonists (rimonabant) for smoking cessation. 4.

Clark, M.M., Hurt, T,R.D., Croghan, I.T., Patten, C.A., Novotny, P., Sloan, J.A., Dakhil, S.R., Croghan, G.A., Wos, E.J., Rowland, K.M., Bernath, A., Morton, R.F., Thomas, S.P., Tschetter, L.K., Garneau, S.K., Stella, P.J., Ebbert, L.P., Wender, D.B., Loprinzi, C.L. (2006). The prevalence of weight concerns in a smoking abstinence clinical trial. *Addictive Behaviors*, 31, 1144–1152.

Cochrane, C., Malcolm, R., and Brewerton, T. (1998). The Role of Weight Control as a Motivation for Cocaine Abuse. *Addictive Behaviors, 23*(2), 207-207.

Cooper, T.V., Dundon, T.M., Hoffman, B.M., Stoever, C.J. (2006). General and smoking cessation related weight concerns in veterans. *Addictive Behaviors,* 31, 722–725.

Curran, H.V. and Robjant, K. (2006). Eating attitudes, weight concerns and beliefs about drug effects in women who use ecstasy. *Journal of Psychopharmacology,* 20 (3), 425-431.

Curran, H.V., and Robjant, K. (2006). Eating attitudes, weight concerns and beliefs about drug effects in women who use ecstasy. *Journal of Psychopharmacology,* 20(3), 425-431.

Gadalla, T., and Piran, N. (2007). Co-occurrence of eating disorders and alcohol use disorders in women: a meta analysis. *Archives of women's mental health, 10,* 133-140.

Fidler, J.A., West, R., Van Jaarsveld, C.H.M., Jarvis, M.J., Wardle, J. (2007). Does smoking in adolescence affect body mass index, waist or height? Findings from a longitudinal study. *Addiction*, 102, 1493–1501.

Forman, V.L. and Morello, P. (2003). Weight concerns, postexperimental smoking, and perceived difficulty in quitting in Argentinean adolescents. *Eating Behaviors*, 4, 41–52.

Jefferey, W.R., Hennrikus, D.J., Lando, H.A., Murray, D.M., Liu, J.W. (2000). Reconciling conflicting findings regarding postcessation weight concerns and success in smoking cessation. *Health Psychology*, 19, 3, 242-246.

Jonas, J. M., Gold, M. S., Sweeney, D., and Pottash, A. L. (1987). Eating disorders and cocaine abuse: A survey of 259 cocaine abusers. *Journal of Clinical Psychiatry*, 48, 47–50.

Krahn, D., Durth, C., Demitrack, M., and Drewnowski, A. (1992). The relationship of dieting severity and bulimic behaviors to alcohol and other drug use in young women. *Journal of Substance Abuse*, 4, 341–353.

Peveler, R., and Fairburn, C. (1990). Eating Disorders in women who abuse alcohol. *British Journal of Addiction, 85*, 1633-1638.

Razavi, D., Vandecasteele, H., Primo, C., Bodo, M., Debrier, F., Verbist, H., Pethica, D., Eerdekens, M., Kaufman, L. (1999). Maintaining Abstinence from Cigarette Smoking:

Effectiveness of Group Counselling and Factors Predicting Outcome. *European Journal of Cancer*, 35, 8, pp. 1238-1247.

Saulesa, K.K., Pomerleaub, C.S., Snedecorb, S.M., Mehringerb, A.M., Shadlea, M.B., Kurthc, C., Krahnd, D.D. (2004). Relationship of onset of cigarette smoking during college to alcohol use, dieting concerns, and depressed mood: Results from the Young Women's Health Survey. *Addictive Behaviors,* 29, 893–899.

Substance Abuse and Mental Health Services Administration. (1995). National Household Survey on Drug Abuse: Main Findings 1993. DHHS Publication No. 95–3020.

Tomeo, C.A., Field, A.E., Berkey, C.S., Colditz, G.A., Frazier, A.L. (1999). Weight Concerns, Weight Control Behaviors, and Smoking Initiation. *Pediatrics,* 104, 918-924.

Von Ranson, K.M., McGue, M., Iacono, W.G. (2003). Disordered Eating and Substance Use in an Epidemiological Sample: II. Associations Within Families. *Psychology of Addictive Behaviors,* 17(3), 193-202.

Wilson, J.R. (1992). Bulimia Nervosa: Occurrence with Psychoactive Substance Use Disorders. *Addictive Behaviors,* 17,603-607.

In: Substance Abuse, Assessment and Addiction                ISBN: 978-1-61122-931-8
Editors: Kristina A. Murati and Allison G. Fischer          © 2011 Nova Science Publishers, Inc.

*Chapter 12*

# ADDRESSING TRAUMA AMONG WOMEN WITH SERIOUS ADDICTIVE DISORDERS: TREATMENT MODELS, PROGRAM FACTORS AND POTENTIAL MEDIATORS

### *Douglas L. Polcin[1]\*, Madhabika B. Nayak[1] and Susan Blacksher[2]*

[1]Alcohol Research Group, Public Health Institute
6475 Christie Avenue, Suite 400. Emeryville, CA 94608-1010
[2]California Association of Addiction Recovery Resources
2921 Fulton Ave., P.O. Box 214127, Sacramento, CA 95821, USA

## ABSTRACT

A large majority of women entering addiction treatment present significant symptoms of trauma related to physical or sexual abuse. Despite research indicating that trauma interventions are integral to women's successful recovery from addiction, many programs do not adequately address violence-related trauma. This chapter provides a review of the literature on trauma among women with addictive disorders and several manual based interventions developed to address co-occurring addiction and trauma-related disorders. One intervention, "Beyond Trauma," which has become increasingly popular among community based programs is described in detail. Beyond Trauma appears to have several advantages over other therapies for treating trauma and addiction in women, including 1) a theoretical foundation that draws on relational theory as a guide to the intervention, 2) a broad based approach that can be utilized by a variety of professional and paraprofessional staff members, 3) a focus that goes beyond treating women with a formal diagnosis of post traumatic stress disorder to include treatment for an array of symptoms and problems associated with trauma, and 4) gender-appropriate

* Phone: (510) 597-3440 Extension 277. Fax: (510) 985-6459. E-Mail: dpolcin@arg.org

use of expressive arts in its curriculum. The chapter also discusses treatment program environment factors that may be critically important to treatment outcome for women: 1) whether the program is gender specific, 2) the degree of emphasis on peer involvement in recovery, 3) program recognition of the value of knowledge-based recovery experience, 4) program facilitation of cohesion, 5) the empowerment of clients in decisions affecting the program and 6) skills training relevant to managing moods, relationships and a variety of problems that women face during recovery. Possible mechanisms of change for Beyond Trauma are explored with particular emphasis on the variety of ways the intervention attempts to impact problem areas experienced by women (e.g., mental health functioning self esteem and social support). Recommendations for future research in the treatment of trauma and addiction-related disorders in women are outlined.

**Keywords**: Trauma, Women, Addiction, Recovery, Post Traumatic Stress Disorder.

# INTRODUCTION

Treatment approaches for addictive disorders have increasingly recognized the need to address co-occurring psychiatric problems. Thus, many treatment programs have made provisions for clients to receive evaluations for psychiatric problems through referrals to outpatient clinics. The integration of treatment for psychiatric symptoms into routine interventions within addiction programs has been more difficult. For example, some peer-oriented approaches to recovery appear to be effective for helping individuals establish abstinence from substances and develop a program of recovery (Kaskutas et al., 1996), but often do not sufficiently address comorbid psychiatric issues comorbid with substance use disorders (Polcin, 2000). Although referrals to mental health professionals outside treatment programs are viable options for many dual diagnosis clients, there are drawbacks to this approach. First, there may be problems motivating clients to attend outside appointments. Second, individuals with substance use disorders are often wary of mental health professionals because of their perception that these professionals do not sufficiently understand addiction problems and view addiction problems as secondary to other psychiatric disorders (Polcin, 1997). Finally, referring to outside professionals can result in disaggregated treatment and precludes addressing the needs of the whole person. The need to integrate psychiatric interventions into addiction recovery programs is therefore critical.

This chapter will review the prevalence and impact of trauma among women in addiction programs beginning with a review of literature that documents the high prevalence of trauma among these women and highlights the insufficiency of trauma related issues being addressed in addiction programs. A broad definition of trauma-related problems is adopted that includes both symptoms of post traumatic stress disorder (PTSD) and other trauma-related symptoms that do not meet PTSD criteria but nonetheless can have a significant impact on the success of sustained recovery. While PTSD has received increased attention in the literature and in treatment programs, less has been devoted to investigating and addressing the impact of trauma in women whose symptoms do not meet diagnostic criteria for PTSD.

Structured treatment interventions for women with histories of trauma have typically been based upon the needs of those who meet DSM-IV Criteria for PTSD. In this chapter we present a manual intervention that was designed to address a broader view of trauma and its effects, "Beyond Trauma: A Healing Journey for Women." In addition to addressing more diverse ways that women have been affected by traumatic experiences, the intervention lends itself to easy integration into addiction recovery programs in the community due to its emphasis on peer-oriented learning. A discussion of how the intervention might interact with program environment characters and possible mechanisms of how it might facilitate improvement of symptoms is included. Although Beyond Trauma is widely used in recovery programs and enjoys anecdotal reports of effectiveness (Messina, 2006), scientific studies that provide rigorous, empirical data to support its effectiveness are lacking. Although two preliminary studies (i.e., Messina, 2005, 2006)testing the efficacy of the intervention are currently underway with criminal justice populations, there is a clear need for additional research that is broader in scope. The chapter closes with a discussion of additional studies that are needed to validate Beyond Trauma.

## PREVALENCE OF TRAUMA AND PTSD AMONG WOMEN WITH SUBSTANCE ABUSE PROBLEMS

While studies vary in their definition and assessment of trauma among women with substance abuse problems, they almost universally report high prevalence rates and detrimental effects on outcome. Over half of all drug-dependent women in treatment report a history of childhood trauma (Haller and Miles, 2004); at least one in four report childhood sexual abuse (Boles et al., 2005; Haller and Miles, 2004). Men and women receiving treatment for substance use disorders who report childhood sexual abuse histories have more co-morbid psychiatric disorders, criminal activities, problem severity, and post treatment relapse than other clients. The harmful effects of childhood trauma among women with substance abuse problems are not limited to those entering treatment. A general population study of 316 Swedish women (Spak et al., 1997) found that sexual abuse prior to age 13 was the strongest predictor of subsequent alcohol dependence/abuse.

Studies also document high rates of lifetime trauma (adult or childhood) in substance abuse treatment samples of women. Najavits et al. (1997) cited studies indicating that a majority of women in substance abuse treatment (55 to 99%) reported a lifetime history of trauma. Treatment seeking women are more likely than men to report any lifetime trauma (Ouimette et al., 2000; Pirard et al., 2005), a larger number of traumatic events, and more sexual, serial, and familial assault (Grice et al., 1995; Kubiak, 2004). Trauma history is associated with co-morbid psychiatric disorders (Grice et al., 1995; Ouimette et al., 2000), severe alcohol-related problems, poly-drug use (Pirard et al., 2005), and greater substance use relapse (Kubiak, 2004).

The role of PTSD in the association between trauma history and substance abuse has received substantial research attention. Several community and epidemiological studies document the incidence of co-morbid PTSD and substance abuse (Chilcoat and Menard, 2003). These studies found individuals with PTSD had a higher risk for drug use disorders, particularly poly-drug dependencies, as well as alcohol dependence and more severe alcohol and drug use related problems. For example, in a study addressing substance use among individuals in the general population with PTSD Breslau (2003) concluded that PTSD increased risk for substance abuse as well as other psychiatric disorders.

A related body of research has examined trauma-related PTSD in treatment seeking substance abusing samples. This research suggests large proportions (30 to 59%) of women with substance use disorders (SUDs) also have PTSD (Grice et al., 1995; Najavits et al., 2003; Najavits et al., 1997). PTSD-SUDs comorbidity is associated with more severe psychological problems and greater use of substance abuse treatment (Najavits et al., 1997). Consistent with community epidemiological data (e.g., Kessler et al., 1995), associations between trauma and PTSD are stronger for women than men in treatment seeking samples (Ouimette et al., 2000).

Despite extensive research documenting the widespread prevalence of PTSD-SUDs co-morbidity, the etiology and treatment of these co-occurring disorders is not well understood (Back et al., 2006). Even less well understood is the relationship between traumatic experiences that do not result in a formal diagnosis of PTSD and their impact on the development of recovery from substance use disorders. A broader understanding of the impact of traumatic experiences and substance use recovery is of great importance because trauma is very common in substance using women. Reynolds et al (2005) reported that while 94% of Australian inpatients with SUDs reported some sort of trauma, only 38.5% of those reporting trauma met PTSD criteria. Close examination of data on women in substance abuse in the United States (Dansky et al., 1996; Dansky et al., 1995; Fullilove et al., 1993; Najavits et al., 1997) also indicates that 40% to 60% of these substance abusing women who report trauma do not meet criteria for current PTSD. Similarly, Najavits et al (2003) reported a high number of lifetime trauma events in cocaine dependent women, even those without PTSD.

The few studies that examined non-PSTD related trauma have reported mixed findings. A recent prospective study of young adult men and women examined the role of trauma in the development of SUD's and found that that PTSD, but not trauma without PTSD, increased risk for drug use (Breslau et al., 2003). However, trauma exposure, regardless of PTSD diagnosis, did not increase risk for alcohol abuse or dependence. However, there may be differences by gender. A retrospective analysis of data from this study examined women only and found that trauma, regardless of PTSD, was associated with higher risk for alcohol use disorders. Clearly, there is a need for more studies on trauma among women to improve our understanding of women's complex and diverse responses to it (Becker-Blease and Freyd, 2005; Brier and Jordan, 2004).

## TREATMENT APPROACHES FOR CO-MORBID PTSD AND SUBSTANCE ABUSE

The substance abuse treatment literature has provided limited information to practitioners about how to address PTSD. In particular, guidance is lacking for how practitioners might address sub-clinical PTSD symptoms in their treatment of women.

The narrower issue of PTSD-SUDs, however, has received some attention and a number of interventions have been developed to address these co-occurring disorders. Treatment models for PTSD-SUDs include Seeking Safety (Najavits, 2001), exposure based therapies (e.g., Triffleman, 2000) and combinations of exposure and cognitive behavioral approaches (for a review see Back et al., 2006). All of these treatments use manual interventions consisting of 16 to 25 individual sessions, with the exception of SS, which has also been used as group treatment. As Back et al. (2006) point out, consensus is lacking as to which approaches are best and whether different approaches have advantages for specific populations. A selection of these interventions is described below along with a description of the limited studies supporting their effectiveness.

SS was designed to treat PTSD-SUDs in men and women in an integrated manner that addresses both PTSD and substance use symptoms. It consists of 25 sessions that focus mainly on the improving the present lives of individuals. Thus, it seeks to help clients develop safety in their relationships, thinking, behavior, and emotions. SS attempts to achieve these goals by 1) using psychoeducation about trauma and addiction, 2) teaching a variety of coping skills, and 3) helping clients make choices to gain more control over their lives. In addition, case management is included as a way of helping clients to access services for other needs they present.

Seeking safety (SS) is clearly the most studied PTSD-SUDs intervention. Research has been conducted in diverse settings and has included including 2 multi-site trials: 1) the Women, Co-Occurring Disorders, and Violence Study WCDVS) (McHugo et al., 2005b) and 2) a study of 200 homeless women (Najavits, in press). Recent studies have also been conducted using controlled trials (Najavits, in press).

SS was also included among the 4 treatments studied across 9 sites in the WCDVS (McHugo et al., 2005b), one of the largest investigations of trauma treatment among women in recovery (see review below). All of the treatments studied, including SS, performed modestly better than treatment-as-usual comparison conditions (Cocozza et al., 2005; Morrissey et al., 2005a). However, no significant differences were reported between (among?) the trauma intervention conditions. Other studies of SS have reported similar findings (Najavits, in press). Overall, studies show that SS outperforms treatment as-usual. Hien et al. (2004) noted that substance use and mental health outcomes associated with SS appear to be comparable to active comparison interventions, such as relapse prevention interventions.

Other interventions for combined PTSD-SUDs use exposure based treatments (see Back et al., [2006] for a review). These techniques use in vivo or imaging procedures to present the client with stimuli associated with their trauma. The therapist works with the client to desensitize traumatic reactions to these stimuli and thereby establish a sense of control and self efficacy. Although exposure based interventions have been shown to be effective for PTSD without substance abuse, they have not been extensively studied for clients who present with both substance use and PTSD disorders (Back et al., 2006). An exception is a study conducted by Triffleman (2000). The intervention consists of twice weekly therapy sessions over a 20 week time period and integrates relapse prevention, coping skills, psychoeducation, and in vivo exposure techniques. Although individuals receiving the intervention appear to improve on PTSD and substance use measures, these improvements are not significantly different from improvements among clients in comparison interventions, such as twelve step facilitation (Back et al., 2006). One potential reason for these findings may be that studies to date have used small sample sizes and may not have sufficient power to detect differences.

A somewhat different exposure based treatment has been described by Back et al. (2006). Known as Concurrent Treatment of PTSD and Cocaine Dependence (CTPCD), this intervention was designed to address combined PTSD with cocaine dependence. The treatment includes sixteen 90-minute therapy sessions delivered once or twice per week. It is delivered in manual format and uses imagined and in vivo exposure therapy for PTSD symptoms and cognitive-behavioral relapse prevention techniques for cocaine dependence. Similar to preliminary studies for other exposure based therapies for PTSD-SUDs, research has shown that individuals who receive the intervention make improvements on substance use and PTSD symptoms. However, larger studies are needed that compare CTPCD with other approaches.

In sum, research provides some support for integrated PTSD-SUD treatment, particularly in terms of reducing symptoms of both substance use and trauma. However, there are several concerns worth noting. First, most of these interventions were not designed to be gender specific and do not address larger gender issues, such as discrimination and prejudice. Rather, they address PTSD among a range of clients with SUDs. For a variety of reasons women may need different interventions than men to heal from the experience of traumatic events. Second, larger studies are needed to assess how trauma informed interventions compare to other substance use interventions. To date, few differences have been found between women receiving PTSD interventions and active comparison interventions, such as 12-step facilitation or relapse prevention. Perhaps most important, to date studies only included individuals with a formal diagnosis of PTSD, thus excluding a large portion of women in recovery who have experienced trauma but do not meet PTSD diagnostic criteria.

## THE WOMEN, CO-OCCURRING DISORDERS AND VIOLENCE STUDY (WCDVS)

A unique study targeting the treatment of women with trauma in multi-service agencies that provided mental health, substance abuse and other community services was conducted by the Substance Abuse and Mental Health Services Administration (SAMHSA) (McHugo et al., 2005b; Veysey and Clark, 2004). The study consisted of a large, multi-site investigation conducted between 2001 and 2003 and examined a broad array of systems and service intervention factors. Nine different multi-service agencies across the United States providing assistance with some combination of substance abuse, mental health, children's services, and healthcare participated as the study's intervention programs. Staff members in these agencies consisted of a variety of professionals as well as peer counselors who were in recovery from addiction and trauma. Treatment programs were diverse and included inpatient, outpatient, mental health, and addiction programs. Four different manualized trauma interventions were used across the 9 intervention programs, including the Trauma Recovery and Empowerment Model (TREM) (Harris and Copeland, 2000), Seeking Safety (Najavits, 2001), Addiction and Trauma Recovery Integrated Model (ATRIUM) (Miller and Guidry, 2001), and 4) TRIAD Women's Group (Fearday et al., 2001). Unlike some of the aforementioned interventions, these were delivered in a group format. Each intervention program selected a local program to serve as a comparison (McHugo et al., 2005b).

One problem with the study from a scientific standpoint was the programs were allowed to adapt interventions to their own needs and it is uncertain how this affected fidelity to the intervention delivered. Some sites also added other trauma specific groups in addition to the above interventions, most commonly domestic violence groups for women. This could obviously contaminate the effects of the targeted interventions. Having the intervention programs select their own comparison programs is also problematic because various biases could have affected the selection. For example, intervention programs may have had a vested interest in showing better outcome relative to comparison conditions. Thus, they may have had an incentive to select comparison programs with which they felt they would compare favorably.

Seeking Safety has already been described above. The other three interventions had noticeable similarities with SS and overlapped with each other to a considerable extent. For example, TREM focused on skill development in multiple areas of functioning and empowerment of the women. Like SS, it used cognitive behavioral and psychoeducation techniques to a significant extent. ATRIUM used a group format to provide psychoeducation about trauma and addiction as well as expressive activities to help women conceptualize their trauma differently. Like SS, developing adaptive strategies in women's current life to mitigate the destructive sequalae of trauma was important. Thus, there were elements that were didactic and process oriented. TRIAD was also a group oriented approach that focused on teaching interpersonal skills such as setting boundaries, as well as improving self acceptance, management of emotions, and tolerance or stress.

A total of 2729 women, 1415 in the trauma-informed intervention condition and 1314 in the treatment-as-usual condition, were enrolled into the study. Study participants were interviewed at baseline, three, six, nine and 12 months post enrollment. Outcome measures were administered at baseline, 6 and 12 month; 2006 and 2026 women completed the 6 month- and 12-month interviews, respectively. Study findings revealed modest effect sizes, with the trauma interventions being more effective than comparison interventions. At the 6-month follow-up, women in the intervention conditions showed greater improvements on measure of PTSD and drug use than those in the control conditions; differences on mental health symptoms were nearly significant but no differences were found for alcohol use (Cocozza et al., 2005; Morrissey et al., 2005a). At 12-month follow-up, small but significant improvements were found for mental health symptoms in the intervention group compared to the control condition; but no effects were found for substance use outcomes (Morrissey et al., 2005). Effect sizes varied across programs, with increased effects for programs that provided more integrated counseling. Specifically, sites at which trauma, mental health and drug use were all addressed in individual or group sessions produced more favorable results on mental health and alcohol and drug problem severity (Cocozza et al., 2005).

Many community based recovery programs do not have professional mental health staff to provide substance abuse and trauma integrated services. Thus, there is a need for trauma interventions that can be integrated into peer oriented community programs that are staffed largely by paraprofessionals. An interesting finding of the WVCDS was that experiential knowledge based on recovery experience appeared to be important in the success of the project. Mazelis (2005) noted that integrating recovering women who had trauma into the intervention was crucial for implementation of both the treatment intervention and collection of data for the research.

The WCDVS is noteworthy as the first large effectiveness study of trauma intervention for treatment seeking women with SUDs and because of its inclusion of person and program level factors. However, several limitations are worth noting. First, the interventions took place in multi-service agencies which included mental health professionals and integration of mental health services was found to be associated with better outcome. As noted above, many community-based alcohol and drug recovery programs do not employ mental health professionals. Second, a variety of factors confound the findings. These include heterogeneity of approaches within intervention and comparison programs (Cocozza et al., 2005) and nonrandom assignment of participants (Noether et al., 2005). Variability in the trauma treatments employed by intervention programs and inconsistent implementation of trauma treatments used within each program (programs adapted manuals as they wished) add to concern about the methods employed (Moses et al., 2003). There was also heterogeneity among sites in both conditions in terms of their integration of mental health, substance abuse, and trauma-specific services, involvement of trauma recovering clients in treatment, and staff training in trauma (McHugo et al., 2005b; Morrissey et al., 2005). Hence, implications of the modest effects found for the trauma interventions require further evaluation.

## THE DIFFICULTY OF ADDRESSING TRAUMA IN SUBSTANCE ABUSE TREATMENT PROGRAMS

Community-based alcohol and drug treatment programs typically do not use the treatment interventions for PTSD-SUDs that are available. One reason is that they are frequently not aware of new interventions for PTSD-SUDs. This underscores the need for improved knowledge transfer strategies to inform programs about new interventions. However, a more salient issue is many of the current interventions were designed to be used by master's level mental health professionals and community based recovery programs employ few such individuals.

While lack of training among staff in most community-based treatment programs (Triffleman, 2003) is clearly a barrier, the terminology used by trauma treatment professionals can also be problematic. Due to their focus on psychiatric disorders and the use of terms such as "clinician," "therapist," and "treatment" in manuals and guidelines (e.g., Najavits, 2001; Najavits, 2004), evidence-based treatments such as "Seeking Safety" are often viewed by community social model programs as necessitating implementation by mental health professionals in psychiatric clinics and, thereby, outside their purview (Susan Blacksher, personal communication, May 15, 2007). Although community programs do address co-morbid problems with outside referrals to mental health services, coordination between caregivers and compliance with recommendations is frequently a problem (McHugo et al., 2005a). Hence, there is a need to integrate trauma services into residential programs and make delivery of those services feasible and responsive to the constraints (such as costs and limited professional training of staff) under which most real-world programs operate.

Because of barriers to disseminating interventions and training staff on the available interventions, programs often experience problems addressing trauma and in general, lack coherent guidelines to inform their treatment approaches. Trauma issues in these programs may be inappropriately confronted, addressed using 12-step recovery principles, or ignored. Confrontational approaches designed to "break down" denial, while popular in some residential programs, are counterproductive for treating trauma (Polcin, 2003). In most cases, such approaches replicate abusive interactions and increase the risk of relapse. Twelve-step recovery principles, a central part of recovery in social model residential programs, also have limitations for trauma treatment. Perhaps most salient is the acceptance of powerlessness and turning over one's life to an external Higher Power (Kaskutas, 1996) which directly contrasts with the emphasis on empowerment and increased self efficacy, recommended and incorporated into most approaches to trauma treatment (e.g., Covington, 2003).

Some community based recovery programs have a history of ignoring or minimizing the symptoms of trauma because they view them as secondary to establishing recovery from addiction. Ignoring trauma and focusing solely on recovery from addiction fails to consider findings that addressing multiple problem areas, especially co-morbid trauma-related psychiatric conditions, is necessary for sustained recovery (National Institute on Drug Abuse, 1999). In addition, women in addiction treatment desire trauma-focused treatment. Najavits et al. (2004) reported that 80% of the 77 women with PTSD and substance abuse problems they recruited for their outpatient treatment study preferred treatment for PTSD alone, or combined PTSD and substance abuse treatment, as opposed to substance abuse treatment alone. In addition, some generic mental health services they received during the prior 30 days, such as individual psychotherapy or medication, were perceived as harmful by a small subgroup of women.

## BEYOND TRAUMA: A HEALING JOURNEY FOR WOMEN

Beyond Trauma was designed to be readily implemented in community based "social model" residential programs and does not require staff to have extensive training in mental health issues. In keeping with recommendations from the WCDVS (Mazelis, 2005) to integrate "Consumer/ Survivor/ Recovering" (CSR) women into treatment for successful outcome, Beyond Trauma also emphasizes active involvement of women recovering from trauma, substance abuse, or both and offers numerous opportunities for workshop participants to contribute to the process and content of the intervention.

Beyond Trauma is an 11-session-manualized group treatment for women based on theory as well as the clinical experiences of the authors. The manual integrates several theoretical models, including relational, addiction, and trauma theories. Relational theory (Miller, 1976) explains women's psychological development as based on connectedness as opposed to separation and individuation. Relational theory helps underscore the complex associations between women's relationships and addiction to substances.

The underlying trauma theory used to develop Beyond Trauma focuses on the need to create an environment of sanctuary for survivors (Bloom, 2000). The intervention includes a three-stage model for building safety and addresses the physiological impact of trauma (Levine, 1997), remembrance and mourning losses associated from traumatic events, and reconnection with oneself and others (Herman, 1997). The manual goes beyond a symptomatic/disorder focus to address broader facets of healing from trauma, including social influences impacting recovery. Thus, Beyond Trauma's uses of a holistic health model of addiction (Covington, 2002; White et al., 2002) which highlights the interconnectedness of trauma, abuse, and ongoing stress in the lives of women. Establishing a recovery program for addiction is viewed as integral to recovery from trauma.

The Beyond Trauma curricula include a "facilitator" manual, participant workbook, and 3 instructional videos (two for facilitators, one for clients). The facilitator's manual has two parts. The first part provides information about trauma for a basic understanding of the depth and complexity of the issues to help facilitators work more effectively with the group. The second part includes lesson plan-like session outlines. The connection between trauma and substance abuse is recognized and integrated throughout the curriculum. The intervention content comprises 3 modules: a) Violence, Abuse, and Trauma; b) Impact of Trauma; and c) Healing from Trauma. The focus on safety and coping skills is exemplified in the use of exercises to help reduce symptoms and to enhance feelings of being grounded and safe. The coping skills component includes the expression and containment of feelings as a critical part of trauma work. Overall, Beyond Trauma promotes a strength-based approach that elicits and enhances the strengths and skills of women.

Beyond Trauma may have advantages over other trauma interventions, such as Seeking Safety, particularly for use in community-based recovery programs for women. Advantages include:

(1) It was designed specifically for use with women and incorporates a gender-appropriate focus on relational theory and expressive arts. The role of gender and relationships in women's trauma and substance abuse has been described previously. Documented evidence for the importance of nonverbal therapeutic material for women (DeYoung, 2003) and for difficulties in verbal expression for some women with childhood traumatic experiences (Wolfe and Kimerling, 1997) supports the use of expressive arts in treatment.

(2) It was developed for use with women in community-based programs and other resource poor settings in which women substance abusers may be treated, such as correctional facilities (Covington, 2003).

(3) It uses a broad-based approach, seen in the use of a variety of techniques, i.e., psycho-education, cognitive-behavioral techniques, expressive arts, mind-body work, and the focus on emotional development and healthy relationships, including sexuality and support for sobriety.

(4) As discussed previously, it does not necessitate implementation by clinicians, instead allowing for implementation by staff with a wide range of training and experience. Congruent with social model recovery programs in which experiential learning via recovered peers and staff is a key feature, the manual does not list educational qualifications or professional training in the description of a "good group facilitator" (Covington, 2002, p. 38), mentioning that the facilitator may be a recovered trauma survivor. Likewise, the materials are designed to be user-friendly, interactive, and self-instructive and include workbooks for participants.

(5) It comprises 11 group sessions compared to the average 20-25 sessions of other trauma interventions. Thus, it may be a better match for resource strained residential programs. Unlike some manual interventions, it is specifically designed to be used in groups, which is an appealing modality for many women. Indeed group therapy, while reported to be infrequently used in the prior 30 days by women with substance abuse and PTSD who are entering treatment, is among treatments viewed positively by trauma survivors (Najavits et al., 2004).

· Notably, interest in Beyond Trauma has increased significantly in recent years among community-based recovery programs for women as evidenced by orders and re-orders of the manual from across the U.S. and a recently state-funded grant to CAARR (Blacksher, 2007 16676) to provide training in Beyond Trauma. Although anecdotal reports of effectiveness abound, scientific investigations have been lacking. Two exploratory NIH funded studies are currently underway (Messina, 2005; Messina, 2006). Both use Beyond Trauma within a larger gender-responsive treatment model for women, one in a prison and in a drug court setting. They have the methodological strengths of employing randomized controlled designs and they assess for treatment adherence.

Additional studies on Beyond Trauma, as for other trauma interventions discussed previously, are needed in a variety of areas. First, studies are need that assess efficacy in non-criminal justice involved populations, such as diverse groups of women found in community based recovery programs. Second, studies also need to examine how the effectiveness of the manual might be affected by characteristics of the social environment where it is delivered. These include characteristics such as the degree of structure provided by the environment, the level of cohesion among clients, the extent to which peer support and peer helping is emphasized, and the degree to which skill training is emphasized, such as strategies for improving communication and self care. Finally, studies need to investigate the mechanisms of how the intervention works. For example, potential mediators might include improved self-efficacy, self esteem, higher recovery related social support, or changes made in interpersonal relationships outside the treatment program. Suggestions for how researchers might co nduct the types of studies needed on Beyond Trauma are reviewed below.

## PROGRAM ENVIRONMENT FACTORS

A variety of researchers have stated that addiction treatment evaluations must go beyond randomized clinical trials to assess social environment characteristics, including the context of the intervention (Moos, 1997; Polcin, 2006). However, program environment variables are both under-studied and under-documented (Moos and King, 1997). There are a number of ways that program variables might interact with Beyond Trauma. For example, programs that are specifically designed for women may reinforce important aspects of the Beyond Trauma intervention, which has also been specifically designed for women. Programs that emphasize issues addressed in the manual might be more effective than programs that do not emphasize them. Thus, programs that are gender specific, emphasize peer involvement in the recovery process, recognize the value of knowledge based on recovery experience, facilitate cohesion, empower clients in decisions affecting the program and teach skills relevant to managing moods and relationships might enhance the positive impact of Beyond Trauma. Because community based social model recovery programs exemplify these characteristics they may be excellent sites for studying the effectiveness of Beyond Trauma. Social model programs may also be excellent venues for studying Beyond Trauma because they treat large numbers of women who have characteristics associated with trauma, such as lower socioeconomic status, history of homelessness, and use of public assistance (Lown et al., 2005; Morrisey et al., 2005). ·

## POTENTIAL MEDIATORS

In addition to studies documenting the overall effectiveness of Beyond Trauma and the types of environments where it is most effective, it would be helpful to investigate the mechanisms of how it works. The Beyond Trauma manual attempts to effect positive changes in a number of ways. There is an attempt to decrease feelings of stigma and low self esteem by normalizing the experience of trauma. This is accomplished by providing information about the prevalence of trauma and its role in substance use disorders. Thus, improved self esteem could be one pathway to better outcome for women receiving the intervention.

Other pathways worth studying center on problems addressed by the skill training interventions within the manual. These include things like helping women improve self efficacy in terms of managing moods, relationships, self care needs and problems that arise during recovery. The resulting increase in self efficacy and skill development in these areas may be critical pathway to better outcome.

Social support for recovery from both trauma and addiction may be key pathways as well. A number of studies suggest that social networks supportive of sobriety prevent substance use relapse, while associating with substance users increases risk for relapse Beattie and Longabaugh, 1997; Billings and Moos, 1983). The development of a recovery-oriented social network in particular predicts abstinence at 6-month and 5-year follow up post outpatient treatment (Weisner et al., 2003).

The role of social support in recovery from co-occurring trauma and substance abuse needs additional study. Building social support from other women who have also experienced traumatic events is an important part of Beyond Trauma. Therefore, it might be an important mediator of long term outcome.

It is also possible that Beyond Trauma impacts women's life experiences after leaving treatment and these may be the key factors associated with outcome. Interpersonal conflicts, including partner violence, infidelity, and mental/physical abuse are frequently associated with women's relapse post treatment (Sun, 2007). Cummings et al. (1980) found that negative emotions, interpersonal conflict, and social pressure covered 72% of all relapses for both men and women. Indeed, for some women with trauma history, interpersonal ties that are destructive may directly contribute to exacerbating trauma-related symptoms (Savage and Russell, 2005). The Beyond Trauma intervention is designed to assist women in developing skills to avoid these types of destructive relationships and the extent to which they are able to succeed in this endeavor after treatment is complete could certainly play a key role in mediating outcome.

## CONCLUSION

Experiences of trauma are common among women with substance abuse problems, yet trauma has often been neglected in their treatment and long term recovery. In recent years a number of manual interventions have been developed to treat trauma among women with addiction problems, including Seeking Safety, other broad based interventions that were used in the Women, Co-Occurring Disorders, and Violence Study (ATRIUM, TRIAD and TREM) and exposure interventions. While some research has shown that women taking part in these interventions make significant improvements, some study designs had significant limitations and others showed no difference compared to other active treatment interventions. In addition, most of the existing studies used manual interventions to specifically study PTSD rather than the broader array of woman impacted by trauma regardless of whether they met diagnostic criteria for PTSD.

Beyond Trauma is a recently developed intervention that addresses many of these concerns (Covington, 2003). It is broad enough in scope to be used to treat women with a variety of trauma histories including those who meet diagnosis for PTSD. Unlike some of the other interventions, Beyond Trauma is specifically designed for women and focuses on gender issues, specifically relationships and addiction for women. Thus, trauma is addressed within the context of issues that are integral for women (e.g., empowerment, self efficacy, peer support from other women who have been victims of trauma, and conceptualization of identity through relationships rather than separation). Beyond Trauma is based on a theoretical foundation that draws extensively on relational theory to guide interventions. Other advantages of this intervention include: 1) It can be utilized by a variety of professional and paraprofessional staff members and 2) It incorporates gender-appropriate use of expressive arts in its curriculum to engage women who are less verbal.

There are currently two randomized trials underway to test the efficacy of Beyond Trauma. Both involve studying women in the criminal justice population. Thus, there is a need to study Beyond Trauma in the broader context of community based recovery programs. Beyond Trauma may be most effective within programs designed for women, but without well designed studies in mixed and single gender programs this remains an open question.

Studies are also needed that address program environment characteristics and how they might interact with the trauma interventions. In particular, the characteristics of social model recovery programs seem to reinforce aspects of the Beyond Trauma intervention, such as empowerment of clients, involvement of clients in the intervention process, and social support. Finally, studies are needed that attempt to depict the mechanisms of how the intervention helps women. As a broad based intervention, Beyond Trauma attempts to help women in many different ways, including improving self efficacy, self esteem, skills to manage a variety of issues, social support for recovery from both trauma and addiction and mobilization of women's existing strengths. In addition, the intervention helps women construct a post treatment lifestyle that avoids the types of destructive relationships and events that can result in relapse. Studying how improvements in all of these areas correlate with long term outcome will be of value to improving substance abuse treatment for women.

## REFERENCES

Back, S. E., Waldrop, A. E., Brady, K. T. and Hien, D. (2006). Evidence-based time-limited treatment of co-occurring substance-use disorders and civilian-related posttraumatic stress disorder. *Brief Treatment and Crisis Intervention,* 6(4), 283-294.

Beattie, M. C. and Longabaugh, R. (1997). Interpersonal factors and post-treatment drinking and subjective well-being. *Addiction,* 92(11), 1507-1521.

Becker-Blease, K. A. and Freyd, J. J. (2005). Beyond PTSD: an evolving relationship between trauma theory and family violence research. *Journal of Interpersonal Violence,* 20(4), 403-411, 2005.

Billings, A. G. and Moos, R. H. (1983). Psychosocial processes of recovery among alcoholics and their families: Implications for clinicians and program evaluators. *Addictive Behaviors,* 8: 205-218.

Blacksher, S. (2007). *Trauma-Informed Services for Women and Girls.* CDADP #06-  00159, California Association of Addiction Recovery Resources.

Bloom, S. (2000). The sanctuary model. *Therapeutic Communities* 21(2), 67-91.

Breslau, N., Davis, G. C. and Schultz, L. R. (2003). Posttraumatic stress disorder and the incidence of nicotine, alcohol, and other drug disorders in persons who have experienced trauma. *Archives of General Psychiatry,* 60(3), 289-294.

Brier, J. and Jordan, C. E. (2004). Violence against women: outcome complexity and implications for assessment and treatment. *Journal of Interpersonal Violence,* 19(11), 1252-1276.

Boles, S., Joshi, V., Grella, C. E. and Wellisch, J. (2005). Childhood sexual abuse patterns, psychosocial correlates, and treatment outcomes among adults in drug abuse treatment. *Journal of Child Sexual Abuse* 14: 39-55.

Chilcoat, H. D. and Menard, C. (2003). Epidemiological investigations: comorbidity of posttraumatic stress disorder and substance use disorder. In: Ouimette, P. and Brown, P. J. (Eds.) Trauma and Substance Abuse: Causes, consequences, and treatment of comorbid disorders. Washington, DC: American Psychological Association, pp. 9-28.

Cocozza, J. J., Jackson, E. W., Hennigan, K., Morrissey, J. P., Reed, B. G., Fallot, R. andBanks, S. (2005). Outcomes for women with co-occurring disorders and trauma: program-level effects. *Journal of Substance Abuse Treatment*, 28, 109-119.

Covington, S. (2003). Beyond Trauma. A healing journey for women. Center City, MN: Hazelden, 2003.

Covington, S. (2002). Helping women recover: creating gender-responsive treatment. In S.L.A. Straussner and S. Brown(Eds.). The Handbook of Addiction Treatment for Women. San Francisco, CA: Jossey Bass, pp. 52-72.

Cummings, C., Gordon, J. R. and Marlatt, G. A. (1980). Relapse: prevention and prediction. In W.R. Miller (Ed.). The addictive behaviors: Treatment of alcoholism, drug abuse, smoking, and obesity. New York, NY: Pergamon, pp. 291-321.

Dansky, B. S., Brady, K. T., Saladin, M. E., Killeen, T., Becker, S. and Roitzsch, J. (1996). Victimization and PTSD in individuals with substance use disorders: gender and racial differences. *American Journal of Drug and Alcohol Abuse,* 22(1), 75-93.

Dansky, B. S., Saladin, M. E., Brady, K. T., Kilpatrick, D. G. and Resnick, H. S. (1995). Prevalence of victimization and posttraumatic stress disorder among women with substance use disorders: comparison of telephone and in-person assessment samples. *International Journal of Addictions*, 30(9), 1079-1099.

De Young, P. (2003). Relational Psychotherapy: A primer. Toronto, Ontario, Canada: Brunner-Routledge.

Fearday, F., Clark, C. and Edington, M. (Eds.) (2001). *Triad Women's Project Group Facilitator's Manual.* Tampa, FL: Louis de la Parte Florida Mental Health Institute, University of South Florida.

Fullilove, M. T., Fullilove, R. E., Iii, Smith, M., Winkler, K., Michael, C., Panzer, P. G. and Wallace, R. (1993). Violence, trauma, and post-traumatic stress disorder among women drug users. *Journal of Trauma and Stress*, 6(4), 533-543.

Grice, D., Brady, K., Dustan, L. and Malcolm, R. (1995). Sexual and physical assault history and posttraumatic stress disorder in substance-dependent individuals. *American Journal of Addictions,* 4, 297-305.

Haller, D. and Miles, D. (2004). Personality disturbances in drug-dependent women: relationship to childhood abuse. *American Journal of Drug Alcohol Abuse*, 30, 269-286.

Harris, M. and Copeland, M. (2000). *Healing the Trauma of Abuse. A woman's workbook.* Oakland, CA: New Harbinger.

Herman, J. (1997). Trauma and Recovery (revised Edition). New York City, NY: Harper Collins.

Hien, D. A., Cohen, L. R., Miele, G. M., Litt, L. C. and Capstick, C. (2004). Promising treatments for women with comorbid PTSD and substance use disorders. *American Journal of Psychiatry*, 161, 1426-1432.

Kaskutas, L. A. (1996). Predictors of self esteem among members of Women for Sobriety. *Addiction Resources.* 4(3), 273-281.

Kaskutas, L. A., Borkman, T. J. and Room, J. (1996). *The Social Model Program: A literature review and analysis.* Center for Substance Abuse Treatment, 1996.

Kessler, R. C., Sonnega, A., Bromet, E., Hughes, M. and Nelson, C. B. (1995). Posttraumatic stress disorder in the National Comorbidity Survey. Archives of General Psychiatry, 5(1), 1-13.

Kubiak, S. (2004). The effects of PTSD on treatment adherence, drug relapse, and criminal recidivism in a sample of incarcerated men and women. *Research on Social Work Practice,* 14, 424-433.

Levine, P. A. (1997). Waking the Tiger: Healing trauma. Berkeley, CA: North Atlantic Books.

Lown, E. A., Schmidt, L. and Wiley, J. A. (2005). Unraveling lives: interpersonal violence among women seeking welfare. Presented at *Research Society on Alcoholism Annual Conference*, June 25–29.

Mazelis, R. (2005). Improving the quality of demonstration research: integrating those with personal experience. *Journal of Substance Abuse Treatment*, 28, 147-148.

McHugo, G. J., Caspi, Y., Kammerer, N., Mazelis, R., Jackson, E. W., Russell, L., Clark, C., Liebschutz, J. and Kimerling, R. (2005a). The assessment of trauma history in women with co-occurring substance abuse and mental disorders and a history of interpersonal violence. *Journal of Behavioral Health Services Research*, 32(2), 113-127.

McHugo, G. J., Kammerer, N., Jackson, E. W., Markoff, L. S., Gatz, M., Larson, M. J., Mazelis, R. and Hennigan, K.(2005b). Women, co-occurring disorders, and violence study: evaluation design and study population. *Journal of Substance Abuse Treatment,* 28, 91-107.

Messina, N. P. (2005). *Gender Responsive Treatment for Women in Prison.* NIH 1 R21 DA18699-01A1.

Messina, N. P. (2006). *Enhancing Substance Abuse Treatment and HIV Prevention for Women Offenders.* NIDA 1R01DA22149-01.

Miller, J. B. (1976). Toward a new psychology of women. Boston, MA: Beacon Press.

Miller, D. and Guidry, L. (2001). Addictions and Trauma Recovery: Healing the mind, body and spirit. New York, NY: W. W. Norton.

Moos, R. H. (1997). *Evaluating Treatment Environments: The quality of psychiatric and substance abuse programs (2nd Edition).* New Brunswick, NJ: Transaction Publishers.

Moos, R. H. and King, M. J. (1997). Participation in community residential treatment and substance abuse patients' outcomes at discharge. *Journal of Substance Abuse Treatment*, 14(1), 71-80.

Morrissey, J. P., Ellis, A. R., Gatz, M., Amaro, H., Reed, B. G., Savage, A., Finkelstein, N., Mazelis, R., Brown, V., Jackson, E. W. and Banks, S. (2005). Outcomes for women with co-occurring disorders and trauma: program and person-level effects. *Journal of Substance Abuse Treatment*, 28: 121-133.

Moses, D., Reed, B., Mazelis, B. and D'Ambrosio, B. (2003). *Creating treatment services for women with co-occuring disorders.* Substance Abuse and Mental Health Services Administration.

Najavits, L. M. (in press). Seeking safety: an evidence-based model for trauma/PTSD and substance use disorder. In K.A. Witkiewitz and G.A. Marlatt, G. A. (Eds.). Evidence-Based Relapse Prevention, Philadelphia, PA: Elsevier Press.

Najavits, L. M. (2001). Seeking Safety: A treatment manual for PTSD and substance abuse. New York, NY: Guilford.

Najavits, L. M. (2003). How to design an effective treatment outcome study. *Journal of Gambling Studies*, 19(3), 317-337.

Najavits, L. M. (2004). Treatment of posttraumatic stress disorder and substance abuse: Clinical guidelines for implementing Seeking Safety therapy. *Alcohol Treatment Quarterly,* 22(1), 43-62.

Najavits, L. M., Weiss, R. D. and Shaw, S. R. (1997). The link between substance abuse and posttraumatic stress disorder in women: a research review. *American Journal of Addiction,* 6(4), 273-283.

National Institute on Drug Abuse. (1999). *Principles of Drug Addiction Treatment: A research-based guide* [NIH Publication No.00-4180], Washington, DC: National Institute on Drug Abuse, National Institutes of Health.

Noether, C. D., Finkelstein, N., Vandemark, N. R., Savage, A., Reed, B. G. and Moses, D. J. (2005). Design strengths and issues of SAMHSA's women, co-occurring disorders, and violence study. *Psychiatric Services*, 56, 1233-1236.

Ouimette, P. C., Kimerling, R., Shaw, J. and Moos, R. H. (2000). Physical and sexual abuse among women and men with substance use disorders. *Alcohol Treatment Quarterly*, 18(3), 7-17.

Pirard, S., Sharon, E., Kang, S., Angarita, G. and Gastfriend, D. R. (2005). Prevalence of physical and sexual abuse among substance abuse patients and impact on treatment outcomes. *Drug and Alcohol Dependence*, 78, 57-64.

Polcin, D.L. (1997). The etiology and diagnosis of alcohol dependence: Differences In The professional literature. *Psychotherapy,* 34(3), 297-306.

Polcin, D. L. (2000). Professional counseling versus specialized programs for alcohol and drug abuse treatment. Journal of Addictions and Offender Counseling. *Journal of Addiction and Offender Counseling*, 21(1), 2-11.

Polcin, D. L. (2003). Rethinking confrontation in alcohol and drug treatment: consideration of the clinical context. *Substance Use and Misuse*, 38, 165-184.

Polcin, D. L. (2006). How health services research can help clinical trials become more community relevant. *International Journal of Drug Policy,* 17(3), 230-237.

Reynolds, M., Mezey, G., Chapman, M., Wheeler, M., Drummond, C. and Baldacchino, A. (2005). Co-morbid post-traumatic stress disorder in a substance misusing clinical population. *Drug and Alcohol Dependence*, 77(3), 251-258.

Savage, A. and Russell, L. (2005). Tangled in a web of affiliation: Social support networks of dually diagnosed women who are trauma survivors. *Journal of Behavioral Health Service Research,* 32(2), 199-214.

Spak, L., Spak, F. and Allebeck, P. (1997). Factors in childhood and youth predicting alcohol dependence and abuse in Swedish women: Findings from a general population study. *Alcohol and Alcoholism,* 32(3), 267-274.

Sun, A. (2007). Relapse among substance-abusing women: components and processes. *Substance Use and Misuse,* 42, 1-21.

Triffleman, E. (2000). Gender differences in a controlled pilot study of psychosocial treatments in substance dependent patients with post-traumatic stress disorder: design considerations and outcomes. *Alcohol Treatment Quarterly,* 18(3), 113-126.

Triffleman, E. (2003). Issues in implementing posttraumatic stress disorder treatment outcome research in community-based treatment programs. In J. Sorenson and R. Rawson (Eds.). Drug Abuse Treatment through Collaboration: Practice and research partnerships that work. Washington, DC: American Psychological Association, 2003, pp. 227-247.

Weisner, C., Ray, G. T., Mertens, J., Satre, D. D. and Moore, C. (2003). Short-term alcohol and drug treatment outcomes predict long-term outcome. *Drug and Alcohol Dependence,* 71, 281-294.

White, W. L., Boyle, M. and Loveland, D. (2002). Alcoholism/addiction as a chronic disease: from rhetoric to clinical reality. *Alcoholism Treatment Quarterly,* 20(3/4): 107-129.

Wolfe, J. and Kimerling, R. (1997). Gender issues in the assessment of posttraumtic stress disorder. In: J.P. Wilson and T.M. Keane (Eds.). Assessing Psychological Trauma and PTSD. New York, NY: Guild, pp. 192-238.

Veysey, B. M. and Clark, C. (2004). Introduction. [Special issue: Responding to Physical and Sexual Abuse in Women with Alcohol and Other Drug and Mental Disorders: Program Building]. *Alcoholism Treatment Quarterly,* 22(3/4): 1-18.

In: Substance Abuse, Assessment and Addiction                ISBN: 978-1-61122-931-8
Editors: Kristina A. Murati and Allison G. Fischer         © 2011 Nova Science Publishers, Inc.

*Chapter 13*

# ANABOLIC STEROID ABUSE: FEDERAL EFFORTS TO PREVENT AND REDUCE ANABOLIC STEROID ABUSE AMONG TEENAGERS

## *Laurie Ekstrand*

## WHY GAO DID THIS STUDY

The abuse of anabolic steroids by teenagers—that is, their use without a prescription—is a health concern. Anabolic steroids are synthetic forms of the hormone testosterone that can be taken orally, injected, or rubbed on the skin. Although a 2006 survey funded by the National Institute on Drug Abuse (NIDA) found that less than 3 percent of 12th graders had abused anabolic steroids, it also found that about 40 percent of 12th graders described anabolic steroids as "fairly easy" or "very easy" to get. The abuse of anabolic steroids and behavioral changes in teenagers.

GAO was asked to examine federally funded efforts to address the abuse of anabolic steroids among teenagers and to review available research on this issue. This report describes (1) federally funded efforts that address teenage abuse of anabolic steroids, (2) available research on teenage abuse of anabolic steroids, and (3) gaps or areas in need of improvement that federal officials and other experts identify in research that addresses teenage anabolic steroid abuse. To do this work, GAO reviewed federal agency materials and published studies identified through a literature review and interviewed federal officials and other experts.

## WHAT GAO FOUND

There are two categories of federally funded efforts that address teenage abuse of anabolic steroids. Efforts are either designed to focus on preventing the abuse of anabolic steroids among teenagers or are broader and designed to prevent substance abuse in general—

which can include abuse of anabolic steroids among teenagers. Two programs that received federal funding during their development and testing, Athletes Training and Learning to Avoid Steroids (ATLAS) and Athletes Targeting Healthy Exercise and Nutrition Alternatives (ATHENA), are designed to focus on preventing or reducing teen abuse of anabolic steroids through use of gender-specific student-led curricula. In addition, there are various research efforts and education and outreach activities that focus on this issue. Two federal grant programs—the Office of National Drug Control Policy's Drug-Free Communities Support program and the Department of Education's School-Based Student Drug Testing program—are designed to support state and local efforts to prevent substance abuse in general and may include anabolic steroid abuse among teenagers as part of the programs' substance abuse prevention efforts. In 2007, about one-quarter of more than 700 Drug-Free Communities Support program grantees reported that they were addressing steroid abuse as one of their program's objectives.

Almost half of the 16 studies GAO reviewed identified certain risk factors and behaviors linked to the abuse of anabolic steroids among teenagers. Several of these studies found connections between anabolic steroid abuse and risk factors such as use of other drugs, risky sexual behaviors, and aggressive behaviors. Most of the other studies were assessments of the ATLAS and ATHENA prevention programs and in general suggested that the programs may reduce abuse of anabolic steroids and other drugs among high school athletes immediately following participation in the programs.

Experts identified gaps in the research addressing teenage abuse of anabolic steroids. Experts identified a lack of conclusive evidence of the sustained effectiveness over time of available prevention programs, for example at 1 year following participants' completion of the programs. Experts also identified gaps in the research on the long-term health effects of initiating anabolic steroid abuse as a teenager—including research on effects that may be particularly harmful in teens—and in research on psychological effects of anabolic steroid abuse.

## ABBREVIATIONS

| | |
|---|---|
| ATHENA | Athletes Targeting Healthy Exercise and Nutrition Alternatives |
| ATLAS | Athletes Training and Learning to Avoid Steroids |
| CDC | Centers for Disease Control and Prevention |
| HHS | Department of Health and Human Services |
| MTF | Monitoring the Future |
| NIDA | National Institute on Drug Abuse |
| NIH | National Institutes of Health |
| ONDCP | Office of National Drug Control Policy |
| SAMHSA | Substance Abuse and Mental Health Services Administration |
| USADA | United States Anti-Doping Agency |
| YRBS | Youth Risk Behavior Survey |

October 31, 2007

The Honorable Henry A. Waxman Chairman The Honorable Tom Davis Ranking Member
Committee on Oversight and Government Reform House of Representatives

The abuse of anabolic steroids [1] by teenagers—that is, their use without a prescription—is a health concern. Anabolic steroids are synthetic forms of the hormone testosterone that can be taken orally, injected, or rubbed on the skin. Although a 2006 survey funded by the National Institute on Drug Abuse (NIDA) showed that less than 3 percent of 12th graders had abused anabolic steroids, the survey also showed that about 40 percent of 12th graders described anabolic steroids as "fairly easy" or "very easy" to get. The abuse of anabolic steroids can cause serious health effects and behavioral changes in teenagers. Under U.S. law, anabolic steroids are controlled substances whose manufacture, possession, and use are regulated by the federal government; [2] they also cannot be sold legally without a prescription.

You asked us to examine federally funded efforts to address the abuse of anabolic steroids among teenagers and to review available research on this issue. In this report, we

1. describe major, federally funded efforts that address teenage abuse of anabolic steroids,
2. describe the available research on teenage abuse of anabolic steroids, and
3. describe gaps or areas in need of improvement that federal officials and other experts identify in research that addresses anabolic steroid abuse among teenagers.

We focused our review on the abuse of anabolic steroids by teenagers in grades 8 through 12. To describe federally funded efforts to address anabolic steroid abuse among teenagers, we reviewed databases of federal grant programs [3]. We also obtained and reviewed pertinent reports and information from the Web sites of agencies within the Department of Health and Human Services (HHS)—the Centers for Disease Control and Prevention (CDC), the National Institutes of Health (NIH), and the Substance Abuse and Mental Health Services Administration (SAMHSA)—as well as the Web sites of the Department of Education (Education) and the Office of National Drug Control Policy (ONDCP). We used these resources to identify federally funded programs, [4] research, and education and outreach activities that address—through efforts to either prevent or reduce—anabolic steroid abuse among teenagers. After identifying these efforts, we interviewed and collected information from federal officials to confirm that these efforts are intended to prevent or reduce anabolic steroid abuse among teenagers. Where available, we requested funding information on the federal efforts that we identified [5].

To describe the available research on teenage abuse of anabolic steroids, we conducted a systematic review of the published literature on this topic. We identified 16 articles that related to teenage abuse of anabolic steroids and were published from January 1995 through June 2007. To select the articles, we conducted a keyword search using the Dialog Database System, [6] a system that searches numerous database files, and reviewed the resulting article titles and abstracts to identify whether the articles focused on teenage abuse of anabolic steroids. We did not select articles that were international works, based on reviews of other articles or research, position papers, policy statements, or federal agency program documents. The references we make to articles refer strictly to those that we reviewed.

To describe the gaps or areas in need of improvement in research that addresses teenage abuse of anabolic steroids as identified by experts, we interviewed experts in anabolic steroid abuse and reviewed relevant literature. We interviewed federal officials from CDC, NIDA, SAMHSA, and Education, as well as other experts from universities and professional associations. We reviewed research articles identifying gaps or areas in need of improvement as part of our systematic review of the literature. We conducted the work for our review from January 2007 through September 2007 in accordance with generally accepted government auditing standards.

## RESULTS IN BRIEF

There are two categories of federally funded efforts that address teenage abuse of anabolic steroids. Efforts are either designed to focus on preventing the abuse of anabolic steroids among teenagers or are broader and designed to prevent substance abuse in general—which can include abuse of anabolic steroids among teenagers. Two programs that received federal funding during their development and testing, Athletes Training and Learning to Avoid Steroids (ATLAS) [7] and Athletes Targeting Healthy Exercise and Nutrition Alternatives (ATHENA), are designed to focus on preventing or reducing teen abuse of anabolic steroids. In addition, there are various research efforts and education and outreach activities that focus on this issue. For example, in addition to steroid-related research, since 2000 NIDA has provided nearly $500,000 in funding for a variety of education and outreach activities including a multimedia educational initiative intended to prevent anabolic steroid abuse among teenagers. Two federal grant programs—ONDCP's Drug-Free Communities Support program and Education's School-Based Student Drug Testing program—are designed to support state and local efforts to prevent substance abuse in general and may include anabolic steroid abuse among teenagers as part of the programs' substance abuse prevention efforts. In 2007, about one-quarter of more than 700 Drug-Free Communities Support program grantees reported that they were addressing steroid abuse as one of their program's objectives.

Almost half of the 16 studies we reviewed identified certain risk factors and behaviors linked to the abuse of anabolic steroids among teenagers. Several of these studies found connections between anabolic steroid abuse and risk factors such as use of other drugs, risky sexual behaviors, and aggressive behaviors. Most of the other studies we reviewed were assessments of the ATLAS and ATHENA prevention programs. In general, these studies suggested that the programs may reduce abuse of anabolic steroids and other drugs among high school athletes immediately following participation in the programs.

Experts identified gaps in the research that addresses anabolic steroid abuse among teenagers. Experts identified a lack of conclusive evidence of sustained effectiveness over time of available prevention programs, for example at 1 year following participants' completion of the programs. Experts also identified gaps in the research on the long-term heath effects of initiating anabolic steroid abuse as a teenager—including research on effects that may be particularly harmful in teenagers—and in the research on psychological effects.

HHS and Education provided technical comments only, which we incorporated into the report as appropriate.

## BACKGROUND

The abuse of anabolic steroids differs from the abuse of other illicit substances. When users initially begin to abuse anabolic steroids, they typically are not driven by a desire to achieve an immediate euphoria like that which accompanies most abused drugs such as cocaine, heroin, and marijuana. The abuse of anabolic steroids is typically driven by the desire of users to improve their athletic performance and appearance—characteristics that are important to many teenagers. Anabolic steroids can increase strength and boost confidence, leading users to overlook the potential serious and long-term damage to their health that these substances can cause. In addition, the methods and patterns of use for anabolic steroids differ from those of other drugs. Anabolic steroids are most often taken orally or injected, typically in cycles of weeks or months (referred to as "cycling"), rather than continuously. Cycling involves taking multiple doses of anabolic steroids over a specific period of time, stopping for a period, and starting again. In addition, users often combine several different types of anabolic steroids to maximize their effectiveness (referred to as "stacking").

While anabolic steroids can enhance certain types of performance or appearance, when used inappropriately they can cause a host of severe, long-term, and in some cases, irreversible health consequences. The abuse of anabolic steroids can lead to heart attacks, strokes, liver tumors, and kidney failure. In addition, because anabolic steroids are often injected, users who share needles or use nonsterile injection techniques are at risk for contracting dangerous infections, such as HIV/AIDS and hepatitis B and C. There are also numerous side effects that are gender-specific, including reduced sperm count, infertility, baldness, and development of breasts among men; and growth of facial hair, male-pattern baldness, changes in or cessation of the menstrual cycle, and deepened voice among women. There is also concern that teenagers who abuse anabolic steroids may face the additional risk of halted growth resulting from premature skeletal maturation and accelerated puberty changes.

The abuse of anabolic steroids may also lead to aggressive behavior and other psychological side effects. Many users report feeling good about themselves while on anabolic steroids, but for some users extreme mood swings also can occur, including manic-like symptoms leading to violence. Some users also may experience depression when the drugs are stopped, which may contribute to dependence on anabolic steroids. Users may also suffer from paranoia, jealousy, extreme irritability, delusions, and impaired judgment stemming from feelings of invincibility.

Two national surveys showed increasing prevalence in teenage abuse of steroids throughout the 1990s until about 2002 and a decline since then (see figure 1). One of these two national surveys, the Monitoring the Future (MTF) survey, is an annual survey conducted by the University of Michigan and supported by NIDA funding [8]. The MTF survey measures drug use and attitudes among students in grades 8, 10, and 12, and asks several questions about the use of and attitudes towards anabolic steroids, such as perceived risk, disapproval, and availability of anabolic steroids. The survey's questions are designed to assess respondents' use of steroids in the last 30 days, the past year, and over the course of the respondent's lifetime. Questions about steroid use were added to the study beginning in 1989. The most recent results from this survey showed that in 2006, 2.7 percent of 12th graders said they had used anabolic steroids without a prescription at least once. The second national survey, the Youth Risk Behavior Survey (YRBS), is a biennial survey conducted since 1991 by CDC [9. The YRBS is part of a surveillance system consisting of national, state, and local surveys of students in grades 9 through 12. These surveys collect information about a wide variety of risk behaviors, including sexual activity and alcohol and drug use.

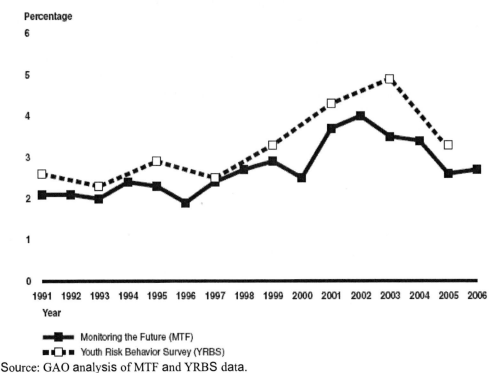

Source: GAO analysis of MTF and YRBS data.

Figure 1. Reported Lifetime Anabolic Steroid Abuse among 12th Graders, 1991-2006.

The most recent available national YRBS survey—conducted in 2005—asked one question related to lifetime steroid use without a prescription, which showed that 3.3 percent of 12th graders had used steroids at least once.

The MTF and YRBS surveys indicate a low abuse rate for anabolic steroids among teenagers [10] when compared with the abuse rates for other drugs [11]. However, the reported easy availability of steroids [12] and the potential for serious health effects make anabolic steroid abuse a health concern for teenagers, particularly among males. In general, the reported rates of anabolic steroid abuse are higher for males than for females (see figure 2). Data from the 2006 MTF survey showed that 1.7 percent of teenage males reported abusing anabolic steroids in the past year, as compared with 0.6 percent of females. Data from the 2005 YRBS survey showed that 4.8 percent of high school males reported abusing steroids in their lifetime, as compared with 3.2 percent of females.

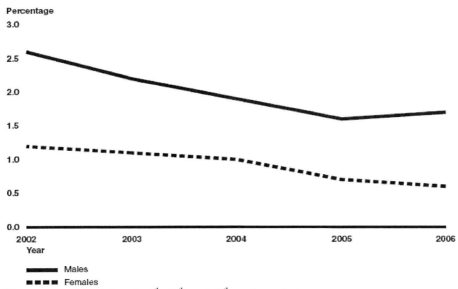

Note: These are combined data for 8th, 10th, and 12th grade students.
Figure 2. Reported Past Year Anabolic Steroid Abuse by Male and Female Adolescents, 2002-2006.

## SOME FEDERALLY FUNDED EFFORTS ARE DESIGNED TO FOCUS ON PREVENTING TEENAGE STEROID ABUSE, WHILE OTHER EFFORTS DESIGNED TO ADDRESS SUBSTANCE ABUSE IN GENERAL MAY INCLUDE TEENAGERS

There are two categories of federally funded efforts that address teenage abuse of anabolic steroids. Efforts are either designed to focus on preventing the abuse of anabolic steroids among teenagers or are broader and designed to prevent substance abuse in general—which can include abuse of anabolic steroids among teenagers. Two programs that received federal research funding for their development and testing, ATLAS and ATHENA, are designed to focus on preventing or reducing teen abuse of anabolic steroids. In addition, there are various research efforts and education and outreach activities that focus on this issue. Two federal grant programs—ONDCP's Drug-Free Communities Support program and Education's School-Based Student Drug Testing program—are designed to support state and local efforts to prevent substance abuse in general and may include anabolic steroid abuse among teenagers as part of the programs' substance abuse prevention efforts. See appendix I for a list of the federally funded efforts discussed below.

### Some Federally Funded Programs, Research, and Activities Are Designed to Focus on Preventing Teenage Anabolic Steroid Abuse

There are various federally funded efforts—programs, research, and educational activities—that address teenage abuse of anabolic steroids. Some of these efforts are designed to focus on preventing or reducing anabolic steroid abuse among teenagers. As part of our review we identified two programs, the ATLAS and ATHENA programs, which received federal research funding during their development and testing and are designed to focus on preventing the abuse of anabolic steroids among male and female high school athletes, respectively.

ATLAS is a student-led curriculum designed to prevent male high school athletes from abusing anabolic steroids and other performance-enhancing substances. The program's intervention strategy relies on peer pressure and providing information on healthy alternatives for increasing muscle strength and size. The ATLAS curriculum is typically delivered during a sport team's season in a series of 45-minute sessions scheduled at the coaches' discretion and integrated into the usual team practice activities. The athletes meet as a team in groups of six or eight students with one student functioning as the assigned group leader. Coaches, group leaders, and student athletes all work from manuals and workbooks, which provide brief, interactive activities that focus on drugs used in sports, sport supplements, strength training, sport nutrition, and decision making.

The ATHENA program is designed to prevent the abuse of body-shaping substances such as diet pills and anabolic steroids, although abuse of the latter is less common in females than in males. Like ATLAS, the ATHENA curriculum is integrated into a sport team's usual practice activities and uses workbooks and student group leaders. The ATHENA curriculum takes into account that female athletes are less likely than males to abuse anabolic steroids but are more likely to have problems with eating disorders and to use drugs such as diet pills and tobacco. As a result, ATHENA's curriculum gives more attention than ATLAS's to addressing these behaviors.

The ATLAS and ATHENA curricula were developed and tested with funding provided by NIDA [13]. From fiscal years 1993 through 2001, NIDA provided more than $3.4 million to fund the research that developed and tested the effectiveness of the ATLAS curriculum. Similarly, from fiscal years 1999 through 2003 NIDA provided $4.7 million in research funding to develop and test the effectiveness of the ATHENA curriculum. While ATLAS and ATHENA were developed and tested with federal funding, the programs are implemented at the local level. Schools in at least 25 states have chosen to implement the programs with local and private funds, and the National Football League and *Sports Illustrated* magazine together have supported the programs in more than 70 schools nationwide [14].

In addition to the ATLAS and ATHENA programs, there are various federally funded research efforts that focus on preventing or reducing anabolic steroid abuse among teenagers. NIDA has funded several research projects examining the factors that influence teenagers to abuse anabolic steroids and the effectiveness of interventions used to prevent teenage steroid abuse. From fiscal years 2000 through 2006, NIDA awarded nearly $10.1 million in grants to support an average of four research projects each year related to anabolic steroid abuse with a specific focus on adolescents [15]. In fiscal year 2006, for example, NIDA awarded a total of nearly $638,000 to three research projects that examined risk factors for anabolic steroid abuse among teenagers or the effects of steroid abuse in this population. Like NIDA, the United States Anti-Doping Agency (USADA)—an independent, nonprofit corporation funded primarily by ONDCP—supports research related to the abuse of anabolic steroids and other performance-enhancing drugs by athletes, including teenage athletes [16]. In fiscal year 2006, USADA spent $1.8 million for research, and an ONDCP official estimated that about one-third of that research funding was directed to anabolic steroids and another performance-enhancing drug, human growth hormone.

In addition to research, there are various education and outreach activities that focus on preventing anabolic steroid abuse among teenagers. Many of these efforts have been supported by NIDA. Since 2000, NIDA has provided nearly $500,000 in funding for a variety of education and outreach efforts in support of this goal [17]. For example, in April 2000, in response to an upward trend in steroid abuse among students, NIDA launched a multimedia educational initiative intended to prevent anabolic steroid abuse among teenagers. Along with several national partners, including the National Collegiate Athletic Association, the American College of Sports Medicine, and the American Academy of Pediatrics, the initiative produced a Web site, a research report on steroid abuse, and postcard-sized messages about steroids for placement in gyms, movie theaters, shopping malls, bookstores, and restaurants in selected areas. By 2007, NIDA funding for this particular initiative totaled about $124,000.

In addition to NIDA, other federal agencies and organizations have supported educational and outreach activities that focus on preventing anabolic steroid abuse among teenagers, as the following examples illustrate.

- ONDCP has funded six informational briefings since 2001 to encourage journalists, entertainment writers, and producers to accurately cover anabolic steroids and drug abuse among teenage athletes. ONDCP also has Web sites for teens and parents with information about anabolic steroids and links to NIDA resources.
- Since 2003, USADA has produced written publications and annual reports on anabolic steroid abuse and has distributed those publications through high schools and state high school associations. In addition, some USADA public service announcements to be aired during televised sports events and movie trailers have targeted anabolic steroid abuse.
- In fiscal years 2007 and 2008, SAMHSA expects to spend a total of $99,000 under a contract to develop and disseminate educational materials addressing the abuse of anabolic steroids by adolescent athletes. These materials, which are intended for use by high school athletic and health science departments, include brochures, a video, and 10 high school outreach seminars.

## Two Federal Grant Programs Designed to Address Substance Abuse May Address Teenage Anabolic Steroid Abuse

As part of our review, we identified two federal grant programs that are designed to support state and local efforts to prevent various forms of substance abuse and that may include teenagers. Grantees of these programs may address teenage anabolic steroid abuse as part of the programs' general substance abuse prevention efforts. The Drug-Free Communities Support program, funded by ONDCP and administered by SAMHSA under an interagency agreement, provides grants to community coalitions to address drug abuse problems identified in their communities [18]. Many community coalitions choose to implement school-based drug prevention programs with their grant funding and are allowed to tailor these programs to address the drug prevention needs of their communities. In 2007, about one-quarter of more than 700 grantees reported that they were addressing steroid abuse as one of their program's objectives [19]. Each community coalition is eligible for grants of up to $125,000 per year, renewable for up to 4 more years, and requiring dollar-for-dollar community matching funds [20]. In 2007, the Drug-Free Communities Support program is providing about $80 million in grants to 709 community coalitions for drug prevention activities based on the needs of the communities.

Another federal grant program that supports substance abuse prevention efforts for teenagers and that may also include efforts to address anabolic steroid abuse in this population is the School-Based Student Drug Testing program in Education's Office of Safe and Drug-Free Schools [21]. Since 2003, this program has provided grants to school districts and public and private entities to establish school-based drug-testing efforts. For fiscal years 2003 through 2007, the Office of Safe and Drug-Free Schools awarded $32.2 million in grants to 87 individual School-Based Student Drug Testing grantees [22]. According to information provided in the grantees' grant applications, 34 of the grantees (representing 180 middle, junior, and high schools and at least 70,000 students) proposed using their grant-supported drug testing to test for anabolic steroids in addition to other substances such as amphetamines, marijuana, and cocaine [23]. Education officials told us that although grantees generally identify the drugs for which they are testing in their annual performance reports, there has been no independent verification by Education staff that confirms that the 34 grantees actually have implemented anabolic steroid testing or whether additional grantees have included steroid testing in their efforts.

## Research Shows Teenage Anabolic Steroid Abuse Is Linked to Certain Risk Factors and That Prevention Programs May Have Some Short-term Effectiveness

Of the 16 studies we reviewed, nearly half focused on linking certain risk factors and behaviors to teenagers' abuse of anabolic steroids, including the use of other drugs, risky sexual behaviors, and aggressive behaviors [24]. Most of the other studies we reviewed were assessments of the ATLAS and ATHENA prevention programs and in general suggested that the programs may reduce abuse of anabolic steroids and other drugs among high school athletes immediately following participation in the programs. Appendix II is a list of the articles we reviewed.

Almost half of the studies we reviewed identified certain risk factors and behaviors linked to the abuse of anabolic steroids among teenagers [25]. Risk factors, such as antisocial behavior, family violence, and low academic achievement, are linked to youths' likelihood of engaging in risky behaviors, including drug abuse. Several studies found that the use of alcohol and other drugs—such as tobacco, marijuana, and cocaine—is associated with the abuse of anabolic steroids among teenagers, including teenage athletes and non-athletes. One 2005 study found that the use of other drugs was more likely to predict anabolic steroid abuse than participation in athletic activities. Several studies we reviewed found no difference between athletes and non-athletes in their abuse of anabolic steroids, and one 2007 study of teenage girls found that female athletes were less likely than female non-athletes to abuse anabolic steroids. A few studies we reviewed found a positive correlation between anabolic steroid abuse and risky sexual behaviors such as early initiation of sexual activity and an increased number of sexual partners. Some studies found that aggressive behaviors such as fighting were related to anabolic steroid abuse by both males and females. Moreover, one 1997 study found that adolescents (both male and female) who reported abusing anabolic steroids in the past year were more likely to be perpetrators of sexual violence. However, the cause-and-effect relationships between anabolic steroid abuse and other risky behaviors, such as violence, have not been determined [26].

About half of the studies we reviewed were assessments of the ATLAS and ATHENA prevention programs, and in general these studies suggested that these programs may reduce abuse of anabolic steroids and other drugs among high school athletes immediately following participation in the programs. Researchers assessing the ATLAS program reported that both the intention to abuse anabolic steroids and the reported abuse of steroids were lower among athletes who participated in the ATLAS program than among athletes who did not participate in the program. The most recent study found that although the intention to abuse anabolic steroids remained lower at follow-up 1 year later for athletes who participated in the ATLAS program, the effectiveness of the program in reducing reported use diminished with time. Similarly, researchers assessing the ATHENA program found that girls who participated in the program reported less ongoing and new abuse of anabolic steroids as well as a reduction in the abuse of other performance-enhancing and body-shaping substances. The authors note that these results are short term, and the long-term effectiveness of the ATHENA program is not known.

The authors of the one study in our review that looked at student drug-testing programs found that the abuse of anabolic steroids and other illicit drugs and performance-enhancing substances was decreased among athletes at schools that implemented mandatory, random drug-testing programs. However, this group of athletes also showed an increase in risk factors that are generally associated with greater abuse of illicit drugs, including anabolic steroids. For example, athletes at schools with drug-testing programs were more likely to believe that peers and authority figures were more tolerant of drug abuse, had less belief in the negative consequences of drug abuse, and had less belief in the efficacy of drug testing. Based on these seemingly inconsistent findings, the study's authors called for caution in interpreting the findings.

## Experts Find There Are Gaps in Research on the Sustained Effectiveness of Prevention Programs and on the Long-term Health Effects for Teenagers

Experts identified gaps in the research that addresses anabolic steroid abuse among teenagers. Experts identified gaps in the current research on the outcomes of prevention programs that focus on anabolic steroids. Experts also identified gaps in the research on the long-term health effects of initiating the abuse of anabolic steroids as teenagers.

According to experts, available research does not establish the extent to which the ATLAS and ATHENA programs are effective over time in preventing anabolic steroid abuse among teenage athletes. Experts acknowledge that both programs appear promising in their ability to prevent the abuse of anabolic steroids among teenage athletes immediately following participants' completion of the programs. Assessment of the effectiveness of the ATLAS program 1 year later, however, found that the lower incidence of anabolic steroid use was not sustained, although participants continued to report reduced intentions to use anabolic steroids. The long-term effectiveness of the ATHENA program has not been reported. The effectiveness of these programs has been assessed only in some schools in Oregon, and therefore experts report that the effectiveness of the programs may not be generalizable. In another example, experts identified the need for additional research to assess the effectiveness of drug-testing programs, such as those funded under Education's School-Based Student Drug Testing program, in reducing anabolic steroid abuse among teenagers [27].

According to experts, there are several gaps in research on the health effects of teenage abuse of anabolic steroids. Experts report that while there is some research that has examined the health effects of anabolic steroid abuse among adults—for example, the harmful effects on the cardiovascular, hormonal, and immune systems—there is a lack of research on these effects among teenagers. There is also a lack of research on the long-term health effects of initiating anabolic steroid abuse during the teenage years. Some health effects of steroid abuse among adults, such as adverse effects on the hormonal system, have been shown to be reversible when the adults have stopped abusing anabolic steroids. Experts point out, however, that it is not known whether this reversibility holds true for teenagers as well. While some experts suggest that anabolic steroid abuse may do more lasting harm to teenagers, due to the complex physical changes unique to adolescence, according to other experts there is no conclusive evidence of potentially permanent health effects. Experts also report that the extent of the psychological effects of anabolic steroid abuse and, in particular, of withdrawal from steroid abuse, is unclear due to limited research. Some experts we consulted noted a need to better inform primary care physicians and pediatricians about anabolic steroid abuse among teenagers, so these providers would be better able to recognize steroid abuse in their patients and initiate early intervention and treatment.

## AGENCY COMMENTS

We provided a draft of this report to HHS and Education for comment and received technical comments only, which we incorporated into the report as appropriate.

As arranged with your offices, unless you publicly announce the contents of this report earlier, we plan no further distribution of it until 30 days after its issue date. At that time, we will send copies of this report to the Secretary of Health and Human Services and to the Secretary of Education. We will also provide copies to others upon request. In addition, the report is available at no charge on the GAO Web site at http://www.gao.gov.

If you or your staff members have any questions regarding this report, please contact me at (202) 512-7114 or ekstrandl@gao.gov. Contact points for our Offices of Congressional Relations and Public Affairs may be found on the last page of this report. GAO staff members who made major contributions to this report are listed in appendix III.

Laurie Ekstrand
Director, Health Care

# APPENDIX I: SELECTED FEDERALLY FUNDED EFFORTS THAT ADDRESS OR CAN ADDRESS ANABOLIC STEROID ABUSE AMONG TEENAGERS

Table 1 lists selected federally funded efforts—including programs, research, and educational and outreach activities—that are designed to focus on preventing or reducing the abuse of anabolic steroids by teenagers (focused efforts), as well as other broader efforts that may address teenage abuse of anabolic steroids as part of the programs' general substance abuse prevention efforts. The list includes programs funded by two departments and the Office of National Drug Control Policy (ONDCP), in the Executive Office of the President.

**Table 1. Selected Federally Funded Efforts That Address or Can Address Anabolic Steroid Abuse among Teenagers**

| Program | Funding for fiscal year 2006 | Program implementers or eligible applicants | Targeted beneficiaries | Program description |
|---|---|---|---|---|
| **Department of Health and HumanS ervices** | | | | |
| National Institute on Drug Abuse (NIDA) | | | | |
| Athletes Training and Learning to Avoid Steroids (ATLAS) | ---[a] | School districts, schools, behavioral health agencies, others | Male high school athletes | Focused effort: program to prevent male high school athletes from abusing anabolic steroids and other performance-enhancing drugs, and to promote healthy strength training and nutrition |
| Athletes Targeting Healthy Exercise & Nutrition Alternatives (ATHENA) | ---[b] | School districts, schools, behavioral health agencies, others | Female high school athletes | Focused effort: program to prevent female high school athletes from abusing body-shaping substances such as diet pills, tobacco, and anabolic steroids, and to promote healthy training and nutrition |
| Research projects | $638,000 | Researchers | Adolescent age group | Focused effort: funding for three steroid-related research projects focused on the adolescent age group in humans and animals |
| Educational and outreach activities | $521,000 | NIDA and its partners, including National Collegiate Athletic Association, American Academy of Pediatrics, American College of Sports Medicine, others | Teenage students, teachers, general public | Focused and broad efforts: to distribute a research report on anabolic steroid abuse to schools; develop steroid abuse posters for schools; and support Scholastic Magazines substance abuse information to schools including anabolic steroids |

## Table 1. (Continued).

| Program | Funding for fiscal year 2006 | Program Implementers or eligible applicants | Targeted beneficiaries | Program description |
|---|---|---|---|---|
| **Substance Abuse and Mental Health Services Administration (SAMHSA)** | | | | |
| Center for Substance Abuse Treatment: What Steroids Can Do to You – The Drug-The Danger- The Deception | ---[c] | SAMHSA contractor | High school teachers, coaches, students | Focused effort: program of print materials, video, and high school assemblies to disseminate accurate information describing the health effects of anabolic steroids |
| **Department ofE ducation** | | | | |
| School-Based Student Drug Testing grants program | $8.6 million | School districts, public and private entities | Students primarily in grades 6 through 12 | Broad effort: as of 2006, 72 grants to support programs that address drug prevention in schools, including anabolic steroid prevention efforts |
| **ExecutiveO ffice of theP resident** | | | | |
| Office of National Drug Control Policy (ONDCP) | | | | |
| Drug-Free Communities Support program | about $80 million | Community coalitions | Various beneficiaries, including school-age youth, depending on community needs assessments | Broad effort: as of 2006, more than 700 grants to communities to support coalitions and grassroots organizations engaged in efforts to prevent use of alcohol, tobacco, and illicit drugs including anabolic steroids |
| ONDCP public information and entertainment industry outreach | $5,000 for 1 event in January 2006 | Medical experts, coaches, teen athletes | Journalists, entertainment writers, producers | Focused and broad efforts: 6 briefings from 2001-2007, including roundtable for a journalists' conference on teen athletes, briefings for magazine staffs, and media roundtables on teen athletes and performance-enhancing drugs |
| United States Anti-Doping Agency (USADA) research projects[d] | $1.8 million | Researchers | Young athletes including teenagers | Focused and broad efforts: grants for research on current and emerging drug issues; estimated one-third of research funding addresses anabolic steroids and human growth hormone |

| Program | Funding for fiscal year 2006 | Program implementers or eligible applicants | Targeted beneficiaries | Program description |
|---|---|---|---|---|
| USADA education and outreach activities[d] | $1.5 million | Public and private organizations | Teenagers, young adult athletes, parents, coaches | Focused and broad efforts: publications about anabolic steroid issues for high schools, public service announcements, and Web sites |

Sources: Agency documents and program officials.

[a]In 2006, NIDA did not provide any funding for the ATLAS program. From 1993 through 2001, however, NIDA funded $3.4 million in research related to developing and testing the ATLAS curriculum.

[b]Similarly, NIDA did not fund research related to the ATHENA program in 2006, but from 1999 through 2003 the agency provided $4.7 million to develop and test the program.

[c]SAMHSA officials reported that the agency expects to spend up to $99,000 on this project. A contract for that amount was awarded on July 6, 2006. As of August 2007, SAMHSA reported that it had made $40,000 in payments under the contract and expects to pay the remaining $59,000 in fiscal year 2008.

[d]USADA is not organizationally part of the Executive Office of the President. However, because it is an independent, nonprofit corporation funded primarily by ONDCP, for purposes of this report we have grouped USADA's activities with ONDCP's.

# APPENDIX II: ARTICLES INCLUDED IN GAO'S REVIEW

Borowsky, I.W., M. Hogan, and M. Ireland. "Adolescent sexual aggression: risk and protective factors." *Pediatrics,* vol. 100, no. 6 (1997): e71-e78.

Dukarm, C.P., R.S. Byrd, P. Auinger, and M. Weitzman. "Illicit substance use, gender, and the risk of violent behavior among adolescents." *Archives of Pediatric and Adolescent Medicine,* vol. 150, no. 8 (1996): 797-801.

DuRant, R.H., L.G. Escobedo, and G.W. Heath, "Anabolic-steroid use, strength training, and multiple drug use among adolescents in the United States." *Pediatrics,* vol. 96, no. 1 (1995): 23-28.

Elliot, D., J. Cheong, E.L. Moe, and L. Goldberg. "Cross-sectional study of female students reporting anabolic steroid use." *Archives of Pediatric and Adolescent Medicine,* vol. 161, no. 6 (2007): 572-577.

Elliot, D., and L. Goldberg. "Intervention and prevention of steroid use in adolescents." *American Journal of Sports Medicine,* vol. 24, no. 6 (1996): S46-S47.

Elliot, D.L., L. Goldberg, E.L. Moe, C.A. DeFrancesco, M.B. Durham, and H. Hix-Small. "Preventing substance use and disordered eating: Initial outcomes of the ATHENA (Athletes Targeting Healthy Exercise and Nutrition Alternatives) program." *Archives of Pediatric and Adolescent Medicine,* vol. 158, no. 11 (2004): 1043-1049.

Elliot, D.L., E.L. Moe, L. Goldberg, C.A. DeFrancesco, M.B. Durham, and H. Hix-Small. "Definition and outcome of a curriculum to prevent disordered eating and body-shaping drug use." *The Journal of School Health,* vol. 76, no. 2 (2006): 67-73.

Fritz, M.S., D.P. MacKinnon, J. Williams, L. Goldberg, E.L. Moe, and D.L. Elliot. "Analysis of baseline by treatment interactions in a drug prevention and health promotion program for high school male athletes." *Addictive Behaviors,* vol. 30, no. 5 (2005): 1001-1005.

Goldberg, L., D. Elliot, G.N. Clarke, D.P. MacKinnon, E. Moe, L. Zoref, E. Greffrath, D.J. Miller, and A. Lapin. "Effects of a multidimensional anabolic steroid prevention intervention: the Adolescents Training and Learning to Avoid Steroids (ATLAS) program." *JAMA,* vol. 276, no. 19 (1996): 1555-1562.

Goldberg, L., D. Elliot, G.N. Clarke, D.P. MacKinnon, L. Zoref, E. Moe, C. Green, and S.L. Wolf. "The Adolescent Training and Learning to Avoid Steroids (ATLAS) prevention program: background and results of a model intervention." *Archives of Pediatric and Adolescent Medicine,* vol. 150 (1996): 713-721.

Goldberg, L., D.L. Elliot, D.P. MacKinnon, E. Moe, K.S. Kuehl, L. Nohre, and C.M. Lockwood. "Drug testing athletes to prevent substance abuse: Background and pilot study results of the SATURN (Student Athlete Testing Using Random Notification) study." *Journal of Adolescent Health,* vol. 32, no. 1 (2003): 16-25.

Goldberg, L., D.P. MacKinnon, D.L. Elliot, E.L. Moe, G. Clarke, and J. Cheong. "The Adolescents Training and Learning to Avoid Steroids Program: Preventing drug use and promoting health behaviors." *Archives of Pediatric and Adolescent Medicine,* vol. 154, no. 4 (2000): 332-338.

MacKinnon, D.P., L. Goldberg, G. Clarke, D.L. Elliot, J. Cheong, A. Lapin, E.L. Moe, and J.L. Krull. "Mediating mechanisms in a program to reduce intentions to use anabolic steroids and improve exercise self-efficacy and dietary behavior." *Prevention Science,* vol. 2, no. 1 (2001): 15-28.

Miller, K.E., J.H. Hoffman, G.M. Barnes, D. Sabo, M.J. Melnick, and M.P. Farrell. "Adolescent anabolic steroid use, gender, physical activity, and other problem behaviors." *Substance Use and Misuse*, vol. 40, no. 11 (2005): 1637-1657.

Naylor, A.H., D. Gardner, and L. Zaichkowsky. "Drug use patterns among high school athletes and nonathletes." *Adolescence*, vol. 36, no. 144 (2001): 627-639.

Rich, J.D., C.K. Foisie, C.W. Towe, B.P. Dickinson, M. McKenzie, and C.M. Salas. "Needle exchange program participation by anabolic steroid injectors." *Drug and Alcohol Dependence*, vol. 56, no. 2 (1999): 157-160.

## ACKNOWLEDGMENTS

In addition to the contact named above, key contributors to this report were Christine Brudevold, Assistant Director; Ellen M. Smith; Julie Thomas; Rasanjali Wickrema; and Krister Friday.

## REFERENCES

[1] We use the term anabolic steroids to refer to anabolic steroids and their precursors, as defined in the Controlled Substances Act. See 21 U.S.C. § 802 (23), (41).

[2] The Crime Control Act of 1990 amended the Controlled Substances Act to include anabolic steroids. 21 U.S.C. § 812(c), Schedule III (e).

[3] We searched both the Catalog of Federal Domestic Assistance, a database of federal grant programs maintained by the General Services Administration, and the Computer Retrieval of Information on Scientific Projects, a database of research grants funded by the National Institutes of Health.

[4] We define federally funded programs as including programs that were developed, implemented, or tested using federal funding.

[5] The efforts that we discuss in this report may not represent all federally funded activities that address anabolic steroid abuse among teenagers but reflect those efforts mentioned by federal officials with whom we consulted. We were unable to determine the extent of total federal funding for programs that address teenage anabolic steroid abuse because, in some instances, funding information covers more than prevention of teenage anabolic steroid abuse.

[6] We searched using the keywords anabolic steroids, abuse, addiction, teen, youth, adolescent, prevent, and treat.

[7] ATLAS—the acronym for the prevention program named Athletes Training and Learning to Avoid Steroids—originally stood for *Adolescents* Training and Learning to Avoid Steroids, which was the title of the NIDA research grants that supported the program's development. For this reason, some published research describing the program, as listed in appendix II, for example, refers to ATLAS as Adolescents Training and Learning to Avoid Steroids.

[8] The MTF survey is administered to nationally representative samples of public and private secondary school students throughout the United States. In 2006, sample sizes

were about 17,000, 16,600, and 14,800 in 8th, 10th, and 12th grades, respectively. In all, about 48,500 students in 410 secondary schools participated in the 2006 survey.

[9]   The sampling frame for the 2005 national YRBS survey consisted of all public and private schools with students in at least one of grades 9 through 12 in the 50 states and the District of Columbia. For the 2005 national YRBS survey, 13,953 questionnaires were completed in 159 schools by a nationally representative sample of students in grades 9 through 12.

[10]  Several researchers conducted an analysis indicating that the prevalence rates of teenage anabolic steroid abuse reported by MTF and YRBS are overestimated and that actual prevalence of teenage anabolic steroid abuse is even lower than these surveys report. See Gen Kanayama et al., "Anabolic Steroid Abuse Among Teenage Girls: An Illusory Problem?" *Drug and Alcohol Dependence*, 88 (2007): 156-162.

[11]  For example, according to the 2006 MTF survey, 42.3 percent of 12th graders reported abusing marijuana at least once, and 8.5 percent reported abusing cocaine at least once.

[12]  In our previous work looking at the availability of anabolic steroids, we found that anabolic steroids were easily obtained without a prescription through the Internet. See GAO, *Anabolic Steroids Are Easily Purchased Without a Prescription and Present Significant Challenges to Law Enforcement Officials*, GAO-06-243R (Washington, D.C.: Nov. 3, 2005).

[13]  The programs originated in investigator-initiated research into the risk factors associated with male and female high school athletes' abuse of anabolic steroids.

[14]  According to NIDA officials, the principal investigators who developed the ATLAS and ATHENA programs signed a contract with the National Football League to place the programs in schools in the vicinity of eight National Football League teams in 2007. The contract was expected to support the training of about 800 coaches and 20,000 athletes.

[15]  For fiscal years 2000 through 2006, NIDA officials reported that they awarded a total of 31 annual grants, many of which were continuation grants for previously-approved projects, for steroid-related research focused on the adolescent age group in humans or animals. Because of the continuity of the projects from year to year, we are reporting the average numbers of projects that were funded and active each year.

[16]  ONDCP officials told us that from fiscal years 2001 through 2007, USADA funding from ONDCP totaled nearly $46 million. In 2007, for example, ONDCP funding was $8.4 million or about 70 percent of USADA's $12 million budget, with the United States Olympic Committee providing the remaining 30 percent.

[17]  In addition to this funding for education and outreach activities specifically focused on anabolic steroid abuse among teenagers, NIDA has contracted with Scholastic Magazines since 2002 to provide information about drug abuse and addiction to students and teachers during the school year. This program, under which Scholastic Magazines receives $500,000 per year for fiscal years 2002 through 2009 for a total of $4 million, supports broader substance abuse prevention activities that have at times included anabolic steroid prevention articles, posters, and other materials.

[18]  Project officers in SAMHSA's Center for Substance Abuse Prevention work with the Drug-Free Communities Support program grantees to provide technical assistance and help them comply with grant requirements.

[19]  An ONDCP official told us that 189 of 702 communities (27 percent) provided information that they were addressing steroids in their grant activities along with other drugs.

[20]  Follow-on grants are also authorized. 21 U.S.C. § 1532(b)(3).

[21]  Education funds no programs specifically targeting steroid prevention for teens. Except for alcohol prevention efforts, the department addresses illegal drug abuse in schools with a comprehensive strategy, not drug by drug.

[22]  Total funding for the School-Based Student Drug Testing program for fiscal years 2003 through 2007 was about $36 million, of which $32.2 million (89 percent) was awarded to grantees. The remainder of the funding supported evaluation and peer review activities.

[23]  During a discussion of Education's program, an ONDCP official said that because testing for anabolic steroids is more expensive than for other drugs—adding $50 to $100 to the cost of a common panel of five drug tests—some schools add steroids to the tests for only a few of the students, as a deterrent. The official said that in some cases, federal funding helps schools afford to add steroids to their usual test panel. The official estimated that about 1,000 schools and school districts across the country were doing some sort of student drug testing and sometimes were including steroids. According to the official, New Jersey requires steroid testing for some athletic teams and Florida and Texas were considering similar legislation.

[24]  We reviewed 16 studies published from January 1995 through June 2007.

[25]  These studies sought to identify a correlation between risk factors and behaviors and anabolic steroid abuse by teenagers. The studies did not identify causation.

[26]  Because aggressive behavior is one of the potential psychological effects of anabolic steroid abuse, anabolic steroids could predispose an individual to aggressive acts, including sexual violence.

[27]  Education officials told us that the agency is currently conducting an evaluation of the effectiveness of the student drug-testing programs implemented by its grantees.

In: Substance Abuse, Assessment and Addiction      ISBN: 978-1-61122-931-8

Editors: Kristina A. Murati and Allison G. Fischer      © 2011 Nova Science Publishers, Inc.

*Chapter 14*

# QUALITY ASSESSMENT OF HERBAL MEDICINE WITH CHROMATOGRAPHIC FINGERPRINT

## *Fan Gong[*a,b], Qing Zhang[c] and Jing Zhang[d]*

[a] Department of Plant Science, Rothamsted Research, Harpenden, Hertfordshire, United Kingdom, AL5 2JQ

[b] Research Center of Modernization of Chinese Herbal Medicines, Institute of Chemometrics and Intelligent Analytical Instruments, College of Chemistry and Chemical Engineering, Central South University, Changsha 410083, China

[c] Department of Economic Management, Hunan City University, Yincheng Southern Road, Yiyang, Hunan 413000, China

[d] Staff Hospital Attached to Central South University, Central South University, Changsha 410083, China

## ABSTRACT

Nowadays, fingerprint analysis based on chromatography has become one of the approaches widely used for quality assessment of herbal medicine. In this paper, chromatographic fingerprint from high performance liquid chromatography-diode array detector (HPLC-DAD) and gas chromatography–mass spectrometry (GC-MS) is investigated. A pragmatic approach combining several well-established chemometric methods is developed for processing the data sets in order to assess the similarity/difference in chromatographic fingerprints obtained. The strategy includes baseline correction, peak alignment, variable selection, correlation analysis, principal co-ordinates analysis (PCO), principal component analysis (PCA) and Procrustes analysis. In order to demonstrate the advantages of chromatographic fingerprint with total profile, a previously used method of fingerprint analysis based on a chromatographic peak table is also investigated in this paper. In the real application to herbal samples of Rhizoma

---

[*] Correspondence should be addressed. Email: fan.gong@bbsrc.ac.uk (F. GONG).

*chuanxiong*, Radix *angelicae*, Cortex *cinnamomi*, Herba *menthae*, Ginkgo *biloba* and Rhizoma *asarum* collected from different sources, fingerprint analysis based on total chromatograms coupled with chemometric data preprocessing and data analysis is a reliable method and thus it should be applicable for quality assessment of herbal medicine.

**Keywords:** Quality assessment; Herbal medicine; Chromatographic fingerprint; Total profile; Peak table; Chemometrics.

## 1. INTRODUCTION

Herbal medicine (HM) has a long therapeutic history over thousand years and is currently still serving many of the health needs of a large population in the world. However, as pointed in Ref.[1], currently existing approaches for quality assessment can not fulfill the practical requirements of the safety and efficacy of HMs. One of these reasons might be that, unlike a chemically synthetic drug with much purity, a HM and/or a HM formula may consist of hundreds of complex phytochemicals. As a result, it becomes very difficult to identify most of chemical components in HM by means of common approaches [2-4]. In general, only a few marker or pharmacologically active components are employed for evaluating the quality and authenticity of a HM, identifying the presence of a HM in a HM preparation, and finding out the quantitative herbal composition of a HM product. Yet, it is a common consent that this approach is barely satisfactory for quality control of a HM and HM products with multiple chemical components [4]. Many other problems specific to the quality assessment of HM have been also investigated in Ref. [4].

In the year of 2004, the Chinese State Food and Drug Administration (SFDA) started to regulate the composition of liquid injection with HM ingredients for assuring stringent quality by chemical assay and standardization. Fingerprints of HMs and HM liquid injection were compulsorily recommended for this purpose. In addition, among the various experimental techniques, chromatographic methods were highly recommended for finding out fingerprints of these products [5-11].

By definition, a chromatographic fingerprint is in practice a total pattern of some common kinds of pharmacologically active and chemically characteristic components in HM [5,11]. This chromatographic profile should be featured by the fundamental attributions of "integrity" and "fuzziness" or "sameness" and "differences" so as to chemically represent the HM investigated [11,12]. Thus, the authentication and identification of HMs can be accurately conducted ("integrity") with chromatographic fingerprints even if the number and/or concentration of chemically characteristic constituents vary from one sample to another ("fuzziness") or, chromatographic fingerprints could successfully demonstrate both the "sameness" and "differences" between a set of herbal samples under study [11,13].

In general, chromatographic fingerprint can be produced by combined approaches of chromatography with spectrometry such as HPLC-DAD, GC-MS, capillary electrophoresis-diode array detection (CE-DAD) and high performance liquid chromatography-mass spectrometry (HPLC-MS) since hyphenated approach could show greatly improved performances in terms of the elimination of instrumental interference, retention time shift correction, selectivity, chromatographic separation abilities, measurement precision [14-16].

If hyphenated chromatography is further coupled with chemometric approaches, more information on quality assessment of HM can be extracted from chromatographic fingerprint. The excellent properties of hyphenated methods are so-called dimension advantages which were proposed by B. R. Kowalski and his colleague [17].

Herbal plants grow in different producing areas and various treating approaches are used during the manufacturing processes. Moreover, during the qualitative and quantitative analysis of HM with a large number of chemical components, chromatographic instruments and experimental conditions are difficult to be reproducible. Thus, fingerprint construction from chromatography is not a trivial task. For example, it is difficult to obtain a chromatographic fingerprint with the complete separation and uniform concentration distribution of all components. On the other hand, as the baseline and retention time shifts exist from one chromatogram to another, several approaches for data preprocessing would be employed [4,18-21].

In this Chapter, several topics on fingerprint analysis from chromatography and its application to quality assessment of HM are discussed. The construction of chromatographic fingerprint based on information theory is firstly investigated [22-24]. Next, some chemometric methods are developed for processing the data sets in order to assess the similarity/difference in chromatographic fingerprints obtained. The strategy includes peak alignment to correct the retention time shift by use of the combined approach of chemometric resolution with cubic spline interpolation [18-19, 25-31], variable selection for selecting significant data points from chromatographic fingerprints [32-40], baseline correction with asymmetric least square [41-42], quality assessment of HMs with similarity index (SI) and linear correlation coefficient (LCC) in correlation analysis [43-48], sample discrimination with PCA and/or PCO [49-54] and comparison of data configurations with Procrustes analysis [55-57]. Finally, a previous fingerprint approach based on a chromatographic peak table is also investigated [58-60]. In the real application to a lot of herbal samples including Rhizoma *chuanxiong*, Radix *angelicae*, Cortex *cinnamomi*, Herba *menthae*, Ginkgo *biloba* and Rhizoma *asarum* collected from different sources in China, it shows that chromatographic fingerprint based on total profiles combined with data preprocessing and data analysis should be a powerful tool for quality assessment of HM.

# 2. METHODOLOGY

## 2.1. Information Theory Applied to Fingerprint Construction from Chromatography

A chromatographic fingerprint, which is in fact a concentration distribution curve including several chromatographic peaks, might be regarded as a continuous signal determined by its chromatographic shape. The information content can be simply expressed as the following [22-23]:

$$\Phi = - \int p_x \log p_x \, dx$$

where $p_x$ is the probability or concentration of chemical components distribution function. In theory, if and only if $p_x$ with unchangeable variance is characterized by normal distribution can its information content $\Phi$ reach its maximum.

Under an ideal situation, all peaks from a chromatogram can be separated completely and each peak confined to a narrow zone might correspond to a normal distribution profile [23-24]. A chromatographic fingerprint with all of peaks just completely separated should be featured by maximal information content. Further separation can not provide more information. On the contrary, if any of chromatographic peaks is overlapped with its adjacent one(s), this peak will surely show non-Gaussian normal distribution and therefore undoubtedly cause a loss of the information content. Thus, the chromatographic shape is closely dependent on the separation degrees of peaks. On the other hand, the concentration distribution of each component can also affect the chromatographic shape.

In this study, fingerprint construction aims at assessing the quality of HM. This evaluation is based on the similarities and/or differences of the chromatographic shapes, or saying the separation degree and concentration distribution of each component from chromatographic fingerprints of HM. As a result, both the separation degrees and concentration distribution of components should be considered for this evaluation. To achieve this goal, some reasonable modification on the information content ($\Phi$) based on Eq.1 is employed here. A chromatographic fingerprint is first normalized with its overall peak area equal to one and then the information content is calculated based on the following Eq.2.

$$\Phi = - \int p_x/(\text{sum}(p_x)) \log p_x/(\text{sum}(p_x)) \, dx$$

where $p_x$ is the real response of each component involved in the chromatographic fingerprint and $\text{sum}(p_x)$ is the sum of $p_x$. In this study, $\Phi$ in Eq.2 is taken as the real information content of a chromatographic fingerprint.

Seen from Eq.2, the total profiles rather than the retention time, peak intensity, peak width, peak area and/or peak height from each peak identified are employed for $\Phi$. Moreover, the identification of chromatographic peaks is unnecessary and the noise might have a little influence on $\Phi$. For an ideal fingerprint, all peaks are separated completely and each peak corresponds to a normal distribution profile. Thus, the information content reaches the maximal.

## 2.2. Peak Alignment

### 2.2.1. Selection of Mark Compounds with Chemometric Resolution Methods

Figures 1a and 2a shows two simulated chromatographic fingerprints (Fingerprint1 and Fingerprint2) with 10 peaks generated by HPLC–DAD. The mesh graphs of their two-dimensional data matrix are shown in Figs.1b and 2b. Figs.1c and 2c, Figs.1d and 2d represent the pure chromatograms and spectra of Fingerprint1 and Fingerprint2, respectively. In comparison with Figs.1a and 2a, the retention time shifts exist in Fingerprint1 and Fingerprint2. Since chromatographic fingerprint is generated from the two-dimensional data matrix which is produced by HPLC-DAD, several chemometric resolution techniques, for example, heuristic evolving latent projections (HELP), evolving factor analysis (EFA), windows factor analysis (WFA), subwindow factor analysis (SFA) and orthogonal projection resolution (OPR), can be used to identify the purity of chromatographic peaks and resolve the data matrix into chromatograms and spectra of the pure chemical constituents [14-15, 19,31]. With the help of chemometric resolution methods, the chromatograms and UV spectra of all 10 components in Fingerprint1 and Fingerprint2 could be obtained. Since there are 7 common components between Fingerprint1 and Fingerprint2, these common peaks are then selected as the mark compounds for the correction of the retention time shifts (Table 1). In general, the markers selected with high signal to noise should span within the whole chromatographic scan region but not concentrate on parts of the regions. Moreover, if a component showing a distinct peak exists in all the chromatographic fingerprints investigated, it is reasonable to select it as one of the markers.

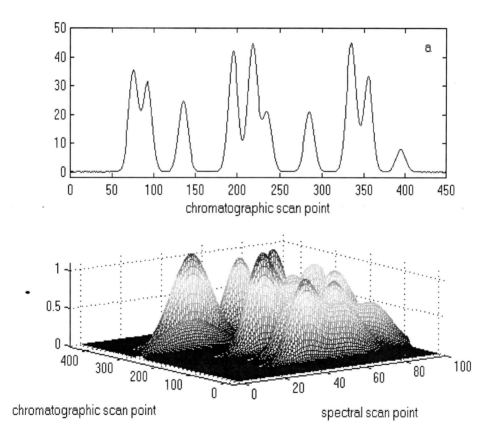

**Table 1. Retention time points of 10 components in Fingerprint1 and Fingerprint2**

| | Retention time point | | | | | | | | | |
|---|---|---|---|---|---|---|---|---|---|---|
| Fingerprint1 | 75 | 92[a] | 135 | 195[a] | 218 | 235 | 285 | 335 | 355[a] | 395 |
| Fingerprint2 | 65 | 88[a] | 145 | 185[a] | 215 | 240 | 275 | 325 | 355[a] | 405 |

[a] Different components between Fingerprint1 and Fingerprint2 simulated.

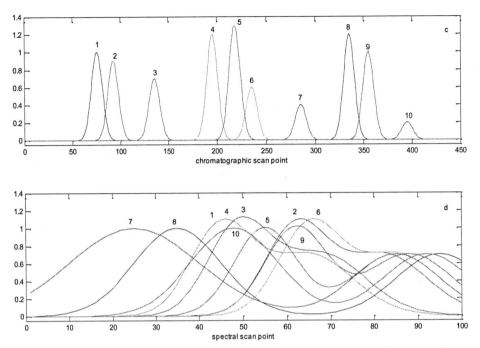

Figure 1. Simulated Fingerprint1(a), mesh graph(b), pure chromatograms(c) and UV spectra(d).

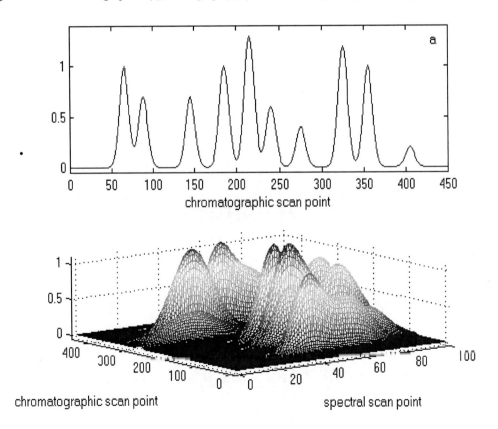

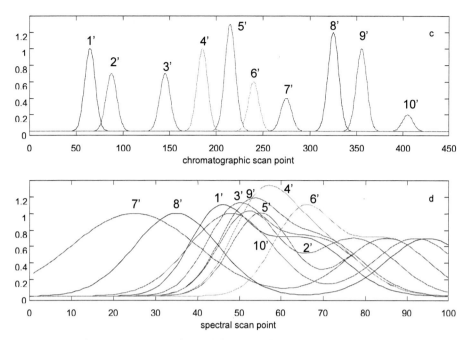

Figure 2. Simulated Fingerprint2(a), mesh graph(b), pure chromatograms(c) and UV spectra(d).

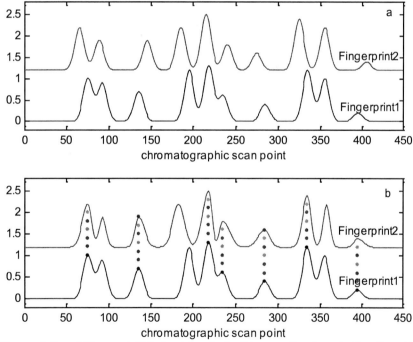

Figure 3. Fingerprint1 and Fingerprint2 before(a) and after(b) correcting the retention time shifts.

## 2.2.2. Correction of Retention Time Shifts and Reconstruction of Chromatographic Fingerprints with Cubic Spline Interpolation

After the marker compounds and the retention times are determined, the retention time shifts might be corrected now. If Fingerprint1 is taken as the target and Fingerprint2 is then aligned with it, the retention time points of the mark compounds in Fingerprint1 might be selected as the fixed points and the time shifts for all points between these fixed points in Fingerprint2 might be calculated by linear interpolation. Thus, new chromatographic scan points of Fingerprint2 with correction could be obtained. Since the new chromatographic scan points of Fingerprint2 are calculated with linear interpolation, these new points might be not integer. For example, the 68th point of Fingerprint2 is adjusted to 77.25 rather than 77 or 78. Clearly, the non-integer should be converted into the integral data as the scan points from chromatography should be integer. In this study, in order to conduct this conversion, the cubic spline data interpolation technique is used to reconstruct Fingerprint2. Figure 3 shows Fingerprint1 and Fingerprint2 with and without correction.

Seen from Figure 3b, the marker components selected from Fingerprint1 and Fingerprint2 have been synchronized after Fingerprint2 is aligned with Fingerprint1. In sum, the steps of the present method for peak alignment could be described as the following:

1) Select some peak clusters with high signal to noise, identify the purity and then resolve the two-dimensional data matrix into pure chromatograms $C$ and UV spectra $S$.
2) In comparison with $C$ and $S$, select several marker compounds. Then, the retention time points of the markers in Fingerprint1 and Fingerprint2 represented by $t\_mark$ and $^l t\_mark$ are obtained.
3) With $t\_mark$ and $^l t\_mark$, linear interpolation is conducted on Fingerprint2 to obtain the new chromatographic scan points $^l t\_new$.
4) Reconstruct a new chromatographic fingerprint ($^l p\_new$) with $^l t\_new$ by means of the cubic spline data interpolation technique.

## 2.3. Variable Selection

### 2.3.1. Methods of Variable Selection

In this study, five approaches for variable selection (forward selection (B4), key set factor analysis, unweighted $w$, weighted $w$ and Fisher coefficient) are used. Among them, both the methods of forward selection and key set factor analysis are based on PCA in chemometrics. For three other approaches of unweighted $w$, weighted $w$ and Fisher coefficient, the inner- and outer-variances, within- and between-group variations of variables are considered [32-40]. All the approaches for variable selection and the criteria to determine the number of representative variables are summarized in Table 2. Here, the size of original data X is $M \times N$ with $M$ samples and $N$ variables. If $p$ variables are retained, the size of the reduced data Y is $M \times p$.

#### 2.3.1.1. Method Forward Selection (B4)

At first, PCA is conducted on the preprocessed data. Method B4 retains variables by starting with the first component and retaining the variable with the highest loading or with the loading closest to zero for each of the first $p$ components.

### 2.3.1.2. Method Key Set Factor Analysis

After PCA is conducted on the preprocessed data, the variable corresponding to the highest loading or the loading closest to zero is selected as the first key variable. Or, among all the variables, the one which is most orthogonal to the mean variable is taken as the first one. The second variable is the one which is most orthogonal to the first variable extracted. The third is the most orthogonal to the plane defined by the first two variables kept. In the same way, other representative variables are determined.

**Table 2. Methods for variable selection and criteria to determine the number of variables retained**

| variable selection method | method of selecting $p$ variables from $N$ original variables | criteria for deciding on the value of $p$ |
|---|---|---|
| forward selection (B4) | Associate $p$ variables with each of the first $p$ components and retain these variables. 1. Select the variables associated with the highest loading for each of the first $p$ components 2. Select the variables associated with the loadings closest to zero for each of the first $p$ components | 1. The number of principal components required to account for some proportion ($\alpha$, here $\alpha$=90%) of the total variance; |
| key set factor analysis | 1. Select the first variable associated with the loading closest to zero 2. Select the first variable associated with the highest loading 3. Select the first variable be most orthogonal to the mean variable | 2. Arbitrarily select $p$ such that the ratio of number of observations to $p$ is 3:1; |
| unweighted $w$ | Calculate the ratio of the mean of the standard deviation of variables in each class to the standard deviation of variables of all samples | 3. The number of chemical factors with the factor indicator function (IND) |
| weighted $w$ | Calculate the ratio of the mean of the weighted standard deviation of variables in each class to the weighted standard deviation of variables of all samples | |
| Fisher coefficient | Calculate the ratio of the between- to the within-class variances | |

### 2.3.1.3. Methods Unweighted and Weighted

For the methods unweighted and weighted $w$, the inner- and outer-variances are used. The coefficient of unweighted $w$ of the $i$-th variable can be calculated based on the following equation:

$$un\_w(i)=\{average[std(i_1), std(i_2)...std(i_n)]\}/ std(i_{all})$$

Here, $std(i_n)$ and $std(i_{all})$ are the standard deviation of the $i$-th variable in the $n$-th group and of all the samples, respectively. average is the mean value.

In most cases, the numbers of samples in each group are different. The coefficient of weighted $w$ of the $i$-th variable is:

$$w(i)=[ std(i_1)\times g_1+ std(i_2) \times g_2 +...+std(i_n) \times g_n]\}/ [std(i_{all}) \times g_{all}] \qquad (4)$$

where $g_n$ is the number of the samples in the $n$-th group and $g_{all}$ is the number of all the samples. For the method of weighted $w$, the standard deviation is weighted with the number of samples in each group. The lower the coefficient of $un\_w$ or $w$, the better the variable.

## 2.3.1.4. Method Fisher Coefficient

For the Fisher method, a coefficient based on the between- and within-group variations is calculated as the following:

between- group variation:

$$SSB(i) = \sum_{k=1}^{g} n_k[i\_average(y_k) - i\_average\ (y)]^2 \ (k=1,2...g)$$

within-group variation:

$$SSW(i) = \sum_{k=1}^{g} \sum_{j=1}^{n_k} [y_{kj} - i\_average(y_k)]^2 \ (k=1,2...g, j=1,2...n_k) \quad (6)$$

Fisher coefficient:

$$F(i) = \{[1/(g-1)] \times SSB(i)\}/\{[1/(n-g)] \times SSW(i)\}$$

where $g$ is the number of groups, $n_k$ the number of samples in the $k$-th group, $i\_average(y_k)$ the mean of the $i$-th variable in the $k$-th group, $i\_average(y)$ the total mean of the $i$-th variable, and $y_{kj}$ the value of the $j$-th sample in the $k$-th group. The higher the value of Fisher coefficient, the better the variable.

### 2.3.2. Determination of Number of Variables Selected

In this study, three criteria are used to determine the number of variables retained (see Table 2). For the first criterion, $p$ is set to be the number of PCs required to account for no less than 90% of the total variance with PCA. We arbitrarily select $p$ such that the ratio of the number of samples to $p$ is 3:1 for the second criterion as in [35]. Finally, IND which has been widely used to determine the number of the chemical ranks in chemometrics is used here. $p$ is equal to the number of the principal factors for the third criterion [39].

### 2.3.3. Evaluation of the Reduced Subsets

#### 2.3.3.1. Procrustes Analysis for Configuration Comparison of Two Datasets

Procrustes analysis is generally used to compare the configurations of two datasets [55-57]. In this study, the configuration differences (D) between the original data X and the reduced subset Y can be calculated as the following.

At first, singular value decomposition is conducted on X and Y,

$$X = U_X \times S_X \times V_X^t$$

$Y = U_Y \times S_Y \times V_Y{}^t$

Taking the first $p$ columns of $U_X$ and $U_Y$ to obtain $U_1$ and $U_2$,

$U_1 = U_X(:,1:p)$

$U_2 = U_Y(:,1:p)$

Then,

$D = \text{trace}\,(U_1{}^t \times U_1 + U_2{}^t \times U_2 - 2\Sigma)$

where $\Sigma$ is the diagonal singular-value matrix of $U_1{}^t \times U_2$ and "trace" means the trace of the matrix.

### 2.3.3.2. Weighted Similarity of Two Data Matrices

In [35], a weighted measure of similarity (Q) between two datasets is used.

$$Q = \frac{\sum_{i=1}^{p} v_i r_i}{\sum_{i=1}^{p} v_i} \quad (i=1,2\ldots p)$$

where $p$ is the number of useful variables retained, $v_i$ the proportion of the total variance explained by the $i$-th principal component of the original data, $r_i$ the correlation coefficient between the $i$-th principal components of the original and reduced datasets.

### 2.3.3.3. Tri-Variate Plot of PCA Scores

The relationship between the samples is visually examined in low dimensional space with PCA. If the grouping of herbal samples can be clearly demonstrated in the first three PC scores plot, the selected subset possibly contains much discriminative information.

## 2.4. Baseline Correction with Asymmetric Least Square

In this study, a chromatographic baseline is modeled with a penalized asymmetric least square (ALS) method [41-42]. If the data size of a chromatographic profile is $m$, an objective function to be minimised is constructed as the following:

$$Q = \sum_{i} v_i\,(y_i - f_i) + \lambda \sum_{i} (\Delta^2 f_i) \quad (i=1,2,\ldots,m)$$

where $y_i$ is a signal sequence to be smoothed and $f_i$ is the smoothed signal sequence. $\Delta^2 f_i$ is the second order differentiation of $f_i$. $v_i$ is a weight function which is non-zero when $y_i$ is observed or allowed to influence $f_i$ and 0 otherwise. The second parameter $\lambda$ controls the roughness of the smoothed signal. The choice of each element in the weight vector $v$ is based on the following rules:

$v_i = p$ if $y_i > f_i$ and $v_i = 1-p$ if $y_i \leq f_i$, with $0 < p < 1$.

The objective function is then optimised by a gradient algorithm. When $p$ is near zero and $\lambda$ approaches a large value, $f$ tends to follow the valleys of $y$ and thus a baseline is estimated.

The complexity of the baseline estimated by ALS is controlled by $\lambda$ and $p$. Here, $\lambda$ needs to be a very large number, usually varied from $10^5$ to $10^8$ while $p$ needs to be close to 0, usually varied from $10^{-3}$ to $10^{-5}$. The higher the contrast of $\lambda$ and $p$, the simpler the estimated baseline [41-42].

## 2.5. Correlation Analysis with Similarity Index (SI) and Linear Correlation Coefficient (LCC)

SI or LCC has been widely used to the similarity search in spectral libraries or the similarity comparison between different spectral or chemical structural vectors [43-48]. The higher the value of SI or LCC, the more similar between the sample and target. SI and LCC between two fingerprints ($x_1$ and $x_2$) can be calculated as the following:

$SI = (x_1' \times x_2) / (\|x_1\| \times \|x_2\|)$
$z_1 = x_1 - \mathbf{1} \times mean(x_1)$
$z_2 = x_2 - \mathbf{1} \times mean(x_2)$
$LCC = (z_1' \times z_2) / (\|z_1\| \times \|z_2\|)$

Here, $\| \|$ is equivalent to the length of the vector of $x_1$, $x_2$, $z_1$ or $z_2$. $mean(x_1)$ and $mean(x_2)$ are the average values of $x_1$ and $x_2$, respectively. $\mathbf{1}$ is a one vector with the same size of $x_1$ or $x_2$.

## 2.6. Principal Co-Ordinates Analysis (PCO) and Principal Component Analysis (PCA)

Besides PCA, PCO is another method to visually inspect the samples in low dimensional space. An important advantage of PCO over PCA is that any distance metric can be used to represent the pattern of the data set. Thus, PCO can give different views on the data if various dissimilarity measures are applied.

Dissimilarity matrix ($D$) is a data matrix showing the dissimilarity between a set of samples. Here, Euclidean distance is used to represent the dissimilarity between chromatographic fingerprints. For $n$ samples studied, the data size of $D$ is $n \times n$. PCO with $D$ is conducted as the following [49-54]:

1). Calculating a square matrix of $D$ represented by $D^{(2)}$.

2). A matrix $A$ is computed:

$$a_{ij} = -1/2d_{ij}^{(2)} \qquad\qquad (i,j=1,2,...,n)$$

3). A matrix $G$ is computed so that

$$g_{ij} = a_{ij} - \bar{a}_i - \bar{a}_j + \bar{a} \qquad\qquad (i,j=1,2,...,n)$$

where $\bar{a}_i$ and $\bar{a}_j$ represent the row and column means of matrix $A$ and $\bar{a}$ the overall mean. Thus, $G$ is the row- and column-centred matrix of $A$.

4). Singular value decomposition is performed on $G$:

$$G = U \times S \times U' + E$$

Thus, a scores matrix $T = U \times S^{1/2}$ can be produced. Keep the first $k$ components related to positive eigenvalues. In analogy to PCA, the inner relationship between the samples can be visually examined in low dimensional space by plotting one column of $T$ against another.

## 2.7. Procrustes Analysis

Please see Section 2.3.3.1 Procrustes analysis for configuration comparison of two datasets.

# 4. EXPERIMENTAL

## 3.1. Materials and Chemicals

Rhizoma *chuanxiong*, Cortex *cinnamomi*, Radix *angelicae*, Herba *menthae*, Ginkgo *biloba* and Rhizoma *asarum* samples were purchased from several pharmaceutical stores, companies and collected from different producing areas in the mainland and in Hong Kong, P. R. China.

$CH_3OH$, $H_3PO_4$, $K_2HPO_4$, $CH_3CN$, isoproanol ($C_3H_8O$), citric acid ($C_6H_8O_7$) and acetonitrile ($CH_3CN$) were of analytical grade. Double distilled water was used.

Standard compounds of cinnamyl alcohol, cinnamaldehyde, cinnamyl acetate and ferulic acid are purchased from Lancaster Synthesis Ltd. (UK) Company, Sigma, Aldrich and National Institute for the Control of Pharmaceutical and Biological Products of China.

## 3.2. Instruments

RT-80 pulverizer made in Taiwan, 5810 centrifuge from Eppendorf Company in Germany , Ultra Turrax T25 basic stirrer from IKA Company in Malaysia, CQ250 ultrasonic cleaner made in Shanghai, Hewlett-Packard HP-1100 HPLC coupled with a G1315A diode array detector, Hewlett-Packard 5890 Series II Gas-chromatography paired with 5972 Series

Mass selective detector and GC-17A Gas Chromatography and QP-5000 Mass Spectrometer from Shimadzu Company were employed in this study.

## 3.3. Extraction

### 3.3.1. Extraction of Raw Materials of Rhizoma Chuanxiong, Cortex Cinnamomi, Radix Angelicae and Herba Menthae

All of the raw materials were dried for about 60 min under $30^{\circ}C$ at first. Then, about 0.5-g amount of dried and pre-pulverized herbal materials were extracted using an Ultra Turrax T25basic stirrer (11,000 rpm) with 30ml of $CH_3OH$ for 2 min. After centrifugation for about 20 min, the upper solution was filtered through a glass filter covered with a filter paper. Next, the solution was evaporated under reduced pressure to about 1ml and then diluted with methanol to 5ml in a volumetric flask. A 1ml volume of this solution was then filtered through a Millipore filtration unit type HV 0.45 μm. A 20μl and 2.5μl volume of this solution were injected into the HPLC and GC-MS systems, respectively.

### 3.3.2. Extraction of Extracts and Products of Ginkgo Biloba

Pre-weighted extracts of Ginkgo biloba were dissolved with 5 mL methanol. A 1 mL volume of this solution was filtered through a Millipore filtration unit type HV 0.45 μm. A 10 μL volume of this solution was injected into the HPLC system.

Raw materials and products pre-weighted were extracted using CQ250 ultrasonic cleaner with 20 mL methanol for 15 min. Keep still for 5 min at room temperature. The solution was then filtered through a glass filter covered with a filter paper. Next, the solution was evaporated under vacuum to about 1mL and then diluted with methanol to 5 mL in a volumetric flask. A 1 mL volume of this solution was then filtered through a Millipore filtration unit type HV 0.45 μm. A 10 μL volume of this solution was injected into the HPLC system.

### 3.3.3. Extraction of Volatile Components from Rhizoma Asarum

About 300g Rhizoma *asarum* was added to a special extractor with over 1000 mL of distilled water till the samples were all swollen and allowed to stand for 30 min. under room temperature. Then, more about 100 mL of distilled water was added. Next, the volatile fractions were extracted by steam distillation as it was found to give a simple and effective method to obtain essential oils from herbs.

### 3.4. Chromatographic Procedure

### 3.4.1. Determination of Raw Materials of Rhizoma Chuanxiong, Cortex Cinnamomi, Radix Angelicae and Herba Menthae with HPLC-DAD

(1)  Column: LiChrosorb RP.18 (Hewlett Packard, 200 × 4.6 mm, I.D.);
(2)  Mobile phase:

I. At the starting time, the mobile phase was composed of A ($CH_3OH$) and B ($H_2O+K_2HPO_4+H_3PO_4$ with pH=3) in the ratio of 40:60 (V/V). Then, this mixed mobile phase was linearly gradient to A : B = 80:20 (V/V) after 50 min;

II. A and B were mixed with 10 : 90 (V/V) at first and then linearly gradient to A : B = 100:0 (V/V) after 60 min.

(3) Flow rate:
I. 0.7 ml/min;
II. 1.0 ml/min.

(4) Column temperature: 25°C;

(5) Wavelength scanning range and step: 190 – 400 nm, 2 nm / step.

### 3.4.2. Determination of Raw Materials of Rhizoma Chuanxiong, Cortex Cinnamomi, Radix Angelicae and Herba Menthae with GC-MS

(1) Column: HP-5MS column (Crosslinked 5% PH MS siloxane, 30 m × 0.25 mm I.D., 0.25 μm film thickness);

(2) Column temperature: maintained at 80 °C for 2 min at first, and then programmed from 80°C to 230 °C at the rate 5 °C/min;

(3) Inlet temperature: 230 °C;

(4) Carrier gas and flow-rate: helium, 1.0 ml/min;

(5) Ionization mode and energy: electron impact ($EI^+$), 70 eV;

(6) Scan range and velocity: 30-400 amu;

(7) Ionization source temperature: 280 °C.

### 3.4.3. Determination of Extracts and of Products Ginkgo Biloba with HPLC-DAD

(1) Column: Spherisorb ODS2 C18 (250 × 4 mm, I.D.);

(2) Mobile phase: At the beginning, the mobile phase consisted of the solvent $H_2O$, $CH_3CN$, isopropyl alcohol and citric acid in the ratio of 1000:200:30:4.92 (W/W). Then, it was linearly gradient to $H_2O$, $CH_3CN$, isopropanol and citric acid in the ratio of 1000:470:50:6.08 (W/W) after 25 min.

(3) Flow rate: 1.0 ml/min;

(4) Column temperature: 25°C;

(5) Wavelength scanning range and step: 200 – 400 nm, 1 nm / step.

### 3.4.4. Determination of Volatile Components from Rhizoma Asarum with GC-MS

(1) Column: OV-17 capillary column (30 m × 0.25 mm I.D., 0.25 μm film thickness);

(2) Column temperature: maintained at 60 °C and then programmed from 60°C to 210 °C at the rate 6 °C/min. Kept 210°C for 30 mins;

(3) Inlet temperature: 230 °C;

(4) Carrier gas and flow-rate: helium, 1.0 ml/min;

(5) Ionization mode and energy: electron impact ($EI^+$), 70 eV;

(6) Scan range and velocity: 20-350 amu;

(7) Ionization source temperature: 230 °C.

# 4. RESULTS AND DISCUSSION

## 4.1. Construction of Chromatographic Fingerprints Based on Information Theory: Rhizoma Chuanxiong and Ginkgo Biloba

### 4.1.1. Selection of A Chromatographic Fingerprint of Rhizoma Chuanxiong

Figure 4 shows two chromatographic fingerprints of the same *Rhizoma chuanxiong* sample detected under two experimental conditions I (Figure 4a) and II (Figure 4b), respectively (see Section 3.4.1). Visually inspecting Figure 4, only 47 chromatographic peaks appear in Figure 4a while there are about 60 ones identified in Figure 4b (See Table 3). Absolutely, Figure 4b might show greatly improved performance in terms of the chromatographic separation degree. On the other hand, the concentration distribution of each peak in Figure 4b is also more uniform than in Figure 4a. So, the detection condition II should be better than the condition I.

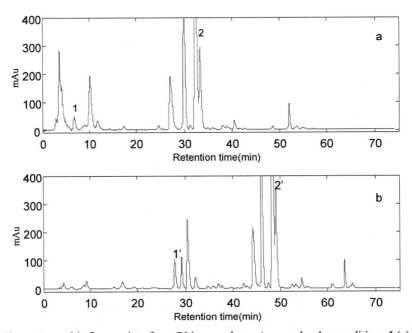

Figure 4. Chromatographic fingerprints from Rhizoma *chuanxiong* under the conditions I (a) and II (b).

**Table 3. Information content and number of peaks identified in chromatographic fingerprints from a Rhizoma *chuanxiong* sample detected under two conditions in Figure 4**

|  | I | II |
|---|---|---|
| $\Phi$ | 7.08 | 7.74 |
| number of peaks | 47 | 60 |

Note: see the experimental section 3.4.1 about the conditions I and II.

Table 3 also displays the information content Φ of Figure 4a and Figure 4b. Seen from Table 3, the information content from Figure 4b is much more than in Figure 4a.

In order to further determine whether chromatographic fingerprints obtained can chemically represent some pharmacologically active and marker compounds existing in *Rhizoma chuanxiong*, several multi-resolution approaches in chemometrics and GC-MS determination are employed here [14-15]. Take the peak clusters 1, 2, 1' and 2' in Figure 4 as examples. Both the peak clusters 1 and 1' are pure peaks representing ferulic acid which is a pharmacologically active and marker compound. However, the peak clusters 2 and 2' are overlapping peaks containing two components, one of which is another pharmacologically active and marker compound of bultylidene dihydro-phthalide. Figure 5 shows the peak clusters 1' and 2' (Figure 5a and Figure 5b) and their resolved chromatograms (Figure 5c and Figure 5d). In Figure 5, the peak A represents ferulic acid while the peak B shows bultylidene dihydro-phthalide. GC-MS determination can further determine these two components (see the experimental section 3.4.2). Their UV obtained directly by HPLC-DAD and mass spectra from GC-MS are showed in Figure 6, respectively. As a result, the chromatographic fingerprint obtained in Figure 4b with more information content could also chemically represent Rhizoma *chuanxiong*. Thus, Figure 4b can be selected as the chromatographic fingerprint of Rhizoma *chuanxiong* for quality assessment of Rhizoma *chuanxiong*.

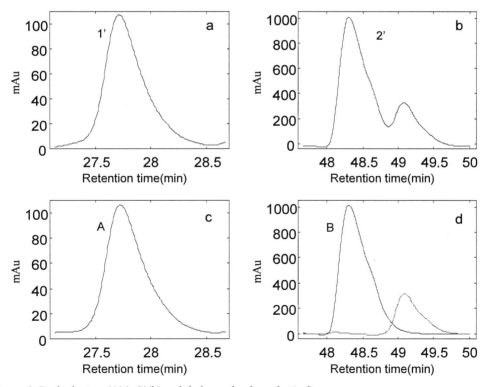

Figure 5. Peak clusters 1'(a), 2'(b) and their resolved results (c,d).

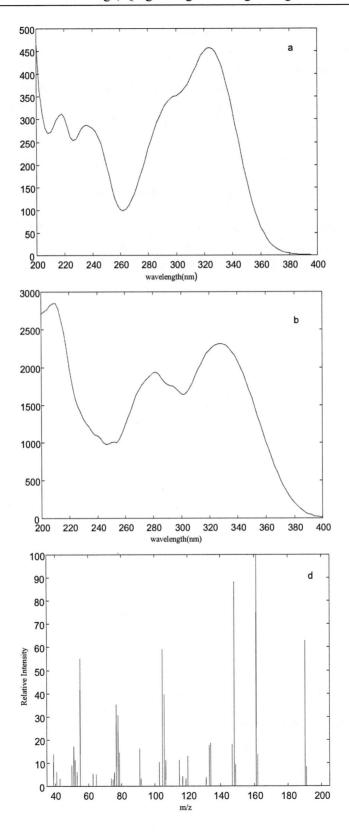

**Figure 6 (Continued)**

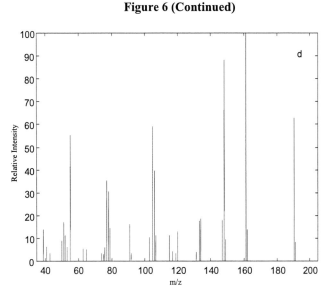

Figure 6. UV and mass spectra of ferulic acid (a and c) and bultylidene dihydro-phthalide (b and d).

### 4.1.2. Determination of Chromatographic Fingerprints of Ginkgo Biloba

Flavonoids are one kind of pharmacologically active and chemically characteristic ingredients from Ginkgo *biloba*. Nowadays, a standard extract denoted by EGb 761, which is a well-defined and beneficial extract from Ginkgo *biloba*, is recognized widely in the world. This standard extract of EGb 761 is mainly composed of thirty-three flavonoids. As a result, the chromatographic fingerprints of Ginkgo *biloba* obtained for quality control should be very similar to that of EGb 761.

Figures7a-c show three chromatographic fingerprints (360 nm) of EGb 761, one extract and one product of Ginkgo *biloba* provided by a pharmaceutical company, respectively. These chromatographic fingerprints are also obtained with HPLC-DAD in this study. In these figures, the peaks denoted by 1 represent rutin (quercetin-3-rutinoside).

Table 4 shows the information content and number of peaks identified from these chromatographic fingerprints obtained. Seen from Table 4, the values of the information content are approximately close to each other, suggesting their same chromatographic shapes or separation degrees and concentration distribution of all chemical components. On the other hand, thirty-four, thirty and twenty-eight chemical components could be identified in Figure 7a, Figure 7b and Figure 7c, respectively. Thus, chromatographic fingerprints obtained in Figure 7a, Figure 7b and Figure 7c should be featured by high separation degrees and uniform concentration distribution of chemical components.

**Table 4. Information content and number of peaks identified of chromatographic fingerprints from three Ginkgo *biloba* samples in Figure 7**

|  | EGb 761 | Ginkgo *biloba* extract | Ginkgo *biloba* product |
|---|---|---|---|
| Φ | 10.98 | 10.79 | 10.67 |
| number of peaks | 34 | 30 | 28 |

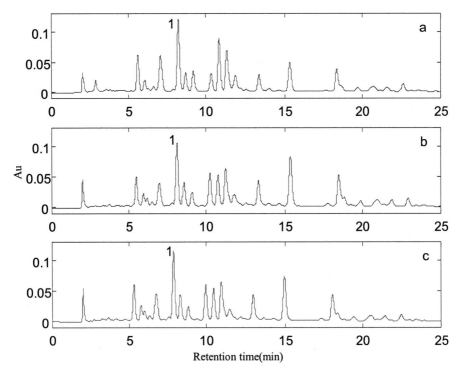

Figure 7. Chromatographic fingerprints of EGb 761 (a), one extract (b) and one product (c) of Ginkgo *biloba* at 360 nm. The peak 1 represents rutin ($C_{15}H_{10}O_6$).

In fact, seen from Figure 7, these chromatographic patterns are very similar to each other. The similarities between these three chromatographic fingerprints are over 0.95, which might be obtained by calculating the correlative or congruent coefficient of these profiles [43-48]. The information content $\Phi$, which is close to each other between these chromatographic fingerprints obtained in Figure 7, might also explain their similarities.

## 4.2. Baseline Correction with Asymmetric Least Square and Peak Alignment: Ginkgo Biloba, Rhizoma Chuanxiong, Radix Angelicae, Cortex Cinnamomi and Herba Menthae

### 4.2.1. Baseline Correction with Asymmetric Least Square: Ginkgo Biloba

In this study, the penalized asymmetric least square (ALS) method is firstly employed to model a chromatographic baseline for fingerprint analysis based on total profiles. In general, the baseline correction for a chromatogram is conducted as the following: (I) Before and after one peak or peak cluster, two points, which contains the background only, are subjectively located; (II) A straight line is modeled with the two points located. This straight line is used to represent the baseline of the peak or peak cluster; (III) The real peak or peak cluster is then obtained by subtracting the baseline from the raw peak or peak cluster. Absolutely, the real peak or peak cluster closely depends on the selection of two background points which are subjectively found. For the ALS method here, a curved baseline can be modeled. Furthermore, the value of the curved baseline modeled at each point is closely dependent on the response of the raw peak or peak cluster as two parameters $\lambda$ and $f$ are adjusted (see Section 2.4). Thus, even if so-called heteroscedastic noise is present in a chromatographic fingerprint, the ALS approach can still work [61].

Figure 8 shows the normalized fingerprints before (blue curve) and after (red curve) baseline correction for the standard extract EGb 761 of Ginkgo *biloba*. The baseline modeled with ALS is also superposed in Figure 8 (green curve). In comparison with the blue and red curves, the baseline shift is corrected successfully.

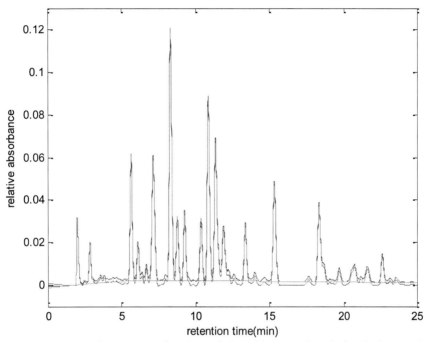

Figure 8. Chromatographic fingerprints of EGb 761 before (blue curve) and after (red curve) baseline correction and the baseline modeled with ALS (green curve).

### 4.2.2. Selection of Mark Compounds in Chromatographic Fingerprints if Real Herbal Medicines with Chemometric Resolution Methods: Rhizoma Chuanxiong, Radix Angelicae, Cortex Cinnamomi and Herba Menthae

Figure 9 shows chromatographic fingerprints (Cfingerprin1 and Cfingerprin2) of Cortex *cinnamomi* from two different sources. Cfingerprin1 and Cfingerprin2 are also the total chromatograms from the response data matrices. Here, the peak clusters denoted by C, D and E in Figure 9a are taken as examples to explain how to select the mark compounds in real chromatographic fingerprints with chemometric resolution approaches.

Figure 10 represents C, D and E peak clusters. Their FSWM plots are shown in Figure 11 [14-15]. Seen from Figure 11a and 11c, two components exist in C while there is only one in E. However, there are possibly two components in D from Figure 11b. In fact, D is also a pure peak of a single component. In Figure 11b, the heteroscedastic noise, which results from a strong absorbance response, has a great effect on the FSWM graph of the D peak cluster.

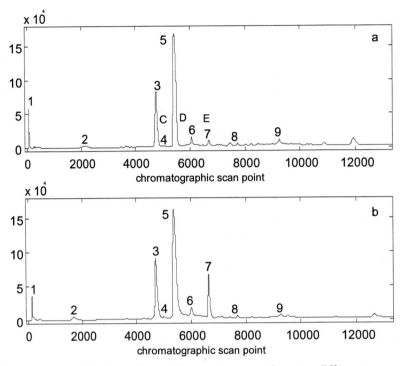

Figure 9. Real chromatographic fingerprints of Cortex *cinnamomi* from two different sources.

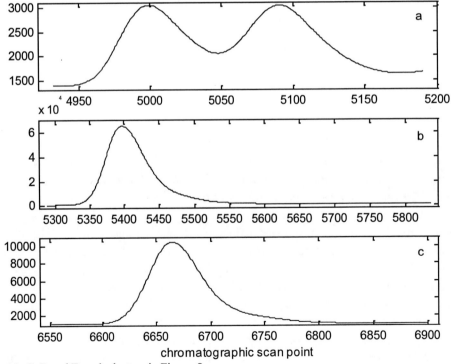

Figure 10. C, D and E peak clusters in Figure 8a.

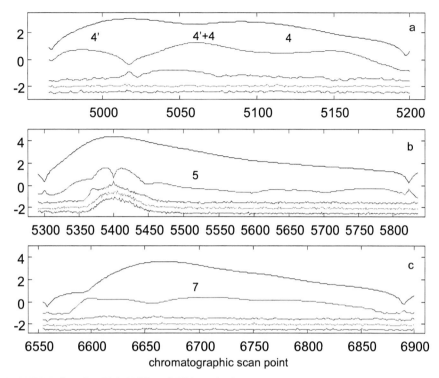

Figure 11. FSWM plots for C(a), D(b) and E(c) peak clusters.

With the help of the chemometric resolution techniques, the resolved chromatographic profiles and UV spectra are shown in Figure 12. With the UV spectra obtained, the 4, 5 and 7 components might be qualitatively determined. They are cinnamyl alcohol ($C_9H_{10}O$), cinnamaldehyde ($C_9H_8O$) and cinnamyl acetate ($C_{11}H_{12}O_2$), respectively. In order to further determine these components, GC–MS analysis has been also employed in this work (see Section 3.4.2). Their mass spectra are shown in Figure 13a–13c, respectively. All these components might be pharmacologically active and marker compounds existing in Cortex *cinnamomi*.

In the same way as described above, the peak purity identification and the resolution into pure chromatograms and UV spectra of components involved in other peaks clusters from these two real chromatographic fingerprints are also conducted (see Figure 9).

With the resolved chromatograms and UV spectra obtained, nine common peaks are selected from the chromatographic fingerprints. These peaks selected might represent the mark compounds (see Figure 9). Their retention time points are listed in Table 5. Seen from Table 5, retention time shifts are surely in existence.

### 4.2.3. Correction of Retention Time Shifts and Reconstruction of Chromatographic Fingerprints of Herbal Medicines with Cubic Spline Interpolation

From above, nine marker compounds are selected and their retention time points are determined. The correction of the retention time shifts could be conducted. In this study, Cfingerprint1 is regarded as the target and Cfingerprint2 is aligned with it.

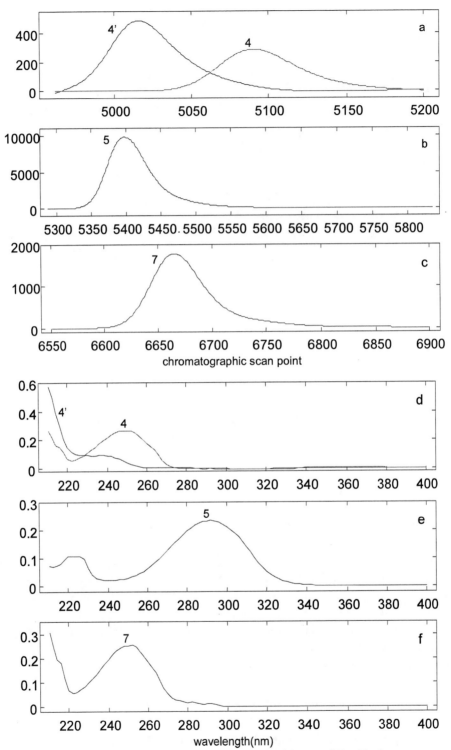

Figure 12. Resolved chromatograms(a,b,c) and spectra(d,e,f) of C, D and E peak clusters.

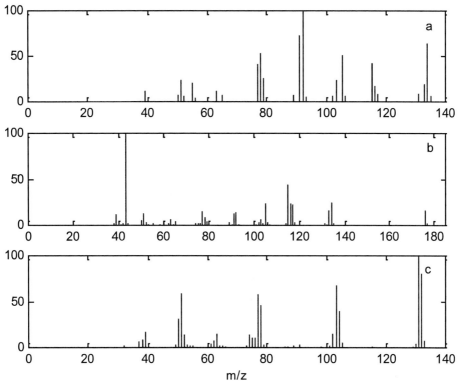

Figure 13. Mass spectra of cinnamyl alcohol(a), cinnamaldehyde(b) and cinnamyl acetate(c).

**Table 5. Retention time points of nine marker compounds in the real chromatographic fingerprints of Cortex *Cinnamomi***

| | | retention time point | | | | | | | | |
|---|---|---|---|---|---|---|---|---|---|---|
| | | 1 | 2 | 3 | 4 | 5 | 6 | 7 | 8 | 9 |
| | Cfingerprin | 5 | 2 | 4 | 5 | 53 | 6 | 6 | 7 | 9 |
| t1 | | 8 | 162 | 756 | 090 | 98 | 039 | 665 | 716 | 253 |
| | Cfingerprin | 1 | 1 | 4 | 5 | 53 | 5 | 6 | 7 | 9 |
| t2 | | 32 | 668 | 710 | 041 | 53 | 992 | 620 | 687 | 271 |

As pointed out in Section 2.2.2, if the chromatographic scan points of Cfingerprint2 are less than 132 (the retention time point of the first marker compound in Cfingerprint2), the retention time shifts for these points will be calculated by linear interpolation between 1 and 58 (the retention time point of the first marker compound in the target). Similarly, the chromatographic scan points of Cfingerprint2 between 9271 (the retention time point of the last marker compound in Cfingerprint2) and its last scan point (13,343 here) are adjusted with linear interpolation between 9253 (the retention time point of the last marker compound in the target) and 13343. However, as for the points between two adjacent fixed points of Cfingerprint2 such as between 5041 and 5353, the retention time shifts are corrected between the corresponding points in the target like 5090 and 5398. After the data treatment like it, new chromatographic scan points of Cfingerprint2 are obtained. Note, most of these new points are not integer.

With the new chromatographic scan points of Cfingerprint2 obtained above, a new chromatographic fingerprint of Cfingerprint2 with the correction of the retention time shifts can be reconstructed by use of cubic spline interpolation. Figure 14 shows Cfingerprint1 and Cfingerpprint2 of two Cortex *cinnamomi* samples before and after peak alignment. Seen from Figure 14b, Cfingerprint2 is aligned with Cfingerprint1 effectively.

Likely, several chromatographic fingerprints from other HMs are aligned with the correction of the retention time shifts. The HMs investigated here include 50 Rhizoma *chuanxiong*, 10 Radix *angelicae* and 17 Herba *menthae* samples from different sources. For all these herbs, the ending chromatographic scan point is 13343. Figure 15 represents the chromatographic fingerprints from one Cortex *cinnamomi*, Rhizoma *chuanxiong*, Radix *angelicae* and Herba *menthae* before and after correcting the retention time shifts, respectively.

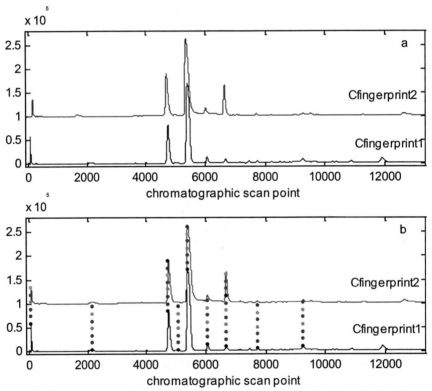

Figure 14. Real chromatographic fingerprints of Cortex *cinnamomi* before (a) and after (b) correcting the retention time shifts.

### 4.2.4. Pattern Recognition Based on Principal Component Analysis before and after Correcting Retention Time Shifts of Chromatographic Fingerprints from Real Herbal Medicines

In order to further assess the reliability and applicability of the approach proposed, this study has attempted to classify the real HMs (79 samples altogether) with chromatographic fingerprints obtained by means of pattern recognition based on principal component analysis (PCA). The profile matrix is constructed by assembling the chromatographic fingerprints as row vectors. The first two principal components PC1 and PC2 are used to provide a convenient visual aid for identifying inhomogenity in the data sets.

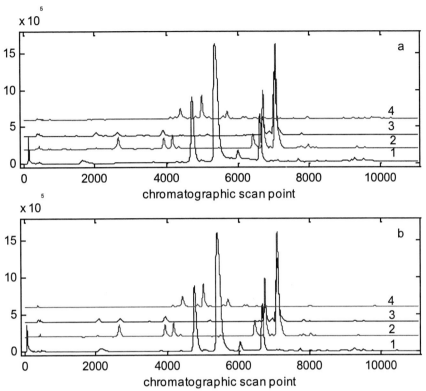

Figure 15. Chromatographic fingerprints from one Cortex *cinnamomi*(1), Rhizoma *chuanxiong*(2), Radix *angelicae*(3) and Herba *menthae*(4) before(a) and after(b) correcting the retention time shifts.

Figure 16 shows the principle component projection plot of PC1 to PC2 before correcting the retention time shifts of 79 chromatographic fingerprints. Clearly, it is very difficult to differentiate Cortex *cinnamomi*, Rhizoma *chuanxiong*, Radix *angelicae* and Herba *menthae* due to the widely scattering projection points (see Figure 16). However, as can be visually seen from Figure 15, the differences are surely in existence between the chromatographic fingerprints from these herbal medicines. Thus, directly conducting PCA on the original chromatographic fingerprints seems unreasonable and unreliable.

On the other hand, if the retention time shifts are corrected, the PC1 to PC2 plot could reveal the segregation of the projection points into four principal clusters (encircled) corresponding to four kinds of herbal medicines (see Figure 17). In comparison with Figs.16 and 17, the retention time shifts have a great impact on the classification and should be corrected before PCA. Unfortunately, there are still two Radix *angelicae* samples (RA1 and RA2) which are classified incorrectly into the cluster of Rhizoma *chuanxiong* (see Figure 18). In fact, the chromatographic fingerprints of RA1 and RA2 seem to be more similar to Rhizoma *chuanxiong* than other *Radix angelicae* due to the high similarity of a large peak cluster between 7006 and 7350 scan points in the chromatographic fingerprints (a compound named bultylidene dihydro-phthalide is involved in this region).

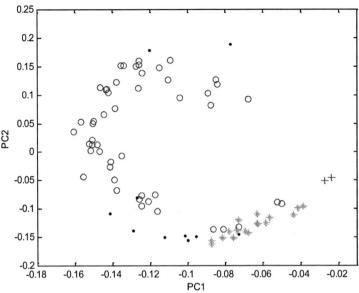

Figure 16. Pattern recognition based on PCA before correcting the retention time shifts of chromatographic fingerprints from seventy-nine herbal medicines ("+" Cortex *cinnamomi*, "o" Rhizoma *chuanxiong*,"." Radix *angelicae*, "*" Herba *menthae*. The variation explained by PC1 and PC2 is 22.42%).

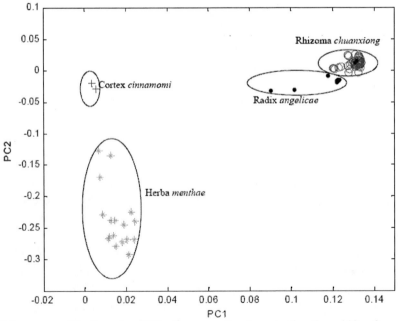

Figure 17. Pattern recognition based on PCA after correcting the retention time shifts of chromatographic fingerprints from seventy-nine herbal medicines ("+" Cortex *cinnamomi*, "o" Rhizoma *chuanxiong*,"." Radix *angelicae*, "*" Herba *menthae*. The variation explained by PC1 and PC2 is 35.09%).

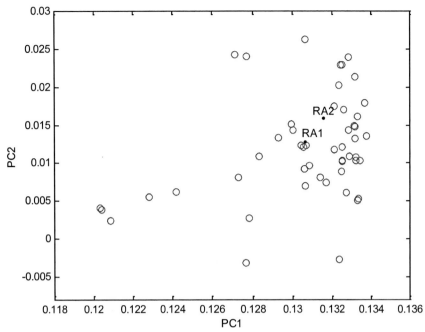

Figure 18. Enlarged plot of the Rhizoma *chuanxiong* cluster in Figure 17 ( "o" Rhizoma *chuanxiong*, "." Radix *angelicae*).

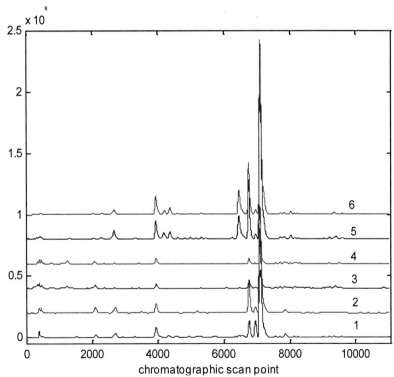

Figure 19. Chromatographic fingerprints of RA1(1) and RA2(2), the mean and median chromatograms of other eight Radix *angelicae* (3,4) and fifty Rhizoma *chuanxiong*(5,6).

If the mean and/or median chromatograms are used to represent the common chromatographic fingerprints from the other eight *Radix angelicae* or fifty Rhizoma *chuanxiong* samples, the similar indices can be obtained [43-48]. The chromatographic fingerprints of RA1 and RA2 surely match well with fifty Rhizoma *chuanxiong* other than eight Radix *angelicae*. Figure 19 represents the chromatographic fingerprints of RA1(1) and RA2(2), the mean and median chromatograms of other 8 Radix *angelicae* (3,4) and 50 Rhizoma *chuanxiong* (5,6). From it, we can see that the simple application of pattern recognition based on PCA is sometimes not satisfactory to the classification of complicated systems. Several data pretreatment processes should be required.

## 4.3. Variable Selection for Selecting Significant Data Points from Chromatographic Fingerprint: Rhizoma Chuanxiong, Radix Angelicae, Cortex Cinnamomi and Herba Menthae

### 4.3.1. Selection of Representative Variables and Determination of Number of Variables Retained

Figure 20 shows four preprocessed fingerprints of Rhizoma *chuanxiong*, Radix *angelicae*, Cortex *cinnamomi* and Herba *menthae*, respectively. Here, the baselines and the retention time shift have been corrected. For each chromatographic fingerprint, there are 11050 data points recorded. Thus, the size of the data matrix is 79×11050 (79 herbal samples and 11050 data points for each fingerprint). Among 11050 variables/data points, some representative ones would be selected.

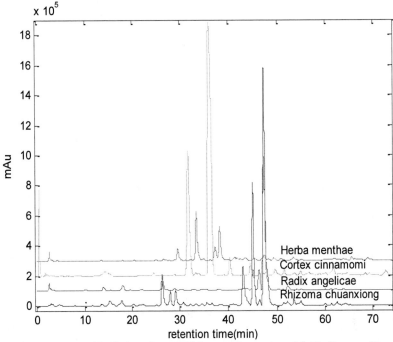

Figure 20. Four chromatographic fingerprints of Rhizoma *chuanxiong* (a), Radix *angelicae* (b), Cortex *cinnamomi* (c) and Herba *menthae* (d).

**Table 6. Number of the variables retained, configuration consensus, weighted measure of similarity between the original and reduced datasets and prediction accuracy with Bayes discrimination analysis for 79 herbal samples**

| method of variable selection | criteria | $p$ | configuration consensus (%) | weighted similarity(%) | prediction accuracy(%) |
|---|---|---|---|---|---|
| B4: the $p$ variables associated with the highest loadings | α=90% | 25 | 71.62 | 54.89 | 86.08 |
| | 3:1 | 27 | 73.80 | 46.78 | 89.87 |
| | IND | 28 | 74.18 | 45.73 | 91.14 |
| B4: the $p$ variables associated with the loadings closest to 0 | α=90% | 25 | 68.27 | 53.27 | 97.47 |
| | 3:1 | 27 | 70.05 | 53.48 | 94.94 |
| | IND | 28 | 70.89 | 53.61 | 96.20 |
| key set factor analysis: the first variable associated with the loading closest to 0 | α=90% | 25 | 74.78 | 1.53 | 96.20 |
| | 3:1 | 27 | 75.27 | 3.37 | 96.20 |
| | IND | 28 | 76.53 | 3.56 | 94.94 |
| key set factor analysis: the first variable associated with the highest loadings | α=90% | 25 | 72.82 | 30.76 | 96.20 |
| | 3:1 | 27 | 74.85 | 30.40 | 97.47 |
| | IND | 28 | 76.83 | 30.65 | 94.94 |
| key set factor analysis: the first variable most orthogonal to the mean variable | α=90% | 25 | 73.05 | 0.55 | 96.20 |
| | 3:1 | 27 | 75.25 | 0.08 | 97.47 |
| | IND | 28 | 76.41 | 0.07 | 96.20 |
| unweighted $w$ | α=90% | 25 | 55.76 | 3.23 | 83.54 |
| | 3:1 | 27 | 56.54 | 2.71 | 83.54 |
| | IND | 28 | 57.36 | 2.14 | 79.75 |
| weighted $w$ | α=90% | 25 | 57.20 | 1.69 | 83.54 |
| | 3:1 | 27 | 59.66 | 1.59 | 88.61 |
| | IND | 28 | 60.07 | 0.49 | 87.34 |
| Fisher coefficient | α=90% | 25 | 57.17 | 2.87 | 87.34 |
| | 3:1 | 27 | 57.60 | 2.16 | 88.61 |
| | IND | 28 | 58.21 | 2.97 | 89.87 |

As shown in Table 2, five approaches are used for variable selection in this study. Moreover, for the method of forward selection (B4), we can select the variables associated with the highest loading or with the loading closest to zero for each of the first $p$ components.

For key set factor analysis, three ways are employed to determine the first variable, 1) the first variable associated with the loading closest to zero; 2) the first variable associated with the highest loading; 3) the first variable being most orthogonal to the mean of all original variables.

In order to determine the number of representative variables retained ($p$), three criteria are used here. For the first criterion, $p$ is equal to the number of PCs required to account for no less than 90% of the total variance with PCA. The second criterion is that we just arbitrarily select $p$ such that the ratio of number of observations to $p$ is 3:1. Finally, IND is used to aid the determination of $p$. In this paper, $p$ is determined to be 25, 27 or 28 with these three criteria, respectively (see Table 6).

**Table 7. Serial number of the original variables retained with two different approaches for variable selection**

| variable selection method | | serial number of original variable retained |
|---|---|---|
| B4: the $p$ variables associated with the highest loadings | 8 | 3542, 3544, 3541, 3525, 3543, 3215, 1971, 2855, 2505, 3214, 3333, 1333, 3567, 1332, 4708, 1331, 1334, 2088. 188, 2083, 3517, 2090, 2124, 2127, 4710, 25, 189, 214 |
| key set factor analysis: the first variable associated with the loading closest to 0 | 8 | 5, 667, 2708, 2847, 3118, 2132, 2800, 619, 803, 995, 2286, 4714, 2072, 3189, 2229, 5435, 1396, 1928, 862, 3307, 4494, 3448, 5123, 111, 2104, 291, 700, 2479 |

Different variables are retained if various approaches for variable selection are used even if $p$ is kept unchanged. For example, Table 8 shows the original serial numbers of the variables retained with the methods of forward selection (B4 with the variables associated with the highest loading for each of the first $p$ components, $p=28$) and key set factor analysis (the first variable associated with the loading closest to zero, $p=28$). Seen from Table 7, the variables selected are different. Figs.21a-21h represent the variables retained for the same samples of Rhizoma *chuanxiong* (21a and 21e), Radix *angelicae* (21b and 21f), Cortex *cinnamomi* (21c and 21g) and Herba *menthae* (21d and 21h) with these two methods, respectively. Clearly, Figure 21 also demonstrates the differences of the variables selected by various methods.

## 4.3.2. Evaluation of the Reduced Datasets Containing Variables Selected

After the representative variables are selected, the original data and reduced subsets are compared with Procrustes analysis and a measure of similarity. Also, the PC1-PC2-PC3 scores plots are used to visually examine the samples with PCA on the representative variables retained. Table 6 also shows the configuration consensus with Procrustes analysis and the weighted similarity between the original and reduced datasets. Seen from Table 6, high configuration consensus does not indicate high weighted similarity.

**Table 8. SI and LCC of chromatographic fingerprints with total profiles and the peak table including 21 peaks identified**

| Sample No. | SI | | | LCC | | |
|---|---|---|---|---|---|---|
| | with total profile | | with peak table | with total profile | | with peak table |
| | before data preprocessing | after data preprocessing | | before data preprocessing | after data preprocessing | |
| 1 | 0.3472 | 0.8765 | 0.9046 | 0.1732 | 0.8628 | 0.8244 |
| 2 | 0.3062 | 0.8917 | 0.9031 | 0.1916 | 0.8819 | 0.8578 |
| 3 | 0.3336 | 0.8573 | 0.8791 | 0.1534 | 0.8234 | 0.6378 |
| 4 | 0.3236 | 0.8777 | 0.9023 | 0.2048 | 0.8636 | 0.8177 |
| 5 | 0.3140 | 0.8769 | 0.8949 | 0.1559 | 0.8505 | 0.7173 |
| 6 | 0.4466 | 0.9750 | 0.9842 | 0.3167 | 0.9705 | 0.9518 |
| 7 | 0.5429 | 0.9912 | 0.9937 | 0.4145 | 0.9893 | 0.9819 |
| 8 | 0.4739 | 0.9733 | 0.9822 | 0.3480 | 0.9686 | 0.9439 |
| 9 | 0.4637 | 0.9895 | 0.9949 | 0.3194 | 0.9877 | 0.9843 |
| 10 | 0.4722 | 0.9386 | 0.9411 | 0.3775 | 0.9320 | 0.9206 |
| 11 | 0.4435 | 0.8827 | 0.8987 | 0.3406 | 0.8648 | 0.8232 |
| 12 | 0.5313 | 0.9645 | 0.9776 | 0.4348 | 0.9567 | 0.9335 |
| 13 | 0.4931 | 0.9020 | 0.9252 | 0.3764 | 0.8826 | 0.8281 |
| 14 | 0.5422 | 0.9573 | 0.9699 | 0.4360 | 0.9478 | 0.9093 |
| 15 | 0.5887 | 0.8561 | 0.9210 | 0.5054 | 0.8276 | 0.7877 |
| 16 | 0.5698 | 0.9166 | 0.9401 | 0.4920 | 0.8982 | 0.8442 |
| 17 | 0.5160 | 0.9264 | 0.9454 | 0.6062 | 0.9119 | 0.8830 |
| 18 | 0.8994 | 0.9136 | 0.9309 | 0.8650 | 0.8939 | 0.7774 |
| 19 | 1.0000 | 1.0000 | 1.0000 | 1.0000 | 1.0000 | 1.0000 |
| 20 | 0.4575 | 0.9504 | 0.9619 | 0.2582 | 0.9394 | 0.8821 |
| 21 | 0.4495 | 0.9495 | 0.9580 | 0.2529 | 0.9382 | 0.8693 |
| 22 | 0.4438 | 0.9509 | 0.9641 | 0.2498 | 0.9400 | 0.8899 |
| 23 | 0.4829 | 0.9555 | 0.9678 | 0.3160 | 0.9457 | 0.9001 |
| 24 | 0.5354 | 0.9489 | 0.9593 | 0.3759 | 0.9375 | 0.8720 |
| 25 | 0.7788 | 0.9470 | 0.9604 | 0.7000 | 0.9351 | 0.8759 |
| 26 | 0.7045 | 0.9391 | 0.9508 | 0.5997 | 0.9254 | 0.8434 |
| 27 | 0.7371 | 0.9533 | 0.9622 | 0.6464 | 0.9429 | 0.8810 |
| 28 | 0.7698 | 0.9084 | 0.9272 | 0.6925 | 0.8874 | 0.7639 |
| 29 | 0.7512 | 0.8762 | 0.9011 | 0.6617 | 0.8472 | 0.6600 |
| 30 | 0.7982 | 0.8933 | 0.9391 | 0.7251 | 0.8692 | 0.7967 |
| 31 | 0.8648 | 0.9396 | 0.9553 | 0.8183 | 0.9266 | 0.8542 |
| 32 | 0.3256 | 0.9430 | 0.9562 | 0.0738 | 0.9302 | 0.8600 |
| 33 | 0.3137 | 0.9421 | 0.9565 | 0.0578 | 0.9291 | 0.8614 |
| 34 | 0.3124 | 0.9472 | 0.960 | 0.0553 | 0.9354 | 0.8773 |
| 35 | 0.2889 | 0.93522 | 0.9522 | 0.0441 | 0.9206 | 0.8488 |
| 36 | 0.3264 | 0.9429 | 0.9594 | 0.0962 | 0.9301 | 0.8702 |
| 37 | 0.3670 | 0.9419 | 0.9605 | 0.1552 | 0.9288 | 0.8787 |
| 38 | 0.4208 | 0.9387 | 0.9594 | 0.2211 | 0.9249 | 0.8739 |
| 39 | 0.4601 | 0.9449 | 0.9633 | 0.2797 | 0.9325 | 0.8872 |
| 40 | 0.4483 | 0.9529 | 0.9649 | 0.2688 | 0.9423 | 0.8901 |

**Table 8. (Continued)**

| Sample No. | SI | | | LCC | | |
|---|---|---|---|---|---|---|
| | with total profile | | with peak table | with total profile | | with peak table |
| | before data preprocessing | after data preprocessing | | before data preprocessing | after data preprocessing | |
| 41 | 0.4457 | 0.9563 | 0.9648 | 0.2598 | 0.9466 | 0.8911 |
| 42 | 0.4373 | 0.9506 | 0.9633 | 0.2437 | 0.9396 | 0.8829 |
| 43 | 0.4305 | 0.9555 | 0.9645 | 0.2425 | 0.9456 | 0.8901 |
| 44 | 0.4264 | 0.9478 | 0.9588 | 0.2387 | 0.9362 | 0.8715 |
| 45 | 0.4085 | 0.9510 | 0.9630 | 0.2134 | 0.9401 | 0.8837 |
| 46 | 0.3713 | 0.9521 | 0.9655 | 0.1625 | 0.9414 | 0.8937 |
| 47 | 0.3257 | 0.8723 | 0.9019 | 0.0603 | 0.8422 | 0.6673 |
| 48 | 0.3771 | 0.9220 | 0.9458 | 0.1507 | 0.9044 | 0.8244 |
| 49 | 0.3203 | 0.8244 | 0.8654 | 0.0541 | 0.7828 | 0.5800 |
| 50 | 0.2887 | 0.7660 | 0.8296 | 0.0268 | 0.7093 | 0.4643 |
| 51 | 0.3441 | 0.9622 | 0.9714 | 0.1105 | 0.9548 | 0.9096 |
| 52 | 0.3127 | 0.9322 | 0.9432 | 0.0936 | 0.9170 | 0.8238 |
| 53 | 0.4369 | 0.9478 | 0.9606 | 0.2357 | 0.9361 | 0.8756 |
| 54 | 0.2696 | 0.9440 | 0.9564 | 0.0436 | 0.9315 | 0.8594 |
| 55 | 0.2875 | 0.9426 | 0.9557 | 0.0686 | 0.9298 | 0.8570 |
| 56 | 0.4172 | 0.9222 | 0.9351 | 0.2224 | 0.9048 | 0.7827 |
| 57 | 0.4039 | 0.9402 | 0.9495 | 0.2074 | 0.9273 | 0.8519 |
| 58 | 0.4575 | 0.9422 | 0.9505 | 0.2556 | 0.9293 | 0.8390 |
| 59 | 0.4755 | 0.9377 | 0.9413 | 0.2731 | 0.9239 | 0.8081 |
| 60 | 0.4394 | 0.9474 | 0.9574 | 0.2460 | 0.9358 | 0.8669 |
| 61 | 0.4082 | 0.9424 | 0.9520 | 0.2460 | 0.9295 | 0.8487 |
| 62 | 0.4200 | 0.9250 | 0.9389 | 0.2231 | 0.9082 | 0.8111 |
| 63 | 0.3854 | 0.9193 | 0.9336 | 0.2162 | 0.9013 | 0.7959 |
| 64 | 0.4035 | 0.9118 | 0.9310 | 0.1898 | 0.8924 | 0.7872 |
| 65 | 0.3870 | 0.8724 | 0.8946 | 0.1610 | 0.8435 | 0.6922 |
| 66 | 0.3792 | 0.8739 | 0.8941 | 0.1457 | 0.8453 | 0.6881 |
| 67 | 0.3936 | 0.9261 | 0.9392 | 0.1756 | 0.9102 | 0.8108 |
| 68 | 0.2513 | 0.9147 | 0.9269 | 0.1177 | 0.8989 | 0.8257 |
| 69 | 0.2683 | 0.9143 | 0.9298 | 0.1153 | 0.8983 | 0.8136 |
| 70 | 0.2888 | 0.9251 | 0.9370 | 0.1014 | 0.9089 | 0.8032 |
| 71 | 0.2901 | 0.9288 | 0.9446 | 0.1109 | 0.9133 | 0.8283 |
| 72 | 0.3098 | 0.9283 | 0.9443 | 0.1260 | 0.9126 | 0.8288 |
| 73 | 0.3800 | 0.9153 | 0.9268 | 0.2008 | 0.9005 | 0.8319 |
| 74 | 0.3876 | 0.9159 | 0.9296 | 0.2040 | 0.9007 | 0.8328 |
| 75 | 0.3737 | 0.9143 | 0.9306 | 0.1930 | 0.9000 | 0.8316 |
| 76 | 0.3608 | 0.8931 | 0.9202 | 0.1775 | 0.8730 | 0.8283 |
| 77 | 0.4582 | 0.9489 | 0.9514 | 0.3040 | 0.9400 | 0.8889 |
| 78 | 0.3206 | 0.8989 | 0.9111 | 0.1222 | 0.8811 | 0.7918 |
| 79 | 0.3041 | 0.8930 | 0.9050 | 0.1141 | 0.8734 | 0.7658 |
| 80 | 0.3287 | 0.8923 | 0.9032 | 0.1403 | 0.8735 | 0.7774 |
| 81 | 0.3206 | 0.8917 | 0.9041 | 0.1176 | 0.8712 | 0.7725 |
| 82 | 0.3176 | 0.9741 | 0.9780 | 0.1717 | 0.9685 | 0.9323 |

Note: a bold face is given to SI or LCC less than 0.85 or 0.80.

Figures 22a-22b show the PC1-PC2-PC3 scores plots of the two reduced data matrices associated with the highest configuration consensus and weighted similarity (76.86% and 54.89%, see Table 2), respectively.

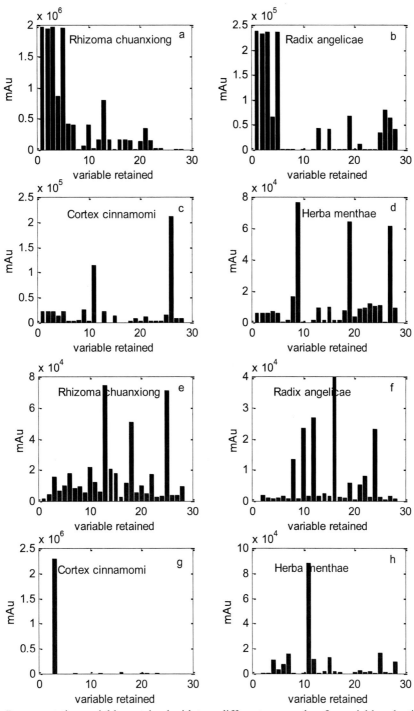

Figure 21. Representative variables retained with two different approaches for variable selection (a,e: Rhizoma *chuanxiong*; b,f: Radix *angelicae*; c,g: Cortex *cinnamomi*; d,h: Herba *menthae*).

Seen from Figures 22a-22b, not all the herbal samples can be separated successfully with the first three PCs of the reduced data sets. Thus, the variables retained are possibly not informative to characterize the PCA model and the number of principal factors of the subsets might be over three here.

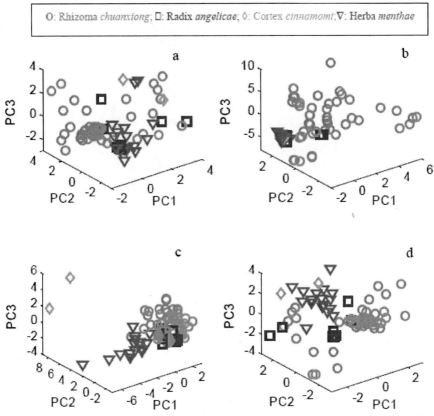

Figure 22. PC1-PC2-PC3 scores plots with the highest values of configuration consensus (a), weighted similarity (b) and prediction accuracy (c, $p=25$; d, $p=27$), respectively.

### 4.3.3. Discrimination of Herbal Medicines with Reduced Subsets by Use of Bayes Discrimination Analysis

In order to further explain the methods of variable selection and the criteria used to determine the number of representative variables selected, 79 real herbs are discriminated with Bayes discrimination analysis in this study. Here, two-thirds of herbs are taken as the training samples and the others as the prediction ones. The prediction accuracy is also list in Table 6. Seen from Table 2, for the methods of forward selection (B4) associating the variables with the loadings closest to zero and key set factor analysis, the prediction accuracy is no less than 94.94% even if $p$ is selected as 25, 27 or 28. However, except the method of forward selection (B4) associating with the variables with the highest loadings and $p=28$, the prediction accuracy is lower than 90.00% for other methods. Thus, the forward selection (B4) associating the variables with the loadings closest to zero and key set factor analysis are preferable for variable selection in this work.

Figures 22c and 22d show the PC1-PC2-PC3 scores plots of the reduced subsets with B4 (the $p$ variables associated with the loadings closest to 0, $p=25$) and key set factor analysis (the first variable associated with the highest loadings, $p=27$), respectively. For both the methods, the prediction accuracy reaches the highest (97.47%). However, as shown in Figures21c and 21d, not all the samples could be separated satisfactorily.

Seen from Table 6, the configuration comparison with Procrustes analysis and a similarity measure between the original matrix and the reduced subsets are not indicative to the discrimination of herbal samples with Bayes discrimination analysis. High matching between the original and reduced datasets does not suggest high prediction accuracy. For example, for the method of key set factor analysis associating with the first variable with the highest loadings, the values of configuration consensus, weighted similarity and prediction accuracy are 72.82%, 30.76% and 96.20% if $p=25$. For $p=27$ and 28, they are 74.85%, 30.40% and 97.47 %, 76.83%, 30.65% and 94.94%, respectively.

## 4.4. Quality Assessment of Hms with Similarity Index (SI) and Linear Correlation Coefficient (LCC) in Correlation Analysis: Ginkgo Biloba

In this study, total flavonoids with pharmacological activities are investigated as they are characteristic markers of Ginkgo *biloba*. For chromatographic fingerprints with total profiles, the entire patterns at 360 nm from HPLC are used.

Figures 23a-23c show the normalized fingerprints with total profiles from the standard extract EGb 761, the 49th and 50th samples of Ginkgo *biloba* investigated in this paper. The 49th and 50th samples are special and it will be explained later. Here, baseline correction and peak alignment have been conducted with the methods described in Sections 2.2 and 2.4.

Seen from Figures 23a-23c, fingerprints with total profiles are in fact complex although only about 20 distinct peaks could be visually detected. Some chemical components with low concentrations are practically involved in the fingerprints produced. Peaks A, C and D in Figures 23a-23c are attributed to rutin (quercetin-3-rutinoside), heteroside A (quercetin cinnamoyl-glycoside) and heteroside B (kaempferol cinnamoyl glycoside), respectively. They are qualitatively identified by comparing the retention times and UV spectra of the reference compounds.

Nowadays, both SI and LCC are used as the measured similarities for quality assessment of herbal samples. However, whether SI is advantageous over LCC or LCC is better than SI is still in the argument and no agreement has been reached in China so far. As EGb 761 is a standard extract of *Ginkgo biloba* which can be commercially available, its fingerprint is taken as the target and the others will be matched with it. Thus, SI and LCC are set to be ones for EGb 761 (the 19th sample) while SI and LCC of other fingerprints are calculated according to Eqs.15-18.

As the sample quality is identified with SI or LCC, a threshold value would be set for SI or LCC at first. A sample with SI or LCC higher than the setting is authenticated to be qualified. Otherwise, it is poor. In our experience, the threshold values of SI and LCC can be set as 0.85 and 0.80, respectively. This setting would be reasonable as it has been investigated by several Chinese herb research groups with a large number of real herbal samples.

If 0.85 and 0.80 are set here, 79 samples are identified as unqualified before data preprocessing. However, SI and LCC are greatly enhanced after data preprocessing (Table 8).

There are only 2 poor samples (Nos. 49 and 50) with SI and LCC less than 0.85 and 0.80 respectively after data preprocessing. Thus, baseline correction and peak alignment are absolutely required for fingerprint analysis based on total profiles.

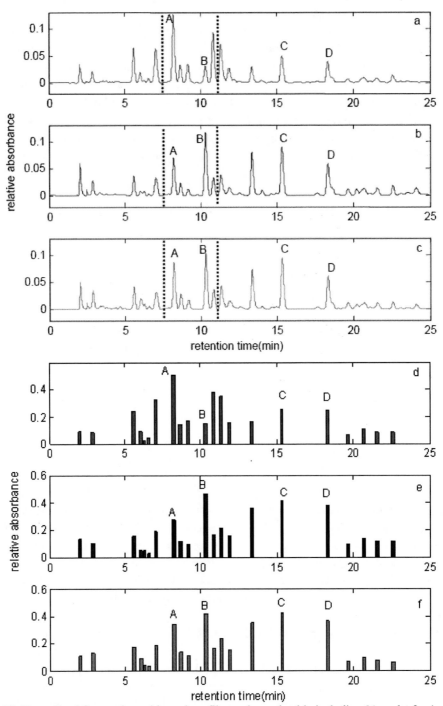

Figure 23. Normalized fingerprints with total profiles and a peak table including 21 peaks for (a, d) the standard extract (EGb 761), (b, e) the 49th and (c, f) the 50th samples of Ginkgo *biloba*.

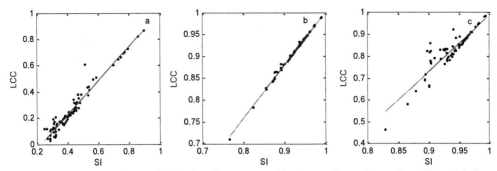

Figure 24. Linear fitting of SI and LCC for chromatographic fingerprints with total profiles (a) before and (b) after data preprocessing, (c) with a peak table including 21 peaks.

As for the 49th and 50th samples which are identified as poor with SI and LCC, their chromatographic fingerprints (Figures 23b and 23c) are surely different from that from EGb 761 (Figure 23a). Especially, within the regions between two dot lines, peak A is higher than peak B in Figure 23a. However, peaks B are more intensive than peaks A in both Figures 23b and 23c.

If the relationship between SI and LCC is further investigated, it is very interesting to examine the linear correlation between SI and LCC for fingerprints with total chromatograms (see Figures 24a and 24b). Especially, SI and LCC are highly linearly dependent after baseline correction and peak alignment.

Thus, if two threshold values 0.85 and 0.80 are set for chromatographic fingerprints based on total profiles, either SI or LCC does work for quality assessment. Moreover, a good linear correlation between SI and LCC can be achieved.

## 4.5. Sample Discrimination with PCO and PCA for Chromatographic Fingerprints with Total Profiles: Ginkgo Biloba

Besides PCA, PCO is another method to visually inspect the samples in low dimensional space. An important advantage of PCO over PCA is that any distance metric can be used to represent the pattern of the data set. Thus, PCO can give different views on the data if various dissimilarity measures are applied.

In this study, 82 Ginkgo biloba samples are in practice from three different groups: commercial Ginkgo biloba extracts and self-prepared extracts from Ginkgo biloba leaves, intermediate and final products of Shuxuening liquid injection, Ginkgo biloba products from Lianbang Pharmaceutical Company and other Ginkgo biloba formula products. Figs.25a-25b and Figs.25d-25e show Dim2-Dim3-Dim4 scores plots with PCO and PC2-PC3-PC4 scores plots with PCA for chromatographic fingerprints based on total profiles before and after data preprocessing. Seen from Figure 25b and Figure 25e, three clusters could be grouped satisfactorily for 82 samples. As a result, both PCO and PCA scores plots can successfully demonstrate the discrimination of 82 samples from various clusters if total profiles with data preprocessing are used. The unqualified 49th and 50th samples are labeled in Figure 25. Unfortunately, they cannot be separated from other samples as shown in Figs.25b and 25e.

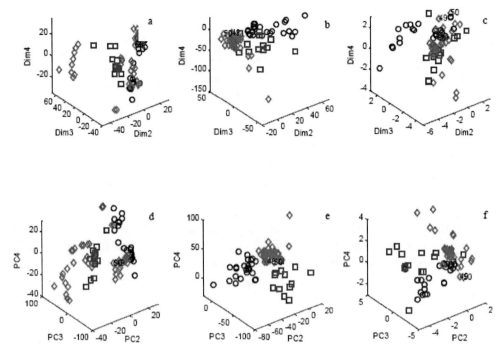

Figure 25. Dim2-Dim3-Dim4 scores plots with PCO and PC2-PC3-PC4 scores plots with PCA for (a, d) and (b, e) chromatographic fingerprints with total profiles before and after data preprocessing, (c, f) chromatographic fingerprints with a peak table including 21 peaks (red square: commercial Ginkgo *biloba* extracts and self-prepared extracts from Ginkgo *biloba* leaves; blue circle: intermediate and final products of Shuxuening liquid injection; cyan diamond: Ginkgo *biloba* products from Lianbang Pharmaceutical Company and other Ginkgo *biloba* formula products.

## 4.6. Comparison of PCO and PCA Configurations with Procrustes Analysis for Chromatographic Fingerprints Based on Total Profiles: Ginkgo Biloba

By comparing SI and LCC, PCO and PCA scores plots (see Figs.24-25), chromatographic fingerprints with total profiles before and after data preprocessing are far different. Seen from Table 9, their differences are clearly shown with Procrustes analysis. Thus, the necessity of baseline correction and peak alignment is further explained by comparing the PCO and PCA configurations with Procrustes analysis.

## 4.7. Chromatographic Fingerprints Based on a Peak Table with 21 Peaks Identified: Ginkgo Biloba

Previously, chromatographic fingerprints of herbal medicines were generally constructed by some peaks selected. With Chemical Station attached to HPLC-DAD, a peak table including 21 distinct peaks is produced. These peaks are detected from the chromatograms at 360 nm and all identified peaks are retained. Each fingerprint is represented by the peak areas of 21 peaks identified. If one peak is missing in a sample, zero substitutes for the peak area. However, it can be sometimes difficult to identify some weak peaks. On the other hand, peak matching is not a trivial task due to retention time shifts.

**Table 9. Difference between PCO and PCA configurations with Procrustes analysis**

| | $PCO_{before}$ | $PCO_{after}$ | $PCO_{peak}$ | | $PCA_{before}$ | $PCA_{after}$ | $PCA_{peak}$ |
|---|---|---|---|---|---|---|---|
| $PCO_{before}$ | / | 0.4333 | 0.6381 | $PCA_{before}$ | / | 0.4844 | 0.6362 |
| $PCO_{after}$ | 0.4333 | / | 0.3336 | $PCA_{after}$ | 0.4844 | / | 0.3028 |
| $PCO_{peak}$ | 0.6381 | 0.3336 | / | $PCA_{peak}$ | 0.6362 | 0.3028 | / |

Note: $PCO_{before}$ and $PCO_{after}$, $PCA_{before}$ and $PCA_{after}$: PCO and PCA configurations of fingerprints with total profiles before and after data preprocessing; $PCO_{peak}$ and $PCA_{peak}$: PCO and PCA configuration of fingerprints with 21 peaks.

Figures23d-23f show the normalized fingerprints based on a peak table containing 21 peaks for the standard extract EGb 761, the 49th and 50th samples. Peaks A, C and D in Figures 1d-1f are also attributed to rutin (quercetin-3-rutinoside), heteroside A (quercetin cinnamoyl-glycoside) and heteroside B (kaempferol cinnamoyl glycoside), respectively. Likely, chromatographic fingerprints of the 49th and 50th samples (Figs.23e and 23f) are different from that of EGb 761 (Figure 23d) especially within the regions between two dot lines.

If correlation analysis is conducted on the data set from the peak table, 1 and 19 samples are identified as poor with SI and LCC, respectively (Table 8). Clearly, some samples are misidentified with LCC. As a result, for fingerprint analysis with a peak table here, LCC is an unreliable index for quality assessment of Ginkgo *biloba* samples. On the other hand, poor linear correlation between SI and LCC is shown in Figure 24c. Seen from Figs.25c and 25f, 82 samples from three clusters can not be completely separated in the PCO and/or PCA scores plots. The unqualified 49th and 50th samples are also labeled in Figs.25c and 25f.

As peak identification and integration are needed for chromatographic fingerprints with a peak table, a large amount of the chromatographic data is discarded even if all the peaks identified are retained. In comparison with the PCO and PCA configurations with Procrustes analysis (see Table 9), the PCO and PCA configurations of chromatographic fingerprints with 21 peaks surely deviate from those based on total profiles. Chromatographic fingerprints with a peak table should provide less information on quality assessment of 82 samples due to the data loss.

# 5. OTHER WORKS ON CHROMATOGRAPHIC FINGERPRINT FOR QUALITY ASSESSMENT OF HERBAL MEDICINE AT OUR GROUP: RHIZOMA *ASARUM*, RADIX *ASTRAGALI*, RHIZOMA *ATRACTYLODIS*, *MACROCEPHALAE*, RADIX *SAPOSHNIKOVIA* AND YUPINGFENG FORMULA

A large number of other herbal samples such as Rhizoma *asarum*, Radix *Astragali*, Rhizoma *Atractylodis*, *Macrocephalae* and Radix *Saposhnikovia* and Yupingfeng formula containing Radix *Astragali*, Rhizoma *Atractylodis*, *Macrocephalae* and Radix *Saposhnikovia* have been also studied at our group. For Rhizoma *asarum*, the volatile components are investigated so as to determine the similarities and/or differences between the chromatographic fingerprints of Rhizoma *asarum* from three producing areas (see Sections 3.3.3 and 3.4.4) [62]. Both the volatile and water-soluble constituents are qualitatively and quantitatively identified for Radix *Astragali*, Rhizoma *Atractylodis*, *Macrocephalae* and Radix *Saposhnikovia* and their Yupingfeng formula. The stabilities and/or changes of chromatographic fingerprints are determined due to the combination of three single herbs to prepare Yupingfeng. On the other hand, in order to facilitate the data preprocessing and data analysis for chromatographic fingerprints with chemometric approaches, a software named "Computer Aided Similarity Evaluation (CASE)" has been developed by our united group. All programs of mathematical algorithms for CASE are coded in MATLAB5.3 based on Windows [43].

# CONCLUSION

In order to demonstrate the reliability and applicability of fingerprint analysis based on total chromatographic profiles for quality assessment of HMs, a lot of real herbal samples are investigated in this study. 82 Ginkgo *biloba* samples are taken as the example for the comparison of fingerprint approaches based on total profiles and a peak table. The result shows that for chromatographic fingerprints based on total profiles, all the samples can be correctly authenticated with similarity index (SI) and linear correlation coefficient (LCC) and good linear relationship between SI and LCC can be achieved. Furthermore, the grouping of 82 samples can be clearly demonstrated with PCO and PCA after data preprocessing. However, if a peak table with 21 chromatographic peaks is used, some samples are wrongly identified with LCC as SI and LCC are not lineally dependent. On the other hand, 82 Ginkgo *biloba* samples cannot be separated satisfactorily in the PCO and/or PCA scores plots. Fingerprint analysis based on total profiles is greatly advantageous over that with a peak table and thus it should be an applicable method for quality assessment of herbal medicine.

However, due to the variability of HMs associated with the producing areas and the manufacturing processes, the irreproducibility of chromatographic instruments and the experimental conditions and the complexity of HMs with a large number of chemical components, fingerprint construction with total profiles and its data preprocessing and data analysis are a little difficult. In this study, several approaches such as information theory, baseline correction, peak alignment, variable selection, correction analysis, principal co-ordinates analysis (PCO), principal component analysis (PCA) and Procrustes analysis are employed to construct and treat chromatographic fingerprints. Their successful application to several HMs such as Rhizoma *chuanxiong*, Radix *agelicae*, Cortex *cinnamomi*, Herba *menthae*, Ginkgo *biloba* and Rizoma *asarum* shows the reasonability and reliability of the chemometric methods employed for fingerprint construction and data preprocessing and data analysis.

## ACKNOWLEDGMENTS

This research work was financially supported by Scientific Research Foundation for the Returned Overseas Chinese Scholars, State Education Ministry of China and Key Laboratory Foundation of State Key Laboratory of Chemo/Biosensing and Chemometrics (No. 200408) and National Natural Science Foundation of China (Grant No. 20175036 and 20235020). We would also like to express our great thanks to Professor Yi-Zeng Liang, Richard Brereton, Ying-Sing Fung, Foo-tim Chau, Pei-Shan Xie and Dr. Yun Xu for their supervision and helpful suggestions.

## REFERENCES

[1] WHO, General Guidelines for Methodologies on Research and Evaluation of Traditional Medicines, 2000, p. 1.

[2] X. J. Yan, J. J Zhou, G. R. Xie and G. W. A. Milne, *Traditional Chinese Medicines: Molecular Structures, Natural Sources and Applications*, Aldershot, Ashgate, 1999, p.1.

[3] P. H. Raven, R. F. Evert and S. E. Eichhorn, *Biology of Plants (sixth edition),* W. H. Freeman and Co., New York, 1999, p. 48.

[4] R. Bauer, *Drug Inform. J.*, 32 (1998) 101.

[5] State Drug Administration of China, Chinese Trad. Pat. Med., 22 (2000) 671

[6] E. S. Ong, *J. Sep. Sci.*, 25(2002) 825

[7] FDA, Guidance for Industry — Botanical Drug Products (Draft Guidance), 2000, VIII, B, 2e; 3e.

[8] P. S Xie, S. B. Chen, Y. Z. Liang, X. H. Wang, R. T. Tian and R. Upton, J. *Chromatogr. A.*, 1112 (2006) 171.

[9] J. D. Philipsom, *British herbal Pharmacopoeia*, British Herbal Medicine Association Publications, 1996, Forward.

[10] P. S. Xie, Trad. *Chinese Drug Res. and Clin. Pharm.*, 12 (2001) 141.

[11] Y. Z Liang, P. S Xie and K. Chan, J. *Chromatogr. B.*, 812 (2004) 53.

[12] W. J. Welsh, W. K. Lin, S. H. Tersigni, E. Collantes, R. Duta, M. S. Carey, W. L. Zielinski, J. Brower, J. A. Spencer and T. P. Layloff, *Anal. Chem.*, 68(1996) 3473.

[13] P. Valentão, P. B. Andrade, F. Areias, F. Ferreres and R. M. Seabra, J. *Agri. Food Chem.*, 47(1999) 4579.

[14] F. Gong, Y. Z. Liang, H. Cui, F. T. Chau and B. T. P. Chau, J. *Chromatogr. A*, 909 (2001) 237.

[15] F. Gong, Y. Z. Liang, Q. S. Xu, F. T. Chau and A. K. M. Leung, J. *Chromatogr. A*, 905 (2001) 193.

[16] F. Gong, Y. Z Liang, Q. S. Xu, F. T. Chau and K. M. Ng, *Anal. Chim. Acta*, 450 (2001) 99.

[17] K. S. Booksh, B. R. Kowalski, *Anal. Chem.,* 66 (1994) 782A.

[18] K. J. Johnson, B. W. Wright, K. H. Jarman and R. E. Synovec, J. *Chromatogr. A*, 996 (2003) 141.

[19] F. Gong, Y. Z. Liang and F. T. Chau, J. *Chromatogr. A.*, 1029(2004) 173.

[20] N.P.V. Nielse, J. M. Carstensen and J. Smedsgarrd, J. *Chromatogr.* A., 805(1998) 17.

[21] G. Malmquist, R. Danielsson, J. *Chromatogr.* A., 687(1994) 71.

[22] Y. Q. Ru, *Information-theoretical Fundamentals of Modern Analytical Chemistry*, Hunan University Press, Changsha, P.R. China, 1996, p. 50.

[23] F. Gong, Y. Z. Liang, P. S. Xie and F. T. Chau, J. *Chromatogr.* A, 1002(2003) 25.

[24] J. Calvin Giddings, Unified Separation Science, John Wiley and Sons. Inc., New York, 1991, p. 86.

[25] N. P. V. Nielsen, J. M. Carstensen and J. Smedsgaard, J. *Chromatogr.* A, 805 (1998) 17.

[26] J. A. Pino, J. E. McMurry, P. C. Jurs, B. K. Lavine, A. M. Harper, *Anal. Chem.*, 57 (1985) 295.

[27] M. E. Parrish, B. W. Good, F. S. Hsu, F.W. Hatch, D. M. Ennis, D. R. Douglas, J. H. Shelton, D. C. Watson, *Anal. Chem.*, 53 (1981) 826.

[28] G. Malmquist, R. Danielsson, J. *Chromatogr.* A, 687 (1994) 71.

[29] D. Bylund, R. Danielsson, G. Malmquist, K.E. Markides, J. *Chromatogr.* A, 961 (2002) 237.

[30] M.D. Hämäläinen, Y.Z. Liang, O.M. Kvalheim, R. Andersson, *Anal. Chim. Acta*, 271 (1993) 101.

[31] E. R. Malinowski, J. *Chemom.* 6 (1992) 29.

[32] I. T. Jolliffe, *Appl. Statist*, 21(1972) 160.

[33] I. T. Jolliffe, *Appl. Statist*, 22(1973) 21.

[34] W. J. Krzanowski, *Appl. Statist*, 36(1987) 22.

[35] J. R. King and D. A. Jackson, *Environmetrics*, 10(1999) 67.

[36] A. D. Shaw, A. d. Camillo, G. Vlahov, A. Jones, G. Bianchi, J. Rowland, D. B. Kell, *Anal. Chim. Acta*, 348(1997) 357.

[37] Q. Guo, W. Wu, D. L. Massart, C. Boucon and S. d. Jong, Chemom. *Intell. Lab. Syst.*, 61(2002) 123.

[38] Q. Guo, W. Wu, D. L. Massart, C. Boucon and S. d. Jong, *Anal. Chim. Acta*, 446(2001) 85.

[39] E. R. Malinowski, *Factor Analysis in Chemistry*, Wiley-Interscience, New York, 2002, p.96.

[40] F. Gong, B. T. Wang, Y. Z. Liang, F. T. Chau and Y. S. Fung, *Anal. Chim. Acta* , 572 (2006) 265.

[41] H. F. M. Boelens, R. J. Dijkstra, P. H. C.Eilers, F. Fitzpatrick and J. A. Westerhuis, J. *Chromatogr.* A, 1057(2004) 21.

[42] R. J. Dijkstra, H. F. M.Boelens, J. A.Westerhuis, F. Ariese, U. A. T. Brinkman and C.Gooijer, *Anal. Chim. Acta*, 519(2004) 129.

[43] F. Gong, B. T. Wang, F. T. Chau and Y. Z. Liang, *Anal. Lett.*, 38(2005) 2475.

[44] I. B. Gornushkin, B. W. Smith, H. Nasajpour and J. D. Winefordner, *Anal. Chem.*, 71(1999) 5157.

[45] C. E.Anderson, R. G.. Nieves, and J. H. Kalivas, *Chemom. Intell. Lab. Syst.*, 41(1998) 115

[46] K. Varmuza, M. Karlovits and W. Demuth, *Anal. Chim. Acta.*, 490(2003) 313.

[47] Z. B. Alfassi, *J. Am. Soc. Mass. Spectrom.*, 15(2003) 262.

[48] A Jurado-López and de Castro M. D. Luque, *Spectrochim. Acta. Part B.*, 58(2003) 1291.

[49] I. Borg and P. Groenen, Modern Multidimensional Scaling, Theory and Applications, Springer-Verlag New York Inc., New York, 1997, p.399.

[50] S. Izrailev and D. K. Agrafiotis, *J. Mol. Graphic. Model.*, 22(2004) 275.

[51] D. M.Rassokhin and D. K.Agrafiotis, *J. Mol. Graphics Model*, 22(2003) 133.

[52] J. C. G. E da Silva, M.A.Ferreira, A. A. S. C Machado and F. Rey, *Anal. Chim. Acta,* 333(1996) 71.

[53] V. Jagadish, J. Robertson and A. Gibbs, *Forensic Sci. Int.*, 79(1996) 113.

[54] J. C. Gower, *Biometrika*, 53(1966) 325.

[55] C. Demir, P Hindmarch and R. G. Brereton, *Analyst,* 121(1996) 1443.

[56] M. Kubista, *Chemom. Intell. Lab. Syst.*, 7(1990) 273.

[57] W. J. Krzanowski, *Principles of Multivariate Analysis: A user's Perspective,* Clarendon Press, Oxford, 1988, p. 27.

[58] Y. Y.Cheng, M. J. Chen and W. J. Welsh, *J. Chem. Inf. Comput. Sci.*, 43(2003) 1959.

[59] S. F. Cui, B. Q. Fu, F. S. C. Lee and X. R. Wang, *J. Chromatogr.* B, 828(2005) 33.

[60] L. H. Zhao, C. Y. Huang, Z. Shan, B. R. Xiang and L. H. Mei, J. *Chromatogr.* B, 821(2005) 67.

[61] H. R. Keller, D. L. Massart, Y. Z. Liang and O. M. Kvalheim, *Anal. Chim. Acta,* 263(1992) 29.

[62] F. Gong, B. T. Wang and F. T. Chau, *Flavour Fragr. J.*, 21(2006) 549.

In: Substance Abuse, Assessment and Addiction     ISBN: 978-1-61122-931-8
Editors: Kristina A. Murati and Allison G. Fischer     © 2011 Nova Science Publishers, Inc.

*Chapter 15*

# HEROIN ADDICTION IN PREGNANCY - ONGOING DEMANDS AND ACTUAL THERAPY MODALITIES

## *Maki Kashiwagi[*], Urs Zimmermann-Baer[**], Margaret Huesler[*] and André Seidenberg[♣]*

[*]University Hospital Zurich, Clinic of Obstetrics,
[**]Kantonsspital Zurich, Winterthur, Department of Pediatrics,
Clinic of Neonatology,
[♣]General Practice, Weinbergstr.9, Zurich, Swetzerland

## ABSTRACT

More than 35 years after its introduction into the therapy of pregnant heroin addicts methadone maintenance continues to be the standard therapy of opiate addiction in pregnancy. Benefit on pregnancy and neonatal outcome compared to the sole abuse of street heroin is evident.

However, there is ongoing need for clinical research to further improve the management of craving during pregnancy as well as the prevention and therapy of neonatal abstinence syndrome.

This chapter intends to review different approaches in improving these problems. Maternal maintenance therapy is discussed under consideration of recent insights into methadone metabolism and the physiological changes during pregnancy as well as under consideration of optimal therapy of concomitant infectious diseases highly prevalent in this risk group. Eventually actual therapy strategies in the management of neonates of opiate addicted women will be illustrated and critically commented.

An overview will be given to allow a better understanding of the specific needs of these women during pregnancy and their affected offsprings.

[*] Corresponding author: Maki Kashiwagi, MD University Hospital Zurich Clinic of Obstetrics, Frauenklinikstr. 10, 8091 Zurich, Switzerland. T.: 0041-44- 255 11 11, Fax: 0041-44 255 44 30, Mail: maki.kashiwagi@usz.ch

## ABBREVIATIONS

| | |
|---|---|
| NAS: | neonatal abstinence syndrome |
| HAART: | highly active antiretroviral therapy |
| IDUs: | injection drug users |
| LAAM: | levoacetylmethadol |
| HCV: | Hepatitis C- virus |
| STD: | sexually transmitted disease |

## 1. INTRODUCTION

According to the 2001 National Household Survey on Drug Abuse (NHSDA) current heroin use was reported by 123,000 Americans which is relatively conforming with data collected in 2000 and lower than the number of 130,000 published in 1998.

Similarly a trend towards a fall in heroin consumption was reported by the European Monitoring Centre for Drugs and Drug Addiction (EMCDDA) in November 2005.

Currently of 1.2-2.1 million problem drug users in the enlarged European Union 850,000 -1.3 million people are likely to be drug injectors. At least 530 000 patients receive substitution therapies.

Since its introduction by Dole and Nyswander in 1965 [1], methadone substitution treatment has been established as the standard therapy for heroin addiction. Randomized studies have demonstrated the benefit of methadone maintenance on illicit drug abuse and mortality of heroin- addicted patients (reviewed in [2]).

For management of opiate addiction in pregnancy methadone has been constituted as standard either. Advantage of the inclusion of a heroin addicted pregnant patient into methadone maintenance therapy has been demonstrated in several studies and is widely acknowledged. Inclusion of these women in any form of treatment programme enables regular medical and psychological follow-up and screening for infectious diseases. Furthermore in comparison to street drug-users it has been further confirmed that methadone maintenance programme positively influences attendance of antenatal pregnancy controls, gestational duration, fetal growth and neonatal birth weight, respectively (3-8].

Nevertheless several issues remain to be particularly considered.

Infection with hepatitis C can be found in up to 55% of the women and HIV in up to 20% [9]. Therefore one major issue is the management of these infections taking pregnancy and methadone maintenance therapy into account.

The other issue, which requires special attention is the development of neonatal abstinence syndrome (NAS), which is known to be more frequent and heavier in neonates after methadone exposure in utero than in neonates exposed to street heroin or street drugs only [7, 10-13].

In the following passages new insights into the course and management of infectious diseases in pregnant opiate abusers are presented. Therapy options in the treatment of addictive behaviour in the light of possible improvement of NAS and the actual recommendations in the treatment of NAS are discussed.

## 2. OPIATE ABUSE AND MATERNAL INFECTIOUS DISEASE

Considering infections in pregnant injection drug users (IDUs) of major concern in the prenatal care are:

- Maternal HIV infection and the possibility of vertical transmission
- Adherence to antiretroviral therapy
- Possible interactions of opioids with antiretroviral therapy
- Maternal hepatitis C infection and the co-infection with HIV
- Other sexually transmitted diseases (especially genital ulcer disease)
- Prevention of preterm delivery
- Improvement of psychosocial aspects

Mother-to-child transmission of HIV near the time of birth is the primary route of HIV infection among infants and young children. In the drug abusing pregnant women transmissible infectious diseases have to be ruled out and if present their vertical transmission has to be prevented.

## 2.1. HIV

Female drug users are particularly vulnerable to HIV infection. Injection drug use plays a key role in the spread of HIV and hepatitis C infection in North and South America, Europe and parts of Asia. Of particular concern is multidrug-using behaviour in female drug users, especially with cocaine and alcohol, which is associated with a significant increase in unprotected sex. A high percentage of heterosexual HIV transmission can be attributed to drug related prostitution and/or a known HIV-infected sex-partner [14]. Drug addicted women who exchange sex for money or drugs often lack control over their working conditions and suffer severe degradation. Thus beside methadone programmes, many countries have introduced needle exchange and "safe sex" programmes [15].

Furthermore there is some evidence supplied by in vitro and animal studies that cocaine and heroin increase HIV- replication and suppress immune function. Epidemiologic studies are inconclusive regarding their effect on the immune system [16]. A study by Thrope et al. (2004) [17] showed a higher risk for nonfatal opportunistic infections in HIV- positive women, especially herpes simplex, pulmonary tuberculosis and recurrent pneumonia.

### 2.1.1. Vertical Transmission

Variables that have been linked to perinatal HIV transmission are high maternal HIV viral load, low maternal CD4 count, increased maternal illness severity, lack of antiretroviral therapy, prolonged rupture of membranes, vaginal delivery, prematurity and eventually illicit drug use. Illicit drug use accounts for prematurity and is moreover associated with intrauterine growth restriction, which is again independently associated with a higher rate of vertical HIV transmission [18]. Postnatal in a study by Abrams et al. (2003) [19] a significant faster rate of disease progression for infants born to women with intravenous drug use was demonstrated.

Over the past decade, significant advances have been made for the prevention of vertical HIV transmission, including the use of single and combination antiretroviral therapy, elective caesarean section as the preferred mode of delivery, weaning and anti-retroviral post-exposition prophylaxis in the newborn. To maximize the benefits to the offspring, therapy is recommended at lower viral load thresholds than for non pregnant adults. For antiretroviral-naïve women, therapy is deferred until the second trimester because of the potential and uncertain risk of teratogenicity and the low risk of transmission during this period [20].

Untreated women might be overrepresented in socially marginalized group and there is need in improving the integration of these women in any kind of management programme, as they are known to be less likely than treated women to receive other prepartum preventive measures either. [21].

### 2.1.2. Highly Active Antiretroviral Therapy (HAART) and Adherence

Highly active antiretroviral therapy (HAART) or synonymously designated as combined antiretroviral therapy (cART) consists of a treatment regimen including the use of two nucleosides with one or more protease inhibitors or a non-nucleoside reverse transcriptase inhibitor. Treatment with nucleosides alone is defined as non- HAART therapy. The introduction of HAART in the mid-1990s has significantly altered the course of HIV-disease, substantially reducing AIDS-related morbidity and mortality.

A high degree of adherence is required to achieve and maintain a successful virologic response, to reduce vertical transmission, to prevent drug resistance and to prevent toxicities associated with opioids and /or antiretroviral agents.

Suboptimal adherence to HAART among IDUs is of significant concern [22]. In a study of Kerr et al. (2004) [22] 66% of HIV infected IDUs were less than 95% adherent. Oblivion (27%) was the most frequently cited reason for missing doses of HAART. Since the introduction of HAART IDUs demonstrated a much higher risk of progression to AIDS than people, who were infected by sexual intercourse (hazard ratio 2.20 [95%,CI 1.30-3.72]) [23]. The most probable explanation is insufficient adherence. Competing non HIV- related morbidity, such as liver disease related to hepatitis C co-infection, may be partially responsible for high numbers of deaths in drug abusers. These co-infections are more common in IDUs and differences in immune recovery following HAART as reported for those co-infected with hepatitis C virus, could also contribute to the increased mortality [24].

In a study by Berg et al. (2004) [25] median adherence among women was significantly lower than among men. Alcohol use, heroin use, significant medication side effects, lack of long-term housing, not belonging to an HIV support group and cocaine use were independently associated with worse adherence [25]. Modified directly observed therapy for patients with HIV disease receiving methadone maintenance therapy can be an option for increasing adherence to HAART [26].

### 2.1.3. Drug Interactions

A certain number of antiretroviral medications are metabolized by cytochrome P 450 enzyme, CYP 3A4. Methadone and also buprenorphine, a newer agent available for the treatment of opioid dependence as discussed below, are likewise primarily metabolized by hepatic cyotochrome P450 enzymes- especially CYP 3A4.

Inhibiting action on CYP 3A4 activity could therefore enhance opioid toxicity or toxicity related to increased exposure to HIV medication. Conversely and clinically more relevant, if an antiretroviral agent is capable of inducing CYP 3A4 activity, an opioid withdrawal syndrome could result, which could place the patient at risk for relapse to illicit drug use.

For methadone significant, in part adverse drug-drug interactions with many antiretroviral medications are described:

## Interaction of Methadone with Protease Inhibitors

In vitro studies showed that protease inhibitors were inhibitors of CYP 3A enzyme activity, which led the manufacturers to include warnings about the potential for methadone-associated opioid toxicity with simultaneous administration [27]. However, in vivo studies showed that concomitant administration of several of the protease inhibitors with methadone showed decreases in serum concentrations of methadone [26]. Treatment with *lopinavir plus ritonavir* (Kaletra®) for example may need an increase in methadone dosage in patients undergoing methadone maintenance therapy. *Lopinavir* is a known inducer of CYP 3A4 and is a potent inducer of methadone metabolism [28]. *Ritonavir* is an inhibitor of CYP 3A4, but is used in subtherapeutic doses in the *lopinavir-ritonavir* combination drug. Therefore in this combination *ritonavir* has no significant effect on methadone exposure.

## Interaction of Methadone with Non-Nucleoside Reverse Transcriptase Inhibitors (NNRTIs)

NNRTIs have significant interactions with methadone. *Nevirapine* is an inducer of CYP 3A. Interaction with methadone can cause severe opioid abstinence syndrome leading to discontinuation of nevirapine therapy or significant increases in daily methadone dose [29]. *Efavirenz* reduces methadone concentrations [20], but it is contraindicated in pregnancy due to proven teratogenicity.

## Interaction of Methadone with Nucleoside Reverse Transcriptase Inhibitors (NRTIs)

NRTIs are unlikely to interact with methadone. In *zidovudine* monotherapy methadone levels were found to be unchanged and only minor effect on opioid therapies including the use of methadone, levoacetylmethadol (LAAM), buprenorphine or naltrexone was observed [26, 30]. The combination of *lamivudine plus zidovudine* had no effect on methadone concentrations in persons undergoing opioid maintenance therapy [31].

Nevertheless one study demonstrated a 41% increase in plasma concentrations of *zidovudine* which produced toxicity in some opioid-dependent patients that were stabilized with methadone [32]. It is to note that application of *zidovudine* during pregnancy is often limited due to its aggravating effect on pregnancy- induced anaemia. Profound knowledge of drug interactions in pregnant methadone-patients treated with antiretroviral medication is thus helpful in anticipating possible complications.

Buprenorphine may have fewer adverse interactions with antiretroviral drugs. It demonstrates significant pharmacokinetic interaction to *efavirenz*, but maybe due to the high affinity and long duration of μ- opioid receptor binding of buprenorphine no significant pharmacodynamic interaction was detected. Simultaneous application of buprenorphine and antiretroviral drugs might be feasible without the risk of inducing opiate withdrawal. This promising finding may simplify the treatment of opioid-dependent patients with HIV disease and improve the patient's outcome [26].

In summary the benefit of HAART can be abolished due to several drug interactions. In HIV positive opiate addicts interactions of opiates and antiretroviral drug therapy can cause toxicities and opioid withdrawal. Consideration of these interactions can improve adherence and HIV outcome for opiate addicts.

## 2.2. Hepatitis C

Hepatitis C virus (HCV) - infection represents a major health problem in pregnancy. Overall vertical transmission rate is 5%. It is highly correlated with maternal hepatitis C-viremia and exposure to maternal blood at delivery [33]. An association between injection drug use during pregnancy and higher perinatal transmission rate has been noted [34].

### 2.2.1. Co Infection HIV, Hepatitis C

The co-infection of HIV and HCV is especially common in IDUs and is frequently correlated with problematic psychosocial settings [35].

The vertical transmission rate of HCV is significantly higher in HIV co-infected pregnant women than in HIV- negative women. It is estimated to be 15-36%. HIV1/HCV co-infected individuals are less likely to clear HCV infection and have frequently higher HCV-RNA levels. Drug injecting during pregnancy may play an important role in terms of reinfection and consecutive increase in viral load [34].

Hence every effort should be made to enrol drug using HCV- and/or HIV- positive pregnant women in drug treatment programmes to stabilize psychosocial circumstances on one hand and to reduce the possibility of vertical transmission on the other hand.

## 2.3. Other Sexually Transmitted Diseases (STD)

Many studies have documented that drug-using women, in particular those using cocaine, have elevated risks for STD compared with either drug-using men or non-drug-using women [36]. Drug using women with drug related prostitution have a higher risk for infection with herpes simplex, syphilis, chlamydia trachomatis, gonorrhoea, and pelvic inflammatory disease. Genital ulcer disease (e.g. herpes simplex and syphilis) increases the likelihood of HIV-transmission by increasing both the infectiousness of, and the susceptibility to HIV-infection [37].

Both clinical and sub clinical reactivation of genital herpes increase the HIV viral load in the genital tract [38]. Clinical genital herpes simplex virus infection during pregnancy in HIV-infected women may be a risk factor for perinatal HIV transmission. If future studies confirm this association, therapy to suppress genital herpes reactivation during pregnancy may be a strategy to reduce perinatal HIV transmission.

# 3. TREATMENT OF ADDICTIVE BEHAVIOUR DURING PREGNANCY

## 3.1. Methadone Maintenance Therapy

For the actual standard therapy using methadone maintenance, analysis of pregnancy course and outcome reveals a persistent high complication rate with frequent presentation of threatened preterm delivery (preterm contractions and cervical insufficiency) partially explained by the higher incidence of genitourinary infections, intrauterine fetal growth retardation and low birth weight [9, 39]. Therefore pregnancy of heroin addicts even under methadone maintenance therapy represents high-risk pregnancy. It requires tight obstetrical follow-ups including regular surveillance of fetal blood supply and fetal growth using doppler-ultrasound.

There remains one major problem in pregnancy of opiate addicts, which could not be resolved by methadone maintenance therapy, that is continued craving and additional illicit use of cocaine, street heroin, psychotropics as benzodiazepines or antidepressants.

Up to two-third of the pregnant women present positive findings in urine screening or self-admit additional drug use [5, 8, 9, 11]. As elucidated in the preceding chapter it is of great importance to restrict illicit drug abuse in consideration of other underlying medical and infectious diseases of the mother. Furthermore illicit drug abuse represent the hazardous factor contributing to fetal malformations or [40] abruptio placentae as specified for cocaine, fetal growth retardation, microcephaly [9, 41] and neonatal withdrawal [42].

Thus efficient pregnancy care in methadone treated women should include urine-drug screening at every antenatal visit. Frequent evidence for illicit drug use should lead to reevaluation and improvement of maintenance therapy under consideration of the patient's individual need, the physiological changes in methadone availability during pregnancy and the potential advantage of alternative therapy options.

It is of interest that a randomized study on 85 methadone treated pregnant women demonstrate that for pregnancy care in these women use of incentives is worth to be reflected as it is apparently capable of enhancing maintenance programme attendance and drug abstinence [43]. Complemented to psychosocial stabilization programmes an overall improvement of pregnancy care could result.

## 3.2. Altered Maternal Methadone Availability During Pregnancy

For pregnancy higher elimination rates and a lower half-life of methadone [44] in comparison to non-pregnant methadone patients and a more rapid fall of methadone blood levels in later stage of pregnancy [45] have been demonstrated. In a study of Pond et al. (1985) [45] methadone trough levels after delivery were significantly higher than during pregnancy.

Beside high tissue binding capacity of methadone and thus "loss" by binding at the growing fetal tissue and the placenta, the change in maternal gastric pH modifying methadone absorption, the increase in plasma volume and in progesteron blood levels are hypothesized mechanisms for the increased methadone demand during pregnancy. Progesteron in turn activates hepatic microsomal oxidation system leading to an increase in methadone metabolization

If half-life of methadone is increased an increase in daily dosage and an increase in application frequency have to be complentated. Splitting of the total daily methadone dose into a twice daily application was recommended from some authors to tackle these prevailing difficulties (reviewed in [2]).

During the last three years research has focused on individual methadone metabolism and changes in the metabolism during pregancy.

As mentioned earlier CYP 3A4 has been identified as the major enzyme responsible for the metabolism of methadone and buprenorphine in human liver and intestine. In addition it has been demonstrated that several isoforms such as CYP2D6, CYP1A2 and possibly CYP2C9 and CYP2C19 are further involved in methadone metabolism (reviewed in [46]). Genetic polymorphism of these enzymes, interindividual variability in enzyme activity or interaction with medication likewise metabolized by CYP enzymes have all been shown to influence the individual´s methadone availability.

Patient's serum methadone levels taking the same amount of daily methadone are varying significantly. For example in a cohort of 20 patients receiving 100mg methadone/day serum levels ranged from 90-520ng/mL (in [46] ).

The key role of CYP acitivity is further comfrimed by a study of Shinderman et al. (2003) [47], who demonstrated that in patients with a need of high doses of methadone cytochrome P450 activity was elevated compared to the activity in patients treated with low methadone doses.

For pregnancy data supporting the need to consider individual variability in methadone metabolism were published by Drozdick et al. (2002) [48]. They compared methadone serum trough levels of 44 asymptomatic and 58 symptomatic methadone- treated pregnant women. Trough levels were measured 20-24 hours after last methadone application. The mean applied methadone dosages in the two groups compared was without significant difference ($101 \pm 42$mg/day versus $114 \pm 43$mg/day), but trough levels in symptomatic pregnant women were significantly lower compared to the asymptomatic group (0.175mg/L versus 0.295 mg/L). The authors therefore concluded that trough level measurements with a recommended cut-off at 0.24mg/L might be of help in regulating methadone dose schemes in pregnant opiate addicts. To achieve this level a methadone dose of 50-150mg or even higher doses in the third trimester can be necessary.

In non-pregnant patients higher doses up to 80-120mg/day have been arrogated to efficiently treat opiate addicts [49-51] thus fear of higher methadone dosages in obstetrics should be likewise revised. Consistent with this postulation in a recent study on 81 pregnant opiate addicts treatment with high doses of $\geq$100mg of methadone resulted in significant lower illicit drug use than in the group treated with $<$ 100mg methadone/day [52]. In 50 pregnant women receiving $\geq$ 80mg methadone/day Berghella et al. (2005) found a similar tendency [53].

In fact first results investigating the role of placental methadone metabolism let presume that further methadone dose adjustment is necessary due to additional placental drug biotransformation. The placental capacity in eliminating xenobiotics is well studied and to a lower amount than in the liver and depending on gestational age the expression of various CYP isoforms have been demonstrated (reviewed in [54] ). More specifically CYP 19 was now found to be the major enzyme catalyzing methadone and also buprenorphine metabolism in placental tissue in vitro [54, 55].

Therefore considering the individual´s methadone metabolism and the specified metabolic aspects of pregnancy arbitrary dose reductions scheme seem to be obsolete, instead prospective management of methadone treated pregnant women should take necessity of dose increase into account.

## Is There a Benefit in Reducing Methadone Dose During Pregnancy?

On behalf of the fetus and as methadone exposed neonates have been reported to develop more frequently and a more intensive and longer lasting NAS than neonates after heroin or cocaine exposure [4, 7, 10-13], the question arised whether a dose reduction towards term would positively influence fetal outcome. Especially the possible benefit for NAS is still matter of actual debate. However published data on this issue are inconclusive.

Main difficulties in interpreting and comparing the study results are the small numbers on which the studies were based on, the constant confounding factor of additional illicit drug abuse and the differences in assessment of NAS.

In a retrospective analysis [42] of a cohort consisting of 70 mothers and their neonates with median maternal methadone dose of 20 mg (range 0-150 mg) 32 infants (46%) were treated for narcotic withdrawal. The authors divided the maternal methadone doses applied in three groups. In the group having received < 20 mg/day (N=25) the necessity of withdrawal treatment was found in 12%, in the group having received 20-39 mg/day (N=25) in 44%, and in the group who received ≥ 40 mg/day of methadone (N=20) in 90%. These differences were significant. Methadone dose correlated with both duration of neonatal hospitalization and neonatal abstinence score. In our own study [39] 100% of the neonates with maternal methadone dose > 80mg/day required treatment for NAS compared to 43% of the neonates after maternal doses < 30mg/day before delivery, but the statistical pitfal might have been the much lower number of 14 mothers treated with methadone doses >80mg/day compared to 40 women in the < 30mg/day group.

In contrast in two recent restrospective studies on large cohorts of 100 and 81 mothers and their offsprings the authors were not able to show a correlation of maternal methadone dose and NAS. The methadone doses used were generally higher and the authors divided into two groups dependent on the daily maternal methadone dose; in a group with <80 (N=50) and >80 (N=50) mg/day and ≥ 100 (N=36) and < 100 (N=45) mg/day, respectively.

In accordance to the latter results Mack et al. (1991) could not find a correlation between maternal methadone dosage, maternal methadone serum levels and neonatal serum levels, nor was there a correlation between neonatal serum level and the severity of NAS [56]. However similar studies analyzing the coherence of methadone blood levels with methadone dose before delivery and the development of NAS do not achieve unanimity either [57, 58].

Considering the individual variability in methadone metabolism in adult opiate addicts the same can be postulated for the fetus and neonate, respectively. Therefore it is to question if maternal methadone dosage rather than neonatal metabolism is the determining factor for the development of NAS.

In our opinion there is requirement for larger prospective studies before generalized recommendations of methadone dose reduction during pregnancy can be advocated.

In addition patients on low-dose methadone or on detoxification programmes are at high risk for relapse as discussed further below.

Actual data are suggestive that maternal methadone dose during pregnancy, maternal methadone blood levels, neonatal methadone blood levels and the development of NAS are all figures depending on multiple factors probably not fully understood so far.

Of interest are recent results investigating placental drug transporting systems. Multidrug resistance proteins MRP1, MRP2 and MRP3 as well as P- Glycoprotein (P-gp) are transmembrane proteins known to be involved in placental drug transfer. P-gp and MRP2 are expressed on the maternal side of the human trophoblast whereas MRP1 and 3 are located on the fetal side.

P-gp possesses ATPase activity that is activated by various drugs. Drug transport occurs unidirectionally facilitating cell efflux. It can be detected in placental trophoblast from the first trimester of pregnancy on and is located in the brush-border membrane. Its importance lies in the capacity of active removal of xenobiotics from the fetal to the maternal side thus protecting the fetus from potential toxic effects (reviewed in [59]).

Using an in-vitro dual placental lobule perfusion system Nekhayeva et al. (2005) and Nanovskaya et al. (2005) showed an asymmetry of methadone transfer with a higher methadone clearance index from the fetal to the maternal direction and after using an P-gp inhibitor an 30% increase of methadone transfer from the maternal to the fetal side [60, 61]. Hence there is evidence for an active P-gp related methadone shift from the fetus´ to the mother´s compartment. It could explain the high discrepancy in postpartum maternal and neonatal methadone plasma levels with relatively low methadone concentrations in the neonatal plasma found by some authors [57, 58] and the lack of correlation between maternal methadone serum level and neonatal methadone level in cord blood reported by Mack et al. (1991) [56].

Nanovskaya et al. (2005) detected a variation in the expression of P-gp in placental brush-border in the 81 term placentas investigated by [60]. Though correlation of the quantity of P-gp expression with P-gp activity is unknown, it is now tempting to presume strong influence of the degree of placental P-gp expression or other variabilities in placental drug transfer on the development of NAS by influencing the degree of fetal methadone exposure. Further perfusion studies on placental lobules will give more informations on this issue.

## 3.3. Alternative Management Options of Addicitive Behaviour During Pregnancy

### 3.3.1. Opioid Detoxification

Idealistically viewed direct detoxification or by preceding transition on maintenance substances seems to be the most reasonable and tempting approach to treat opiate addiction in pregnancy. Longer duration of pregnancy, normalized birth weight and head circumference, improved respiratory status and lower incidence of NAS are the reported benefits after complete detoxification [62, 63]

However, withdrawal in the mother can be critical for the fetus. During maternal methadone dose reduction Zuspan et al. (1975) [64] found increased norepinephrine values in amniotic fluid. During the last years it has been confirmed that there is fetal hypothalamic-pituitary-adrenal response to stress independent of maternal responses [65]. It gives strength to the conclusion of Zuspan et al. (1975) that their findings represent signs of fetal distress rather than increased transmission of catecholamines from a withdrawing mother.

In rats Lichtblau et al. (1981) induced an increase in the rate of stillbirth after continuous naloxone administration in pregnant rats pretreated with LAAM [66].

Nevertheless MEDLINE- search presents two published studies questioning the fetal risk, if detoxification is performed cautiously in selected cases [62, 67].

One study is a retrospective data analysis of 101 cases on a 21day in-patient detoxification using methadone [67]. All patients revealing illicit drug use were discharged from the programme leading to a preselection of data. Finally 42/101 patients (41.6%) completed the detoxification programme. There are no data on fetal monitoring and investigated end-points were restricted to the number of miscarriages and preterm deliveries.

In only five cases detoxification was carried out during the first trimester of pregnancy of which one ended in miscarriage. In summary data from this study cannot assure safety for methadone detoxification for early pregnancy nor does it provide data on fetal wellbeing during detoxification procedure in second and third trimester.

For fetal monitoring Dashe et al. (1998) [62] reported the use of a "qualitative" assessment of daily fetal "activity" and once a fetus had reached gestational age of 24 weeks gestation a fetal heart rate monitoring semiweekly in 34 gravidas. Thus fetal distress had been monitored rather punctually than continuously. As much as recent research focus on the significance of "fetal programming" in determining chronic diseases in adulthood comprehensive safety for the fetus during detoxification should be guaranteed and is not convincingly demonstrated in the two studies presented.

Frustrating adding concern is the high relapse rate of 40-60% during pregnancy [6, 9, 62, 67]. Finnegan (1991) reports of her personal experience of nearly 100% failure [6] and as relapsing patients are at risk of consuming illicit street-drugs the benefit of detoxification attempts on fetomaternal outcome is unsure. Indication for detoxification should be based on each individual´s case and overall prognosis.

### 3.3.2. Morphine Maintenance

Morphine has a duration of action of 4-6 hours. With its short acting property it was discussed as an alternative for maintenance therapy presuming a beneficial effect on neonatal abstinence syndrome. In maintenance therapy oral morphine sulphate is used provided as a slow-release formula with prolonged plasma level and lack of accumulation.

In 1999 Fischer et al. [68] conducted a randomized open study treating 24 pregnant women with slow- release morphine and 24 women with methadone. The appliance of morphine has been proven to be equally suitable in the treatment of pregnant opiate addicts. Mean applied morphine dose at delivery was 300.4 ±137.5 mg/day (range: 13-120mg). Women of the morphine group demonstrated a statistically significant reduction in illicit benzodiazepine and additional opiate consumption, but not in cocaine consumption. Whereas Fischer et al. (1999) did not find a difference in duration and intensity of NAS in the two groups compared, NAS developed in 28 of 30 (93%) neonates after morphine hydrochloride maintenance in the continued study evaluated by Rohrmeister et al. (2001) [69]. In addition Rohrmeister et al. (2001) [69] compared the neonates after morphine hydrochloride exposure to 42 neonates after maternal methadone maintenance therapy and 16 neonates after maternal buprenorphine treatment. Incidences of NAS in the latter groups were significantly lower (76% and 19%). Therefore the negative impact of morphine maintenance on NAS overweighs benefit in reduction of illicit benzodiazepine and opiate use.

In a recent double-blind, double-dummy study on 18 pregnant patients the transition from short-acting morphine maintenance to methadone or buprenorphine maintenance has been shown to be comfortable and safe during the second trimester of pregnancy [70].

### 3.3.3. Buprenorphine Maintenance

Buprenorphine is a partial μ-opioid receptor agonist. Acute doses act as an agonist on opioid receptors while chronic application produces effective blockade of opioid agonists. Buprenorphine is metabolized by direct glucuronisation and by oxidation involving CYP 3A4 to norbuprenorphine, its active metabolite. Buprenorphine has a poor oral bioavailability and is administered as a sublingual tablet.

Clinical studies on non-pregnant addicts confirmed that buprenorphine is effective for maintenance treatment most useful in highly-motivated patients resulting in a decrease of illicit drug use during the treatment programme (reviewed in [2] ).

In pregnant patients doses applied vary from 0.4-24mg/day. During the last decade observational and retrospective studies confirmed the safety of buprenorphine treatment during pregnancy with no negative impact on fetomaternal outcome [71-75]. In fact there is some evidence that in comparison to methadone maintenance the rate of preterm deliveries could be lower after buprenorphine [75].

In addition data from preliminary studies led to the assumption that buprenorphine could cause less severe NAS.

In a literature review Johnson et al. (2003) [74] evaluated 21 published reports on buprenorphine use during pregnancy. Of these reports two were open-label controll studies, five prospective studies and 14 were case reports. Summarizing reported numbers of NAS in a total of 309 buprenorphine exposed neonates NAS appeared in 62% of the infants with 48% requiring treatment. However, detailled analysis of the Johnson et al. showed that 40% of these cases were confounded by illicit drug use, therefore actual benefit on NAS is presumed to be better.

In 2005 Lejeune et al. [75] published the largest prospective observational study on 159 buprenorphine treated versus 101 methadone treated opiate-dependent mothers. Mean daily buprenorphine doses were 5.4 ± 4.5 mg/d (range 0.4-24) and mean daily methadone dose was 57 ± 30.4 mg/d (range 10-180). A difference in the frequency of severe NAS in the two substitution groups could not be registered.

Up to now there is only one randomized, double-blind, double-dummy controlled study investigating the benefit of buprenorphine over methadone during pregnancy [75]. The investigators like in all studies on opiate addicted individuals had to struggle with a high drop-out rate. Of 30 randomized women, ten did not complete the study and finally 9 buprenorphine treated versus 11 methadone treated pregnancies were compared in view of the neonatal abstinence syndrome. Between the two groups there was no statistically significant difference in percentage of neonates treated for NAS, but total amount of opioid-agonist medication administered to treat NAS and length of hospitalization was significantly higher in the neonates exposed to methadone.

In summary actual literature surely do not show any disadvantages of buprenorphine in comparison to methadone in maintenance treatment of pregnant opiate addicts and favourable tendencies have not been ruled out yet.

### 3.3.4. Naltrexone

Naltrexone is an opiate receptor antagonist. It differs from naloxone by a longer half-life and longer lasting effect of 42-48 hours and more than 24 hours respectively. It has been approved for the treatment in opioid abuse by the US Food and Drug administration (FDA) in 1985. High rates of relapses and high rates of sudden death after scheduled and unscheduled termination of therapy discredited naltrexonebased therapy in non-pregnant patients. Experience with naltrexone treatment in pregnancy is limited. In a recent trial Hulse et al. (2004) reported of 17 pregnant heroin user who were managed with a naltrexone implant [76]. There were no differences in gestational length or birthweight compared to 90 women treated with methadone maintenance but a tendency for higher birthweight in the naltrexone treated group. Though of minor value as a predictor for neonatal survival and neurological development than Apgar Score at 5 minutes, Apgar Score at 1 minute was significantly higher in the naltrexone exposed compared to the methadone exposed newborn.

### 3.3.5. Heroin

In Switzerland heroin assisted treatment within the bounds of a psychosocial treatment programme has been established since 1994. It consists of controlled heroin supplementation to an underlying methadone maintenance as for the short half-life of action of heroin.

Data evaluated demonstrated a significant improvement of participant´s health status, a high retention rate and a reduction in criminal activity and illicit cocaine and/or heroin abuse [77]. Practically the use is however restricted to the more "difficult" cases, thus the four cases we medically accompanied during pregnancies [9, 39] were patients with reduced health condition and chaotic multidrug-using behaviour before inclusion into heroin assisted treatment.

In two of our cases the patients were switched to heroin assisted treatment at 33 and 34 weeks gestation and one of the women being enrolled before conception was able to cease heroin completely at 32 weeks gestation. Average methadone dose before delivery was 80 ± 59 mg/day and heroin doses ranged from 0-270mg/day. All neonates born to these women were term deliveries and all had birthweights within normal ranges. NAS occurred in all neonates. It is to be discussed if earlier embedding to heroin assisted treatment with lesser need of methadone doses and early suppression of multidrug-using behaviour would have positive impact on NAS. Unfortunately the use is limited by the more severe course of withdrawal in the detoxifying adult.

# 4. CURRENT MANAGEMENT STRATEGIES OF THE NEONATAL ABSTINENCE SYNDROME

Managing newborn infants of a drug dependent mother is a multi-task challenge. Neonatal course is complicated not only by the effects of maternal substance abuse itself but also by poor health and social conditions of the mother. To improve long term outcome of children born to illicit drug addicted mothers, beside medical treatment, psychological, social and child protection strategies must be prospectively planned in neonatal management of these children.

## 4.1. Fetal, Perinatal and Neonatal Risk Factors in Infants Born to Illicit Drug Dependant Mothers

Infants born to illicit drug addicted mothers are at risk for several fetal, perinatal and neonatal problems. Given the absent evidence of teratogenic effect of opiates in the human fetus [78-80], nevertheless newborns to opiate addicted mothers have to be carefully examined for congenital malformations. The reason is that up to 80% of opiate dependent mothers are taking other potentially teratogenic substances, i.e., alcohol, cocaine or antidepressants [5, 8, 9, 11, 80-82]. In the offspring of these mothers prematurity, microcephaly and inappropriate growth for gestational age but also viral and bacterial infections are well known perinatal risk factors, which has already been discussed in part in the chapters above. Neonatal adaptation is more often disturbed in infants born to illicit drug dependent mothers [79, 83, 84]. As a consequence, opiate addicted mothers should give birth in specialized perinatal centers, where both, the mother and the newborn can be adequately managed.

## 4.2. Diagnosis of Neonatal Abstinence Syndrome (NAS)

Neonatal Abstinence Syndrome (NAS) was first described in the 1970s. In 1975 L. P. Finnegan proposed a scoring system to describe the intensity of NAS [85]. Clinical signs of NAS were classified into four groups: central nervous system symptoms, gastrointestinal symptoms, vegetative symptoms and tachypnoea. Since the original Finnegan score consists of 31 items, it was modified for clinical use. *Figure 1* shows the modified Finnegan Score as it is applied in the Swiss Neonatal Abstinence Study. Up to now neither the validity of the original nor of the modified Finnegan score has been investigated. Normative data of the adapted Finnegan score in healthy newborns are currently under evaluation by a member of our study group. These Data are not yet published. An alternative withdrawal score in newborns was proposed by Lipsitz [86]. Both, Finnegan's and the Lipsitz' scoring system enables semi-objective description of the intensity of withdrawal symptoms. An objective way to describe the intensity of NAS was lately proposed by O'Brian and colleagues. They measured the movements of the newborn by a portable motion detector (actigraph) and found them to be positively correlated with the intensity of NAS [87]. Whether this tool will provide a benefit for the management of newborns with NAS has to be proved in the future years.

Since symptoms of narcotic withdrawal lack specifity, NAS is a diagnosis of exclusion. Infection, intraventricular hemorrhagia, hypoglycemia, inborn errors of metabolism and others may mimic symptoms of NAS and have to be carefully excluded as differential diagnosis.

When NAS is suspected upon clinical presentation, laboratory investigations have to further confirm the diagnosis. Residues of opiates and other illicit substances can be detected in amniotic fluid, in the newborn's urine, meconium and hair.

| Modified Finnegan Score<br>Swiss Study on Detoxification in Newborns (SSDN) | | | | | | | |
|---|---|---|---|---|---|---|---|
| | Date | | | | | | |
| | Time | | | | | | |
| **CNS Symptoms** | | | | | | | |
| High pitched cry | 2 | | | | | | |
| High pitched cry > 2 h | 3 | | | | | | |
| Sleeps less than 3 h after feeding | 1 | | | | | | |
| Sleeps less than 2 h after feeding | 2 | | | | | | |
| Sleeps less than 1 h after feeding | 3 | | | | | | |
| Mild tremors when disturbed | 1 | | | | | | |
| Marked tremors when disturbed | 2 | | | | | | |
| Mild tremors when undisturbed | 3 | | | | | | |
| Marked tremors when undisturbed | 4 | | | | | | |
| Increased muscle tone | 2 | | | | | | |
| Excoriation of skin | 1 | | | | | | |
| Myoclonic jerks in sleep | 3 | | | | | | |
| Generalized convulsion | 5 | | | | | | |
| **Vegetative Symptoms** | | | | | | | |
| Sweating | 1 | | | | | | |
| Temperature 37.5 – 38.0 °C | 1 | | | | | | |
| Temperature > 38.0 °C | 2 | | | | | | |
| Frequent yawning | 1 | | | | | | |
| Mottling | 1 | | | | | | |
| Nasal stuffiness | 2 | | | | | | |
| Sneezing | 1 | | | | | | |
| **Gastrointestinal Symptoms** | | | | | | | |
| Frantic sucking | 1 | | | | | | |
| Poor feeding | 2 | | | | | | |
| Regurgitation | 2 | | | | | | |
| Projectile vomiting | 3 | | | | | | |
| Loose stools | 2 | | | | | | |
| Watery stools | 3 | | | | | | |
| **Respiratory Symptoms** | | | | | | | |
| Tachypnea | 1 | | | | | | |
| Tachypnea with retractions | 2 | | | | | | |
| **Total Score** | | | | | | | |

Figure 1. Modified Finnegan Score as it is used in the Swiss Study on Detoxification in Newborns (SSDN). Every eight hours the infant is checked for withdrawal symptoms. For each symptom presented the corresponding score is added. If total score exceeds 9 points twice, pharmacological treatment is started.

Urine testing is easily available and commonly used in adults. In diagnosing NAS, urine analysis however has strong limitations. Positive findings after opiate consumption persists for only a few days, thus negative urine results can not rule out the development of NAS [88-90].

Residues of maternal illicit drug abuse during pregnant state are retained in the fetus' meconium during the last trimester. Therefore analysis of the newborn's meconium provide the more reliable retrospective information on maternal drug consumption during pregnancy [88, 89, 91, 92]. Positive results are associated with a highly increased risk of the development of NAS and should lead to close and careful clinical monitoring of the neonate.

As much as any laboratory test, meconium analysis has its pitfalls. Testing for instance should be solely performed using the first two meconium probes of the neonate. In later stool probes already a minimal degree of fermentation is capable in falsifying test results.

Residues of opiates are also retained in the newborn's hair. Hair analysis enables drug screening even after the first days of life, when meconium passage is completed [93]. However, hair analysis is difficult to put into practice as the amount of hair needed to perform the test is considerable. Some newborns lack enough hair for testing; in fact in some, complete shaving of the scalp hair would be necessary to achieve the demanded amount for reliable testing. This is in turn hardly accepted by both parents and nursing staff.

As a result we suggest that for the diagnosis of NAS meconium analysis by an experienced laboratory should be considered to become the gold standard.

## 4.3. Therapy of Neonatal Abstinence Syndrome (NAS)

Since the first study results in the 1970´s there is general agreement that NAS should be treated. Early diagnosis and adequate treatment of neonatal abstinence syndrome is required to prevent the infant from substantial morbidity such as dehydration, electrolyte abnormalities, poor weight gain, aspiration or seizures [79, 94]. However, in some neonates the course of narcotic withdrawal may be mild without requiring any specific therapy. In any case infants born to substance dependent mothers should be monitored closely for withdrawal symptoms [79, 94, 95] using a defined symptom score scale with determination of an upper score limit. Once the evaluated score exceeds the upper limit, therapy should be initiated immediately.

For the treatment of NAS basically two therapy options exist, which should be used in supplementation, general supportive treatment and pharmacological treatment.

### 4.3.1. Supportive Treatment

There is broad consensus that supportive treating strategies such as minimal handling and optimal feeding help to minimize neonatal withdrawal symptoms and therefore prevent the newborn from suffering [95]. Only a few groups have studied nursing interventions properly. Ostrea et al. (1976) showed that withdrawal symptoms can be minimized by loosely swaddling the newborn in a quiet, dimly lit room [7]. A positive effect of non-oscillating waterbeds was demonstrated by Oro et al. (1988) [96].

Withdrawal symptoms are associated with a huge energy burden for the metabolism of the newborn. A considerable number of newborns with NAS are small for gestational age and need supplemental energy to catch up growth. Gastrointestinal withdrawal symptoms (excessive sucking, poor feeding, regurgitation or vomiting, loose or watery stools) interfere with the required uptake of adequate amounts of energy and fluids. Supportive strategies to preserve adequate caloric and fluid intake help to allow the infant a normal daily weight gain and are therefore of great importance [79, 95, 97]

### 4.3.2. Pharmacological Treatment

Several drugs and several drug application strategies are used to treat NAS. Only a few studies compare the efficacy of these different pharmacological regimens.

#### 4.3.2.1. Opiates

Opiates in use for treatment of NAS are *tincture of opium, morphine, methadone,e* and *paregoric,* which contains anhydrous morphine with antispasmodics, camphor, 45% ethanol and benzoic acid. There are no prospective randomized controlled trials, which compare efficacy and safety between these opiates. Although *paregoric* was one of the first substances used for treatment of NAS, there are many concerns about its use today, because of the known and potential toxic effects of some these ingredients [90].

The aim of using an opiate in NAS is to control symptoms provoked by opiate withdrawal. Therefore most authors titrate the therapeutic opiate amount by stepwise increasing the dose until symptoms release [82, 90, 98, 99]. Once the symptoms are controlled, the dose of the substituted opiate is decreased step by step. While some author increase the dose until symptoms are controlled others start augmenting a sedative drug as soon as a certain ceiling limit of opiates is reached. Some authors prefer to give a fixed dose of opiate and add a sedative, if opiate alone fails to control symptoms [81].

There is neither consensus on the starting dose of opiates nor on its upper therapeutic limit.

There is futher no evidence whether one of these above mentioned strategies is safer or more effective than the other.

Some authors claim concerns about the potential harm of prolonged administration of opiates to the developing brain. These objections are mainly based on animal studies [100]. In humans, no negative effect of opiate therapy on long term outcome was reported so far. But one must keep in mind that this issue is extremely difficult to study. Long term outcome in infants born to drug dependent mothers may be already influenced by confounding factors, such as maternal co-morbidities and/or unprivileged socioeconomic background, to name only a few. Studies on this topic must therefore include a sufficient number of patients to achieve adequate statistical power.

#### 4.3.2.2. Sedatives

Sedatives used to treat neonatal narcotic withdrawal are *phenobarbitone, diazepam,* and *chlorpromazine.* The rational for using sedatives in NAS is twofold. On one hand, the most prominent symptoms of NAS are signs of neurological excitability, which can be improved with sedatives. On the other hand up to 80% drug addicted mothers demonstrate multi-drug addiction and consume other drugs than opiates. Hence in these cases monotherapy with opiates are of limited value.

*Phenobarbitone*

Phenobarbitone effectively ameliorates hyperactive behavioural state in the newborn suffering from narcotic withdrawal, but does not treat gastrointestinal symptoms [90, 94]. When high doses of phenobarbitone are used to control NAS, the resulting central nervous depression affects also sucking reflex either [98], which subsequently leads to impaired feeding.

Rapid tolerance to the sedative effect, a long half-life time (up to 200 hours in newborns) and induction of drug metabolism are further disadvantages of phenobarbitone [90].

Several administration strategies are described. Some authors propose a loading dose followed by a lower maintenance dose [90, 101]. Other authors prefer to refrain from loading dose, but instead increase the dosage stepwise until symptoms are controlled or an upper dosage limit is reached [94, 98, 101, 102]. After stabilization of withdrawal symptoms the dosage is subsequently reduced stepwise. Finnegan reported that symptoms of NAS were controlled within a significantly shorter time when - in contrast to the titration strategy – therapy was initiated with a loading dose [103]. In contrast Kaltenbach (1986) could not confirm the advantage of loading over titration strategy [101].

*Diazepam*

Although signs of withdrawal resolve rapidly when treated with diazepam, the sole use of benzodiazepine in the treatment of NAS proved to be insufficient in almost cases [101]. Other concerns in its use include the infant's limited capacity of metabolization and excretion of diazepam [104], the sedative effect, reports of its negative impact on sucking [101, 105] as well as reports of its association with late onset seizures [106]. Therapy with diazepam has therefore become obsolete. However, French colleagues lately raised the question whether diazepam has been abounded to quickly. Based on their local experience they enforced the need for a new prospective trial on this subject [107].

*Chlorpromazine*

Symptoms of affected central nervous system as well as gastrointestinal signs of NAS are well controlled by chlorpromazine [108, 109]. While in some European medical centres chlorpromazine is commonly used, the American Academy of Pediatrics (AAP) has strong concerns about this medicament because of its very slow elimination in newborns and because of numerous potential side effects such as cerebellar dysfunction, decreased seizure threshold and hematological problems [90]. There is only one small prospective controlled trial including 38 infants that studies the efficacy of chlorpromazine [108]. In this study by Kahn et al. (1969) NAS treatment with chlorpromazine was compared to treatment with phenobarbitone and no significant differences in outcome were found.

Nevertheless, chlorpromazine remains widely used to control neonatal withdrawal symptoms [109, 110]. In MEDLINE no report on adverse effects of chlorpromazine in newborns can be found.

### 4.3.2.3. Clonidine

Clonidine is a non narcotic, non sedative substance which acts as a presynaptic α2-blocker. It has been demonstrated to effectively reducing opiate withdrawal signs in adults and also in newborns [111]. Up to now there is no randomized, controlled trial that studied efficacy and safety of clonidine use in NAS. An ongoing trial by Agthe et al. will elucidate this issue, but results are not yet available [112]. Presently, in the absence of controlled trials, the use of clonidine in NAS cannot be recommended.

## 4.4. Comparative Studies

Nine randomized controlled or comparative trials on different treatment strategies for NAS are published so far. Due to methodological limitations in particular insufficient control of confounding variables none of these studies is able to answer the question of efficacy and safety of a single treatment strategy definitely. Even systematic reviews fail to elucidate this question [112, 113].

This is in our view explained by the complexity of the population studied. Uncontrolled maternal illicit drug use, differences in maternal socio-economic and health condition and the huge variety of morbidities presented by the newborns of drug using mothers may all contribute to different courses of neonatal withdrawal. Individual adaptation of treatment strategy is thus essential.

In addition studies on the pharmacological treatment efficacy of NAS have to deal not only with different medicaments but also with different regimens of drug application and different evaluation of NAS.

Nevertheless, survey of the few randomized controlled trials published on this issue are of interest:

Kandall et al. (1983) [98] compared the efficacy of *paregoric* and *phenobarbitone*. 153 infants of opiate addicted mothers were enrolled. Severity of NAS was assessed by Lipsitz score. Neonates were randomly allocated to treatment with *paregoric* (titration strategy) or *phenobarbitone* (no loading dose, but titration strategy). No significant differences in terms of duration of hospital stay and severity of NAS symptom were found. Seizures were reported in 7 of 62 infants treated with *phenobarbitone* while there were no seizures in the *paregoric* group. The author speculated later that this difference may be explained by the *phenobarbitone* dosage, which was probably sufficiently high to control NAS symptoms but not high enough to prevent seizures [94]. The main methodical limitation of this study is the lack of blinding of treatment.

At the same time Carin et al. (1983) [99] compared *paregoric* versus *phenobarbitone* for NAS treatment in a small study of 38 neonates. The primary outcomes of this study were physical and biochemical variables such as respiratory rate, blood pressure, blood gases and thrombocyte counts. No significant group differences were found in these parameters analyzed, but clinical relevance of these parameters as indicator for efficient NAS treatment is to be questioned. Interestingly, the authors found a significantly longer treatment duration in the *paregoric* group compared to the *phenobarbitone* group. The evidence of this finding, however, remains unclear. On the one hand treatment was not blinded, on the other hand there were significantly more multi-drug using mothers in the *paregoric* compared to the *phenobarbitone* treating group.

Comparative studies of different treatment strategies were extended to the analysis of *diazepam* by Kaltenbach et al. (1986) [101]. The authors were interested in the question, whether the performance of six month old infants assessed by Bayley Scale of Mental Development (BSMD) differed when treated with either *paregoric* (dose not reported), *phenobarbitone* (loading dose strategy versus titration strategy) or *diazepam* (dose not reported). Outcome analysis of allocated treatment groups was limited as only *paregoric* appeared to be sufficient as a mono-therapy. *Diazepam* mono-therapy had to be combined with *pheobarbitone* or *paregoric* as second line medicaments in all cases. Of the infants initially treated with *phenobarbitone* 50% required the addition of a second medicament. By retrospectively regrouping the infants considering the medicaments received the authors did not find a difference in performance on BSMD at 6 month of age. However clinicians are discordant regarding the value of BSMD as a predictive value for later mental development.

Insufficiency of *diazepam* as a mono-therapy in NAS was endorsed by Finnegan et al. (1984) [103], though study cohort appears to overlap with the cohort reported by Kaltenbach et al. (1986). Of major interest, this is the only study where treatment analysis was performed under consideration of the confounding factor of maternal multidrug-using behaviour during pregnancy. Compared to *phenobarbitone paregoric* demonstrated a significant lower rate of treatment failure in infants of mothers with a sole abuse of opiates.

In a randomized study Madden et al. (1979) [82] investigated the treatment success of *methadone* (titration strategy), *phenobarbitone* (no loading dose and no titration strategy) and *diazepam* in 102 newborns of narcotic addicted mothers. Treatment was initiated upon clinical judgement. The authors found no significant differences in duration of treatment or hospitalisation. Main limitations of this study are the lack of blinding of treatment and that there was no standardized scoring system used to judge the severity of NAS.

Similarly Khoo et al. (1995) [114] compared the application of opiate (*morphine*) to *phenobarbitone* with no difference in the duration of treatment or rate of treatment failure.

In contrast in a more recent study (2004) Jackson reported of a significant reduction of duration of treatment in infants treated with *morphine* compared to those treated with *phenobarbitone* [81]. Several methodological aspects possibly explain the differences in the results annotated above. Titration strategy for *morphine* and *phenobarbitone* was applied in Khoo's trial whereas fix dose scheme for *morphine* and *phenobarbitone* was applied in the study of Jackson et al. (2004). It is conceivable that Jackson utilized these rather unusual treatment strategies to facilitate blinding of therapy regimens. In our opinion this exceptional strategy leads to limited clinical evidence.

In 2002, Coyle analyzed the question whether a combined treatment with diluted *tincture of opium (DTO)* and *phenobarbitone* is superior to the treatment with *DTO alone* [115]. 21 infants of opiate using mothers with elevated Finnegan scores were treated with *DTO* (titration strategy). They were randomly allocated to receive additionally either *phenobarbitone* (loading dose strategy) or placebo. In both groups, there was no treatment failure. Infants additionally treated with *phenobarbitone* had a significant reduction of maximal daily dose of *DTO*. A significant reduction of the duration of hospitalisation in this combined treatment group was noted either. Since infants treated with *phenobarbitone* were unlike the *morphine* treated group discharged home on *phenobarbitone*, it is unclear, if the reduction of the hospitalisation time depends on discharge policy or if it can interpreted as a valid outcome parameter.

Currently we have knowledge of four further ongoing trials on NAS treatment analysis. Beside Agthe's trial on *clonidine* as mentioned above[112], there is report of a trial on the effect of *phenobarbitone* on developmental outcomes in infant with methadone withdrawal [116] and of a study on neurobehavioral effects of treatment for opiate withdrawal [117]. Detailed results of these latter two studies are not yet available.

Finally our group initiated a prospective randomized controlled trial, in which efficacy of *morphine, phenobarbitone* and *chlorpromazine* in NAS is compared (Swiss Neonatal Abstinence Study). It is a Swiss multi-centre study including 120 infants born to opiate-dependent mothers in which treatment is fully blinded. Results are not yet available.

In summary currently there is not enough evidence to recommend one or another medicament to treat NAS. The above cited studies must be interpreted under consideration of the local situation and policy.

In our opinion it is crucial that a standardized scoring system is applied to evaluate and interpret withdrawal symptoms and that the once chosen medicament is given in a well defined regimen. In our institution we prefer to treat NAS with an opiate. Severity of withdrawal symptoms is judged by an adapted Finnegan score, the Swiss modified Finnegan Score (Figure 1), every 8 hours. If the score exceeds 9 points twice in a row or 14 points once, *morphine* is started in a relatively high dose (0.25mg/kg) to achieve quick control of the symptoms. *Morphine* is given every 4 hours. If the score remains > 9, the *morphine* dose is augmented (+0.05mg/kg/dose). Once the score is < 8 three times in row, we keep the *morphine* dosage constant for 3 days. Subsequently we reduce the *morphine* dose daily, if the median of the last three scores is < 8. If the *morphine* dose applied comes to exceed a total of 0.5mg *morphine phenobarbitone* treatment is initiated.

One must be aware, that in NAS the obvious effect of pharmacological treatment is only of short term. Treatment with a pharmacological agent improves clinical signs and prevents the infant from suffering. To the best of our knowledge none of the randomized controlled studies were aligned to evaluate long term outcome. No data exist about the impact of NAS treatment on addictive behaviour in later adulthood. This is very disappointing, since some authors argue that by observing physicians giving a medicament to their distressed infant, parents learn to treat signs of infant's discomfort with drugs instead of behavioural interventions. In this sense, treating NAS in an infant might be speculated to be a feasible risk factor for later addictive disease.

## 4.5. Breastfeeding

Whether infants of opiate dependent mothers should be breastfed remains a controversial issue and should not be discussed here in detail. Multiple studies demonstrated that the amount of opiates in maternal milk is low. Studies on the infant's plasma methadone level after breastfeeding in relation to the methadone level in the maternal milk however assert the relevance of inidividual methadone metabolism capacity. Such studies will further clarify the value of recommendations based solely on drug concentration in maternal milk. In our opinion, the decision whether an infant born to a drug dependent mother should be breastfeed or not, should be made on the basis of multiple factors considering diversity of maternal illicit drug use, maternal nutrition and health status (e.g. coexisting infectious disease) as well as psychological and child protection aspects [118].

## 4.6. Social and Child Protection Interventions

Beside prevention of the infant's suffering during neonatal period, improvement of the infant's long term outcome must always be considered as the ultimate goal. All decisions concerning treatment interventions or non-interventions should intend to support the child's normal development. All therapists involved assume responsibility to pave the way for a healthy, socially well integrated and happy childhood, adolescence and eventually adulthood.

There is to the best of our knowledge no prospective randomized controlled trial aligned to study long term impact of social or child protection interventions on these variables.

However it is worthwhile to discuss the important retrospective study by Ornoy et al. (1996) from Jerusalem [119]. Developmental problems were evaluated using *Bayley Developmental Scales* in children at the age of 0.5 to 2.5 years and *McCarthy Scales for Children's Abilities* in children at the age from 2.5 to 6 years. 83 children born to heroin addicted mothers were compared to 76 children born to heroin addicted fathers and to 3 matched control groups: 50 children with environmental deprivation, 50 children from families of moderate or high socioeconomic class without environmental deprivation and 80 healthy children from kindergartens.

While only newborns of heroin addicted mothers demonstrated physical growth restriction with lower birth weight and lower head circumference than controls, children of heroin addicted mothers as much as children of heroin addicted fathers showed a high incidence of hyperactivity, inattention and behavioural dysfunction.

Lowest DQ or IQ was found in children with environmental deprivation, followed in range by children born to heroin addicted fathers and finally in children born to heroin addicted mothers.

As a matter of particular interest after dividing children born to heroin-dependent mothers in two further groups, those, who were adopted at very young age and those raised by their mothers, the adopted children performed similarly to the healthy and non environmentally deprived controls. In contrast those raised by their mothers had significantly lower DQ/IQ's.

These results strongly suggests that child development depends much more on the environmental situation the child is exposed to then on the particular substance abused by the mother during pregnancy. We hope that our colleagues from Israel will follow up their cohort's to adolescence and provide these data on health and development status as well as addiction behaviour in these children in near future. We speculate that pharmacological NAS treatment strategy may also contribute relatively little to long term outcome in comparison to the potentially much more powerful effect of the environmental situation.

The stabilisation of the environmental situation must therefore be the main target in the care of drug dependent mothers and their children.

## CONCLUSION

Taking care of pregnant heroin addicts and their newborns is an challenging issue that requires an interdisciplinary and professional approach. The benefit of maintenance programmes remains undoubted.

Recent research results lead to the conclusion that optimal management of maternal comorbidities including pharmacological interventions and optimal management of maternal opiate addiction require profound knowledge on drug interactions, drug metabolism and furthermore the physiological changes of pregnancy.

For the neonate any intervention should be performed in a context that not only considers improvement of short term outcome but also intends to stabilize the environmental situation of mother and child in particular the health and socioeconomic status.

It is crucial that the professionals involved are unanimous about the main support strategy. We therefore strongly recommend establishing local interprofessional working groups. Consensus about obstetrical, perinatal and neonatal, as well as social and juridical support strategy should be achieved based on the local eventualities and evidence based medicine.

# REFERENCES

[1] Dole, V. P. and Nyswander, M. A Medical Treatment for Diacetylmorphine (Heroin) Addiction. A Clinical Trial with Methadone Hydrochloride. *Jama* 1965;193:646-50.

[2] Weaver, M.F., Rose, B. D. and Rush, J. editors. Heroin and other opioids. (2005). Available from: UpToDate® online 2006. 2005.

[3] Fischer, G. Treatment of opioid dependence in pregnant women. *Addiction* 2000;95(8):1141-4.

[4] Giles, W., Patterson, T., Sanders, F., Batey, R., Thomas, D., Collins, J. Outpatient methadone programme for pregnant heroin using women. *Aust N Z J. Obstet Gynaecol* 1989;29(3 Pt 1):225-9.

[5] Hagopian, G. S.,Wolfe, H. M., Sokol, R. J., Ager, J. W., Wardell, J. N., Cepeda, E. E. Neonatal outcome following methadone exposure in utero. *J. Matern Fetal. Med.* 1996;5(6):348-54.

[6] Finnegan, L. Treatment issues for opioid-dependent women during the perinatal period. *J. Psychoactive Drugs* 1991;23(2):191-201.

[7] Ostrea, E. M., Chavez, C. J., Strauss, M. E. A study of factors that influence the severity of neonatal narcotic withdrawal. *Pediatrics* 1976;4(1):642-645.

[8] Edelin, K.,Gurganious, L.,Golar, K.,Oellrich, D.,Kyei-Aboagye, K.,Hamid, M. Methadone Maintenance in Pregnancy: Consequences to Care and Outcome. *Obstet. Gynecol.* 1988; 71(3):399-404.

[9] Kashiwagi, M.,Arlettaz, R.,Lauper, U., Zimmermann, R., Hebisch ,G. Methadone Maintenance Program in a Swiss Perinatal Center: I. Management and Outcome of 89 Pregnancies. *Acta Obstet. Gynecol. Scand.* 2005;84:140-44.

[10] Fischer, G.,Bitschnau, M., Peternell, A., Eder, H., Topiz ,A. Pregnancy and substance abuse. *Archives of Women's Mental Health* 1999;2:57-65.

[11] Brown, H. L., Britton, K. A., Mahaffey, D., Brizendine, E., Hiett, A. K., Turnquest M. A. Methadone maintenance in pregnancy: a reappraisal. *Am. J. Obstet Gynecol* 1998;179(2):459-63.

[12] Malpas, T. J., Darlow, B. A., Lennox, R., Horwood, L. J. Maternal methadone dosage and neonatal withdrawal. *Aust N Z J Obstet. Gynaecol.* 1995;35(2):175-7.

[13] Wilson, G. S., Desmond, M. M., Wait, R. B. Follow-up of methadone-treated and untreated narcotic-dependent women and their infants: Health, development and social implications. *J. Pediatr.* 1981;98:716-722.

[14] Ellerbrock ,T. V., Harrington, P. E., Bush, T. J., Schoenfisch ,S. A.., Oxtoby ,M. J., Witte ,J. J. Risk of human immunodeficiency virus infection among pregnant crack cocaine users in a rural community. *Obstet Gynecol* 1995;86(3):400-4.

[15] Mesquita, F., Doneda, D., Gandolfi, D., Nemes, M. I., Andrade ,T., Bueno, R., Piconez e Trigueiros, D. Brazilian response to the human immunodeficiency virus/acquired immunodeficiency syndrome epidemic among injection drug users. *Clin Infect Dis* 2003;37 Suppl 5:S382-5.

[16] Adler, M. W., Geller ,E. B., Rogers, T. J., Henderson, E. E., Eisenstein, T. K. Opioids, receptors, and immunity. *Adv. Exp. Med. Biol.* 1993;335:13-20.

[17] Thorpe, L. E., Frederick, M., Pitt ,J., Cheng, I., Watts, D. H., Buschur, S., Green, K., Zorrilla, C., Landesman, S. H., Hershow ,R. C. Effect of hard-drug use on CD4 cell percentage, HIV RNA level, and progression to AIDS-defining class C events among HIV-infected women. *J. Acquir. Immune Defic Syndr.* 2004;37(3):1423-30.

[18] Soepatmi, S. Developmental outcomes of children of mothers dependent on heroin or heroin/methadone during pregnancy. *Acta Paediatr. Suppl.* 1994;404:36-9.

[19] Abrams, E. J., Wiener, J., Carter, R., Kuhn, L., Palumbo, P., Nesheim, S., Lee, F., Vink, P., Bulterys M. Maternal health factors and early pediatric antiretroviral therapy influence the rate of perinatal HIV-1 disease progression in children. *Aids* 2003;17(6):867-77.

[20] Mofenson, L. M. U.S. Public Health Service Task Force recommendations for use of antiretroviral drugs in pregnant HIV-1-infected women for maternal health and interventions to reduce perinatal HIV-1 transmission in the United States. *MMWR Recomm. Rep.* 2002;51(RR-18):1-38.

[21] Mayaux,, M. J., Teglas, J. P., Blanche, S. Characteristics of HIV-infected women who do not receive preventive antiretroviral therapy in the French Perinatal Cohort. *J. Acquir. Immune Defic Syndr.* 2003;34(3):338-43.

[22] Kerr, T., Palepu, A., Barness, G., Walsh, J., Hogg, R., Montaner, J., Tyndall, M., Wood E. Psychosocial determinants of adherence to highly active antiretroviral therapy among injection drug users in Vancouver. *Antivir Ther.* 2004;9(3):407-14.

[23] Porter, K., Babiker, A., Bhaskaran, K., Darbyshire, J., Pezzotti, P., Walker, A. S. Determinants of survival following HIV-1 seroconversion after the introduction of HAART. *Lancet* 2003;362(9392):1267-74.

[24] Greub, G., Ledergerber, B., Battegay, M., Grob, P., Perrin, L., Furrer, H., Burgisser, P., Erb, P., Boggian, K., Piffaretti, J. C., Hirschel, B., Janin, P., Francioli, P., Flepp, M., Telenti, A. Clinical progression, survival, and immune recovery during antiretroviral therapy in patients with HIV-1 and hepatitis C virus coinfection: the Swiss HIV Cohort Study. *Lancet* 2000;356(9244):1800-5.

[25] Berg, K. M., Demas, P. A., Howard, A. A., Schoenbaum, E. E., Gourevitch, M. N., Arnsten, J. H. Gender differences in factors associated with adherence to antiretroviral therapy. *J Gen. Intern. Med.* 2004;19(11):1111-7.

[26] McCance-Katz, E. F. Treatment of opioid dependence and coinfection with HIV and hepatitis C virus in opioid-dependent patients: the importance of drug interactions between opioids and antiretroviral agents. *Clin. Infect. Dis.* 2005;41 Suppl 1:S89-95.

[27] Iribarne, C., Berthou, F., Carlhant, D., Dreano, Y., Picart, D., Lohezic, F., Riche, C. Inhibition of methadone and buprenorphine N-dealkylations by three HIV-1 protease inhibitors. *Drug Metab. Dispos.* 1998;26(3):257-60.

[28] McCance-Katz, E. F., Rainey, P. M., Friedland, G., Jatlow, P. The protease inhibitor lopinavir-ritonavir may produce opiate withdrawal in methadone-maintained patients. *Clin. Infect Dis.* 2003;37(4):476-82.

[29] Clarke, S. M.,Mulcahy, F. M., Tjia ,J., Reynolds, H. E., Gibbons, S. E., Barry, M. G., Back, D. J. Pharmacokinetic interactions of nevirapine and methadone and guidelines for use of nevirapine to treat injection drug users. *Clin Infect Dis* 2001;33(9):1595-7.

[30] Schwartz, E. L., Brechbuhl, A. B., Kahl, P., Miller, M. A., Selwyn, P. A., Friedland, G. H. Pharmacokinetic interactions of zidovudine and methadone in intravenous drug-using patients with HIV infection. *J. Acquir. Immune. Defic. Syndr.* 1992;5(6):619-26.

[31] Rainey, P. M., Friedland, G. H., Snidow, J. W., McCance-Katz, E. F., Mitchell, S. M., Andrews, L., Lane, B., Jatlow, P. The pharmacokinetics of methadone following co-administration with a lamivudine/zidovudine combination tablet in opiate-dependent subjects. *Am. J. Addict.* 2002;11(1):66-74.

[32] McCance-Katz, E. F., Rainey, P. M., Jatlow, P., Friedland, G. Methadone effects on zidovudine disposition (AIDS Clinical Trials Group 262). *J. Acquir Immune Defic. Syndr Hum. Retrovirol.* 1998;18(5):435-43.

[33] Gibb, D. M., Goodall, R. L., Dunn ,D. T., Healy, M., Neave, P., Cafferkey, M., Butler K. Mother-to-child transmission of hepatitis C virus: evidence for preventable peripartum transmission. *Lancet* 2000;356(9233):904-7.

[34] Nikolopoulou, G. B., Nowicki, M. J., Du, W., Homans, J., Stek A., Kramer, F., Kovacs, A. HCV viremia is associated with drug use in young HIV-1 and HCV coinfected pregnant and non-pregnant women. *Addiction* 2005;100(5):626-35.

[35] Sulkowski, M. S. and Thomas, D. L. Perspectives on HIV/hepatitis C virus co-infection, illicit drug use and mental illness. *Aids* 2005;19 (Suppl 3):S8-12.

[36] Edlin, B. R., Irwin, K. L., Faruque, S., McCoy, C. B., Word, C., Serrano, Y., Inciardi, J. A., Bowser, B. P., Schilling, R. F., Holmberg, S. D. Intersecting epidemics--crack cocaine use and HIV infection among inner-city young adults. Multicenter Crack Cocaine and HIV Infection Study Team. *N Engl. J. Med.* 1994;331(21):1422-7.

[37] Corey, L., Wald, A., Celum, C. L., Quinn, T. C. The effects of herpes simplex virus-2 on HIV-1 acquisition and transmission: a review of two overlapping epidemics. *J Acquir Immune Defic. Syndr.* 2004;35(5):435-45.

[38] Chen, K. T., Segu, M., Lumey, L. H., Kuhn, L., Carter, R. J., Bulterys, M., Abrams, E. J. Genital herpes simplex virus infection and perinatal transmission of human immunodeficiency virus. *Obstet Gynecol* 2005;106(6):1341-8.

[39] Arlettaz, R., Kashiwagi, M., Kundu, S., Fauchere, C., Lange, A., Bucher, H. Methadone Maintenance Program in a Swiss Perinatal Center: II. Neonatal Outcome and Social Resources. *Acta Obstet. Gynecol. Scand.* 2005;84:145-50.

[40] Kashiwagi, M., Chaoui, R., Stallmach, T., Huerlimann, S., Lauper, U., Hebisch, G. Fetal Bilateral Renal Agenesis, Phocomelia, and Single Umbilical Artery Associated with Cocaine Abuse in Early Pregnancy. *Birth Defects Research (Part A)* 2003;67:951-952.

[41] Hulse, G. K., Milne, E., English, D. R., Holman, C. D. The relationship between maternal use of heroin and methadone and infant birth weight. Addiction 1997;92(11):1571-9.

[42] Dashe, J. S., Sheffield, J. S., Olscher, D. A., Todd, S. J., Jackson, G. L., Wendel, G. D. Relationship between maternal methadone dosage and neonatal withdrawal. *Obstet Gynecol.* 2002;100(6):1244-9.

[43] Jones, H. E., Haug, N., Silverman, K., Stitzer, M., Svikis, D. The effectiveness of incentives in enhancing treatment attendance and drug abstinence in methadone-maintained pregnant women. *Drug Alcohol. Depend* 2001;61(297-306).

[44] Jarvis, M. A. E., Wu-Pong, S., Kniseley, J. S., Schnoll, S. H. Alterations in Methadone Metabolism During Late Pregnancy. *J. Add Dis.* 1999;18(4):51-61.

[45] Pond, S. M., Kreek, M. J., Tong, T. G., Raghunath, J., Benowitz, N. L. Altered methadone pharmacokinetics in methadone-maintained pregnant women. *J. Pharmacol Exp. Ther.* 1985;233:1-6.

[46] Leavitt, S. B., Shinderman, M., Maxwell, S., Eap, C. B., Paris ,P. When "enough" is not enough: new perspectives on optimal methadone maintenance dose. *Mt. Sinai J. Med.* 2000;67(5-6):404-11.

[47] Shinderman, M., Maxwell S.. Brawand-Amey, M., Golay, K. P., Baumann ,P., Eap, C. B. Cytochrome P450A4 metabolic activity, methadone blood concentrations, and methadone doses. *Drug Alcohol. Depend.* 2003;69:205-211.

[48] Drozdick, J. r., Berghella, V., Hill, M., Kaltenbach, K. Methadone Trough Levels In Pregnancy. *Am. J. Obstet Gynecol.* 2002;187:1184-8.

[49] Borg, L., Broe, D. M., Ho, A., Kreek, M. J. Cocaine Abuse Sharply Reduced in an Effective Methadone Maintenance Program. *J. Add Dis.* 1999;18(4):63-73.

[50] Strain, E. C., Bigelow, G. E., Liebson, I. A., Stitzer, M. L. Moderate-vs high-dose methadone in the treatment of opioid dependence: a randomized trial. *JAMA* 1999;281:1000.

[51] Dole, V. P. Implications of methadone maintenance for theories of narcotic addiction. *Jama* 1988;260(20):3025-9.

[52] McCarthy, J. J., Leamon, M. H., Parr, M. S., Anania, B. High-dose methadone maintenance in pregancy: Maternal and neonatal outcome. *Am. J. Obstet Gynecol* 2005;193:606-10.

[53] Berghella, V., Lim, P. J., Hill, M. K., Cherpes, J., Chennat ,J., Kaltenbach, K. Maternal methadone dose and neonatal withdrawal. *Am. J. Obstet Gynecol.* 2003;189(2):312-7.

[54] Deshmukh, S. V., Nanovskaya, T. N., Ahmed, M. S. Aromatase Is the Major Enzyme Metabolizing Buprenorphine in Human Placenta. *J. Pharmacol. Exp. Ther.* 2003;306(3):1099-1105.

[55] Nanovskaya, T., Deshmukh, S., Nekhayeva, I., Zharikova, O., Hankins, G., Ahmed, M. Methadone metabolism by human placenta. *Biochemical Pharamacology* 2004;68:583-591.

[56] Mack, G., Thomas, D., Giles, W., Buchanan, N. Methadone levels and neonatal withdrawal. *J Paediatr Child Health* 1991;27:96-100.

[57] Doberczak, T. M., Kandall, S. R., Friedmann, P. Relationship between maternal methadone dosage, maternal-neonatal methadone levels, and neonatal withdrawal. *Obstet. Gynecol* 1993;81(6):936-40.

[58] Harper, R. G., Solish, G. I., Feingold, E., Gersten-Woolf, N. B., Sokal ,M. M. Maternal ingested methadone, body fluid methadone and the neonatal withdrawal syndrome. *Am J. Obstet. Gynecol.* 1977;129:417-24.

[59] Gedeon, C., Koren, G. Designing Pregnancy Centered Medications: Drugs Which Do Not Cross the Human Placenta. *Placenta* 2005.

[60] Nanovskaya, T., Nekhayeva, I., Karunaratne, N., Audus, K., Hankins, G. D., Ahmed, M. S. Role of P-glycoprotein in transplacental transfer of methadone. *Biochem Pharmacol* 2005;69(12):1869-78.

[61] Nekhayeva, I. A., Nanovskaya, T. N., Deshmukh, S. V., Zharikova, O. L., Hankins, G. D., Ahmed, M. S. Bidirectional transfer of methadone across human placenta. *Biochem. Pharmacol.* 2005;69(1):187-97.

[62] Dashe, J. S., Jackson, G. L., Olscher, D. A., Zane, E. H., Wendel, G. D. Opioid Detoxification in Pregnancy. *Obstet. Gynecol.* 1998;92:854-8.

[63] Maas, U., Kattner, E., Weingart-Jesse, B., Schäfer, A., Obladen, M. Infrequent neonatal opiate withdrawal following maternal methadone detoxification during pregnancy. *J. Perinat. Med.* 1990;18:111-118.

[64] Zuspan, F. P., Gumpel, J. A., Mejia-Zelaya, A., Madden, J., Davis, R. Fetal stress from methadone withdrawal. *Am. J. Obstet. Gynecol.* 1975;122(1):43-6.

[65] Gitau, R., Fisk, N. M., Teixeira, J. M., Cameron, A., Glover, V. Fetal hypothalamic-pituitary-adrenal stress responses to invasive procedures are independent of maternal responses. *J. Clin. Endocrinol. Metab.* 2001;86(1):104-9.

[66] Lichtblau, L. and Sparber, S. B. Opiate withdrawal in utero increases neonatal morbidity in the rat. *Science* 1981;212(4497):943-5.

[67] Luty, J., Nikolaou, V., Bearn, J. Is opiate detoxification unsafe in pregnancy? *J Subst Abuse Treat* 2003;24(4):363-7.

[68] Fischer, G., Jagsch, R., Eder, H., Gombas, W., Etzersdorfer, P., Schmidl-Mohl, K., Schatten, C., Weninger, M., Aschauer, H. N. Comparison of methadone and slow-release morphine maintenance in pregnant addicts. *Addiction* 1999;94(2):231-9.

[69] Rohrmeister, K., Bernert, G., Langer, M., Fischer, G., Weninger, M., Pollak, A. [Opiate addiction in gravidity - consequences for the newborn. Results of an interdisciplinary treatment concept]. *Z Geburtshilfe Neonatol* 2001;205(6):224-30.

[70] Jones, H. E., Johnson, R. E., Jasinski, D. R., Milio, L. Randomized controlled study transitioning opioid-dependent pregnant women from short-acting morphine to buprenophine or methadone. *Drug Alcohol. Depend* 2005;78:33-38.

[71] Jernite, M., Viville, B., Escande, B., Brettes, J., Messer, J. Burenorphine and pregnancy. Analysis of 24 cases. *Arch Pédiatr* 1999;6:1179-85.

[72] Fischer, G., Etzersdorfer, P., Eder, H., Jagsch, R., Langer, M., Weninger, M. Buprenorphine maintenance in pregnant opiate addicts. *Eur. Addict. Res.* 1998;4 Suppl 1:32-6.

[73] Marquet, P., Chevrel, J., Lavignasse, P., Merle, L., Lachatre, G. Buprenorphine withdrawal syndrome in a newborn. *Clin. Pharmacol. Ther.* 1997;62(5):569-71.

[74] Johnson, R. E., Jones, H. E., Fischer, G. Use of buprenorphine in pregnancy: patient management and effects on the neonate. *Drug Alcohol. Depend.* 2003;70(2 Suppl):S87-S101.

[75] Lejeune, C., Simmat-Durand, L., Gourarier, L., Aubisson, S. Prospective multicenter observational study of 260 infants born to 259 opiate-dependent mothers on methadone or high-dose buprenophine substitution. *Drug. Alcohol. Depend.* 2005.

[76] Hulse, G., O'Neil, G., Arnold-Reed, D. Methadone maintenance vs. implantable naltrexone treatment in the pregnant heroin user. *Int. J. Obstet. Gynecol.* 2004;85:170.

[77] Rehm, J., Gschwend, P., Steffen, T., Gutzwiller, F., Dobler-Mikola, A., Uchtenhagen, A. Feasibility, safety, and efficacy of injectable heroin prescription for refractory opioid addicts: a follow-up study. *Lancet* 2001;358(9291):1417-23.

[78] Smeriglio, V. L. and Wilcox, H. C. Prenatal drug exposure and child outcome. Past, present, future. *Clin. Perinatol.* 1999;26(1):1-16.

[79] Bauer, C. R. Perinatal effects of prenatal drug exposure. Neonatal aspects. *Clin. Perinatol.* 1999;26(1):87-106.

[80] LaGasse, L. L., Seifer, R., Lester, B. M. Interpreting research on prenatal substance exposure in the context of multiple confounding factors. *Clin. Perinatol.* 1999;26(1):39-54.

[81] Jackson, L., Ting, A., McKay, S., Galea, P., Skeoch, C. A randomised controlled trial of morphine versus phenobarbitone for neonatal abstinence syndrome. *Arch. Dis. Child Fetal Neonatal Ed.* 2004;89(4):F300-4.

[82] Madden, J. D., Chappel, J. N., Zuspan, F., Gumpel, J., Mejia, A., Davis ,R. Observation and treatment of neonatal narcotic withdrawal. *Am. J. Obstet. Gynecol.* 1977;127(2):199-201.

[83] Doberczak, T. M., Thornton, J. C., Bernstein, J., Kandall, S. R. Impact of maternal drug dependency on birth weight and head circumference of offspring. *Am. J. Dis. Child* 1987;141(11):1163-7.

[84] Ostrea, E. M. and Chavez, C. J. Perinatal problems (excluding neonatal withdrawal) in maternal drug addiction: a study of 830 cases. *J. Pediatr.* 1979;94(2):292-5.

[85] Finnegan, L. P., Kron, R. E., Connaughton ,J. F., Emich, J. P. Assessment and treatment of abstinence in the infant of the drug-dependent mother. *Int. J. Clin. Pharmacol Biopharm* 1975;12(1-2):19-32.

[86] Lipsitz, P. J. A proposed narcotic withdrawal score for use with newborn infants. A pragmatic evaluation of its efficacy. *Clin. Pediatr. (Phila)* 1975;14(6):592-4.

[87] O'Brien, C., Hunt, R., Jeffery, H. E. Measurement of movement is an objective method to assist in assessment of opiate withdrawal in newborns. *Arch. Dis. Child Fetal Neonatal. Ed* 2004;89(4):F305-9.

[88] Dahlem, P., Bucher, H. U., Ursprung, T., Mieth, D., Gautschi, K. [Detection of drugs in meconium]. *Monatsschr Kinderheilkd* 1992;140(6):354-6.

[89] Ostrea, E. M., Brady, M. J., Parks, P. M., Asensio, D. C., Naluz, A. Drug screening of meconium in infants of drug-dependent mothers: an alternative to urine testing. *J. Pediatr.* 1989;115(3):474-7.

[90] American Academy of Pediatrics. Committee on Substance Abuse. Tobacco, alcohol, and other drugs: the role of the pediatrician in prevention and management of substance abuse. *Pediatrics* 1998;101(1 Pt 1):125-8.

[91] Dahlem, P., Bucher, H. U., Cuendet, D., Mieth, D., Gautschi, K. [Prevalence of drugs in meconium]. *Monatsschr Kinderheilkd* 1993;141(3):237-40.

[92] Ryan, R. M., Wagner, C. L., Schultz, J. M., Varley, J., DiPreta ,J., Sherer, D. M., Phelps, D. L., Kwong, T. Meconium analysis for improved identification of infants exposed to cocaine in utero. *J. Pediatr.* 1994;125(3):435-40.

[93] Vinner, E., Vignau, J., Thibault, D., Codaccioni, X., Brassart, C., Humbert, L., Lhermitte, M. Neonatal hair analysis contribution to establishing a gestational drug exposure profile and predicting a withdrawal syndrome. *Ther. Drug Monit.* 2003;25(4):421-32.

[94] Kandall, S. R. Treatment strategies for drug-exposed neonates. *Clin. Perinatol.* 1999;26(1):231-43.

[95] Kulig, J. W. Tobacco, alcohol, and other drugs: the role of the pediatrician in prevention, identification, and management of substance abuse. *Pediatrics* 2005;115(3):816-21.

[96] Oro, A. S. and Dixon, S. D. Waterbed care of narcotic-exposed neonates. A useful adjunct to supportive care. *Am J Dis Child* 1988;142(2):186-8.

[97] Weinberger, S. M., Kandall, S. R., Doberczak, T. M., Thornton, J. C., Bernstein, J. Early weight-change patterns in neonatal abstinence. *Am J Dis Child* 1986;140(8):829-32.

[98] Kandall, S. R., Doberczak, T. M., Mauer, K. R., Strashun, R. H., Korts, D. C. Opiate v CNS depressant therapy in neonatal drug abstinence syndrome. *Am. J. Dis. Child* 1983;137(4):378-82.

[99] Carin, I., Glass, L., Parekh, A., Solomon, N.,Steigman, J., Wong, S. Neonatal methadone withdrawal. Effect of two treatment regimens. *Am. J Dis. Child* 1983;137(12):1166-9.

[100] Malanga ,C. Jr. and Kosofsky, B. E. Mechanisms of action of drugs of abuse on the developing fetal brain. *Clin. Perinatol.* 1999;26(1):17-37.

[101] Kaltenbach, K. and Finnegan, L. P. Neonatal abstinence syndrome, pharmacotherapy and developmental outcome. *Neurobehav. Toxicol. Teratol.* 1986;8(4):353-5.

[102] Pacifico, P., Nardelli, E., Pantarotto, M. F. Neonatal heroin withdrawal syndrome; evaluation of different pharmacological treatments. *Pharmacol. Res.* 1989;21 (Suppl 1):63-4.

[103] Finnegan, L. P., Michael, H., Leifer, B., Desai, S. An evaluation of neonatal abstinence treatment modalities. In: NIDA, editor. NIDA Research Monograph; 1984. p. 282-8.

[104] Morselli, P. L., Principi, N., Tognoni, G., Reali, E., Belvedere, G., Standen, S. M., Sereni, F. Diazepam elimination in premature and full term infants, and children. *J. Perinat. Med.* 1973;1(2):133-41.

[105] Kron ,R. E., Litt, M., Eng D., Phoenix, M. D., Finnegan, L. P. Neonatal narcotic abstinence: Effects of pharmacotherapeutic agents and maternal drug usage on nutritive sucking behavior. *J. Pediatr.* 1976;88(4 Pt. 1):637-41.

[106] Kandall, S. R. and Gartner, L. M. Late presentation of drug withdrawal symptoms in newborns. *Am. J. Dis. Child.* 1974;127(1):58-61.

[107] Autret, F., Mucignat, V., De Montgolfier-Aubron, I., Blond, M. H., Ducrocq, S., Lebas, F., Gold, F. [Use of diazepam in the treatment of opioid neonatal abstinence syndrome.]. *Arch. Pediatr.* 2004;11(11):1308-13.

[108] Kahn, E. J., Neumann, L. L., Polk, G. A. The course of the heroin withdrawal syndrome in newborn infants treated with phenobarbital or chlorpromazine. *J. Pediatr.* 1969;75(3):495-500.

[109] Morrison, C. L. and Siney, C. A survey of the management of neonatal opiate withdrawal in England and Wales. *Eur. J. Pediatr.* 1996;155(4):323-6.

[110] Levy, M. and Spino, M. Neonatal withdrawal syndrome: associated drugs and pharmacologic management. *Pharmacotherapy* 1993;13(3):202-11.

[111] Hoder, E. L., Leckman, J. F., Poulsen, J., Caruso, K. A., Ehrenkranz, R. A., Kleber, H. D., Cohen, D. J. Clonidine treatment of neonatal narcotic abstinence syndrome. *Psychiatry Res* 1984;13(3):243-51.

[112] Osborn, D. A., Jeffery, H. E., Cole, M. J. Sedatives for opiate withdrawal in newborn infants. *Cochrane Database Syst. Rev.* 2005(3):CD002053.

[113] Osborn, D. A., Jeffery, H. E., Cole, M. Opiate treatment for opiate withdrawal in newborn infants. *Cochrane Database Syst. Rev.* 2005(3):CD002059.

[114] Khoo, K. T. The effectiveness of three treatment regimes used in management of neonatal abstinence syndrome. [PhD Thesis]: University of Melbourne; 1995.

[115] Coyle, M. G., Ferguson, A., Lagasse, L., Oh, W., Lester, B. Diluted tincture of opium (DTO) and phenobarbital versus DTO alone for neonatal opiate withdrawal in term infants. *J. Pediatr.* 2002;140(5):561-4.

[116] Bier, J. B., Ferguson, A. E., Grenon, D., Mullane, E., Coyle, M. The effect of Phenobarbital on developmental outcomes in infants with methadone withdrawal: results of a randomized trial. *Pediatric Research* 2000; 47:175A.

[117] Ferguson, A., Coyle, M., LaGasse, L., Liu, E., Lester, B. Neurobehavioral effects of treatment for opiate withdrawal. *Pediatric Research* 2001;49:18A.

[118] Kashiwagi, M., Schaefer, C., Kaestner, R., Vetter, K., Abou-Dakn, M. Opiate Addiction and Breastfeeding- Review of the Literature and Recommendations. *German J. Obstet Gynecol.* 2005;65:938-41.

[119] Ornoy, A., Michailevskaya, V., Lukashov, I., Bar-Hamburger, R., Harel, S. The developmental outcome of children born to heroin-dependent mothers, raised at home or adopted. *Child Abuse Negl.* 1996;20(5):385-96.

In: Substance Abuse, Assessment and Addiction                ISBN: 978-1-61122-931-8
Editors: Kristina A. Murati and Allison G. Fischer        © 2011 Nova Science Publishers, Inc.

*Chapter 16*

# ALCOHOLISM AND PREGNANCY

## *Jorge Eduardo Montesinos Balboa**
## *and Angélica Calderón Alvarez***

*Psychiatrist. Hospital General de Zona N° 1. IMSS.
Tapachula Chiapas México
**Physician. Consejo Mexicano de Medicina General.

## ABSTRACT

In this section we review historical aspects of the use of alcohol by women. Social and cultural characteristics are mentioned about of the ingestion of alcohol in different regions all over the world. Statistics figures are pointed out that give an image of the alcohol consumption in the general population and in women more specifically. The interactions among the biological, psychological and social traits of women are emphasized. It is analysed the pregnancy in adolescents and its relation with the pregnancy of high risk.

It is examined the fetal alcohol syndrome that is the first avoidable cause of mental retardation in U.S. Data about the use of alcohol during the pregnancy are revealed. We mention the problems in the diagnosis of the alcohol use, mainly during the pregnancy. It is proposed and justified the use of tests to the diagnosis of alcoholism. Treatment and ethical aspects are treated.

## INTRODUCTION

It is said that from immemorial time are known the intoxicant effects of some nature products put under fermentation. The oldest alcoholic drink is the beer. The alcoholic

---

* Correspondence:4° Avenida Norte 88c, col: centro Tapachula de C y O Chiapas México. C.P: 30700. Tel: 962 – 62 – 5- 91-32.. E-mail: montesinos_eduardo@hotmail-com

ingestion has been a common practice among men since the agriculture beginning, its consumption and consequences are described in several cultures.

In the Vatican Codex II, it is described as the Quetzalcoatl dynasty was defeated by the excessive consumption of alcohol, when one of the women of the dynasty learnt, thank to gods, to prepare the drinking called "octli", which is "the neutle" or "the pulque" [1]. Quetzalcoatl was the agriculture god, who intoxicated had a incestuous relationship with his sister and this act provoked his own ruin [2].

The clinical entity was described in the 19th century by Swedish Doctor Magnus Hauss, who named it alcoholism in 1849 taking as a base the Esquirol's description of "the delirium drinkers"[3].

He defined it like the group of morbid accidents produced by the alcoholic drinks.

The alcoholism recognized like a disease came up with the Industrial Revolution, at first it was considered like something dirty or immoral.

## STATISTICS

With certain genetic influence the alcoholism is considered a social and cultural phenomenon.

When considering it this way is convenient to comment that it is spoken of different types of cultures with relation to the permissiveness in the alcohol use: Abstinent civilizations like the Islamic. Ambivalent in which Protestantism has influence, for example US and England. Moderated permissive for example, Italia. Permissive unconditional, for example France, Chile. Alcoholism prevalence varies according to the cultural context [3, 4].

The WHO reports that there are 70 millions people dependent on alcohol [5].

Eight of each ten people inhabitants of Europe and the American continent refer to have drunk alcohol, throughout the life. In a study of the ECA, using DSM III, found and average prevalence of abuse or alcohol dependency of 13.6%, Blazer and cols discovered a greater prevalence of alcoholism in rural regions and in low educative levels. The rates of separation and divorce are increased by this pathology [4].

According to DALY unit (Disability Adjusted Life Years) there are four mental diseases among the ten first causes of disability, first of them is depression, second is the alcohol consumption [6].

Using this same unit the alcoholism explains the 9.7% of all lost DALY in 2000 in the American Continent [7].

Every year in US 85,000 deaths are attributed to the alcohol use. Observational studies indicate that men younger than 34 years old and women younger than 45 years old who refer not to ingest alcohol display a lower mortality [8].

In accordance with the health report 2002, the alcohol abuse, is the risk factor that influences more the load of diseases in American Continent.(10% or more of the general morbidity load), causes multiple deceases and is the factor that contributes more to accidents and death by external injuries and violence, generating also several chronic diseases [9].

In spite of increase in consumption of illicit drugs alcohol consumption continues being the main problem because of is the one of greater use. Being like this is considered that the repercussion of alcohol abuse in health and social welfare is enormous in the region, these facts motivated to the Pan Americans Organization of Health (OPH) to participate with the

WHO to translate and to publish the report "Neuroscience of consumption and psychoactive substance dependence" [9].

In an epidemiological study carried out from 1999 to 2003 using the data base Latin - American and the Caribbean (LILACS) on studies of population in South America the prevalence, use or alcohol dependence oscillated between 4 and 12%.[10].

According to OPH the higher alcohol prevalence happens the American continent, although regional differences exist, the average consumption is 50% higher in the American continent than in the world in general, the way to drink of inhabitants in this continent is erratic [7].

## ALCOHOLISM AND GENDER

Searching this phenomenon in Mexico in the 19th century some numbers of affected subject were reported; in these statistics in the female sex were not mentioned. The social condition women and the customs of that time, promoted that the suffering related to morality and sexuality were diagnosed too much late.

The international literature medical of the 19ht century did not make reference to the alcoholic pathology in female sex [11].

During the decade of seventies in the 20th century increased the number of alcoholic women that looked for or were referred for treatment this increase was relativity greater than the alcoholic men. Some possible factors of this increase were considered between which it emphasizes a greater tolerance to women's behaviours of drinking alcohol. It was observed that women usually restrict the alcohol ingestion to home, because in that case the social pressure that sanctions the intoxication is lesser [12].

It has been found that nowadays a greater number of women attends to the meetings of the groups of anonymous alcoholics. [13].

At the present time there is a greater percentage of alcohol use by women.

With a proportion between men and women that marks a great difference among different nations, for example from 2 to 1 en US and from 28 to 1 in Korea [4] (Figure 1).

Women tend to display a greater degree of intoxication that men, even drinking the same amount of alcohol by unit of corporal weight.

This greater sensibility of women can be explained by a smaller activity of the enzyme alcohol deshydrogenase, a greater amount of greasy tissue and a smaller amount of water in women's body; women reach greater alcohol levels in blood, because they have less total corporal liquid, that allows to dilute the alcohol. It is considered that a man drinks strong when he ingests four or more glasses at a day, a woman drinks strong when she takes two or more glasses at a day [14].

In a study of Mariño et al, in Mexico it was found that men drink more distil drink followed of tequila, mezcal and alcohol of 96ª. However women prefer pulque, then beer and finally distil drinks.In other studies in the country it is reported a greater frequency of alcohol dependency in men and a greater amount of consumption by women when they show dependency [15].

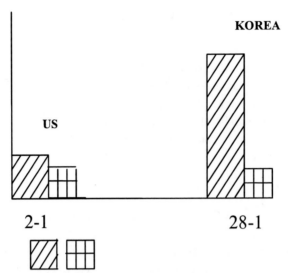

Figure 1. Proportion between men and women in the use of alcohol.

Complications like ulcer peptic, hepatic disease, anaemia, and cortical atrophy have an accelerated presentation in the female sex, and the death possibility is also higher than in men.

Specifically gynaecological and obstetric problems are presented such as breast cancer, menstrual disorders, frequent miscarriage, sterility, difficult childbirth and sexual difficulties. [16,17].

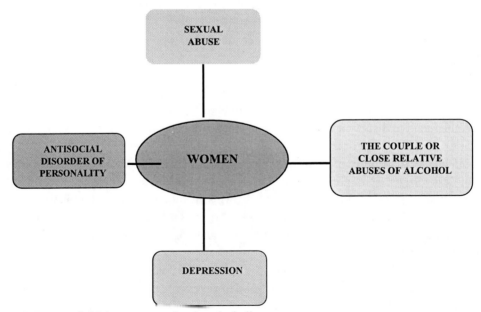

Figure 2. Factors of risk in women to develop alcoholism.

In the general population there are a minor amount of dependent women to alcohol.

This phenomenon has been tried of explaining because of a greater predisposition of men to the alcohol dependency [13]. A high sensibility of women to look for medical aid in front of alcoholism problems, this maybe must be to the social intolerance front to the alcoholic women. Perception of gravity of alcoholism is different in both genders. It is likely that there is a greater social rejection to women drink because the alcohol consumption is incompatible with the traditionally rolls assigned to woman, one of the most important the children rising.

Risk factors in women that are considered to develop alcoholism: sexual abuse, abuse of illicit substances, antisocial disorder of personality and depression. [14] (Figure 2)

It is considered also the high risk that the couple or a close relative abuses of alcohol. Depression usually precedes to alcoholism. Some women drink alcohol like it was a medicine to avoid the annoyances of the premenstrual syndrome. [4]

## HIGH RISK PREGNANCY

The pregnancies of high risk reach a 30% of the pregnancies all over the world. The pregnancy of high risk can be divided in two great categories: medical and psycho - social.

The Women who uses substances during the pregnancy does of this a pregnancy of high risk. The use of substances has become a problem of public health. When it happens in the pregnant women the approach changes from the individual medical care to attention of the mother and the fetus [18].

In 1986 it was calculated that the abuse of substances by pregnant women reach a rank of 16, this rank increased until 46% at the beginning of nineties. It is esteemed that 27% of women who drink alcohol do it a least once a week [18].

Nowadays there is a double risk; the use of substance during pregnancy to which the pregnancy in adolescents is added.

Nearly 50% of students in the U.S. have had experiences of alcohol consumption at the age of 13 years old that is increased to 81.7% at the age of 17 years old.

In Canada 78% of people of 15 years old or older are consuming alcohol at the moment, 12% of men and 3% of women enter in the risk category. [19]

A risk factor that influences that adolescents use substances is the fact that some people think is a normal behaviour during that period of the development. [20]

In U.S. the adolescents between 12 to 17 years old have tasted alcohol at least once in their life and 25% among them are described as regular consumers. [21]

In Mexico it has been found an increase in the alcohol consumption between people younger than 30 years old. [22]

Pregnancy in this young group of people has become more frequent. Gestation to this age is already in it self a factor of high risk; it has been observed in these adolescent mothers and their babies psychological disorders, social and economical problems. [23]

The consumption of substances by adolescents has raised, it has been observed that pregnant adolescents raise the consumption and acquire a compulsive pattern during the first trimester. [18]

Madden mentions that Sclare in 1975 described three way of alcohol abuse by women according to theirs age: Adolescents and women between 20 to 30 years old, drink in excess with their couples. Medium - aged adults with children adults have a drink model similar to the masculine one. Women in half of life who present frustrations because they don't have a couple or because they feel their couple doesn't take care enough of them, these women drink in excess. [12]

# FETAL ALCOHOL SYNDROME (FAS)

When a pregnant women consumes alcohol, this directly affects the brain tissue of the fetus, because the substance is very soluble in lipids and brain is rich in these [6].

Alcoholic women's children have a greater risk of: presenting different pathologies; attention disorder with hyperactivity and impulsiveness, a higher tendency to develop alcoholism; being the victim of a deficient education, living in a impoverished social ambient, suffering from negligence or mistreat: They have a greater possibility of display deficiencies in the social and cognitive functioning, a greater risk of, develop substance consumption and criminal behaviours.

The fetal alcoholic syndrome is reported by some authors like the first well - known and avoidable cause of mental retardation in U.S., other authors mention it like one of the main causes [24,25,26].

It is a congenital syndrome represented by an ample spectrum of anomalies. When the syndrome does not appear complete then we talk about fetal alcoholic effects or prenatal exposition to alcohol [27].

It can happen unnoticed because physicians omit to ask about the maternal alcohol use and not to know the effect of alcohol n the neurodevelopment [26].

The FAS has a worldwide incidence of 1.9 x 1000 alive been born. [19] The risk of the an alcoholic woman's child develops the syndrome is of 6% [4].

The FAS is presented among 0.1 to 0.03 of the normal births [19].

The first description was elaborated by scientifics in France ad U.S. at the end of 1960 and the beginning of 1970. Its presence is due to the alcohol effect on developing cell. The cellular growth factors diminish their effect in the growth and cellular differentiation.

It is probable that there is genetic predisposition to present it. Probably free radicals are produced that allow accumulation of calcium in cells which generates a smaller size in the brain and a smaller thickness of the external layers of the cerebral cortex caused by a diminished number of cellularity within the neuropathologica findings the dendritic thorns are affected phenomenon that also happens in the Down Syndrome, it has been found hypodevelopment or absence of the corpus callosum. It is possible that alcohol influences migration of the damage cells [19, 27].

In the mechanism of damage is mentioned the presence of factors like placental dysfunction and nutritional deficiency, acetaldehyde presence, neonatal hypoxia, and prostaglandins influence [28].

Swyze, Johnson et al. found the presence in studies of Magnetic Resonance a spectrum of abnormalities in the midline of brain, most of them related to abnormalities of the neural tube closure that occur during craniofacial and brain development in the embryonic and early fetal periods; studies that support the findings of pathology the effect depends on the moment of the maximum exposure to alcohol (the trimester of gestation) and the dose. The earlier and the greater doses of alcohol ingest a pregnant woman the more gravity in the presentation o the syndrome [29].

It has not been determined yet the exact dose of alcohol necessary to cause the syndrome but it is necessary to indicate that a safe dose has not settled down either that avoids its presentation.

The clinic data are: lack of growth pre- and post-natal, mental retardation of different degrees. Facial malformations characteristic: Approximately 50% present congenital anomalies in eyes, ears and heart. Attention disorders: Slowness in the processing of information. motor clumsiness, disorder of the language, difficulty in the fine motivity. Academic disorders (problems), mainly in the apprenticeship of mathematics. Autistic characteristics have been described. Agenesis of the corpus callosum, also, it has been found a displacement of the same one, that it is correlated to performance in verbal learning tests. [19, 27]

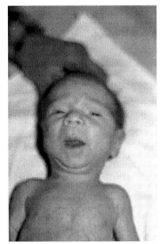

Picture 1.

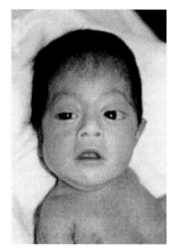

Picture 2.

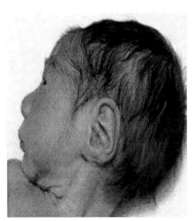

Picture 3.

Pictures 1, 2, 3. FAS. Courtesy MD: Rocìo Baez (Genetista del Instituto Nacional de Perinatologìa, México).

There are some morphogenetic markers that must be looked for ultrasound, being these: restriction in the uterine growth, diminution of the cephalic circumference, cleft lip and, or cleft palate, cardiopathy, diminution of fetal movements.

Some biochemical markers can be searched in maternal blood, umbilical cord and meconium.

These markers are: fat acids eter etilics (FAEE), gamma glutamyl transpeptidase, acetaldehyde, alcohol deshydrogenase, aldehide deshydrogenase, N acetyl aspartate [28].

It is interesting to mention that some neuropsychological alterations like to which occur in the FAS has been found in children who do not fulfil all the criteria to FAS but who were exposed to alcohol in the prenatal period.

It is necessary to emphasize that this syndrome can be prevented to which it is required to educate the population.

Children with this syndrome need an early educative attention the treatment starts with the treatment of the parents. The physical and behavioural characteristics of the children who suffer from this syndrome most be discussed. it is possible that familial therapy be required. [19,27]

The use of alcohol during the lactation can be dangerous because the alcohol passes to maternal milk and the babies brain has not matured yet [27]. It must be insisted in this aspect since there are some communities where it is considered that alcoholic drinks like the pulque rise the amount of maternal milk.

It must be emphasized that the only preventive measure safe to avoid the FAS is he total abstinence of ingestion of alcohol during pregnancy. [19,24,27]

## ALCOHOLISM DIAGNOSTIC

Alcoholism is a diagnostic problem, it has been considered like syphilis or AIDS a great imitator because it causes signs and symptoms to which physician looks for a diverse etiology or considered them like idiopathic. It is usual that the alcoholic patient complains of slight physical malaises. Diagnosis is difficult if it is not thought about it.

A physician must think in a routinely way in the possibility of alcoholism in a patient with hypertension especially when it is resistant to treatment, depression, insomnia, pyrosis, anaemia, thrombocytopenia, injuries, problems of the social life or at work, abnormal hepatic enzyme levels, approximately a 50% of the cases of cirrhosis, non ischemic cardiomyophaty cancer of the esophagus, larynx and mouth can be attributed to alcohol [8].

Usually it happens that alcoholism is not diagnosed and the patients are not treated because they resist to get a treatment and avoid the physicians by shame, we can add problems with the authority figures and lack of self care [4].

It has been found that physicians only identify between 20 to 50% of the alcoholics that attend to consultation and 25% of the diseases that deserve hospitalization are related with alcoholic consumption.

The medical interrogation and the physical exploration orient the diagnosis, although the signs and the symptoms of alcoholism are no easily recognizable. In the services of health, there are no widely spread programs to detection of addictions [30].

Specific tests to alcoholism detection have been developed, they are screening tests which are the fundamental part of the strategy to detect patients who ingest alcohol. The instruments used to conduct this detection are questionnaires that allow suspect the use, abuse and the dependency to alcohol some of them are MAST (Michigan Alcoholism Screening Test). CAGE. T - ACE and AUDIT (Alcoholism Use Disorder Identification Test) [31, 32].

The WHO developed a useful instrument in primary medical attention to detect people who consume alcohol in a excessive, dangerous or harmful way. the elaborated instrument is the AUDIT, it is considered a useful test with transcultural validity, congruent with the International Classification of Disease (ICD 10) it can be applied in a fast and flexible way. It consists of 10 questions and it is an instrument of complementary clinic evaluation [31].

Laboratory test are also utilized that in case of being positives they orient to think the patient presents problems by alcohol use, each one has a specific weight, when the results of these tests are related some with others the diagnosis is more probable. Example of these tests are: Gamma glutammil transferase, (GGT), mean corpuscular volume, uric acid, cholesterol of high density (HDL), triglicerides and liver panel. [33]

## ALCOHOLISM DURING PREGNANCY

Alcoholic is a teratogenic substance. As it has been commented before the nervous system is one of the target organs to alcohol.

The FDA has divided drugs in five categories according to damage that they can cause:

Category A:  Medicaments safe during pregnancy.
Category B:  Medicaments that have not shown risks in studies with animals, but they have not been studied in humans.
Category C:  The studies in human beings not have been definitive.
Category D:  Cases where exists evidence of risk.
Category X:  The risk for the fetus is well established. This drug would be contraindicated in pregnant women. [18,25]

Alcohol is in the X category.

Some occasions a woman does not know that is pregnant, if she dinks can follow using alcohol, without having conscience of the danger for the fetus.

In the studies made with pregnant women the lack of control of variables has been critized forgery of memory in the interviewed women, differences in quantification of the exposition to alcohol and mistakes in the classification of cases [34].

The prevalence of use of any amount of alcohol between pregnant women was of 12.8% in U.S.

Some factors associated with increase of alcohol consumption are mentioned; among others; a greater education, desires of drink in social situation, history of previous ingestion or consumption during long periods of time an a greater alcohol prenatal ingestion at the time of investigation [32].

Studies have been made to look for detect the alcohol use during gestation, most of them are retrospective.

In 1988 in the study of the National Survey Addiction it was asked about alcohol use during gestation and adverse answers; his survey. using logistic regression found: low weight when being born and premature childbirths [35].

In a study of the author of this chapter, 132 pregnant women were studied, all them went to the service of Enfermeria Materno Infantil (EMI) in TheGeneral Hospital of the Zone of Tapachula Chiapas, that belong to region coast of the state of Chiapas in Mexico, it is know that in tropical regions like this the ingestion of beer can be greater because of the high temperature.

It was applied a descriptive survey. The population was select by non probabilistic sampling by quotas. The AUDIT was used to identify, use, abuse, dependency and the physical or mental damage caused by the alcohol. It was found a frequency of 45.5% of pregnant women with positive consumption and a case of dependence. None of the cases was identified by the family physician.

We concluded that the population studied presents a high alcohol consumption, even greater than the general population in non pregnant women. The emitted recommendations were: To use tests of detection like the AUDIT. To implement measures for training and sensitization of the health staff to take to the detection of this problem.

According to the commented data, we can infer that the alcohol use by pregnant women is an under estimated problem that causes multiple problems in their children [36].

## TREATMENT

Like in other clinic entities related to alcohol, it is recommended according to the gravity of the case: Brief interventions that include the pregnant women´s partner. Attendance to self-help groups. Specialised treatment. Management of alcohol withdrawal. Pharmacotherapy [16].

Chang et al, in a research in 2005, using the T - ACE confirm other studies in which the brief interventions that includes the woman's partner, reduce the use of alcohol by woman who has a high level of use [32].

In the cases where comorbidity is presented it is convenient to establish a strategy to face it, for example pregnant women with depression and alcohol use must get attention to both problems.

## CONCLUSION

According to this review, we consider that the use of alcohol by pregnant women, is not adequately diagnosed.

The alcohol is a teratogenic substance, whose use must be avoided during pregnancy as recommend both the American Academy of paediatrics and the American College of Obstetricians and Gynaecologists to pregnant and preconceptional women [32].

Ideally the measures must be prevention specifically education for health to avoid he pregnant women use alcohol during gestation. This situation is contradicted with the findings that inform about the education dos not have influence to diminish the alcohol use in population. [16] It must be insisted on the necessity that the health professionals know and utilize the instruments of detection of alcoholism, this recommendation is promoted by the US Preventive Service Task Force that advises the use of the AUDIT or the CAGE.

The measures that have shown to be effective to reduce the alcohol ingestion in population are of political type, [16] it is probable that it happens these same in the case of pregnant women in risk of ingesting alcohol.

A measurement would be to place a label on the bottles that reports that the alcohol is injurious for the product of pregnancy. Another measurement could be forbid the alcohol sale to pregnant women.

From the ethical point of view a serious of dilemmas is generated: Must be recommended the abortion to a pregnant woman who use, abuse or has alcohol dependency?

Since in case of dependency the treatment with the medicaments of recent appearance, acamprosate and naltrexone. Others researchers have proposed, ondansetron and topiramate, [37, 38] that help to the alcoholic, but are not allowed to be used during pregnancy. Must they be used in spite of the risk of teratogenia?

This and other questions must be solved by the members of the health team.

## REFERENCES

[1]     Sánchez. H. *La lucha en Mèxico contra las enfermedades mentales.* 1ª Mèxico: Fondo de Cultura Econòmica; 1974.

[2]     *www.alcmeon.com.ar/10/38/index,htm.*

[3]     Vidal.G. Alarcón.R. Lolas.F. *Enciclopedia Iberoamericana de psiquiatrìa.* 1ª.Argentina. Panamericana. 1995.

[4]     Hales. R. Yudofsky.S. Talbott. J. *Tratado de psiquiatrìa*; DSM IV. 3ª España; Masson. 2000.

[5]     *(www.who.int/dsa/justpub/whr2001.pdf.2001)*

[6]     Andreasen.N. *Un cerebro feliz.* 1ª. Barcelona; Psiquiatrìa Editores, S.L. 2004.

[7]     Rehm. J. Monteiro. M. (2005). Alcohol consumption and burden of disease in the Americas: Implications for alcohol policy. *Revista Panamericana de Salud Pùblica.* 1814, 5, 241 – 247.

[8]     Saitz.R. (2005). Unhealthy Alcohol Use. *The New England Journal of Medicine.* 352, 6, 596 – 607.

[9]     Roses. P.M. (2005). La salud mental: Una prioridad de salud pùblica en las Amèricas. *Revista Panamericana de Salud Pùblica.* 1814, 5, 223 – 225.

[10]    Silva de L. Garcìa de Oliveira. S. Mari. J. (2004). Investigación epidemiològica sobre salud mental en Amèrica del Sur: Hallazgos recientes. *World Psychiatry.* 2, 2, 120 -122.

[11]    Ramos de V. M. (2001). La mujer y el alcoholismo en el Siglo XIX. *Salud Mental.* 24, 3, 24 – 28.

[12]    Madden. J.S. *Alcoholismo y Farmacodependencia.* 2ª Mèxico; El Manual Moderno. 1986.

[13]    Mariño. M. Berenzon. S. Medina. M. M. (2005). Síndrome de dependencia al alcohol: comparación entre hombres y mujeres. *Salud Mental.* 28, 4, 33-39.

[14]    Ontiveros. U. M. Lara. M. (2002). Diferencias de gènero y cerebro. *Programa de Actualizaciòn Continua en Psiquiatrìa (PAC).* 1, 3, 9 -48.

[15]  Barragán. T. Gonzàles. V. Medina. M. Ayala. V. (2005). Adaptación de un modelo de intervención cognoscitivo – conductual para usuarios dependientes de alcohol y otras drogas a población mexicana: Un estudio piloto. *Salud Mental.* 28, 1, 61 – 71.

[16]  Roam. R. Babor. T. Rehm. J. (2005). Alcohol and public health. *The Lancet.* 365, 5, 519 – 530.

[17]  Pèrez. H. Rubio. A. *Antologìa de la Sexualidad Humana.* 2ª. Mèxico; Miguel Angel Porrua Grupo Editorial.

[18]  Corlay. N.I. (2004). Depresiòn y Embarazo. *Programa de Actualizaciòn Continua en Psiquiatrìa (PAC).* 4, 5, 157 -206.

[19]  Gelder. G.M. Lòpez- Ibor.J.J. Andreasen. N. *Tratado de psiquiatrìa.* 1ª. España; Psiquiatrìa Editores, S. 2003.

[20]  Swadi.H. (2000). Abuso de sustancias en adolescentes. *Avances en psiquiatrìa.* 6, 3.35 – 43.

[21]  Kaplan. H. Sadock. B. Grebb. J. *Sinopsis de psiquiatrìa.* 7ª. Argentina; Editorial Mèdica Panamericana. 1996.

[22]  Mora–R. Natera. G. Juàrez. F. (2005). Expectativas relacionadas con el alcohol en la predicciòn del abuso en el consumo en jóvenes. *Salud Mental.* 28, 2. 82 – 90.

[23]  Barriguete. M. J. (203). Psiquiatrìa perinatal e intercultural. *Programa de Actualizaciòn Continua en Psiquiatrìa (PAC).* 1, 11- 63.

[24]  Kotulak. R. *El cerebro por dentro.* 1ª.Mèxico; Diana. 2003.

[25]  Flaherty. J. Channon. R. Davis. J. Psiquiatrìa. 1ª. Argentina; *Editorial Medica Panamricana.* 1991.

[26]  Kaplan. Sadock. *Sinopsis de psiquiatrìa.* 8ª. Madrid; Editorial Medica Panamericana. 2001.

[27]  *http:/db-doyma.es/egi/bin/wdbegi.exe/doyma/mrevistapdf*

[28]  *Comunicacion personal dra:* Baez. R. Genetista del Instituto Nacional de Perinatologìa. Mèxico.

[29]  Swayze. V. Jonson. V. James. Piven. (1997) J. Magnetic Resonance Imaging of Brain Anomalies in Fetal Alcohol Syndrome. *Pediatrics.* 99, 2. 232 – 239.

[30]  Divisiòn Tècnica de Informaciòn Estadìstica en Salud. (2005). *revista medica del IMSS* .43, 5. 449 -456.

[31]  De la Fuente.J. (1994). Detecciòn oportuna del paciente alcohòlico. Problemas psiquiatricos en la pràctica mèdica. *Temas de Medicina Interna.* 2, 3. 477 – 483.

[32]  Chang. G. Tay. M. Orav. E. (2005). Brief Intervention for Prenatal Alcohol Use: A Randomized Trial. *Obsterics and Gynecology.* 105, 5. 991 – 998.

[33]  Schuckit. M. Irwin. M (1988) Diagnòsticos difìciles: Diagnòstico de alcoholismo.*clìnica mèdicas de norteamerica.* 5. 1205 – 1221.

[34]  Borges. G.(1988). Consumo moderado de bebidas alcohòlicas por mujeres embarazadas: una controversia epidemiològica. *Salud Pùblica de Mèxico.* 30, 1. 14 – 24.

[35]  Borges. G. Tapia. R. Medina – Mora. M. (1997). Alcohol consumption and pregnancy in the Mexican nacional addiction survey. *Cuadernos de Salud Pùblica.* 13, 2. 205 – 211.

[36]  Montesinos. B. Altuzar. M. Benitez. C. (2004). Alcoholismo durante el embarazo: un problema de salud subestimado. *Ginecología y Obstetricia de México.* 72, 10. 508 – 514.

[37]  Johnson. B. Rooache. J. Javors. M.(2000). Ondansetron for Reduction of Drinking among Biologically Predisposed Alcoholic Patients. *JAMA,*. 284, 8.963 – 971.

[38]  Johnson. B Daoud. N. Bowden. C. Oral topiramate for treatament of alcohol dependence a randomised controlled trial *Lancet.* 361. 1677 – 1685.

# INDEX

## C

## D

## E

# H

# I

## J

## K

## L

# O

# Q

# R

**T**